Disclaimer

This publication is a summary of selected developments in the area of employment law in 2015. Case reports and summaries of decisions are based solely on the publicly available copies of the relevant judgments, recommendations and determinations. There may be cases reported in this publication which, unknown to the authors and the publishers, have been appealed and/or overturned, or subsequently settled.

Whilst every care has been taken to ensure the accuracy of this work, this publication is not a definitive statement of the law and is not intended to constitute legal advice. The authors, editors and publishers do not accept any liability or responsibility for errors or omission. No responsibility for loss occasioned by any person acting or refraining from action as a result of any statement in the publication can be accepted by any of the authors, editors or the publishers.

Arthur Cox
Employment Law
Yearbook 2015

Bloomsbury Professional

Published by
Bloomsbury Professional
Maxwelton House
41–43 Boltro Road
Haywards Heath
West Sussex
RH16 1BJ

Bloomsbury Professional
The Fitzwilliam Business Centre
26 Upper Pembroke Street
Dublin 2

ISBN 978 1 78451 182 1

© Arthur Cox

British Library Cataloguing-in-Publication Data
A catalogue record for this book is available from the British Library

Typeset by Marie Armah-Kwantreng, Dublin, Ireland
Printed and bound in the United Kingdom by CPI Group (UK) Ltd, Croydon, CR0 4YYL

i.m. Dr Mary Redmond (RIP)

1950–2015

Our colleague and friend Dr Mary Redmond passed away in April 2015. The Arthur Cox Employment Law Yearbook was Mary's idea and she was the principal author and editor of the first two volumes in 2011 and 2012.

Mary was one of the finest lawyers of her generation, a distinguished academic, a noted author, a leader in business, a true philanthropist and was devoted to her family.

Mary was a wonderful colleague and she is greatly missed.

i.m. Declan Drislane (RIP)

1957–2015

The former Head of our Pensions Group, Declan Drislane also passed away at the end of 2015. Declan was a valued contributor to the Arthur Cox Employment Law Yearbook.

Declan was a founder member of the Association of Pension Lawyers in Ireland as well as a formidable corporate lawyer. His plain-speaking courtesy, generosity of spirit, constant good humour and sense of fun are greatly missed.

INTRODUCTION

This is the fifth volume of the *Arthur Cox Employment Law Yearbook* which is designed to set out the latest developments and information on areas that affect employment law in Ireland in 2015. The *Arthur Cox Employment Law Yearbooks* are a unique resource for lawyers, human resource professionals, management, public and private sector employers, employees and trade unionists, for whom keeping up to date in employment law is an ever-present challenge.

Significant changes have occurred in 2015 to the workplace dispute resolution landscape with the enactment of the Workplace Relations Act and the establishment of the Workplace Relations Commission. There continues to be a high volume of employment litigation in the Employment Appeals Tribunal, the Equality Tribunal and in the Labour Court. There have also been many employment cases of note in the civil courts including applications for judicial review and interlocutory injunctions.

The material for the *2015 Yearbook* has been carefully selected by experienced Arthur Cox lawyers in the fields of employment law, data protection, freedom of information, pensions and taxation.

The opening chapter of the *2015 Yearbook* is a mini-version of the Yearbook itself. It outlines in sequence the content which follows in subsequent chapters, and is intended to assist the reader by providing a synopsis of the 2015 content with brief comments thereon.

The *2015 Yearbook* includes a number of new chapters on the employment law aspects of the Companies Act 2014, judicial review, the Workplace Relations Act 2015, developments in Northern Ireland and a contribution on the doctrine of curial deference and the Labour Court by employment barrister Tom Mallon BL.

The line for inclusion in the *2015 Yearbook* was drawn as of 1 December 2015. Where we are aware that cases are being appealed, this is noted in the text. Work on the sixth *Arthur Cox Employment Law Yearbook* is already in progress.

Among those deserving special thanks are Sarah Sheehy of Bloomsbury Professional, whose encouragement and assistance were much valued, Tessa Robinson BL for editing, Andrew Turner for indexing, Marie Armah-Kwantreng for typesetting and tabling and to Siobhan Mulholland for her expertise and guidance.

Sincere thanks also to all those in Arthur Cox who contributed to this Yearbook but in particular to Niamh Hanratty and Michelle Leamy, in the Arthur Cox Library.

Elaine Mettler, Arthur Cox Editor

February 2016

PRACTICE AREAS INVOLVED IN THE ARTHUR COX EMPLOYMENT LAW YEARBOOK 2015

Employment and Industrial Relations

Séamus Given
Kevin Langford
Cian Beecher
Gill Woods
Elaine Mettler, Arthur Cox Editor
Michael Doyle
Louise O'Byrne
Deborah Delahunt
Sarelle Buckley
Zelda Cunningham
Grace Gannon
Michelle Maloney
Fran Moran
Niamh Fennelly

Pensions

Philip Smith
Catherine Austin
Sarah McCague
Michael Shovlin
Marie McQuail

Taxation

Conor Hurley
Caroline Devlin
Fintan Clancy
Ailish Finnerty
Anne Corrigan

Edel Hargaden
Aisling Burke
David Kilty
Aoibhin O'Hare
Diyu Wu
Patricia McCarvill
Clodagh Power
Kevin Mangan
Christine Lynch
Dearbhla O'Gorman

Technology and Innovation

John Menton
Rob Corbet
Pearse Ryan
Colin Rooney
Bob Clark
Iseult Mangan
Olivia Mullooly
Chris Bollard
Claire O'Brien
Joanne Neary
Colm Maguire

Arthur Cox Belfast

Rosemary Lundy
Emma-Jane Flannery
Chris Fullerton

Contents

Contents

Contents

TABLE OF CASES

C

D

E

F

G

H

I

J

K

L

M

N

O

P

TABLE OF STATUTES

TABLE OF STATUTORY INSTRUMENTS

TABLE OF EUROPEAN LEGISLATION

TABLE OF CONSTITUTIONS

Chapter 1

INTRODUCTION

[1.01] This introductory Chapter provides a snapshot of selected employment law and related developments contained in this Yearbook. Readers are encouraged to delve into each themed chapter where the developments have been carefully selected, reviewed and summarised to provide a user-friendly guide to the employment law environment in Ireland in 2015.

CONTRACT OF EMPLOYMENT
Employment status

[1.02] CHAPTER 2 notes a number of important decisions in 2015 on employment status.

In *Beirne v Board of Management of Loughlynn National School*[1] the claimant, who taught the tin whistle to primary school children as part of an extracurricular music class, was held to be an independent contractor. In *Blake v Grand Circle LLC*[2] the EAT concluded that a tour guide was not an employee and in *Forde v Newspread Ltd*[3] a newspaper delivery man was held to be self-employed. In *Comerford v Health Service Executive*[4] the claimant, who performed maintenance duties at a high-security centre for children, was held to have the status of an independent contractor.

Employment status was also considered by the Court of Appeal in England in *Halawi v WDFG UK Ltd (t/a World Duty Free)*[5] which concluded that the claimant, a beauty consultant selling cosmetics in a duty free outlet in Heathrow, was not an employee of the respondent for the purposes of a claim of discrimination on grounds of race and religion under the Equality Act 2010.

Income protection

[1.03] Whether or not there is a contractual right to benefit from an income protection plan was considered by the High Court in *Holohan v Friends First Life Assurance Co Ltd*.[6] The High Court considered the eligibility of the plaintiff to benefit from the plan and whether he was totally disabled by reason of sickness or accident as required by the plan rules.

---

1. *Beirne v Board of Management of Loughlynn National School* TE22/2015.
2. *Blake v Grand Circle LLC* UD620/2013.
3. *Forde v Newspread Ltd* UD1699/2013.
4. *Comerford v Health Service Executive* UD466/2014, MN195/2014, WT70/2014.
5. *Halawi v WDFG UK Ltd (t/a World Duty Free)* [2014] EWCA Civ 1387.
6. *Holohan v Friends First Life Assurance Co Ltd* [2014] IEHC 676.

Performance-related pay

[1.04] The legality of a decision to withhold a performance-related bonus from a CEO was considered by the High Court in *Gunning v Coillte Teoranta*.[7]

The contractual nature of an employee handbook

[1.05] Whether or not an employee handbook is contractual in nature is often considered. The High Court in England looked at this question in *Sparks & Ors v Department for Transport*[8] where the staff handbook had been amended unilaterally by the employer.

Flexibility clauses

[1.06] In *Norman and Douglas v National Audit Office*[9] the UK EAT held that in order for a flexibility clause to be effective, it must clearly and unambiguously identify a right for the employer to vary the employment unilaterally.

Unilateral contractual amendments

[1.07] In *Cartwright & Ors v Tetrad Ltd*[10] the UK EAT affirmed the decision of the employment tribunal that the appellants had accepted a unilateral change in their pay by continuing to work without protest for months after its implementation.

Introduction of restrictive covenants after employment begins

[1.08] In *Reuse Collections Ltd v Sendall & Anor*[11] the High Court in England considered the requirement to provide consideration to an employee if restrictive covenants were introduced by an employer after the inception of the employment relationship. The extent to which an employee owes a duty of loyalty to an employer and whether this is a fiduciary duty was also examined by the Court.

COMPANIES ACT 2014 – EMPLOYMENT LAW ISSUES

[1.09] The law relating to companies in Ireland has been significantly overhauled by the enactment of the long-awaited Companies Act 2014, which came into force on 1 June 2015. In **CH 3**, we look at the impact of the 2014 Act on employment law and

---

7.   *Gunning v Coillte Teoranta* [2015] IEHC 44.
8.   *Sparks & Ors v Department of Transport* [2015] EWHC 181 (QB). Note: under appeal.
9.   *Norman and Douglas v National Audit Office*, Appeal No UKEAT/0276/14/BA.
10. *Cartwright & Ors v Tetrad Ltd* Appeal No UKEAT/0262/14/JOJ.
11. *Reuse Collections Ltd v Sendall & Anor* [2014] EWHC 3852 (QB).

specifically consider key changes in relation to the appointment and removal of directors, service contracts and remuneration of directors, directors' duties and compensation for loss of office.

DATA PROTECTION

[1.10] 2015 saw continued developments in data protection on an international scale, with the Court of Justice of the European Union (CJEU) invalidating the Safe Harbor mechanism approved by the European Commission in 2010 for the transfers of personal data from the European Union to the United States.[12] **CHAPTER 4** analyses the implications of the CJEU judgment in *Schrems* and notes that this case forms part of a line of European cases which have firmly enshrined the principles of necessity, proportionality and transparency in European data protection law, and will need to be equally borne in mind in processing of personal data in the workplace.

Two recent case studies from the Office of the Data Protection Commissioner concerning the workplace are detailed in **CH 4** along with a recent EU judgment *Weltimmo v Nemzeti*,[13] which concerned the place of establishment of a data controller.

There is also consideration of new legislation, which makes it an offence to hire a private investigator that is not licensed by the Private Security Agency.[14]

EMPLOYMENT EQUALITY

[1.11] **CHAPTER 5** details the amendments to equality legislation made by the Equality (Miscellaneous Provisions) Act 2015. **CHAPTER 5** also contains a broad selection of complaints considered by the Equality Tribunal and the Labour Court on appeal in 2015. The protected grounds that feature most often in the case law are gender, race and nationality, disability and age. **CHAPTER 5** also includes two important cases on religion.

A preliminary issue which often arises is whether or not the parties are bound by a valid pre-existing settlement agreement which precludes a case from proceeding. This was considered by the Equality Tribunal in *A Chef v A Hospital*[15] and in *McGrath and Ryan v Athlone Institute of Technology*.[16]

---

12. *Schrems v Data Protection Commissioner* (Case C–362/14).

13. *Weltimmo v Nemzeti* (Case C–230/14).

14. Private Security Services Act 2004 (Commencement) Order 2015 (SI 194/2015); and Private Security (Licensing and Standards) (Private Investigator) Regulations 2015 (SI 195/2015).

15. *A Chef v A Hospital* DEC–E 2015–054.

16. *McGrath and Ryan v Athlone Institute of Technology* DEC–E2015–114.

Gender—pregnancy and maternity leave

[1.12] The number of equality decisions in 2015 which relate to pregnancy and maternity leave is striking and highlights the ongoing difficulties that many female employees have in the workplace on notification of pregnancy and, in particular, on return from maternity leave. A selection of these decisions of the Equality Tribunal, which are noteworthy for the high levels of awards made against the relevant employers, is included in **Ch 5**.

In *Gacek v Pagewell Concessions (Ilac) Ltd t/a €uro 50 Store Ilac Centre*[17] the Equality Tribunal described the treatment of the complainant during pregnancy and on her return from maternity leave as the second worst case of working conditions that had ever come before it. In upholding claims of harassment, discrimination and victimisatory constructive dismissal and awarding compensation equivalent to 30-months of salary, the Tribunal noted the complainant worked in an environment of aggression, excessive surveillance and under-payment.

The timing of a dismissal which was facilitated by a pregnancy-related absence was held to be discriminatory in *A Worker v A Catering Business*.[18] In *Sobczyk v SAMI SWOI Ltd*,[19] the treatment of the complainant in relation to her working conditions, a reduction in hours and a purported disciplinary issue which was not pursued, led the Tribunal to conclude that she was discriminated against on grounds of gender, and that her subsequent dismissal which was influenced by the fact she was pregnant was discriminatory.

In *A Worker v An Insurance Company*[20] an award of €70,000 was made by the Tribunal to the complainant arising from the less favourable treatment of her on her return from maternity leave due to her gender and family status.

The decision of an employer in *Gilman Bennet v Elaine Byrne's Health and Beauty Clinic*[21] to place a pregnant employee on health and safety leave against her wishes following a risk assessment that the complainant disputed, and the consequent failure of the respondent to make any distinction between generic risks and specific risks, was held by the Tribunal to constitute prima facie discrimination. The Tribunal made an award of €12,000.

The requirements on receivers and those tasked with managing companies in the course of restructurings and other business change were emphasised by the Equality Tribunal in *Murphy v Browell Ltd t/a The Four Roads (In Receivership)*.[22]

A failure to top-up State maternity benefit to match salary levels was held to constitute discrimination on grounds of gender and family status in *Duggan and Barry v*

---

17.   *Gacek v Pagewell Concessions (Ilac) Ltd t/a €uro 50 Store, Ilac Centre* DEC–E2015–29.

18.   *A Worker v A Catering Business* DEC–E2015–037.

19.   *Sobczyk v SAMI SWOI Ltd* DEC–E2015–016.

20.   *A Worker v An Insurance Company* DEC–E2015–022.

21.   *Gilman Bennet v Elaine Byrne's Health and Beauty Clinic* DEC–E2015–059.

22.   *Murphy v Browell Ltd t/a The Four Roads (In Receivership)* DEC–E2015–050.

Waterford Area Partnership.[23] The Tribunal ordered that arrears of pay be paid as though the top-up had been made and awarded compensation of €2,500 to each complainant.

Gender—promotions, training, conditions of employment

[1.13] The conduct of an internal recruitment process for the appointment of an emergency medical controller and the operation of regional and national recruitment panels was considered by the Equality Tribunal in *O'Leary v Health Service Executive South*[24] in the context of complaints by a female complainant that her failure to be appointed to the role constituted discrimination of her on grounds of gender.

However, contrast the outcome of *Smolinska v Webroot International Ltd*[25] where the dismissal of the complainant for performance reasons from employment, in what was described by the Tribunal as a very tough and demanding sales culture, was held not to be related to her race, nationality or gender.

Sexual harassment

[1.14] *An Employee v An Employer*[26] is illustrative of the difficulties that can be faced in claims of sexual harassment or harassment where there are no third-party witnesses and there is contradictory evidence from both parties on all aspects of the case. In *C v A Multi-National Grocery Retailer,*[27] the Equality Tribunal held that the employer had failed to take reasonable steps to prevent the sexual harassment of the complainant in the workplace and that even less was done to reverse its effects on the complainant.

Race and nationality

[1.15] The failure to re-employ the complainant in his role after security contracts were taken over by the respondent was held to be prima facie discrimination on grounds of race in *Maciukas v G4S Secure Solutions Ltd.*[28] Noting its view that a transfer of undertaking had taken place, the Tribunal found the explanations provided by the respondent for the non-employment of the complainant to be vague and inadequate.

There can rarely be a more overt example of workplace discrimination than that seen in *Naqui v Vantry International*[29] where the complainant, who was a British national of Asian origin, was told in an email response to a job application that the recruiter was only looking for Irish nationals because they wanted someone with knowledge of Irish companies and the Irish accounting system. Despite the respondent's best efforts to

---

23.   *Duggan and Barry v Waterford Area Partnership* DEC–E2015–064.
24.   *O'Leary v Health Service Executive South* DEC–E2015–019.
25.   *Smolinska v Webroot International Ltd* DEC–E2015–074.
26.   *An Employee v An Employer* DEC–E2015–052.
27.   *C v A Multi-National Grocery Retailer* DEC–E2015–079.
28.   *Maciukas v G4S Secure Solutions Ltd* DEC–E2014–095.
29.   *Naqui v Vantry International* DEC–E2015–063.

distance itself from these initial emails on the basis that they were sent by a contractor and not one of its employees, it was held to have discriminated against the complainant on grounds of her nationality.

Jansen v Allied Irish Banks,[30] a claim of race discrimination by an agency worker, should be noted for the finding of the Equality Tribunal that the fact that the complainant had made assertions supported only by speculation was not sufficient to establish a prima facie case of discrimination. Also the Tribunal was clear that the proper comparators in this case were other relevant agency staff and not the permanent employees of the respondent.

Race – harassment

[1.16] The response of an employer to a once-off serious incident where a line manager made a derogatory comment to the complainant which was linked to his race was considered in *Bains v Maotham Ltd t/a Mao*.[31]

Race – language and foreign workers

[1.17] The obligations on an employer to made adequate provision for the employment rights of foreign workers with poor English was emphasised by the Equality Tribunal in *Mikoliuniene v Halcyon Contract Cleaners Ltd*.[32]

In *Zdzalik and Rospenda v Helsinn Birex Pharmaceuticals Ltd*[33] the Equality Tribunal considered the respondent's requirement that all employees speak English at work. While the Tribunal accepted the validity of a language policy, the 'zealous' application of this to the Polish complainants in this workplace was held to be less favourable treatment of them on grounds of their nationality.

In *Delanowski v Kellsydan Ltd t/a McDonalds Restaurant*[34] the Equality Tribunal considered the respondent's employee handbook which confirmed that English was the business operational language. The Tribunal noted the three reasons put forward by the respondent namely health and safety, to ensure inclusion and to ensure business efficiency and held that any one of these reasons justified the use of a business language.

Disability

[1.18] The challenges for an employer where there are legacy disability issues but current performance concerns can be seen in *A Post Person v A Postal Service*.[35] The

---

30.   *Jansen v Allied Irish Banks* DEC–E2015–077.
31.   *Bains v Maotham Ltd t/a Mao* DEC–E2015–030.
32.   *Mikoliuniene v Halcyon Contract Cleaners Ltd* DEC–E2015–036.
33.   *Zdzalik and Rospenda v Helsinn Birex Pharmaceuticals Ltd* DEC–E2015–047.
34.   *Delanowski v Kellsydan Ltd t/a McDonalds Restaurant* DEC–E2015–072.
35.   *A Post Person v A Postal Service* DEC–E2015–026.

employer had sought expert medical opinion which established that the performance issues were not linked to the disability. The Tribunal noted that had the employer raised the issue of disability every time there was a performance concern, this of itself could have been discrimination.

In *Kozak v Eirtech Aviation Ltd and Firefly Management Services Ltd*,[36] the complainant, who suffered an acute anxiety attack following an alleged severe bullying and a harassment incident, was held by the Tribunal to have a disability and a subsequent decision to dismiss him was influenced by what had happened.

A decision to move an employee with multiple sclerosis from her role to another part of the business on an assumption that she was unable to undertake her duties because of her disability but without any medical evidence to support this and against the employee's wishes was held to be discriminatory treatment of her on grounds of disability.[37]

The actions of an employer in how it handled a resignation received over the telephone from an employee on sick leave who was known to have depression and to be self-harming, and that employer's failure to ascertain the level and extent of her disability and failure to make reasonable accommodation was criticised by the Tribunal in *A Complainant v A Restaurant Ltd and Mr A t/a A Restaurant*.[38]

A Worker v An Employer[39] demonstrates the difficulty faced by a small retail business in accommodating an employee with a serious back condition who was restricted in terms of her capacity for physical movement and her need to work significantly reduced hours.

In *Clavin v Marks & Spencers (Ireland) Ltd*[40] the Equality Tribunal upheld the claim of discriminatory dismissal on grounds of disability and awarded compensation of €40,000, the equivalent to 18 months salary to the complainant who was dismissed on ill-health grounds. The Tribunal was critical of the respondent and held that it had fallen far short of best practice in its treatment of the complainant.

[1.19] The decision of an employer to dismiss a pregnant employee who, separate to her pregnancy, was suffering symptoms suggestive of multiple sclerosis, and who was on sick leave on grounds of incapacity and due to go on maternity leave, and its failure to follow medical advice and reports, led the Equality Tribunal to uphold claims of discrimination on grounds of disability and victimisation.[41]

---

36. *Kozak v Eirtech Aviation Ltd and Firefly Management Services Ltd* DEC–E2015–028.
37. *A Complainant v A Healthcare Company* DEC–E2015–009.
38. *A Complainant v A Restaurant Ltd and Mr A t/a A Restaurant* DEC–E2015–015.
39. *A Worker v An Employer* DEC–E2015–058.
40. *Clavin v Marks & Spencers (Ireland) Ltd* DEC–E2015–055.
41. *Hoey v White Horse Insurance Ireland Ltd* DEC–E2015–066.

Age

[1.20] In *NUI Maynooth v Keane*[42] the Labour Court considered the refusal to permit the complainant to return to work on a contract or on an occasional basis following retirement and held that it did not amount to age discrimination.

Border, Midland and Western Regional Assembly v Lavelle[43] is a noteworthy decision of the Labour Court which held that the refusal to grant 'e-working' arrangements to a complainant was influenced by his age. The Court confirmed that if a motive for wishing to e-work or work remotely disclosed by a worker is related to a protected ground under the Acts, the rejection of the validity of that motive by an employer is sufficient to raise an inference of discriminatory treatment.

In *Butler-Duffy v Boots Ireland Ltd*,[44] the Equality Tribunal did not uphold claims of age discrimination by a prospective employee who attended for interview for the role of health-care assistant.

Whether or not an employee can be bound by a retirement age contained in a staff handbook introduced after employment had commenced in circumstances where the employee had no knowledge of the staff handbook was considered by the Labour Court in *Earagail Eisc Teoranta v Lett*.[45]

Religion

[1.21] Whether the protected ground of religion and religious belief extends to the right to manifest one's religion, in relation to religious teaching or observance, was considered by the Labour Court in *Tipperary County Council v McAteer*.[46] The Court upheld the claim and affirmed the original award of €70,000.

St Nathy's College v Burke[47] is an unusual case where the Labour Court considered a claim of discrimination on grounds of religion arising from an internal promotional process. The complainant was not shortlisted and one of the reasons given was that she had failed to provide evidence of a commitment to the school's Catholic or Christian ethos. The complainant asserted that the respondent had imputed to her an absence of religious belief or that she was not an adherent of the Catholic religion; however the complainant's evidence was that she was in fact a Catholic. The Court held that the complainant had failed to overcome the prima facie test.

---

42.   *NUI Maynooth v Keane* EDA158.
43.   *Border, Midland and Western Regional Assembly v Lavelle* EDA 154.
44.   *Butler-Duffy v Boots Ireland Ltd* DEC–E2015–012.
45.   *Earagail Eisc Teoranta v Lett* EDA1422.
46.   *Tipperary County Council v McAteer* EDA153.
47.   *St Nathy's College v Burke* EDA1512.

Multiple grounds

[1.22] It is not uncommon for complainants to bring claims of discrimination and/or victimisation on multiple protected grounds.

In *A Teacher v A National School*[48] a complaint of discrimination in relation to access to employment and promotion on grounds of age, religion and sexual orientation arising from an interview process, was upheld by the Tribunal which awarded the complainant €54,000, the equivalent to one year's remuneration. On appeal to the Labour Court, the Court disallowed the appeals on the age and religion grounds but upheld the appeal on grounds of sexual orientation. The compensation award was affirmed by the Court.

In *Adejumo v Noonan Services Group Ltd*,[49] a case of alleged discrimination on grounds of religion and family status, the Equality Tribunal held that mere assertions are insufficient to discharge the complainant's initial probative burden.

Equal pay

[1.23] *Savel v Workforce International Contractors Ltd*[50] is a reminder of the requirement to choose a valid and appropriate comparator in an equal pay claim. Similarly, in *Aleksandrovs, Sidorov, Rikmanis, Timofejus and Sinicins v Roskell Ltd*[51] the Labour Court considered whether the work performed by the complainants and their chosen comparator was of equal value to justify equal pay in circumstances where the comparator performed additional duties.

Selected equal status cases

[1.24] CHAPTER 5 contains four important cases under the Equal Status Acts 2000 to 2015 on four different protected grounds concerning sports leagues,[52] educational admission policies[53] and the refusal of services in a barber shop.[54]

---

48. *A Teacher v A National School* DEC–E2014–097.
49. *Adejumo v Noonan Services Group Ltd* DEC–E2015–023.
50. *Savel v Workforce International Contractors Ltd* DEC–E2015–075.
51. *Aleksandrovs, Sidorov, Rikmanis, Timofejus and Sinicins v Roskell Ltd* EDA1519.
52. *Turner v Basketball Ireland* DEC–S2014–029.
53. *Christian Brothers High School Clonmel v Stokes (on behalf of John Stokes a minor) and the Equality Authority (Amicus Curiae)* [2015] IESC 13; *A (on behalf of her daughter B) v A Girls' Secondary School* DEC–S2015–001.
54. *Carroll v Gruaig Barbers* DEC–S2015–005.

EMPLOYMENT RELATED TORTS

[1.25] CHAPTER **6** considers an extremely important decision of the Court of Appeal[55] published in late 2015 which considered the law on bullying and, in a majority decision, overturned a High Court award of damages in May 2014[56] in the sum of €255,276 to a special needs assistant on foot of her claim of personal injuries arising out of alleged bullying in the course of her employment.

EUROPEAN UNION LAW

[1.26] CHAPTER **7** notes a recent decision[57] of the CJEU relating to posted workers in which the Court clarified the concept of 'minimum rates of pay' for posted workers. The CJEU determined that the laws and agreements in respect of pay and conditions in the host Member State applied to posted workers and determined the allowances that constitute minimum rates of pay in Council Directive 96/71/EC.

FIXED-TERM WORKERS
Contract of indefinite duration

[1.27] In CH **8**, there are several cases relating to contracts of indefinite duration.

The Labour Court has continued to apply the test enunciated by the CJEU in *Adeneler*[58] and has focused on whether the work undertaken was to fulfil the fixed and permanent needs of the employer or was for the purpose of meeting a temporary or transient need.

When an objective justification must be ascertained was emphasised by the Labour Court in *Galway County Council v Canavan*.[59]

Two academic research cases of note are included. In *O'Doherty v UCD*[60] the Labour Court found that participation of the complainant in a research careers framework was an objective ground to justify successive fixed-term contracts. In *University of Limerick v Haverty*[61] the Court considered whether the complainant's work on a specific research project was temporary in nature and held that it was a stand-alone project and was not part of the fixed and permanent needs of the respondent university. Thus the decision to

---

55. *Ruffley v The Board of Management of St Anne's School* [2015] IECA 287.
56. See *Arthur Cox Employment Law Yearbook 2014* at [5.02]; *Ruffley v The Board of Management of St Anne's School* [2014] IEHC 235.
57. *Sähköalojen Ammattiliitto ry v Elektrobudowa Spółka Akcyjna (Reference for a preliminary ruling, Finland)* (Case C–396/13).
58. *Adeneler & Ors v Ellinikos Organismos Galaktos* (Case C–212/04).
59. *Galway County Council v Canavan* FTD1513.
60. *O'Doherty v UCD* FTD 159.
61. *University of Limerick v Haverty* FTD158.

provide the complainant with a further specified purpose contract as opposed to a contract of indefinite duration was objectively justified.

In *Health Service Executive v Doherty*[62] the High Court held that it had no authority to interfere with findings of fact made by the Labour Court in holding that a claimant was entitled to a contract of indefinite duration under the 2003 Act.

Terms of a contract of indefinite duration

[1.28] The question as to what a contract of indefinite duration must contain was addressed by the Labour Court in *Kerry County Council v Walsh & Ors*.[63]

CJEU decision

[1.29] In *European Commission v Grand Duchy of Luxembourg*[64] the CJEU considered whether Luxembourg had fulfilled its obligations to prevent the abusive use of successive fixed-term contracts in accordance with the Framework Agreement on Fixed-Term Work (Annex to Council Directive 1999/70/EC).

FREEDOM OF INFORMATION

[1.30] CHAPTER 9 details the developments in the law relating to the freedom of information in 2015.

HEALTH AND SAFETY

[1.31] CHAPTER 10 notes a selection of cases relating to health and safety at work.

[1.32] The extent of an employer's statutory obligations to train its employees was considered by the High Court in *Meus v Dunnes Stores*,[65] a personal injuries action.

[1.33] In *Gillane v Focus Ireland Ltd*[66] the High Court considered whether there was negligence and breach of statutory duty in the configuration of the plaintiff's workstation and concluded that defects in the plaintiff's workstation were a contributory factor in the onset of her chronic inflammatory condition.

---

62. *Health Service Executive v Doherty* [2015] IEHC 611.
63. *Kerry County Council v Walsh & Ors* FTD 154.
64. *European Commission v Grand Duchy of Luxembourg* (Case C–238/14).
65. *Meus v Dunnes Stores* [2014] IEHC 639.
66. *Gillane v Focus Ireland Ltd* [2015] IEHC 478.

[1.34] In *Besenyei v Rosderra Irish Meats Group Ltd and Rosderra Meats Group*[67] the dismissal of the claimant for the principal reason of his refusal to wear arm-length safety gloves, which were designed for use by boners on the production line, was held to be not unfair. The EAT noted the high level of risk inherent in this type of production operation and held that compliance with health and safety regulations was paramount.

[1.35] A decision to dismiss following a physical altercation on a factory floor near industrial equipment was upheld by the EAT in *Hanlon v Smurfit Kappa Ireland Ltd t/a Smurfit Kappa Dublin*[68] which noted the right to work in a safe environment.

[1.36] In *Katherine Gordon & Co Ltd v Crowley O'Toole*[69] the Labour Court found that the complainant's decision to report a workplace accident to the Health and Safety Authority had not been an operative factor in the respondent's decision to dismiss the complainant.

HUMAN RIGHTS

[1.37] CHAPTER 11 contains a note of the decision of the European Court of Human Rights in *Boyraz v Turkey*.[70] The Court held that the dismissal of the applicant from a security officer role on the basis of her female gender and the fact that she had not completed military service was a breach of Art 14 (prohibition of discrimination) and Art 8 (right to respect to private and family life) of the European Convention on Human Rights.

The length of time it took to prosecute the applicant's claims in the Turkish Courts, a period of eight years, was criticised by the ECHR as being excessive. The ECHR further held that the Turkish Supreme Court's failure to provide adequate reasoning for its decisions in circumstances where it had simply endorsed the judgment of the Administrative Court was contrary to Art 6(1) of the Convention.

IMMIGRATION

[1.38] CHAPTER 12 looks at legislative and case law developments in the area of immigration in 2015 to include revised Regulations under the Employment Permits Acts to provide for certain skills shortages in a number of industries and revised immigration registration arrangements for holders of critical skills or green card employment permits. We also note the Trusted Partner Initiative, which was introduced on 12 May 2015 to bring in a streamlined system of registration for employment permits which is available to certain employers who are designated with Trusted Partner status.

---

67. *Besenyei v Rosderra Irish Meats Group Ltd and Rosderra Meats Group* UD37/2014.
68. *Hanlon v Smurfit Kappa Ireland Ltd t/a Smurfit Kappa Dublin* UD388/2014.
69. *Katherine Gordon & Co Ltd v Crowley O'Toole* HSD155.
70. *Boyraz v Turkey* Application No 61960/08.

INDUSTRIAL RELATIONS

Industrial Relations (Amendment) Act 2015

[1.39] A key development in 2015 was the enactment of the Industrial Relations (Amendment) Act 2015, which became effective on 1 August 2015. **CHAPTER 13** sets out the key provisions of the Act which creates a new regime for registered employment agreements (REAs), makes provision for sectoral employment orders (SEOs) and amends the Labour Court's jurisdiction to make legally binding determinations affecting non-union employees, first established by the Industrial Relations (Amendment) Act 2001.

Selected cases

[1.40] **CHAPTER 13** also contains a selection of cases under the Industrial Relations Acts and/or concerning collective bargaining issues in 2015.

Dispute resolution clauses in collective agreements

[1.41] In *ACC Loan Management Ltd v A Worker*[71] the Labour Court confirmed that where a collective agreement provides for a dispute resolution clause, it must be adhered to.

Introduction of GPS systems

[1.42] The installation of a GPS vehicle management system in a commercial fleet was upheld by the Labour Court in *UPC Ireland v Unite Services Industrial Professional Technical Union*.[72]

Trade union recognition

[1.43] In circumstances where the trade union, Unite, represented 20 employees, the Labour Court in *Mount Tabor Care Centre & Nursing Home v Unite*[73] recommended that the employer recognise Unite for collective bargaining purposes and that the parties should meet with a view to concluding a collective agreement.

Acting-up

[1.44] The entitlements of an employee who is acting-up in their role and their request for regularisation was considered by the Labour Court in *HSE West v A Worker*.[74]

---

71. *ACC Loan Management Ltd v A Worker* LCR 20902.
72. *UPC v Unite Services Industrial Professional Technical Union* LCR20938.
73. *Mount Tabor Care Centre & Nursing Home and Unite* LCR 20987.
74. *HSE West v A Worker* LCR21002.

Promotion

[1.45] In *IBM Ireland v A Worker*[75] the Labour Court was asked to consider whether the claimant had been unfairly overlooked for promotion where he was deemed to be ineligible to apply for internal roles, because his position was in scope for a transfer within the business.

Demotion

[1.46] The demotion of the claimant following a failed health and safety audit was considered by the Labour Court in *Keelings Logistics Solutions v A Worker*.[76] The Court concluded that the sanction, which was indefinite demotion, was excessive and recommended the claimant be reinstated in his role.

Performance management

[1.47] In *Matheson Solicitors v A Worker*[77] the Labour Court considered the introduction of a new performance management system by the respondent employer for its legal personal assistant staff.

Reassignment of employees

[1.48] In *HSE West v A Worker*,[78] the Labour Court considered the decision to reassign an employee to another position following deterioration in the working relationship between the employee and his colleagues such that their work was being adversely affected.

Elimination of night shift

[1.49] A proposal to eliminate a night shift and the consequent reduction in hours for three staff members was the subject of a referral to the Labour Court in *Kerry Women's Refuge & Support Services v Services Industrial Professional Technical Union (SIPTU)*.[79]

---

75. *IBM Ireland v A Worker* LCR 21019.
76. *Keelings Logistics Solutions v A Worker* AD1516.
77. *Matheson Solicitors v A Worker* LCR20931.
78. *HSE West v A Worker* AD1518.
79. *Kerry Women's Refuge & Support Services v SIPTU* LCR21042.

Transfer and redistribution of work

[1.50] In *An Post v CPSU*[80] the Labour Court considered whether the transfer and redistribution of work to employees based in Sligo was legitimate in circumstances where the respondent was in a position to offer voluntary redundancies to employees in Dublin.

INJUNCTIONS

[1.51] CHAPTER 14 contains a selection of High Court judgments delivered in 2015 to include an application to restrain picketing, an application to restrain a reassignment of position which proceeded to a full plenary hearing, and an application to restrain a dismissal.

University College Cork v Services Industrial Professional Technical Union and Irish Federation of University Teachers[81] is an important interlocutory decision of the High Court in relation to industrial action. The Court granted an injunction restraining the defendant trade unions from engaging in industrial action on the main campus of the plaintiff university in circumstances where they had an ongoing pay claim in respect of its members employed at the Tyndall Institute, a research institute situated 1km from the plaintiff's main campus. A key issue in the case was the extent to which the defendant unions had called on union members (who were employed at the main campus and were not party to the secret ballot) to engage in picketing.

In *Earley v The Health Service Executive*[82] the plaintiff sought to restrain a reassignment of her from her position as area director of nursing for the Galway Roscommon Mental Health Services. She also sought to restrain any appointment of a replacement to her role. The High Court granted the applications sought. In the plenary action[83] the plaintiff sought a declaration that the defendant's decision to temporarily reassign her from her role to an allegedly lesser role was unlawful. The Court rejected the plaintiff's claims and concluded that the defendant had acted in accordance with both its contractual entitlements and statutory obligations.

Boyle v An Post[84] is illustrative of the high bar facing plaintiff employees to seek to restrain the termination of their employment. In this case, the plaintiff, who was dismissed for misconduct under what he claimed were unfair procedures, failed to produce any evidence of bias against him and thus failed the *Maha Lingham*[85] test of a strong case that is likely to succeed.

---

80.   *An Post v CPSU* LCR 20929.
81.   *University College Cork v SIPTU and IFUT* [2015] IEHC 282.
82.   *Earley v The Health Service Executive* [2015] IEHC 520.
83.   *Earley v The Health Service Executive* [2015] IEHC 841.
84.   *Boyle v An Post* [2015] IEHC 589.
85.   *Maha Lingham v Health Service Executive* [2006] 17 ELR 140.

INSOLVENCY

[1.52] In *Glegola v The Minister for Social Protection Ireland and the Attorney General*,[86] an application for judicial review, which is noted in **CH 15**, the High Court considered whether the applicant was entitled to receive an award in respect of unfair dismissal and arrears of remuneration from the Insolvency Payments Scheme, in circumstances where there was a dispute before the Court as to whether the employer company had been placed in liquidation or whether it continued to trade.

JUDICIAL REVIEW

[1.53] **CHAPTER 16** notes several judicial review cases from 2015 which are relevant to employers and employees.

A recommendation of the Labour Court was challenged in *Mullally & Ors v The Labour Court and Waterford County Council (Notice Party)*[87] where it was asserted that the Court had failed to investigate a trade dispute.

In *Fassi v Dublin City University*[88] the High Court considered whether there existed a sufficient public element in the relationship between a PhD student and a university to render a decision about academic studies progression amenable to judicial review.

[1.54] In *Noel Recruitment (Ireland) Ltd v The Personal Injuries Assessment Board and Issak, otherwise known as Michael Chapwanya (Notice Party)*[89] the High Court considered whether the applicant was entitled to an order of *certiorari* where two separate authorisations were granted by the respondent to the notice party arising from the same workplace accident.

[1.55] In *Conroy v Board of Management of Gorey Community School*[90] the High Court considered whether the decision to remove the applicant from his position as chaplain of the school, and certain other restrictions placed on the applicant with regard to his interaction with students, had any public law element.

---

86. *Glegola v The Minister for Social Protection, Ireland and the Attorney General* [2015] IEHC 428.
87. *Mullally & Ors v The Labour Court and Waterford County Council (Notice Party)* [2015] IEHC 351.
88. *Fassi v Dublin City University* [2015] IEHC 38.
89. *Noel Recruitment (Ireland) Ltd v The Personal Injuries Assessment Board and Issak, otherwise known as Michael Chapwanya* [2015] IEHC 20.
90. *Conroy v Board of Management of Gorey Community School* [2015] IEHC 103.

LEGISLATION

[1.56] CHAPTER 17 contains a selection of legislation of relevance to employment, equality and industrial relations law, including Acts, Statutory Instruments and Bills published in 2015.

LITIGATION

Failure to give reasons for a decision

[1.57] The requirement on High Court judges to give reasons for their decisions was reiterated by the Court of Appeal in *Bank of Ireland Mortgage Bank v Heron and Heron*,[91] which is noted in CH 18.

Statute of Limitations

[1.58] In *Stapleton v St Colman's (Claremorris) Credit Union Ltd*[92] the High Court considered whether personal injury proceedings for occupational stress could be struck out for being statute barred where the plaintiff had been certified as unfit to work due to stress more than two years prior to the proceedings being commenced.

Claims in parallel

[1.59] In *Culkin v Sligo County Council*[93] the High Court considered s 101(2)(a) of the Employment Equality Acts 1998 to 2015 and whether the plaintiff's personal injury proceedings should be struck out as an abuse of process and/or a duplication of the plaintiff's equality claim.

Want of prosecution

[1.60] In *McLoughlin v Garvey*[94] the Court of Appeal considered whether the plaintiff's proceedings, which concerned allegations of sexual abuse against her defendant brother, should be struck out for want of prosecution because of inexcusable and inordinate delay. The Court was asked to consider whether the delay was excusable where the plaintiff cared for her son who had a serious and debilitating medical condition.

---

91. *Bank of Ireland Mortgage Bank v Heron and Heron* [2015] IECA 66.
92. *Stapleton v St Colman's (Claremorris) Credit Union Ltd* [2015] IEHC 510.
93. *Culkin v Sligo County Council* [2015] IEHC 46.
94. *McLoughlin v Garvey* [2015] IECA 80.

Frivolous and vexatious claims

[1.61] In *Harvey v The Courts Service & Ors*[95] there was an application to strike out proceedings initiated by a lay litigant on a number of grounds including that the procedures contained within the Rules of the Superior Courts had not been complied with and that the proceedings were frivolous and vexatious. The High Court addressed the administration of proceedings involving lay litigants, confirming that lay litigants are required to adhere to the legislative procedures in the same fashion as litigants with legal representation.

PART-TIME WORK

Pension rights

[1.62] CHAPTER 19 notes *Minister for Education and Science v The Labour Court (respondent), Boyle and the Committee of Management of Hillside Park Pre-School (Notice Parties)*,[96] which concerned a judicial review of a Labour Court decision. The High Court considered whether the claimant, a part-time teacher in a grant-aided school for children of the Traveller Community, was less favourably treated when she was not admitted to the National Teachers Superannuation Scheme. This decision involves extensive consideration of who the claimant's employer was under the Protection of Employees (Part-Time Work) Act 2001. The Court concluded that the Labour Court, in directing that the claimant be admitted to the Scheme, had gone beyond requiring an employer to cease less favourable treatment and therefore had acted *ultra vires*.

Pro rata temporis

CHAPTER 19 contains two decisions of the CJEU in relation to part-time workers and in relation to the principle of *pro rata temporis*.

In *Österreichischer Gewerkschaftsbund v Verband Österreichischer Banken und Bankiers*[97] the CJEU considered whether the calculation of a dependent child allowance, which was provided for in a collective agreement and paid to part-time employees in accordance with the principle of *pro rata temporis*, was in breach of the Framework Agreement on Part-Time Work.[98] In *Greenfield v The Care Bureau*[99] the CJEU

---

95. *Harvey v The Courts Service & Ors* [2015] IEHC 680.

96. *Minister for Education and Science v The Labour Court (respondent), Boyle and the Committee of Management of Hillside Park Pre-School (Notice Parties)* [2015] IEHC 429.

97. *Österreichischer Gewerkschaftsbund v Verband Österreichischer Banken und Bankiers* (Case C–476/12).

98. Framework Agreement on Part-Time Work annexed to Council Directive 97/81/EC concerning the Framework Agreement on Part-Time Work amended by Council Directive 98/23/EC.

99. *Greenfield v The Care Bureau* (Case C–219/14).

considered the application of the principle of *pro rata temporis* to annual leave entitlements.

PENSIONS

[1.63] CHAPTER 20 notes the key pensions-related policy and legislative developments in 2015 including the Government's annual Budget statement and the Finance Bill 2015, the Occupational Pension Scheme (Section 50 and 50B) (Amendment) Regulations 2015 and the Occupational Pension Schemes (Revaluation) Regulations 2015. Consideration is also given to the guidance provided by the Pensions Authority and the Revenue Commissioners in 2015.

CHAPTER 20 also contains a detailed synopsis of the material pensions cases determined in Ireland, the CJEU and in the UK. They cover topics as diverse as: age discrimination; an employer's liability to contribute to scheme in wind-up; the impact of the FEMPI legislation on a transferred-in pension pot; disability discrimination; sexual orientation/civil partner discrimination; changes to pensionable salary; the consequences of breach of the duty of good faith; personal liability of trustees; the meaning of accrued benefits; and the transfer of pensions-related data outside of the European Union.

PROTECTIVE LEAVE

[1.64] Whether or not there is an entitlement to paid maternity leave was considered by the Labour Court in *A Worker v Cork Association for Autism*,[100] which is noted in CH 21. The respondent employer had unilaterally withdrawn paid maternity leave as a cost-saving measure. The Court noted the claimant's express contractual entitlement to paid maternity leave benefit and recommended that payment be made.

The entitlement to a payment equivalent to maternity benefit or adoptive benefit from the Department of Social Protection, in circumstances where an employee becomes a parent by reason of a surrogacy arrangement, was considered by the High Court on appeal from the Circuit Court and the Equality Tribunal in *G v Department of Social Protection*.[101]

PUBLIC SERVANTS

[1.65] CHAPTER 22 notes a wide range of cases involving employees of public bodies and the State.

In *McEnery v Commissioner of An Garda Síochána*[102] the High Court was asked to review the decision to summarily dismiss a garda sergeant from employment following

---

100. *A Worker v Cork Association for Autism* LCR20906.
101. *G v Department of Social Protection* [2015] IEHC 419.
102. *McEnery v Commissioner of an Garda Síochána* [2014] IEHC 545.

her conviction for assault on a member of the public. The Court refused the application sought. However, Kelly J in the Court of Appeal[103] allowed the appeal and granted an order of *certiorari* quashing the decision of the Garda Commissioner to summarily dismiss the appellant garda.

Whether a redundancy was a breach of the Public Service Agreement was considered by the Labour Court in *Trinity College Dublin v Irish Federation of University Teachers*.[104]

In *Nic Bhrádaig v Employment Appeals Tribunal and Mount Anville Secondary School, Minister for Expenditure and Reform and Minister for Education and Skills (Notice Parties)*[105] the High Court, in a point of law appeal, affirmed the conclusion of the EAT that the claimant, an employee in a fee-paying private school, was a 'public servant' for the purposes of the Financial Emergency Measures in the Public Interest (No 2) Act 2009.

Two cases where the Labour Court was asked to consider whether roles are analogous for the purposes of determining appropriate rates of pay and previous service are noted in **CH 22**. In *National University of Ireland Galway v A Worker*[106] the Labour Court considered the roles of university fellow and university lecturer. In *University College Cork v A Worker*[107] the Court considered the roles of dental nurse and registered general nurse.

The practice of affording 'bank time' to local authority employees and a proposal to unilaterally end such a practice were considered by the Labour Court in *Dublin City Council v SIPTU & Anor*.[108]

In *Hosford v Minister for Social Protection*[109] the High Court considered whether the transfer of the applicant, a higher executive officer in the Department of Social Protection, from one position to another was *ultra vires* and unlawful.

A claim to have locally-agreed enhanced on-call rates restored was heard by the Labour Court in *St Vincent's University Hospital v Irish Nurses' and Midwives' Organisation (INMO)*.[110]

Whether or not the terms of the Circular on Revised Annual Leave Arrangements for Staff employed in Universities and Schools applied to staff of the Royal Irish Academy of Music was considered by the Labour Court in *Royal Irish Academy of Music v Services Industrial Professional Technical Union (SIPTU)*.[111]

---

103. *McEnery v Commissioner of an Garda Síochána* [2015] IECA 217.
104. *Trinity College Dublin v Irish Federation of University Teachers* LCR 20962.
105. *Nic Bhrádaig v Employment Appeals Tribunal and Mount Anville Secondary School, Minister for Expenditure and Reform and Minister for Education and Skills (Notice Parties)* [2015] IEHC 305.
106. *National University of Ireland Galway v A Worker* AD1529.
107. *University College Cork v A Worker* AD1540.
108. *Dublin City Council v SIPTU & Anor* LCR 20950.
109. *Hosford v Minister for Social Protection* [2015] IEHC 59.
110. *St Vincent's University Hospital v Irish Nurses' and Midwives' Organisation* CD/15/186; LCR21049.
111. *Royal Irish Academy of Music v SIPTU* CD/15/187; LCR21048.

Whether Government Ministers are entitled to restrict pension payments to a retired public servant was considered by the High Court in *The Minister for Education & Skills & Anor v The Pensions Ombudsman & Anor.*[112]

The assessment criteria used for an interview process to appoint an associate professor were examined by the Labour Court in *Trinity College Dublin v A Worker.*[113]

REDUNDANCY

[1.66] As the Irish economy recovered in 2015, there appears to be a welcome reduction in the numbers of large scale plant/firm closures and collective redundancies. Similarly the volume of redundancy cases appears to have levelled off.

Existence of a genuine redundancy

[1.67] The willingness of the EAT to look behind a redundancy to establish the underlying facts and to determine whether a genuine redundancy situation exists can be seen in several cases in **CH 23**.

In *Quinn (Junior) v Quinn Insurance Ltd*[114] the EAT considered the impersonal nature of a redundancy and held that the claimant's redundancy was not genuine, when viewed against the background of antagonistic relations between the parties.

In *Melia v M & J Gleeson & Co*[115] the EAT was satisfied that the stated reason for the redundancy, which was the loss of a major contract, was not a genuine redundancy in circumstances where the respondent did not actually lose the contract for another eight months after the dismissal took place.

In contrast, in *McDonald v Computer Placement Ltd*[116] the EAT accepted that a genuine redundancy situation did arise because of a reduction in the demand for health and safety consultancy services which necessitated a restructuring of the respondent's consultancy business.

In *Meekel v Delmec Engineering Ltd*[117] the EAT accepted the respondent was undergoing financial difficulties and required significant cost-cutting measures. However the EAT did not accept that the claimant's dismissal was wholly or mainly due to redundancy.

---

112. *Minister for Education & Skills & Anor v The Pensions Ombudsman & Anor* [2015] IEHC 792.
113. *Trinity College Dublin v A Worker* AD1552.
114. *Quinn (Junior) v Quinn Insurance Ltd* UD2415/2011.
115. *Melia v M & J Gleeson & Co* UD1569/2012.
116. *McDonald v Computer Placement Ltd* UD1551/2012.
117. *Meekel v Delmec Engineering Ltd* UD653/2013, PW265/2013.

Fair procedures

[1.68] *Kerrigan v Smurfit Kappa Ireland Ltd, c/o Smurfit Kappa Group*[118] is a redundancy case where the EAT considered a multiplicity of issues concerning the fairness of the procedures used by the employer, the selection criteria and also the validity of a settlement agreement signed by the claimant prior to the claim being initiated.

Voluntary redundancy/*ex-gratia* redundancy

[1.69] The legitimacy of an employer's decision to refuse an application for voluntary redundancy was considered by the Labour Court in *Business Mobile Security Ltd t/a Senaca Group v A Worker*.[119]

[1.70] In *Ages and Stages Crèche Dundalk v SIPTU*[120] the Labour Court recommended that the employer, which had closed because of financial difficulties but which was funded via a number of public agencies, should pay its staff *ex-gratia* redundancy payments of three weeks' pay per year of service. The Court recommended that the employer approach its funding agencies to source funding to meet these redundancy costs.

Conduct of an employee during a redundancy process

[1.71] *McDonnell v Barclays Insurance Dublin t/a Barclays Assurance Dublin Ltd*[121] is a case where the EAT considered the conduct of the employee during the redundancy process. The EAT noted that while the claimant had been given copious opportunities to prevent his redundancy, the employer was forced to take a stand at an end of a long period of 'prevarication' by the claimant and thus the subsequent redundancy was not unfair.

Selection for redundancy

[1.72] CHAPTER 23 includes several claims of unfair selection for redundancy. In each case the EAT shows a willingness to examine the selection criteria (if any) adopted by the employer and gives consideration as to whether the individual claimants were fairly selected for redundancy.

In *Dolan v Bruscar Bhearna Teoranta t/a Barna Waste*[122] the EAT was critical of the lack of any selection procedure and held the dismissal to be unfair.

---

118. *Kerrigan v Smurfit Kappa Ireland Ltd, c/o Smurfit Kappa Group* UD1921/2011.
119. *Business Mobile Security Ltd t/a Senaca Group v A Worker* AD151.
120. *Ages and Stages Crèche Dundalk v SIPTU* LCR 21017.
121. *McDonnell v Barclays Insurance Dublin t/a Barclays Assurance Dublin Ltd* UD 799/2013.
122. *Dolan v Bruscar Bhearna Teoranta t/a Barna Waste* UD762/2014.

In *Coad v Eurobase Ltd*[123] the EAT considered the selection criteria used by the employer in effecting redundancies and evaluated its stated need to retain key skills as a basis for selection. The EAT accepted that the employer had acted in good faith but noted that the procedures used were rushed and held that the claimant was unfairly selected.

A contrast can be seen in *Cranitch v Matflo Engineering Ltd*[124] where the EAT accepted that the respondent's redundancy selection was based on the needs of the business and that the four best workers with essential skills were retained. As the claimant's role as foreman was no longer required, his selection for redundancy was fair.

In *O'Connor v Cove Brewers Ltd t/a Cove Bar*[125] the EAT upheld the claim of unfair selection for redundancy and noted the lack of consultation with the claimant and the fact she had no opportunity to present alternatives. The fact that a new employee was hired prior to the claimant's dismissal was also noted by the EAT, who awarded compensation of €6,000.

The lack of any consultation with the claimant and any objective selection criteria were noted by the EAT in upholding the claim of unfair dismissal in *Morris v Callan Tansey Solicitors*.[126] The EAT noted that an alternative full-time role in Sligo, 48km from the claimant's home, was a not a viable proposition for the claimant, a part-time legal secretary.

[1.73] In *MacEvilly v KOD/Lyons Solicitors,*[127] the EAT considered the selection process used for redundancy where there was a merger of two law firms. The EAT concluded that the selection criteria were unfair.

Entitlement to a redundancy payment

[1.74] The entitlement to a redundancy payment in circumstances where the claimant was placed on suspension while his role ceased to exist was upheld by the EAT in *Ruane v Bridie Lyons t/a C Lyons Tractor Sales*.[128]

Offers of alternative employment

[1.75] Whether the offer of a position in another location was suitable alternative employment was examined in *Essalhi-Ferenc v Fitzers Holdings Ltd*.[129] It is noted that the EAT considered a variety of factors put forward by the claimant as to why the

---

123. *Coad v Eurobase Ltd* UD1138/2013.
124. *Cranitch v Matflo Engineering Ltd* UD1368/2013.
125. *O'Connor v Cove Brewers Ltd t/a Cove Bar* UD464/2014.
126. *Morris v Callan Tansey Solicitors* UD143/2014.
127. *MacEvilly v KOD/Lyons Solicitors* UD805/2013.
128. *Ruane v Bridie Lyons t/a C Lyons Tractor Sales* RP159/2012, MN174/2012.
129. *Essalhi-Ferenc v Fitzers Holdings Ltd* RP94/2014.

alternative role was not suitable such as location, travel time, travel costs and childminding arrangements.

The timing of an offer of alternative employment, which came in the course of a 30-day consultation period but after the claimant regarded himself as having been made redundant, was considered by the EAT in *McBride v Ladbroke (Ireland) Ltd.*[130]

Termination of employment at the end of an apprenticeship

[1.76] Is there an entitlement to a redundancy payment at the end of an apprenticeship training programme? This was considered by the EAT, in *Toomey v Hemblestan Ltd t/a Dungarvan Nissan,*[131] which did not uphold the claim for the payment.

Collective redundancy

[1.77] CHAPTER 23 notes an opinion from an Advocate General and three decisions of the CJEU on collective redundancy law.

The Opinion of the Advocate General in *Lyttle & Ors v Bluebird UK Bidco 2 Ltd*[132] is significant for its consideration of what was the exact scope of the concept of 'establishment' referred to in art 1(a)(ii) of Directive 98/59/EC.[133] In its judgment, the CJEU subsequently confirmed that the concept of establishment must be construed in the same way in both sections of art 1(a) of the Directive.

A similar outcome can be seen in the '*Woolworths*'[134] case and in *Canas v Nexea Gestion Documental SA, Fondo de Garantia Salarial.*[135]

TAXATION RELATING TO EMPLOYMENT

[1.78] CHAPTER 24 considers developments in tax law relative to employment in 2015.

Key changes to note include the Budget for 2016, which was announced by the Minister for Finance on 13 October 2015 (Budget Day 2015) and which changed USC rates and thresholds, introduced a PRSI tiered credit system for lower income workers and extended the USC exemption for employer contributions to PRSAs. Other developments include the introduction of the Employment and Investment Incentive

---

130. *McBride v Ladbroke (Ireland) Ltd* RP788/2014.
131. *Toomey v Hemblestan Ltd t/a Dungarvan Nissan* RP1071/2013; MN779/2013.
132. *Lyttle & Ors v Bluebird UK Bidco 2 Ltd* (Case C–182/13); *Rabal Canas v Nexea Gestion Documental SA, Fondo de Garantia Salarial* (Case C–392/13); and *Union of Shop, Distributive and Allied Workers, Wilson v WW Realisation 1 Ltd & Ors* (Case C–80/14).
133. Council Directive 98/59/EC on the approximation of the laws of Member States relating to Collective Redundancies.
134. *Union of Shop, Distributive and Allied Workers (USDAW), Wilson v WW Realisation, No 1 Ltd in Liquidation, Ethel Austin Ltd and Secretary for State for Business, Innovation and Skills* (Case C–80/14).
135. *Canas v Nexea Gestion Documental SA, Fondo de Garantia Salarial* (Case C–392/13).

Scheme and changes introduced by the Finance Act 2015 in relation to the expenses of non-Irish Resident Non–Executive Directors.

TEMPORARY AGENCY WORK

[1.79] CHAPTER 25 notes cases that consider the definition of pay in the Protection of Employees (Temporary Agency Work) Act 2012 and whether subsistence pay and pay in respect of travel time could be offset against arrears of wages. Those are the Labour Court decisions in *Paul Doyle Hire Services Ltd v Furlong*[136] and *Paul Doyle Hire Services Ltd v Stafford*.[137] Both cases also considered whether the time limits for bringing a claim under the 2012 Act could be extended in each case for reasonable cause.

TRANSFER OF UNDERTAKINGS

[1.80] CHAPTER 26 notes the decision of the CJEU in *da Silva e Brito & Ors v Estado Portugues*[138] relating to intra-group transfers.

In *Brady v McNamara*[139] the EAT considered preliminary and substantive issues as to whether the claimant, a court messenger with the Sheriff for County Cork, transferred to the newly appointed County Sheriff. These cases are significant as they contain detailed reasoning by the EAT on various aspects of the 2003 Regulations, addressing the circumstances which may constitute a transfer under the 2003 Regulations, and the obligations upon a transferor and a transferee under the applicable Irish law.

In *Deveci & Ors v Scandinavian Airlines System Denmark-Norway-Sweden*[140] the EFTA (European Free Trade Agreement) Court considered whether a transferee was permitted to apply its own collective agreement to transferring employees, on cessation of the collective agreement which was applicable to those employees, where this resulted in pay reductions for those employees.

Salmon v Castlebeck Care (Teesdale) Ltd & Anor[141] is an important decision of the UK EAT which considered who had the contractual obligation to hear and determine a disciplinary appeal of a dismissal effected pre-transfer. The UK EAT also examined the effect of a successful appeal in such circumstances where the transfer had taken effect, and held that the effect of the appeal was to revive the contract of employment.

Ansari v Lodge Services Dublin Ltd and Albany House[142] is a case where the parties disputed whether a transfer of undertakings occurred. The EAT examined the evidence

---

136. *Paul Doyle Hire Services Ltd v Furlong* AWD1512.
137. *Paul Doyle Hire Services Ltd v Stafford* AWD1513.
138. *da Silva e Brito & Ors v Estado Portugues* (Case C–160/14).
139. *Brady v McNamara* TU36/2014.
140. *Deveci & Ors v Scandinavian Airlines System Denmark-Norway-Sweden* (Case E–10/14).
141. *Salmon v Castlebeck Care (Teesdale) Ltd (In administration) & Anor* [2015] IRLR 189.
142. *Ansari v Lodge Services Dublin Ltd and Albany House* UD792/2014, MN403/2014.

and held that a transfer did not take place and thus the decision to dismiss the claimant was unfair.

UNFAIR DISMISSAL
Preliminary issues

[1.81] A wide variety of preliminary issues have again been raised in unfair dismissal cases. CHAPTER 27 notes a number of such claims from 2015, including whether the claimant is an employee or self-employed contractor;[143] whether a break of eight days between employment contracts was sufficient to break continuous service;[144] whether the claim is statute barred when the complaint form was submitted one day outside the statutory time limit;[145] whether the medical condition of the claimant constituted exceptional circumstances to extend the time limit to bring a claim;[146] whether a failure on the part of the claimant's solicitor to prosecute the claim within the statutory time limits justifies an extension of the time limit;[147] and whether a claim lodged in advance of the date of dismissal can be heard.[148]

Agency workers – section 13 of the Unfair Dismissals (Amendment) Act 1993

[1.82] CHAPTER 27 notes two important cases which consider s 13 of the Unfair Dismissal (Amendment) Act 1993, a much overlooked statutory provision.

Dunphy v Industrial Temps Ltd t/a Industrial Temps & Anor[149] is a reminder to all end-user companies to take control of any investigation or disciplinary process that might ultimately result in liability under the 1993 Act and to ensure an appropriate commercial agreement is in place with an employment agency which contains indemnification in respect of such liability.

In *Granaghan v DSV Solutions Ltd*[150] the wrong entity (the employment agency) was named on the original complaint form and was subsequently released by the EAT in recognition of s 13. However a subsequent attempt by the claimant to have the form corrected against the end user company (some 18 months after the original claim) in reliance on s 13 was rejected by the EAT.

---

143. *Kearney v Seel Publishing Ltd (in liq) t/a North County Leader* UD258/2013.
144. *Kenyon v Macxchange Ltd t/a Compu B* UD132/2014.
145. *Ali Raza Khan v Deeal Retail Ltd* UD1722/2013.
146. *Cronin v Rigney Dolphin* UD589/2015.
147. *Duffin v St James's Hospital* UD924/2014.
148. *Neeson v John O'Rourke & Seán O'Rourke Chartered Accountants* UD2049/2011.
149. *Dunphy v Industrial Temps Ltd t/a Industrial Temps & Anor* UD718/2014, MN986/2012.
150. *Granaghan v DSV Solutions Ltd* UD1249/2013.

Involvement of third parties

[1.83] What does an employer do when one of its employees is refused access to a site by a client following an incident? The difficulties faced by the respondent in this situation were noted by the EAT in *Kelly v Kelco Services Ltd*.[151]

Expiry of a fixed-term contract

[1.84] In *Simpson v Applus Car Testing Service Ltd t/a National Car Testing Services Ltd*[152] the EAT considered whether the expiry and non-renewal of a fixed-term contract was an unfair dismissal.

Dismissals on grounds of performance or capability

[1.85] The obligations and challenges facing an employer when contemplating a dismissal on grounds of performance and/or capability are evident from the selected 2015 cases in **CH 27**.

In *Counter Products Marketing (Ireland) Ltd v Mulcahy*[153] the EAT found that the dismissal of an employee for consistent failure to meet performance targets was unfair. Similarly in *Noreika v The Printed Image Ltd*[154] the dismissal of the claimant following a progressive set of disciplinary warnings arising from his work performance, attitude, aggressive behaviour and conduct towards his work colleagues was held to be procedurally unfair insofar as he was not represented at disciplinary meetings, had no opportunity to confront his accusers, and was offered no right of appeal.

A contrast can be seen in *Corbett v Harvey Norman Trading (Ireland) Ltd*.[155] a case which clearly shows the requirements on an employer to fairly dismiss on performance grounds. In that case, the EAT held that the respondent had acted fairly and reasonably and refused to uphold the claim. In *Morrison v Tesco Ireland Ltd*[156] the dismissal of the claimant was held to be reasonable in circumstances where the claimant was unable to perform his job to the requisite minimum work standards.

Dismissals on grounds of capacity or illness

[1.86] While the right to dismiss on grounds of capacity is recognised in the Unfair Dismissals Acts 1977 to 2015, **CH 27** notes three cases which emphasise that employers

---

151. *Kelly v Kelco Services Ltd* UD638/2014, MN298/2014.
152. *Simpson v Applus Car Testing Service Ltd t/a National Car Testing Services Ltd* UD72/2013.
153. *Counter Products Marketing (Ireland) Ltd v Mulcahy* UD1419/2013.
154. *Noreika v The Printed Image Ltd* UD245/2013.
155. *Corbett v Harvey Norman Trading (Ireland) Ltd* UD1626/2013.
156. *Morrison v Tesco Ireland Ltd* UD1470/2013.

must obtain expert medical opinion before taking any action to bring employment to an end.

In *Hayes v Boliden Tara Mines Ltd*[157] the EAT considered the dismissal of the claimant in circumstances where he was medically unfit to engage in mining duties and was not fit for any alternative duties that required physical or manual handling tasks or normal shift hours. *Hoey v White Horse Insurance Ireland Ltd*[158] is an example of a case where an employer's failure to consider medical advice when deciding to dismiss an employee on grounds of incapacity was criticised by the EAT. Similarly, in *Ward v Coverall Courier Services Ltd*[159] the respondent's failure to obtain its own medical evidence prior to the dismissal of the claimant for incapacity, in circumstances where the claimant was certified fit to work by his own medical team, was held to be an unfair dismissal.

The duty on an employer to make contact with an employee, who had been on certified sick leave but stopped putting in medical certificates, was considered by the EAT in *Cunningham v Premco Distributors Ltd*.[160]

Retirement

[1.87] The legitimacy of a decision to terminate employment on reaching the age of 65 was considered by the EAT in *O'Connor v Beaufield Mews Ltd t/a Beaufield Mews Restaurant*[161] where it, in a majority decision, held the dismissal not to be unfair.

Automatically unfair dismissals—pregnancy

[1.88] *O'Brien v Thomas Kiely t/a Thomas Kiely Catering*[162] is an example of a case where the respondent employer was able to establish that the claimant was not dismissed by reason of her pregnancy.

Dismissal on grounds of conduct

Misuse of email/suspension

[1.89] The most notable unfair dismissal case of 2015 was the High Court decision in *The Governor and Company of the Bank of Ireland v Reilly*[163] where an order of reinstatement was made. The claimant was dismissed following the discovery of inappropriate material on his work email account contrary to the Bank's email policy.

---

157. *Hayes v Boliden Tara Mines Ltd* UD1218/2014.
158. *Hoey v White Horse Insurance Ireland Ltd* UD1519/2013, MN118/2014.
159. *Ward v Coverall Courier Services Ltd* UD1263/2013.
160. *Cunningham v Premco Distributors Ltd* UD1666/2013.
161. *O'Connor v Beaufield Mews Ltd t/a Beaufield Mews Restaurant* UD556/2013.
162. *O'Brien v Thomas Kiely t/a Thomas Kiely Catering* UD325/2013.
163. *The Governor and Company of the Bank of Ireland v Reilly* [2015] IEHC 241.

Noonan J's decision is particularly noteworthy for the guidance it provides for employers on how to handle an investigation and disciplinary process in circumstances of suspected or alleged misconduct. Particularly noteworthy is the finding of the High Court that, because of its potential impact on an employee's reputation, suspension on full pay pending the outcome of an investigation should only be used when the circumstances warrant it and should not be a blanket step in every investigative process.

Gross misconduct

[1.90] CHAPTER 27 contains a wide range of examples of gross misconduct cases decided in 2015. What is clear from the case law is that the establishment of gross misconduct remains difficult for employers and such a finding should not be arrived at lightly, without due regard to the proportionality of the sanction in the context of the particular conduct at issue. The requirements of fair procedures continue to be examined carefully by the EAT and Superior Courts and it is noted that orders of reinstatement and re-engagement continue to be made, even in cases involving gross misconduct where some time has elapsed since the initial decision to dismiss.

Altercations/assault

[1.91] In *Harris v Tesco Ireland Ltd*[164] the EAT upheld the dismissal of the claimant who had a physical altercation with a customer. A similar outcome can be seen in *Cooper v Johnston Mooney & O'Brien Bakeries*[165] which involved an altercation between colleagues. A contrast in approach is evident in *Kinsella v Securitas Security Services Ltd*[166] and *Lewental v Securitas Security Services Ltd*[167] where the EAT held that the dismissal of two security officers for an alleged misuse of force was unfair.

Breach of trust/dishonesty

[1.92] CHAPTER 27 includes a range of employment cases which concern allegations of dishonesty,[168] the removal of food items[169] and breach of trust and confidence.[170]

The potentially serious consequences of a decision to cover for a colleague who had left his work station was noted by the EAT in *Kalinins v ISS Ireland Ltd t/a ISS Facility Services*.[171]

---

164. *Harris v Tesco Ireland Ltd* UD1661/2012.
165. *Cooper v Johnston Mooney & O'Brien Bakeries* UD169/2014.
166. *Kinsella v Securitas Security Services Ltd* UD1119/2012.
167. *Lewental v Securitas Security Services Ltd* UD1124/2012.
168. *Cullen v McGrath t/a The Bridgend Bar* UD1298/2013.
169. *Cottingham v Wine Street Bakeries t/a O'Hehirs Bakery* UD211/2013; *Fogarty v Byrne t/a Gala Service Station* UD453/2013, UD358/2013.
170. *Byrne v St Pauls Garda Medical Aid Society* UD397/2013; *Akinfaye v Tesco Ireland Ltd* UD630/2012.
171. *Kalinins v ISS Ireland Ltd t/a ISS Facility Services* UD1508/2012.

Breach of cash-handling procedures

[1.93] *Oney v Persian Properties t/a O'Callaghan Hotels*[172] and *Pender v Woodies DIY Ltd t/a Woodies DIY and Garden Centres Arena*[173] are two similar cases before the EAT in relation to breaches of cash-handling procedures which had contrasting outcomes.

Breach of confidentiality

[1.94] *Forder v AV Pound & Company Ltd*[174] concerned a dismissal for sending emails containing confidential company information to a competitor. The EAT considered the claimant's duty of confidentiality, the duty not to establish a competing business, her failure to follow reasonable management instructions and the breach of her duty of fidelity to her employer.

The EAT decision in *Anderson v O'Connor & O'Connor t/a OCPM Property Consultants*[175] is noteworthy as it is critical of the conduct of both employer and employee in a summary dismissal. The employee's actions in downloading the respondent's software and removing files and the respondent's procedural failures resulted in a finding of unfair dismissal with no compensation awarded.

Garda vetting

[1.95] **CHAPTER 27** contains several important cases relating to the disclosure of pre-existing criminal convictions and the responses of each employer.[176]

One such case is *Donoghue v Dublin West Home Help Ltd*[177] where the EAT found that the dismissal of a home help carer was reasonable in light of the fact that the employee had failed to disclose prior convictions and the fact that three convictions had been imposed during the course of her employment. The EAT made this finding on the basis that the employer had acted reasonably (despite some procedural defects at appeal stage) and despite the fact that the employee had committed the offences under duress from her husband.

Unauthorised use of internet

[1.96] The challenges facing employers in managing the use of computers and social media in the workplace can be seen in **CH 27**. A decision to dismiss for unauthorised use

---

172. *Oney v Persian Properties t/a O'Callaghan Hotels* UD543/2014.
173. *Pender v Woodies DIY Ltd t/a Woodies DIY and Garden Centres Arena* UD460/2014.
174. *Forder v AV Pound & Company Ltd* UD927/2011, MN1057/2011, WT385/2011.
175. *Anderson v O'Connor & O'Connor t/a OCPM Property Consultants* UD954/2013, WT169/2015.
176. *O'Connell v An Post, General Post Office* UD47/2014; *Keogh v Cloverland Healthcare Ltd* UD439/2013; *Stynes v Cloverland Healthcare Ltd* UD384/2013.
177. *Donoghue v Dublin West Home Help Ltd* UD691/2014.

of the internet on a restricted computer in the course of a night shift was held to be unfair because of procedural failings in *Dempsey v Righpur Ltd t/a Boru Stoves.*[178]

Social media

[1.97] In *Brown v The Mountview/Blakestown/Hartstown/Huntstown Community Drugs Team Ltd t/a Adapt*[179] a dismissal for allegedly unacceptable use of Facebook by the claimant was held to be unfair although the EAT was critical of the claimant's actions which were described as reckless and a serious error of judgment.

Use of iPad while driving

[1.98] In *Purcell v Last Passive Ltd t/a Aircoach*[180] a decision to dismiss the claimant for using an iPad while driving an Aircoach was upheld.

Falling asleep at work

[1.99] CHAPTER 27 notes two cases where the claimants, one a care assistant in a psychiatric hospital/care home,[181] and the other a call centre operative responsible for answering emergency 999 calls,[182] were both alleged to have fallen asleep while at work and were subsequently dismissed. The EAT upheld both claims of unfair dismissal.

Persistent absenteeism

[1.100] In *Wall v Paul Doyle Hire Services Ltd*[183] the claimant was dismissed for consistent absenteeism and failure to adhere to the respondent's procedures for absenteeism. The EAT concluded that the respondent should have been a little more considerate in its dealings with the claimant and specifically around the challenging circumstances that contributed to the claimant's absence that led to his ultimate dismissal. The EAT concluded that, while an employer might have considered that some sanction was necessary, a reasonable employer would not have applied a sanction of outright dismissal on that occasion. However, the EAT did have regard to the claimant's own contribution to his ultimate dismissal when measuring the compensation awarded.

---

178. *Dempsey v Righpur Ltd t/a Boru Stoves* UD204/2014.
179. *Brown v The Mountview/Blakestown/Hartstown/Huntstown Community Drugs Team Ltd t/a Adapt* UD1447/2014.
180. *Purcell v Last Passive Ltd t/a Aircoach* UD1223/2014, MN745/2013.
181. *Malijs v Bloomfield Care Centre Ltd* UD1164/2013, TE158/2013.
182. *Marshall v Conduit Enterprise Ltd* UD1293/2013.
183. *Wall v Paul Doyle Hire Services Ltd* UD 458/2014.

Breach of company procedures

[1.101] The requirement to observe company procedure exists in every workplace; however, the EAT has recognised that in certain industries and sectors, such procedures are safety critical. In two featured cases from 2015,[184] both of which concern the aviation sector, the EAT recognised the importance of the employer's procedures in each case and the fact that said procedures were known to each employee and that training had been provided in respect of same. The EAT upheld the decision to dismiss as being fair in each case.

The dismissal of the claimant in *Gould* for his failure to conduct security searches of an aircraft before a transatlantic flight in accordance with policy and statutory procedure was held not to be unfair, despite there being some procedural deficiencies in the disciplinary process. In *Ijusonuwe* the dismissal of the claimant for his breach of the respondent's check-in and safety procedures was similarly held to be not unfair in all of the circumstances.

Lack of engagement

[1.102] In *Finegan v PhoneWatch Ltd*[185] the Circuit Court upheld an EAT finding that the claimant's failure to engage with his employer and its grievance and disciplinary procedure and his failure to comply with new roster arrangements meant that his dismissal for gross misconduct was not unfair. A similar outcome can be seen in *Kearns v Provident Personal Credit Ltd,*[186] where the EAT was critical of the claimant for his refusal to provide an explanation to his employer for an unusual transaction to which he was party. The EAT held that the claimant's failure to engage with his employer in a sensible way left the respondent with no option but to assume the worst and to dismiss him for gross misconduct, which was not unfair.

In *McNamara v Board of Management of St Joseph's National School*[187] the employee had been on sick leave for a prolonged period and refused to engage with the employer. The EAT had no hesitation in finding the termination of the claimant's contract with the respondent was not unfair, but wholly and completely justified.

Drug and alcohol screening

[1.103] A dismissal for a refusal to participate in random drug and alcohol screening was held to be unfair by the EAT in *Wojciechowski, Olszewski, Smiecinski v PRL Group.*[188]

---

184. *Gould v ICTS Ireland Ltd and ICTS UK Ltd* UD301/2013, MN154/2013, WT38/2013; *Ijisonuwe v Aer Lingus Ltd* UD27/2013.
185. *Finegan v PhoneWatch Ltd* Circuit Court Record No 006752/14 (Note: under appeal).
186. *Kearns v Provident Personal Credit Ltd* UD1652/2013.
187. *McNamara v Board of Management of St Joseph's National School* UD846/2012.
188. *Wojciechowski, Olszewski, Smiecinski v PRL Group* UD1543/2013, UD1551/2013, UD1565/2013.

Fair procedures

[1.104] Employers continue to have difficulty with the rigorous requirements of fair procedures. CHAPTER 27 contains a selection of 2015 decisions which demonstrate areas where employers have struggled in this area.

Employers who fail to use any process and procedures in effecting a dismissal will almost certainly be the subject of an adverse finding. *Frawley v Lionbridge International*[189] is an example where, in the absence of any procedures, the claimant was awarded €94,000 in compensation.

The role of human resources departments in a disciplinary process and the extent to which advice was provided to a decision-maker in a disciplinary process was considered in a noteworthy case by the UK EAT in *Ramphal v Department for Transport.*[190] The UK EAT concluded that there had been improper influence on the decision-maker by the human resources department which led to a change in the outcome of the investigation process and the sanction imposed.

The importance of transparency in any investigation and disciplinary process cannot be emphasised enough. Employees must be provided with all relevant materials related to the issue of concern.[191]

Murphy v DWG Refrigeration Wholesale Ltd[192] is a case where a full re-hearing at appeal stage was held by the EAT to have cured the defects in the original disciplinary process.

Employees must be advised of the potential adverse outcome of an investigative or disciplinary process in advance.[193]

Where an employer dismisses for gross misconduct, there must be evidence of wrongdoing on the part of the claimant and a process must be afforded to the claimant.[194]

Previous involvement of decision-makers

[1.105] The fact that a claimant did not participate in a disciplinary process because he regarded it as unfair was not fatal to his unfair dismissal claim in *Young v Tower Brook Ltd t/a Castle Durrow House Hotel.*[195] The EAT noted that the process was conducted by the two members of management who were involved in a previous altercation with the claimant and thus the claimant could not be faulted for not engaging with a fundamentally flawed process.

---

189. *Frawley v Lionbridge International* UD1627/2013.
190. *Ramphal v Department for Transport* UKEAT/0352/14/DA.
191. *Old v Palace Fields Primary Academy* UKEAT/0085/14/BA.
192. *Murphy v DWG Refrigeration Wholesale Ltd* UD 215/2013, MN128/2013.
193. *Fahavane Ltd v Flood* UD1719/2013.
194. *O'Halloran v Ballykisteen Hotel Ltd* UD625/2013, MN322/2013.
195. *Young v Tower Brook Ltd t/a Castle Durrow House Hotel* UD1598/2013, MN783/2013.

Delay

[1.106] Fair procedures require an expeditious process. In *Godsland v Applus Car Testing Ltd*[196] a delay of 12 months between the incident of misconduct and the subsequent investigation and disciplinary process, which was not explained by the respondent, were held by the EAT to have undermined the decision to dismiss. In *Dubrowski v Strathroy Dairy*[197] the EAT held that a delay of 18 months from the time of being made aware of alleged issues and the decision to dismiss, had dissipated the reasonableness of taking action against the claimant.

Trade union representation

[1.107] A failure to allow trade union representation in a disciplinary process was criticised by the EAT in *Leigh v SpeedKing Couriers Ltd t/a Fastway Couriers (Midlands)*.[198]

Need to ensure claimant comprehends process

[1.108] The decision of the claimant to sell alcohol to a minor in a Garda test purchase led to her dismissal which was challenged in *Perenc v Dunnes Stores*.[199] However the EAT was critical of the respondent's investigative and disciplinary process and was particularly concerned that the claimant appeared to have difficulty with the English language and was extremely passive in each of the meetings held with her. The EAT noted that the claimant's lack of confidence with English raised doubts as to whether she understood the severity of the consequences she faced and hampered her ability to articulate her position.

Appropriateness and proportionality of sanction of dismissal

[1.109] The appropriateness and proportionality of any disciplinary sanction must be carefully considered. In *Sadowska v Players Leisure Ltd t/a Players Leisure Ltd,*[200] the failure to take into account the claimant's length of service and to consider alternatives to dismissal was criticised by the EAT.

In *Rafter v Connaught Gold Co-Op-Aurivo Co-Op Society Ltd t/a Aurivo Co-Operative Society Ltd*[201] the EAT held that the claimant's dismissal was unfair because

---

196.   *Godsland v Applus Car Testing Ltd* UD1422/2013.
197.   *Dubrowski v Strathroy Dairy (ROI)* UD468/2014, MN196/2014.
198.   *Leigh v SpeedKing Couriers Ltd t/a Fastway Couriers (Midlands)* UD28/2014, MN484/2014.
199.   *Perenc v Dunnes Stores* UD1441/2013.
200.   *Sadowska v Players Leisure Ltd t/a Players Leisure Ltd* UD1658/2013, MN707/2013.
201.   *Rafter v Connaught Gold Co-Op-Aurivo Co-Op Society Ltd t/a Aurivo Co-Operative Society Ltd* UD48/2014.

the evidence in relation to his alleged gross misconduct was inconclusive. The dismissal was also considered to be disproportionate when viewed in light of the claimant's long and unblemished employment history with the respondent.

Custom and practice

[1.110] It is often the case that employees will explain their conduct by reference to custom and practice. Two such cases where the conduct of each employee resulted in dismissals that were held by the EAT to be unfair were *Coady v Oxigen Environmental*[202] and *Casserley and Foy v AGI Media Packaging (Dublin) Ltd*.[203]

Constructive dismissal

[1.111] There has been a noticeable increase in the volume of constructive dismissal cases. The bar remains extremely high for an employee to prove he or she was justified in resigning. However 2015 has seen a considerable number of important claims of constructive dismissal which have been upheld.

The most significant of these cases was *Smith v RSA Insurance Ireland Ltd*.[204] It is not often that an EAT decision will make the front page of the national media but this case is probably the most widely reported dismissal case of 2015. In this constructive dismissal claim by the former CEO of the respondent, the EAT, in a lengthy and detailed decision, was critical of the respondent for its treatment of Mr Smith, particularly with regards to its decision to announce the suspension of Mr Smith on television. Mr Smith's claim was upheld by the EAT and he was awarded compensation of €1.25 million, a decision which was appealed to the Circuit Court.

When it comes to wages it is clear from *Kilkerr v Burke Fabrications Ltd*[205] that part-payment and even late payment of wages may be regarded as a fundamental breach of contract which can justify a decision to resign. In *Lai v Brophy & Co Chartered Accountants*[206] the EAT confirmed that a failure to pay the claimant's salary on an ongoing basis, which resulted in significant back pay owing to him, justified the claimant's decision to terminate his employment and his claim for constructive dismissal succeeded. In *Lynch v Donegal Highland Radio Ltd t/a Highland Radio*[207] a unilateral reduction in salary amounted to a constructive dismissal.

Where there are unilateral changes to terms and conditions of employment a constructive dismissal situation may arise in certain circumstances. Factors such as

---

202. *Coady v Oxigen Environmental* UD1048/2013.
203. *Casserley and Foy v AGI Media Packaging (Dublin) Ltd* UD520/2013, MN291/2013, UD521/2013, MN292/2013.
204. *Smith v RSA Insurance Ireland Ltd* UD1673/2013. (Note: Appealed to Circuit Court.)
205. *Kilkerr v Burke Fabrications Ltd* UD470/2013, WT70/2013.
206. *Lai v Brophy & Co Chartered Accountants* UD281/2014, RP115/2014, MN105/2015, WT38/2014.
207. *Lynch v Donegal Highland Radio Ltd t/a Highland Radio* UD1599/2013, MN758/2013.

whether there was a lack of engagement by the employer,[208] a lack of consultation with employees, and/or whether the change in terms is less favourable or amounts to a demotion will be relevant.[209] Whether or not the employee has agreed or affirmed the changes will need to be considered. Note that in *Adjei-Frempong v Howard Frank Ltd*[210] the UK EAT held that an employee should not have been considered to have 'affirmed' the unilateral change to his terms and conditions of employment in circumstances where he was out of work on sick leave for a period of time before his resignation. What is stated in the contract of employment will also be relevant.

In *Hart v St Mary's School (Colchester) Ltd*[211] the UK EAT overturned the finding of the employment tribunal that the wording of the appellant's contract of employment was sufficiently clear as to confer a power of unilateral variation on the respondent. In S*mith v Campbell Wallcoverings Ltd t/a House of Tiles*[212] a unilateral change in the place of work was held to amount to constructive dismissal.

Can a decision to refuse full-time work justify a decision to resign and claim constructive dismissal? In *O'Grady v Kellysdan Ltd t/a McDonalds*[213] the reasonableness of the employer in handling the request was considered.

Performance management

[1.112] **CHAPTER 27** notes three cases[214] where employees chose to resign and claim constructive dismissal in the course of a performance management process, of which only one claim was upheld by the EAT.[215] These cases demonstrate the importance of managing performance in accordance with a clearly defined process or procedure.

Failure to deal with complaints

[1.113] The onus on an employer to investigate any complaints of which it has notice was emphasised by the EAT in *Ogbulafor v Laois County Childcare Committee Ltd*[216] where the employer's failure to deal with a bullying complaint and the subsequent resignation of the claimant was held to be constructive dismissal.

The high bar on claimants in proving constructive dismissal cases was emphasised by the EAT in *Byrne v Horwath Bastow Charleston Wealth Management Ltd*[217] which

---

208. *O'Connell v Melvyn Hanley Solicitors* UD75/2014, MN33/2014.

209. *McCarthy v O'Shea, O'Lionaird Parnership t/a Bebé Crèche* UD2050/2011, MN2072/2011.

210. *Adjei-Frempong v Howard Frank Ltd* UKEAT/0044/15/DM.

211. *Hart v St Mary's School (Colchester) Ltd* UKEAT/0305/14/DM.

212. *Smith v Campbell Wallcoverings Ltd t/a House of Tiles* UD1520/2013.

213. *O'Grady v Kellysdan Ltd t/a McDonalds* UD338/2013.

214. *Young v Bioshell Teoranta* UD988/2012; *Rock v Irish Custom Extruders Ltd* UD614/2013; *Ojha v Harry Corry Ltd* UD848/2013.

215. *Young v Bioshell Teoranta* UD988/2012.

216. *Ogbulafor v Laois County Childcare Committee Ltd* UD1479/2013.

217. *Byrne v Horwath Bastow Charleston Wealth Management Ltd* UD67/2014.

concerned the decision of the claimant to resign having raised a grievance and complaint of bullying and harassment against her manager. The EAT noted that the claimant had not exhausted all internal avenues before resigning and that the respondent had made reasonable and genuine attempts to resolve the situation.

Unworkable employment relationship

[1.114] *Obst v Bodyblast Fitness Ltd t/a Women's Fitness Plus*[218] is a case where the EAT described the employment relationship between the parties as unworkable, but stopped short of upholding the claim of constructive dismissal.

Procedural failings in an investigation

[1.115] In *Rawski v Callan Bacon Company Ltd*[219] the EAT determined that, in all of the circumstances, the claimant was entitled to resign and that it was reasonable for him to do so. The EAT was critical of the respondent's investigation and communications with the claimant who was not a native English speaker. The EAT stated that it was simply unacceptable that, in a workplace where there is a multi-national workforce, employees would be denied access to copies of documents fundamental to their contractual relationships with their employer in their respective native languages.

Lack of support

[1.116] Constructive dismissal can also arise by reason of omissions on the part of an employer. *Hawkins v Arvagh Area Childcare Ltd t/a Busy Bees*[220] illustrates that the failure of an inexperienced management team to support the claimant in her employment did amount to constructive dismissal.

Flawed recruitment process

[1.117] The way in which an internal recruitment process was conducted, which led to the claimant being forced into accepting a retirement package, was sufficient to give rise to a constructive dismissal situation in *Healy v Kerry County Council (formerly Killarney Town Council)*.[221]

---

218. *Obst v Bodyblast Fitness Ltd t/a Women's Fitness Plus* UD196/2013.
219. *Rawski v Callan Bacon Company Ltd* UD529/2014.
220. *Hawkins v Arvagh Area Childcare Ltd t/a Busy Bees* UD638/2013.
221. *Healy v Kerry County Council (formerly Killarney Town Council)* UD730/2012.

Where the fact of resignation is in doubt

[1.118] CHAPTER **27** includes several cases where the fact of resignation was in doubt.[222]

Redress for unfair dismissal

[1.119] The EAT has continued to order reinstatement and re-engagement of claimants as an alternative to compensation in dismissal cases. In *Jones v Bulmers Ltd,*[223] the EAT ordered the re-engagement of the claimant following a procedurally flawed dismissal. *Mahon v eircom Ltd*[224] is a Circuit Court decision (under appeal to the High Court) which ordered the claimant to be re-engaged with pay backdated to 1 January 2015.

In *Stapleton v St Colman's (Claremorris) Credit Union Ltd*[225] the claimant was reinstated in a majority decision of the EAT.

Mitigation

[1.120] Employees who claim unfair dismissal have a statutory obligation to mitigate their loss. In *Murphy v Independent News and Media*[226] the EAT was critical of the claimant for having only searched for future employment within a specific field of expertise.

WAGES

[1.121] In *Devlin v Electricity Supply Board*[227] which is noted in CH **28**, the EAT considered the nature of a discretionary performance-related bonus and whether its non-payment was an unlawful deduction under the Payment of Wages Act 1991.

The entitlement to be paid in cash was considered by the Labour Court in *Britvic Ireland Ltd v A Worker,*[228] which held that the employer's proposals to move the last remaining employee over to an electronic funds transfer payroll was reasonable.

The most significant payment of wages case in 2015 was the High Court decision in *Earagail Eisc Teoranta v Doherty & Ors*[229] where the High Court effectively ruled that the comments made by Edwards J in *McKenzie & Anor v Minister for Finance &*

---

222. *Prestige Foods Ltd v Gutauskiene* UD880/2012; *Durkin v McSweeney Assets Group Holdings Ltd* UD996/2012; *Delaney v The Phone Store t/a Lorat Trading Ltd* UD373/2013, MN200/2013, WT55/2013.
223. *Jones v Bulmers Ltd* UD423/2014, UD587/2014.
224. *Mahon v eircom Ltd* Circuit Court Record No 2015/00085. Note this case is under appeal to the High Court.
225. *Stapleton v St Colman's (Claremorris) Credit Union Ltd* UD1776/2012.
226. *Murphy v Independent News and Media* UD 841/2013.
227. *Devlin v Electricity Supply Board* PW550/2011.
228. *Britvic Ireland Ltd v A Worker* LCR20966.
229. *Earagail Eisc Teoranta v Doherty & Ors* [2015] IEHC 347.

Anor,[230] previously regarded as authority for the proposition that a reduction of wages was not a deduction, were *obiter.*[231] The High Court also distinguished *McKenzie* insofar as it related to a reduction in motor and travel subsistence allowances as opposed to a reduction in salary or wages, which was at issue in this case. The High Court held that the reduction in wages in this case was unlawful and did constitute a breach of the 1991 Act.

In *Bord na Móna v Murphy, McKenna, O'Neill, Garrett, Smyth*[232] the EAT was asked to consider whether the employer's action in placing the claimants on lay-off was unlawful and therefore an illegal deduction from their wages under the Payment of Wages Act 1991.

WHISTLEBLOWING

[1.122] CHAPTER 29 notes the developments in the law on whistleblowing since the enactment of the Protected Disclosures Act in 2014.

The 2014 Act has been amended by the Workplace Relations Act 2015 and there have been two Statutory Instruments.[233] To date, there has been very little Irish case law: just one Circuit Court written judgment which concerned an application for interim injunctive relief, *Philpott v Marymount University Hospital and Hospice Ltd.*[234]

CHAPTER 29 also summarises a number of 2015 decisions[235] on the equivalent provisions of the UK Employment Rights Act 1996, which are instructive as to the interpretation of the 2014 Act.

WORKING TIME

[1.123] In CH 30 we note cases on working time.

---

230. *McKenzie & Anor v The Minister for Finance & Anor* [2010] IEHC 461.
231. *Obiter dictum*: words or opinion expressed by a judge which are unnecessary for the decision of the case and therefore not legally binding as a precedent.
232. *Bord na Móna v Murphy, McKenna, O'Neill, Garrett and Smit* PW6/PW7/PW8/PW9/PW10/2014.
233. (i) The Protected Disclosures Act 2014 (Disclosure to Prescribed Persons) Order 2015.
    (ii) The Industrial Relations Act 1990 (Code of Practice on Protected Disclosures Act 2014) (Declaration) Order 2015.
234. *Philpott v Marymount University Hospital and Hospice Ltd* [2015] IECC 1.
235. *Barton v Royal Borough of Greenwich* UKEAT/0041/14/DXA; *Schaathun v Executive & Business Aviation Support Ltd* UKEAT/0227/12/LA; *McKinney v Newham London Borough Council* [2015] ICR 495, UKEAT/501/13/0412.

Road haulage

[1.124] In *Cosgrave Transport (Limerick) Ltd v Bonczak*[236] the Labour Court held that the period of time during which the truck driven by the claimant was being loaded or unloaded was not reckonable as working time for the purposes of the European Communities (Road Transport) (Organisation of Working Time of Persons Performing Mobile Road Transport Activities) Regulations 2012, rather it was a 'period of availability'.

Travelling time

[1.125] A significant development in Europe was seen in the *Tyco*[237] case where the CJEU concluded that for workers with no fixed or habitual place of work, the time spent travelling between their homes and the premises of their first and last customers did constitute working time.

Annual leave and holiday pay

[1.126] In *Sparantus Ltd t/a Highfield Healthcare v Jemiola*,[238] a case concerning the accrual of annual leave during sick leave, the Labour Court considered whether the Working Time Directive[239] could have direct effect in a case involving private sector employees in Ireland and held it could not.

The calculation of holiday pay and specifically whether non-guaranteed overtime, radius allowances and travel expenses should be taken into account was examined by the UK EAT in *Bear Scotland Ltd & Ors v Fulton*.[240]

Non-consultant hospital doctors

[1.127] The treatment of non-consultant hospital doctors in terms of their working time was considered by both Advocate General Bot and the CJEU in *European Commission v Ireland*.[241] Although the Advocate General was critical of Ireland's failure to fulfil its obligations under the Working Time Directive[242] in relation to doctors in training, the CJEU dismissed the action and held that there was no evidence adduced by the

---

236. *Cosgrave Transport (Limerick) Ltd v Bonczak* RTD158.
237. *Federación de Servicios Privados del Sindicato Comisiones Obreras (CCOO) v Tyco Integrated Security SL, Tyco Integrated Fire & Security Corporation Servicios SA* (Case C–266/14).
238. *Sparantus Ltd t/a Highfield Healthcare v Jemiola* DWT14110.
239. Directive 2003/88.
240. *Bear Scotland Ltd & Ors v Fulton & Ors; Hertel (UK) Ltd v Woods & Ors; AMEC Group Ltd v Law & Ors* UKEATS/0047/13/BI, UKEAT/0160/14/SM, UKEAT/0161/14/SM.
241. *European Commission v Ireland* (Case C–87/14).
242. Directive 2003/88.

Commission that showed that Ireland had failed to fulfil its obligations under the Directive.

Rest breaks

[1.128] The adequacy of rest breaks continues to be a topical issue. CHAPTER 30 notes two decision of the Labour Court where it examined the adequacy of the rest breaks afforded to a chef (*Nutweave Ltd t/a Bombay Pantry v Kumar*)[243] and to a security guard (*P&J Security Services Ltd v Chitii*).[244]

Appeals on quantum

[1.129] There has been an increasing number of appeals on quantum in respect of Rights Commissioner awards under the 1997 Act. CHAPTER 30 contains a selection of the 2015 cases in this area to include *C & F Tooling Ltd v Cunniffe*[245] where the Labour Court clarified the obligations of a statutory tribunal in relation to calculating quantum of awards of compensation and also *B Brothers Foods Ltd v Furmanczyk*,[246] *Zafer Bars Ltd (in liq) v Csaba*[247] and *Wicklow Recreational Services Ltd t/a Shoreline Leisure Centre v Marciniuk*.[248]

Maximum working hours

[1.130] In *Andrzej Gera t/a Family Bakery Samo Zdrowie v Krawczyk*[249] the Labour Court preferred the complainant's evidence as to his working hours and how he was regularly required to work 70 to 90 plus hours a week, far in excess of the statutory limits.

Working time records

[1.131] The obligation on an employer to prove compliance with statutory requirements in the absence of any working time records was emphasised by the Labour Court in *Blue Thunder Fast Foods Ltd t/a Blue Thunder v Oleniacz*.[250]

---

243. *Nutweave Ltd t/a Bombay Pantry v Kumar* DWT 1537.
244. *P&J Security Services Ltd v Chitii* DWT 1556.
245. *C & F Tooling Ltd v Cunniffe* DWT15125.
246. *B Brothers Foods Ltd v Furmanczyk* DWT1540.
247. *Zafer Bars Ltd (in liq) v Csaba* DWT14120.
248. *Wicklow Recreational Services Ltd t/a Shoreline Leisure Centre v Marciniuk* DWT14123.
249. *Gera (Andrzej) t/a Family Bakery Samo Zdrowie v Krawczyk* DWT 1585.
250. *Blue Thunder Fast Foods Ltd t/a Blue Thunder v Oleniacz* DWT15124.

WORKPLACE RELATIONS ACT 2015

[1.132] 2015 has seen a significant reform of the employment law dispute resolution structures in Ireland with the enactment of the Workplace Relations Act 2015 and the establishment of the Workplace Relations Commission (WRC). **CHAPTER 31** sets out in detail the key changes made by the 2015 Act and is intended to be a practical guide to the WRC for those who will be availing of its services.

NORTHERN IRELAND – 2015 IN OUTLINE

[1.133] **CHAPTER 32** sets out a contribution from Arthur Cox Northern Ireland on the key developments in Northern Ireland employment law in 2015.

CURIAL DEFERENCE AND THE LABOUR COURT

[1.134] In **CH 33** Tom Mallon BL considers the application of the doctrine of curial deference in light of the Workplace Relations Act 2015 and the consolidation of the dispute resolution structures to provide for a single point of appeal to the Labour Court.

Chapter 2

CONTRACT OF EMPLOYMENT

EMPLOYMENT STATUS

[2.01] *Beirne v Board of Management of Loughlynn National School[1]—Employment Appeals Tribunal—Terms of Employment (Information) Acts 1994 to 2012— preliminary issue—whether claimant an employee or an independent contractor of respondent national school*

The claimant's evidence was that following the death of her husband she took over the duties of teaching music to the children in the respondent national school in 1987. She maintains she was an employee of the respondent. Each year she was asked by the school principal if she was available to teach music and she taught the children every Wednesday for two hours. She was paid generally by cheques but occasionally in cash. She did not receive a contract of employment or payslips and did not receive holidays. The claimant gave evidence that she provided her own tin whistle but did not provide tin whistles for the children. She never missed a class due to illness but conceded that her daughter had replaced her on one occasion due to her having another engagement. She further conceded that she also gave private classes to some children in their homes.

Evidence was given by the respondent principal that music was taught in the classroom as part of the school curriculum by mainstream teachers. Separately, however, the school arranged for the provision of extracurricular activities based on the outcome of a parental ballot. The funding for these activities was provided by the parents who had also organised fundraising events to help with this. The respondent's evidence was that the claimant was paid to teach music as an extracurricular activity to school children. She was paid for her services solely from parental funding and was engaged as an independent contractor. She was paid generally by cheque and very occasionally in cash. She was not given a contract of employment, pay slips or holidays as she was not an employee. She chose her own content for the music classes and, as school principal, the witness had no input into the classes.

The EAT held itself satisfied that the claimant was not an employee but was engaged as an independent contractor. She provided services to the school and was engaged by the school under a contract for service. As the claimant was not an employee within the meaning of the Act, the EAT held that it had no jurisdiction to hear the appeal. The EAT held similarly in a related unfair dismissals claim.[2]

---

1. *Beirne v Board of Management of Loughlynn National School* TE22/2015.
2. *Beirne v Board of Management of Loughlynn National School* UD 1141/2014.

[2.02] *Blake v Grand Circle LLC[3]—Employment Appeals Tribunal—Unfair Dismissals Acts 1977 to 2015—whether claimant an independent contractor and thus not entitled to redress—employment status—unfair dismissal*

A preliminary issue was raised whereby the respondent submitted that the claimant was an independent contractor and therefore had no entitlement to bring a claim under the Acts. The respondent is a tour operator and had engaged the claimant to act as a tour guide/programme director from 2007. Evidence was given that the claimant had signed a written contract as an independent contractor with the respondent in February 2008 and this contract was entitled 'Independent Contractor Agreement'. Like other programme directors, the claimant was given a handbook and some training. He was required to submit a list of block-off dates when he would not be available for work and he was then allocated tours outside of those dates.

The EAT held that the description of the claimant as an independent contractor in the written contract was not determinative of the issue. The EAT noted the landmark Supreme Court decision in *Henry Denny & Sons v Minister for Social Welfare[4]* where the Court held that regard must be had to all the circumstances of employment. *Castleisland Cattle Breeding Society Ltd v Minister for Social and Family Affairs[5]* was cited with approval, where it was held that:

> … the adjudicating body is bound to examine and have regard to what the real
> arrangement on a day to day basis between the parties was.

Reference was made by the respondent to a previous High Court case of *Murphy v Grand Circle Travel[6]* which is was submitted was binding on the EAT. In that case it was held that the claimant, a programme director and former colleague of the claimant in this case was an independent contractor. In this case, the claimant challenged the assertion and claimed that the mutuality of obligation missing in the *Murphy* case was present in his work relationship with the respondent and that it, as well as an increased level of control over how he did his work, distinguished his case from that of *Murphy*. The EAT freshly considered the issue of mutuality of obligation.

The EAT noted the claimant's evidence that subsequent to his colleagues leaving employment, the level of work commitment required of him had increased. When he became a senior programme director he had to promise services for a minimum number of assignments and days per year and, in this regard, he signed an addendum with the respondent committing him to a minimum of 60 days, comprising of at least five tours per year at an increased rate of pay until 2010. The claimant asserted that the respondent required more and more from him and, because of his level of commitment, he did not have free time to work for other tour companies. He had to provide a service personally and only work for the respondent. The EAT noted further evidence from another senior programme director whose position was more senior than the claimant's. Her evidence

---

3.   *Blake v Grand Circle LLC* UD620/2013.

4.   *Henry Denny & Sons v Minister for Social Welfare* [1998] 1 IR 34.

5.   *Castleisland Cattle Breeding Society Ltd v Minister for Social and Family Affairs* [2004] IESC 40.

6.   *Murphy v Grand Circle Travel* [2014] IEHC 337.

was that senior programme directors like herself guaranteed such a level of commitment because the respondent paid the best and required a high level of service. If a programme director does a good job he/she will be assigned more work and priority is given to senior programme directors. The EAT noted that this witness regarded herself as an entrepreneur, in business on her own account.

The EAT concluded that the claimant could have accepted other work, had he wanted to. The EAT noted the claimant's own evidence that he had reduced his level of commitment when he had adopted a baby and there was no evidence that this was done under the statutory scheme for employees. The respondent's submission that it could not guarantee a minimum number of tours to a programme director but, if it had tours, it would assign them was noted by the EAT. It was further noted that the respondent could at any time unilaterally terminate the addendum agreement. On the balance of probability, the EAT concluded that mutuality of obligation was not present. The EAT noted the legal position that, although mutuality of obligation is an essential element and the irreducible minimum that has to be present for a contract for service to exist, its presence is not determinative of the issue, it was necessary in this case to examine the relationship further (Edwards J in *Minister for Agriculture and Food v Barry & Ors*).[7] The EAT stated that even if it was wrong in its conclusions as to mutuality of obligation, it determined, having examined the relationship further, that it was a contract for services. The EAT noted from the contract the high level of residual control retained by the respondent and in such a context the EAT did not accept the claimant's argument that the 2011 guidelines (which were not produced) were of significance.

The claimant's written contract provided for payment on a daily basis. There was no entitlement to holidays, sick pay or pension. There was no provision for payment if a tour was cancelled. The claimant was required to look after his own tax and social insurance. The EAT noted that the claimant was compliant in this regard and had declared himself to be self-employed to the Revenue Commissioners. The EAT noted that there was no evidence the respondent had a disciplinary policy. Tips were high, sometimes exceeding pay, and these were not collected by the respondent. All these suggested a contract for service.

The EAT noted that in the *Castleisland Cattle Breeding*[8] case, Geoghegan J had found the fact that the worker was self-assessed for tax purposes, claimed allowances as a self-employed person, carried his own insurance and was not entitled to any pension was overwhelming evidence that he was an independent contractor. The EAT noted that the evidence as to insurance cover was not clear in this case; however, having regard to the evidence before it, including the contra indicators, such as the duty to provide personal service, the EAT held on balance of probability that the claimant was engaged under a contract for service and was not an employee. The claim could not proceed.

---

7. *Minister for Agriculture and Food v Barry & Ors* [2008] IEHC 216 at 230.
8. *Castleisland Cattle Breeding Society Ltd v Minister for Social and Family Affairs* [2004] IESC 42.

[2.03] *Forde v Newspread Ltd[9]—Employment Appeals Tribunal—Unfair Dismissals Acts 1977 to 2015—preliminary issue—whether claimant engaged as an independent contractor on a contract for service or was an employee of the respondent—unfair dismissal*

A preliminary issue arose where the EAT was asked to consider whether the claimant was an independent contractor, engaged on a contract for services or whether he was an employee of the respondent, a newspaper distribution company delivering publications countrywide. The EAT considered the agreement between the parties and heard evidence from the claimant that he was engaged to deliver newspapers in the Co Clare region for 27 years. He was required to collect the newspapers at a set time daily and was given a list of shops to make deliveries to. He was paid a fixed daily rate of €120 per day. It was noted the claimant provided his own vehicle and was responsible for taxing, insuring and fuelling the vehicle. He was registered for VAT and reclaimed VAT for diesel expenses incurred. In the event that he was unable to carry out deliveries he was required to provide relief cover but this person had to be pre-approved by the respondent. The claimant was paid directly into his bank account without payslips or a P60. He had his own accountant who looked after his own tax affairs and calculated his VAT liability. The EAT considered copies of the claimant's invoices, which the claimant asserted were generated by the respondent. The claimant asserted that he did not receive holidays although he believed he had an entitlement to holidays. It was accepted that the claimant made deliveries for other newspaper groups and was paid separately for these deliveries.

The EAT held itself satisfied that the claimant was employed under a contract for services. The EAT noted that the claimant had provided and fuelled his own vehicle and also taxed and insured his vehicle. He was registered for VAT and his accountant looked after his tax affairs and his income tax was returnable at the end of each year. The claimant did not receive and did not seek to be paid for holidays. The EAT noted that the claimant had a service agreement with the respondent and at the same time had service agreements with other newspaper groups.

The EAT concluded that the claimant was self-employed under a contract for services and declined jurisdiction.

[2.04] *Halawi v WDFG UK Ltd (t/a World Duty Free)[10]—England and Wales Court of Appeal—Equality Act 2010—whether claimant an employee for purposes of Equality Act 2010, s 83(2)—meaning of employment—meaning of employee—discrimination on grounds of race and religion—mutuality of obligations—contract personally to do work—freedom to refuse work assignment—requirement of subordination—power of substitution inconsistent with personal performance of services*

The respondent operated a duty free retail outlet at Heathrow airport. The claimant was a beauty consultant who provided her services at an outlet, which was managed by the

---

9.   *Forde v Newspread Ltd* UD1699/2013.

10.   *Halawi v WDFG UK Ltd (t/a World Duty Free)* [2014] EWCA Civ 1387.

respondent through a limited company, for the purpose of selling Shiseido cosmetic products. The claimant was not an employee of the respondent for the purposes of the Equality Act 2010. She had, however, signed 'WDF business partner guidelines' which included references to the health and safety and confidentiality policy of the respondent. Shiseido is a cosmetics company and the claimant wore a Shiseido uniform and sold Shiseido products at the outlet, under an agreement between Shiseido and the respondent. Shiseido further had an agreement with another company, CSA, pursuant to which CSA provided management services to Shiseido. Management services included the organisation of the staffing of the outlet. The claimant initially worked at the outlet through an agency, with the assistance of CSA, but subsequently incorporated her own limited company, which then invoiced CSA for her time and services at an hourly rate. The hourly rate was set by CSA and CSA, in turn, invoiced Shiseido.

The claimant required two authorisations to ensure her entitlement to work. Firstly, she required a formal approval from the respondent, which stated that the claimant had approval to work in that outlet. Secondly, the respondent sponsored an airport pass for the claimant, which was issued to her by the British Airports Authority. The dispute arose in circumstances where the airport pass was withdrawn by the respondent. This, in turn, prevented the claimant from continuing her work in the outlet. The claimant then commenced proceedings against the respondent and CSA on the basis that the withdrawal of the pass from the claimant was discriminatory on the grounds of race and/ or religion. The claimant characterised the withdrawal of the airport pass as an effective dismissal from employment.

In the first instance, the UK EAT had to determine whether the claimant was an employee under a contract personally to do work for either the respondent or CSA and for the purposes of the Equality Act 2010. The UK EAT found that the claimant had no relevant contract of employment with the respondent or CSA and that if a contract had existed, it would not have been a contract 'personally to do work'. The UK EAT found that neither the respondent nor Shiseido had provided the claimant with work and that CSA had not been under an obligation to provide work to the claimant and further, the claimant had always been free to refuse any work assignment. There was no mutuality of obligations in the relationship between the claimant and the respondents. The UK EAT also found that the respondent did not have any level of control over the claimant beyond its control over the physical outlet at which the claimant worked. The claimant appealed the decision of the UK EAT to the Court of Appeal, citing only WDF as the respondent. The principal grounds of appeal were that the UK EAT judge had erred in law as his decision did not give effect to EU law providing that employment has an autonomous meaning under EU law and that a relationship of employment existed where the claimant was in a relationship of subordination and that personal service was not required as a criteria.

The Court of Appeal confirmed that the relevant provisions of the Equality Act 2010 must be interpreted so as to be compatible with EU law; that there existed an autonomous meaning in EU law of the term 'employee' and that Member States did not have the power to diminish this meaning.

The Court of Appeal found that the claimant was not an employee of the respondent for the purposes of s 83(2) of the Equality Act 2010. The Court confirmed that the criteria in respect of an employment relationship must generally be referred to under EU law, the employee must agree personally to perform services for the employer and further, the employee is generally bound to act on the employer's instructions. The existence of the relationship of employment does not depend on whether the parties entered into a formal contract which would be recognised in domestic law as constituting employment, but whether it meets the criteria set down by EU law. In determining whether the relationship is one of employment, the Court must look at the substance of the relationship.

In dismissing the appeal, the Court of Appeal agreed with the UK EAT that the claimant had possessed a power of substitution which had been inconsistent with the personal performance of services. The Court of Appeal noted that, despite the fact that the power of substitution was rarely used by the claimant, the power of substitution was found not to be a sham or a power that could be disregarded. The Court of Appeal also agreed with the UK EAT in finding that the requirement for subordination does not need to be qualified and that the requirement must be satisfied for employment to be found to exist. The Court of Appeal noted that the lack of subordination is consistent with the claimant's lack of integration in the respondent's business. The Court of Appeal also noted that there was no requirement or obligation to refer the case to the CJEU for a preliminary ruling on the requirements and integration of EU law.

[2.05] *Comerford v Health Service Executive[11]—Employment Appeals Tribunal— Unfair Dismissals Acts 1977 to 2015—Organisation of Working Time Act 1997— Minimum Notice and Terms of Employment Acts 1973 to 2005—whether claimant an employee or an independent contractor—appropriate test to be applied—'enterprise' test—'control' test, 'integration' test and 'mutuality of obligation' test—combination of factors to be considered—each case to be decided on own facts*

The claimant maintained that he was an employee of the respondent. The respondent disagreed, maintaining that the claimant's status was that of a self-employed contractor.

The claimant performed maintenance duties at the respondent's premises (the Ballydowd Special Care Unit), a high security centre for children aged 12 to 17 years with serious emotional and behavioural difficulties. The claimant was advised in August 2012 of the need for public liability insurance but stated that he could not afford it and, despite meetings throughout 2013, failed to obtain the insurance. It was on this basis that the respondent made the decision to end its relationship with the claimant on 15 November 2013. The claimant was referred to the scope section of the Department of Social Protection, which identified him as self-employed. The claimant failed to appeal this decision within the required 21 days, though he did appeal it in August 2015, almost one year later, because, he placed importance on it for the purposes of the EAT case.

The claimant usually worked from 8 am to 4 pm on Monday to Friday; however this arrangement was not strictly adhered to. He was provided with a maintenance list by the acting deputy director of operation, though he was not instructed in relation as to how to carry out the work. The respondent supplied paint and heavy hardware equipment in

---

11. *Comerford v Health Service Executive* UD466/2014, MN195/2014, WT70/2014.

order to enable the claimant to carry out his duties. The claimant submitted a daily invoice of €220, which was processed by the respondent's accounts payable department rather than payroll. The accounts varied depending on the days worked by the claimant. The respondent was under the impression that it could not decline a request for a day off from the claimant. The claimant was not paid for holidays or sick days, nor was he required to present medical certs. He did, however, advise the respondent when he planned to take holidays, as a matter of courtesy.

The acting director of the Special Care Unit gave evidence that the claimant had originally worked for a company which provided services to the respondent. Once that company ceased to provide services to the respondent the claimant commenced his role; however he was not provided with a contract of employment. He signed in and out of the respondent's premises every day on which he worked. He received induction training and was trained on fire safety. The claimant also carried out regular fire checks on the premises and was a member of the health and safety committee. The acting director of the Special Care Unit told the EAT that it was his understanding that the claimant operated as an independent contractor. He added that the claimant had never been subject to disciplinary proceedings with the respondent during his tenure. The general manager of the respondent's finance department gave evidence that the claimant paid relevant contract tax (RCT), a tax deduction system for subcontractors, on his income. Although the claimant was not the subject of public service cuts, he was requested to take a 10 per cent pay cut.

It was the claimant's evidence that he had originally been employed by Mr M, who provided contracting maintenance services to the centre. An issue arose between Mr M and the respondent, which resulted in the claimant being asked to take over Mr M's work. The claimant told the EAT that, although he had requested a contract of employment on two separate occasions, the respondent had told him that this was not possible. He maintained that he was paid the same sum per month, regardless of whether he missed a day of work or whether there had been a bank holiday that month. The claimant told the EAT that the respondent provided him with the powered equipment he used in the performance of his work. The claimant stated that the issue of public liability insurance had not been broached by the respondent until late 2012. The claimant queried why this was suddenly a requirement, when, according to him, all factors pointed to him being an employee of the respondent. During cross-examination the claimant agreed that he had previously been subject to the PAYE tax system and that employees do not register for VAT. The claimant had submitted tax clearance certificates and engaged the services of an accountant since 2006.

Following the termination of the claimant's engagement with the respondent, he was told by the Department of Social Protection that he was not due any payments from them. However, a few weeks later, he began receiving €41.00 each week.

The EAT noted that the claimant was not subject to HSE control or direction. Rather, he was engaged by the Ballydowd Centre. While he reported to Ballydowd management in relation to the maintenance work he conducted, he was not instructed on how it was to be done.

The EAT noted that the claimant's hours of work could vary and that he was not precluded from working for other employers, as he did work for a local school from time to time. There was no contract of employment between the parties, though the claimant stated that he had requested one twice, and he was registered for VAT. The EAT further noted that the claimant did not object to the RCT arrangement; that he was required to provide annual tax clearance certificates; that he was not paid for holidays or sick days nor did he require the respondent's permission to take time off. The claimant paid class S social welfare insurance, which is a self-employed designation, and was not subject to public service cuts. Finally, the EAT considered that the claimant was deemed to be self-employed by the Department of Social Welfare and failed to object to this designation within the necessary 21 days.

The EAT concluded that the claimant was hired on a contract for services basis. The *dicta* of Keane J in *Henry Denny & Sons (Ireland) Ltd v Minister for Social Welfare*[12] were cited as authority for the proposition that each case depends on its own particular circumstances. *Barry & Ors v Minister for Agriculture and Food*,[13] in which Charlton J noted that a self-employed relationship could, over time, develop into an employment relationship, was also considered by the EAT in reaching its conclusion. The EAT considered the view of Edwards J in *Minister for Agriculture and Food v Barry*[14] that there was no single composite test for determining whether an employment relationship existed. He stated that the 'enterprise test' could not be determinative. While it could be relied upon as an aid to draw appropriate inferences, it should not be applied in a formulaic way. Edwards J stated that the general principles emanating from case law such as 'enterprise', 'control', 'integration' and 'mutuality of obligation' do not represent an exhaustive list and each case is ultimately decided on its own facts. The EAT also had regard to the decision in *Hayes v Business & Shopping Guide Ltd*,[15] in which the EAT had concluded that a sales agent was a self-employed contractor. In reaching this decision the EAT had taken account of the fact that there was no signed contract in place and that the sales agent paid his own tax and PRSI contributions. Finally the EAT had regard to the decision in *McCotter v Quinn Insurance Ltd*,[16] in which it was emphasised that it was not the sum total of factors but the overall effect that was important in determining employment status.

In accordance with its determination that the claimant was hired on a contract for services basis, the EAT held that it had no jurisdiction to hear his claims under the various Acts.

---

12. *Henry Denny & Sons (Ireland) Ltd v Minister for Social Welfare* [1998] 1 IR 34.
13. *Barry & Ors v Minister for Agriculture and Food* [2015] IESC 63.
14. *Minister for Agriculture and Food v Barry & Ors* [2008] IEHC 216.
15. *Hayes v Business & Shopping Guide Ltd* UD177/2010.
16. *McCotter v Quinn Insurance Ltd* UD242/2011.

INCOME PROTECTION

[2.06] *Holohan v Friends First Life Assurance Co Ltd*[17]—*High Court—White J— whether defendant in breach of contract of insurance—entitlement of plaintiff to benefit of income protection plan—whether plaintiff totally disabled by reason of sickness or accident as required by the plan conditions—fibromyalgia*

The plaintiff sought a declaration that the defendant was in breach of a contract of insurance. The plaintiff had been employed as an insurance broker/financial advisor since September 2005 and had a consistent work record and history of continuous employment, without issue, for approximately 19 years before ceasing work in April 2009 due to medical difficulties.

He entered into a contract of insurance with the defendant for an income protection policy with effect from March 2006 which would cover him financially through a period of disability if he was totally unable to carry out his normal occupation due to a recognised illness or accident, and during which the insured was not involved in carrying out any other occupation for a reward, profit or remuneration.

Evidence was given that the plaintiff began to have medical symptoms in 2007. He visited his GP in September/October 2008 complaining of breathlessness, pains in his chest, arms, back, neck and legs together with dizzy spells and irritable bowel symptoms. He was referred to a cardiologist who excluded heart disease and, in April 2009, he was subsequently diagnosed with fibromyalgia. The plaintiff was certified unfit for work by his GP from April 2009 and he claimed on the policy. In September 2009, the defendant asserted that, based on medical evidence, there was an expectation that the treatment of the symptoms would result in the claim being of short duration; once medical investigations were complete the claim would be reviewed further. The policy had a deferral period of 26 weeks so the benefit commenced from October 2009, payable at four-weekly intervals in arrears.

Having carried out various investigations, the defendant wrote to the plaintiff in 2010 confirming that its chief medical officer had considered a recent medical report from an occupational specialist, together with all medical evidence received, and the defendant had decided it was unable to consider the plaintiff totally disabled by reason of sickness or accident from the occupation of insurance broker. As such, the terms of the policy were no longer satisfied and the benefit would be terminated after payment of 50 per cent of the benefit for a period of four weeks. As this was disputed by the plaintiff, the defendant arranged a further examination with the occupational specialist and also a Chronic Pain Abilities Determination test (CPAD) which was carried out over a two-day period in May 2011. Subsequently the defendant wrote to the plaintiff in June 2011 confirming that he was not suffering from disability as defined by the policy and that the decision to terminate the claim remained unchanged.

These proceedings were commenced by way of plenary summons in June 2012. White J heard detailed medical evidence from both sides. He noticed that there was a detailed and robust cross-examination of the plaintiff by the defendant's counsel,

---

17.   *Holohan v Friends First Life Assurance Co Ltd* [2014] IEHC 676.

especially in relation to the detailed medical history taken by experts who administered the CPAD test. White J noted that the results of the test were put to the plaintiff and that he had denied exaggerating his symptoms; however mistakes had been made in the course of the test, as he was nervous and was subsequently not allowed to change his responses.

The plaintiff stated that he would like to return to work but he physically could not do so as he was in a lot of pain sitting and could not hold a pen. He denied that he had misrepresented his ability, but accepted that he had only attended two or three sessions of physiotherapy and had only seen a psychologist on one occasion in 2009 as he was worried about costs. The plaintiff's spouse gave evidence to the Court that he was a hard worker with a good personality and that he enjoyed work. The managing director of the defendant gave evidence that he had been head hunted from his previous role and was employed from 2005, looking after senior sales, meeting clients and advising clients on investments, which was a responsible job. The defendant was sorry to lose him as he was a loyal employee and was in a responsible position but confirmed that he would now be out of touch with the market and that his qualifications were not up to date. The evidence was that the defendant could not take the plaintiff back in his present state or condition.

White J summarised the medical evidence which had been given on both sides and noted that the onus was on the plaintiff to show that he was totally unable to carry out his normal occupation due to a recognised illness.

White J held that if a misrepresentation is made by an insured person it can be taken into consideration even though it arises subsequent to the initial claim being made and its initial refusal. If, during the course of a review of the claim, a misrepresentation is made which the Court finds to be consciously or recklessly made to mislead the insurer, it should be taken into account.

White J distinguished this case from *Haghiran v Allied Dunbar Insurance*[18] and held that the evidence in this case went beyond the erroneous, albeit genuine, belief on the part of the plaintiff that he was totally unable to carry out his normal occupation, due to recognised illness or accident. White J noted that three separate medical witnesses, two of whom are experts in the field, had given sworn evidence that the plaintiff was suffering from a recognised illness and was unable to carry out his normal occupation due to that illness. The Court noted there was a genuine difference between two of the medics and one of the occupational specialists as to the appropriate approach to take in the plaintiff's case. However, it was noted by the Court that all of the medical experts accepted that the plaintiff was suffering from a recognised illness, namely fibromyalgia, and it was further accepted that this can be a very debilitating condition and have a wide spectrum of symptoms, ranging from minor to severe.

The Court placed significance on the fact that the plaintiff had an excellent work history and had worked consistently since 1990 and had no relevant medical history prior to 2008. The Court noted that three individual medical witnesses had all separately formed the opinion that the plaintiff was genuine and was not exaggerating his symptoms, while accepting that a vital part of the diagnosis of fibromyalgia is based on

---

18.   *Haghiran v Allied Dunbar Insurance* [2001] 1 All ER (Comm) 97.

subjective symptoms and medical history provided by the individual. The Court did not accept that there were inconsistencies in the CPAD testing, particularly in respect of cognitive testing of the plaintiff. The Court noted that the plaintiff had given evidence that he was on substantial medication at the time of his test and that some mistakes were made and he had informed the expert carrying out the test of these mistakes.

White J concluded, based on the evidence of the plaintiff and his wife and on the medical evidence provided, that the plaintiff did not deliberately or recklessly attempt to misrepresent his condition as worse than it actually was. The Court noted that the medical expert called on behalf of the defendant was a creditable witness and had given a genuine opinion that the plaintiff was fit for work and that many, if not most sufferers from fibromyalgia, can undertake their chosen profession. However, it was noted that two of the other medical witness had stated that this was a spectrum and that there are some cases of such severity that an individual is unable to carry out their chosen professions. On the balance of probabilities, and notwithstanding the misgivings the Court had in relation to the CPAD testing, White J concluded that the plaintiff did come within the scope of the policy and he was entitled to the relief sought. The Court held that the appropriate relief was one of specific performance in respect of future payments of the benefits which accrued under the policy.

PERFORMANCE-RELATED PAY

[2.07] *Gunning v Coillte Teoranta[19]—High Court—Kearns P—contractual performance-related pay—withholding on foot of Ministerial directive—whether Ministerial directive can retrospectively cancel contractually-earned, performance-related pay*

The plaintiff was employed as CEO of the defendant on a fixed-term contract from 1 February 2006 to 19 March 2013. Under the terms of his written contract of employment with the defendant, the plaintiff was entitled to receive performance-related pay if he met specified performance targets on an annual and three-yearly basis. It was noted that it was evident from the relevant documentation and correspondence between the parties and the Department of Agriculture, Food and the Marine (the Department), that the plaintiff was successful in the performance of his duties as CEO, and, as a result, he earned significant performance-related bonuses.

It was uncontested that between 2008 and 2012, the plaintiff earned performance-related pay in the sum of €299,001.

Following the economic downturn in 2008, the Minister for Agriculture, Food and the Marine (the Minister) wrote to the defendant's then chairman in relation to the plaintiff's performance-related pay. In his letter of 23 June 2009, the Minister acknowledged that there was no legal basis for him to request or insist that the performance-related payment be withheld from the plaintiff. The Minister stated that while he accepted that the payment was a contractual matter between the defendant and the plaintiff, having regard to the economic crisis, he was of the view that in the best

---

19. *Gunning v Coillte Teoranta* [2015] IEHC 44.

interests of the defendant and the public interest, the defendant should cancel the proposed bonus for 2008. Kearns P noted that the plaintiff had voluntarily agreed to the deferral of his 2008 performance-related pay and had voluntarily waived his entitlement to bonus for the years 2009 and 2010 in response to the appeal by the Department to recognise the financial crisis.

The Minister wrote to the chairman of the defendant again on 26 January 2011, reiterating that, although there was no legal basis for him to insist that the performance-related pay be withheld from the plaintiff, he was astonished that the remuneration committee and the board of the defendant could consider that the payment was appropriate in the prevailing economic climate.

The Court heard how in mid-August 2012, the defendant had entered into discussions with the plaintiff for a second term as CEO of the defendant. It was noted, in order for his reappointment to be satisfactory to the Minister, the plaintiff's remuneration would be revised and he would be required to forego any entitlement to performance-related pay arising under his current contract over and above that which had already been paid to him. The plaintiff did not seek reappointment and subsequently sought that the outstanding balance of the performance-related pay owed to him be paid by the expiry of his fixed-term contract.

The defendant's remuneration committee met on 5 March 2013 to discuss the award of the plaintiff's performance-related pay. The meeting was attended by the Assistant General Secretary from the Department, who was the Minister's representative. The minutes of the meeting recorded the Assistant General Secretary stating that both the Minister and the Minister for Finance had reaffirmed the view that, in line with government policy, performance-related pay should not be paid to the chief executive of any State commercial company and that this policy superseded the defendant board's contractual obligations to the plaintiff. The Assistant General Secretary continued that the plaintiff had the right to legal redress should the board decide not to award the outstanding performance-related payment.

The remuneration committee nonetheless awarded the payment to the plaintiff.

On 8 April 2013, the Minister wrote to the chairman stating his disapproval of the any performance-related bonuses to CEOs of State commercial companies, and stated:

> I understand that clause 5.13 of the CEO's contract specifically allows the Company to make changes to the bonus arrangements and it has therefore been open to the Company to alter or to cancel them. In view of this express power of the Board to cancel the performance arrangements and the duties of the Board to comply with section 36 of the Forestry Act 1988, as well as the general obligations to implement Government pay policy under the Code of Practice, referred to above, I have been advised that the Board would be in defiance of Government policy on remuneration, as outlined above, if it intends to proceed to award a performance payment to Mr. Gunning.

Section 36 of the Forestry Act 1988 (the Act) provides in relation to the 'staff of company' that:

> ... the company, in determining the remuneration or allowances for expenses to be paid to its officers or servants or the terms or conditions subject to which such officers or servants hold or are to hold their employment, shall have regard to

Government or nationally agreed guidelines which are for the time being extant, or to Government policy concerning remuneration and conditions of employment which is so extant, and in addition to the foregoing, the company shall comply with any directives with regard to such remuneration, allowances, terms or conditions which the Minister may give from time to time to the company with the consent of the Minister for Finance.

The defendant determined that this letter constituted a Ministerial directive under s 36 of the Act to withhold the performance-related pay from the plaintiff.

The defendant wrote to the plaintiff advising him that, under the Ministerial directive on 8 April 2013, it could not make the payment to him. The Court noted, however, that the Minister's letter on 8 April 2013 did not explicitly state that the Minister was making a directive, and the letter did not make reference to the Minister for Finance's consent to such a directive, as required by s 36 of the Act. Kearns P stated that given the penal nature of s 36, the defendant would have to show strict compliance with the requirements of s 36, which was not demonstrated in this instance.

The Court noted that the Act did not provide for retrospective forfeiture of remuneration earned by either the chief executive or any member of staff of the company. Kearns P also noted that the Minister's letter was issued after the plaintiff's term of employment with the defendant had ended. He held that if s 36 of the Act were exercised during the currency of the plaintiff's contract of employment, a Ministerial directive could direct the defendant to cease or vary its performance-related pay programme and withhold unearned and unpaid bonuses; however, it could not deprive the plaintiff of his already accrued bonus entitlements.

The Court referred to *Clancy & Anor v Ireland*[20] and *Cox v Ireland*,[21] both of which provided that the State cannot retrospectively require forfeiture of citizens' vested property as to do so would violate the constitutional right to property. In applying this principle to s 36 of the Act, Kearns P held:

> ... as s.36 does not provide in any way for the forfeiture of vested property rights, and given further that in construing s.36 the Court must apply the presumption of constitutionality and in this regard must apply the double construction rule, the construction contended for by the defendant would offend Article 40.3.2 of the Constitution which requires the State to vindicate the property rights of every citizen.

In finding in favour of the plaintiff, Kearns P stated that he was satisfied that the plaintiff was entitled to the performance-related pay earned during his employment and that the defendant was not entitled rely on the Minister's letter of 8 April 2013 to deprive the plaintiff of his accrued entitlements.

---

20.   *Clancy & Anor v Ireland* [1988] IR 326.
21.   *Cox v Ireland* [1992] 2 IR 503.

THE CONTRACTUAL NATURE OF AN EMPLOYEE HANDBOOK

[2.08] *Sparks & Ors v Department for Transport[22]—High Court of England and Wales—whether provisions of employee handbook are incorporated into claimants' employment contracts—whether employer entitled to vary terms of staff handbook unilaterally—whether all employee handbook provisions are apt for incorporation into employment contracts—whether court should grant declaration in circumstances where staff handbook has been amended unilaterally—extent of such declaratory relief*

The claimants were employed by one of seven individual bargaining agencies for which the defendant was responsible. A departmental staff handbook existed to cover all of the agencies for which the claimants worked and contained specific provisions relating to attendance management. The claimants applied to the High Court seeking a declaration relating to their terms of employment in relation to the introduction by the defendant of a new attendance management policy in July 2012. The seven agencies had adopted their own terms and conditions in respect of attendance management but there existed very similar conditions across all agencies. Globe J noted that it was common ground that the resolution of all issues would have the same consequences for all claimants and that there was no requirement to conduct a detailed analysis of all seven processes and respective amendments. He further noted that the key provision of the handbook in dispute was para 10.1.18 of Pt A of the handbook which originally provided that, in any 12-month period, where a number of short terms absences had been taken as sick leave and such absences exceeded 21 working days, the line manager would discuss the attendance record with the employee. Where such thresholds had been exceeded and the line manager perceived a problem with attendance, he would address the matter in accordance with the procedures set out in the handbook, 'Maintaining Satisfactory Standards of Attendance'. However, in July 2012, that provision was replaced by a new provision, which contained disciplinary procedures relating to conduct, performance and attendance issues. The procedure provided that stage 1 could result in a formal written warning, stage 2 could result in a final written warning and stage 3 could result in dismissal. The amended procedures were not wholly dissimilar to the previous procedure but did contain references to disciplinary issues. This unilateral amendment to the policy was the subject of the proceedings.

Globe J noted that the case raised three issues for determination. Firstly, Globe J had to determine whether the previous and amended attendance management provisions contained in the handbook had been incorporated into the claimants' employment contracts. He noted that the claimants' contracts provided that the handbook was divided into Pt A (terms and conditions) which were explicitly incorporated into the employment contracts and Pt B (procedures and guidance) which were relevant to the operation of the contract terms and conditions. Globe J further noted that it was well

---

22. *Sparks & Ors v Department of Transport* [2015] EWHC 181 (QB). Note – this case is under appeal.

established that an employee handbook can be incorporated into an employee's contract of employment and referred to previous authorities in support of this. Globe J provided a summary of what the status of the attendances policy was prior to the employer's amendment to the handbook in July 2012. He noted that the handbook provided that it was the intention that all of the provisions of the handbook that applied to an employee and were apt for incorporation should be incorporated into the employee's contract of employment. The generality of that provision was qualified by another provision, in that it separated out Pts A and B of the handbook. All of Pt A and all annexes of Pt A that applied to the employee and which were apt for incorporation were to be incorporated. Part B of the handbook merely contained procedures and guidance relevant to the operation of the contractual terms and conditions. Annex A of Chap 1 provided each of the agencies of the defendant with the discretion to adopt their own terms and conditions for attendance management. The Part relevant to the dispute was contained in Chap 10, Pt A of the handbook.

Globe J noted that no clear evidence was presented as to when the handbook was first created or circulated and that he had not seen a complete handbook in its original pre-July 2012 hard copy form. Globe J noted that part of the confusion about the form of the handbook related to the decision by the defendant and its agencies to stop producing hard copies of the handbook and instead to produce electronic versions. Any subsequent changes to a handbook involved an exercise in overwriting a previous version and, as such, there was a lack of archive material to trace back to earlier copies or versions. The defendant had previously sought to highlight certain provisions in Pt A of the handbook to indicate which provisions would be 'contractual'. This led to some confusion and the defendant's HR department subsequently issued a notice to all employees at the end of July 2012 stating that the 'contractual highlighting' would be removed and that the whole of Pt A of the handbook would be contractual going forward and not just the highlighted parts. The intention that the entirety of Pt A would be contractual was further supported by the defendant's response on 10 July 2014, to a freedom of information request as to the contractual effect of the highlighted provisions. The response was included in the following passage which stated that 'The Department's position is that all of Pt A of the staff handbook is apt for incorporation'.

Globe J noted that it could never have been the situation that the whole of Pt A was contractual or that all of it was apt for incorporation. Globe J referred to certain provisions contained therein which were never meant to be contractual, including provisions regarding sick pay, requirements for employees to inform line managers of absence through illness before 10 am, the provision of self-certification or medical certificates within set periods of time and requirements for line managers to keep confidential information about illnesses or medical conditions of employees. Globe J noted that in the current instance, a number of provisions were entirely inapt for incorporation into employment contracts. Globe J noted that it would have been inapt for a breach of contract to occur where a call was made after 10 am, a medical certificate form produced a day late or for guidance provisions for line managers to be terms of the contract. Globe J noted that it was necessary to look beyond the contents of the HR bulletin and the response to the freedom of information request and to examine the specific wording of the relevant provision. He noted that its contents were clearly and precisely set out. Simply stated, an employee had the right not to have the procedures in Annex A implemented until there had been more than 21 days in short-term absences as sick leave in any 12-month period. The procedures in Annex A that would then be triggered had originally been called 'Maintaining satisfactory standards of attendance'. The defendant had changed the title of the Annex to 'Disciplinary Procedures'. Whichever title was used, Globe J noted that the potential consequences of the procedures were serious. They were capable of leading to formal processes that could have resulted in written warnings and dismissal. However, Globe J found that while many of the provisions surrounding it were not apt for incorporation, the relevant provision was capable of having a life of its own and was therefore apt to be incorporated into the claimant's employment contracts.

The second issue was whether or not the defendant was entitled to unilaterally vary the terms of employment by virtue of amending the attendance management policy. Globe J noted that the handbook provided that contracts of employment could not be changed detrimentally without the employee's agreement. The handbook also provided that the defendant would not change any terms and conditions of a contract without the consent of an employee or recognised trade union. By letter dated 6 July 2012, following unsuccessful negotiations, the defendant informed the claimants' trade unions that it would be imposing a new attendance management procedure across the agencies from 9 July 2012. Globe J noted that two sub-issues arose in these circumstances with regard to whether the defendant was entitled unilaterally to vary the terms at all and whether the defendant was entitled unilaterally to vary the terms to the extent that they were varied. Globe J found that the meaning that para 1.3.1 as a whole would have conveyed to a reasonable person was that any proposals affecting a change in an employee's terms and conditions should first of all have been the subject of consultation through the Whitley Council system, with a view to reaching agreement. In the absence of agreement, unilateral changes could then have been made, but only if they were not detrimental to the employee. Globe J noted that the language of the provision was sufficiently clear, unambiguous and certain as to be interpreted as amounting to the reservation by the defendant of the right to impose unilateral changes to terms and conditions that were not detrimental to an employee. Globe J then had to determine whether or not the variation was detrimental to the claimants and referred to the dictionary definition of detrimental in addition to previous authorities. The defendant submitted that the variation was beneficial as it enabled both management and employees to deal with any issues arising from sickness absence and to attempt to address such issues at the earliest opportunity, so as to enable the employee to provide effective service. The aim was to ensure that an employee's absence is supportively managed to enable the employee to return to work at the earliest possible opportunity. Globe J noted that the reasons for the changes may have been motivated by appropriate principles, but that the amendments were fundamentally different to the previous processes. Globe J found that material differences existed between the two sets of processes and that while circumstances may not have arisen at the time to demonstrate the detriment in a clearly identifiable manner, any reasonable worker would take the view that the amended provisions were to his or her detriment. Globe J found that the defendant was not entitled to unilaterally amend the terms of the claimants' contract in these circumstances.

Globe J determined the third issue as to whether the Court should grant a declaration in the circumstances of the case and noted that, in accordance with the provisions of Civil Procedure Rule 40.20, the Court has a discretionary power to grant a binding declaration whether or not any other remedy is claimed but that in order to do so, there should exist a real and present dispute between the parties. Each party must also be affected by the Court's determination of the issues. The Court may give declaratory relief in respect of a 'friendly action' or where there is an 'academic question', if all parties accede. This may occur in circumstances of a 'test case' or where it may affect a significant number of other cases and it is in the public interest to decide the issue. Assuming all the other tests are satisfied, Globe J noted that the Court should ask whether a declaration is the most effective way of resolving the issues raised. The defendant submitted this was not a suitable case for declaratory relief given the lack of any actual detriment and the lack of any specific case by which the court can test the issue. Globe J noted that these objections were insufficient to preclude the making of a declaration if there was a useful purpose in granting a declaration.

Globe J noted that the defendant had known about the objection to the new disciplinary process from its inception, but continued to operate the new policy in any event. He noted that the defendant had done so at its own risk. Globe J found that the issue was of sufficient importance and, taking into account justice on both sides, he found that a declaration would serve a useful purpose and there existed no reasons not to grant a declaration. Globe J granted a declaration stating that the terms of the claimants' contracts of employment would be as requested by the claimants, the new procedures implemented by the defendant were not effective to implement any variation to those terms and were not contractually binding on them. The declaration also provided that by imposing the new procedures, the defendant and/or its agencies had committed an anticipatory breach of contract and if the new procedures were applied in any individual case, the defendant and/or its agencies would be committing a breach of contract.

VARIATION OF TERMS

[2.09] *Norman and Douglas v National Audit Office*[23]—*UK employment appeal tribunal—appeal from decision of employment tribunal—contract of employment—implied terms—unilateral variation—construction of terms*

The appellants worked in the National Audit Office and were members of the Public and Commercial Services Union.

This appeal originated as a claim for breach of contract to an employment tribunal, brought by the appellants when their employer, National Audit Office, attempted to impose a unilateral variation on their leave and sick pay entitlements. When the union refused consent to these changes, which were to the appellants' detriment, the employer implemented them unilaterally. The appellants were informed of the changes by way of letter and policy circular.

---

23.   *Norman and Douglas v National Audit Office*, Appeal No UKEAT/0276/14/BA.

Before the tribunal, the appellants sought to assert that their existing terms and conditions relating to paid sick leave and privileged holidays remained unchanged and had not been affected by the unilateral changes made by the employer. The employer disagreed and maintained that the contractual agreement between the parties included the right of the employer to alter or vary the terms of the agreement, irrespective of whether the appellants agreed to such an alteration or variation or not, ie a power or right of unilateral variation. In this regard they sought to rely on cl 2 of the appellants' offer letters, which provided as follows:

> subject to amendment: any significant changes affecting staff in general will be notified by Management Circulars, Policy Circulars or by General Orders, while changes affecting your particular terms and conditions will be notified separately to you.

The employer further relied on sections of its HR Manual, which it maintained were incorporated into the appellants' contracts. In particular they sought to rely on a section entitled 'Settlement of Disputes', which provided as follows:

> Wherever possible, management and the TUS will try to reach agreement before implementing any changes which affect staff. Changes to working practices or terms and conditions will not be implemented whilst negotiations are taking place, or whilst the issue is under referral to ACAS, unless management considers this essential to the operation of the National Audit Office.

The tribunal held in favour of the employer on the basis that the combination of cl 2 of the appellants' offer letters and the section of the HR manual entitled 'Settlement of Disputes' gave the employer the right of unilateral variation.

The UK EAT noted that the task which faced them was a matter of pure construction as to whether cl 2 clearly and unambiguously provided for or identified a right of the employer to vary the contract unilaterally in the manner in which it had done. After consideration of the matter in detail, the UK EAT concluded that the wording in cl 2 came 'nowhere near' being clear and unambiguous. It was considered that the relevant wording established nothing more than the potential for amendment. The UK EAT held that for a flexibility clause to be effective, it must clearly and unambiguously identify a right for the employer to vary the employment unilaterally.

In its judgment, the UK EAT stated that it encountered the most difficulty in deciding whether the provision in the HR manual had in fact been incorporated into the appellants' contracts. It concluded that this provision had not been so incorporated, on the basis that it was not a particular of conditions of service. While it noted that some parts of the HR manual did relate to particulars of service, this could not be said to be the case in relation to the section entitled 'Settlement of Disputes'. The UK EAT stated that the alternative view of this, which they did not favour, was that while much of the detail of collective bargaining was not part of the individual terms and conditions of employment of the appellants, where a right arises under that negotiating machinery to implement changes in advance of the negotiations having been concluded and with that agreement having been reached, the right to implement does become part of the appellants' contract of employment. The UK EAT added that, even if it was wrong in this regard and that a limited or qualified right of the employer to vary unilaterally did indeed exist, there were two reasons why the employer could not succeed, as follows:

- it was never maintained by the employer that the variation was essential to the operation of the employer; and

- this argument had not been advanced before the tribunal.

The UK EAT concluded that the appellant's appeal must be allowed. Accordingly, the appellants' original terms of employment were reinstated.

UNILATERAL AMENDMENT TO CONTRACT OF EMPLOYMENT

[2.10] *Cartwright & Ors v Tetrad Ltd*[24]*—UK employment appeal tribunal—appeal from decision of employment tribunal—unilateral change to terms and conditions of employment—whether pay cut constituted unilateral deduction from wages— requirement to raise formal objections and grievances—acceptance of variation through conduct—allegation of bias on behalf of employment tribunal*

The appellants' claims against their employer, the respondent, for unlawful deductions from their wages had failed before the employment tribunal.

The respondent, a furniture manufacturer, encountered financial difficulties. On 19 April 2012 it was decided to impose a 5 per cent pay cut on its unionised workforce (which included the appellants) without its express consent. The change was to take effect from 20 April 2012. The first affected pay statements were issued on 10 May 2012. On 20 April 2012 a meeting took place between management and union representatives. The tribunal had held that, at this meeting, the union full-time officer had been 'equivocal' as to whether or not his members would agree to a pay cut. The tribunal had concluded that the appellants did not give their express consent to the pay reduction. In relation to the question of whether the appellants had impliedly consented to the pay reduction, the tribunal considered that, although a union meeting was held on 20 May 2012, no outcome was ever communicated to management. Notwithstanding that further meetings took place over the summer, the first indication of objection received by the respondent had been by letter from the union's solicitor dated 23 October 2012. In circumstances where no formal objection had been lodged by the union in relation to the change of pay and no individual objections had been raised by the appellants, the employment tribunal concluded that the appellants had accepted the variation by their conduct and therefore no unauthorised deductions had been made from 10 May 2012.

The appellants appealed to the UK EAT, maintaining that the tribunal had failed to consider the material evidence before it. In particular the appellants cited an allegation that the respondent had obstructed the union's ability to consult with its members by not allowing meetings during working hours on the premises. The UK EAT accepted the

---

24. *Cartwright & Ors v Tetrad Ltd* Appeal No UKEAT/0262/14/JOJ.

respondent's evidence in this regard, ie that such meeting were permitted during break times. The approach of Elias J in *Solectron (Scotland) Ltd v Roper*[25] was applied by the UK EAT in consideration of the question of whether, on the facts found, the tribunal had been entitled to conclude that by continuing to work without protest until 23 October 2012 the appellants had accepted the change in their pay. The UK EAT held that the answer to that question was in the affirmative and the appellants' grounds for appeal in this regard were accordingly dismissed.

The appellant's final ground for appeal had been an allegation of bias on behalf of the judge in the tribunal. The UK EAT applied Lord Hope's test in *Porter v Magill*[26] in this regard and asked whether a fair-minded and informed observer, having considered the facts, would conclude that there was a real possibility that the tribunal was biased? The UK EAT concluded that there was no such possibility and the appellants' appeal on this basis was also dismissed.

INTRODUCTION OF RESTRICTIVE COVENANT AFTER EMPLOYMENT BEGINS

[2.11] *Reuse Collections Ltd v Sendall & Anor*[27]*— High Court of England and Wales—Davies J—contracts of employment—duty of loyalty—requirement to provide consideration by employer if restrictive covenants introduced after inception of employment relationship—whether employee owes fiduciary duty to employer*

Reuse Collections Ltd (the plaintiff) was a glass recycling business which had been founded in 1922 by the grandfather of the first defendant, Keith Sendall (KS). KS had been a director of the family-run business until it was transferred into the ownership of the plaintiff in the 1990s, at which time he became employed by the plaintiff as the manager of its Dagenham depot. He had no written contract of employment. In October 2012, the plaintiff gave him a draft written contract of employment which included, for the first time, provisions in relation to confidential information and post-termination restrictions. KS received a pay rise at the same time.

In 2011, KS contemplated the setting up of a business to compete with the plaintiff and from November 2012 his plans became more serious. By February 2013 he was actively contacting the plaintiff's suppliers, and at least one of its customers, with a view to winning their custom for his new business, May Glass Recycling Ltd (May Glass), the second defendant. From January 2013, he was spending a significant amount of his time, while at work for the plaintiff, on matters relating to May Glass, and in March 2013 he gave three month's notice of resignation.

Upon discovering the existence of May Glass, the plaintiff suspended KS with immediate effect, pending the conclusion of disciplinary proceedings. KS asserted that the treatment which he had received in this regard amounted to constructive dismissal and he refused to participate in the disciplinary process. The plaintiff subsequently

---

25.   *Solectron (Scotland) Ltd v Roper* [2004] IRLR 4.

26.   *Porter v Magill* [2002] 2 AC 357.

27.   *Reuse Collections Ltd v Sendall & Anor* [2014] EWHC 3852 (QB).

wrote to him stating that it regarded him as having resigned with immediate effect, failing which he would have been dismissed for gross misconduct in any event. By the end of April, May Glass had begun actively trading in competition with the plaintiff.

The plaintiff brought proceedings against KS and May Glass. The plaintiff also sought an injunction, contending that the breaches of duty by both defendants had the effect of giving the defendants a 'springboard advantage'. An interlocutory injunction was granted by the High Court.

It was not disputed that KS, as an employee of the plaintiff, owed the usual implied duty of fidelity and good faith; however, the main issue which arose was whether he also owed a fiduciary duty. The plaintiff argued that the covenants had been supported by consideration because they had been introduced as part of a package under which benefits had been conferred, including a pay rise. KS countered that the pay rise had not had anything to do with the restrictive covenants.

The plaintiff's alternative argument was that consideration could have been found by its continued employment of KS after the move to the new contract.

Davies J summarised the issues as follows:

- Did KS owe a fiduciary duty to the plaintiff in addition to an (admitted) duty of fidelity and good faith?

- Were certain restrictive covenants contained in the contract of employment signed by the KS on 22 February 2013 binding upon him? In particular:

- Did the KS receive consideration for undertaking the covenants?

- Were the covenants unreasonably wide and thus void as being contrary to public policy?

- Was KS discharged from the covenants by reason of his being constructively and wrongfully dismissed by the plaintiff?

- To what extent was KS involved in setting up the competing business established as May Glass, and did that involvement put him in breach of his obligations to the plaintiff?

- Was May Glass liable for inducing or procuring KS to breach his contract with the plaintiff or for conspiring with KS for him to do so?

- On the basis of the facts, was the plaintiff entitled to the interlocutory injunction that it obtained on 4 June 2013?

- What if any loss and damage has the plaintiff suffered as a result of such unlawful conduct on the part of KS and/or May Glass? and

- Had KS established his counterclaim?

Davies J concluded that:

- KS did not owe any fiduciary duty to the plaintiff;

- The plaintiff did not provide consideration, and the covenants were of unreasonable duration, but if they had applied KS would not have been discharged because he was not constructively dismissed;

- KS was directly and intimately involved in setting up the competing business established by May Glass, and was in breach of his duty of fidelity and good faith as a result;

- May Glass was liable for conspiring with KS to breach his contract with the plaintiff;

- The plaintiff was entitled to the interlocutory injunction that it obtained on 4 June 2013 as against both KS and May Glass;

- The plaintiff suffered loss and damage that it was entitled to recover against KS and May Glass, which was quantified in the total sum of £51,822.20.

- Because KS was not wrongfully dismissed by the plaintiff his counterclaim failed.

In relation to implied obligations, Davies J stated that it was not disputed that KS, as an employee of the plaintiff, owed it the usual implied duty of fidelity and good faith. He stated that in the case of a senior employee such as KS that would include a duty not to compete with the plaintiff during the duration of his employment, even in the absence of an express contractual term to that effect. He further stated that obligations would also be implied in relation to the unlawful misuse of what genuinely amounts to confidential information.

Davies J noted that there was no express provision for, or reference to, any fiduciary duty in the contract of employment and therefore he did not believe it was possible for such a duty to be imposed by reference to the contract. He did not consider it possible for a fiduciary duty to be imposed by reference to the wider factors relied on by the claimant either.

Davies J then considered the express contractual restrictions, which fell into two categories: restrictions in relation to confidential information; and restrictions in relation to post-termination conduct. He noted that the restrictive covenants required consideration to be enforceable, since they were introduced after the inception of the employment relationship and thus amounted to a variation of an existing contractual relationship. Counsel for KS referred to *Brearley & Bloch's Employee Covenants and Confidential Information*[28] in support of his argument that, in a case such as the present, where an employer seeks to impose substantial new obligations on an existing employee, the consideration must comprise 'some real monetary or other benefit (promotion for example) conferred on the employee for the purpose of causing the employee to agree to the restrictive covenant' and that it must be 'substantial and not nominal'.

So far as the package of benefits conferred on KS under the contract of employment was concerned, Davies J found that the majority of these benefits were already enjoyed

---

28.   *Brearley & Bloch's Employee Covenants and Confidential Information* (3rd edn, Bloomsbury Professional, 2009) at [11.3].

by KS prior to his entering into a formal contract of employment. In relation to the pay increase which he received at the time of signing the contract, he held that Reuse had failed to produce any satisfactory evidence that this salary increase was specific to either KS or to the other senior employees who were being asked to enter into a formal contract of employment, or that it was made clear to KS that the increase was conditional upon his accepting the contract of employment, or even that in some more general sense it was linked with the introduction of the new contract of employment. Davies J found that, in the circumstances, this could not be said to amount to consideration for the post-termination restrictions. Regarding the plaintiff's alternative argument that it had provided consideration by continuing to employ KS, Davies J held that this could not be said to amount to consideration either, particularly without the plaintiff having sought to link its continued willingness to employ KS with his willingness to sign the contract of employment.

There were no separate submissions as to whether or not the same requirement of consideration also applied to the incorporation of the express confidentiality clause. However, Davies J stated that, in principle, it would appear that it should, and that this was particularly so in the instant case by reason of the very wide definition of confidential information set out in the contract and the potentially substantial obligation which it imposed on KS.

Davies J went on to consider the question of the proper construction and the reasonableness of the clauses at issue and adopted the summary of principles relating to non-competition clauses generally set out in the judgment of Haddon-Cave J in *QBE v Dymoke & Ors.*[29]

In relation to the 12-month non-setting-up covenant, Davies J found that this clause was far too wide to be reasonable and that the plaintiff had wholly failed to establish how a 12-month restriction on setting up in competition could be justified, in circumstances where it appeared to accept only six months' restriction was required in relation to the other restrictive covenants. As to the reasonableness of the other clauses (non-solicitation and non-dealing), it was held that a restriction of more than three months maximum had not been objectively demonstrated as being necessary or reasonable and Davies J stated that he would have refused to enforce these covenants on that basis.

Although the issue of constructive dismissal did not arise directly for decision before Davies J, given his primary conclusions, he stated that he should deal with it as it had been fully argued and involved a need to make findings on conflicting evidence. Having considered the evidence, Davies J stated that if he had needed to decide on the issue, the constructive dismissal defence would have failed.

The Court then turned to the issue of whether KS was in breach of his obligations to the claimant by reason of his involvement in setting up the competing business carried on by May Glass. Davies J held that KS's conduct, which included arranging bank finance for May Glass; becoming its director and major shareholder; actively contacting suppliers and at least one customer with a view to winning their business for May Glass; making arrangements for the necessary skips and vehicles to be obtained for May Glass

---

29.   *QBE Management Services Ltd v Dymoke & Ors* [2012] IRLR 458 HC.

to use as a competing business; and spending a significant amount of his time, while at work, on matters relating to May Glass, amounted to a clear breach of his duty of fidelity and good faith.

So far as any implied duty of confidentiality was concerned, Davies J stated that given the narrow ambit of what the law would regard as genuinely confidential information, he did not find that KS had breached that duty. He stated that, even if he had found that KS was subject to the express confidentiality clause, he would not have held that it had been breached by KS as there was no evidence that any of the information in question was genuinely confidential.

The plaintiff also contended that May Glass was liable for intentionally inducing or procuring KS's breaches of his duties owed to the plaintiff and had engaged in an unlawful means conspiracy with KS. Davies J found that the plaintiff had failed to make out its case so far as establishing the tort of inducing or procuring breaches of contract, however he was satisfied that they had made out a case so far as establishing the tort of unlawful means conspiracy. Davies J relied on the reasons given by Morgan J in *Aerostar Maintenance International v Wilson*[30] in stating that he was satisfied that it was possible in law for there to be an unlawful means conspiracy involving a breach of the implied duty of fidelity and good faith. He was also satisfied that the other necessary ingredients of the tort of conspiracy had been made out and therefore the substantive claim against May Glass succeeded.

With regard to whether the plaintiff was entitled to an interlocutory injunction, Davies J held that the plaintiff was entitled to seek injunctive relief against KS on the basis of his breach of the implied duty of good faith and fidelity. He stated that the plaintiff would have been entitled to invite the Court to grant injunctive relief against KS on the springboard basis. The plaintiff was also found to have been entitled to seek injunctive relief against May Glass.

Finally, Davies J found that the plaintiff was entitled to damages for loss of profit suffered in the first three months after the termination of KS employment, from May 2013 to 1 August 2013.

See also *Forder v AV Pound & Company Ltd*[31] in **CH 28**, *Unfair Dismissal*.

---

30. *Aerostar Maintenance International v Wilson* [2010] All ER (D) 364 (Jul) HC.
31. *Forder v AV Pound & Company Ltd* UD927/2011, MN1057/2011, WT385/2011.

Chapter 3

COMPANIES ACT 2014: EMPLOYMENT LAW ISSUES

INTRODUCTION[1]

[3.01] The Companies Act 2014 (the Act) was enacted on 23 December 2014. The Act came into force on 1 June 2015.

The Act introduced changes to the corporate governance rules regarding directors. In this chapter we focus on the rules and the key changes that are of particular relevance from an employment perspective, under the following headings:

(a) appointment of directors;

(b) service contracts and remuneration of directors;

(c) directors' duties;

(d) removal of directors; and

(e) compensation for loss of office.

BACKGROUND

[3.02] Under the Act the old private company limited by shares is replaced by two new types of private company limited by shares:

(a) the new model private company limited by shares (the LTD); and

(b) the designated activity company (the DAC).

The other existing types of company – a public limited company (PLC), a company limited by guarantee and not having a share capital (CLG) and an unlimited company (UC) are largely replicated under the Act. The focus of the Act is on the LTD and the majority of the reforms in the Act apply to it.

APPOINTMENT OF DIRECTORS

[3.03] Previously, every company was required to have at least two directors. Under the Act an LTD is permitted to have just one director.[2] Every other type of company must continue to have at least two directors.

---

1. This chapter is focused on relevant company law provisions and so does not address any additional rules that may apply to listed or regulated companies.
2. Companies Act 2014, s 128(1).

A company must still have a secretary, who may be one of the directors;[3] however where the company has only one director, that director cannot also hold the office of secretary.[4]

The old rules as to whom a company can and cannot appoint as director are largely replicated in the Act: a company cannot appoint a body corporate;[5] an undischarged bankrupt;[6] or a person or individual who is listed as a restricted or disqualified director.[7] In addition, the Act expressly prohibits the appointment of a person of less than 18 years of age[8] (which was previously precluded in practice but not directly by law) or an unincorporated body of persons.[9]

Section 136 confirms that there is no statutory obligation on a company to require directors to hold any share qualification. In those rare cases where a company's constitution requires such a share qualification, this section operates to require a director to vacate office if the share qualification is not met within two months of appointment or if the director ceases to hold the share qualification thereafter.

As was previously the case, at least one director of a company must be resident in an EEA state, save in cases where a company obtains a certificate from the Registrar of Companies that it has a real and continuous link with one or more economic activity in Ireland, or holds a bond in the prescribed form to the value of €25,000 (rounded down from €25.394.76). The Act restates the old provisions for determining whether a director is resident in the State.[10]

The maximum number of companies of which a person can be a director remains 25.[11] However, as was previously the case, there are some exceptions to this rule, for example this number does not include some types of company (eg PLCs), and where a person is director of two or more companies, one of which is the holding company of the other(s), these shall be counted as one company in determining this number. Any purported appointment as a director in contravention of the limitation will be void.

Any appointment of a person as a director of a company without his or her consent is void.[12] This consent must include a statement by the person being appointed acknowledging the legal duties and obligations that they will have as a director under the Act and otherwise.[13]

The first directors of a company are those determined by the subscribers of the constitution or the majority of them.[14]

---

3.   Companies Act 2014, s 129(1).
4.   Companies Act 2014, s 129(6).
5.   Companies Act 2014, s 130(1).
6.   Companies Act 2014, s 132.
7.   Companies Act 2014, Pt 14, Chs 3 and 4.
8.   Companies Act 2014, s 131.
9.   Companies Act 2014, s 130(1).
10.   Companies Act 2014, s 137–141.
11.   Companies Act 2014, s 142.
12.   Companies Act 2014, s 144(1).
13.   Companies Act 2014, s 223(3).
14.   Companies Act 2014, s 144(2).

One of the innovations in the Act generally is that provisions which were previously set out in the model regulations (eg Table A model regulations), and typically adopted by companies, are now set out as statutory defaults, which apply unless the company's constitution provides otherwise.

One example of this is that directors (other than the initial directors) can be appointed by the members of the company in a general meeting, unless the company's constitution provides otherwise. In that case, a non-retiring director will only be eligible for election where notice from a voting member of the intention to propose him or her is left at the company's registered office not less than three or more than 21 days before the day appointed for the meeting and the proposed director consents to the appointment.[15]

Similarly, unless the constitution provides otherwise, the directors of a company may appoint directors to fill vacancies or add additional directors (subject to the maximum number permitted under the constitution of the company) but they will hold office only until the next following AGM and then shall be eligible for re-election.[16]

In single-member companies, the sole member may appoint a director by serving notice on the company.[17] It might be noted in this respect that any company is permitted to have just one member (whereas previously a PLC or CLG was required to have at least seven members and a UC to have two members).

As was previously the case, the appointment of directors must be voted upon individually unless a resolution that a motion for the appointment of two or more persons as directors of the company by single resolution has first been agreed by the meeting without any votes against it.[18]

The requirement on appointment of a director that certain personal details (including the director's home address) be set out in the register of directors and notified to the Companies Registration Office (CRO) (resulting in that information being publicly available) continues to apply under the Act, but one notable change in this respect is that the Minister may make regulations exempting a director or secretary from disclosing his or her home address in cases where this is warranted by circumstances concerning the safety or security of that person.[19]

SERVICE CONTRACTS AND REMUNERATION OF DIRECTORS

[3.04] A company must continue to keep copies of contracts or memoranda of contracts of service with directors of the company and of its subsidiaries and all variations to same, and the so-called 'rights of inspection' apply to these contracts. This requirement

---

15. Companies Act 2014, s 144(3)(a) and (e) and (4).
16. Companies Act 2014, s 144(3)(b).
17. Companies Act 2014, s 144(5).
18. Companies Act 2014, s 145.
19. Companies Act 2014, s 150(11).

only applies to contracts of greater than three years' duration or which cannot be terminated by the company within three years without paying compensation.[20]

Unless a company's constitution provides otherwise:

(a) the remuneration of the directors must be determined by the board of directors of the company; and

(b) the directors of a company may also be paid all travelling, hotel and other expenses properly incurred by them in attending and returning from: (i) meetings of the directors or a committee of directors; (ii) general meetings of the company; or (iii) otherwise in connection with the business of the company.

The exception to this is for a PLC, where the default provision is that unless the constitution provides otherwise, the remuneration of the directors must be determined by the members in general meeting.

Section 156 of the Act restates the old prohibition on a company making tax-free payments to directors.

DIRECTORS' DUTIES

[3.05] Part 5 of the Act sets out certain important fiduciary duties of directors previously only stated in case law, and consolidates statutory duties that were scattered across the Companies Acts 1963 to 2013. As noted above, directors are obliged to acknowledge their duties and obligations when consenting to act.[21]

Chapter 1 of Pt 5 provides that many of the duties set out in Pt 5 are owed by more than just persons who have been appointed as directors of a company (so-called '*de jure* directors', whose appointments are formally notified to the CRO). Accordingly, 'shadow directors' (persons in accordance with whose directions or instructions the directors of a company are accustomed to act)[22] and '*de facto* directors' (persons who occupy the position of director who have not been formally appointed as such)[23] will each be treated as directors of a company for the purposes of Pt 5.

Ensure compliance with the Act[24]

[3.06] Directors have a duty to ensure that the Act is complied with by the company. The breach of this duty will not invalidate any contract or other transaction or affect the enforceability of same (other than by the director in breach) but this is without prejudice to the principles of liability of a third party who has been an accessory to a breach of duty or who has knowingly received a benefit therefrom.

---

20. Companies Act 2014, s 154.
21. Companies Act 2014, s 223(3).
22. Companies Act 2014, s 221.
23. Companies Act 2014, s 222.
24. Companies Act 2014, s 223.

Regard to employees' interests[25]

[3.07] While directors are required to have regard, in the performance of their functions, to the interests of the company's employees in general as well as the interests of its members, this duty is owed to the company alone and is enforceable by the company alone. As set out below, this duty means that where there is more than one way of effecting an action which is in the best interests of the company, the directors can have regard to the interests of employees (and members) in deciding which way is preferable.

Directors' compliance statement[26]

[3.08] Directors of all PLCs and of large LTDs, DACs and CLGs (with a balance sheet total exceeding €12.5m and turnover exceeding €25m) are required to include a directors' compliance statement in the directors' report. This has been dealt with in detail in an Arthur Cox briefing;[27] it is important that companies required to prepare such a statement seek appropriate advice as to the scope of their specific obligations.

Fiduciary duties of directors

[3.09] The Act sets out for the first time in statute eight principal duties of directors (including shadow and *de facto* directors), which have been developed by the courts. The duties are expressed to be owed by directors to the company and to the company alone.[28] The breach of directors' duties will not invalidate any contract or other transaction or the enforceability of same (other than by the director in breach) but this is without prejudice to the principles of liability of a third party who has been an accessory to a breach of duty or who has knowingly received a benefit therefrom.[29] A director must:

(a) *act in good faith in what the director considers to be the interests of the company* – this imposes a subjective test on a director to act in what he or she believes to be the interests of the company and implicitly recognises that two directors can, legitimately, have different opinions as to what is in a company's best interests;

(b) *act honestly and responsibly in relation to the conduct of the affairs of the company* – this was not a common law duty but has been considered in great detail by the courts in the context of defending applications to have directors restricted;

---

25. Companies Act 2014, s 224.
26. Companies Act 2014, s 225.
27. See Arthur Cox Companies Act microsite at http://www.arthurcox.com/companies-act-home/ in the analysis of Pt 5 of the Act.
28. Companies Act 2014, s 228.
29. Companies Act 2014, s 227.

(c) *act in accordance with the company's constitution and exercise his or her powers only for the purposes allowed by law* – this requires directors to be compliant with the company's constitution and to exercise their powers in the interests of the company only;

(d) *not use the company's property, information or opportunities for his or her own or anyone else's benefit unless this is expressly permitted by the constitution or approved by resolution of the members in general meeting* – this reflects the common law position that directors are similar to trustees and control property owned by someone else (ie, the company). Directors cannot use or benefit from company property, including business opportunities, by diverting them to themselves or companies controlled by them or other third parties. Companies, acting by their members in general meeting, can release directors from, or relax, this duty;

(e) *not agree to restrict the director's power to exercise an independent judgment unless this is expressly permitted by the company's constitution or the director believes in good faith that it is in the interests of the company to fetter his or her discretion* – this recognises that directors must be independent and bring an independent judgment to decisions facing the company. It recognises, however, that in some cases it will be in the company's interests to agree to do something or refrain from doing something at a future point in time and so permits this;

(f) *avoid any conflict between the director's duties to the company and his or her other (including personal) interests unless the director is released from this duty in accordance with the constitution or by a resolution of the members* – this provides that directors must avoid conflicts of interest, eg taking a decision as to the company's position on a particular matter where the direct or indirect effect of that position is to the benefit or detriment of the director. Again the company, acting by its members in general meeting, can release directors from this duty or the constitution can provide for particular conflicts and release directors from this duty in those circumstances;

(g) *exercise the care, skill and diligence which would be exercised in the same circumstances by a reasonable person having the knowledge and experience that may reasonably be expected of a person in the same position as the director and the knowledge and experience which the director has* – this requires directors to perform their functions with care, skill and diligence. The standard by which a director is to be judged in relation to this duty is a quasi-objective standard. While the test is that a director must exercise the same care, skill and diligence as a reasonable person would exercise, that reasonable person is to be taken to be someone with that director's knowledge and experience. Therefore, and by way of example, a director who is an accountant is expected to exercise the same skill as a reasonable person who is an accountant; and

(h) *in addition to the general duty owed to employees under s 224, have regard to the interests of its members* – this requires directors to have regard to members' interests; members being the owners of the company. This duty also demonstrates that it is permissible to have regard to various parties' interests but still be required to act in the best interests of the company. This means that where it is in a company's interests to do something which can be achieved in two or more ways, and one of those ways is more in the interests of the members or the employees, then that way is preferable. While directors are required to have regard to the interests of employees and members, they may have regard to other peoples' interests too. Provided that they first and foremost act in the interests of the company, there is no prohibition on having regard to other people's interests. Directors are also permitted to have regard to the interests of a particular member where that director has been appointed or nominated for appointment by that member on foot of his or her entitlement under the constitution or a shareholders' agreement.[30]

Other interests of directors

[3.10] Directors are permitted, subject to the constitution of the company, to become an officer of, or otherwise interested in, any company promoted by the company or in which it is interested as shareholder or otherwise, but without prejudice to the director's fiduciary duties.[31]

Power to act in a professional capacity for the company

[3.11] Subject to a company's constitution, a director is permitted to act in a professional capacity for the company and be entitled to be remunerated.[32]

Duty to disclose interest in contracts

[3.12] A director who is in any way, directly or indirectly, interested in a contract or proposed contract with his or her company, has a duty to declare the nature of that interest at a meeting of the directors. While this provision is in the main a restatement of s 194 of the Companies Act 1963, it contains two very important clarifications:

(a) the duty applies only in respect of a contract where the decision whether to enter into that contract is taken, or falls to be taken, by the board of directors or a committee of which the director in question is a member; and

(b) the duty to disclose applies only in relation to an interest that can reasonably be regarded as likely to give rise to a conflict of interest.[33]

---

30.   Companies Act 2014, s 228(3).
31.   Companies Act 2014, s 229.
32.   Companies Act 2014, s 230.
33.   Companies Act 2014, s 231.

Breaches of duties: liability to account and indemnify

[3.13] The breach of certain directors' duties can result in the director and others being liable to account to the company for any gain made by him or her and liable to indemnify the company for any loss incurred by it as a result of such a breach.[34] This section also sets out the consequences for breaching other sections contained in Pt 5, such as those in connection with substantial property transactions and loans to directors (which have been analysed in an Arthur Cox briefing).[35]

Power of court to grant relief

[3.14] The court may grant relief to an officer in any proceedings brought for negligence, default, breach of duty or breach of trust, where the officer is shown to have acted honestly and reasonably.[36]

Anticipated claims

[3.15] A director may seek to be relieved of liability where he or she has acted honestly and reasonably in relation to an anticipated future claim for negligence, default, breach of duty or breach of trust.[37]

Exclusion of liability and indemnities

[3.16] Any provision in a contract or the company's constitution will be void where it purports to exempt or indemnify an officer from any liability which would otherwise attach in respect of any negligence, default, breach of duty or breach of trust, save in situations where, in defending proceedings, a director is given judgment in his or her favour or he or she is acquitted; or in connection with s 233 or s 234 proceedings. This provision also addresses related matters, including directors' and officers' liability insurance and cases where companies are re-registered in Ireland.[38]

Duty to ensure that secretary has necessary skills or resources

[3.17] The Act places a new duty on directors of a company (other than a PLC) to ensure that the person appointed as secretary has the skills or resources necessary to

---

34. Companies Act 2014, s 232.
35. See Arthur Cox Companies Act microsite at http://www.arthurcox.com/companies-act-home/ in the analysis of Pt 5 of the Act.
36. Companies Act 2014, s 233.
37. Companies Act 2014, s 234.
38. Companies Act 2014, s 235.

discharge his or her statutory and other duties.[39] The qualifications necessary to act as secretary of a PLC largely replicate the old law.

REMOVAL OF DIRECTORS

[3.18] A director of a company may be removed by the members by ordinary resolution,[40] and 28 days' notice must be given to the company of the intention to move such a resolution, save in circumstances where the directors have resolved to submit it.[41] This reflects the old law, save that the term 'extended notice', which was previously used to refer to this 28-day period, is not used in the Act. The company must give notice to the director concerned (and to its members), and the director concerned (whether a member of the company or not) is entitled to be heard on the resolution at that meeting.[42] A vacancy created by the removal of a director in this manner may be filled at the same meeting for the remainder of the removed director's term.[43]

The office of director is vacated if a director becomes bankrupt or disqualified and, unless the constitution otherwise provides, where the director resigns, becomes of unsound mind, is restricted, sentenced to a term of imprisonment for an indictable offence or is absent for six months without permission.[44] This largely reflects the provisions previously set out in this regard in the Table A model regulations.

Where a director is removed from office, he will not be precluded from seeking any remedy to which he might be entitled under his contract of employment.[45]

A multi-member company cannot pass a unanimous written resolution to remove a director.[46] The Act introduced new decision-making mechanisms for shareholders. Majority written resolutions can be passed as ordinary resolutions (more than 50 per cent of total voting rights) or special resolutions (75 per cent or more of total voting rights) and will take effect seven or 21 days, respectively, after the last member has signed. This is in addition to the old system where written shareholder resolutions must be unanimous and take immediate effect, which option is still available to companies. A company may not use the new majority written resolution to remove a director.[47] Accordingly, it remains the case that a company *cannot* remove a director by passing a written resolution.

Section 196(2) expressly provides that a written decision of the sole member of a single-member company can be used to remove a director. The European Communities

---

39. Companies Act 2014, s 129(4).
40. Companies Act 2014, s 146(1). Note that s 146(1) does not authorise the removal of a director for life.
41. Companies Act 2014, s 146(3)(a).
42. Companies Act 2014, s 146(3)(b).
43. Companies Act 2014, s 146(1) and (11).
44. Companies Act 2014, s 148.
45. Companies Act 2014, s 147.
46. Companies Act 2014, s 193(11).
47. Companies Act 2014, s 195(1).

(Single-Member Private Limited Companies) Regulations 1994[48] (the 1994 Regulations) previously allowed for written decisions of the sole member. However, s 196(2) includes a new provision which states that this power of removal 'is without prejudice to the application of the requirements of procedural fairness to the exercise of that power of removal by the sole member' and without prejudice to s 147 regarding compensation (referred to at para **[3.06]** above). The reference to 'procedural fairness' would imply that one cannot simply, without due process, remove a director of a single-member company by written decision with immediate effect, as has been done under the 1994 Regulations.

Companies must maintain a register of directors and secretaries, must file changes in the register and particulars of directors must be shown on business letters.[49] As noted above, there is the possibility for an exemption from the requirement to disclose a director's home address, where warranted by concerns for his or her safety or security. Where companies have failed to notify the CRO that persons have ceased to be directors or secretaries, those persons can self-report, as was previously the case.[50]

As an alternative to removal by the members, the constitution may provide that the directors may remove a director and may set out the process to be used by the directors for that purpose.

COMPENSATION FOR LOSS OF OFFICE

The old law on payments to directors as compensation for loss of office

[3.19] Sections 186 and 189(3) of the Companies Act 1963 provided that payment of compensation for loss of office as director or, while director, of any other office in connection with the management of a company's affairs (except any bona fide payment by way of damages for breach of contract or by way of pension in respect of past services) is unlawful, unless pre-approved by the shareholders of the company in general meeting.

The primary purpose of s 186 was to protect the company and, indirectly, its shareholders, from abuse by directors of their position of trust by using company funds to make generous termination payments to one of their number on removal, resignation or retirement.

The new law: s 251 of the Act

[3.20] The Act recasts the restriction in s 186 in markedly more precise terms. Section 251, in conjunction with s 254(5), provides that it shall not be lawful for a company to

---

48. European Communities (Single-Member Private Limited Companies) Regulations 1994 (SI 275/1994).

49. Companies Act 2014, ss 149–151.

50. Companies Act 2014, s 152.

make a payment by way of compensation for loss of office (including a management office) to a director unless the following conditions are satisfied:

(a) the particulars relating to the proposed payment (including the amount of it) are disclosed to the members of the company; and

(b) the proposal is approved by resolution of the company in general meeting.

Sections 221 and 222 of the Act apply Pt 5 to shadow directors and *de facto* directors respectively, and, therefore, payments for loss of office made to such individuals are also caught by s 251. The prohibition in s 251 also extends to payments to former directors.[51]

While the marginal note to s 251 refers to payments by a company to directors or directors' dependents for loss of office, there is no reference to directors' dependents in the Act. Accordingly, payments to dependents for loss of a director's office are prima facie not caught by s 251 but if the payments were to be made for the director's benefit, they would be caught by s 251.

Section 254(5) brings under the ambit of s 251 payments by way of compensation for loss of a management office (eg, the post of CEO or finance director) where the individual losing that office is also a director of the company and possibly continues to hold that directorship.

Section 254(5) also provides that a payment made bona fide in discharge of an existing legal obligation does not fall within s 251. Section 254 defines an 'existing legal obligation' as one that was not entered into in connection with or in consequence of the event giving rise to the payment for loss of office in question. This statutory carve-out had not been provided for previously and its introduction owes its origin to case law, in which a distinction has been drawn between a termination payment that a company has a pre-existing legal obligation to make, for example because it is provided for in a contract of employment, and one that it does not. Case law from the UK,[52] Australia and New Zealand[53] confirms that prior shareholder approval is only required in respect of the latter. Unfortunately there is no decision of the High Court in Ireland on s 186.

Section 254(5) provides that s 251 does not apply to any bona fide payments by way of damages for breach of contract or pension in respect of past services.

Section 232(3) provides that where a company makes a payment to a director in breach of s 251, that director shall be liable:

(a) to account to the company for any gain which he or she makes directly or indirectly from the payment;

(b) to indemnify the company for any loss or damage resulting from the payment; or

(c) to do both of those things as the circumstances may require.

---

51. Companies Act 2014, s 254(7).
52. In *Re Duomatic Ltd* [1969] 2 CH 365, *Mercer v Heart of Midlothian plc* [2001] SLT 945 Court of Session (Outer House), *Gooding & Anor v Cater & Ors*, 13 March 1989, English High Court.
53. *Taupo Totara Timber Co Ltd v Rowe* [1977] 3 All ER 123, [1978] AC 537.

This provision provides clarification as to the legal consequences of a payment made in breach of that section and the position and duties of the recipient of such payment.

Chapter 4

DATA PROTECTION

Rob Corbet, Partner & Olivia Mullooly, Associate

INTRODUCTION

[4.01] The year 2015 saw continued developments in data protection on an international scale, with the Court of Justice of the European Union (CJEU) invalidating the Safe Harbour mechanism approved by the European Commission in 2010 for the transfers of personal data from the European Union to the United States (discussed in more detail below). This decision again stresses that the right to protection of personal data is 'guaranteed' by the Charter of Fundamental Rights of the European Union (the Charter) and that the Data Protection Directive (the Directive)[1] and the roles of national supervisory authorities in protecting this right are to be applied in light of the Charter. This continues a line of CJEU cases which were decided on similar principles in 2014,[2] which referred extensively to the Charter in support of the Court's decision. The principles of necessity, proportionality and transparency are now firmly enshrined in European data protection law and will need to be equally borne in mind when processing personal data in the context of the workplace. The Office of the Data Protection Commissioner (ODPC) has in the past identified these principles as important components of compliance for processing employee data, where consent is viewed as an insufficient legitimiser when the processing is otherwise excessive or disproportionate.

On a domestic basis, the Data Protection Commissioner, Helen Dixon, has, since taking up office in 2014, expanded the resources of her office to include an office in Dublin, as well as the base in Portarlington. In her first annual report for 2014,[3] she noted that the largest single category of complaints related to data subject access requests, and the Commissioner was particularly critical of delays on the part of the data controllers in responding to access requests within the 40-day statutory timeframe. Employers should be mindful of this when dealing with these requests, particularly if the response to the request is likely to result in a complaint to the ODPC. 2014 also saw a large increase in the number of data breaches being notified to the ODPC.

---

1.   Directive 95/46/EC.
2.   Judgment in *Google Spain SL, Google Inc v Agencia Española de Protección de Datos, Mario Costeja González* (Case C–131/12); judgment in *Digital Rights Ireland and Seitlinger & Ors* (Joined Cases C–293/12 and C–594/12).
3.   Twenty-sixth Annual Report of the Data Protection Commissioner, 2014 dated 23 June 2015.

RELEVANT LEGISLATION

Hiring of private investigators

[4.02] Pursuant to the Private Security Services Act 2004 (Commencement) Order 2015[4] and the Private Security (Licensing and Standards) (Private Investigator) Regulations 2015,[5] it is now an offence to engage or employ a private investigator who is not licensed by the Private Security Authority. This is important from a data protection perspective where the ODPC has, in the past, conducted investigations and prosecuted businesses arising out of their use of private investigators in a manner that breached the Data Protection Acts 1988 and 2003.

RELEVANT CASE LAW

[4.03] *Weltimmo v Nemzeti*[6]—*concept of 'establishment' under art 4(1) of the Directive—place of establishment of data controller*

Another notable decision of the CJEU issued in October 2015 in the judgment in *Weltimmo v Nemzeti*, whereby Weltimmo, a company registered and headquartered in Slovakia, that operated a website that provided services to residents in Hungary, was found to be 'established' in Hungary for the purpose of the Directive; Weltimmo did not have a branch or office in Hungary and none of the other bases for the application of Hungarian law under the Directive was applicable.

The CJEU noted the data protection law of a Member State applies to data processing activities 'where the processing is carried out in the context of the activities of an establishment of the controller on the territory of the Member State'. However, in applying art 4(1) of the Directive, which governs the determination of establishment for data protection compliance purposes, the Court observed, following on from its decision in *Google Spain*, that establishment is a flexible concept which 'extends to any real and effective activity – even a minimal one – exercised through stable arrangements'.

One of the factors that the CJEU took into account was the presence of a single representative in Hungary. The Court found this was sufficient to create an establishment of the controller in that Member State. This decision is potentially significant for businesses that maintain even a minimal presence in another EU state whereby that state's laws will apply to processing undertaken in the context of that local establishment. Any business that employs or engages representatives in other EU Member States, even in the absence of an established agency or branch in that state, should bear in mind the potential implications of this decision.

---

4.   Private Security Services Act 2004 (Commencement) Order 2015 (SI 194/2015).
5.   Private Security (Licensing and Standards) (Private Investigator) Regulations 2015 (SI 195/2015).
6.   *Weltimmo v Nemzeti* (Case C–230/14).

The agreed text of the General Data Protection Regulation changes this position as the Regulation includes detailed provisions governing the so-called 'one-stop shop' for companies operating in several jurisdictions across the EU. The Regulation was agreed in December 2015 with the conclusion of the 'trilogue' legislative process between the European Commission, the European Parliament and the European Council. Although the text of the Regulation was agreed, the Regulation was not yet published in the Official Journal at the time of writing (with publication of the final text expected in Q1 of 2016). The Regulation will have a two-year lead-in period and looks set to significantly change the data protection regulatory environment for employers as 'data controllers'. Employers are likely to see these changes most prominently in respect of legitimising the processing of personal data, increased record-keeping obligations and the updated breach notification mechanism, among other developments.

[4.04] *Schrems v Data Protection Commissioner[7]—CJEU—data protection—safe harbor*

This landmark European data protection law case of 2015 was handed down in October 2015 and rendered the Commission Decision underpinning the Safe Harbor regime (Commission Decision 2000/520/EC, the Decision) invalid. The case was instigated by Mr Schrems who made a complaint to the Irish Data Protection Commissioner (DPC) alleging that Facebook Ireland's data transfers to Facebook Inc. (located in the US) were not compliant with EU data protection laws. The transfer of this data occurred pursuant to Facebook's 'Safe Harbor' certification. The DPC rejected Mr Schrems' complaint and Mr Schrems appealed this decision to the Irish High Court which, in turn, referred a query as to the legality of the Safe Harbor regime to the CJEU.

The CJEU held that the Safe Harbor regime was invalid for two reasons: a) the Decision failed to sufficiently examine the data protection standards in the US to ensure, by reason of US domestic law or its international commitments, a level of protection of fundamental rights which were equivalent to those guaranteed in the EU; and b) the Decision potentially deprived data subjects of their rights of access to Data Protection Supervisory Authorities who are vested with the authority to exercise independent oversight of data controllers within their jurisdiction.

The judgment in *Schrems v Data Protection Commissioner* had immediate consequences for the over 4,000 companies who have self-certified under the Safe Harbor regime and to all of their customers and other contractors who have relied on that certification to legitimise transfers of personal data to the US. The European Commission stated that it hoped to resolve this issue with a reformed version of the Safe Harbor framework and estimated that this would be agreed upon by early February 2016. At the time of writing, a 'Safe Harbor II' was not yet agreed. However, as the Irish DPC acknowledged, there are other legal methods (for example, data subject consent, the use of binding corporate rules or model contracts) by which international data transfers may be legitimised by data controllers and data processors in the interim.

---

7.   *Schrems v Data Protection Commissioner* (Case C–362/14).

CASE STUDIES OF THE OFFICE OF THE DATA PROTECTION COMMISSIONER

In 2014, two case studies relevant to the workplace were published by the ODPC in its Twenty-sixth Annual Report dated 23 June 2015.

[4.05] *Case Study 11 of 2014: failure to meet statutory timeframe for processing access request*

A staff member of eircom made a complaint to the ODPC arising from the alleged failure of eircom to comply with an access request. The staff member had sought a particular document and eircom argued that it had already provided the requester with this document prior to him making the access request that was the subject of the complaint. Eircom then re-sent the document to the staff member but, as the 40-day timeframe had then expired, the ODPC found that eircom had breached s 4(1)(a) of the Data Protection Acts 1988 and 2003 by failing to provide the requester with a copy of the requested personal data in response to his access request. This finding demonstrates that the ODPC will not tolerate a failure to respond to an access request within the 40-day period, even if the personal data in question has already been released to the requester in advance of the access request.

The ODPC used this example to criticise the failure of data controllers to respond either appropriately or in a timely manner to access requests, which had accounted for over 50 per cent of the complaints in 2014 with a 'common theme' being a failure to respond within the 40-day statutory timeframe and, in some cases, not at all. The ODPC noted that 'far too many data subjects are experiencing barriers and access denying tactics on the part of data controllers'.

In light of the high level of complaints to the ODPC arising from data access requests, it is important that employers thoroughly consider the scope of personal data that falls within the request and any relevant exemptions, and issue the relevant response within the 40-day timeframe, as the ODPC is likely to take a dim view of failure to meet this timeframe in the event that a complaint is made.

[4.06] *Case Study 14 of 2014: Employee of financial institution resigns taking customer data*

In this case study, the Commissioner reported that a departing employee had emailed a spreadsheet containing customer details to his or her personal email account. It subsequently transpired that the employee had commenced operating a new business and was therefore handling the personal data as a data controller. The ODPC questioned the ex-employee as to the basis of consent for processing the personal data in this new business. The ex-employee informed the ODPC that, as part of his or her employment, he or she had been asked to use his or her own laptop and personal phone for all business dealings. The ex-employee confirmed that he or she had not used the data contained in the spreadsheet and that all copies had been deleted.

Although the financial institution in question did have appropriate data protection clauses in the contract of employment, the ODPC noted that as employees were using their own personal equipment for business purposes, the financial institution had little or no control over the data held on that equipment. The institution introduced additional policies and procedures including the introduction of software to password protect any data records that were being emailed. The institution also introduced a policy that all employees must sign an undertaking on termination of employment that all data has been returned and will not be further processed.

AUDITS AND INVESTIGATIONS

[4.07] The ODPC has, in the last number of months, investigated 40 sample organisations for compliance with s 4(13) of the Data Protection Acts 1988 and 2003, which makes it unlawful for employers to require employees or applicants to make an access request of another organisation (eg An Garda Síochána), seeking copies of personal data which is then made available to the employer or prospective employer. In light of a continued high number of access requests being made to An Garda Síochána, the Commissioner has announced that her office will 'vigorously pursue and prosecute any abuse detected in this area'. Employers are reminded that this method of vetting employees and prospective employees is an offence and that recruitment processes should be checked for confirmation that this practice is not used in the recruitment of individuals.

Chapter 5

EMPLOYMENT EQUALITY

EQUALITY (MISCELLANEOUS PROVISIONS) ACT 2015

[5.01] The Equality (Miscellaneous Provisions) Act 2015 (the '2015 Act') was enacted on 10 December 2015 and was commenced with effect from 1 January 2016.[1]

The 2015 Act makes numerous amendments to employment equality legislation and of particular note are the introduction of the statutory obligation to objectively justify compulsory retirements and the issuance of fixed-term contracts to employees over the compulsory retirement age for the employment concerned. In addition, the 2015 Act restricts certain derogations from equality laws which are available to religious-run education and medical institutions and it amends the Equal Status Act 2000 to add an additional ground of discrimination.

Compulsory retirements

[5.02] Section 10 of the 2015 Act amends s 34 of the Employment Equality Act 1998 by substituting a new subsection for subsection (4), which now provides that it shall not constitute discrimination on the age ground to fix different ages for the retirement (whether voluntarily or compulsorily) of employees or any class or description of employees, if same is objectively and reasonably justified by a legitimate aim and the means of achieving the aim are appropriate and necessary. This amendment brings the legislation relating to compulsory retirement into line with case law from the Court of Justice of the European Union.[2] While the amendment does not impact on an employer's ability to set a compulsory retirement age, it does impact the ability to enforce that retirement age, in that the employer may be required to justify retirement at that age by reference to the statutory test.

Section 4 of the 2015 Act amends s 6 of the Employment Equality Act 1998 by substituting a new paragraph (c), which provides that it shall not constitute discrimination on the age ground to offer a fixed-term contract of employment to a person over the compulsory retirement age for that employment (or to a particular class or description of employees) if the fixed term contract is objectively justified by a legitimate aim and the means of achieving that aim are appropriate and necessary. One of the practical consequences of this is that if an employer offers a fixed-term contract to an employee in respect of their continued employment beyond their retirement age, it will have to be able to objectively justify its decision to do so and its failure to allow the

---

1. Equality (Miscellaneous Provisions) Act 2015 (Commencement) Order 2015 (SI 610/ 2015).

2. For a concise summary of the key decisions of the CJEU, see the excerpt from the judgment of Hale J in the UK Supreme Court decision in *Seldon v Clarkson Wright & Jakes* [2012] UK SC 16 on p 365 of the *Arthur Cox Employment Law Yearbook 2013*.

employee continue in permanent employment beyond the employee's retirement date. Furthermore, on expiry of such a fixed-term contract, the employer may have to be in a position to objectively justify a decision not to renew the fixed-term contract for a further fixed-term.

Impact for religious-run educational and medical institutions

[5.03] Section 11 of the 2015 Act amends s 37 of the Employment Equality Act 1998 by inserting new subsections (1A), (1B) and (1C) so as to limit the religious discrimination exemption previously available to religious-run educational and medical institutions.

Subsection (1A) provides that where an educational or medical institution is maintained, in whole or in part, by public monies, more favourable treatment on the religion ground given by that institution to an employee or prospective employee shall be taken to be discrimination unless (a) the treatment does not constitute discrimination on any of the other discriminatory grounds; and (b) by reason of the nature of the institution's activities or the context in which the activities are being carried out, the religion or belief of the employee or prospective employee constitutes a genuine, legitimate and justified occupational requirement having regard to the institute's ethos.

Subsection (1B) provides that where an educational or medical institution is maintained, in whole or in part, by public monies, an action taken by that institution which is reasonably necessary to prevent an employee or prospective employee from undermining the religious ethos of the institution shall be taken to be discrimination unless by reason of the nature of the employment concerned or the context in which it is carried out (a) the action is objectively justified by the institution's aim of preventing the undermining of the religious ethos of the institution and (b) the means of achieving that aim are appropriate and necessary.

Subsection (1C) provides that an action referred to in subsection (1B) shall not be objectively justified unless the action is (a) rationally and strictly related to the institution's religious ethos; (b) a response to conduct of the employee or prospective employee undermining the religious ethos of the institution rather than a response to that employee's or prospective employee's gender, civil status, family status, sexual orientation, age, disability, race or membership of the Traveller community; and (c) proportionate to the conduct of the employee or prospective employee having due regard to (i) any other action the employer make take in the circumstances, (ii) the consequences of that action for that employee or prospective employee, (iii) the employee's or prospective employee's right to privacy, and (iv) the actual damage caused to the religious ethos of the institution by the conduct of that employee or prospective employee.

Housing assistance ground

[5.04] Section 13 of the 2015 Act amends the Equal Status Act 2000 so as to add an additional ground of prohibited discrimination (to be known as the housing assistance ground) such that discrimination on that ground against persons in receipt of a statutory rent supplement, housing assistance or any payment under the Social Welfare Acts is prohibited. This is to prohibit discrimination in the area of the letting of dwelling houses.

PRELIMINARY ISSUES

[5.05] *A Chef v A Hospital[3]—Equality Tribunal—Employment Equality Acts 1998 to 2015—Safety, Health and Welfare at Work Act 2005—alleged discrimination on grounds of race, religion, disability, harassment and salary—preliminary point— whether Equality Tribunal had jurisdiction where parties entered into written settlement of certain statutory employment claims*

The Equality Tribunal considered the preliminary issue as to its jurisdiction. The respondent stated that a final settlement between the parties was agreed and signed on 17 February 2014, subsequent to this claim being initiated. The agreement stated that the complainant had accepted an agreed sum as a final settlement of all claims arising from her employment both at common law and under statute. The settlement agreement went on to provide that the sum was inclusive of any entitlement or claims under certain listed statutes to include the Employment Equality Acts 1998–2015 and all other relevant legislation. The respondent submitted that the agreement was accepted by the complainant following time to reflect on its contents and to take professional advice. The complainant and her SIPTU official signed their acceptance of the agreement and the consideration was paid and accepted. It was submitted by the respondent that the complainant did not have a right to take this claim under the Acts. The complainant maintained that while SIPTU was representing her on a health and safety matter, she had separate legal representation dealing with this equality issue. The consideration that was agreed with the respondent was in respect of a complaint under the Safety, Health and Welfare at Work Act 2005 and in particular a loss of earnings claim.

Reference was made to a letter from the employer dated 6 February 2014 which provided for the payment of the amount for the health and safety claim. The complainant maintained that while she and her representative had signed the settlement terms, the reference to equality was slipped in by the employer. The Equality Tribunal noted the wording of the settlement agreement, particularly the reference to the statutory claims listed. Reference was also made by the Tribunal to the acknowledgement within the agreement that the complainant had read the document and had it explained to her prior to signing and that she had been given the opportunity to seek legal or trade union advice prior to signing same and that she understood and accepted the contents in full.

The Tribunal noted the High Court decision in *Sunday Newspapers Ltd v Kinsella and Bradley[4]* and the Supreme Court decision in *Doran v Thompson.[5]* The Tribunal concluded that a final settlement means that it is final and that the settlement was subsequent to the presentation of the claim before the Tribunal. The Tribunal found that the complainant had the benefit of professional representation, she had time to reflect on

---

3. *A Chef v A Hospital* DEC–E 2015–054.
4. *Sunday Newspapers Ltd v Kinsella and Bradley* [2007] IEHC 324.
5. *Doran v Thompson* [1978] IR 223.

the terms of the agreement and she signed an agreement which explicitly stated that it was in final agreement and that it encompassed the Employment Equality Acts. The Tribunal concluded that the complainant could not now ignore the obligations placed upon her by signing that agreement and thus the Tribunal did not have jurisdiction to hear this case in accordance with s 79(6) of the Acts.

Validity of a compromise agreement

[5.06] *McGrath and Ryan v Athlone Institute of Technology*[6]*—Equality Tribunal—Employment Equality Acts 1998 to 2015, s 6(2)(f), s 74(2)—discrimination on ground of age—victimisation—whether terms of compromise agreement precluded the bringing of claims in question— significance of independent legal advice—key elements of victimisation*

The complainants lodged separate complaints, which were jointly heard by the Equality Tribunal. The complainants maintained that they had been discriminated against on the ground of age, contrary to s 6(2)(f) of the Acts. They maintained that this discrimination was evident in the fact that the respondent had offered their younger colleagues re-training and grade progression while they had not been afforded these opportunities; and in the fact that reassignment was offered to their younger colleagues whereas they had been redeployed. The complainants further claimed that they had suffered victimisation within the meaning of s 74(2) of the Acts.

The respondent made a preliminary application to the Equality Tribunal, maintaining that the Tribunal lacked jurisdiction to hear the claims on the basis of a binding settlement agreement signed by the complainants on 19 January 2012.

By way of background, the complainants had been engaged by the respondent as assistant lecturers in 2005, under a series of specific-purpose contracts. Eventually, the prevailing economic conditions caused the trades courses on which the complainants were teaching to be discontinued. When the respondent sought to make the complainants redundant, they brought claims under the Protection of Employees (Fixed-Term Work) Act 2003. While these claims were initially rejected by a Rights Commissioner, on appeal the Labour Court awarded the complainants contracts of indefinite duration. Further litigation ensued between the complainants and the respondent, amounting to four different proceedings before the High Court and one before the Supreme Court. These claims, in their entirety, were compromised by the signing of the agreement. The agreement was executed by the complainants and witnessed by their solicitor. It was executed on behalf of the respondent by the HR manager.

The Tribunal examined the terms of the agreement. It was noted that while cl 8 struck out the various sets of proceedings which had been pending in the High Court and the Supreme Court, cl 9 of the agreement provided:

> Mr McGrath and Mr Ryan may prosecute claims pursuant to the Industrial Relations Acts in respect of grade progression and while they must institute such

---

6.   *McGrath and Ryan v Athlone Institute of Technology* DEC–E2015–114.

claims prior to their redeployment the bringing of such claims shall not interfere
or delay such redeployment.

Additionally, cl 13 of the agreement contained a full and final settlement clause in the
following terms:

The foregoing constitutes full and final settlement between the employees named
at 1 above the employer of all claims of whatsoever nature and disputes arising
from the cessation of the trades courses and their resulting redeployment.

After the signing of the agreement the complainants applied to the respondent for grade
progression, from the position of assistant lecturer to lecturer. As the information
submitted did not meet the requirements, their applications were refused by the
respondent. The complainants brought claims under the Industrial Relations legislation.
As a result, a Right Commissioner recommended that the complainants be allowed the
opportunity to review the respondent's decision to refuse their applications for grade
progression. The respondent facilitated such a review. The complainants wrote to the
respondent alleging that they had been 'singled out, bullied, discriminated, victimised
and excluded' by named employees of the respondent. They requested an open and
transparent enquiry through the grievance procedure. The respondent replied to the
complainants, referring them to terms of the agreement and explaining that their
applications for grade progression were being dealt with under a separate process.
Numerous pieces of correspondence were exchanged between the parties. The
complainants continuously suggested that they had been subject to exclusion, ageism,
victimisation, bullying and discrimination.

Ultimately the respondent awarded the complainants progression to the position of
lecturer.

The complainants subsequently raised an issue with their placement on the lecturer
scale. While they had been placed on point one of the scale, they argued that certain
named co-workers had been placed on point two of the scale. As these colleagues were
20 years younger than them, the complainants alleged that this was further proof of
ageism and discrimination on the part of the respondent. The respondent replied, setting
out information regarding increment dates and how they were calculated. Subsequently,
the complainants were both placed on point three of the lecturer scale. The complainants
received retrospective payment for the weeks in respect of which they were on the
incorrect scale.

The respondent redeployed the complainants to Kildare Wicklow Education and
Training Board and Laois Offaly Education and Training Board, where they work as
Resource Persons for Youth Reach. The complainants told the Equality Tribunal that,
while their pay terms did not change on account of this redeployment, they now work in
positions which are seven grades below their previous positions as lecturers.

The complainants' union representative (JOC) gave evidence on their behalf before
the Equality Tribunal. He stated that there had been no effort to reassign the
complainants and that none of his representations to keep the complainants in
employment in the Institute had been entertained by the respondent. By way of evidence
that this treatment of the complainants was attributable to their age, JOC produced an
email dated 10 June 2014 from the respondent's HR manager. This email suggested that

the complainants should look at retirement opportunities or even a voluntary redundancy package that was available. JOC stated that this email was proof that the actions of the respondent, in not internally reassigning the complainants, were solely based on ageism and victimisation. It was alleged that younger workers had not been asked to accept retirement. Further evidence was given by witnesses on behalf of the complainants in relation to younger colleagues who had been retrained and reassigned, as opposed to redeployed.

The complainants stated that they had been adversely treated in four separate respects:

- retraining had been offered to their younger colleagues and not to them;

- reassignment had been offered to their younger colleagues, while they had been redeployed;

- they had been put on the wrong pay scale following grade progression; and

- they had been isolated, bullied and harassed.

Although the complainants had agreed that they had signed the agreement with the benefit of legal advice, they disagreed that they had waived any future claims that they could bring in relation to their employment.

On the other hand, the respondent's case was that the complainants simply had no right to bring these claims. The agreement had been drafted by the parties' counsel. The respondent relied in particular on cl 13 of the agreement, which stated that the complainants had compromised their entitlement to bring any future claim if it arose out of the cessation of the trades courses or the redeployment of the complainants. The wording of cl 13 referred to 'all claims of whatsoever nature and dispute arising'. The respondent told the Tribunal that the language of the agreement had been carefully negotiated, on account of the fact that the litigation between the parties leading up to its signing was 'fractious and difficult'. The respondent maintained that the failure to list the various Acts of employment legislation in the agreement was not fatal. Furthermore, the respondent maintained that, on account of the fact that the redeployment of the complainants was through the Department of Education Scheme, it had no control over where the complainants were redeployed to. In addition, the complainants had been given the opportunity to appeal their redeployment. The respondent stated that it was a matter of public policy that parties should be encouraged to settle proceedings. The respondent stated its view that the courts would uphold such compromises unless it could be shown that the agreement reached was somehow reached by unlawful means, which was not applicable in this case.

The respondent maintained that the complainants had merely made assertions and had not provided primary facts from which the presumption of discrimination on the ground of age could be drawn. The comparators named by the complainants were differentiated from them in that they had academic degrees which allowed them to be considered to teach other courses. This was not the case in relation to the complainants, as they did not have the requisite qualifications. Finally, in relation to the email of 10 June 2014, the respondent stated that this email had no relevance to the case and was not evidence of ageism. The HR manager was entitled to form the view that the complainants had been uncooperative.

In its decision on the preliminary issue, the Tribunal referred to cl 13 of the agreement. The Tribunal stated that, in accordance with the terms of the agreement, the only proceedings which could be brought were those 'carved out' of the agreement by cl 9, ie those in respect of grade progression under the Industrial Relations Acts. The Tribunal commented on the obvious hostility which existed between the parties. It noted that although the complainants exhausted all remedies available to them in relation to their grade progression, they had ultimately been unsuccessful. The Tribunal stated that it was bound by the decision of Smyth J in *Sunday Newspapers Ltd v Kinsella and Bradley.*[7] It stated that the question of whether or not rights had been compromised was a matter for the proper construction of the agreement itself. The Tribunal noted that the agreement had been entered into after a long series of claims, on legal advice and following extensive negotiation in relation to the wording of the agreement. Accordingly, it concluded that the complainants were bound by the agreement and estopped from bringing the claims insofar as they related to retraining and reassignment.

The Tribunal found that the grade progression claim was not excluded by the agreement. However, it concluded that there was no evidence of any alleged treatment of the complainants by the respondents that could be attributed to their age in this regard.

Furthermore the Tribunal held that the claim of victimisation was not covered by the agreement. It noted the definition of victimisation contained in s 74(2) of the Acts and stated that the key elements of this definition, as per *Department of Defence v Barrett,*[8] were:

- the employee had taken action of a type referred to at s 74(2) of the Acts, ie a protected act;

- the employee was subjected to adverse treatment by the respondent; and

- the adverse treatment was in reaction to the protected action having been taken by the employee.

The Tribunal noted that the definition of 'proceedings' as set out in the Acts, ie 'proceedings before the person, body or court dealing with a request or reference under this Act by or on behalf of a person'. The Tribunal also cited *Department of Foreign Affairs v Cullen,*[9] which stated that s 72(2) is expressed in terms of there being both a cause and effect, in the sense that there must be a detrimental effect on the employee which is caused by him or her having undertaken a protected act of a type referred to in s 72.

The Tribunal considered the totality of the evidence proffered by the complainants in relation to their alleged victimisation and concluded that there was no evidence that, arising from the protected act, the complainants suffered adverse treatment or

---

7.   *Sunday Newspapers Ltd v Kinsella and Bradley* [2007] IEHC 324.

8.   *Department of Defence v Barrett* EDA1019.

9.   *Department of Foreign Affairs v Cullen* EDA116.

victimisation. It considered that the first allegation of ageism was made on 30 October 2012. The agreement, which had been signed before this on 19 January 2012, clarified that there was no obligation to provide training to the complainants. Furthermore, the complainants were in the process of redeployment in advance of this allegation. The issues relating to placement on the pay scale were linked to the complainants' start dates in 2005 and corresponding increments due. Finally, the Tribunal held that it had not been presented with any evidence of isolation, bullying or harassment of the complainants by the respondent due to the making of their claim of ageism.

GENDER

Pregnancy and maternity leave

[5.07] *Gacek v Pagewell Concessions (Ilac) Ltd t/a €uro 50 Store, Ilac Centre*[10]— *Equality Tribunal—Employment Equality Acts 1998 to 2015—gender, family status, race discrimination—constructive dismissal—treatment during pregnancy and onreturn from maternity leave—exploitation of foreign workers—requirement to work long hours without payment or transport home—excessive monitoring of toilet breaks—promotion—training—harassment—conditions of employment —victimisation—compensation equivalent to 30 months' salary awarded*

The complainant was employed with the respondent, initially, as a general sales assistant. She was paid the minimum wage and received overtime if she worked over 40 hours a week. The complainant submitted that she was often requested to clock out earlier than her actual finish time to avoid becoming eligible for overtime payments.

In November 2011, the complainant was promoted to the role of trainee manager with an annual salary of €22,000, but no overtime. The complainant submitted that she worked an average of 60 to 70 hours per week, which meant that she earned significantly less than what she had earned as a sales assistant. On 8 December 2011, she signed a management handover form with the former store manager, Mr B, which she submitted meant that she had become the *de facto* store manager. As a result of this handover, her responsibilities changed and included staff, layout, deliveries and training as well as any problems or irregularities. The complainant submitted that Mr B had told her that her salary would be increased at her next review to reflect her increase in responsibilities.

In February 2012, the complainant informed the respondent of her pregnancy. She submitted that she was instructed to take all ante-natal appointments outside of work hours and that she was discouraged from taking regular toilet breaks. The complainant gave evidence that it was extremely difficult to arrange medical appointments in circumstances where she was working 70 hours per week. An email was submitted as

---

10.   *Gacek v Pagewell Concessions (Ilac) Ltd t/a €uro 50 Store, Ilac Centre* DEC–E2015–29.

evidence of the poor treatment she received while pregnant as well as further evidence that she was the *de facto* store manager. The email from Mr B stated:

> I can understand that you are pregnant but I can still show you time sheets of other managers that were pregnant and still were doing 60-80 hours a week and worked till the last day. Only last year two managers nearly got their baby in the store, they finished in the afternoon and in the evening they were in labour. Also their stores are much more difficult than yours. This is the commitment they are giving to us, we didn't ask them.
>
> I hope that you understand that you are the manager, not the staff anymore and you have much more responsibility to your staff and the store.

The complainant claimed that she was told she would only be paid as a store manager after she returned from maternity leave as the respondent did not want to pay her higher salary during her leave period. The complainant gave evidence that the area manager, Mr A had referred to her maternity leave as her 'maternity holiday'.

While on maternity leave, the complainant claimed that an employee, Ms C, acted as the store manager. The complainant emailed the respondent on 20 November 2012 to say that her maternity leave finished on 1 January 2013 and that she was available to return to work the following day. At this stage, the complainant claims that she was instructed to take 14 days' annual leave out of her 20 day allowance which would leave her with only one week's holidays for the remaining 11 months of the year. On her return to work, the complainant claimed that her working conditions changed dramatically and she was now reporting to Ms C who was junior to her prior to maternity leave. Her responsibility had also changed and she was no longer given keys to the office or codes to the safe.

The complainant raised a grievance regarding this change in working conditions and the outcome of this process was communicated to her by letter dated 11 February 2013, which denied that there was any promotion from her position as trainee manager to the position of store manager. Therefore, the respondent submitted that the complainant was in the position of a trainee manager when she went on maternity leave and she had returned to the same position. The letter requested the complainant to provide any documentary evidence to show that her position was anything other than a trainee manager at the time of her maternity leave. Following this, the complainant provided a copy of the Manager Handover Form which she claims proved she was a store manager. As a result of submitting this document to the respondent, the complainant was subjected to a disciplinary process in relation to an alleged breach of the Data Protection Acts for providing company documentation. She received a written warning as a result of the disciplinary process and the complainant submits that, at this stage, she felt that she had no choice but to resign. The respondent submitted that the disciplinary matter was a serious matter that warranted dismissal but instead the complainant was given a written warning. The complainant also submitted that the respondent had refused to pay her annual leave entitlements on termination which she submitted was victimisation although the respondent claims that this was an administrative error and subsequently paid the annual leave entitlements.

The respondent denied that the complainant was a store manager but argued that, in her role as a trainee manager, she was expected to take responsibility including opening or closing the store. It was also denied that the complainant was expected to work 70 hours per week and instead was submitted that her average hours worked were 46 hours per week. The respondent accepted that the complainant was denied annual leave immediately prior to the commencement of her maternity leave, but it submitted that this was due to operational reasons and annual leave was within the gift of the employer. The respondent also sought to use Ms C, who replaced the complainant while she was on maternity leave, as a comparator, as Ms C was a Polish female who was also pregnant at the time she took on the complainant's role. The respondent submitted that Ms C was also a trainee manager and was given the responsibilities of an assistant manager and not a store manager, as alleged by the complainant. The respondent submitted that the complainant was disappointed that somebody at the same level was promoted ahead of her.

The Equality Tribunal considered the witness evidence of Mrs D, a witness for the complainant as crucial. Mrs D was Irish and not a mother. Mrs D was also a trainee manager at the time that the complainant was the *de facto* store manager and she corroborated the evidence given by the complainant of her working conditions and ill-treatment. Mrs D left the employment of the respondent while the complainant was on maternity leave as she stated that she was not willing to put up with the working conditions. She claimed that the respondent's approach was to promote good employees to trainee manager as it saved them money on overtime in the long run. Mrs D also gave evidence of working until late hours but not being provided with a taxi home. Mrs D claimed that, as a manager, she expected to work longer hours than staff but that the conditions under which the employees of the respondent worked were exploitative. Mrs D submitted that no Irish person would put up with these conditions on a long-term basis.

The Equality Tribunal considered whether to uphold the complaint on discrimination regarding her conditions of employment, promotion and/or training on the grounds of race, gender and family status as well as whether the complainant was harassed in relation to any of the discriminatory grounds.

In this regard, the Equality Tribunal noted that this was the second worst case of working conditions that had come before the Tribunal. The Equality Tribunal found that respondent had violated their duty of care to employees by expecting them to work past midnight and not to receive any payment or even transport home. The Equality Tribunal accepted Mrs D's account that the appointment of trainee managers was a 'scam' to avoid paying overtime. The Equality Tribunal agreed with Mrs D that Irish people would not have put up with such working conditions on a long-term basis and that, because the complainant was not Irish, she felt she had no choice but to remain in her role. The Equality Tribunal found that the treatment of the complainant was unwanted conduct connected to the ground of race. This had the effect of creating an intimidating and degrading work environment and therefore fell within the definition of harassment under the Acts. No facts were submitted by the respondent to rebut the presumption of harassment.

Furthermore, the Equality Tribunal noted that less favourable treatment linked to pregnancy and/or maternity leave is discrimination on the grounds of gender. The Equality Tribunal accepted the complainant's evidence of excessive monitoring of toilet breaks and lack of accommodations for pregnant women. Although, the Equality Tribunal agreed that granting annual leave is within the gift of the employer, it referred to the Supreme Court judgment in *Berber v Dunnes Stores Ltd* [11] which stated that:

> ...There is implied in a contract of employment a mutual obligation that the employer and employee will not, without reasonable and proper cause, conduct themselves in manner likely to destroy or seriously damage the relationship of confidence and trust between them. The term is implied by law and is incident to all contracts of employment unless expressly excluded.

The Equality Tribunal found that the respondent's treatment of the complainant during her pregnancy and maternity to be less favourable treatment linked to her pregnancy and therefore found that the complainant was discriminated against in relation to her conditions of employment on the grounds of gender. Furthermore, the Equality Tribunal found that by requiring the complainant to take two thirds of her annual leave allowance immediately after her return from maternity leave, notwithstanding that the complainant had given sufficient notice as 'callous and unnecessary', and therefore found that it was discriminatory on the grounds of family status as a parent. The Equality Tribunal made particular reference to the attitude of the respondent to pregnancy and new mothers as being encapsulated by Mr B's repeated references to maternity leave as a 'maternity holiday'.

The Equality Tribunal also accepted the complainant's evidence that she was told her salary would reflect her new responsibilities on return from maternity leave but that this did not happen. In relation to the presentation of Ms C as a comparator for the complainant as she was also pregnant, the Equality Tribunal found that this was disingenuous by the respondent as Ms C was not actually pregnant at the time of being appointed as a manager. The evidence adduced by the respondent at the hearing showed that Ms C became pregnant long after she had become the manager in charge. Ms C was not brought as a witness to the hearing and no evidence was adduced to show whether she was treated more or less favourably than the complainant. The Equality Tribunal found that the respondent deliberately omitted to promote the complainant and that this was linked to her pregnancy. Accordingly the Equality Officer found that the complainant had raised a prima facie case of discrimination regarding promotion on the grounds of gender and family status which was not rebutted by the respondent.

The Tribunal did not make a finding as to discrimination in relation to training as the complainant had not established a nexus to the grounds of race and family.

The Tribunal also considered whether the complainant had been victimised within the meaning of the Acts leading to a constructive victimisatory dismissal. The Equality Tribunal considered this to be a classic case of victimisation particularly in relation to the complainant's treatment during the grievance procedure and the subsequent disciplinary process in respect of an alleged breach of the Data Protection Acts. The

---

11.   *Berber v Dunnes Stores Ltd* [2009] IESC 10.

Equality Tribunal found that the written warning imposed on the complainant was disproportionate and the series of events had 'eviscerated' the complainant's trust and confidence in her employer. The Equality Tribunal noted that the complainant had exhausted all internal avenues with her employer and therefore, having evaluated all the evidence, the Equality Tribunal found that the complainant had established facts of sufficient significance to raise the presumption of victimisatory constructive dismissal. No evidence was tendered by the respondent to rebut this.

Turning to the question of redress, the Equality Tribunal noted that the maximum award which could be awarded was two years of salary for discrimination and two years of salary for victimisation. The Equality Tribunal was cognisant of a number of considerations, namely that the complainant had worked in an environment of aggression, excessive surveillance and under-payment. The Tribunal awarded the sum of €33,000 (the equivalent of 18 months' salary) in compensation for the harassment and discrimination in relation to conditions of employment and promotion. A further €22,000 (the equivalent of one year's salary) was awarded as compensation for the distress caused by victimisatory dismissal.

[5.08] *A Worker v A Catering Business[12]—Equality Tribunal—Employment Equality Acts 1998 to 2015—pregnancy and gender discrimination—absence on sick leave following miscarriage—timing of redundancy facilitated by pregnancy-related absence—whether discriminatory intent—redundancy—discriminatory dismissal*

The complainant was employed by the respondent as a delicatessen chef. She contended that she informed the respondent of her pregnancy but she subsequently miscarried; during this period she was on certified sick leave. Shortly after her return to work, following her sick leave, she contended that she was dismissed from her employment with one week's notice. The complainant claimed that her dismissal was discriminatory on the grounds of her gender and family status.

The respondent submitted that it had operated the catering business since March 2003. In and around August 2012, the respondent submitted that the level of trade could not sustain operating costs and therefore the staff numbers would need to be reduced. Around this time, the complainant sought to return to work following her miscarriage, however it was submitted that due to the continuing downturn in business, there was no option but to give her one week's notice of the termination of her employment as per her contract of employment. The respondent submitted that it terminated the employment of another male employee from the front of house team at this time and the duties of both were assumed by the respondent. No additional recruitment took place, and subsequently the business finally closed in December 2013 with significant outstanding debts.

The Equality Tribunal accepted the reduction in staff numbers by the respondent was objectively justified as all staff members were eventually laid off due to economic downturn and subsequent failure of the business. The Tribunal accepted that the complainant would have been laid off in due course, regardless of whether or not she

---

12. *A Worker v A Catering Business* DEC–E2015–037.

had been pregnant and miscarried. However, the Equality Tribunal noted that the complainant was actually laid off at the time when she was returning to work post-pregnancy miscarriage and that no consultations or discussions took place with the complainant regarding how her dismissal could be avoided. The Equality Tribunal noted that it is established EU and national law that a dismissal during pregnancy on its face is sufficient to establish a prima facie case of discrimination, as a woman enjoys special protection during her pregnancy (and her maternity leave). The Equality Tribunal concluded that the complainant's absence on sick leave was due to a miscarriage and therefore it related directly and intrinsically to her pregnancy. The Equality Tribunal found that the complainant was laid off earlier than she would have been had she not suffered a miscarriage and noted that the respondent had continued trading for one year after the complainant's dismissal. Therefore, although the Equality Tribunal was satisfied that there was no discriminatory intent and there was no doubt that the complainant's role would eventually have been made redundant, the timing of her dismissal was, in the opinion of the Equality Tribunal, facilitated by her pregnancy-related absence and the respondent had not rebutted the inference of discrimination.

The Equality Tribunal upheld the complaint of discrimination on the grounds of gender. In considering redress, the Equality Tribunal accepted that there was little or no prospect of the complainant actually receiving any financial compensation due to the bankruptcy of the respondent but that this was not a consideration in making the finding and accordingly awarded compensation in the sum of €12,000 for the effects of the discriminatory treatment.

[5.09] *Sobczyk v SAMI SWOI Ltd[13]—Equality Tribunal—Employment Equality Acts 1998 to 2015, s 6(2) and s 8—gender and family status—pregnancy—discriminatory treatment—discriminatory dismissal—whether claims part of settlement agreement executed by the parties*

The complainant was employed as a shop assistant on a full-time permanent basis in one of the respondent's retail outlets which stocked Polish products. No written submissions were made by the respondent in this matter nor did they attend the hearing before the Equality Tribunal.

The complainant learned that she was pregnant in October 2012 and, because of a medical matter relating to that pregnancy, she provided her employer with early confirmation of her pregnancy, and subsequently furnished a medical certificate from her GP setting out her expected date of confinement. The complainant became unwell mid-December 2012 and attended her GP, who certified her unable to work due to pregnancy-related illness until 31 December 2012. The complainant returned to Poland for the Christmas. On 1 January 2013 she sent a text message to her manager to enquire as to when she was next rostered to work, as her sick certificate had now expired, but no reply was received. The following day she received a phone call from her manager to inform her that she was being dismissed and when she challenged this decision she submitted that she was advised 'if you were loyal to the company this would not be an

---

13.   *Sobczyk v SAMI SWOI Ltd* DEC–E2015–016.

issue'. The complainant asserted that the decision to dismiss her from employment was made in the absence of any legitimate reason or fair procedures and she did not receive any written confirmation of this decision.

The Equality Tribunal noted that instead of a replying submission from the respondent, it received correspondence from the respondent enclosing a copy of a settlement agreement which purported to settle this claim. The Equality Tribunal made reference to the settlement agreement which purported to settle a number of claims listed for hearing before a Rights Commissioner on 1 October 2013. With reference to dismissal, the agreement provided that: 'the unfair dismissal claim was being withdrawn as the claimant was proceeding with the claim for dismissal before the Equality Tribunal. The balance of the claims having being compromised in consideration of a net payment of (three figure sum) as a termination payment to the claimant from the respondent.'

It was submitted by the respondent to the Tribunal in correspondence that the settlement agreement amounted to a compromise of the matters before the Equality Tribunal. However, the complainant advised the hearing that the settlement agreement referred only to those claims which were before a Rights Commissioner on 1 October 2013, namely a payment of wages claim and a working-time claim. The complainant explained to the Tribunal that she had originally submitted a claim under the Unfair Dismissal Acts but this was withdrawn because of her intention to proceed with the claim before the Equality Tribunal. The complainant submitted that the settlement agreement did not relate to any claim under the Acts nor did it refer to any settlement in relation to those outstanding claims.

The Tribunal noted that the respondent was not present at the hearing to provide any direct evidence on this matter. The Equality Tribunal stated that the settlement agreement submitted did not preclude it from examining the complaints of discrimination or of discriminatory dismissal on grounds of gender and family status and thus those claims before the Tribunal could proceed.

The Equality Tribunal made reference to s 85 of the Acts, which sets out the burden of proof applying to a claim of discrimination. The Tribunal noted that the entire period of pregnancy and maternity leave constituted a special protected period as noted by the CJEU in *Webb v EMO Air Cargo (UK) Ltd, Brown v Rentokil Ltd and Dekker v Stichting Vormingscentrum*.[14] The Equality Tribunal noted that the Labour Court had found[15] that only the most exceptional circumstances, not connected with the condition of pregnancy, allow a woman to be dismissed while pregnant. It is equally settled law that the dismissal of a pregnant woman raises a prima facie case of discrimination on gender grounds. Once such a case had been raised the burden of proof shifts and it is for the respondent to prove that the discriminatory dismissal did not take place.

The complainant asserted that there had never been any issues with her performance prior to her informing the respondent of her pregnancy. She had chosen to inform her employer of her pregnancy at an early stage as she had a related medical condition and,

---

14.   *Webb v EMO Air Cargo (UK) Ltd* (C–32/93), *Brown v Rentokil Ltd* (Case C–394/96) and *Dekker v Stichting Vormingscentrum* (Case C–177/88).

15.   *Intrum Justitia v McGarvey* EDA 095.

as a result, she needed to take precautions and act with due care in the workplace. She had also informed the respondent that she had previously suffered a miscarriage and that she was anxious about her pregnancy. The complainant's evidence was that there was an immediate reduction in her hours by the respondent following notification of her pregnancy but, when she queried whether this was related to her pregnancy, she was restored to normal working hours. The complainant further asserted that there had been an attempt to give her a written warning on the day of notification of her pregnancy as there was a problem with the fridge, for which she was blamed. It was subsequently confirmed that the fridge was broken and that the problem was not the complainant's fault. Ultimately she refused to sign any warning, or modification of the warning and no warning was ever issued or put on file for her.

The Equality Tribunal was satisfied that the complainant had raised an inference of discriminatory treatment on grounds of her gender, in relation to her working conditions, the reduction in her hours and in respect of her treatment regarding the fridge. In the absence of any arguments from the respondent to rebut this case, the Equality Tribunal found in favour of the complainant and held that the complainant had been discriminated against on grounds of gender. The Equality Tribunal further held that it was satisfied that the respondent was aware of the complainant's pregnancy when she was dismissed and therefore the dismissal was influenced by the pregnancy. The Equality Tribunal held that it was guided by *Company v A Worker*,[16] one of the first cases to be decided under the Acts, where the Labour Court found that no complaint was made about the complainant's work until she informed her employer that she was pregnant. The Labour Court in that case referred to the special protection for pregnant workers under the Equal Treatment Directive[17] and the Pregnancy Directive[18] and stated that: 'A worker cannot be discriminated against or be dismissed whilst pregnant except in exceptional grounds only connected with the pregnancy. In addition such grounds must be clear and stated in writing.'

In this case, the respondent attempted to issue the complainant with a written warning on the day she notified it of her pregnancy. The complainant was advised a few months later that her contract was not going to be renewed and that she was being dismissed. The only explanation given to her was a lack of loyalty to the company and further it was noted that the complainant received no letter of dismissal or grounds for her dismissal in writing. The Equality Tribunal was satisfied that the complainant had established a prima facie case of discrimination on grounds of gender in relation to her dismissal. The Equality Tribunal noted that the complainant's contract did have an end date of 31 December 2012. However, the Equality Tribunal was satisfied that the complainant had demonstrated a prima facie case of discriminatory treatment and the Tribunal found in her favour. The Tribunal held that the complainant had not established a prima facie case of discrimination on grounds of family status as she produced no evidence in support of her claim on this ground and provided no evidence of a comparator with a different family status. The Equality Tribunal considered the

---

16. *Company v A Worker* ED/01/1.
17. Directive 2000/78/EC.
18. Directive 92/85/EEC.

circumstances of the case, the rate of remuneration to which the complainant was in receipt of at the relevant time and her length of service and awarded her compensation of €10,000.

[5.10] *A Worker v An Insurance Company[19]—Equality Tribunal—Employment Equality Acts 1998 to 2015, s 6(1)(a)—Directive 2006/54/EC on the Principle of Equal Treatment of Men and Women (the Recast Directive)—European Convention on Human Rights Act 2003—gender—family status—maternity leave—promotion—discrimination—victimisation*

The complainant asserted discrimination on the grounds of gender and family status in relation to performance rating and non-promotion following a period of maternity leave. The complainant also submitted that she suffered victimisation following raising her grievance with the respondent.

The complainant commenced employment at the respondent's European operation in Dublin in April 2005 as a HR 'generalist' at tier/grade 9. She had several years of experience, she held a certificate in Personnel Practice and she also completed a degree in HR Management in 2006. By 2007 the complainant had been promoted to a tier/grade 8, one grade below management and stated that she was on track for promotion to management level.

The respondent had a scaled bonus plan and performance review in operation. In her first three years of employment, the complainant received a grade 2 (exceeds expectations). In 2008 the complainant went on her first maternity leave and did not receive a performance review for that period but was given a 3 rating (meets expectations) by the HR Director on the basis that he was unable to assess her performance as she was out on maternity leave. As a result, her bonus was reduced for that year. The following year her grade and bonus returned to grade 2 standards. The following year the complainant was on a second maternity leave and again received no review and a lower grade 3 rating and bonus.

Another employee, Ms F, was hired as a tier/grade 9 in 2007 before the complainant went on her first maternity leave and the complainant worked closely with her in order to ensure a smooth handover for her maternity-leave period.

The complainant stated that, before going on her second maternity leave, she had been asked for her view on taking up a HR management role on her return, but during that maternity leave, when speaking to management, she was asked a series of questions about how she was going to cope with work and three children, etc and she stated that she was offered the option to have a severance package arranged for her at that time.

The complainant made a request during her maternity leave for parental leave on her return to work on a one day per week basis; but this request was refused. She was permitted to take the leave as part-time leave but this had knock-on effects for her annual leave entitlements. The complainant contended that the respondent had granted this form of parental leave and other family-friendly arrangements on other occasions.

---

19. *A Worker v An Insurance Company* DEC–E2015–022.

On her return from maternity leave it was announced that the complainant's junior colleague, Ms F, was to be appointed to the role of interim HR manager. When this interim position was subsequently made permanent, Ms F was recommended for the role by management.

Given the representations that the complainant claimed had been made to her about a potential management role, she sought clarification about the criteria used in making this decision but did not receive any clarification about the criteria used and her queries were overlooked. The complainant subsequently raised an allegation of discrimination with the CEO due to the fact that she had not been given the opportunity to apply for the permanent HR manager role. She asserted that the selection process clearly disadvantaged her on the basis of her maternity leave and the lower grade 3 performance rating she received during those periods; and no proper objective transparent selection process and scoring criteria had been used.

A series of further meetings between the complainant and the CEO took place in the following months, in which the complainant indicated her feelings that she had been discriminated against as a result of her maternity leave. The complainant contended that these meetings were intimidating and she felt she was being threatened not to pursue her allegation of discrimination any further. The complainant also alleged victimisation following her allegation of discrimination and that she had had significant and sensitive tasks taken away from her range of duties. In December 2011, the complainant submitted a request for redundancy due to her feelings of upset and intimidation over how her grievances had been handled. The complainant's request for redundancy was refused and she was informed that she would have to exhaust internal grievance procedures before she could pursue the matter externally with the Equality Tribunal. The complainant was finally granted redundancy in December 2013.

When the complainant's case finally came before the Equality Tribunal, the respondent raised the preliminary issue of delay in the processing of the complaint. The Tribunal concluded that while the delay was undesirable, it was not unreasonable or unlawful in the context of the European Convention on Human Rights.

In considering the substantive issue, the Tribunal determined that the complainant had established a prima facie case of discrimination on gender grounds and that the respondent had failed to rebut this inference. In reaching this decision, the Tribunal noted that s 85A of the Acts provides for a shift in the burden of proof to the respondent in circumstances where the complainant establishes facts from which it may be presumed that there has been discrimination. The Tribunal concluded that the fact that the complainant's performance rating was lowered because she was on maternity leave, coupled with the fact that the appointment of Ms F to the interim HR manager role was made less than a week before the complainant was due to return from maternity leave, established a prima facie case of discrimination, which, under s 85A, placed the onus on the respondent to rebut the inference.

In considering the discrimination itself, the Tribunal noted that the Directive defines discrimination as any less favourable treatment of a woman relating to pregnancy or maternity leave. The Equality Tribunal noted that the job for the Tribunal was not to consider whether the complainant was a more suitable candidate for the position, but was simply whether the respondent could show that the gender and family status of the complainant did not influence the decision to appoint Ms F to the role in preference to the complainant. The Tribunal concluded that the respondent had failed to demonstrate that the appointment was wholly unconnected and on that basis, the complainant's case was successful.

On the issue of victimisation, the Tribunal concluded on balance that the complainant had not been victimised.

The complainant was awarded €70,000 in compensation, equating to approximately one year's gross salary and performance bonus.

[5.11] *Gilman Bennet v Elaine Byrne's Health and Beauty Clinic[20]—Equality Tribunal—Employment Equality Acts 1998 to 2015, ss 6(2) and 8—Safety, Health and Welfare at Work Act 2005—gender discrimination—risk assessment—pregnancy*

The complainant was employed on a permanent contract as general manager of the respondent's health and beauty clinic in August 2011. She informed the respondent that she was three months pregnant on 2 December 2011. On 13 December 2011, the respondent informed the complainant that she would be placed on health and safety leave, due to the risks arising from a risk assessment the complainant signed, allegedly on the instruction of the respondent, on 9 December.

The complainant claimed that the respondent discriminated against her by removing her prematurely from her role and failing to offer her alternative employment or sourcing alternative employment for her. She further claimed that the risk assessment did not point out any risks that could not be carried out by another employee without undue burden to the respondent and claimed it amounted to as little as 2 per cent of her working month.

The complainant also claimed that the respondent breached its duty under the Safety Health and Welfare at Work Act 2005 to take all preventative measures which would allow her to continue in her employment, and cited *Doorty v UCD*[21] in which the Tribunal stated that 'creative solutions to an undoubted problem' were required to ensure an employee could remain in his/her post.

The respondent submitted that the risk assessment was signed after a discussion with the complainant and the most notable risk identified was the use of chemicals in spray tanning, training in which the complainant was obliged to provide to other staff because of her role as general manager. The respondent submitted that another pregnant employee was not a relevant comparator as she was employed in a different role and denied placing the complainant on leave prematurely, stating that it was not practical, due to the standalone nature of the complainant's role, for another employee to take up her duties. The respondent denied that she refused to accept any of the alternatives put forward by the complainant and noted that the complainant did not avail of a chance to advance her grievance after she wrote an initial letter to the respondent on 29 December 2011.

---

20.   *Gilman Bennet v Elaine Byrne's Health and Beauty Clinic* DEC–E2015–059.
21.   *Doorty v UCD* DEC–E2004–43.

The Tribunal noted that the entire period of pregnancy and maternity leave constitutes 'a special protected period'[22] and any discriminatory treatment during that period raises a 'prima facie case of discrimination on the gender ground'. The Tribunal accepted that the respondent was, at the relevant time, undergoing financial difficulty and was particularly focused on cutting costs, but also accepted that the complainant was placed on health and safety leave, against her wishes, for reasons which could be used to exclude almost all pregnant employees. The complainant had therefore established facts from which discrimination could be inferred and shifted the burden of proof to the respondent.

The Tribunal found no evidence that a distinction between many generic risks and two serious risks listed in the risk assessment was made by the respondent when discussing it with the complainant. The Tribunal further found no evidence that the respondent attempted to limit exposure to the generic risks identified in the risk assessment or gave any consideration to finding alternatives to the two specific risks identified there. The Tribunal ruled that the complainant established a prima facie case of discrimination, which the respondent had failed to rebut. The complainant was awarded €12,000 compensation.

[5.12] *Murphy v Browell Ltd t/a The Four Roads (In Recelvership)[23]—Equality Tribunal—Employment Equality Acts 1998 to 2015—gender—maternity leave— alleged discrimination—receivership—preliminary issue whether without prejudice discussions that took place between the parties could be admitted in evidence— maternity leave*

The complainant was employed as a senior bar person and was later promoted to assistant manager. In November 2012 she went on maternity leave. On 2 December 2012 the complainant was informed that the respondent was being put into receivership. The major shareholder informed the receiver that the complainant was on maternity leave and was due back in May 2013. A letter was issued to the complainant from the receiver confirming her status as an employee. The long-term strategy of treating the business as a going concern was pursued by the joint receivers and managers. A pub management company was appointed to take over the running of the respondent's pub. Correspondence passed between the respondent and the Revenue Commissioners. A manager was appointed by the management company and was given responsibility for running the pub. He attended on a periodic basis and the complainant made efforts to communicate with him, beginning in April 2013, with regard to a return to work in May. She failed to receive a satisfactory response. On 9 May she attended the pub and was informed that she was not on the roster as no instructions had been received to put her on the roster. Further attempts by her to contact management of the pub were unsuccessful.

---

22. Decisions of the European Court of Justice in *Webb v EMO Air Cargo (UK) Ltd* (Case C–32/93), *Brown v Rentokil Ltd* (Case C–394/96) and *Dekker v Stichting Vormingscentrum* (Case C–177/88).

23. *Murphy v Browell Ltd t/a The Four Roads (In Receivership)* DEC–E2015–050.

The complainant applied to the Department of Social Protection for social welfare payments. A social protection officer contacted the pub and was informed by management that there was no longer any work for the complainant at the pub. The non-issue of a P45 was put down to the difficulties management had when scheduling meetings with pub management. The complainant's evidence was that additional staff had been employed in the pub since her last working year to include one individual in the same role as her. The complainant had obtained subsequent employment and when she was established on her new employer's payroll they were informed by Revenue that she ceased employment with the respondent in December 2012. It was submitted by the complainant that she was either dismissed in December 2012 or, without prejudice to this, was dismissed in May 2013 by the respondent's failure to roster her for work on return from maternity leave.

She was claiming constructive dismissal arising from the conduct of the respondent. Evidence was given on behalf of the respondent that the complainant's employment situation could have been better handled but that the receivership situation had created a lot of confusion for all concerned. It was accepted that the complainant had been contacted by the Department of Social Protection and that it was submitted that no one behaved inappropriately towards the complainant.

The Tribunal noted the evidence before it and that the facts of the case were largely agreed. A witness from the pub management company explained that he had been given only a brief handover from his predecessor and that the initial details of staff lists did not include the complainant. When contacted by the complainant he passed matters to the receiver.

The Equality Tribunal first considered the preliminary issue as to meetings between the parties which took place after 9 May 2013. The Tribunal noted that these meetings were an effort by the receiver to effect a settlement of the claim and, as such, they could not be advanced as major elements of the defence for events that occurred before 9 May. The Tribunal concluded that whether these meetings were without prejudice, or were solicitor/client confidential matters (and thus inadmissible), became irrelevant when they were spoken about by various witnesses. However the Tribunal noted that the situation before 9 May was clear cut and well supported by evidence. The complainant was clearly employed and her employment situation had been confirmed by the receiver in a letter of 3 December, by email communications to the pub management and by the accepted common knowledge of staff that she was on maternity leave. The complainant had made reasonable efforts to contact management from the middle of April 2013 regarding her return dates. While the new management could be forgiven for some confusion, an experienced pub manager should have been well capable of handling the situation and likewise a prestigious firm such as the receiver company was not a novice in this area.

The Equality Tribunal concluded that confusion about responsibilities among parties on the respondent's side, albeit in a receivership situation, was not a credible defence. The Tribunal held that the complainant was, in effect, dismissed by default and this qualified as discriminatory dismissal on grounds of gender because she was on maternity leave. The Tribunal noted the legal submissions that had been put before it, particularly by the complainant with reference to *O'Brien v Persian Properties t/a*

O'Callaghan Hotels.[24] The Tribunal noted the precedents in these cases and commented that maternity leave has a special protected status. The Tribunal concluded that the complainant had been dismissed in a discriminatory manner and awarded the complainant compensation for the discriminatory dismissal in the amount of €17,500, being the equivalent of 26 weeks' pay.

[5.13] *Duggan and Barry v Waterford Area Partnership*[25]—*Equality Tribunal—Employment Equality Acts 1998 to 2015, ss 6(2)(a) and (c), and 74(2)—maternity leave—discrimination on grounds of family and gender status—salary top-up of maternity benefit—custom and practice—alleged victimisation*

The complainants took three claims against their employer for discrimination on the grounds of gender and family status on the basis of not being paid a top-up payment in addition to maternity benefit contrary to their terms of employment. Ms Barry also complained of victimisation.

Ms Duggan commenced work in 1999 in a community development organisation which was absorbed into the respondent organisation in January 2011. She stated that all her terms and conditions of work were protected in that transfer. In 2011, Ms Duggan became pregnant and in November 2011 she enquired about her maternity pay, as full maternity pay was one of her terms and conditions of employment. On 31 January 2012, she received a letter from the respondent CEO in which she was told that there was no finance for her maternity pay due to cutbacks in public funding. Ms Duggan commenced her maternity leave on 3 February 2012.

On 21 March 2012 a meeting took place at the respondent organisation where it was declared that there was a saving made, due to two staff members being on maternity leave and one being on carer's leave, and the workers were asked what those savings should be spent on.

Ms Barry commenced employment for the respondent in 2006. She, too, became pregnant in 2011 and, like Ms Duggan, did not receive paid maternity leave and was told it was due to financial difficulties in the organisation, again due to cutbacks in public funding. However, in Ms Barry's case, she received another letter from the respondent's general manager on 6 March 2012, in which it was suggested that the reason given in his letter of 31 January 2012 was incorrect and that the correct reason for not getting fully-paid maternity leave was that the arrangements pertaining to the complainant's maternity leave had been decided in June 2008, and that according to the respondent, the complainant had only been appointed to her role in December 2009.

Ms Barry was the other staff member on maternity leave whose leave brought about savings for the organisation referenced above. Ms Barry further complained that she had since had another pregnancy in which, likewise, she did not receive any maternity pay from the respondent.

---

24. *O'Brien v Persian Properties t/a O'Callaghan Hotels* DEC–E2012–010; *Assico Assembly Ltd v Corcoran* EED033.

25. *Duggan and Barry v Waterford Area Partnership* DEC–E2015–064.

Both complainants maintained that not topping their maternity benefit to the levels of their salaries amounted to discrimination on the ground of gender.

The respondent denied discriminating against the complainants as alleged or at all. It submitted that the decision by the respondent's board not to pay Ms Duggan and Ms Barry maternity pay was solely due to the budget cutbacks which the organisation, as a publicly-funded body, experienced between 2008 and 2012.

The respondent company is a social enterprise government-funded agency. It works in the areas of information and training, education, enterprise and employment, and community development. It was merged with the Ballybeg Community Development Project in 2011, following a Ministerial directive aimed at streamlining these social enterprises. Ballybeg is a deprived area in Waterford city. The respondent did have its funding reduced in line with the budget reductions imposed in the recession. In terms of the employment situations of the complainants and their comparator, it transpired that the comparator, Ms C, was never an employee of the respondent. Ms Duggan was her colleague in Ballybeg Community Development Project, and transferred into the respondent's employment when the merger happened, whereas Ms C did not. Only Ms Barry was employed by the respondent.

The Equality Tribunal heard considerable arguments from both sides on whether paid maternity leave could be regarded as part of the complainants' terms and conditions of employment, or whether it was in the discretion of the employer. The Tribunal also heard considerable argument between the parties as to whether there had been a board decision in 2008 to cease maternity pay, whether it was minuted and how it was communicated to staff. The updated staff handbook simply stated the legal position.

There was no dispute that prior to the maternity leaves of the two complainants, it had been the practice of the respondent to pay staff during maternity leave, ie, to top up their maternity benefits to the level of their salary. According to the local SIPTU representative, Mr W, who was present at the relevant meetings in 2008 and who gave evidence at the hearing, it was nowhere explicitly stated that the practice of making these top-up payments would cease. Mr W further stated that if such a decision had been explicitly communicated to staff, there would have been resistance. The minutes only speak of 'updated procedures' and the updated staff handbook then simply reflected the law. This is also what was circulated to staff. Nowhere was it highlighted that a decision had been taken not to top up maternity benefit any longer. Accordingly, there were no adverse responses from staff.

The Tribunal was satisfied that neither staff nor their union representative were ever expressly told of, never mind consulted on, the decision the respondent claims to have made in 2008 not to top up maternity benefit any longer.

The Tribunal also found that another detail which cast doubt on the respondent's evidence was that the original response received by complainants from the respondent, when they wrote to enquire about their top-up pay, was that it could not be paid due to financial constraints. At the hearing of the complaint, the respondent's CEO claimed to have written these letters in haste, and they did not reflect the correct position. The Tribunal found this position doubtful and in its decision stated that it seemed more likely overall that he tried to save face with his second letter, in which he referred to the disputed 2008 decision, because by then it had become known that the respondent would indeed have had the means to pay the top up.

The Tribunal noted that while the case law on discrimination in connection with pregnancy has mostly focused on dismissal during pregnancy, the repeated statement by the CJEU (see, for example, *Brown v Rentokil*),[26] that pregnancy and maternity leave constitute a specially protected period, has taken on the extended meaning that terms and conditions of a pregnant worker, or a worker who is on maternity leave, ought not be changed except in extenuating circumstances unconnected with the pregnancy. This normally means extenuating financial circumstances.

The Tribunal noted that employers have no legal obligation to top up a staff member's maternity benefit to the level of her salary. However, without a clearly communicated, express policy change, which would include a meaningful consultation with staff, the Tribunal found that resiling from a continuation of custom and practice, in the absence of extenuating financial circumstances, constituted a less favourable treatment of a worker during a specially protected period of her employment, and, in line with long-standing CJEU jurisprudence, was *ipso facto* discrimination on the ground of gender.

With regard to the respondent's ability to pay these top-ups, the complainants presented two important pieces of evidence. The first of these was a draft budget spreadsheet which was given to the local SIPTU representative, from which it was clear that neither worker was replaced during her maternity leave, and that the salary for each was budgeted as normal. This was the case, despite the overall exchequer-funding reductions to which the respondent had been subjected. The respondent confirmed the authenticity of the spreadsheet, but argued that it was simply a draft budget. The Tribunal accepted that it may have been a draft proposal and that it represented one particular spending proposal, but was satisfied that it reflected the overall financial position of the respondent. The Tribunal held that to simply top up the State maternity benefit to the level of each complainant's salary would still have saved the respondent money, since it would have had to pay only a part of each salary.

The second piece of evidence was the minutes of the meeting of 21 March 2012 which recorded a meeting after the two complainants had gone on their maternity leave. In the minutes, the savings achieved as a result of their absence were highlighted and the respondent's employees were canvassed to suggest projects on which the saved money could be spent. The Tribunal found that these two pieces of evidence, taken together, wholly undermined the respondent's contention that it was unable to top up the complainants' maternity pay in line with previous practice and that the complainants were therefore entitled to succeed.

The Tribunal held that the respondent had discriminated against the complainants in their terms and conditions of employment on the ground of gender. The Tribunal held that the respondent did not victimise Ms Barry within the meaning of the Acts.

The Tribunal ordered that the respondent pay each complainant their arrears of pay, that is, the pay they would have received if their State maternity benefits would have been topped up to reach their normal salaries in line with previous practice. The

---

26. *Brown v Rentokil* (Case C–394/96).

Tribunal further ordered that the respondent pay each complainant €2,500 in compensation for the effects of the discrimination. These awards took into account the exchequer-funded, non-profit nature of the respondent's undertaking.

Promotion, training, conditions of employment

[5.14] *O'Leary v Health Service Executive South[27]—Equality Tribunal— Employment Equality Acts 1998 to 2015—discrimination on grounds of gender— promotion, training, conditions of employment*

The complainant alleged that the respondent discriminated against her on the grounds of gender regarding access to promotion to emergency medical controller, training and conditions of employment.

The complainant commenced employment with the respondent as a ward assistant in September 1999. She was employed as a paramedic in the Ambulance Service since 2001 and completed all mandatory training. She was also seconded to the National Ambulance Service for a year as a training officer.

In May 2009, the complainant applied for the position of emergency medical controller. She was successful and subsequently empanelled – she came first on the Cork panel, first on the Kerry panel and first on the Limerick panel. When these regional panels were amalgamated, she was third on the national panel. She was offered positions in Donegal and Dublin but she submitted that she could not relocate so far away from her family. The complainant submitted that it was her understanding that she would be trained on the job. This is because the job specification said 'the person(s) employed will receive full training and will work with a team of skilled and dedicated personnel on a shift work basis to ensure appropriate staffing is provided on a 24 hour/ 365 day basis'. After being placed on the panel, she was regularly told that training by local personnel would have to be done in her own time. In December 2011, an emergency medical controller retired and a male was placed in his position. There was an interview for this role.

The complainant submitted that she was next on the national panel and, therefore, she should have been appointed to this role. Having raised a grievance, the respondent acknowledged that the complainant was third on the panel but that the first two persons on the panel above her would have to be offered the position first. When the complainant contacted the national recruitment centre, they were not aware that there was a vacancy in Cork. She submitted that the male comparator was given the position, even though he was not on the active recruitment panel. She submits that there was a female (apart from the complainant) with more experience than the male comparator and she did not receive the acting up position. The respondent advertised for relief emergency controllers in May 2012 despite the complainant being on a panel for same and the male comparator in the acting capacity retained the position.

---

27.   *O'Leary v Health Service Executive South* DEC–E2015–019.

The complainant also submits that this was indirectly discriminatory.

In June 2013, the control centre in Cork was shut down and the complainant submitted that the people in it retained their grade and salary and were redeployed. The complainant submitted that she missed this opportunity to become an emergency medical controller as family circumstances did not allow her to move out of Cork. The complainant submits that the continued refusal to allow her finish her advanced paramedic training was further discrimination on the gender ground.

The respondent denied any allegation of discrimination on grounds of gender. It submitted that ambulance personnel are required to retain their skills. The complainant was provided access to all such mandatory training relevant to her contract of employment as an emergency medical technician. In addition, the complainant had applied for training as an advanced paramedic. She commenced this training on two occasions in 2007 and again in 2008. Her attendance was infrequent both times and, because of the cost of the course (€120,000 per participant), she had been refused the third time. She was granted a secondment to the role of ambulance officer (training and development) in the National Ambulance Training Board Dublin for a year (Grade VI). She received an increase in her remuneration and was facilitated with the continuation of her cardiac allowance. In relation to the 'on the job' training in the control room, the HSE submitted that the custom and practice was that people interested in becoming a controller sit in the control room on their own time (on a supernumerary basis) to learn how it works. This option remained available to the complainant at all times. It was only following a significant period of this on the job training that personnel are offered an opportunity to undergo the Advanced Medical Priority Dispatch System training (AMPDS) which is the system the Ambulance Service use to take and prioritise calls.

The Ambulance Service in HSE South (Cork and Kerry) has 18 stations with a front-line staff of approximately 200 to serve a population of 745,000. The male to female ratio in Cork is 4.1:1 (123:30). The emergency control room is similar, at 4:1, ie eight men and two women. Like many areas of the public sector it has undergone significant change – the HIQA standards for emergency response times, phasing out of on-call allowances and centralisation of the control and command centres. That has meant that the Cork control centre closed in May 2013.

The panel for which the complainant applied expired on 18 February 2013 and she was notified of this. It was suggested by letter (including the application form) that she should apply for the new national recruitment campaign for emergency medical dispatcher (the new title for emergency medical controller). In 2012, following the retirement of a staff member in the Cork control centre, the respondent was granted sanction to fill this post temporarily. It was filled based on the 2010 HSE Circular 'Policy on Acting Up in a Higher Capacity' which states:

> The employee who is selected for the acting up position must have all the competencies, qualifications, experience and if necessary the appropriate registration, to enable them to carry out the acting up role effectively.

The respondent submitted that it identified seven HSE South Ambulance staff from the emergency medical controller relief panel that were trained, had their Advanced Medical Priority Dispatch System (AMPDS) licence and had experience working as an emergency medical controller as potential candidates to fill the acting role. These staff members had been providing relief cover in the Cork control centre for periods of off-duty, annual leave, etc, on a rotational basis. These seven people were invited to express an interest. Two did so – a man and a woman – both of whom had over four years of experience as full-time controllers. Both names were put into a hat. The respondent submitted that both people agreed to this selection process in advance. The person selected happened to be a man and he was appointed on a temporary basis from 2 January 2012. He continued to hold this post until the control centre in Cork closed on 16 May 2013.

The complainant raised a grievance, and the respondent met with her and her SIPTU representative on 27 February 2012 and explained the difference between the relief panel and the national panel. The respondent submitted that the purpose of the national panel was to fill long-term vacancies while the purpose of the relief panel was to address relief requirements that may arise from time to time. They suggested that she upskill by sitting in the control room on a supernumerary basis. Following this, she did sit in the control room to enhance her skills in that area. She was facilitated on 16 occasions between 2 July 2012 and 26 March 2013.

The respondent admitted that it did advertise for relief personnel in May 2012 but submitted that was because they initially thought the control centre would be closing in May 2012. When it was to remain open until May 2013, they advertised the position. Preference was given to people who had a month's experience sitting in the control room and were available attend the next Advanced Medical Priority Dispatch System course. The person already acting up retained the position until May 2013. He reverted to his previous position when the control centre closed.

The respondent denied the allegation that advertising for relief emergency medical controllers was indirectly discriminatory when the complainant was next on the permanent panel. The respondent reminded the Equality Tribunal that this occurred during one of the worst recessions to hit Ireland and during the resultant public sector moratorium. All vacancies could only be temporary as it was Government policy to close the control centre in Cork. Therefore the respondent submitted that it was both appropriate and necessary (given the importance of the position) to appoint people (on an acting basis) who were already qualified and experienced.

The Equality Tribunal held that there was a clear difference between the permanent national panel, to which the complainant was appointed following a competition, and a local relief panel to cover short-term absences. Had the male comparator been made permanent as an emergency medical controller on the basis of being picked out of a hat when there was a national panel extant, it is likely this case would have taken a different turn. Had the other woman on the relief panel who expressed an interest in the emergency medical controller role and who had more experience than the male comparator taken a case, the result of the complaint may also have been different.

The complainant and the male comparator were both aware that the Cork control centre was due to close. The deadline for closure was extended but the temporary vacancy that the male comparator filled remained a temporary vacancy. It was never a permanent vacancy; therefore the complainant had not established a prima facie case of direct discrimination.

The complainant argued that neutral provision of appointing the male comparator as emergency medical controller was indirectly discriminatory, however the Equality Tribunal accepted that there was a public sector moratorium, the male comparator was trained and experienced (while the complainant was not) and as it was a post that had to be filled urgently, the Equality Tribunal found that the respondent had objectively justified their approach to filling this position, and consequently did not find that the complainant was indirectly discriminated against regarding access to promotion.

The complainant correctly stated that if she were appointed in a permanent capacity, she would receive full training. However, for short-term urgent vacancies, the respondent did not have the time or resources to train people up. People were only sent on the Advanced Medical Priority Dispatch System course after watching how the control room worked as the course would not make sense otherwise, this was not discriminatory. Not allowing the complainant to continue the advanced paramedic course was harsh, but there was no evidence adduced on how it was less favourable treatment on the ground of gender.

The Equality Tribunal found that there was no evidence that the complainant was discriminated against on the ground of gender in relation to her conditions of employment, and she did not establish a prima facie case of discrimination in relation to her conditions of employment.

[5.15] *Smolinska v Webroot International Ltd*[28]—*Equality Tribunal—Employment Equality Acts 1998 to 2015, s 6(2) and s 8—direct discrimination—discriminatory dismissal—gender and race*

The complainant alleged that she was discriminated against by the respondent on the grounds of race and gender and suffered a discriminatory dismissal.

The complainant commenced employment in April 2012 and her employment ended in February 2013. The complainant was employed as an insider sales representative. The complainant submitted that she was selected for dismissal on the grounds that she was of Polish nationality and was a woman and that other named employees with the same or shorter service and of a different gender and nationality continued in employment. The complainant disputed the assertion by the respondent that her employment was terminated because of low sales quota achievement.

The respondent submitted that the complainant's responsibilities included generating sales leads, negotiating and closing sales opportunities and processing these opportunities within the customer relationship management software system. From the outset of her employment there were ongoing issues with complainant's sales performance. The complainant failed to reach her agreed sales targets for the three consecutive quarters of her employment. She failed to properly record her sales activities or build a future pipeline for the respondent company.

---

28. *Smolinska v Webroot International Ltd* DEC–E2015–074.

The respondent took a decision to terminate the complainant's employment for performance reasons and her dismissal was wholly unconnected to her race or gender. The respondent submitted that the complainant was subject to, and fully aware of, the respondent's Sales Plan and Policy. During the period of the complainant's employment a number of her colleagues failed to achieve their sales targets and two of these resigned.

The respondent submitted that it afforded all employees a reasonable period in which to improve performance and reach targets. However, where a sales employee did not achieve targets over a substantial period of time and it became unlikely that the employee would do so in the long term, the respondent was required to evaluate the employee's performance at that stage.

The respondent submitted that it was committed to equality and diversity in the workplace and was an equal opportunities employer. All managers received training on equality, including race and gender issues. Out of a total of 28 employees in the Dublin office, 11 were non-Irish and 12 were women. The complainant's immediate line manager was non-Irish (Swedish) and a woman.

The respondent recognised that, in valuing diversity, it catered to a customer base of growing diversity and also ensured that colleagues were treated with respect and dignity. The respondent asserted that the complainant had not produced credible prima facie evidence of any kind to support a race or gender basis for the ending of her employment. All sales employees were treated equally and assessed by reference to their targets irrespective of race or gender.

At the hearing, the complainant submitted that she had successfully concluded her six-month probationary period without negative incident but her employment was terminated three months later, effectively without warning.

In response, the respondent stated that the complainant was seeking to make an unfair dismissal claim (she did not have the requisite service) under the guise of an equality claim.

The respondent further submitted that the complainant lacked the requisite 'prima facie evidence' to support an equality claim and that the sales performance figures clearly supported the respondent's case of a performance-related termination.

In *Valpeters v Melbury Development Ltd*[29] the Labour Court stated:

> In this case, it was submitted that the complainant was treated badly by the respondent and the Court was invited to infer that he was so treated because of his race. Such an inference could only be drawn if there was evidence of some weight from which it could be concluded that persons of a different race or nationality were or would be treated more favourably. All that has been proffered in support of that contention is a mere assertion unsupported by any evidence.

The respondent submitted that it had a vigorous sales performance system for sales staff – the staff turnover figures produced was clear evidence of this fact. In the period from June 2012 to January 2014 the employment of seven staff was terminated (involuntarily) for performance issues. Of the seven in question three were Irish with one Polish, one

---

29.   *Valpeters v Melbury Development Ltd* EDA0917.

Italian, one French and one German making up the balance. The respondent produced evidence which it asserted clearly identified a negative sales performance question for the complainant. The respondent submitted that sales performance was the key factor in employment retention.

The complainant also raised an issue in the context of the then sales manager's methodology by which sales leads were distributed to staff, including the complainant, by the then manager. The complainant alleged that sales leads were unfairly given to male colleagues. The Tribunal concluded that, from an examination of the total leads statistics provided by the respondent, it was hard to find any major disparities to the disadvantage of the complainant.

The complainant gave evidence that she successfully completed her probationary period and was confirmed in employment after the initial six-month period only to be let go after a further three months. The Tribunal noted that this was not a highlight of the respondent's defence; however, it could not see any required prima facie evidence of racial/nationality or gender discrimination in this matter.

The Tribunal concluded that the complainant and all her colleagues, irrespective of varying racial origins and different genders, were employed in a very tough and demanding sales culture. The Tribunal found that there was no doubt but that she lost out in this sales culture but there was no credible evidence, to the standards identified in the legal precedents widely accepted in equality matters of this nature, that there was any racial, nationality or gender aspects to her termination of employment.

The Tribunal found that the complainant had failed to establish a prima facie case of discrimination on the grounds of race or gender. The Tribunal also found that the complainant failed to establish a prima facie case of discriminatory dismissal in terms of s 8 of the Acts.

Sexual harassment

[5.16] *An Employee v An Employer*[30]*—Equality Tribunal—Employment Equality Acts 1998 to 2015—sexual harassment—discriminatory dismissal—alleged inappropriate verbal comments and physical contact*

The complainant alleged that she was sexually harassed by the respondent. She commenced employment with the respondent as a hairdresser/barber in December 2012 and her evidence was that, in April 2013, the respondent began to make vulgar jokes and comments about her relationship status. The complainant gave evidence that the respondent began to engage in inappropriate physical contact and touching of her and that banter of a sexual nature continued on a regular basis. The complainant made further allegations that while she was on holidays at home in Bulgaria she received a number of telephone calls from the respondent with a strong sexual overtone in the messages and that he had made inappropriate comments regarding Bulgarian women.

---

30. *An Employee v An Employer* DEC–E2015–052.

On her return from holidays, the complainant alleged that the inappropriate comments continued, coupled with many incidents of physical touching. The complainant's evidence was that she had repeatedly asked the respondent to stop his unwanted physical contact and verbal comments.

In August 2013 a dispute arose, which broadened into a significant verbal exchange, where alleged inappropriate sexual language was used by the respondent. This incident culminated in the complainant being verbally dismissed and leaving the premises.

The respondent gave evidence through an interpreter and completely rejected all claims of improper physical contact and allegations of inappropriate language. He noted that, as a Turkish man, all who knew him would agree that he was loud in normal conversation but never inappropriate. He noted that he himself was of an ethnic minority in Ireland and was in the course of applying for citizenship and thus would never be insulting to another person on ethnic or sexual grounds. He engaged in harmless humour and joking with the complainant and stated that there was never any harm or offence intended.

He noted the fact that the complainant had never reported the alleged matters to the local garda station which was close to the shop and he further submitted that the basis of the complainant's case was entirely financial and that her motivation was to get money from a small trader. Subsequent to the complainant's last day at work, the respondent made contact with the complainant's father to meet him to try and resolve the matter.

The Equality Tribunal noted the requirements of s 85A setting out the burden of proof necessary in claims of discrimination. The Tribunal further noted the definition of sexual harassment in s 14A and the contention from the complainant that the respondent had engaged inappropriately in verbal and physical behaviour on a number of occasions.

The Equality Tribunal noted that the language spoken in the shop was Turkish and that the inappropriate physical contact alleged occurred only on occasions when the complainant and respondent were alone in the shop together. The Equality Tribunal noted that the only other possible witness was a staff member of Eastern European origin and did not speak Turkish. Thus the Tribunal concluded that there was little to be gained in calling that individual to give evidence. The Tribunal noted that there was contradictory evidence from both parties on almost all contentious elements of the case and therefore it was necessary to decide on balance which version of events was more credible. The Tribunal concluded that the complainant was a solid witness who gave evidence with clarity and conviction and had a clear recollection of the disputed events to which she averred. Her version of events was preferred by the Equality Tribunal.

The Tribunal noted that the respondent's evidence was strongly emotional but lacked any actual substance that could be relied upon to defend a claim. He admitted phoning the complainant on a number of occasions in Bulgaria and maintained that in a barber shop brushing hair off a colleague's clothes by hand was a normal practice. The repeated use of verbal humour was also accepted by him. The Tribunal found that the confirmation of the brushing and verbal banter, even if not intended to be consciously upsetting, favoured the complainant's version of events. The Tribunal noted also the factual vagueness in the respondent's written submission and the lack of any written employment contracts which did not aid the respondent's position.

The Tribunal concluded that, on the balance of probabilities, the respondent had made the comments attributed to him and that these comments fell within the definition of sexual harassment. On the balance of probabilities, the physical elements also took place. The Tribunal noted that for the alleged behaviour to constitute sexual harassment under the Acts, it must occur in the workplace or in the course of the complainant's employment. As all of the primary incidents did take place on the respondent's premises, save for the phone calls to Bulgaria, the Tribunal found that the harassment did occur in the course of the complainant's employment and thus she had established a prima facie case of sexual harassment.

The Tribunal further concluded that given the vigorous verbal exchange in August 2013 and a lack of any substantive evidence presented to justify her dismissal, it had to favour the complainant and hold that a discriminatory dismissal did take place. The Tribunal ordered the respondent to pay the complainant the sum of €6,500 as compensation for the distress and effects of the discrimination and sexual harassment, equating to approximately 16 weeks' pay. The respondent was further ordered to provide a very basic written employment handbook appropriate for a small business with suitable sections on equality and the prevention of discrimination.

[5.17] *C v A Multi-National Grocery Retailer[31]—Equality Tribunal—Employment Equality Acts 1998 to 2015, s 14A and s 74—discrimination—terms and conditions of employment—gender—whether employer had taken reasonable steps to prevent harassment or reverse its effects—victimisation by employer*

The complainant submitted that she had been sexually harassed in the workplace by another employee (Mr X). The complainant claimed that the respondent discriminated against her on grounds of gender in terms of her conditions of employment. She further claimed that she had been victimised.

The complainant had been employed by the respondent as a cashier since 2003, before her promotion to team leader in June 2011. On 8 November 2011, the complainant alleged that she was sexually harassed when Mr X, a security guard, followed her into the store room and 'started feeling her buttocks in a massaging motion'. The complainant submitted that when she initially complained to the personnel manager in her store, her complaint was not taken seriously. When the complainant stated that other employees had been the victims of similar assaults by Mr X before, her manager asked her to obtain statements from these other victims herself. Although the complainant considered this demand inappropriate, she went to considerable efforts to obtain their statements. The complainant contended that her complaint was still not taken seriously by the respondent, citing the fact that she was 'met with a bored response' and that Mr X was allowed to see her statement even though she had not been allowed to see his. The respondent concluded in a meeting held on 29 November 2011 that '[a]fter conducting a full investigation, I must advise you that all we can do is to put a comment on Mr X's file to say that there have been allegations made against him but due to lack of evidence we cannot prove he is guilty'. The complainant was not offered

---

31. *C v A Multi-National Grocery Retailer* DEC–E2015–079.

an appeal and subsequently spent six weeks out of work while suffering from depression.

Upon her return, the complainant successfully applied for a promotion to supervisor. This required her to be responsible for the money run to supply other tills with cash. Despite assurances to the contrary, she was forced to work with Mr X on one such money run and subsequently became visibly distressed. The complainant contacted her union official and made a complaint regarding how unsupported she had felt since her initial complaint, but was only made to make a second comprehensive statement repeating her initial complaint. Further, the complainant argued that a separate grievance raised by her against Mr X was not dealt with and that the respondent eventually suggested she should move to the bakery and lose her promotion to avoid contact with him. Further, the complainant was removed from her responsibilities on the cash run on a subsequent occasion. The complainant ultimately became physically ill with bronchitis, which her GP ascribed to her immune system being depleted due to work-related stress.

The respondent argued that it had followed procedures when investigating the complaint and it could not uphold the complainant's complaint as her evidence was disputed by Mr X and there were no other witnesses to prove her account of events. The respondent contended that it had treated her fairly, promoting her after her extended period of sick leave. The respondent further submitted that the fact the complainant was not asked to do the cash run on one occasion was due to it being the busiest day of the retail year and not as a punishment. The respondent also claimed that it had treated the complainant with concern and empathy, offering her counselling services and a move to another store, both of which she refused.

Before addressing sexual harassment and victimisation, the Equality Tribunal disposed of some preliminary issues raised by the respondent. First, the Tribunal concluded that the complainant's ticking of the harassment box as opposed to the sexual harassment box on the EE1 form did not breach the complainant's right to natural justice. The Tribunal noted the EE1 form was not a statutory form, that the defences to harassment and sexual harassment under the Acts are identical and that the complainant had previously complained of sexual harassment in her initial statement to the respondent. Second, the Tribunal also rejected the respondent's argument that the Tribunal could not investigate incidents prior to 24 October 2011 (six months prior to the lodging of the complaint with the Tribunal). The Tribunal relied on the Labour Court decision in *County Cork VEC v Hurley*[32] and the High Court decision in *County Louth VEC v Equality Tribunal and Brannigan*[33] as authority for doing so. In the present circumstances, the Tribunal was satisfied the incidents that occurred since the original incident in November 2010 were sufficiently linked so as to make them part of a continuum and thus admissible.

The Tribunal next addressed the complaint of discrimination on foot of the alleged sexual harassment. The Tribunal was satisfied that the conduct complained of constituted sexual harassment as defined in the Acts and the respondent was not entitled

32. *County Cork VEC v Hurley* EDA1123.
33. *County Louth VEC v Equality Tribunal and Brannigan* [2009] IEHC 370.

to avail of the s 14A defence in circumstances where little was done to prevent sexual harassment and even less was done to reverse its effects on the complainant, certainly falling short of the 'reasonable' threshold required. The Tribunal concluded that the respondent's investigation of the complaint was inadequate. First, the managers involved appeared to believe the criminal standard of proof (ie, beyond a reasonable doubt) applied despite their own 'Dignity at Work' policy stating that they should apply the civil standard of proof, ie, balance of probabilities. Second, these managers had not received training in sexual harassment investigations. Third, the Tribunal accepted the complainant's evidence that the manager she initially complained to treated her complaint as an inconvenience from the beginning.

The Tribunal commented that the whole investigation was weighted against the complainant and proceeded to highlight several flaws in the investigation. These included that Mr X's barely credible explanation of events was not probed, that the complainant did not have the opportunity to view Mr X's statement and that no appeal was offered in breach of the 'Dignity at Work' policy. The Tribunal noted that while the respondent's 'Dignity at Work' policy was adequate, this did not save the respondent in a situation where it was not implemented effectively.

The Tribunal finally addressed the issue of victimisation. The Tribunal believed that if the respondent had investigated the complaint properly, it would never have ended up before the Tribunal. A number of the respondent's actions were found to constitute victimisation including the fact that a later grievance by the complainant against Mr X was 'completely ignored', that the complainant was made to 'feel like the accused rather than the victim' and that the complainant was forced to work with Mr X unless she gave up her promotion. The Tribunal noted that for an employer of the respondent's means, the respondent had options such as moving Mr X to a different premises or not scheduling him to do cash runs with the complainant. The respondent chose not take these and failed to rebut the prima facie case of victimisation raised by the complainant.

The Tribunal concluded that, the respondent did discriminate against the complainant by not taking reasonable and practicable steps to prevent her sexual harassment contrary to s 14A of the Acts. The Tribunal further concluded that the respondent did victimise the complainant within the meaning of s 74 of the Acts.

The Tribunal ordered that the respondent pay the complainant €33,000 (comprising one year's salary for the harassment suffered and six month's salary for the victimisation suffered). The Tribunal further ordered that the respondent conduct a review of its policies and procedures in relation to its employment practices to ensure compliance with the Acts and that all managers should to be trained accordingly. The respondent should then provide a progress report to the Irish Human Rights and Equality Commission within one year of the date of the decision.

RACE AND NATIONALITY

Access to employment

[5.18] *Maciukas v G4S Secure Solutions Ltd[34]—Equality Tribunal—Employment Equality Acts 1998 to 2015—alleged discrimination in access to employment— whether transfer of undertakings had taken place—inadequate explanation by respondent—prima facie case*

The complainant, a Lithuanian national, was employed as a security guard at Athlone Direct Provision Centre by Bridgestock Ltd for a total of seven years. In May 2012, the respondent took over the security contracts. All employees, including the complainant, were invited to apply for their old positions in the respondent. On 13 June 2012 the complainant was advised that his application to the respondent had not been successful. The complainant submitted that all other employees who applied, with the exception of his brother, were reemployed in the respondent. He maintained that a transfer of undertakings had occurred and therefore he should not have had to apply for his job. The complainant cited *Redmond Stichting v Bartol[35]* in support of his argument that a transfer of undertakings had taken place. Without prejudice to that contention, the complainant submitted that the fact that he was not reemployed was discriminatory on the ground of race.

The complainant stated that he was very physically fit and therefore well-qualified for his job as a security guard. He explained that he had been very disappointed to have lost his job. He made reference to some of the Irish people that had been given positions in the new company, objecting that some of them had disciplinary records. In contrast, the complainant maintained that both he and his brother had outstanding work records.

The respondent, a licensed security provider of static guarding services to Irish customers, submitted that it had been advised that a transfer of undertakings did not apply at the time of the awarding of the contract. *Süzen v Zehnacker Gebäudereingung GmbH[2][36]* was cited in support of the contention that a transfer of undertakings did not take place. It was submitted that the reason that neither of the brothers was reemployed in the new company was the result of a request from their client, Athlone Accommodation Centre. It was further submitted that those reemployed consisted of both Irish and non-Irish nationals. Finally the respondent contended that it was well aware of its obligations regarding the Acts and that it adhered to its own equality policy.

The Equality Tribunal considered s 6(1) of the Act, which sets out when discrimination will be considered to have occurred. The Tribunal stated that it must first consider whether the complainant had established a prima facie case pursuant to s 85A of the Acts and cited *Melbury Developments Ltd v Valpeters[37]* in this regard. The Tribunal agreed with the complainant that a transfer of undertakings did in fact take place. This conclusion was reached on the basis that a major part of the workforce in

---

34. *Maciukas v G4S Secure Solutions Ltd* DEC–E2014–095.
35. *Redmond Stichting v Bartol & Ors* (Case C–29/91).
36. *Süzen v Zehnacker Gebäudereingung GmbH[2]* (Case C–13/95).
37. *Melbury Developments Ltd v Valpeters* EDA0917.

terms of numbers and skills had transferred, as *per Süzen*, and the fact that the activities carried out were similar to work carried out previously. The Tribunal commented that the respondent had been very vague about the reasons Athlone Accommodation Centre did not want the complainant and his brother retained. The Tribunal noted that, if performance issues were at play, their employment would have been terminated at an earlier stage. The Tribunal placed emphasis on the fact that no evidence had been presented to back up the assertion that the complainant was not retained on the request of the respondent's client. On this basis, the Tribunal found this reason 'too convenient' for the respondent and held that the evidence of the complainant was to be preferred. On the basis that those retained were six Irish nationals and one Romanian, the complainant was found to have established a prima facie case of discrimination on the ground of nationality. The Tribunal held that the respondent had failed to rebut this presumption.

The Tribunal took account of the fact that the maximum award that could be given in a case relating to access to employment was €13,000, as *per* s 82(4). On this basis the Tribunal concluded that €6,500 was an appropriate award in the circumstances, ie half of the maximum award that could be made. It was held that the respondent did discriminate against the complainant regarding access to employment on the ground of race.

[5.19] *Naqui v Vantry International[38]—Equality Tribunal—Employment Equality Acts 1998 to 2015, s 6 and s 8(1)(a)—nationality—race—discrimination—access to employment—prospective employee—where complainant informed respondent it was looking for Irish nationals only in a recruitment process—employment agency—vicarious liability—actions of talent account manager engaged as consultant on contract for services—complainant advised that decision not to progress her application was because she was not Irish*

The complainant, a British national of Asian origin living and educated in Ireland, applied for a finance position (Corporate Finance Executive) based in Dublin and advertised by the respondent on LinkedIn for a client. As she did not receive a response to her application, she contacted a representative of the respondent in August 2013, seeking an update. She received an email response thanking her for her application and advising her that they were only looking for Irish nationals. The complainant responded to this email highlighting that this was a discriminatory position to take against non-Irish applicants and would be illegal in Ireland. A response was sent by email apologising but setting out an explanation that the client was looking for Irish people because they wanted people with a vast knowledge about Irish companies and the Irish accounting system, which is not the same as in other countries.

As a consequence of these email responses, the complainant lodged her complaint claiming that she had been discriminated against on the basis of her nationality where it was decided by the respondent that, as she was not an Irish national, she was excluded from being considered for the role. She noted that the decision of the respondent was based purely on nationality and not on whether she was qualified for the role or if she

---

38. *Naqui v Vantry International* DEC–E2015–063.

had appropriate work experience. Having submitted her complaint, the complainant gave evidence at the hearing that she was subject to a series of phone calls from the respondent to pressurise her to withdraw her complaints and she was offered the amount of £1,000Stg as redress. The respondent acknowledged the email from the complainant, but noted that the person who sent the emails in response was not an employee, but was only supplying services to it under a consultancy agreement. It was submitted that this consultant was responsible for the delivery of the services and thus the respondent was not accountable or responsible for the consultant's actions. The respondent submitted that the complaint should be directed to the consultant and thus the Equality Tribunal was not entitled to hear a complaint against the respondent.

On this jurisdictional point, the Equality Tribunal noted ss 2 and 11 of the Acts. The Equality Tribunal was satisfied that the evidence presented to it confirmed that the respondent agency had advertised for the position on behalf of another person, and when responding to the position advertised, the complainant had sought the services of the respondent to obtain employment. The Tribunal held that it did have jurisdiction to hear and make findings in relation to the complaint. Section 11(1) of the Acts state that, without prejudice to its obligations as an employer, an employment agency shall not discriminate against any person who seeks the services of the agency to obtain employment with another person.

The Equality Tribunal noted that the contract for services with the consultant was signed by both parties. Reference was made to the contract which indicated that the consultant was referred to as a talent account manager with responsibility to supply recruitment services as notified by the respondent. The Tribunal was satisfied that the person was acting on behalf of the respondent in relation to the recruitment for the position for a client. The Tribunal noted the provisions of s 15(2) of the Acts in relation to vicarious liability and was satisfied that the respondent was answerable under the Acts for the actions of the talent account manager, in relation to the sourcing and the decisions made on the appointment for the role that was advertised, on the authority of the respondent for its client.

The Equality Tribunal then turned to consider whether the complainant was discriminated against. It considered s 6 of the Acts. The Tribunal held that the emails that the complainant had received were contrary to s 6(2). Upon questioning the respondent's rationale, the respondent further stated in an email that they were looking for Irish people. The Tribunal noted arguments made by the respondent that, in their second email to the complainant, they had clarified that the client would accept any nationality provided they had relevant working experience in Ireland and further that the message from the talent account manager to the complainant was a miscommunication due to the poor English of the talent manager. The Tribunal noted that it was significant that the respondent had stated that they were aware that the talent account manager had not conducted recruitment advertisements in English previously. It was further noted by the Tribunal that the complainant had acknowledged, in cross examination, that the job advertisement stated that applicants were required to be fully qualified accountants with a minimum of three years' experience in corporate finance and she conceded that she was not a qualified accountant. The complainant however submitted that the decision of the respondent to disregard her application because of her nationality denied her a fair opportunity to be considered for the position stating that she had been successful in applying for accountancy jobs previously without being qualified.

The Tribunal found that the respondent did advise the complainant on two occasions that the decision not to progress her application was because she was not Irish. The Tribunal noted that while the respondent appeared to have been aware of the lack of experience of the talent account manager in relation to advertising in English, it did not present in its defence any steps taken to prevent the manager from referring to the nationality of the complainant with regard to the selection for employment. Rather the respondent had contended that the talent account manager operated on her own initiative, that the actions taken were not its responsibility and that, in any event, the talent account manager had terminated the contract for services shortly after the event and no longer provided services to the respondent.

The Tribunal concluded that the respondent, through the actions of the talent account manager and contrary to s 8 of the Acts, had discriminated against the complainant on grounds of race (nationality) in relation to access to employment.

With regards to the allegation that the complainant had been pressurised by the respondent as a consequence of making her complaint, reference was made to s 74(2) of the Acts relating to victimisation. It was submitted by the respondent that it had contacted the complainant to advise her that the basis of the decision was not related to her nationality but was due to the fact that she was not qualified. The offer of compensation was to redress the offence that was caused by the emails which were written by a person whose native language was not English and to explain that what had happened amounted to a miscommunication. The Equality Tribunal noted s 14A(2) of the Acts which provides a defence for the employer who can prove they took reasonable steps to prevent the victim from being treated differently in the workplace or otherwise in the employment. The Tribunal, while acknowledging the complainant found the attempts to contact her about the complaint offensive, was satisfied that the respondent, in offering her compensation, was reversing the situation and the offence caused to her by the email. It is clear the complainant was not qualified for the position, and as such, it would not have been reasonable for the respondent, by way of reversing the effects of discrimination, to appoint her to the role. As the complainant did not lodge a specific equality complaint of being harassed or victimised following her initial complaint, as was required to under s 77, no specific finding could be made on this issue.

The Tribunal concluded by noting that the complainant was not qualified for the job and, had her application been considered beyond the fact she was not an Irish national, it is highly unlikely she would have been found suitable. She did not meet the criteria requiring her to be a fully-qualified accountant with a minimum of three years' experience. The Tribunal noted that, once proscribed treatment occurs, the respondent is fixed with liability unless the defence provided for at s 15(3) of the Acts is successfully made out. In accordance with the Acts, the respondent must show that it took such steps as are reasonably practicable to prevent discrimination. This means that an employer or recruitment agency must be conscious of the possibility of discrimination occurring and have in place reasonable measures to prevent its occurrence. This requires the respondent to show at a minimum that a clear anti-discrimination policy was in place before the discrimination occurred and the policy was effectively communicated to all employees and consultants providing recruitment services.

In this case the respondent's defence was that they were not responsible for the actions of a consultant, or person they appointed to supply the services. The respondent further failed to demonstrate any awareness of their obligations in this regard. The Tribunal held that it was not sufficient for the respondent to 'wash their hands' of the actions of their service provider as to do so would demonstrate a disregard for their obligations under the Acts. The Tribunal concluded that had the talent account manager been conversant with the equality legislation in Ireland, it is unlikely that discrimination would have occurred. The Tribunal did not accept the defence provided for by the respondent under s 15(3) could apply, thus the complainant was entitled to succeed. The Equality Tribunal ordered the respondent to pay the complainant €2,000 as redress for the infringement of the complainant's statutory rights.

While the respondent demonstrated clear and blatant discrimination on grounds of nationality, the Tribunal held that the complainant was not qualified for the job and would not have been appointed had all matters been considered. The respondent was ordered to provide up-to-date policies and procedures to prevent the occurrence of further discrimination by its employees and consultants; to ensure all contracts for services issued in future require consultants engaged by the respondent to adhere to the requirements of the Acts; and to ensure that all employees and consultants receive appropriate and adequate training on the obligations under the Acts.

Agency worker

[5.20] *Jansen v Allied Irish Banks*[39]*—Equality Tribunal—Employment Equality Acts 1998 to 2015, s 6—discrimination on grounds of race—agency worker—discriminatory dismissal*

The complainant brought a claim to the Equality Tribunal alleging that she was subject to discrimination by the respondent on the grounds of race, contrary to s 6 of the Acts when she was dismissed from her employment.

The complainant was engaged as an agency worker with the respondent from 7 November 2011 in an administrative role. The complainant's contract was renewed for a further 10 months on 23 December 2011 to work in a different administrative area (Area A) of the respondent's operations. The complainant submitted that during the course of her employment the bank failed to provide comprehensive training to her similar to that received by Irish nationals. She submitted that for a time she was working in a small cramped room away from other staff. The complainant submitted that the respondent provided her with a computer which was too slow to allow her to work effectively, and inferior to computers provided to other employees, which forced her to contact the IT department on a daily basis.

The complainant submitted that her supervisor in Area A (Ms A) treated one member of her team (Mr B) more favourably than others due to an interpersonal

---

39. *Jansen v Allied Irish Banks* DEC–E2015–077.

relationship and overlooked his poor work performance. The complainant submitted that on one occasion Mr B made an offensive racial remark to the general office. This remark caused great offence to the complainant but she did not report it to anyone. The complainant claimed that, on 7 March 2012 she received a text from the recruitment agency informing her that she was not to return to work for the respondent. The complainant says that the respondent failed to give her any reason for her sudden dismissal.

The respondent rejected all aspects of the complaint. The respondent submitted that the claims made by the complainant were entirely without merit. The respondent submitted that the complaint was out of time as the last date of discrimination should be the complainant's last day of employment on 2 March 2012. The respondent submitted that the complainant was supplied to them as an agency worker with effect from 7 November 2011, with an expectation that her assignment would last 10 months. In December the complainant was one of 22 agency staff who were transferred to a specific administrative area (Area A) of the bank. The respondent submitted that the complainant was trained in exactly the same way as other agency staff.

The respondent submitted that PCs were assigned to agency workers from an available pool of PCs and that the complainant was not singled out in any way when computers were assigned. The respondent acknowledged that the IT department was contacted to rectify issues and obtain extra memory/storage, but that these issues were not experienced only by the complainant. The respondent submitted that the speed of any computer could not account for the performance difficulties which resulted in the termination of her arrangement with the bank. The respondent submitted that workers in Area A of the bank's operations worked under strict regulatory requirements and that it was vital that they follow established strict rules and procedures at all times. The respondent submitted that the complainant consistently:

— challenged and refused to implement the bank's rules and procedures;

— failed to use check lists;

— refused to accept explanations as to why procedures were in place;

— failed to follow management instructions; and

— made repeated errors and refused management feedback.

The respondent submitted that Ms A sought to support the complainant and to coach her in order to assist her in reaching an acceptable level of performance in her assignment. Ms A provided feedback to the complainant in relation to her progress and the matter was escalated to senior management. The respondent submitted that the complainant's performance failed to improve and the respondent lawfully exercised its right to end the complainant's assignment.

The respondent submitted that two other agency staff (Irish nationals) also had their assignments terminated.

The Tribunal had to decide if the complainant was discriminated against by the respondent, on the ground of race, in relation to her conditions of employment and dismissal when the respondent dispensed with her services as an agency worker. The

Tribunal made it clear at the outset of the hearing that it considered the proper comparator in this case to be other relevant agency staff and not permanent employees of the respondent. The Tribunal had to consider whether all aspects of the complaint were referred within the statutory time limits in accordance with s 77(5) and whether the matters complained of constituted a chain of linked events or if all of the instances were separate events.

The respondent contended that the complainant's employment ended on 2 March 2012 and that the referral of the complaint was therefore outside the required six months. Central to the instant case was the complainant's contention that the respondent's deliberate refusal to communicate her dismissal and the manner of the dismissal was motivated by the ground of race and resulted in serious determent to her for a number of months after her employment ended. Regardless, the complainant specifically stated in the original complaint that discrimination continued until 26 March. This brought the complaint within time for referral as set out in the Acts.

The complainant put forward her evidence of alleged discrimination during her entire time working with the respondent, which only amounted to some six months. The complainant offered only one example of an occasion on which overt discrimination took place (the use of a racial insult) while all other alleged instances of discrimination related to her receiving inferior training, equipment, accommodations and management. The Tribunal also heard direct evidence from most of the key personnel who dealt with the complainant, including her supervisor (Ms A), regarding the respondent's procedures.

The Tribunal found that when the complainant was questioned directly at hearing about the training provided by the respondent to other agency staff, the complainant could give no specifics to back up her allegation that she received different training from other staff. On the contrary she stated that during the induction everyone got the same training and that she was 'not treated differently from other people'. The only available evidence was that all agency staff were inducted in the same manner. As the complainant was only in Area A for three months, worked only with a small group of others and had no knowledge of training provided to others, the Tribunal was satisfied that her assertions that she was excluded from particular training to be pure speculation, unsupported by any evidence.

In relation to the issue of the PC, the Tribunal accepted the complainant's account that she had problems with her PC, but there was no evidence that this was linked to her race. The Tribunal preferred the account put forward by the respondent, that a number of agency workers had the same problem and that it was dealt with through normal procedures. The Tribunal found that the complainant was simply speculating in this regard.

For a number of weeks the complainant was one of seven people working in a back room. The Tribunal found no evidence of less favourable treatment or any connection to the ground of race.

The respondent contended that the complainant was not a cooperative worker. At the hearing, the complainant persisted in arguing with the respondent about the efficiency of their established administrative procedures. The complainant insisted that she had a better way of doing things. The Tribunal accepted the respondent's account that the complainant refused to implement established procedure and refused to take direction from management. The Tribunal found that it was clear that the respondent had a reason other than the ground of race for dispensing with the complainant's services as an agency worker.

The Tribunal examined all of the instances of alleged discrimination put forward by the complainant and found that in each instance (with the exception of the incident of the racial slur) the complainant made assertions backed up purely by speculation.

As an agency worker, it was a matter for the employment agency to inform the complainant of the status of her assignments and no fault lay with the respondent in this regard. The Tribunal examined all aspects of the conditions of employment put forward by the complainant and found no evidence of less favourable treatment; and that the complainant had failed to establish a prima facie case. The Tribunal found that the complainant was not subject to discrimination on the ground of race and her conditions of employment were not affected and she was not subject to discriminatory dismissal.

Race—harassment

[5.21] *Bains v Maotham Ltd t/a Mao*[40]—*Equality Tribunal—Employment Equality Acts 1998 to 2015, s 6 and s 14A—Employment Equality Acts 1998 (Code of Practice) (Harassment) Order 2012*[41]—*discrimination on grounds of race—harassment— verbal abuse—derogatory comment linked to race*

The complainant was employed in the Dundrum branch of the respondent's chain of restaurants. It was accepted by both parties that the complainant left his employment following an incident at work on 31 August 2012 and had not returned to work since that date. On the day in question, the complainant claimed that his line manager greeted him with foul language, had physically tried to kick him and degraded him in front of other staff members. The complainant further submitted that his line manager had told him, in the context of cleaning a fryer, that 'it was dirty like your f*****g face'. The complainant left the workplace in shock and contended that the derogatory comments about his skin colour amounted to harassment on grounds of his race.

On the day after the incident, the store manager of the respondent met with the complainant and the line manager. At this meeting, the line manager explained that her comments were made in jest, and were not intended to cause offence and she attempted to apologise to the complainant; but this was not accepted by the complainant. The complainant submitted that he had sought not to work with the line manager again or that either he or his line manager be redeployed elsewhere but that this was refused by the respondent and therefore this amounted to a further act of discrimination. Subsequent attempts to facilitate the complainant's return to work were unsuccessful and the respondent then involved its area manager and director of operations.

---

40. *Bains v Maotham Ltd t/a Mao* DEC–E2015–030.
41. Employment Equality Acts 1998 (Code of Practice) (Harassment) Order 2012 (SI 208/ 2012).

Although the complainant had not lodged an official complaint, the respondent instigated an investigation into the incident, which culminated in a final written warning for the line manager for use of bad language, chastising an employee in front of staff and for passing a racist remark in relation to the complainant. A letter of apology was also offered to the complainant but was refused by him. The respondent contended that it explained to the complainant that it was not possible to move the line manager but explored other options, which included an arrangement where the complainant would not have to work directly with the line manager or to transfer the complainant to another restaurant. These options were not acceptable to the complainant. Subsequently, the respondent advised the complainant that it had dealt with the matter and sought his return to work on 16 September 2012. The complainant did not return to work on this date and his pay ceased. Even after the complainant had failed to return to work, further proposals were made to him to facilitate his return to work but the complainant failed to engage with the respondent from that point onwards.

The respondent submitted that it had taken the incident seriously and had attempted to immediately resolve the matter with the complainant. When this failed, it conducted an internal investigation which upheld the complaint and imposed a serious disciplinary sanction on the line manager.

In relation to training, the respondent stated that, during induction, all staff are trained on their obligation not to engage in verbal abuse, intimidation or any form of harassment and informed that threatening or abusive behaviour will not be tolerated. The respondent submitted that its actions against the line manager demonstrated that it applied reasonable measures to address the situation.

The Equality Tribunal found that the respondent had been subjected to a verbal comment from his line manager that was directly attributable to the colour of his skin. The Equality Tribunal further found that this remark was made publicly and was derogatory in nature and not disputed by the respondent. Accordingly, the Equality Tribunal was satisfied that comments made to the complainant constituted harassment on the grounds of race within the meaning of s 14A.

The Equality Tribunal then considered if the defence in ss 14A(2) and 15(3), that an employer took such steps as were reasonably practical so as to prevent an employee from behaving in a harassing manner, was available to the respondent. The Equality Tribunal noted that the respondent did not have a written code of practice or policy in place to address harassment within the workplace as recommended in the Employment Equality Acts 1998 (Code of Practice) (Harassment) Order 2012[42] notwithstanding that training was provided to all staff in an induction. However, the Equality Tribunal did note that the employer had proactively dealt with the matter, instigating an investigation and upholding the incident as serious misconduct.

The Equality Tribunal found that while the incident was a once off that was managed reasonably by the employer, it did create an intimidating, hostile, degrading, humiliating and offensive environment for the complainant. In order to avail of the defence to harassment, the Equality Tribunal concluded that the obligation is on employers to take

42. Employment Equality Acts 1998 (Code of Practice) (Harassment) Order 2012 (SI 208/2012).

reasonably practical steps of a preventative nature and therefore it is not sufficient for an employer to show that measures were taken to prevent a recurrence of harassment after it had already taken place. The Equality Tribunal noted that an employer must be conscious of the possibility of harassment occurring and, at a minimum, should have a clear anti-harassment or dignity at work policy in place prior to the occurrence of any harassment and to communicate this policy effectively to all employees. Furthermore, the Equality Tribunal noted that management personnel should be trained to deal with incidents of harassment and to recognise its manifestations. Accordingly, the Equality Tribunal found that the complainant had suffered harassment and the respondent was not entitled to avail of the defence provided in the Acts.

The complainant contended that he was not treated fairly following the investigation and the respondent had not addressed the matter reasonably in requiring him to return to work with the same manager who had harassed him and this amounted to further discrimination. The Equality Tribunal found that the complainant was not treated differently in the workplace or otherwise in the course of his employment by reason of rejecting the harassment and found that he was subject to a fair and reasonable investigation procedure and that attempts were made by the respondent to secure his return to work. The Equality Tribunal also noted that, notwithstanding the complainant was absent during the course of the investigation, he was paid for a total of 16 days and his wages only ceased when he remained absent after he had been provided with time to consider the situation.

On balance, the Equality Tribunal found that if an anti-harassment policy had existed, the respondent would have behaved reasonably in attempting to address and reverse the effects of the harassment. The fact that the employee was not satisfied with the process does not in itself amount to discrimination. The Equality Tribunal ordered that compensation of €500 be paid to the complainant.

Race—language and foreign workers

[5.22] *Mikoliuniene v Halcyon Contract Cleaners Ltd[43]—Equality Tribunal—Employment Equality Acts 1998 to 2015—Terms of Employment (Information) Act 1994, s 3—gender and race discrimination—duty of care of employer to foreign employees—whether obligation to ensure employment documents translated—obligation to make provision for employment rights of foreign workers*

The complainant was employed by the respondent as a cleaner from 19 December 2007 to 19 January 2012. The complainant claimed that she was discriminated against in that she did not receive any proper contract and the documentation she received was in English only, which put her at a disadvantage as she had a poor command of English. She submitted that she did not receive any proper health and safety documentation or

---

43.   *Mikoliuniene v Halcyon Contract Cleaners Ltd* DEC–E2015–036.

training and she was required to work seven days a week, which Irish workers did not. The complainant further submitted that she was not paid holiday pay.

The complainant contended that special measures may be necessary in the case of a foreign national to ensure that they are advised of their basic employment law rights and that the failure to do so amounts to discrimination. The complainant had also taken a Rights Commissioner case in relation to the Organisation of Working Time Act 1997, which was not attended by the respondent. The complainant was awarded a sum of €5,000 by the Rights Commissioner but she was required to secure a decision from the Labour Court in order to enforce this award.

The complainant referred to *58 Named Complainants v Good Concrete Ltd,*[44] which provides that there is an obligation on employers to provide a contract of employment in a language understood by the complainant. The respondent submitted written evidence to the Tribunal stating that the complainant had received a copy of her contract of employment and that it was open to her to request her supervisor to translate it if necessary. It was further submitted that it was the respondent's choice to work seven days a week. Further issues regarding pay and holiday pay occurred as a result of an administrative error on two occasions. The respondents submitted that these errors arose from time to time in a company employing a large workforce and were not discriminatory.

The Equality Tribunal found that, in respect of contracts, documentation and training, the complainant received the same treatment from her employer as persons of any other race or nationality. The complainant asserted that the complainant's poor English language skills put her in a materially different situation than a notional Irish comparator and therefore to treat her the same amounts to indirect discrimination. The Equality Tribunal referred to s 3 of the Terms of Employment (Information) Act 1994 and noted that it was incorrect to assert that there is a legal requirement under this Act to provide foreign nationals with documentation in a language likely to be understood by them. However, the Equality Tribunal noted that all employers have a duty to ensure that the rights of their employees are not violated and, in some cases, where facts support such an approach, documentation may need to be translated. However, facts supporting such an inference must be provided by the complainant. In the current case, no such difficulties had been raised by the complainant and therefore the Tribunal found that the facts did not show that the complainant was in a situation that was materially different to a person of a different race or nationality and concluded that she was treated in the same way as other employees in a comparable situation would have been treated.

The Equality Tribunal commented that the record of the respondent in its treatment of the complainant was a poor one. The Tribunal found that it was a matter of concern that the respondent had engaged a large number of foreign workers without having translated employment contracts or health and safety information and had left it to individual employees to take the initiative to obtain translations. The Equality Tribunal was unimpressed by the lack of engagement by the respondent with the Rights

---

44.   *58 Named Complainants v Good Concrete Ltd* DEC–E2008–020.

Commissioner Service. The Equality Tribunal referred to the Labour Court's comments in *A Company v A Worker*,[45] as follows:

> ... the Court is also satisfied on the balance of probabilities the treatment of the worker by the manager, and the almost complete non-implementation of relevant legislation, was due to the fact that it regarded the worker as someone of different nationality, who would not have the capability to stand on their legal rights and that by its actions ... it discriminated against her on the grounds of her nationality.

The Equality Tribunal also referred to the decision in *Campbell Catering Ltd v Rasaq*[46] and the principle that, in some cases applying the same procedural rules to foreign workers as apply to Irish workers can, in itself, amount to discrimination:

> It is clear that many non-national workers encounter special difficulties in employment arising from a lack of knowledge concerning statutory and contractual employment rights together with differences of language and culture.

In the current case the Equality Tribunal found that the respondent had not made adequate provision for the employment rights of this foreign worker who was disadvantaged by a poor command of English. The Tribunal found that the actions and omissions of the respondent had put her at a particular disadvantage compared to a hypothetical Irish employee. The Equality Tribunal upheld the complaint of discrimination that the respondent had failed in its duty of care to foreign employees. The sum of €5,000 was ordered as compensation for the effects of the discrimination.

[5.23] *Zdzalik and Rospenda v Helsinn Birex Pharmaceuticals Ltd*[47]*—Equality Tribunal—Employment Equality Acts 1998 to 2015—race—conditions of employment—constructive discriminatory dismissal—requirement that complainants stop speaking their native language, Polish, while at work—language policies— interpretation of sensible policy not sustainable if it results in less favourable treatment of Polish workers*

The complainants were employed as general operatives for a number of years when both resigned in June 2013, in circumstances which they claimed amounted to constructive discriminatory dismissal.

The respondent is a small privately-owned pharmaceutical group with production facilities in Co Dublin employing 180 staff in total. In its production facility it employs 60 staff; of which 43 are Irish, 11 Polish, 3 Lithuanian, 2 Italian, and 1 Romanian. The respondent noted that both complainants had been assessed with regards to their English language ability prior to being hired, which should have alerted them to the requirement of speaking English in the workplace. It was noted that no issue had ever been raised by the complainants from the start of their employment in 2006 until 2012. According to the respondent's language policy, English must be spoken while at work and in any of

---

45.   *A Company v A Worker* EED024.
46.   *Campbell Catering Ltd v Rasaq* EED048.
47.   *Zdzalik and Rospenda v Helsinn Birex Pharmaceuticals Ltd* DEC–E2015–047.

the production areas, whereas staff are free to use their native language during break times, as long as other workers are not feeling excluded.

The complainants' evidence was that they and other Polish workers were engaged in mundane and repetitive tasks on the respondent's production line and they talked to each other in Polish while working. They asserted that their manager forbade them to speak Polish to each other, regardless of the fact that workers of other nationalities were allowed to have conversations in their native language. Further evidence was given by the complainants that management interrupted their conversations and threatened them with disciplinary sanctions if they did not stop speaking Polish.

The complainants made a written complaint and, while their manager met with them, they never received a written response. They initiated a written grievance in which they listed details of instances where they were prohibited from speaking Polish and other inappropriate actions by management. The response did not deal with the grievances but set out the rationale for the prohibition on speaking any language other than English. The complainants ultimately resigned.

The respondent submitted that in November 2012, following the complaint that had been received, a company briefing was held with all staff, at which the language policy was outlined. It was reiterated that English was the business language to be spoken when in the workplace; but not during breaks or in places like the canteen. It was acknowledged that this was not a formal written policy but was well established through custom and practice. It was further submitted that there had been no need to promulgate the policy prior to the complainants' grievances because it had not been an issue before.

With regard to the complainants' resignations, the respondent noted that they had been offered alternative positions in another company and wished to commence their employment within one week of leaving employment. However, for operational reasons, the respondent could not facilitate this and a notice period of three weeks each was mutually agreed. It was noted that the investigation of the grievance ultimately concluded in July 2013 and the respondent did not uphold the grievance.

The Equality Tribunal considered whether the complainants had established a prima facie case under s 85A of the Acts. Firstly it considered whether to describe the dispute between the parties as harassment within the meaning of the Acts or as a matter of the complainants' terms and conditions of employment. The Tribunal noted the evidence from the respondent that all of its regulatory documentation including business processes and all standard operating procedures were in English. The Tribunal noted the respondent's evidence that regulators can visit the company at any time and that any production floor operative can be asked any question by a regulator and thus it was essential that production operatives are trained in standard operating procedures in English and are proficient in the English language. It was however noted that this approach was only semi-formalised and promulgated after consultation with IBEC and in the wake of the complaints. This was not disputed by the complainants. It was noted by the Tribunal that the situations in which the complainants were reprimanded for speaking Polish did not arise in this context and that these related to conversations in the gowning room when they were getting ready for their shift, chatting on the production floor at the end of a shift when the line had been switched off and chit chat while they were sitting next to each other on the production line packaging pharmaceuticals. It was noted by the Tribunal that the complainants had never been formally disciplined for speaking Polish to each other. However both asserted that they had been threatened in this regard by their immediate supervisor many times. The Tribunal noted the discipline carried out against them remained on the level of verbal counselling but according to the complainants it was constant and also arose in situations where no other workers were around, except two Polish employees exchanging a short sentence in Polish and the intervening supervisor.

The Tribunal held that, given the complainants had worked for a number of years to the respondent's satisfaction, it appeared that this issue escalated when specific supervisors started applying particular zeal to this question in 2012. In terms of colleagues being left out by the use of Polish, the Tribunal held it important to note that one of the complainants acknowledged that she was asked many times by non-Polish speaking colleagues to speak English.

The Tribunal noted that employers generally have a great deal of leeway in setting language policies which meet their needs for both operational reasons and those of workforce integration. However it was impossible to link the valid operational objectives underpinning the respondent's overall language policy with the kind of situations in which the complainants were constantly admonished for using their native language. The complainants' evidence was that their use of Polish was for small talk at the beginning and end of the working day and during long hours of repetitive packaging work and this was accepted by the Tribunal. The Tribunal noted that an Irish person whose native language is English would not run the same risk of discipline for the same small talk while being engaged in what was generally agreed to be repetitive, boring packaging work.

The Tribunal concluded that such a zealous interpretation of an overall sensible policy was not sustainable and allegedly was less favourable treatment of any worker whose native language was not English. This constituted less favourable treatment in the complainants' conditions of employment rather than harassment. The Tribunal held that discipline by way of a verbal counselling can only be harassment if it contains clear references to a protected ground, but no such detail was put in evidence. It was viewed therefore by the Tribunal as an unequal application of discipline in that only non-native speakers of English could ever be in a position to be disciplined for normal small talk situations, while workers who conducted the same small talk in English would not be disciplined. The complainants were therefore entitled to succeed in this part of their complaint.

The Tribunal concluded that the complainants' resignations at the end of their employment did not constitute constructive dismissal, either discriminatory or victimisatory. Evidence was given by the respondent that they were contacted by another company for references in respect of both complainants on the day of their meeting with management. The Tribunal concluded that the respondent had discriminated against the complainants in their conditions of employment on grounds of their nationality, but they were not dismissed in a discriminatory or victimisatory fashion. The Tribunal ordered the respondent to pay each complainant €1,500 in compensation.

[5.24] *Delanowski v Kellsydan Ltd t/a McDonalds Restaurant[48]—Equality Tribunal— Employment Equality Acts 1998 to 2015, ss 6(1) and (2)—use of English language while at work—allegation of discrimination based on race*

The complainant brought a claim against his employer to the Equality Tribunal for discrimination based on race due to the respondent's policy, which prohibits the use of any language other the English.

The complainant was a Polish national and commenced employment with the respondent in November 2005. At the time of the hearing before the Tribunal he was employed as a shift manager. The basis for the complaint was that his employer, the respondent, insisted on the use of the English language at all times and refused the complainant the opportunity of conversing in any other language. The complainant viewed this as being discriminatory treatment based on race.

The complainant informed the Tribunal that the insistence by the respondent of using English only was not just restricted to the restaurant floor, but also the kitchen area and in meetings with management in the office area. Such meetings with management included disciplinary hearings where disputes arose in respect of translation, during the course of same.

The complainant contended that there were no objective grounds for the respondent's English-only policy and referred to *Noonan Services Ltd v A Worker[49]* where it was held that:

> it is clear that a requirement to have competency in English is likely to place persons whose native language is other than English at a disadvantage relative to persons whose native language is English. Hence, prima facie, a requirement of competency in English is indirectly discriminatory unless it is objectively justified.

The respondent operates four McDonalds restaurants throughout Limerick and employs 188 employees from 15 different countries. The respondent submitted that it promotes anti-discrimination within the company in accordance with the company handbook. The respondent outlined that in the company policy there is no outright ban on speaking a language other than English in the workplace. The respondent stated that the policy recognised that it may at times be appropriate for employees to converse in a language other than English should a customer initiate a conversation in another language. It was also stated that employees were also permitted to use a language other than English while on a break, provided that no other employee was being excluded.

The respondent stated that it did use English as its business language and that this decision was objectively justified for a number of reasons. In this case the complainant was employed in client-facing roles which required a proficiency in English. Also the respondent was required to maintain a high level of health and safety standards in line with Hazard Analysis Critical Control Point (HACCP). The respondent submitted that all safety signs, documentation and records were in English and food safety audits were

---

48.   *Delanowski v Kellsydan Ltd t/a McDonalds Restaurant* DEC–E2015–072.

49.   *Noonan Services Ltd v A Worker* EDA1126.

conducted in English. The respondent further submitted that the use of the English language was deemed necessary based on the need for all staff members to be able to communicate and understand one another, so as not to exclude any other member of staff based on the diversity of the workforce,

The respondent referred to *Mitchell v Southern Health Board*[50] in which it was found that 'the first requirement is that the claimant must establish facts from which it may be presumed that the principle of equal treatment has not been applied to them'. They also referred to *Andvzejeczak and 7 others v Microsemi*[51] where the Tribunal found that Microsemi had objective grounds to justify the policy.

Section 85A of the Acts sets out the burden of proof which applies to claims of discrimination. It requires the complainant to establish, in the first instance, facts from which discrimination may be inferred. It is only where such a prima facie case has been established that the onus shifts to the respondent to rebut the inference of discrimination raised.

The respondent stated that under its Employee Handbook, English is identified as the business operational language and that:

> ... every day in our business there are times when a common language is needed and in Ireland this language is English. There are many sensible benefits to this when dealing with customers and colleagues to ensure the best teamwork, customer service, food quality and safety. As a result, our employees are encouraged to speak English when working and when talking with customers. However, we recognise that at times another language may be more appropriate. In fact, we are proud of our ability to speak to our customers in their native tongue whenever and wherever appropriate.

The respondent stated that the reasoning behind the use of a business language was three-fold: for health and safety purposes, to ensure inclusion, and to ensure business efficiency. The respondent claimed that it was important for it that all employees should be able to understand the health and safety notices and instructions issued by supervisors and managers and, given that it had different nationalities employed, it had to be able to ensure that instructions were understood and followed by all employees.

The Tribunal was satisfied that any one of these reasons justified the use of a business language and more so when the three reasons were taken into account. The Tribunal was satisfied that this practice was objectively justified.

In considering the allegation for discrimination, the Tribunal concluded that the complainant had not established a prima facie case of discriminatory treatment in relation to conditions of employment.

This finding was also reached in the almost identical case *Pajak v Kellsydan Ltd t/a McDonalds Restaurant.*[52]

---

50. *Mitchell v Southern Health Board* [2001] ELR 201.
51. *Andvzejeczak and 7 Others v Microsemi* DEC–E2013–086 and EDA157.
52. *Pajak v Kellsydan Ltd t/a McDonalds Restaurant* DEC–E2015–073.

DISABILITY

Reasonable accommodation

[5.25] *A Post Person v A Postal Service[53]—Equality Tribunal—Employment Equality Acts 1998 to 2015, ss 16(1), (3) and 77(5)—disability—alleged discrimination— failure to provide reasonable accommodation—performance issues—discriminatory dismissal—victimisation—preliminary issues—importance of medical evidence*

The complainant was employed by the respondent as a general postal worker. In 2002, the complainant was diagnosed with schizophrenia and was hospitalised due to his illness in 2003 and 2005. On the complainant's discharge from hospital, he requested that the respondent put in place a rehabilitation programme to facilitate his return to work. The respondent duly implemented such a programme notwithstanding that there was no medical basis for same. The same programme was also put in place following the complainant's second period of hospitalisation in 2005.

In April 2008, following a number of performance issues including failure to deliver items of mail, failure to attend for duty and failure to notify the office of inability to attend for duty, the respondent imposed a serious warning on the complainant. Subsequently, in September 2008, further absences, unsatisfactory attendance and poor performance continued and the respondent informed the complainant by writing that they were considering disciplinary action, including dismissal. The complainant responded, by letter, that he was extremely anxious to continue with employment and assured them of his commitment to his employment duties. As a result, he was given a further six months to demonstrate his commitment to his duties. During the hearing before the Tribunal, the complainant claimed that this letter was written under the influence of his disability and therefore not credible. Unfortunately, due to further issues with his disability, the complainant had additional late and sick absences. By letter in February 2009, the respondent recommenced a disciplinary process with a recommendation of the complainant's dismissal. The complainant claimed that the reactivation of this disciplinary process against him amounted to discrimination and a failure to offer him reasonable accommodation. The complainant further claimed that the respondent had dismissed a request to consider night-shift working or working indoors, because if this was afforded to him, the complainant believed he would not have had any issues with his absence record. The respondent contended that this request was later withdrawn by the complainant and documentary evidence was provided to the Tribunal supporting this.

The complainant attended an oral hearing in April 2009 accompanied by his union representative. At this meeting, the respondent was informed of the complainant's underlying medical condition and asked to give him another chance. The respondent then referred the complainant to the chief medical officer (CMO) for assessment. Arising from the assessment of the CMO, a decision was made to retire the complainant on the grounds of ill health. This decision was appealed by the complainant and the appeal was successful. The complainant claimed that the result of the successful appeal

---

53.   *A Post Person v A Postal Service* DEC–E2015–026.

was withheld by the respondent from him for a period of two years, which amounted to a form of victimisation.

The respondent submitted that while the complainant had a number of absences related to medical matters, the absences were not the cause of the performance issues that were the subject of the disciplinary process. The respondent submitted that the performance issues were due to late attendances and failure to notify his inability to attend work and there was no medical evidence that the complainant's disability caused these performance issues. The respondent submitted that the complainant was certified as fully fit for work following his hospitalisation in 2003. The issue of alternative duties was not discussed with the complainant at times when he was certified as fit for work. The respondent submitted that it was only at the disciplinary hearing in April 2009 that the complainant claimed the reason for his difficulties at work was due to an underlying medical condition. On becoming of aware of this, the respondent referred the matter to the CMO. The respondent submitted that it was entitled to terminate the complainant's employment on ill-health grounds in light of the evidence and the CMO's medical report and that the process leading up to this decision was fair and reasonable. The delay in issuing the appeal decision to the complainant was based on a number of reasons, including the complexity of the case and an unfortunate administrative error. The respondent submitted that if the disciplinary process continued, following the decision of the Equality Tribunal, the complainant would be offered an opportunity to put forward medical evidence and reasonable accommodation could be considered at that stage.

It was agreed by both parties that the complainant suffered from a disability within the meaning of the Acts. The Equality Tribunal considered a preliminary issue as to whether the complaints were referred within the statutory time limits and considered s 77(5) of the Employment Equality Acts 1998 to 2015 as to whether there was ongoing discrimination. The Tribunal referred to *County Louth VEC v Johnson*[54] which provided that:

> ... in certain circumstances, the Court may take into consideration previous occasions in which a complainant was allegedly discriminated against on the same ground i.e. where the alleged acts can be considered a separate manifestation of the same disposition to discriminate and the most recent occurrence was within the time period specified in the Act.

In the current case, the Equality Tribunal considered all instances of the alleged treatment of the complainant with regard to his disability to be linked.

The Tribunal referred to s 16(1) of the Acts which provides that an employer is not obliged to retain an employee who is not fully competent and capable of doing the job he or she is required to do. The Equality Tribunal also referred to s 16(3) which provides that a person with a disability is regarded as fully competent and fully capable of undertaking duties if reasonable accommodation is the only difference between being able to do the job and not being able to do the job. The Equality Tribunal then referred to

---

54. *County Louth VEC v Johnson* EDA0712.

the Labour Court's comments in *Humphreys v Westwood Fitness Club*[55] regarding the obligations of an employer in relation to a dismissal on grounds of incapacity:

> The nature and extent of the enquiries which an employer should make will depend on the circumstances of each case. At a minimum, however, an employer should ensure that he or she is in full possession of all material facts concerning the employee's condition and that the employee is given fair notice that the question of his or her dismissal for incapacity is being considered. The employee must be allowed an opportunity to influence the employer's decision.

> In practical terms, this will normally require a two-stage enquiry, which looks firstly at the factual position concerning the employee's capability including the degree of impairment arising from the disability and its likely duration. This would involve looking at the medical evidence available to the employer either from the employee's doctors or obtained independently.

> Secondly, if it is apparent that the employee is not fully capable s.16(3) of the Act requires the employer to consider what if any special treatment or facilities may be available by which the employee can become fully capable. The section requires that the cost of such special treatment or facilities must also be considered. Here, what constitutes nominal cost will depend on the size of the organisation and its financial resources.

> Finally, such an enquiry could only be regarded as adequate if the employee concerned is allowed a full opportunity to participate at each level and is allowed to present medical evidence and submissions.

In the current case, the Tribunal noted that the respondent had provided a full extensive record of the complainant's medical history and supporting documentation and details of all of their processes employed in dealing with the complainant's numerous health issues during the employment. The Equality Tribunal accepted the CMO's evidence that the respondent's attitude to the complainant's disability was that it had been treated in 2003 and 2005 and the complainant had been certified as fit for work. Accordingly, the respondent had drawn a line under the disability and considered it as something that had occurred in the past. Subsequently, when performance issues arose in 2008, the respondent took account of the complainant's medical records and obtained medical advice that the performance issues were not linked to his disability. The Tribunal found that the respondent had, at the relevant times, made more than adequate enquiries to establish the factual position relating to the complainant's capacity and had demonstrated that they considered the complainant's disability at the appropriate times. Furthermore, the Tribunal noted that, given the long period of time that the complainant had been working without incident for the respondent, and taking into account relevant medical advice, it was reasonable for the respondent not to raise the issue of his disability with the complainant every time there was a performance issue, as to do so could, in itself, be construed as discrimination. The Tribunal accepted that the respondent did provide a return-to-work programme for the complainant even though it was not required by medical advice and therefore found that the allegations by the

---

55. *Humphreys v Westwood Fitness Club (Health and Fitness Club v A Worker)* EED037.

complainant that the programme was not properly implemented could not in itself be considered as failure to provide reasonable accommodation.

The Equality Tribunal found that the complainant had been allowed a full opportunity to participate at all stages of the disciplinary process and had been allowed to present relevant medical evidence and submissions. The Tribunal noted that the respondent had immediately halted the disciplinary process once the complainant raised the issue of his disability and sought expert medical advice. The decision to retire the complainant on the grounds of ill health was based on an independent medical assessment and their decision was reasonable based on the findings of that assessment. Accordingly, the Tribunal found no evidence of discriminatory dismissal.

In relation to the claim of victimisation, the Tribunal noted that a decision not to release the medical assessment was reasonable based on further medical advice and therefore did not amount to discrimination or victimisation under the Acts. The Tribunal further noted that it is well established that individuals with a disability are subject to the disciplinary procedures of their employers as long as their employers take proper account of that disability, if necessary. Accordingly, the Tribunal found that the complainant had failed to establish a prima facie case of discriminatory dismissal or discriminatory treatment and dismissed the complaint.

[5.26] *Kozak v Eirtech Aviation Ltd and Firefly Management Services Ltd*[56]*— Equality Tribunal—Employment Equality Acts 1998 to 2015, s 2, s 16—disability and race—discrimination—failure to provide reasonable accommodation—whether or not complainant an employee or an independent contractor*

The complainant was engaged by the first respondent as an aircraft spray painter. The complainant gave evidence that on 18 August 2011 he received a number of documents, including an Eirtech start pack, a B10 Change of Directorship Form, an Eirtech Aviation memo, a Form 12A, an Agent Link Notification Form and an EU Essentials Form along with a request to complete and return these documents.

Subsequently, in January 2012, the complainant was informed that there was work to be carried out in the Czech Republic and he volunteered to go there to assist. The complainant and other employees were provided with a document entitled 'New Paint Facility in Ostrava Czech Republic opening January 2012' and that document set out the pay and conditions for employees who would be going to the Czech Republic. The first respondent denied that this document applied to the complainant and claimed that it was only in respect of permanent employees and that the complainant was not considered as an employee of the first respondent.

The complainant travelled to the Czech Republic on 19 January 2012 and gave evidence that he was subjected to severe bullying and harassment by employees and supervisors at the premises of the first respondent, which resulted in him having an acute anxiety attack. It was claimed by the complainant that following an incident on 25 January 2012, he was taken to a psychiatric unit at a local hospital. The complainant was discharged from hospital on 30 January 2012 and flew home to Ireland. On his arrival in

---

56. *Kozak v Eirtech Aviation Ltd and Firefly Management Services Ltd* DEC–E2015–028.

Ireland, the complainant attended his GP and psychiatrist and he was certified as unfit to work due to stress.

The complainant lodged a complaint with the first respondent and was advised that an investigation would be carried out. Subsequently, on 21 May 2012, a letter was sent to the complainant informing him of the finding that his complaints were not upheld. The same letter also informed the complainant there was no longer any work for him with the first respondent due to seasonal factors and that he was not entitled to any compensation as he had worked under a contract for services. Evidence was submitted to the Tribunal by the complainant that, notwithstanding the assertions of seasonal factors, there was an advertisement in FÁS from the respondent seeking an aircraft spray painter. The complainant submitted that he was not furnished with any of the procedures regarding the alleged investigation and at no stage was he consulted during the course of the investigation. The complainant alleged that the treatment of him during the period up to, and including, his dismissal amounted to discrimination on grounds of race and disability in relation to his working conditions and also claimed discriminatory dismissal.

As a preliminary issue, the respondent denied that the complainant was an employee and submitted that he was an independent contractor engaged by his own company, the second-named respondent, who was provided to the first-named respondent through Parc Aviation Ltd (which was not named in the proceedings). The commercial agreement for the provision of maintenance contract services between the first-named respondent and Parc Aviation Ltd was submitted to the Tribunal as evidence. The complainant had named both respondents on his claim form. The complainant submitted that he had applied for the position advertised by the first-named respondent and was interviewed and offered the role by the first-named respondent. He then worked for the first-named respondent at their plant in Shannon and again in the Czech Republic. The complainant submitted that he had no contact with anyone from the second-named respondent but that his name had appeared on a B10 Change of Directorship Form which was provided to him by the first-named respondent. The names of both respondents appeared on his payslips.

The Tribunal considered the definitions in s 2 of the Employment Equality Acts 1998 to 2015 in relation to 'contract of employment', 'employer', 'employee', 'agency worker' and 'providers of agency work'. The Tribunal examined the documents provided to the complainant for signing, one of which was a B10 Form naming the complainant as a director of a company called Firefly Management Services. The complainant stated that he did not understand these documents but had signed them as instructed. The complainant was then issued with a contract stated to be between the complainant, Firefly Management Services and Parc Aviation Ltd. The P60s issued to the complainant gave the employer's name as 'Firefly Management Services–Eirtech'. The Tribunal deduced from the evidence that the second respondent is a company set up by the first respondent in order to effect payment of the complainant's wages through that company and the complainant was made a director of the second respondent. The Tribunal found that the respondent had put in place a complicated series of relationships between a number of intertwined companies and was satisfied that the complainant would not have understood the procedures set out in the documentation provided to him.

The Equality Tribunal carried out an assessment in relation to the status of the complainant as either an independent contractor or an employee of either or both of the respondents. The Tribunal referred to the judgment of the Supreme Court in *Castleisland Cattle Breeding Society Ltd v Minister for Social and Family Affairs*[57] and the precedent set in that case that an assessment of the real arrangement, on a day-to-day basis, between the parties is required. The Equality Tribunal also referred to the guidance of Keane J in *Henry Denny and Sons Ireland Ltd v The Minister for Social Welfare*[58] that:

> It is accordingly clear that while each case must be determined in the light of its particular facts and circumstances, in general a person will be regarded as providing his or her services on a contract of service and not as an independent contractor where he or she is performing those services for another person and not for himself or herself. The degree of control exercised over how the work is to be performed, although a factor to be taken into account, is not decisive. The inference that a person is engaged in business on his or her own account is more readily drawn where he or she provides the necessary premises or equipment or some other form of investment, where he or she employs others to assist in the business and where the profit which he or she derives from the business is dependent on the efficiency with which it is conducted by him or her.

The 'enterprise test' as set down in *Minister for Agriculture and Food v Barry & Ors*[59] and the question of mutuality of obligation was also considered by the Tribunal.

Taking the foregoing into account, the Equality Tribunal noted that the complainant was issued a security card by Eirtech to clock in and out of work. He was required to work a set number of hours each day which were set by Eirtech and during his work, he was controlled and supervised by Eirtech. The complainant had to carry out personally the tasks assigned to him and could not nominate or send a replacement. It was noteworthy for the Tribunal that the complainant's application to go to the Czech Republic was submitted and accepted in the same process as other employees of the first-named respondent who were chosen for Ostrava. Furthermore, the Equality Tribunal noted that the remuneration received by the complainant for his work did not vary depending on how fast or slowly he carried out his work and therefore the complainant could not derive any profit from the arrangement or minimise his losses.

In relation to the involvement of Parc Aviation Ltd, the Tribunal referred to *Brook Street v Dacas*[60] which stated that:

> … in ascertaining the overall legal effect of the triangular arrangements on the status of Mrs Dacas, the Employment Tribunal should not focus so intently on the express terms of the written contracts entered into by Brook Street with Mrs Dacas and the Council that it is deflected from considering finding facts relevant to a possible implied contract of service between Mrs Dacas and the Council in respect

---

57. *Castleisland Cattle Breeding Society Ltd v Minister for Social and Family Affairs* [2004] IESC 40.
58. *Henry Denny and Sons Ireland Ltd v The Minister for Social Welfare* [1998] 1 IR 34.
59. *Minister for Agriculture and Food v Barry & Ors* [2008] IEHC 216.
60. *Brook Street v Dacas* [2004] EWCA Civ 217.

> of the work actually done by her exclusively for the Council at its premises and
> under its control, until it took the initiative in terminating that arrangement. The
> formal written contracts between Mrs Dacas and Brook Street and between Brook
> Street and the Council relating to the work to be done by her for the Council may
> not tell the whole of the story about the legal relationships affecting the work
> situation. They do not, as a matter of law, necessarily preclude the implication of a
> contract of service between Mrs Dacas and the Council. There may be evidence of
> a pattern of regular mutual contact of a transactional character between Mrs Dacas
> and the Council, from which a contract of service may be implied by the tribunal.

The Equality Tribunal was satisfied that the totality of the evidence demonstrated that
the complainant was an employee of the first respondent and that, notwithstanding the
existence of a written contract between the complainant, the second respondent and Parc
Aviation Ltd, he was employed under an implied contract of service by the first
respondent. The Equality Tribunal was therefore satisfied that the first respondent was
the correct respondent, being the entity that made the decision to hire and terminate the
employment of the complainant. The second respondent should not have been named in
the proceedings.

A further preliminary issue arose as to whether or not the complainant had a
disability, which was known to the respondent, for the purposes of the Acts. Following
the alleged treatment he suffered in the Czech Republic, the complainant informed the
Tribunal that he had been diagnosed as having suffered an acute anxiety attack. The
complainant's GP diagnosed him as suffering from stress and he submitted medical
certificates to the respondent, citing stress as the reason for his non-attendance at work.
The Equality Tribunal accepted that the complainant appeared to become physically
upset and shook when providing his account of the night in question. The Equality
Tribunal was satisfied that the complainant fell within the definition of a person with a
disability under s 2 of the Acts. The Equality Tribunal also found that the respondent
was aware of the complainant's disability on the date of termination of the complainant's
employment.

The respondent submitted that the complainant was dismissed due to seasonal
factors within the industry, but, the Tribunal noted that Mr R (on behalf of the
respondent), in response to a direct question, gave evidence that the complainant was let
go as he was considered unsuitable because of what happened in Ostrava. Mr R went on
to state that the job involved expensive machinery and planes and that he could not be
sure that the complainant was suitable for this type of work given what happened in
Ostrava. The Equality Tribunal noted that this directly contradicted the respondent's
earlier evidence that the complainant was let go solely due to seasonal factors. The
evidence from the respondent was that the Ostrava incident had influenced a decision to
let the complainant go. On that basis, the Tribunal inferred that the complainant's
disability had influenced the decision to dismiss him and found that the complainant had
established a prima facie case of less favourable treatment on grounds of disability in
relation to his dismissal.

As to the question of whether reasonable accommodation was considered, the
Tribunal stated that there was an obligation on the employer to make a proper and
adequate assessment of the situation before taking the decision to dismiss and referred

to the Labour Court decision in *A Health and Fitness Club v A Worker.*[61] The Tribunal noted that the Labour Court had interpreted s 16 of the Acts to be a process-orientated approach which places an obligation upon an employer to embark on a process of ascertaining the real implications of the employee's ability to do the job. This process would involve taking appropriate expert advice; consulting with the employee concerned; and considering with an open mind what special treatment or facilities could realistically overcome any obstacles to the employee doing the job for which he or she is otherwise competent and assessing the actual costs and practicality of providing that accommodation. The Equality Tribunal found that the respondent did not make any enquiries to ascertain the extent of the complainant's condition and failed to look at any measures which might facilitate his return to work. In the circumstances, the Equality Tribunal found that the complainant's disability was the factor which contributed to respondent's decision to dismiss him and that the respondent had failed to provide him with reasonable accommodation within the meaning of the Acts. On that basis, the Tribunal upheld the complaint of discrimination and awarded compensation in the sum of €28,000. Corresponding claims on the grounds of race and in relation to conditions of employment were not upheld.

[5.27] *A Complainant v A Healthcare Company*[62]*—Equality Tribunal—Employment Equality Acts 1998 to 2015—disability—multiple sclerosis—whether complainant subjected to discriminatory treatment in working conditions on grounds of disability—whether respondent failed to provide her with reasonable accommodation*

The complainant had been employed with the respondent for 36 years, initially as an assembler and, since 2002, with the respondent's bio clean team. In 2006, the complainant was diagnosed with multiple sclerosis (MS) and the respondent was fully aware of her condition at all times.

After two periods of absence as a result of her illness, the respondent referred the complainant for a medical assessment in December 2012. In the course of her examination, the complainant intimated to the company's doctor that there were concerns in respect of her job on occasions when extra work was required of the team for operational reasons. The respondent maintained that this intermittent imbalance of workload was giving rise to disquiet among the workers in the 'bio clean' area as, when peaks occurred, the added work was unevenly distributed. It was the contention of the respondent that the complainant intimated to the doctor that she believed this exacerbated the symptoms of her MS, but she clearly stated that she did not want to formalise the issue as a complaint or grievance. At that time, she was considered unfit to return to work and a review was scheduled for January 2013.

The complainant maintained that the company's doctor appeared to take it upon himself to ask the Occupational Health Adviser to 'informally have discussions with management regarding the issue of concern within the workplace to evaluate measures

---

61. *A Health and Fitness Club v A Worker (Humphreys v Westwood Fitness Club)* [2004] 15 ELR 296.

62. *A Complainant v A Healthcare Company* DEC–E2015–009.

to try and lessen any tension within the group as a consequence of (the complainant's) inability to cope with extra work'.

In his report of January 2013, the company doctor stated that the complainant should meet with the respondent to resolve any issues of concern before she returned to work. The company doctor recommended that the complainant work half shifts for a two-week period but stated that thereafter she should be able to work on a full-time basis, without restriction.

On her return to work, the complainant was invited to attend a meeting with management. The complainant contended that the purpose of the meeting was to inform her that the respondent had decided to move her to another part of the business. The complainant queried whether the move was as a result of her condition and was told that if she did not have MS she would not be removed from the area. She stated that, due to the relocation, she suffered an injury and was caused extreme stress. She lost a lot of responsibility and connections and that her new post was not a job which was suitable to her vast experience and knowledge with the respondent. She further stated that the respondent had failed in its obligations and duties towards her under ss 6 and 16 of the Acts.

The respondent stated that the objective of the meeting was to review options that might have less onerous physical demands for the complainant, eliminating the likelihood of the symptoms of fatigue that presented with her illness while, at the same time, alleviating the workload imbalance within the bio-clean area. The respondent stated that the identified area was a suitable alternative for the complainant and that there was no decrease or diminution in her remuneration or conditions of employment. It was further stated that the proposal in respect of the complainant was reasonable and effective and that there was no detriment whatsoever associated with her transfer.

The Equality Tribunal noted that s 85A requires the complainant to establish a prima facie case of discrimination and, only if she succeeds in doing so, is it for the respondent to prove the contrary. It was noted that the Labour Court has held consistently that the facts from which the occurrence of discrimination may be inferred must be of 'sufficient significance' before a prima facie case is established.

The Tribunal noted that both parties had accepted that the complainant's condition was a disability within the meaning of the Acts, and it agreed that it fell within that definition. The Tribunal then turned to consider whether the respondent had provided the complainant with appropriate measures in accordance with s 16 of the Acts. The Tribunal was guided by the Labour Court determination in *Humphreys v Westwood Fitness Club*[63] which was upheld by the Circuit Court. In its determination, the Labour Court stated:

> At a minimum, however, an employer should ensure that he or she is in full possession of all the material facts concerning the employee's condition … In practical terms this will normally require a two-stage enquiry, which looks firstly at the factual position concerning the employee's capability including the degree of impairment arising from the disability and its likely duration. This would involve looking at the medical evidence available to the employer either from the

---

63.   *Humphreys v Westwood Fitness Club (Health and Fitness Club v A Worker)* EED037.

employee's doctors or obtained independently. Secondly, if it is apparent that the employee is not fully capable, Section 16(3) of the Act requires the employer to consider what if any special treatment or facilities may be available by which the employee can become fully capable. The Section requires that the cost of such special treatment or facilities must also be considered. Here, what constitutes nominal cost will depend on the size of the organisation and its financial resources.

Finally, such an enquiry could only be regarded as adequate if the employee concerned is allowed a full opportunity to participate at each level and is allowed to present relevant medical evidence and submissions.

The Tribunal noted that Dunne J in the Circuit Court appeal in the *Humphreys* case had stated that there is a legal obligation under the Employment Equality Acts for an employer to take advice from either the complainant's own doctor, or an independent doctor, where there are concerns in relation to the health of a worker.

The Tribunal considered the reports of the doctor and the evidence in relation to the meeting held between management and the complainant on her return to work and found that prima facie evidence of discriminatory treatment on grounds of disability had been established and that the burden of proof shifted to the respondent to rebut the evidence.

The Tribunal stated that the respondent made the decision to move the complainant without any medical evidence and on the basis of an assumption that the complainant was unable to undertake the duties of her position due to her disability. The Tribunal found that there had been no consideration of reasonable accommodation or appropriate measures by the respondent. There was no evidence that the area in which the complainant worked was not suitable due to her MS and it was evident that the complainant was not afforded any opportunity to participate in an assessment of her needs. The Tribunal concluded that the decision to move the complainant was ill-considered and ill-thought out.

It was noted that in *An Employer v A Telecommunications Company*,[64] the Equality Tribunal was particularly critical of the employer's misinterpretation of or failure to follow the findings of its medical report. The Tribunal concluded that this decision was very pertinent and applicable in the instant case and found that the approach of the respondent, in failing to ensure that the complainant was appraised at all stages of the evidence ran contrary to what is required, having regard to the decision in *Humphreys v Westwood*.[65]

Reference was also made by the Tribunal to the decision of the Labour Court in *McCrory Scaffolding Ltd v A Worker*,[66] where it was established that assumptions of a health and safety nature towards employees with a disability, without the benefit of receiving or assessing the medical evidence, constitute discrimination on grounds of disability. It was further noted that in *A Worker v An Employer*[67] it was held that a proper and adequate assessment has to be made of the situation of an employee with a disability

---

64. *An Employer v A Telecommunications Company* DEC–E2009–073.
65. *Humphreys v Westwood Fitness Club (Health and Fitness Club v A Worker)* EED037.
66. *McCrory Scaffolding Ltd v A Worker* EED055.
67. *A Worker v An Employer* (2005) 16 ELR 159.

before decisions which may be to the detriment of the employee are taken. The Tribunal stated that there was an absence of any such assessment by the respondent here.

In the instant case, the complainant had made it clear in the meeting with management that she was not unable to undertake her duties and that she was entirely unhappy with the proposal for her transfer. At this juncture, the respondent ought to have considered further medical evidence and invited the complainant to furnish medical advice or opinion, given the divergent views expressed at the meeting. There was also no attempt by the respondent to deal with the tensions on the team, as requested by the occupational doctor.

In the case of *A School v A Worker*[68] the Labour Court stated that:

> the duty imposed on an employer to provide reasonable accommodation carries with it a concomitant obligation to make an informed and considered decision on what is or is not possible reasonable and proportional. If all the options that may be available are not adequately considered, the employer cannot form a bona fide belief that they are impossible, unreasonable or disproportionate.

The Tribunal found that, in the instant case, the respondent had not complied with its duty and obligations to the complainant in this regard.

The Tribunal held that a prima facie case of discrimination on grounds of disability had been made out by the complainant and that the respondent had failed to rebut this evidence. The Tribunal also found that the respondent failed to provide the complainant with reasonable accommodation in accordance with s 16 of the Acts.

The Tribunal directed that the complainant be reinstated in the Bio-Clean area and directed that an award of compensation of €20,000 be made (which equated to six months' salary).

[5.28] *A Complainant v A Restaurant Ltd and Mr A t/a A Restaurant*[69]*—Equality Tribunal—Employment Equality Acts 1998 to 2015—disability—discrimination contrary to s 6(2)(g) and discriminatory dismissal contrary to s 8—failure to provide complainant with reasonable accommodation—where complainant suffering from depression and self-harming—whether there had been a resignation*

The complainant was employed as a waitress in the respondent's restaurant since October 2009. It was submitted that the complainant had been diagnosed with depression as a teenager and through the years suffered episodes of depression but had not informed her employer of this fact. The complainant suffered a serious bout of depression on 19 November 2011 and, as a result, missed work on 19, 20, 24 and 25 November 2011. The complainant notified her employer by text on 18 and 23 November that she would be unable to attend work due to illness but she did not cite depression as the reason for her non-attendance. A member of the respondent's staff visited the complainant at home on 24 November and became aware of her condition. The complainant had been self-harming and told her colleague about this and her history of depression. On 25 November the complainant's friend called to her place of work and

---

68. *A School v A Worker* EDA1413.

69. *A Complainant v A Restaurant Ltd and Mr A t/a A Restaurant* DEC–E2015–015.

informed the respondent about her condition and said that she was seeking medical treatment for same. On 15 December 2011 the complainant met with her manager at the respondent's premises and disclosed full details of her condition.

Medical certificates were provided by the complainant to the respondent on 22 December, and again in January 2012, stating that her absence was due to depression. She met with the respondent on 20 January and was told that she had finished working there. She received a P45 in the post which was drawn up on 19 January 2012 and which confirmed her employment had ended on 20 November 2011, the second day of her sick absence.

The respondent advised the Tribunal that the staff member who visited the complainant in her home on 24 November reported that the complainant was suffering from the effects of having taken intoxicating substances and that she had asked for cigarettes and alcohol to be purchased for her. The respondent further submitted that on the evening of 24 November 2011, the complainant had phoned the respondent at night time and asked for her wages and further asked that alcohol be purchased for her and delivered to her home. It was submitted that, in the course of this phone call, the complainant had advised the respondent that she would not be returning to work and had resigned. When the complainant's friend advised the respondent that she was seeking medical treatment for her condition, the respondent assumed the complainant was suffering from alcoholism and that she was seeking treatment in that regard. The respondent accepted that at the meeting which occurred before Christmas the complainant had apologised for her behaviour over the past few weeks and explained the history of her illness and how it had resulted in self-harming. The complainant stated that she had 'lost' about eight or nine days during the period of her depression and apologised for letting down the respondent. In the course of this conversation, the respondent mentioned the phone call that it had received from the complainant and the text on 23 November stating that she was unable to attend work on the following day. The complainant stated she had no recollection of the text or indeed the phone call and referred to the black outs that she had experienced.

The Tribunal accepted that the complainant had suffered from depression since early 2000 and had been receiving medical treatment since that time, to include prescribed antidepressants, regular GP visits and also psychiatric treatment. The Tribunal was satisfied that the complainant did have a disability within the meaning of s 2 of the Acts.

The Tribunal then considered whether the respondent was on notice of the complainant's disabilities. The Tribunal concluded that the respondent was aware of the complainant's depression at least after the December meeting, but was aware from 25 November that the complainant was suffering from a condition for which she was seeking treatment, which was assumed to be an addiction of some sorts. The respondent had also become aware, following its staff member's visit to the complainant's home on 24 November that the complainant had been self-harming. The Tribunal noted the provisions of s 85 of the Acts which set out the burden of proof which applies in a claim of discrimination. The Tribunal considered whether the complainant had established a prima facie case. The Tribunal noted the disputed facts about the complainant's purported resignation. The complainant's evidence was that she has lost eight or nine days in the period of depression and did not recall any text or phone call during the week of 23 November. In the course of her meeting with the respondent in December 2011, she advised the respondent that she was receiving treatment for her depression but was currently unable to work. The complainant's position was that she was advised by the respondent not to worry about work, that there was plenty of cover available for the Christmas period and that she should look after herself and they would talk again in the New Year. A medical certificate was subsequently handed in by the complainant, covering the period from the 21 December along with a note wishing the respondent a happy Christmas and stating that she would see them in the New Year. The complainant advised the Tribunal that when she went to the respondent's premises on 19 January 2012, she was informed that the manager was too busy to talk and so she called again the next day and, in the course of that conversation, she was advised she was finished working there.

The complainant had no recollection of the alleged resignation in the course of the purported telephone call on 24 November 2011. The Tribunal noted that when asked why the respondent had not raised the purported resignation with the complainant in the December meeting, the respondent's witness had replied that they hadn't wanted to upset the complainant so close to Christmas. The Tribunal noted that the complainant's P45 was not drawn up until 19 January 2012 despite the fact that she had allegedly resigned on 24 November 2011. The Tribunal held that while it was not a delay in issuing a P45 which was at issue in the case, it was relevant that the respondent submitted the complainant resigned on 24 November 2011, but did not issue any documentation relating to her termination of employment until 20 January 2012. The Tribunal considered the evidence given by the respondent with regard to the purported resignation by the complainant in the course of the phone call on 24 November 2011. The Equality Tribunal noted that this had not been followed up by any letter or documentation confirming the complainant's termination of employment. The Tribunal further noted that, in the course of the hearing, when questioned, the respondent stated that the complainant had, in the alleged phone call, seemed to be under the influence of alcohol; but the respondent nevertheless accepted that the complainant wished to resign. The Tribunal concluded that the complainant's version of events in relation to the period from November to January 2011 was honest and consistent. The Tribunal accepted the complainant's evidence that she had suffered a 'black out' and had lost eight or nine days due to her illness. The Tribunal held it was difficult to comprehend that although the respondent allegedly received a phone call from the complainant resigning, they did not mention this to her in the subsequent meeting of December 2011 and instead allowed the complainant to believe that she would be returning to work in the New Year. The Tribunal held that it was hard to believe that the respondent accepted this alleged phone call as the complainant's resignation and took no follow-up action to clarify the situation especially as the respondent's evidence was that the complainant seemed to be under the influence of alcohol during the call. Furthermore, the day after the alleged call, the respondent was informed that the complainant was seeking treatment and hospitalisation for a medical condition, which the respondent assumed was an addiction of some sorts. Two days after the alleged phone call, the respondent was advised by a staff member who had visited the complainant at home that the complainant had been self-harming and seemed to be suffering the effects of alcohol. The Tribunal noted that the complainant had received no contact from the respondent notifying her that her employment had ended. She came to the respondent's premises three weeks later and had a detailed discussion with the respondent about the illness and about the treatment she was receiving. The complainant also submitted medical certificates at this stage. The respondent did not, at this point, contradict the complainant but instead told her to go home and get better and not to worry about work.

The Tribunal then considered whether the alleged phone call of 24 November 2011 amounted to a resignation by the complainant. It held that, in general, it is established law that a resignation is a unilateral act which, if expressed on unambiguous terms, brings a contract of employment to an end. The Tribunal, however, noted there were exceptions to this general rule and made reference to the Labour Court determination in *Millett v Shinkwin*.[70] The Equality Tribunal made further reference to the Labour Court's determination in *Reilly v Meath County Council*[71] where the Court held:

> the decision of the Court of Appeal for England and Wales in *Sothern v Franks Charlesly & Co*[72] is authority for the proposition that where unambiguous words of resignation are used by an employee and are so understood by the employer, the employee thereby brings his or her employment to an end. There are however recognised exceptions to this general rule.

The Equality Tribunal noted that the test which had been followed in many cases, both in this jurisdiction and in the UK, was whether the words of resignation used by the employee, taken in the context in which they are used, represented his or her true and considered intention or whether they were a heat of the moment response to some occurrence. The Tribunal noted the decision of the Court of Appeal in England and Wales in *Willoughby v CF Capital plc*[73] where the Court of Appeal had to consider the application of this principle in deciding whether the claimant had resigned from her employment or had been dismissed and held that 'the principles of contract law ordinarily require that a person's intentions are ascertained not by reference to a subjective intention but objectively by a reference to how a reasonable man would interpret them'.

In this case the respondent submitted that the complainant had resigned via phone call, which the respondent claimed was not denied by the complainant. The complainant, however, stated that she could not confirm or deny it as she was suffering from a depressive illness at the time and had a blackout which lasted for eight or nine days. The complainant did however notify the respondent that the day after the phone call she was seeking treatment for a medical condition and the respondent was told the following day that the complainant had been self-harming. Three weeks later the complainant attended the respondent's premises and disclosed details of her depression and the fact that she had blacked out for a number of days; she also submitted medical

---

70. *Millett v Shinkwin* EED044.
71. *Reilly v Meath County Council* FTC 1230.
72. *Sothern v Franks Charlesly & Co* [1981] IRLR 278.
73. *Willoughby v CF Capital plc* [2011] EWCA Civ 1115.

certificates for the forthcoming period, citing depression as the reason for her absence from work. The complainant had received no contact from the respondent to the effect that her employment had ended. The Equality Tribunal held that is was clear that the complainant's alleged resignation on 24 November 2011, which was made while she was suffering from depression, falls into the 'special circumstances' cited in the authorities. In addition, the respondent was subsequently provided with information that the complainant was treated for a medical condition and had been self-harming. The Tribunal held that a prudent employer, before accepting the resignation of an employee in such circumstances, would have requested the resignation in writing or would at least have ensured that the employee fully understood what she was saying and doing. The Tribunal noted that there was no written confirmation of the notice of termination of her employment nor was there any written record of the phone call. In addition the respondent in the December meeting with the complainant made no reference to the fact that the complainant had resigned and did not mention it to the complainant until a month later in the meeting of 20 January. The Tribunal concluded that the alleged resignation did not in fact amount to an unconditional and unambiguous resignation and was invalidated by the special circumstances of this case.

The Equality Tribunal concluded that the complainant's employment was terminated and it was satisfied that it was terminated by the respondent for reasons connected with her disability. The Tribunal was not satisfied that the respondent had rebutted the inference of discrimination raised by the complainant.

The Equality Tribunal then considered the provisions of s 16(1)(b) of the Acts which provide an employer with a complete defence to a claim of discrimination on the disability grounds if it could be shown that the employer formed a bona fide belief that the complainant was not fully capable of performing the duties for which he or she was employed. The Equality Tribunal noted the Labour Court's process-orientated approach, which it detailed in *A Health and Fitness Club v A Worker*.[74] This approach placed an obligation on the employer to embark on a process of ascertaining the real implications for the employee's ability to do the job, taking appropriate expert advice, consulting with the employees concerned and considering with an open mind what special treatment or facilities could realistically overcome any obstacles to the employee doing the job for which he or she is otherwise competent and assessing the actual cost and practicality of providing that accommodation. The Tribunal noted that this decision had been upheld on appeal by Dunne J in the Circuit Court who found that an employer who has failed to go through that process-orientated approach will have breached the requirements of the Acts, even if the employer might reasonably have supposed, without checking further, that the disability is serious enough to render the employee not fully capable of undertaking their duties under s 16(1) of the Act.

Applying this case to the facts, the Equality Tribunal held that it was clear that there was an obligation on the respondent to ascertain the level and extent of the complainant's disability. In this case, the respondent, when faced with the situation where the employee was absent from work due to her disability, did not make enquiries to ascertain the extent of the complainant's condition and failed to look at any measures

---

74. *A Health and Fitness Club v A Worker (Humphreys v Westwood Fitness Club)* EED037.

which might facilitate her in returning to work. The Tribunal concluded that the respondent was obliged to make further enquiries, when it became aware that the complainant was absent from work due to her disability, to ascertain whether any special measures could be taken to assist her in returning to work. The Tribunal noted that it was open to the respondent to request documentary evidence from the complainant's doctor or to refer her for a medical examination in order to assess the extent of her disability. The respondent was obliged to look at suitable measures and accommodation and, if it concluded that there were no suitable measures or accommodation which would enable the complainant to return to work, it should have advised the complainant that she was now being considered for termination. In this case, the complainant was not afforded any opportunity to participate or influence the decision-making process that resulted in her dismissal. The Tribunal concluded that the respondent could not rely on the defence in s 16(1)(B) of the Acts. The complainant's disability was a factor which contributed to the decision to dismiss her and the respondent failed to provide her with reasonable accommodation within the meaning of the Acts. The Equality Tribunal awarded compensation of €18,000 to the complainant for the discriminatory dismissal and the failure to provide her with reasonable accommodation.

[5.29] *A Worker v An Employer*[75]—*Equality Tribunal—Employment Equality Acts 1998 to 2015, s 6 and s 8—disability—back condition—conditions of employment—discriminatory dismissal—whether provision of reasonable accommodation a disproportionate burden on a small retail shop*

The complainant was employed by the respondent, a small employer with less than 10 staff and part of a chain of three retail shops, as a sales assistant and later as an assistant manager. In January 2013 she suffered a disc tear, which necessitated spinal surgery. In February 2013 she took three months unpaid leave and returned to work in May 2013 on a full-time basis but was put on light duties. In September 2013, the complainant sought further medical advice with regard to her back condition and was advised to work few hours and perform light duties in the hope that her back condition might improve.

It was noted by the Equality Tribunal that reasonable efforts were made during this period to facilitate the complainant's back condition. It was noted that the premises operated on two floors, a retail floor and a stock room accessible by stairs. The nature of the work involved a fair degree of movement from floor to floor with deliveries and the need to obtain additional stock and clothing sizes that may not be in the immediate retail display. The respondent gave evidence that it was clear that on her return to work the complainant was not to carry any boxes or materials up and down the stairs. The parties met in September 2013 to discuss the complainant's medical situation. The respondent asked for full medical reports from the complainant, which were provided. These confirmed the medical condition of the complainant was serious, she had a scoliosis condition, and the reports indicated there was no likelihood of an immediate or full

---

75.   *A Worker v An Employer* DEC–E2015–058.

recovery. The complainant advised the respondent that she wished to continue working and was confident that if she were afforded reasonable accommodation, in terms of lighter duties or reduced hours, her situation would improve. Further medical evidence was provided by a physiotherapist report which also recommended lighter duties.

The evidence to the Tribunal was that the respondent did consider the medical reports and the nature of the complainant's work. It concluded that it was not possible for an assistant manager to work part-time in the shop, as the role required her to be on her feet at all times and that the medical restrictions sought would impose a very high degree of inflexibility on the complainant's duties and her possible working hours. The respondent was sympathetic to the complainant but met with her in October 2013 and advised her that they could not accommodate her employment on a part-time basis and therefore her full-time employment was being terminated with immediate effect.

It was submitted by the complainant that the respondent discriminated against her because she was unable to work on a full-time basis and noted that there was no exploration or discussion of alternative options at any stage. It was submitted by the respondent that to facilitate the complainant in the manner sought by her, would have placed a disproportionate burden on the respondent as it would have had to employ someone else on an assistant manager's salary to carry out the duties of the complainant on a part-time basis. To take on such a part-time resource with the necessary time flexibility to work in tandem with the complainant would not have been operationally feasible.

The Tribunal noted the obligations of s 85A of the Acts which sets out the burden of proof in claims of discrimination. The complainant was required to establish facts from which discrimination may be inferred and it was only where such a prima facie case was established that the onus shifted to the respondent to rebut the inference of discrimination raised. The Tribunal was satisfied that the parties were aware that the complainant had a serious back condition that required major spinal surgery in Poland. The Tribunal noted that she was put on light duties on a return to work and reasonable efforts were made to facilitate her. The Equality Tribunal noted that the respondent was a small employer and made reference to details of its total turnover which were provided at the hearing. The Tribunal noted that the respondent could not be described as an employer with access to large financial resources.

Reference was made to the Labour Court's approach in *A Health and Fitness Club v A Worker*[76] which sets out the required procedures in these types of cases. The Equality Tribunal held that in relation to the first stage of an employer's enquiry it was satisfied that the respondent had made adequate enquiries as to the complainant's condition to establish the factual position. The Tribunal noted that the respondent did not seek an independent opinion on the complainant's condition, however the Tribunal accepted that the nature and extent of the medical evidence presented by the complainant was such that an independent medical review could scarcely have materially altered the factual

---

76.　*A Health and Fitness Club v A Worker (Humphreys v Westwood Fitness Club)* EED037.

position. The complainant was confirmed to be suffering from lumber scoliosis and had major spinal surgery. The Tribunal noted that the need for independent medical review, while possibly procedurally advisable, would not really have added to a situation where the complainant's position was accepted.

The Tribunal concluded that the respondent was fully appraised by the complainant of all medical evidence. It was noted by the Tribunal that the respondent was sympathetic to the complainant and did not in any way seek to hastily terminate her employment, without full consideration of the evidence. The Tribunal then considered what appropriate measures could be taken by the respondent and noted that the costs of those measures must be taken into account. The Tribunal highlighted that the respondent had provided light work since the post-operative return of the complainant from Poland, but this light work, albeit on a full-time basis, did not seem to have helped the complainant's medical condition. The Tribunal noted that the nature of the work required the complainant to stand up and be on her feet all day. It was clear that the only form of reasonable accommodation would have been for the complainant to work significantly reduced hours and it was further noted that the physiotherapy report restricted the type of physical movements available to the complainant. There was a further requirement for medical appointments and follow up which were quite extensive. The Tribunal held that the reduced hours in the full assistant manager role would have involved the respondent sourcing another part-time employee of assistant manager calibre. The Tribunal held it necessary to bear in mind the small scale and limited resources of the respondent's business. There was also the practical issue of the uncertainty and inflexibility of the complainant's working times and the difficulty of securing another employee flexible enough to effectively partner her while not increasing the cost base of the business.

If the complainant were to accept a reduced role as a sales assistant, the physical restrictions and uncertain limited hours, in what was essentially a standard retail role, would have been very difficult for a small retail outlet to cope with. It was submitted by the respondent that the period since the complainant returned from surgery, when she was facilitated as best as possible, had provided sufficient time to demonstrate that accommodations, short-term working and change of roles would simply not work either medically for the complainant or operationally for the business.

The Tribunal concluded that the evidence given by the respondent's manager was credible and the Tribunal noted s 16(3)(c) of the Acts. The Tribunal held that the financial resources of the respondent operating in the clothing retail sector did not lend themselves to additional costs; thus the basic reality was that, in a small shop, the opportunities for accommodation or revised roles as sought by the complainant would have been a disproportionate burden on the respondent. The Tribunal concluded that it found the disproportionate burden argument had merit. It concluded that the complainant was not dismissed for discriminatory reasons on grounds of gender or disability and the lack of accommodation was based on sound reasons and not connected to discrimination.

[5.30] *Clavin v Marks & Spencers (Ireland) Ltd*[77]—*Equality Tribunal—Employment Equality Acts 1998 to 2015—Directive 2000/78/EC—disability—alleged discriminatory dismissal where complainant dismissed for being absent for in excess of nine months—whether reasonable accommodation—multiple failures by respondent—significant redress awarded*

The complainant was employed as a sales advisor with the respondent in its Dundrum store. Following an injury outside of work, the complainant was diagnosed with severe tendonitis which required surgery and a period of rehabilitation. She was on certified sick leave from March 2011. In June 2011 she received a phone call from the respondent's Occupational Health Advisor (OHA), a nurse based in the UK, and in the course of this call the complainant advised the nurse that she had been referred to a specialist because of complications with her condition. The Equality Tribunal noted that at no time was the complainant requested to attend a meeting or visit a medical examination with the occupational health advisor. The complainant gave permission for the OHA to contact her medical consultants, who provided a report to the OHA.

In the report, the orthopaedic surgeon stated that the complainant intended to attend another consultant in the hospital. He gave no opinion in this letter on her prognosis to return to work.

In September 2011, the respondent's HR manager wrote to the complainant inviting her to a meeting. The Tribunal noted that the medical consultant was misquoted by the respondent's HR manager, in that letter because he stated that the medical consultant had been unable to advise of a likely date of return to work. The Tribunal noted that the consultant did not write this in his letter. The complainant did not receive this letter in time to attend the meeting as she had undergone further surgery and was recuperating at a relative's home following the operation. The complainant then made contact with Human Resources as soon as she returned to her own home and attended a subsequent meeting. She contacted her subsequent consultant surgeon for the purpose of obtaining medical reports, but he had not returned from his Christmas break. It was noted by the Tribunal that the complainant was not advised to bring someone to the meeting with her but she had prudently brought her trade union shop steward to the meeting. The Tribunal considered the minutes of the meeting and noted the complainant's submission that at no stage during the meeting was it proposed to refer her to OHA. The only occupational assessment that was conducted by the respondent's occupational health team was by way of a telephone conversation with a nurse based in England, six months previously. No proper opportunity was given to the complainant to provide medical evidence to support her case. It was noted the complainant had changed consultants since the occupational report and had subsequent surgery, yet her orthopaedic surgeon was not allowed to contribute in any way with his expertise, prior to the decision to dismiss her.

Thereafter the complainant contacted HR to request more time to meet with her consultant as he had not returned from Christmas holidays. This phone call was not returned. Furthermore the complainant's request to allow her consultant to provide further medical reports was ignored. In January 2012 the complainant was dismissed on

---

77. *Clavin v Marks & Spencers (Ireland) Ltd* DEC–E2015–055.

ill-health grounds and it was submitted by the complainant that the respondent had deliberately misquoted her in this dismissal letter, ie she had advised she was no longer attending her specialist and that she was attending her GP and the pain management doctor. Reference was made to the respondent's own notes of the meeting, which contradicted this and where it was clearly said by the complainant that she would be attending her consultant in the New Year. The complainant's evidence was that she made a good recovery from surgery and would have been in a position to return to work six months later.

The Tribunal noted that significant issues arose between the parties after the complainant's dismissal, in that she did not receive payment in lieu of holidays and notice period for five months after the issuing of the letter of dismissal. Also, she was never informed by the respondent that she could apply for an ill-health pension from the respondent's pension provider. The Tribunal noted that, to date, she had not had the benefit of this pension, despite having made pension contributions towards this eventuality. The complainant asserted that the respondent had failed to assess her needs in respect of her employment and had failed to consult adequately with her regarding what measures it could have taken to allow her to return to work. The respondent repeatedly informed the complainant that they were unable to keep her role open indefinitely and submitted at the Tribunal that it was entirely reasonable to dismiss an employee who was no longer able to fulfil duties which they are employed to undertake. Regarding her pension entitlements, the respondent provided evidence that the complainant had cashed out her pension. The respondent's position was that it had examined potential reasonable accommodation but the complainant was not fit to return to work in the short term and this was not disputed. The respondent submitted that they did make adequate enquiries as to whether the complainant was able to return to work.

The Equality Tribunal considered the definition of a disability in s 2 of the Acts and noted that this definition included temporary disabilities. It was therefore not in dispute that severe tendonitis, requiring an operation, was a disability within the meaning of the Acts. The Tribunal quoted extensively from the test for discriminatory dismissal on grounds of disability as determined by the Labour Court in *A Health and Fitness Club v A Worker.*[78] The Tribunal noted that the required level of assessment was an onerous process for employers but that it was important to bear in mind why the burden was placed on them. Reference was made to recital 16 of Directive 2000/78 which states that:

> ... the provision of measures to accommodate the needs of disabled people in the workplace plays an important role in combating discrimination.

The Tribunal noted that it had not been denied by the respondent that it had dismissed the complainant on ill-health grounds. The respondent had gone through some of the motions necessary to defend its discriminatory dismissal; but the Tribunal concluded that it fell far short of best practice as follows:

(1) Human Resources had misquoted the complainant's first specialist, hence the inquiry as to factual position of the complainant's prognosis was inadequate;

---

78. *A Health and Fitness Club v A Worker (Humphreys v Westwood Fitness Club)* EED037.

(2)   The decision to dismiss on ill-health grounds was mainly based on only one telephone conversation with a nurse six months before the dismissal and this significantly weakened the respondent's defence. The occupational health report was a 'cookie cutter' response and not tailored to the complainant's condition. It was noted by the Tribunal that in the time that had elapsed between the report and the dismissal, the complainant had changed consultants and had had an operation but was not allowed to provide medical evidence from the relevant consultant, ie the one that had operated on her.

(3)   The two days' notice that was given to the complainant for the meeting regarding her dismissal was inadequate and no recommendation was given to her to bring medical evidence to the meeting. It was noted that the complainant had clearly stated that she was due to attend her consultant shortly thereafter but the respondent was not prepared to wait.

(4)   It was profoundly discourteous to an employee of nearly seven years standing to ignore her request for an extension of time because her consultant had not returned from Christmas holidays.

(5)   No real exploration of reasonable accommodation was made. The Tribunal noted that an appropriate measure may have been to allow the complainant recover from her operation and explore a return to work based on medical advice in a few months subsequent to the meeting. The Tribunal expressed the view that, had the job been kept open for the complainant for another six months, it was highly probable that she would have been able to return to work as she had made a good recovery. It was further noted that as the complainant was not in receipt of any sick pay, the decision to leave the job open for her to return would have been a nominal cost to the employer.

(6)   No appeal of the dismissal was allowed which was not in line with fair procedures.

(7)   By encouraging the complainant to resign rather than be dismissed, the respondent was asking the complainant to waive her rights, as constructive discriminatory dismissal is harder to prove than actual dismissal. The Tribunal also noted that this was contradictory to the respondent's own procedures.

(8)   The complainant was misquoted by Human Resources in the letter of dismissal.

While insufficient on its own to shift the burden of proof to the respondent, the Tribunal held that the failure to pay the complainant her statutory entitlement to notice pay and annual leave was indicative of the callous approach that the respondent took towards the complainant.

The Tribunal noted that to avail of a s 16(3) defence, an employer must show genuine engagement with the process of finding alternative and practical measures to allow an employee to return to work. In this case, the respondent did not make adequate enquiries nor was it in full possession of material facts regarding the complainant's disability before a decision was taken to dismiss her. It was further noted that the complainant was not allowed to influence this decision and she was not allowed enough time to produce medical evidence from the relevant consultant. The Tribunal held that the appropriate measure in this case would have been to extend the recuperation period but this was not explored. The Tribunal again noted that the complainant was not in receipt of sick pay while on sick leave and therefore it would not have been a disproportionate burden on the respondent, given its significant revenues. The Tribunal therefore held that the complainant had established a case of discriminatory dismissal on grounds of her disability and that the respondent was not entitled to avail of the statutory defence.

With regard to the complainant's pension, the Tribunal held that this issue would have been more appropriately taken as a complaint under the Pensions Acts 1990 to 2014. The Tribunal decided not to award any redress on the issue. The Tribunal however did take account of the effect the dismissal had on the complainant, including the financial and social implications; particularly the fact that the complainant was in her fifties when this dismissal occurred, the time of life when employment opportunities are lessened.

Regard was also had by the Tribunal to the fact that the respondent had lost a discriminatory dismissal case in almost identical fashion in 2013. In that case, the Equality Tribunal had ordered that all staff employed in Human Resources functions receive relevant training on equality matters. In this case, it was admitted by HR that this had not occurred. The Tribunal noted that penalties are required to be effective, proportionate and dissuasive.

The Equality Tribunal upheld the claim of discriminatory dismissal on grounds of disability and awarded the complainant €40,000 (the approximate equivalent of 18 months' salary) in compensation for the breaches of the Acts. The Tribunal made a further order as per s 82(1)(e) of the Acts that the respondent must conduct a review of its policies and procedures to ensure that they are in compliance with the Acts and especially on disability grounds. The Tribunal ordered that unless the decision was overturned on appeal, a report of the progress of this review must be made to the Irish Human Rights and Equality Commission within one year of the date of the decision. If this is not done, the Irish Human Rights and Equality Commission may, with the consent of the complainant, apply to the Circuit Court for the enforcement of the order under s 91(4)(b) of the Acts.

[5.31] *Hoey v White Horse Insurance Ireland Ltd[79]—Equality Tribunal— Employment Equality Acts 1998 to 2015—discrimination—victimisation— pregnancy—reasonable accommodation—dismissal for incapacity*

The complainant was employed by the respondent in April 2008 as a claims controller and was dismissed on 1 August 2013 due to incapacity. The complainant had been on medical leave and was due to go on maternity leave from 28 August 2013. Her internal appeal was rejected on 16 August 2013. The complainant brought a number of claims against the respondent, including claims for equal pay, discriminatory dismissal,

---

79.   *Hoey v White Horse Insurance Ireland Ltd* DEC–E2015–066. See related claim in **CH 27** at **[27.16]**.

victimisation and a failure to make reasonable accommodation, though she only proceeded with her claims for discrimination and victimisation.

The complainant claimed that the respondent discriminated against her by not making a reasonable accommodation for disability, and subsequent pregnancy-related illness, pending a full medical report relating to the initial symptoms she suffered, prior to her pregnancy. The complainant further claimed that the investigations into her health were suspended when she became pregnant and were not resumed.

The complainant also claimed that she was victimised for raising grievances related to her disability, first internally (November 2012) and later externally (January 2013). She claimed that her sick pay was stopped after four months, as opposed to eight months for a comparable employee; that she was not paid her maternity benefit by the respondent; that she was dismissed by the respondent to avoid making this payment; and that she was victimised by weekly phone calls from the respondent relating to her medical conditions (a level of communication she claimed was not made to comparable colleagues on sick leave).

The respondent claimed that the complainant was lawfully dismissed due to ongoing incapacity, that she was paid four months sick pay, in excess of her five-day entitlement, that she was issued with a final warning in May 2013 instructing her to return to work and warning her that a failure to do so would result in her dismissal and that she was not victimised.

The Tribunal concluded that the complainant had succeeded in establishing facts from which a failure to make reasonable accommodation and victimisation may be inferred and the burden of proof was therefore shifted to the respondent.

The Tribunal noted that in May 2013, the complainant requested a list of her proposed duties from the respondent, which the respondent failed to provide and thereby breached its duty to accommodate the complainant's disability. The respondent also failed to follow medical advice that the complainant could resume her medical tests for a long-term illness (MS) after she had given birth and it could then make its decision regarding her capacity. The respondent was also found to have ignored the advice in a medical report dated 5 July 2013 in which it was advised that the complainant would not be in a position to return to work for three to six months and additional medical reports advised that she be reassessed after the birth of her child, which was not facilitated by the respondent.

The complainant's claims of victimisation were also upheld. The claimant was awarded €12,000 as compensation for discrimination and victimisation.

AGE

Post retirement employment

[5.32] *NUI Maynooth v Keane*[80]*—Labour Court—appeal from decision of Equality Tribunal—Industrial Relations Acts 1946 to 2015—Employment Equality Acts 1998 to 2015, s 83—alleged discrimination on grounds of age—where complainant not permitted to return to work on contract or occasional basis following retirement*

This was an appeal by the complainant against a decision of the Equality Tribunal which found that the respondent's retirement policy was objectively justified. The complainant was employed by the respondent as an executive assistant from 2000 until she retired on 30 September 2010 in accordance with the respondent's pension scheme, which provided for retirement to take effect on 30 September following an employee's 65th birthday. The complainant sought to return to the respondent university after her retirement as an occasional or contract employee and claimed that other members of staff were facilitated in the past. The respondent conceded that a small number of staff were re-employed after retirement in exceptional circumstances which related to the nature of the work in which they were engaged. The complainant contended that there was a significant shortfall in her pension entitlements (by reason of her relatively short service) and she wished to work up to age 66, the age at which the state pension is payable. The Labour Court noted that the Equality Officer had stated that the complaint was 'that the complainant was not allowed to work past retirement age and was forced to retire on 30 September 2010 and this amounted to age discrimination'.

The Labour Court held that the characterisation of the complaint before the Equality Tribunal as being for the continuation of employment after reaching retirement age was not an entirely accurate interpretation of the complaint under the Acts. However, it was noted that the Equality Tribunal proceeded to hear the case on that basis. It was further noted that the respondent sought to rely on the Employment Control Framework as a justification for the imposition of a mandatory retirement age. The Labour Court noted that the complainant was not professionally represented, either at the hearing before the Equality Tribunal or before the Labour Court.

At the outset of the appeal hearing, the Labour Court sought clarification from the complainant as to the exact nature of her complaint and it was confirmed to the Court that the substance of the complaint was that the complainant's request to return to work on a casual or occasional basis after retirement was turned down by the respondent in a situation where others, over the age of 65 and post-retirement, were allowed to do so. It was confirmed by the complainant that she was not claiming that the termination of her employment by way of retirement was unlawful and discriminatory.

The Court noted that before a claim of discrimination on grounds of age can be made out, the Court must be satisfied that the complainant was treated differently and less favourably than another person in comparable circumstances is, was or would be treated. Therefore, the Court must examine the treatment afforded in similar circumstances to a comparator, actual or hypothetical. The Court noted that the complainant relied upon

---

80.   *Keane v NUI Maynooth* EDA158.

actual comparators who were also 65 years old, and therefore discrimination on the age ground did not arise. The complainant's allegation was that others aged 65 were allowed to continue working after retirement but she was not. The Labour Court held that a person of the same age as the complainant does not constitute a valid comparator within the meaning of the Acts, which in s 6(2)(f), expressly states that a comparator must be a person of a different age. The Court noted s 85 of the Acts, which provides that it is for the complainant to establish the primary facts upon which her complaint is based. The Court concluded that no evidence of less favourable treatment on age grounds had been proffered to the Court; and, while the refusal to allow the complainant to return to work on a casual or occasional basis may or may not be considered unfair, this was not a basis upon which the Court could draw an inference of discrimination.

The Court concluded that the complainant had failed to establish facts of sufficient significance to raise an inference of discrimination on grounds of her age and thus her claim could not succeed. The appeal was disallowed and the decision of the Equality Tribunal was varied accordingly. The Court noted, by way of addendum, that it made no finding on the respondent's reliance on the Employment Control Framework as a justification for the imposition of a mandatory retirement age.

Access to remote working

[5.33] *Border, Midland and Western Regional Assembly v Lavelle[81]—Labour Court— appeal from decision of Equality Tribunal—Employment Equality Acts 1998 to 2015—alleged discrimination on grounds of age—whether refusal to allow complainant to avail of e-working policy discrimination on grounds of age*

In this case the complainant alleged that he was discriminated against on grounds of his age, contrary to ss 6(2)(f) and 8(1) of the Acts, when the respondent refused to allow him to avail of its e-working policy which allowed its employees to work partially from home. The Equality Tribunal found that the respondent had discriminated against the complainant regarding the conditions of employment on grounds of age. The Tribunal ordered the respondent to facilitate the e-working for a minimum of one day per week for a period of one year with a review meeting on the feasibility of the arrangement at the end of that period and with compensation of €2,000 This was appealed by the respondent.

The Labour Court noted that the respondent's e-working policy had been in operation informally since 2004 and formally since 2010. Applicants are required to apply each year to avail of the policy and approval is given at the discretion of the respondent's director. In November 2010, the complainant made an application to be allowed to e-work for two days per week during 2011 only. This request was refused. The complainant unsuccessfully appealed this decision. One of the reasons given by the complainant for his request was that e-working might assist him in making the transition to retirement from a social perspective in case he opted for early retirement under the Public Service Agreement 2010 to 2014 (which provided an incentive to those over 50

---

81.   *Border, Midland and Western Regional Assembly v Lavelle* EDA 154.

years of age opting for early retirement up to December 2011). The Labour Court noted that the complainant did not ultimately avail of the early retirement scheme.

The respondent's decision on the complainant's application specified the reasons for the refusal, ie the nature of the work and responsibilities of the applicant did not lend themselves to working alone. His position required the overseeing of various administrative activities requiring him to be office-based to ensure the effective performance of those duties by staff. Secondly, the respondent held that the justification for the complainant's application which was to enable him to plan and adjust to retirement was not valid as e-working arrangements did not give rise to a reduction in the responsibilities, workload or working hours of an applicant. However, the respondent suggested in its correspondence that the complainant may be interested in participating on a retirement planning programme as a means of planning and transitioning to retirement at some stage over the coming years, or in the alternative, an arrangement such as a shorter working year could also be considered an appropriate transition to the retirement mechanism. The application was not approved as the role was not suitable to working remotely and because planning for retirement is not compatible with the spirit of working remotely. This decision was appealed but it was not overturned. The response from the assistant director to the complainant's appeal stated that facilitation of e-working by employees was not intended to be a prelude or transition to retirement for employees.

Evidence was given by the complainant's trade union official that, over the course of these policies, five employees had applied for e-working; three applicants aged less than 50 years of age (all were 40 at the time) were approved whereas the complainant and one other applicant, who was over 50 at the age of application, were refused. The trade union official contended that the criteria which applied to those granted e-working was primarily based on reasons other than the work carried out. He noted that in respect of the three named comparators whose applications had been approved, one was on an identical grade to the complainant, and two were on a similar grade to him. All three named comparators were granted e-working arrangements due to the distances involved in travelling to work and family circumstances rather than the type of work they were engaged in. It was submitted that there was no consistency between the criteria applying to the complainant in refusing his request for e-working and the criteria specified in the policy itself. It was submitted that there was a complete lack of transparency and a general unfairness in the selection process as to how the three younger employees were granted e-working. It was submitted by the trade union official, that the primary reason for not granting e-working to the complainant was based on the view that he sought to have a phased withdrawal from the office environment in preparation for eventual retirement which was viewed by both the director and assistant director of the respondent as an insufficient, if not improper motive for e-working. The rejection of the validity of such a motive which was directly related to age, coupled with the fact that the older employees who applied were refused while three younger employees were granted e-working was sufficient evidence to raise an inference of discriminatory treatment within the meaning of the Acts.

It was further submitted that the exclusion of the complainant, based on the reasons he sought the e-working arrangement, placed a particular disadvantage on older employees as typically it would be older employees who would seek e-working in preparation for eventual retirement. It was disputed that the complainant was responsible for overseeing various administrative activities undertaken by staff; instead it was contended that all 13 staff of the respondent organisation had a definite reporting structure supervised by their line managers, and the complainant had only one employee reporting directly to him. It was asserted on behalf of the complainant that he had sought an e-working arrangement to assist with the planned and gradual alienation and separation from the interaction with other employees and not to seek a diminution in his work, his duties or his responsibilities. The complainant made reference to a decision of the Labour Court in *Portroe, Stevedores v Nevins, Murphy, Flood*[82] where the Court determined that 'evidence of discrimination on the age ground will generally be found in the surrounding circumstances and facts of particular case'. The respondent's rationale for assessing the complainant's suitability for e-working was challenged and it was noted by the complainant's representative that the respondent had failed to observe the requirement to complete an assessment based on a detailed questionnaire as contained in the revised national guidelines for local authorities on e-working.

It was submitted by the respondent that e-working was not an appropriate arrangement to facilitate a transition to retirement and, on that basis, the nature of the complainant's work did not lend itself to e-working. These were the reasons why the application was rejected. The respondent's representative stated that the principle of e-working was based on providing a facility to employees on occasions when such type of working suited the exigencies of the organisation and it was not primarily a family-friendly initiative. The family reasons may be taken into account in terms of allowing e-working, but only in circumstances where the work was suited to working remotely from the office. It was noted that the complainant had been offered the option to avail of a shorter working year scheme, which it was suggested was the most appropriate family-friendly policy available to an individual who wished to ease their way to retirement, without having to attend the office every day. It was further stated that the decision not to grant e-working was based entirely on the incompatibility of the complainant's duties as HR officer and his responsibilities for running the organisation's corporate affairs. It was contended that, if the complainant's request had been granted, then due to incompatibility of his duties to e-working, there would have been a *de facto* reduction in his workload and it was noted that the e-working policy expressly stated that it was intended to retain skilled staff that might otherwise leave, not to facilitate the phased withdrawal of staff from work responsibilities. The rationale for the initial application by the complainant was fundamentally at variance with the objective of the respondent's e-working policy and it was for these reasons alone that the complainant's application was refused.

The Labour Court noted that the legal principles applicable in this type of case were enunciated by the Court in *O'Higgins v University College Dublin*.[83] They noted the provisions of s 85 of the Acts, whereby the burden of proving the absence of discrimination on the normal civil standard rested on the respondent. The Labour Court

---

82. *Portroe, Stevedores and Nevins, Murphy, Flood* EDA 051.
83. *O'Higgins v University College Dublin* EDA 131.

noted that it had been pointed out in *McCarthy v Cork City Council*[84] that, at the initial stage, the complainant is seeking to establish a prima facie case, hence it is not necessary to establish that the conclusion of discrimination is the only, or indeed the most likely, explanation that can be drawn from the facts proved. It is sufficient that the presumption is within the range of inferences which can reasonably be drawn from the facts.

The Court noted that it had been asserted by the complainant that his application for e-working was refused due to his age, where his younger colleagues were approved for e-working. The Court held that it must firstly consider whether the facts relied on by the complainant are of sufficient significance to raise an inference of discrimination and if that issue is decided is in favour of the complainant, the Court must then consider whether the respondent can prove, as a matter of probability, that the complainant's age was in no sense whatsoever a factor influencing the decision to refuse him the facility for e-working. The Court noted the respondent's view that the fundamental reason for the complainant's requirement to work from home for two days per week revolved around consideration of his retirement which rationale it held was at variance with the objective of its e-working policy, however the respondent held the view that the complainant's duties were incompatible with the e-working arrangements and as the facility for e-working was not a guaranteed benefit, it retained the right to refuse it on that ground.

However, when the complainant was rejected for e-working, he was instantly informed that he could apply for the shorter working year scheme that would have seen him being out of the office for blocks of between two and 12 weeks of unpaid leave, in addition to his annual leave. The Labour Court noted the fact that the respondent was a small organisation of 13 employees. The Labour Court concurred with the Equality Tribunal's conclusion that the respondent's argument was weakened considerably by its offer to apply the short working year scheme to the complainant in lieu of approving e-working. The respondent stated that such an offer was made on the basis that the short working year scheme was an unpaid arrangement whereas e-working was a paid benefit.

The Labour Court noted that it had been concluded by the Equality Tribunal that the complainant's motive for his application, which was clearly related to his age, was expressly rejected by the respondent and accordingly found that the complainant had succeeded in establishing a prima facie case that the refusal to let him ework amounted to discriminatory treatment on the grounds of age. The Labour Court further concluded that, insofar as a motive for wishing to e-work or work remotely is disclosed by a worker which is related to a status protected by the Acts, the rejection of the validity of such a motive by an employer is sufficient to raise an inference of discriminatory treatment, within the meaning of s 85 of the Acts.

The Labour Court concurred with the Equality Tribunal's final conclusion that even if the respondent had concerns that the complainant's work performance would drop as a result of working from home, it could have easily agreed to a trial period and the Labour Court noted that this or any other new working options were not suggested to the complainant. The Labour Court held it was satisfied that age was more than a trivial

---

84.   *McCarthy v Cork City Council* EDA 0821.

influence in the respondent's decision not to approve the complainant's application for e-working and accordingly the complainant had established a prima facie case of discrimination. The reasons advanced by the respondent were not sufficient to discharge this onus and thus the complainant must succeed.

The Court ordered the respondent to amend its e-working policy to align it closer to the national guidelines contained in the Local Authorities template, which include application forms and guidelines on identification of suitable jobs and awareness of potential equality implications. The Court further determined that if the complainant makes a further application for e-working arrangements, his application should be assessed in accordance with these national guidelines, based on the nature of the duties and responsibilities of his role at the time of application. The Labour Court upheld the Equality Tribunal's decision to award compensation of €2,000 for the effects of the discrimination. The Court concluded that while it varied the decision of the Equality Tribunal in terms of the determination, the appeal must be disallowed.

Access to employment

[5.34] *Butler-Duffy v Boots Ireland Ltd*[85]*—Equality Tribunal—Employment Equality Acts 1998 to 2015—age—access to employment—recruitment—whether complainant less favourably treated on grounds of her age in recruitment process*

The complainant (aged 56) had applied online for the position of a health care assistant with the respondent for their new store in Galway shopping centre. When she attended for interview the respondent's manager asked her for a form of identification and the complainant presented her driver's licence, which contained her date of birth. The complainant submitted that she felt that the respondent's manager was going through the motions during the interview once they were aware of her age. She submitted that a question asking her how to recommend the purchase of suntan lotion to an older person was strange, no notes were taken in the course of the interview, and she was interrupted in the course of a shop floor test by the relevant manager. The complainant submitted that it was no surprise when she heard her application was unsuccessful and submitted that this was because of her age. She subsequently requested the interview notes which stated twice, incorrectly, that she had previously worked in Roches Stores but she had never worked for that employer.

The respondent submitted that the age profile of its employees is between 16 and 70 and that it is an equal opportunities employer. It confirmed its policy is to look for some form of identification, but denied that this is for the purpose of confirming an applicant's age. An in-store exercise was conducted as part of the interview for the purpose of assessing the complainant and whether she could adapt her advice to be relevant to the customer and to see her selling skills. The respondent's manager denied she had abandoned the interview, but merely had assisted a customer with a query when the complainant could not. The respondent found the complainant's selling skills and her merchandising ability to be weak and these were the reasons she was unsuccessful in

---

85.   *Butler-Duffy v Boots Ireland Ltd* DEC–E2015–012.

obtaining the position. With regards to the purported error in the interview notes, the respondent noted that the complainant had worked in the past in a concession store within the shopping centre that contained Roches Stores and that locally that shopping centre was known as 'Roches'.

A table was submitted to the Equality Tribunal showing the demographic of people working for the respondent in August 2014 and, while it was acknowledged by the respondent that its work force tended to be younger, it contended that this was no different from other pharmacy retailers and was a reflection of the demographic of the application for the roles.

The Tribunal considered whether the complainant had established a prima facie case in accordance with s 85 of the Act. It did not find the respondent's request for proof of identification to be discriminatory nor did the Tribunal consider the scenario presented to the complainant, where she was asked to recommend sun screen for mature skin, to be an ageist question. The Tribunal noted that the interviewer had made a mistake in the notes about where the complainant had previously worked but this was an understandable error in the circumstances of this case and was not sufficient to shift the burden of proof of discrimination.

The Tribunal accepted the respondent's explanation that its manager had not abandoned the interview, but merely tried to assist a customer when the complainant, through no fault of her own, could not. The Tribunal had accepted that all the respondents' employees had received diversity training and that, having considered of the interview notes of all the candidates for the position, there was no evidence that the process was tainted by discrimination. The Tribunal concluded that the complainant had failed to establish a prima facie case of discrimination on grounds of age and the complaint was not upheld.

Retirement age

[5.35] *Earagail Eisc Teoranta v Lett*[86]*—Labour Court—appeal and cross-appeal of decision of Equality Tribunal—Employment Equality Acts 1998 to 2015, s 34(4)— Directive 2000/78/EC—discrimination on grounds of age—retirement age—quantum*

This was an appeal by the complainant, of a decision of the Equality Tribunal under Section 83 of the Employment Equality Acts and a cross appeal by the respondent. The case arose from the termination of the complainant's employment on reaching his 66th birthday. The complainant contended that his dismissal constituted discrimination on the grounds of age. The complainant appealed the quantum of the compensation award and the respondent cross-appealed against the totality of the Tribunal decision.

The complainant was a director and shareholder of the Lett Group – companies engaged in a family business of fish processing and distribution. In 1988 or 1989 the Lett Group acquired the shareholding in the respondent. It appears the complainant became a director of the respondent and continued in that capacity until 1998, when there was a restructuring of the business.

---

86.   *Earagail Eisc Teoranta v Lett* EDA1422. See also **[20.16]**.

In 2007 the respondent was acquired by the Navid Group and as consideration for the acquisition, Navid Group took on the liabilities of the respondent. It was also a condition of the acquisition that the respondent undertook to employ the complainant as a fish buyer and engineering consultant. On foot of this agreement, the complainant was engaged on a contract for service for a period of two years from 2007. On expiry of the contract, the complainant continued employment although his fixed-term contract was not formally renewed at that time.

In 2010 the respondent furnished the complainant with a draft fixed-term contract expressed to commence in 2009 and to run for a period of 18 months from that date. It was accepted in evidence that the end date of this draft contract coincided with the complainant's 65th birthday. The complainant refused to sign the contract but nonetheless continued his employment.

Neither the 2007 nor the 2010 draft contract contained an express term stipulating a retirement age but the respondent produced a staff handbook in which normal retirement age for all staff was expressly stated to be 65. The respondent's pension scheme rules stipulated that a pension can be paid at any time between 60 and 75 and the complainant was a trustee of the scheme.

In February 2011 the respondent wrote to the complainant informing him that in the course of the business restructuring his position had been identified as superfluous, and that a decision would be made on the continued viability of his position. The letter also set out the 7 September 2011 as his retirement date (his 66th birthday) and advised that he would be reduced to a three-day week from 28 February 2011. The complainant's employment was terminated with effect from 28 February 2011.

The complainant contended that he was not contractually required to retire at any particular age and he denied that a compulsory retirement age was every introduced. He also contended that other named employees continued to work beyond the age of 66. In particular he named one person who he claimed worked to 70 and another to 67.

The complainant also claimed that the first time he had sight of the company handbook was in 2011 in the course of the Equality Tribunal proceedings. He also claimed that other members of his family, who were not retained following the restructuring, received a compensatory package and he had expected a similar package if his services were not being retained.

The respondent contended that the complainant knew or ought to have known that retirement was fixed at 65 and his retirement was delayed until the end of the year in which he turned 65 because of a view taken as to what was meant by the wording of the company handbook. The respondent provided the details of all employees whose employment came to an end by retirement in since 2006, none of whom had remained after the age of 66. The respondent argued that the validity of a retirement age is not dependent upon the employee to which it applies having knowledge thereof.

The Chairman of the respondent between 1990 and 2014 gave evidence that the issue of retirement age would have been a matter for management but he was personally unaware of whether management had put such a retirement age in place. He also gave evidence that he had never seen the company handbook but that he would have expected management to have produced such a booklet.

The current chief executive of the respondent gave evidence that it was in the course of 2007 that the decision was taken to introduce a staff handbook. He gave evidence that the handbook was discussed with all staff members. He did concede that it was possible that the complainant had not had sight of the handbook but he would have become aware of its existence through his involvement with the Board. His evidence was that the retirement age in the handbook reflected the respondent's existing practice.

In assessing the complainant's claim, the Labour Court emphasised that s 34(4) of the Acts allows an employer to fix a retirement age without contravening the prohibition on age discrimination and that retirement, ie the coming to an end of employment pursuant to a condition of employment which limits an employee's tenure to the point to which they attain a specific age, should be distinguished from dismissal on the grounds of age. Section 34(4) authorises an employer to apply such a condition of employment and the term can be provided in the conditions of employment either expressly or by implication, or it can be incorporated in some other document to be read in conjunction with the contract of employment.

The Court took the view that such a condition of employment could only arise where the policy is promulgated in such a manner that the employees to whom it applies either know or ought to have known of its existence.

The Court referred to *McCarthy v HSE*[87] on whether the retirement age could be viewed as an implied term of the contract of employment. The Court also considered *Calor Teoranta v McCarthy*[88] and the focus on whether the individual in question has reached his or her agreed or contractual retirement age.

It was accepted by the Court that as the complainant did not have an express term as to retirement age, the question for consideration was whether the handbook could have attained contractual status. The Court accepted that the complainant neither had sight of nor knew of the handbook until it was produced at the Equality Tribunal hearing. The Court also rejected the contention that the fact the draft contract from 2010 would have ended on his 65th birthday would have implied that the complainant's tenure was fixed to age 65. The Court labelled it as 'remarkable' that the contract made no reference to the company handbook or any policy on retirement age if it was intended that either would have contractual effect.

The Court also rejected the contention that the existence of a policy could attract immunity from liability for a unilateral termination of employment on the grounds of age. The Court accepted the principle that a policy can take effect as a contractual term if it is promulgated in such a manner that those to whom it applies either know or ought to have known of its existence but the Court rejected that this had happened in the present case.

The Court concluded that the complainant had neither actual nor constructive knowledge of the handbook or the fixed retirement age. On that basis, the complainant should be deemed to have been dismissed because of his age.

In considering the adequacy of the redress awarded by the Equality Tribunal it was noted that there was no evidence to suggest that on the restructuring of the business the

---

87. *McCarthy v HSE* [2010] IEHC 74.
88. *Calor Teoranta v McCarthy* [2009] IEHC 139.

parties intended or envisaged that the complainant would remain in employment for as long as he wished. In light of the economic and commercial circumstances of the business it was accepted that had the respondent not mistakenly believed that the complainant could be compulsorily retired, he would as a matter of probability have been dismissed on the grounds of redundancy. This would have significantly reduced his potential loss arising from the dismissal. The Court's finding differed from the decision of the Equality Tribunal in that it found the complainant did not suffer any discrimination in being placed on a three-day week.

The Court concluded that the award of €24,000 as compensation was fair and equitable in the circumstances and that award was not in the nature of remuneration. The complainant's appeal was disallowed and the respondent's cross-appeal was allowed in part.

RELIGION

[5.36] *Tipperary County Council v McAteer[89]—Labour Court—appeal from decision of Equality Tribunal—Employment Equality Acts 1998 to 2015—Directive 2000/78/ EC[90]—Charter of Fundamental Rights of the European Union—discrimination on grounds of religious beliefs—indirect discrimination of complainant, an Evangelical Christian—whether religion includes manifestation of religion—appeal on quantum*

The complainant was employed as a civil engineer assigned to Clonmel Borough Council. He was dismissed in July 2010 resulting from his failure to obey lawful instructions and following several warnings. It was asserted by the complainant, an Evangelical Christian, that the underlying reason for his dismissal was practice by him of a central tenet of his religion, namely the requirement to speak to others about Jesus and to share the Gospel with them. The Labour Court noted that complaints were received about the complainant engaging in preaching in the office and he was instructed to desist from this practice. The complainant also preached to members of the public during his lunch breaks. Initially the respondent sought to deal with the complaints by way of counselling of the complainant, as opposed to a disciplinary process. The complainant was advised that his conduct was unacceptable during working hours, including his lunch break. He was advised that he was a representative of the respondent and his activities had the potential to bring the respondent into disrepute. In subsequent meetings, the complainant was asked to confine sharing his beliefs to outside of his work area. The complainant repeatedly stated that he would find this difficult to adhere to.

In 2008, the complainant was observed engaging a member of the public in conversation on the street while assisting in traffic management to facilitate an event, and shortly thereafter he was observed talking to two minors in school uniform about Jesus. The Labour Court noted that neither the minors nor the young man had made any

---

89.   *Tipperary County Council v McAteer* EDA153.
90.   Directive 2000/78/EC of 27 November 2000 establishing a general framework for equal treatment in employment and occupation.

complaint to the respondent, from which it could be construed that neither the integrity nor the standing of the respondent had been compromised by the conduct of the complainant. The complainant was issued with a written warning in which he was required to cease the preaching of personal religious beliefs to members of the public during normal working hours. Further complaints were received in 2009, which resulted in the complainant being suspended without pay for a period of two months; he was also instructed to undergo counselling to assist him in controlling the compulsion to speak to others about religion. A further complaint was made against the complainant in May 2010 to the effect that he had spoken about religion to a contractor working for the respondent. The Labour Court noted that, as with previous such occurrences, the person to whom the complainant spoke made no complaint but rather the complainant's conduct had been observed by others. This incident ultimately resulted in the dismissal of the complainant in July 2010.

The complainant contended that the respondent's actions amounted to an interference with the practice of his religion. He asserted that he had been treated less favourably because of his religious beliefs.

The Labour Court noted that the Employment Equality Acts and Directive 2000/78/EC prohibit discrimination against an employee by an employer on grounds of his or her religious beliefs. The Labour Court noted that the issue in this case is whether religion includes the manifestation of one's religion. The Labour Court noted that both Acts and the Directive are silent on this, however art 10.1 of the Charter of Fundamental Rights of the European Union provides that everyone has the right to freedom of thought, conscience and religion. This right includes freedom to change religion or belief, either alone or in community with others, and in public or in private to manifest religion or belief in worship, teaching, practice and observance. The Court noted that the Charter has the same legal standing as the Treaties and therefore is part of the primary legislation of the European Union and so the Directive must be read in harmony with the Charter. The Court further noted that art 10.1 of the Charter corresponds to art 9(1) of the Convention for the Protection of Human Rights and Fundamental Freedoms and thus the jurisprudence of the European Court of Human Rights (ECHR) on the interpretation of the Convention applies in determining the ambit to be ascribed to the Charter. The Labour Court held that it followed that the right to manifest religion *inter alia* in teaching and observance is inherent in the notion of religion itself.

Consequentially if a person is treated less favourably on grounds relating to religious teaching or observance, they are discriminated against on grounds of their religion. Reference was made by the Labour Court to the decision of the ECHR in *Eweida v United Kingdom*,[91] where it was held that an employer can restrict the right to manifest religious beliefs in the workplace (as opposed to the holding of religious beliefs) where the restriction is proportionate. The Court noted that while the restriction on holding or professing a religious belief cannot be justified in an employment context, there cannot be an unfettered right to engage in the practice or manifestation of religion. Logic dictates that the right must be subject to the rights of others and it cannot be exercised in

---

91. *Eweida v United Kingdom* [2013] ECHR 37—see *Arthur Cox Employment Law Yearbook 2013* at [10.02].

a way that is restrictive of the business of the employer or constitutes an interference with the legitimate interests of the employer. While the complainant had urged the Court to consider the treatment of him as direct discrimination, the Labour Court held that the restriction placed on the complainant was more properly classifiable as indirect discrimination. The Court noted that where indirect discrimination is alleged, it should consider if the restriction bears more heavily on a class of persons of which the complainant is one than it does on another body or class of persons whose circumstances are similar, other than in respect of the impact on them of the impugned measure.

The Court held that the complainant, a person who was enjoined by his religious beliefs to speak to others about Jesus and the Gospels, was prohibited by his employer from so doing during work hours, to include his lunch breaks. This placed the complainant at a disadvantage relative to a hypothetical class of persons to whom the same restriction might be applied but whose religious beliefs do not enjoin them to evangelise in the same manner as the complainant.

The Court was satisfied that the prohibition against discussing matters relating to religion was intrinsically liable to place persons of the same religious belief as the complainant at a disadvantage, relative to those of no religious belief or those of a different religious belief; hence the measure was prima facie indirectly discriminatory on grounds of the complainant's religion. The Court then considered whether there was any objective justification for the measure. The Court noted the respondent's position in the case was that the complainant was dismissed for refusing to obey a legitimate instruction not to engage in preaching during working hours. It sought to justify that instruction on the basis that the complainant's conduct with members of the public had the potential to bring the respondent into disrepute. However the Labour Court noted that no evidence had been tendered which indicated that any of the persons to whom the complainant had spoken considered his conduct to be disreputable, or that it had adversely affected the perception of the respondent; nor was there any evidence to show the complainant's evangelism impacted adversely on his capacity to perform the duties for which he was employed. The Labour Court noted that while it was perfectly legitimate for the respondent to seek to protect itself from damage, there was nothing before the Court to show that its reputation was in anyway imperilled by the complainant's activity. The Court further noted that the respondent had gone further than merely prohibiting the complainant from discussing matters of religion while at work; he was also prohibited from so doing during his lunch break. The Labour Court noted that other employees were not so monitored or restricted as to how they spent their time while on lunch break and in that regard the complainant was treated differently than others. The Court was satisfied that the complainant was subjected to indirect discrimination on grounds of his religion and thus the finding of the Equality Tribunal was affirmed.

On the issue of redress, the Court noted the complainant had been awarded compensation of €70,000 by the Equality Tribunal which the respondent submitted was grossly excessive. The Court noted that the complainant had been in receipt of a salary of €54,000 per annum at the time of his dismissal and that he was in permanent employment with the benefit of a public sector defined benefit pension. While he had obtained alternative employment, he was earning half his previous salary. The Labour Court held that the award made by the Equality Tribunal could not be regarded as excessive and affirmed the award. The appeal was disallowed.

Promotion

[5.37] *St Nathy's College v Burke*[92]—*Labour Court—appeal from decision of Equality Tribunal—Industrial Relations Acts 1946 to 2015—Employment Equality Acts 1998 to 2015, s 83—religion—alleged discrimination as result of internal promotional process—whether complainant discriminated against for not providing evidence of commitment to ethos of school—whether respondent imputed to complainant an absence of religious belief or that she was not an adherent of the Catholic religion when in fact she was Catholic*

This was an appeal by the complainant of the decision of the Equality Tribunal in a claim against her former employer for discrimination on grounds of religion. The complainant was employed as a teacher from September 1987 until she retired in February 2012. In September 2011 she applied for a post as deputy principal but was not shortlisted for interview for the position. There were 12 applicants for the post and a shortlist of four candidates proceeded to interview. Before considering applications, the selection board adopted criteria against which the shortlist would be selected. These included a requirement that candidates submit a properly completed application form and that the candidates show evidence of their commitment to the school ethos and their vision for the school. When the complainant sought feedback as to why she had not been shortlisted, she was informed by the chairperson of the selection board that she had not met the criteria in two respects. Firstly, it was claimed that a written application was not well presented and was not typed, and secondly it was claimed that in her application she had failed to provide clear evidence of a commitment to the school's ethos. It was accepted by the parties that reference to ethos was a reference to the Catholic or Christian ethos of the school.

The complainant contended that the real reason for not shortlisting her for interview was that the board of the respondent imputed to her an absence of religious belief or that she was not an adherent of the Catholic religion. However, the complainant gave evidence that she was in fact a Catholic. The respondent denied any such imputation. The respondent maintained the position that the complainant was not shortlisted because her recent application was not well presented and she failed to adequately demonstrate a commitment to upholding the school ethos. The respondent pointed out that the complainant and those shortlisted were also Catholics and that in the absence of comparators having a different religious belief to that of the complainant, her claim could not succeed.

The Labour Court considered the complainant's application form which was put in evidence. The Court concluded that the criticism directed at its quality was harsh and

92.   *St Nathy's College v Burke* EDA1512.

unjustified. The Court made reference to *Mulcahy v Waterford Leader Partnership*[93] where O'Sullivan J pointed out that there was no principle in either law or logic on which to hold that because a person offers a bad reason for an impugned decision this necessarily means that the bad reason is not the real one. The Court summarised that this case was not concerned with the objective fairness of the respondent's decision; the only issue before it was whether that decision was tainted with unlawful discrimination on the grounds of the complainant's religion or religious belief.

The Labour Court noted that unlawful discrimination arises when one person is treated less favourably than another because they have a particular characteristic that the law regards as relevant. The scheme of the Acts is based on comparison. The complainant's discrimination must be grounded by reference to the treatment afforded to a comparator, actual or hypothetical, who does not have the protected characteristic relied upon. In the case of discrimination on the grounds of religion, s 6(2)(e) of the Acts provides that the comparison would be between persons, one of whom has a different religious belief from the other, or between one who has a religious belief and another who has not. For the purpose of the Acts, the Court noted that religious beliefs included religious background or outlook. The Court noted that s 6(1) of the Acts provides that discrimination may arise where a protected characteristic (a) exists; (b) existed but no longer exists; (c) may exist in the future; or (d) is imputed to the person concerned.

The Court noted that in this case the complainant was treated less favourably in not being shortlisted for the post. It was, however, clear that the complainant professes the Catholic faith and each of those shortlisted are also of that religion. This fact alone indicated to the Court that the less favourable treatment, of which the complainant complains, could not have arisen because of her religious belief. Faced with this difficulty, the complainant then contended that the import of the decision conveyed to her by the chairperson of the selection board imputed to her a religious belief other than that of the Catholic faith. The Court noted that no evidence was proffered by the complainant to support that contention; this could not be accepted by the Labour Court. Candidates were not asked to disclose their religion in the application form, but the Court noted that in her application the complainant had indicated that she was a member of the parish Council of her home parish in the Archdiocese of Tuam and she nominated, as one of her referees, a Catholic parish priest. The Court said that this could reasonably be taken to negate any imputation that she was not a Catholic.

The Court noted that the respondent selection board clearly did not believe the complainant had provided enough information in the narrative of her application form to demonstrate how she might promote the Catholic ethos of the school. This may or may not have been a reasonable conclusion in the circumstances but this, in the view of the Court, did not amount to an imputation that the complainant professed any religious belief other than the one she in fact does possess.

The Court noted s 85A of the Acts providing for the allocation of the burden of proof in cases involving allegations of discrimination. The Court noted that the central primary fact upon which the complainant was relying in this case to ground her

---

93.   *Mulcahy v Waterford Leader Partnership* [2002] 13 ELR 12.

complaint of discrimination was that the respondent had imputed to her a religion other than Catholicism. The Court was satisfied that the complainant had failed to prove this as a fact and therefore her claim could not succeed. The appeal was disallowed and the decision of the Equality Tribunal was affirmed.

MULTIPLE GROUNDS

Age, religion, sexual orientation

[5.38] *A Teacher v A National School[94]—Equality Tribunal—Employment Equality Acts 1998 to 2015, ss 2, 6(2)(d) to (f) and 37—discrimination in relation to access to employment and promotion on grounds of age, religion and sexual orientation— 'religious outlook'—rating two differently qualified candidates as 'equally qualified'—inappropriate interview questions—whether complainant succeeded in establishing a prima facie case of discrimination*

The complainant, a primary school teacher alleged that the respondent discriminated against her on the grounds of age, religion and sexual orientation in terms of access to employment and promotion, contrary to the Employment Equality Acts 1998 to 2015 (the Acts).

The complainant qualified as a primary school teacher in 1987 and had occupied the role of deputy principal in the respondent since 2003. The complainant applied for the position of principal in June/July 2011. The initial interview process she attended was found to be flawed and therefore invalid. This was due to breaches of regulations contained in a document entitled 'Boards of Management of National Schools— Constitution of Boards and Rules of Procedure'. The position was subsequently re-advertised and the complainant re-applied for the role of principal. The complainant was surprised to meet an identical interview board at her second interview, comprised of a Sr B, Mr B, and Mr C. The complainant submitted that the presence of Mr C, in particular, was in contravention of the procedures. The complainant contended that a prima facie case of discrimination on the ground of age arose from this breach, coupled with the fact that the successful candidate was considerably younger and less experienced than the complainant. Accordingly, she argued, the burden of proof should shift to the respondent.

The complainant also took issue with the alleged lack of transparency in how the criteria for assessment of the interview applications were applied. There were nine criteria in total. The complainant submitted that the following criteria were not utilised—'Teaching Experience and Reports on Competence', 'Other Relevant Experience' and 'References'. Further, the complainant submitted that Sr B posed inappropriate questions during her interview, including asking her about her thoughts on INTO's submission on the Forum on Patronage and Pluralism. The complainant stated that the only reason she had mentioned the Forum in her application was that it was a current issue in education. She had responded to Sr B's question by stating that she had

---

94. *A Teacher v A National School* DEC–E2014–097.

read the INTO submission and also the submission of the Irish Human Rights Commission, which referred to children opting out of religion. She commented that the respondent school was already accommodating children of different faiths and of no faith at all. The claimant stated that Sr B followed up with another inappropriate question when she asked her about 'homos'. The complainant indicated in her submission that these questions had unsettled and upset her.

When the complainant was unsuccessful in her application, her trade union raised objections to the interview process with the respondent. The union was told that the issues were 'rebutted substantively' by the board of the respondent. Nevertheless, the respondent extended an offer to allow the complainant to interview again. The complainant declined this offer because she had lost faith in the process and the successful candidate was already working in the respondent.

The respondent denied discriminating against the complainant in any shape or form. While acknowledging that minor irregularities occurred in the interview process, it was submitted that they affected both candidates equally. The judgment of Quirke J in *Brown v the Board of Management of Rathfarnham Parish National School*[95] was cited, in which it was held that 'non-compliance with the minute detail of the agreed procedures will not invariably invalidate affected decisions'. On this basis, the respondent disputed that the non-compliance, along with the age difference between the candidates, established a prima facie case of discrimination which would be for the respondent to rebut.

In relation to the complaint of age discrimination, the respondent explained that the complainant simply did not perform well enough during her interview to be successful in securing the role of principal. The respondent did not agree with the complainant's assertion that her qualifications and experience were disregarded. It was maintained that both candidates were awarded equal marks for their qualifications and experience. In relation to the complaint of discrimination on the ground of religion, the respondent denied that Sr B asked the complainant about the INTO submission. Rather she had been asked about her personal views on the Patronage and Pluralism of the respondent, as this is a very topical issue. The respondent submitted that the complainant was herself Roman Catholic; therefore she lacked a comparator to demonstrate less favourable treatment by the board of the Catholic National School. In relation to the complaint of discrimination on the ground of sexual orientation, the respondent stated that Sr B's denied asking the complainant about 'homos', or indeed making any statements regarding sexual orientation. The respondent further maintained that the complainant's sexual orientation was unknown to it.

The Equality Tribunal noted that, although the issue for determination was whether the complainant was discriminatorily treated in terms of access to employment and promotion within the meaning of the Acts, it must first consider whether the complainant had established a prima facie case under s 85A of the Acts. The Tribunal noted that the Labour Court had consistently stated that the facts from which the occurrence of discrimination may be inferred must be of 'sufficient significance' before

---

95.   *Brown v the Board of Management of Rathfarnham Parish National School* [2006] IEHC 178.

a prima facie case could be held to have been made out. In relation to the protected grounds of age, religion and sexual orientation, the complainant was heterosexual, born in 1966 and a Roman Catholic.

The Tribunal was satisfied that the complainant had succeeded in establishing a prima facie case of discrimination on the ground of age in terms of access to promotion. In coming to this decision the Tribunal considered that the complainant's comparator (and the successful candidate) did not have a primary degree in primary teaching, nor did she hold a postgraduate degree, nor did she have any work experience at deputy principal level such as the complainant had. Emphasis was placed on the significant difference in qualifications and experience which existed between the candidates and the fact that the interview board saw fit to rate both candidates as equally qualified regardless of this fact. The Tribunal also noted that the respondent did not dispute the fact that the successful candidate was considerably younger than the complainant in coming to the decision that a prima facie case had been made out. However, as the complainant had already been in the employment of the respondent, the Tribunal concluded that no case arose in relation to access to employment.

The Tribunal noted that the respondent's witnesses, who were members of the interview board, did not seek to maintain the argument that the candidates were equally qualified in their evidence. The Tribunal identified several irregularities and poor practices in terms of the respondent's hiring and promotion process. These included the fact that interview criteria for the candidates were not drawn up in advance of the interview board meeting; the fact that the interview board met for the first time one hour before the interviews started; and the fact that one interview board member stated that he had thrown his interview notes away. The Tribunal rejected the respondent's substantive argument during the hearing, which was that the complainant's additional qualifications and experience were irrelevant because the only minimum requirement for the role was to be a qualified primary school teacher. If this were the case, there would be no need to award the candidates marks. The Tribunal concluded that the respondent had failed to rebut the complainant's prima facie case of discrimination on the ground of age in relation to access to promotion. Accordingly, the complainant was entitled to succeed.

The Tribunal then considered the questions which Sr B allegedly put to the complainant at interview. In relation to inappropriate questions asked during job interviews on grounds other than gender, complainants enjoy protections which are equal to those long enjoyed by women in the workforce, in accordance with the EAT decision in *MacGabhainn v Salesforce.com*.[96] The Tribunal further noted that s 2 of the Acts states that the ground of religion includes 'religious background or outlook'. The Tribunal interpreted the wording of this section to protect persons who are converts to a specific faith (ie 'background'), in addition to specific attitudes which go with a religious belief (ie 'outlook'). The Tribunal considered the complainant's evidence that she had been left feeling very insecure after Sr B asked her about her personal opinions on the Forum on Pluralism and Patronage in her interview. It was noted that any change of patronage was in fact the gift of patrons rather than that of the staff, meaning that the

---

96.   *MacGabhainn v Salesforce.com* DEC–E2007–048.

personal opinions of staff on such a matter were largely irrelevant. Sr B had agreed that she had asked the complainant about her personal opinions on the Forum on Pluralism and Patronage. She stated that she did this because she wanted to ascertain the complainant's position on the Catholic ethos of the school and to form a general view of her 'philosophy of education'. However, the Tribunal placed emphasis on the fact that the 'philosophy of education' was not part of the interview marking scheme. Sr B stated that she was concerned about what the complainant would do with children whose parents do not want them to participate in the religious programme. The Tribunal concluded that Sr B's question did not relate to any specific challenges which the complainant may have faced as principal.

Although the respondent did not seek to invoke its rights as a religious employer under s 37 of the Acts, it was appropriate to consider the interview situation in light of those rights. The Tribunal stated that it was satisfied that Sr B's question had no connection to broader questions relating to the ethos of the school, therefore the protections of the Acts did not cover it. The Tribunal further noted that no evidence had been adduced by the respondent that any problem relating to the complainant maintaining the ethos of the school had arisen during her eight-year tenure as deputy principal. It was concluded that Sr B's questions were outside the remit of the exemptions of s 37 and intruded into the protected sphere of personal belief identified in the Acts as 'religious outlook'. The complainant was accordingly entitled to succeed in this part of her complaint.

Finally the Tribunal addressed Sr B's question 'what about the homos'. The Tribunal noted the fact that both Sr B. and the other interview board members denied that Sr B had asked such a question. The Tribunal remarked that Sr B's insistence on her general lack of memory of this line of questioning stood in marked contrast to her remarkably precise recollection of her interview questions relating to educational philosophy. The Tribunal stated that a variety of circumstances arose which combined to limit the credibility of the respondent witnesses in the course of his investigation. The Tribunal concluded that it was satisfied that Sr B had asked the question 'what about the homos?'. The respondent made the argument that as it did not know the complainant's sexual orientation, it could not have discriminated against her on the ground of sexual orientation. The Tribunal did not accept this argument, as it was settled law that inappropriate interview questions in order to be unlawful did not require specific knowledge on the part of the interviewer as to the position of the interviewee on the protected grounds. The Tribunal stated that it was precisely because the interview board did not know the complainant's sexual orientation, that it interpreted Sr B's question as an attempt to ascertain the complainant's sexual orientation without asking the question directly. The Tribunal was satisfied that Sr B's question was unlawful on the ground of sexual orientation and accordingly the complainant was also entitled to succeed in this part of her complaint.

The Tribunal concluded that, the respondent had discriminated against the complainant on the grounds of age, religion and sexual orientation in terms of promotion to principal, contrary to s 8(1) of the Acts. In accordance with s 82 of the Acts, it was ordered that the respondent pay the complainant €54,000, which was equal to one year's salary, in compensation for the effects of discrimination.

This was appealed to the Labour Court – see **[5.39]** below for a summary of the Court's decision.

[5.39] *A National School v A Teacher*[97]*—Labour Court—appeal from decision of Equality Tribunal—Industrial Relations Acts 1946 to 2015—Employment Equality Acts 1998 to 2015, ss 6(2)(d), (e) and (f), 37 and 85A*

The respondent employer appealed the decision of the Equality Tribunal at **[5.38]** above, which held that the respondent had discriminated against the complainant, in relation to access to promotion on the grounds of age, religion and sexual orientation contrary to s 6(2)(d), (e) and (f) of the Acts.

The respondent maintained that there was no breach of procedure in this case, and if there was, it was relatively minor in nature and of no consequence for the purposes of the Acts. It asserted that the selection panel was properly constituted. The panel consisted of three experienced people, who had conducted the interview process both fairly and honestly. The person considered most suitable for the position had been awarded the role. The respondent strongly denied that any discrimination of any nature had taken place.

On the other hand, the complainant maintained that the selection process was tainted with discrimination on the grounds of age, religion and sexual orientation. In relation to the age ground, she gave evidence to the Court that she was some 10 years older than the successful candidate. The complainant maintained that she had substantially more teaching experience and qualifications than the successful candidate. In relation to the religion ground, the complainant maintained that her views on matters relating to religious patronage and pluralism in the school were canvassed. In relation to the sexual orientation ground, the complainant alleged that she was asked a question which was intended to adduce her view on the employment of homosexual teachers in the respondent school.

By way of her oral evidence to the Labour Court, the complainant explained that she had qualified as a primary school teacher in 1987. Since then she had earned a Master's degree and further expanded her skills as a teaching assistant in Boston College. She had been working in the respondent's school since 2003, in the role of deputy principal. She explained that she had a number of staff reporting to her in the absence of the principal and frequently carried out functions for the principal which required her to handle difficult situations, including the representation of the respondent in court cases. The complainant told the Labour Court that the successful candidate only had four years' teaching experience, compared with her 12 years. On this basis she said that it was remarkable that the selection panel had declined to score her higher than the successful candidate under any of the headings in the interview process. She added that the successful candidate had not held a position of responsibility in her previous school. In relation to the alleged line of questioning in relation to her religious views, the complainant told the Court that she found this unsettling and uncomfortable. She explained that she had been asked about her views on the INTO Submission to the

---

97.   *A National School v A Teacher* EDA1515.

Forum on Patronage and Pluralism and her thoughts on religion. The complainant responded to the question by saying that the respondent was already accommodating children of different faiths, and indeed of no faith. The complainant further gave evidence that she had been asked, 'what about the homos'? She told the Court that she did not know how she was supposed to answer this question. She assumed that the question related to homosexual teachers, as opposed to children, and therefore said in reply 'they're already there'. By way of summary, the complainant told the Court that she regarded the lines of questioning described above as unacceptable and discriminatory. She believed that they placed her at a disadvantage in the interview process.

The respondent denied that considerations relating to religion had played any part in the appointment of the successful candidate instead of the complainant. The respondent did however point out that it was a Catholic school under the patronage of a Catholic Archbishop and that the maintenance of the religious ethos of the school was a matter of legitimate interest in filling the vacant post. The respondent denied that any questions relating to homosexuality were put to the candidates at interview. The respondent stated that the only mandatory qualification for the post in question was qualification as a primary school teacher. The respondent's case was that the complainant had failed to ground her claims of discrimination on the grounds of religion and sexual orientation by reference to a valid comparator. Accordingly, the respondent maintained that her claims could not succeed.

All three members of the selection panel gave oral evidence to the Court on behalf of the respondent. Mr H was the deputy chairperson of the respondent's board of management. Sr C was a retired primary school teacher and Mr C was a teacher at second level. Mr H told the Court that the rules regarding the conducting of the interviews were set down by the Department of Education and Skills, which specified the factors to be taken into account when assessing candidates. These factors included professional qualifications, teaching experience and reports on competence, in addition to other relevant experience. The candidates received notice of the criteria under which they would be assessed in advance of the interview. Mr H described to the Court his impression of both candidates. He said that while the successful candidate had been positive, confident and willing to give her own opinions instead of reciting policy, the complainant had been quieter and less sure of herself. Under cross examination Mr H admitted that the complainant was more qualified than the successful candidate. He said that he could not explain why this was not reflected in the marks awarded to the complainant. Sr C told the Court that she considered the complainant's qualifications and experience were inferior to those of the successful candidate, as they had been obtained in America. Sr C further gave evidence that the complainant's role in the school, ie that of deputy principal, was 'meaningless'. She told the Court that this had been discussed by the selection panel before the complainant's interview. Mr C gave evidence that the successful candidate had come across as capable of making quick and clear decisions, compared with the complainant who had come across as ultra-cautious. All three witnesses spoke about the questioning of the candidates in relation to the submission. They were consistent in their evidence that Sr C had asked both candidates for their views on the submission. However, all three witnesses also agreed that the complainant had not been asked about religion. None of the three witnesses could remember how the complainant had answered Sr C's question about the submission. All three witnesses agreed that the question 'what about the homos' had definitely not been asked of the complainant. They agreed that it would have been wholly inappropriate to ask such a question, which had no bearing on the interview. In relation to interview notes, Sr C told the Court that she had destroyed her notes on the evening of the interview. Similarly, Mr C's notes were unavailable, as he had destroyed them three and a half years after the interviews and prior to his knowledge of the complaint to the Equality Tribunal. Mr H gave evidence that his interview notes had been vague and that he had not had time to take notes verbatim.

The Labour Court considered the relevant statutory provisions in this case. It was considered that s 8 of the Acts contained a general prohibition on discrimination by an employer, which extends to discrimination in relation to promotion or regrading. Section 6(1)(a) of the Acts provides a definition of discrimination. Section 6(2) sets out the protected grounds under the Acts, which include sexual orientation, religious beliefs and age. The Court considered that the expression 'religious belief' is defined by s 2 of the Acts as including religious background or outlook. Section 28 of the Acts provides that a claim of discrimination must be grounded by reference to a comparator. Section 6(1)(a) of the Acts makes it clear that this comparator may be actual or hypothetical. The Court considered the relevance of s 37 of the Acts, which provides a saver or exception to the prohibition of discrimination on grounds of religion.

In considering the applicable legal principles, the Court considered s 85A of the Acts, which provides that where facts are established from which discrimination can be inferred, the onus of proving the absence of discrimination rests on the respondent. The case of *A Worker v A Hotel*[98] was cited in this regard. The Court noted that the approach to be adopted in relation to cases involving the filling of posts could be discerned from a line of previous decisions, which began with the determination in *Moore Walsh v Waterford Institute of Technology*.[99] In that case the Court held that in dealing with cases involving the filling of posts, it was not the function of the Court to substitute its own views on the relative merit of candidates for those of the designated decision makers. Rather, the role of the Court was to ensure that the selection process had not been tainted by unlawful discrimination. Accordingly, the Court considered that it would not normally look behind a decision other than in the presence of clear evidence of unfairness in the selection process or manifest irrationality in the result. However, the Court noted that preferring a less qualified candidate over one whose qualifications were superior is suggestive of irrationality and would normally be regarded as a fact of sufficient significance to raise an inference of discrimination. *Wallace v South Eastern Education and Library Board*[100] was cited in this regard. In relation to the idea that discrimination is often routed in the subconscious thought process of the discriminator, the House of Lord's decision in *Nagarajan v London Regional Transport*[101] was cited.

98.   *A Worker v A Hotel* [2010] 21 ELR 72.

99.   *Moore Walsh v Waterford Institute of Technology* EDA 042.

100. *Wallace v South Eastern Education and Library Board* [1980] IRLR 193.

101. *Nagarajan v London Regional Transport* [2001] UKHL 48.

The Court noted that this House of Lords decision had been followed and applied by the Labour Court in *Nevins, Murphy, Flood v Portroe Stevedores Ltd.*[102]

In relation to the composition of the selection panel, the Court held that it was not concerned with the extent to which it complied with the rules and procedures for the filling of vacancies for the post of principal in primary schools set out by the Department of Education and Skills. It concluded that the issue for it to decide was whether the respondent infringed on the complainant's rights under the Acts.

In relation to religious outlook and patronage/pluralism, the Court considered whether the questions put to the complainant could properly be regarded as relating to her religious belief, as that expression was statutorily defined. In that context, the Court observed that religious belief includes religious outlook. The Court concluded that when viewed in its proper context, a person's opinion on religious patronage of schools and on pluralism and education were matters that could properly be regarded as pertaining to that person's religious outlook, and consequently to his/her religious belief.

The Court considered the complainant's need for a comparator in making the claims as alleged. It held that insofar as the complainant's claim was related to age, the treatment of the successful candidate for the post could be relied upon, as she was 10 years younger than the complainant. However, the position in relation to the complaints on the grounds of religion and sexual orientation were less straightforward. Although the Court noted that the complainant was a practising Catholic, it further considered that no evidence had been proffered on either side concerning the religion or sexual orientation of the successful candidate. The Court noted that in relation to the complaint on grounds of religion, the complainant did not base her claim on her own adherence to a particular religious denomination. Rather, the complaint was based on the weight which she alleges the selection panel gave to her own private views on the question of religious control, or patronage, and pluralism in education. The Court noted that in the submission, a certain view on the subject of religious control, or patronage, and pluralism in education was advocated. That view could be said to differ somewhat from what some would regard as the 'orthodox stance' of the Catholic Church on the importance of religious control of education and the centrality of religion in education. Rather, the submission advocated a broader acceptance of religious diversity and education. The Court concluded that it appeared to be reasonable to infer from the evidence that the complainant had not answered the question posed in a way that Sr C, or her colleagues, had considered satisfactory. Furthermore, there was no evidence of how the successful candidate had answered the same question. In these circumstances the Court accepted that the complainant, in advancing her claim on the grounds of religious belief was entitled to rely on a hypothetical comparator, whose views on religious patronage and pluralism were also canvassed but whose answer to that question was more in line with the orthodox position of the Catholic Church, or in line with what the selection panel considered to be appropriate.

The Court took account of the respondent's position, in the alternative, that if matters relating to religious belief were taken into account in a selection process, s 37 of the Acts allowed them to do so without infringing the principle of equal treatment on

---

102. *Nevins, Murphy, Flood v Portroe Stevedores Ltd* [2005] 16 ELR 282.

grounds of religion. The Court noted that s 37 of the Act does not provide an employer to which the section applies with an unfettered right to prefer one candidate over another by reference to their religious belief. At best, it allows for religious belief to be taken into account only where it is reasonable to do so in order to maintain the religious ethos of the school. The Court further held that s 37 of the Acts must be interpreted and applied in conformity with Directive 2000/78/EC, which establishes a general framework for equal treatment in employment and occupations. The Court held that s 37 of the Acts and art 4 of the Directive constituted exceptions to the general prohibition of discrimination on grounds of religious belief. Accordingly, it held that it should be ascribed 'narrow ambit' and that it could only be availed of by an employer in limited circumstances. The Court held that the respondent had failed to adduce evidence on which the Court could hold that the canvassing of the candidate's private views on the issue of religious patronage and pluralism was reasonable or necessary in order to maintain the religious ethos of the school. For this reason the Court concluded that the line of questioning to the complainant on her opinions on religious patronage and pluralism was a primary fact of sufficient significance to raise an inference of discrimination on the ground of religious belief.

In relation to the claim made on the ground of sexual orientation, the Court held that it could not find any basis upon which the claim could be sustained. It took account of the fact that the complainant's evidence regarding the question that had allegedly been put to her ('what about the homos?') had been uncorroborated. In any event, the Court held that even had such a question been asked, it could not imply discrimination against the complainant on grounds of her sexual orientation. The complainant was not homosexual and no such orientation was alleged to have been suggested. In relation to the question of the complainant's qualifications, the Court considered that if the complainant was successful in establishing, as a matter of fact, that she was the better qualified candidate, the relevant authorities indicated that this would be sufficient to shift the probative burden to the respondent. The Court had heard evidence that while the complainant had 12 years' experience as a teacher, the successful candidate had only four. In addition, unlike the complainant, the successful candidate had no experience in a position of responsibility. Furthermore, the complainant held a Master's degree, while the successful candidate held a post-graduate diploma in education. The Court commented that it found it extraordinary and somewhat incredulous that Sr C would dismiss the relevance of the complainant's academic attainment on the basis that it was obtained in the US. Furthermore, they considered it 'puzzling' that the selection panel would dismiss her role and experience as deputy principal as having no significance. The Court concluded that it preferred the complainant's evidence that she was the better qualified candidate for the role.

As the Court was satisfied that a less qualified candidate was preferred for appointment over the complainant, it was held that an inference of discrimination on grounds of both age and religious belief was within the range of reasonable inferences that could be drawn from that primary fact. The Court noted that as the complainant had managed to establish facts from which discrimination on grounds of religious belief and age could be inferred, it was for the respondent to discharge the burden of proof, in accordance with s 85A of the Acts. The case of *O'Higgins v University College*

Dublin[103] was cited in this regard. In that case it was held that where the probative burden shifts to the respondent, that places a requirement on the respondent to show a 'complete dissonance' between the relevant discriminatory grounds and the act which it alleged constitutes discrimination. In its determination as to whether the respondent had managed to discharge the probative burden that it bore in the circumstances, the Court carefully evaluated the evidence before it in relation to how the decision for the successful candidate was reached. It commented that the notes taken by the members of the selection panel had not been retained. The Court held that the testimony given by members of the selection panel in relation to the reasons for their decision had been couched in vague and general terms.

The Court ultimately held that no clear explanation had been provided to them as to why the successful candidate had been preferred over the complainant, who was clearly better qualified. In the circumstances, the Court held that the respondent had failed to establish the absence of discrimination on either the age or religious belief ground. Accordingly the appeal, insofar as it related to the finding of discrimination on grounds of religion and age, was disallowed. However the appeal, in relation to the claim of discrimination on grounds of sexual orientation, was allowed. The award of €54,000 to the complainant for the effects of discrimination suffered by her was upheld.

Religion and family status

[5.40] *Adejumo v Noonan Services Group Ltd*[104]*—Equality Tribunal—Employment Equality Acts 1998 to 2015, ss 6, 8 and 14A—religion—family status—discriminatory treatment—harassment*

The complainant, a married man with children and a Christian, commenced working as a security operative with a security company in July 2008. He transferred under TUPE[105] to the respondent in November 2010 after the company at which he worked lost a security contract to the respondent. He claimed that he had been discriminated against and harassed by the respondent on the grounds of his family status and religion, when his hours of work were reduced shortly after the transfer.

The complainant asserted that his initial employment contract, signed in September 2007, and his second contract, signed on the actual commencement of work (delayed due to permit difficulties), were both full-time, permanent contracts and that he was entitled to work 40 hours per week. This was subject to his availability as he shared childcare arrangements with his wife, who worked as a nurse. He could not remember if his employer at that time guaranteed him a certain number of hours per week.

The complainant asserted that his hours were reduced shortly after the transfer. The complainant raised this issue with Mr X, an employee of the respondent, in January 2011 and claimed that he was advised that the reduction in hours was due to his limited

---

103. *O'Higgins v University College Dublin* EDA131.
104. *Adejumo v Noonan Services Group Ltd* DEC–E2015–023.
105. European Communities (Protection of Employees on Transfer of Undertakings) Regulations 2003 (SI 131/2003).

availability. After a meeting to discuss the issue, the complainant's hours varied from week to week until he went on long-term sick leave.

The complainant returned to work in November 2011 and cited two colleagues, Mr R (no children) and Mr S (whose family status was unclear) to evidence the alleged discrimination, claiming that changes to the shift patterns were of benefit to them and disadvantageous to the complainant.

He made a complaint to the respondent and received what he considered to be an unsatisfactory reply. He appealed this and met with two other employees of the respondent and though he was again dissatisfied with the outcome, he did not complain further internally as he had already made this complaint to the Tribunal.

In October 2012, the complainant was informed that the client at the site where he worked had requested a change of staff. During the hearing, the complainant stated that he was the only employee to be so treated but later admitted that he did not know if this was the case. He was also offered shifts at another site but declined as the location was not suitable. He then went on annual leave and sick leave and never returned to work.

Finally, the complainant alleged that the meeting with Mr X in October 2012 constituted harassment on the grounds of family status, as he was prevented from earning and providing for his family. He also alleged that on using the phrase 'as God is my witness' to corroborate his story, Mr X responded 'let's leave God out of this', constituting harassment on the grounds of religion.

The respondent accepted that the complainant transferred to its employment under TUPE and stated that its information was that the complainant was a permanent employee with 24 weekly working hours. It also stated that it was happy to accommodate the complainant's childcare arrangements but asserted that he was, as a result, treated more favourably than any other employee.

Mr X gave evidence that, at the January 2011 meeting to discuss the complainant's hours, the complainant was informed that those full-time employees with set hours each week had to be accommodated and it was difficult to accommodate the complainant due to his restricted availability. Mr X also stated that the respondent was honouring the complainant's terms of employment as they were communicated by the previous employer. The respondent noted that the complainant was generally rostered for 30 to 40 hours per week, in excess of the number of hours it believed it was obliged to provide for him.

The respondent stated that the role of security operatives at the site changed to a customer focus role and, at the request of the client, after failing a number of audits the complainant and a number of other employees were removed. The complainant was offered other employment but declined and subsequently went on annual leave followed by sick leave.

Mr X denied harassing the complainant on religion grounds and rejected making the comments regarding God that had been attributed to him by the complainant. He also noted that the complainant was aware of the Dignity at Work Policy but did not avail of it at the time of the alleged comment, nor did he refer to the comment in subsequent emails or letters.

The Tribunal noted the requirements of s 85A of the Acts and noted that the complainant made reference to two colleagues, compared to whom he contended he was treated less favourably. The respondent claimed they were not in similar circumstances as each was entitled to 36 hours per week. In addition, Mr S had children and his family status was equivalent to that of the complainant. The Tribunal was therefore satisfied that there were reasons unconnected with the complainant's family status to offer a 'credible non-discriminatory explanation' for differences in treatment.

The Tribunal noted that the respondent could be described as offering more favourable treatment to the complainant, in comparison with his colleagues, as his shifts were not assigned to him until he confirmed his availability. The Tribunal found it difficult to accept that an employer offering more favourable treatment on the grounds of family status would also discriminate on the grounds of family status.

The Tribunal noted that mere assertions are insufficient to discharge the initial probative burden to prove inequality. The Tribunal found that the alleged incident of harassment on the grounds of religion was outside the time limit prescribed in the Employment Equality Acts and therefore statute barred. Further, allegations of harassment on the grounds of family status occurred after the complaint was referred to the Tribunal and could not therefore be investigated. The Tribunal examined the meeting of October 2012 at which the complainant was informed that the client had requested his removal from the site, but after which he was offered work at an alternative location. The Tribunal noted that the complainant's contract of employment included a mobility clause which could be exercised at the discretion of the employer, based on operational requirements. The complainant refused this offer and the respondent stated that it therefore had no alternative but to give the complainant notice of short-time work. The complainant produced no evidence that he was treated any differently to an employee in similar circumstances and therefore failed to discharge the initial probative burden.

The Tribunal noted that the complainant offered no further details in support of his claim of harassment on the grounds of family status and therefore the mere assertion on the part of the complainant was insufficient to surmount the initial burden of proof. The complaints were rejected.

EQUAL PAY

[5.41] *Savel v Workforce International Contractors Ltd*[106]*—Equality Tribunal— Employment Equality Acts 1998 to 2015, ss 29, 29(3) and 6(2)(h)—race—direct discrimination—equal pay—proper comparator—'comparable circumstances'— indirect discrimination in pay—no prima facie case*

The complainant brought a claim against his employer for discrimination based on grounds of race contrary to s 6(2)(h) of the Employment Equality Acts 1998 to 2015, in terms of his right to equal remuneration.

The complainant submitted that a named colleague, who was Hungarian and who was based in Weeze, Germany, was receiving more pay than him for the same work. At the time of the hearing before the Tribunal, the complainant was based in Budapest.

---

106. *Savel v Workforce International Contractors Ltd* DEC–E2015–075.

Both the complainant and his named comparator were employed by the respondent as aircraft cabin crew.

The complainant further submitted that provisions in various pieces of EU legislation which express the goal of achieving comparable living standards across the EU ought to be read as mandating employers to pay their staff the same wage for like work, regardless of location.

The respondent denied discriminating against the complainant as alleged or at all. It submitted that the pay rates offered reflected the local costs of living. It further submitted that it employed two Slovak nationals at the same German base as the complainant's Hungarian comparator and workers of four different nationalities at Budapest, who were all treated equally. It submitted that the complainant had not established a prima facie case of discrimination in remuneration on the basis of race.

The issue for decision by the Tribunal was whether the complaint, as presented, was validly before the Tribunal and if it was within the provisions of the Acts, and if so, whether the complainant was discriminated against in terms of his right to equal remuneration within the meaning of the Acts.

The Tribunal considered whether the complainant had established a prima facie case under s 85A of the Acts. The Labour Court has held consistently that the facts from which the occurrence of discrimination may be inferred must be of 'sufficient significance' before a prima facie case is established and the burden of proof shifts to the respondent.

The complainant maintained that the fact that the respondent's employees on cabin crew contracts, who were based in Budapest, were paid less than its employees in places like Weeze on the Dutch-German border, or in Charleroi in Belgium, was discriminatory. He expressed the opinion that the lower pay was related to the fact that both the location and the staff were Eastern European. He also cited a remark made to him by an unnamed respondent staff member, that life was much cheaper in Budapest than in locations in Western Europe. He stated that when he applied for a transfer to Budapest, he was warned that the pay would be less than what he had earned before.

When presented with a list of respondent staff who also worked from Budapest, the complainant confirmed that these were his colleagues, but stated that there were also some other staff, who were brought in on a short-term basis for a few weeks, who earned more than he and his colleagues.

The respondent stated that the complainant's comparator was not a valid comparator, since there were several Hungarian nationals at the Budapest base who would have been suitable comparators for a complaint on the basis of race. The complainant confirmed that the people in question were employed alongside him in Budapest. He also spoke of general dissatisfaction among the staff there about the pay rate.

The Supreme Court, in *National University of Ireland Cork v Ahern & Ors*,[107] has established the important principle that in complaints of equal remuneration, complainants are not entitled to choose a comparator more favourable to their case when other comparators are available who are more representative of the situation complained of. The Tribunal noted that if the complainant wished to complain of being paid less

---

107. *National University of Ireland Cork v Ahern & Ors* [2005] IESC 40.

than someone of Hungarian nationality, there would have been several regular respondent employees in Budapest, who were cabin crew like the complainant, and Hungarian nationals, which he could have chosen as his comparators.

On this basis, the Tribunal acceded to the respondent's argument that the complainant's comparator was not valid. The Tribunal also stated that it was not clear during the hearing of the complaint, what exactly the complainant was arguing as he had even stated that he felt it was more of a scenario of indirect discrimination on the ground of race, in that staff in the Budapest location were paid considerably less than staff elsewhere, and that the Budapest staff were mostly Eastern Europeans. The complainant did not confirm in oral evidence that his complaint was one of individual discrimination in respect of remuneration, on the ground of race, notwithstanding that this is what all of his submissions were based on.

With regard to a possible case of indirect discrimination, it became clear from the complainant's own evidence that Eastern European nationals also worked in Western European locations and in the UK. The complainant had done this himself, having applied to transfer to Budapest, despite warnings that the pay would be less, again according to his own evidence. Based on the complainant's evidence that people of any nationality could apply to work anywhere and be paid according to whatever rate was paid in that location, the Tribunal did not accept that this practice of paying remuneration in line with local costs of living was in any way linked to staff of a particular nationality being subjected to a particular disadvantage within the meaning of the Acts. The Tribunal was satisfied that the complainant's evidence in this matter did not amount to a prima facie case of indirect discrimination in terms of remuneration on the ground of race within the meaning of the Acts.

The Tribunal also addressed the point of whether it was unfair or discriminatory in general, to pay staff in different countries according to the local cost of living. To do so is a long-established principle of both public and private employers. The Tribunal noted that such a practice is not connected to any of the protected grounds, as it is everyone in a particular location, regardless of the presence or absence of any protected characteristic, who is paid these rates. The Tribunal did not accept the complainant's argument that social policy aims enshrined in EU legislation could be literally binding on employers. The Tribunal in its decision stated that if any public or private employer paid all staff in all locations the same rates, despite wide varieties in the cost of living, ie when the purchasing power of wages or salaries were much bigger in one place than another, this would in itself give rise to some very unfair situations and cause possible problems in staffing certain locations. The Tribunal further noted that whether a particular salary range in a particular location is in line with local cost of living is essentially an industrial relations matter.

The Tribunal found that due to the complainant's choice of an invalid comparator, and a general lack of compatibility in circumstance as referenced in s 29(3) of the Acts, that the complaint of direct discrimination with regard to equal remuneration on the ground of race was misconceived in law and that the Tribunal had no jurisdiction to investigate it.

[5.42] *Aleksandrovs & Ors v Roskell Ltd[108]—Labour Court—appeal from decision of Equality Tribunal—Employment Equality Acts 1998 to 2015, s 6(2)(h)—equal pay—alleged discrimination on grounds of race*

In this appeal, the complainants alleged that they were discriminated against by the respondent on the grounds of race arising from the respondent's failure to remunerate them on the same basis as a named Irish comparator.

The complainants alleged that the comparator performed the same work as the complainants, ie, picking fruit and vegetables from bulk delivery in order to fulfil orders for individual stores. One of the complainants gave evidence on behalf of all of the complainants and stated that he had first-hand knowledge of the work done by the comparator, notwithstanding that the comparator worked from time to time in a building some 50 metres from where the complainants worked. The complainant witness accepted that, in addition to picking duties, the comparator was responsible for picking a small number of orders for flowers.

The respondent accepted there was a disparity of pay between the comparator and the complainants but submitted that the difference in pay was attributable to the additional responsibilities undertaken by the comparator. The respondent alleged that the comparator was responsible for:

(i)   checking the bulk product each day before individual orders were picked;

(ii) ensuring there was sufficient product available to meet the daily orders and liaised with retailers if a shortfall occurred;

(iii) liaising with a supplier if a difficulty arose in connection with the delivery of an order; and

(iv) supervising and directing pickers on the Northern Irish line.

The Court noted that it was presented with two diametrically opposing views of the key issues and facts. Notwithstanding this, the Court concluded that the complainants failed to establish that they performed work of equal value to that of the named comparator. The Court accepted that the disparity in rate of pay arose as a consequence of additional duties undertaken by the named comparator. The appeal was refused.

---

108.   *Aleksandrovs & Ors v Roskell Ltd* EDA1519.

SELECTED EQUAL STATUS CASES

Race—access to services

[5.43] *Turner v Basketball Ireland[109]—Equality Tribunal—Equal Status Acts 2000 to 2015, ss 3(1)(a), 3(2)(h), 5(2)(f) and 6(1)—race—access to service—categorisation as 'Category 2' basketball player—inference of discriminatory treatment on grounds of complainant's race and national origin—whether difference in treatment objectively justified by legitimate aim—whether means of achieving that aim were appropriate and necessary—need for survival and growth of basketball in Ireland*

The complainant, a professional basketball player, alleged that he was being discriminated against on grounds of race, contrary to s 3(2)(h) of the Equal Status Acts 2000 to 2015 (the Acts).

The complainant's team, Killester Basketball Club, played in the Irish Men's Super League. The complainant, who was originally from America, came to Ireland in 2003 and attained Irish citizenship in June 2012. He is married to an Irish citizen and has two children. The complainant submitted that the respondent was in breach of its own Code of Conduct by allowing a system of discriminatory categorisation of authorised players to operate within the league. As a result, the complainant submitted that he had been prevented from being recognised as a Category 1 Irish player and/or Category 1 EU player.

The respondent is the body responsible for the promotion and administration of the sport of basketball throughout Ireland. The responsibilities of this role include the regulation of the league competition. The respondent was required to review and update its policies and procedures in line with FIBA, who are the governing body for basketball associations. There were two categories of players, according to the regulations of Basketball Ireland, at the time the complainant lodged his complaint. Category 1 consisted of any player resident in Ireland for a minimum of three months (ie 90 days), provided they fulfilled the requirements as a 'FIBA Europe Developed Player'. Category 2 was comprised of any player not qualifying for a Category 1 licence. The League's Competition Regulations prevents more than one Category 2 player being on court at any one time during the game. The Players must be registered and licensed to play with a particular club in order to participate in the League. The licence is applied for, and held by, the relevant club, as opposed to the individual player. The respondent submitted that Category 2 players, such as the complainant, are paid as professional basketball players. It is open to Category 2 players to play every week, if selected. It was stated that Killester Basketball Club had applied on behalf of the complainant, and in advance of the 2012/2013 season, for a Category 1A licence in respect of the complainant. The licence was refused on the basis that the complainant did not meet the criteria for such a licence. In order to qualify as a Category 1 player, the applicant has to be a locally-trained player and must have spent at least three years at a primary or secondary level school in Ireland. The respondent further submitted that the

---

109. *Turner v Basketball Ireland* DEC–S2014–029.

complainant did not qualify for a Category 1B or Category 1C licence, as he had not spent at least three years at primary or second level school in the EU.

This meant that the complainant was prevented from playing on a weekly basis for his local basketball club. The complainant believed that this constituted direct and/or indirect discrimination on grounds of race. He claimed that that the respondent rejected his legal and actual nationality without just cause. He maintained that the respondent had ascertained his nationality on the basis of the duration of primary and/or second-level schooling within Ireland and/or the European Union. The complainant contended that the respondent had changed its rules in 2012 in order to allow a group of Lithuanians who played for an Irish club to play in the League. However, the respondent maintained this was necessary on the basis of EU Directives. The complainant maintained that he had worn the Irish jersey and played in Latvia on the European National Team in early August 2014. Therefore, he stated, the respondent had regard to his Irish passport only when it suited them. In relation to the complainant's argument that he wore an Irish jersey and played on the European National Team in August 2014, the respondent stated that the complainant had been one of the players eligible to play for Ireland under the FIBA rules for this European competition. It was not a full international competition and, as yet, was still experimental.

The complainant contended that the respondent was offering the opportunity to play basketball in its leagues and competitions as a Category 1 player to the vast majority of Irish citizens and European citizens. The complainant himself was being denied participation on that basis because he was born in America and was not educated in Ireland. The complainant submitted that, as he was now in his early forties, he may not have much playing time left. He stated that he should be given categorisation as a Category 1 Irish player on the basis that he had attained Irish citizenship in June 2012. He submitted that he would never be in a position to meet the academic requirements imposed by the respondent to be considered a Category 1 Irish player, due to his US origin. He maintained that the respondent was in violation of his fundamental personal rights as enshrined in the Irish Constitution including Art 40.1. Specifically, he submitted that the respondent was in breach of s 3(c)(iii) of the Acts, as the respondent had imposed a condition which was directed specifically at the complainant which could only affect a tiny proportion of the population. It was further maintained by the complainant that the respondent was acting in breach of s 5 of the Acts, since it was engaged in providing a service where that service could be availed of only by a section of the public.

The respondent denied in the strongest terms that it discriminated, directly or indirectly, against the complainant on the race ground. The respondent submitted that any difference in treatment was objectively justified by a legitimate aim. This aim was the respondent's efforts to ensure the survival and promotion of basketball at the highest level in Ireland. The respondent highlighted the fact that the complainant had failed to employ the National Appeals Committee in respect of his grievance. This was an internal mechanism within the sport of basketball, charged with examining disputes. The complainant also declined the option of mediation.

The respondent accepted that the complainant was an Irish and an EU citizen. Accordingly, the respondent stated, he was categorised as a 'Category 2-Irish player'. It was explained that not all Irish or EU citizens qualify as Category 1 players either, due to the reasonable requirement of being locally schooled. The respondent stated that in some respects the Category 2 players are in a superior position to Category 1 players. While Category 2 players are paid, it is not the customary in the League to pay Category 1 players. In addition, while Category 1 players can only apply to transfer clubs at the beginning of the season, Category 2 players can apply to transfer right up to the last few weeks of the end of the season. The CEO of Basketball Ireland explained the history of the development of basketball in Ireland to the Equality Tribunal. He explained that under the old rules, three Category 2 players were allowed in a club at any one time. This caused clubs financial difficulties and was causing certain clubs to go out of business. As a result, the rules were changed in early 2000 so as to only allow one Category 2 player on the court at any time. The respondent stated that the complainant was campaigning for a change in the rules just to suit him. He was not considering the greater good of the sport, in relation to the development of individual players and of the game itself. It was stated that the respondent organisation needed to be cognisant of the wider impact that any change of rule could potentially have on the sport.

The respondent contended that any difference in treatment of the complainant was objectively justified by a legitimate aim and that the means of achieving that aim were appropriate and necessary by virtue of s 5(2) and in particular s 5(2)(f) of the Acts. The respondent submitted that such differences as existed in relation to the complainant were reasonably necessary to ensure the survival and promotion of basketball at a local level. These differences were required in order to afford locally trained players the opportunity to play basketball at the highest level in Ireland. This ensured a high quality of locally trained players and, as a result, the survival of the sport in Ireland.

The Tribunal considered s 3(1)(a) of the Acts, which defines the circumstances in which discrimination of the ground of race will be considered to have occurred. It noted that it was up to the complainant to establish a prima facie case of discriminatory treatment. The Tribunal stated that it was satisfied that the respondent was providing a service within the meaning of s 2 of the Acts. The Tribunal considered the meaning of indirect discrimination under the Acts and stated that it was satisfied that the complainant had demonstrated that he was disadvantaged by an apparently neutral provision on account of his race. This was due to the fact that, on account of his US origin, he could not fulfil the requisite requirements to be a Category 1 player. Therefore, the Tribunal considered that the complainant had succeeded in establishing an inference of discriminatory treatment on grounds of his race and national origin. Thus, the onus shifted to the respondent to establish that the provision was objectively justified on the basis that there was a legitimate aim involved; the means of achieving that aim were appropriate; and the means of achieving that aim were necessary in the circumstances.

The Tribunal was persuaded by the respondent's arguments that its rules regarding the categorisation of players constitute a legitimate aim, and that the means of achieving that aim were appropriate and necessary in the circumstances. The aim of the respondent was stated to be to safeguard and foster the amateur sport of basketball in Ireland. The Tribunal was also persuaded by the points made by the respondent in regard to the implications and repercussions of a rule change, as requested by the complainant.

Emphasis was placed by the Tribunal on an example offered by the respondent, where a change, such as requested by the complainant, could result in a situation where professional basketball players approaching the end of their careers in the US decide to come and play here, given their knowledge of the situation in Ireland. Due to the fact that these players are professional and are paid, the enforcement of a rule change, such as requested by the complainant, would detrimentally change the dynamics of the amateur status of the sport in Ireland. This could impede the development of locally trained players. The Tribunal further noted that it could also have serious detrimental effects in terms of the financial viability of the clubs in question and could result in some clubs going out of business. The Tribunal concluded that the rule change in question would result in a disproportionate impact overall on clubs in the League and ultimately on the growth of the game of basketball in Ireland. While the Tribunal agreed that the complainant had established a prima facie case of indirect discrimination on grounds of race, it was equally satisfied that the respondent had established objective justification for the difference in treatment.

In addition, the Tribunal held that the respondent was entitled to rely on the exemption laid down in s 5(2)(f) of the Acts where it allows for 'differences in the treatment of persons, *inter alia*, on the basis of nationality or national origin in relation to the provision or organisation of a sporting facility or sporting event to the extent that the differences are reasonably necessary having regard to the nature of the facility or event and are relevant to the purpose of the facility or event'. The Tribunal concluded that the respondent did treat the complainant less favourably on grounds of race in terms of the manner in which it categorised him as a Category 2 Irish player. However, the respondent had objectively justified its actions in terms of s 3(1)(c) of the Acts. Additionally, the respondent was entitled to rely on the exemption laid down in s 5(2)(f) of the Acts.

Admission policies—member of the Traveller Community

[5.44] *Christian Brothers High School Clonmel v Stokes (on behalf of John Stokes a minor) and the Equality Authority (Amicus Curiae)*[110]*—Supreme Court—Hardiman and Clarke JJ—appeal from decision of High Court —Equal Status Acts 2000 to 2015—whether appeal validly lay to Supreme Court—concept of indirect discrimination—membership of Traveller Community—school admissions policy— concept of particular disadvantage*

This case concerned an application made on behalf of the complainant for admission to the respondent secondary school, which was ultimately unsuccessful. The school's admission policy gave preferential access to applicants who met all of the following criteria:

(1)   whose parents are seeking to submit their son to a Roman Catholic education;

---

110.   *Christian Brothers High School Clonmel v Stokes (on behalf of John Stokes a minor) and the Equality Authority (Amicus Curiae)* [2015] IESC 13.

(2) who already had a brother who attended or was in attendance of the school, or is a child of a past pupil, or who has close family ties with the school;

(3) who attended his primary education in one of the local schools listed within the locality or demographic area of the school.

The complainant was the eldest child in his family and his father had not attended secondary school. Thus he did not meet the second of the three criteria as he was neither a sibling of a present or past pupil or was a child whose father had attended the school. As applications to the school were oversubscribed a lottery was carried out to allocate the remaining 47 places to the remaining 84 applicants who did not meet the above criteria. The complainant was unsuccessful in this lottery and his subsequent internal appeal under the school's admission policy was unsuccessful, as was a further appeal to the Department of Education and Skills. A complaint was made to the Equality Tribunal to the effect that both the school and the Department of Education had indirectly discriminated against the complainant on the basis that, as a member of the Traveller Community, it was much less likely that his father would have attended secondary school and thus he was disproportionally disadvantaged by the relevant admissions policy.

The Tribunal upheld the claim of discrimination and concluded that, on the parental rule, the operation of the policy disadvantaged members of the Traveller Community more than non-Travellers. The Tribunal took into account evidence in relation to the attendance levels at secondary school of members of the Traveller Community in the complainant's father's generation. The Tribunal compared the chances of the complainant getting a place under the present policy with what they would have been if the parental rule was not applied and found the probability of getting a place in the latter scenario would have been 70 per cent which was an increase from 15 per cent under the present policy. The Equality Tribunal concluded that the complainant was at a particular disadvantage compared to non-Travellers as a result of the preferential treatment afforded to children of past pupils. The Equality Tribunal rejected the objective justification grounds submitted by the school.

A *de novo* appeal was heard before Teehan J in the Circuit Court. It was noted that an application was made at this point to have the appeal dismissed on the basis that the Tribunal did not have jurisdiction to hear the claim as the time limits for bringing a complaint were not complied with. This procedural issue was not raised before the Tribunal nor was it expressly pleaded in the notice of appeal. The Circuit Court dismissed the application and held the complaint was within time, as the time only ran when the appeal to the Department of Education and Skills concluded. The Court also concluded that the respondent school had acquiesced throughout the Tribunal proceedings.

Teehan J concluded that the parental rule was discriminatory against members of the Traveller Community, to the extent that members of the Community, such as the complainant, were at a particular disadvantage. However, the Circuit Court upheld the appeal and set aside the decision of the Equality Tribunal holding that the rule was objectively justified.

In an appeal to the High Court on a point of law, McCarthy J concluded that there was no particular disadvantage and, on that basis, the subsequent question of objective justification did not arise. The appeal to the High Court was dismissed.

The majority judgment of the Supreme Court was given by Clarke J. He considered firstly whether an appeal could be taken to the Supreme Court in light of s 28 of the Equal Status Act 2000 which provides as follows 'No further appeal lies, other than an appeal to the High Court on a point of Law'. Clarke J concluded that an appeal did lie. In his minority judgment on this point, Hardiman J held there was no appeal to the Supreme Court in light of the clear statutory provisions.

Clarke J then went onto consider whether the claim was out of time, as raised by the respondent when the matter was before the Circuit Court but not before the Equality Tribunal. Clarke J noted that no issue of time limits was raised at the Tribunal and he concluded that to permit the respondent to rely on this time point now, would be to deprive the complainant of the opportunity to persuade the Equality Tribunal to extend the time for bringing the complaint. This would, in the view of Clarke J, be a manifest injustice. He concluded that the respondent was precluded from raising a time bar issue.

Clarke J then considered whether a 'particular disadvantage' had been made out. He noted that both the Equality Tribunal and the Circuit Court were satisfied that a particular disadvantage had been made out, but this was not upheld in the High Court. Clarke J concluded that the High Court was mistaken in its view and that the Circuit Court judge's conclusion must stand. Clarke J held that in light of the requirement in s 3(2) of the Equality Act 2004, the particular disadvantage had to be established. He opined that there must be at least a disadvantage and this must be considered by comparing the differential effect of the relevant measure on the competing categories of persons. In order for a protected category of persons to be said to be at a disadvantage, compared to an alternative category, it is necessary to attempt to analyse the effect of the measure on both of the categories.

Clarke J considered what was meant by the Oireachtas in its use of the word 'particular'. Clarke J held that he was satisfied that the term 'particular' requires, as a matter of law, that it must be established that the extent of any disadvantage is significant or appreciable. He noted that if it was intended that a slight disadvantage could give rise to a finding of indirect discrimination, the word 'particular' would not have been included in the statutory provisions.

Clarke J held that the scale of any disadvantage must be known in order to determine whether it could be said to place the relevant protected group at a particular disadvantage. The scale of such disadvantage may well be relevant in assessing whether any objective justification meets the 'appropriateness' test. Clarke J concluded that, as a matter of law, the Equality Tribunal or Court, when considering whether a particular disadvantage has been established, must carry out a proper analysis of the extent of any disadvantage at which a protected group has been placed by reason of the ostensibly neutral measure so as to determine whether that level of disadvantage is sufficient to meet the particular disadvantage test.

Clarke J looked at how disadvantage is analysed and noted that a proper analysis of disadvantage will normally require sufficient numbers to make that analysis meaningful. Looking at the position of a single individual does not really add much to an analysis of disadvantage. Clarke J held that firstly it is necessary to identify the group to whom it can be reasonably said that the challenged provision or measure applies; and secondly, it is necessary to conduct an analysis of a sufficiently large number of people to form a realistic view as to whether the protected group is truly at a measurable disadvantage by reference to its counterpart.

Clarke J went on to consider whether it was appropriate to look at the parent rule in isolation, or whether it was necessary to look at the cumulative effect of the overall admissions policy. He concluded that the question was: what was the 'provision' that could be said to give rise to the disadvantage? Clarke J concluded that where a number of alternative means are provided for complying with the qualifying measure, and where it is only necessary to qualify under one heading then 'the provision' must mean the totality of the alternative measures available. In this case, the second aspect of the qualification criteria could be met where either the applicant pupil has a sibling who attended or is in attendance at the school or where the parental rule is met or where there applicant has close family ties to the school. The Supreme Court noted that any one of those criteria allowed the second leg of the admissions policy to be met and thus must be considered as a whole. Where there are alternate means of qualification, then it did not seem to Clarke J that one could sever one possible means of qualification, without having regard to all of the others.

He then also considered the question of identifying the relevant group of persons from a geographical perspective for the purpose of assessing any differential effect on members of the Traveller Community on one hand and non-Travellers on the other. Clarke J noted it was a matter for the decision maker, whether the Equality Tribunal or Circuit Court, to form a view as to the appropriate group to be assessed. He noted that in this case, one might look at only those who sought a place in Clonmel High School or those who were within a geographical area where it might be expected that they might wish to apply. Clarke J noted that it was always necessary to consider, in cases involving persons making an application in order to qualify, that one of the effects of a potentially discriminatory measure might be that people do not even apply in the first place, thus distorting any figures generated by reference to those applicants.

Clarke J then referenced the proper question which should be asked in order to determine whether there is a disadvantage in a case such as this, between a protected group and its counterpart, and for the measurement of the extent of that disadvantage. He stated that he was not satisfied that either the Equality Tribunal or the Circuit Court judge asked the correct question or carried out an appropriate analysis to answer the question. The appropriate starting point was to determine the differential effect of the combination of the sibling and parental rules on potential Traveller applicants to Clonmel High School and potential non-Traveller applicants respectively.

This question was not addressed at all because of the failure to have regard to alternative means of qualification by virtue of having had a sibling in the school. Apart from that, and allowing for reasonable discretion as to the definition of group to which the analysis should be applied, the analysis did not really address the question of the effect of the rule on a typical applicant or potential applicant for the school. While the analysis of the effect on potential non-Traveller applicants was adequate the analysis of the effect on potential Traveller applicants, which was confined to one applicant, the complainant, fell a long way short of being adequate.

Clarke J concluded that there was no evidence or material on which any realistic assessment could have been made of the chances of a typical Traveller applicant to the school meeting the parental rule by itself, let alone meeting the combination of the sibling and parental elements of the overall rules. Clarke J held that it was not open to the Circuit Court to conclude that any disadvantage, let alone a particular disadvantage, had been established. Clarke J held that for this reason, and not for the reasons given by McCarthy J, the High Court was correct to overturn the decision of the Circuit Court on the question of particular disadvantage.

Clarke J noted that it was not the case that applicants were excluded because they did not qualify but instead they were entered into a draw for places. Hence, the effect of the measure was that qualification meant that one certainly got a place, but lack of qualification meant that one only had a chance of getting a place. Clarke J then considered the argument as to whether the risk of not getting a place was the sort of measure that could give rise to indirect discrimination. A measure, which significantly reduces the chances of a person from a protected group of qualifying places, that person at a natural disadvantage. If the level of that disadvantage is sufficiently large or appreciable then the person will have been placed at a particular disadvantage and thus will, in the view of Clarke J, meet the statutory test.

Clarke J held it was important to emphasise one aspect of the proper analysis of the question of disadvantage. Once a member of the Traveller Community went into the draw for one of the remaining places (on the basis of not having qualified for an automatic place) then the chances of that member of the Traveller Community getting a place were exactly the same as any other person in the draw. There was no doubt about this fact. The area where potential disadvantage arose for a member of the Traveller Community was in relation to qualification for an automatic place, rather than arising from random selection of those who did not automatically qualify.

Clarke J concluded that the overall analysis of the level of disadvantage suffered by a member of the Traveller Community would have required two matters to be calculated. Firstly, it would have been necessary to determine the chances of a member of the Traveller Community of qualifying under the parent or sibling rule for automatic enrolment entitlements. Clarke J noted that the Court was satisfied that there was not sufficient information before either the Equality Tribunal or the Circuit Court to enable any proper analysis or approximation of that probability to have been calculated. Secondly, it would have been necessary to calculate the chances of a member of the non-Traveller Community qualifying. Clarke J held that, in addition, it would have been necessary to calculate the extent of the disadvantage caused by failing to obtain automatic qualification and to factor that into an overall assessment of the degree of disadvantage. The fact that there was no certainty about getting a place even if one did not qualify for an automatic enrolment was required to be taken into account.

Clarke J held that there was no reason, in principle, why particular disadvantage could not be established by statistical analysis. The fact that indirect discrimination can be established by proper statistical analysis emphasises the need for such analysis to be robust enough to sustain a determination on the extent of the disadvantage caused by the impugned provision. Clarke J held that the case should have failed before the Circuit Court on the question of particular disadvantage, by reason of the absence of adequate evidence to allow a proper analysis to be carried out and it followed that it was unnecessary and inappropriate to go on to consider whether the provision might be considered to be objectively justified.

Clarke J held that he was not satisfied that there was sufficient evidence or material before the Equality Tribunal or the Circuit Court to enable a proper assessment to be carried out as to whether there was, in fact, particular disadvantage. The existence of such evidence and materials, and the approach adopted in their analysis, are essential matters to enable a sustainable decision of particular disadvantage to be made. The absence of sufficient evidence, materials and analysis gave rise to an error of law which required the decision of the Circuit Court judge on particular disadvantage to be overturned. Clarke J held that asking the right question and going about seeking the answer to that question in the right way is, in substance, a matter of law and a failure to follow this process requires that the decision be overturned in an appeal on a point of law.

Admission policies—foreign adopted children

[5.45] *A (on behalf of her daughter B) v A Girls Secondary School[111]—Equality Tribunal—Equal Status Acts 2000 to 2015, ss 3(1), 3(2)(c) and (h)—Education Act 1998, s 15(2)(d)—alleged discrimination on grounds of race and family status— whether respondent's admissions policy, which ranked applications in accordance with date of application, discriminatory—impact of admissions policy on foreign adopted children—indirect discrimination on grounds of race*

The complainant brought a complaint on behalf of her daughter, who was born in June 2003 in China, and adopted, by the complainant at 16 months, and who returned to Ireland in October 2004. The adoption was admitted to the Register of Foreign Adoptions in November 2004. The complainant applied for a secondary school place for her daughter on 15 March 2005. In October 2012, the respondent advised the complainant that the application on behalf of her daughter was unsuccessful and that all places had already been offered to pupils. She was further advised that her daughter's name was on a waiting list but was so far down the waiting list that it was clear that she would not be offered a place. The complainant asserted that the admissions policy, which applied to the date of application to the school, discriminated against her daughter on grounds of family status and/or race. The complainant was unable to make an earlier application for her daughter due to the fact that she was born in China and was then selected for foreign adoption, after which she came to Ireland. It was submitted by the complainant that the respondent's admission policy placed her daughter at a disadvantage, compared to an Irish child living in the care of their biological parents whose application could have been submitted immediately following their birth. The

---

111. *A (on behalf of her daughter B) v A Girls' Secondary School* DEC–S2015–001.

complainant could not have applied at such an early stage as the complainant had no rights of custody of her daughter prior to her adoption aged 16 months.

It was noted by the Tribunal that the respondent's admission policy operated a two-tier system of the priority group and a standard group. In the case of each group, the applicants were ranked in the order in which their completed application forms and birth certificates were received. The Tribunal noted that the priority list was limited to sisters of current pupil attendees of a named feeder school and children of current staff. The Tribunal confirmed that the complainant had no claim in respect of this aspect of the policy. The second category of the policy, category 2, included all applicants who did not fall into category 1. The category 2 applications were ranked in accordance with their application date, and all applicants irrespective of their race, colour or national origins were required to submit an application form. Their application was then ranked in accordance with the date the application was received. The Tribunal noted that, in order to gain a place on the list, all applications should be submitted as early as possible and, in some cases, shortly after the birth of the child. The Tribunal noted that the complainant's daughter, an adopted child who was of Chinese national and ethnic origins, was not in a position to submit an application to the respondent as early as other applicants of Irish national origin who were not adopted. The complainant advised the Tribunal that her daughter was disadvantaged due to the fact that she was adopted; as a result, the complainant, as an adoptive parent, was unable to apply for a place close to her birth date, as the adoption process was not concluded until she was 16 months old. The complainant further submitted that the majority of the adoptions that take place in Ireland are inter-country adoptions and specific reference was made to the level of adoptions in 2004, the year the complainant's daughter was adopted, which indicated that there were 486 non-family adoptions in total; 82 per cent (398) of those adoptions were inter-country adoptions involving children of a different race.

In considering whether there was discrimination on grounds of race and/or family status, the Tribunal noted that the Acts did not differentiate between the biological parent of the child born to them and remaining in their care and an adoptive parent. Both have the same 'family status' under s 3(1), (2)(c) and (2)(h) of the Equal Status Acts 2000 to 2015. The Tribunal was satisfied that it did not have jurisdiction to examine a complaint on the grounds of adoptive status and that this aspect of the complaint must fail.

The Tribunal set out the provisions of the Acts relating to indirect discrimination. The Tribunal noted that it was for the complainant to prove, on the balance of probabilities, that these criteria, ie placing applications on a list in accordance with their date of application, put the complainant's daughter, as an adoptive child who was of Chinese national and ethnic origin, at a particular disadvantage. If she succeeded in this, the burden of proof shifted to the respondent to prove that the criteria were objectively justified by a legitimate aim and that the means of achieving that aim were appropriate and necessary. The Tribunal was satisfied that the complainant had demonstrated that her daughter was disadvantaged by an apparently neutral provision, on account of her foreign adoptive status. Thus she had established prima facie evidence of discriminatory treatment in relation to the admissions policy that applied to applicants who fell into the non-priority list or category 2, which the respondent was required to rebut.

The Tribunal noted that the respondent had declined to elaborate on the objective justification of the policy. It had been submitted prior to the hearing by the respondent that the aim of the policy was to have a fair and reasonable application policy, consistent with the goals and ethos of the school. The non-priority list was operated on the basis of the date of application only, which was totally transparent. The Equality Tribunal was satisfied that the aim of the policy was to have a fair and reasonable application process consistent with the goals and ethos of the school. This did constitute a legitimate aim, but it was necessary to examine whether this aspect of the policy was appropriate and necessary. The Tribunal noted that a provision is 'necessary' where there is no alternative less discriminatory way of advancing the respondent's aim. It was noted by the Tribunal that the respondent did not provide any examples of any other means of achieving this aim which that may have been considered and disregarded. The respondent submitted that the policy was reviewed on several occasions and that it was of the view that this aspect of the policy was fair, reasonable, appropriate and entirely in keeping within the requirements of the Education Act 1998. The respondent had submitted that it was conscious of s 15(2)(d) of the 1998 Act, which provided that the respondent must ensure the right of parents to send their child to a school of the parent's choice are respected, but as was noted by O'Keeffe J in *Lucan Educate Together National School v The Department of Education and Science & Ors*,[112] there was no parental right to send a child to the school of their choice.

The Tribunal noted that the respondent had a maximum intake of 120 students every year, but the number of applicants usually greatly exceeded this figure. Hence, in any given year, many applicants did not get a place. The respondent had submitted that it framed a policy which was objectively justified and not discriminatory. The Tribunal noted the complainant's arguments that the majority of adopted children were from other countries and were clearly at a disadvantage, if their parents are not in a position to lodge an application immediately following the date of birth, as the adoption process can take up to two years on average. The Tribunal noted that the admission policy made no provision for exceptional circumstances, for example where the child may experience a change of circumstances, a change of address due to a loss of parent; or a change of parenting arrangements. The policy also made no provision for children in foster care.

The Tribunal noted the evidence provided by the complainant as to steps that other schools had taken to change their policies to accommodate adopted children of other national origins. Specific example was given of a named school, whose policy had been amended to make provision for foreign adopted children by allowing applications to be backdated to take account of the amount of time which had elapsed between the child being born and the adoption date thus putting the parents of an adopted child in a similar position of that of biological parents who could submit an application for their child as soon as he or she was born. The complainant also advised the Tribunal that other schools operated a single cut-off date of applications each year and that this cut-off date was taken as the date of application for each applicant and then places were allocated by means of a lottery. The Tribunal noted that this approach took into account the changing

---

112. *Lucan Educate Together National School v The Department of Education and Science & Ors* [2011] IEHC 86.

demographics of Irish society in recent years, with the increase of immigration resulting in children of foreign or migrant workers moving to Ireland from other countries and requiring school places, for which they would not have been in a position to apply, prior to their moving to Ireland.

The Tribunal noted there was an absence of any evidence provided by the respondent at the hearing in support of the objective justification test. The complainant had advised of other options which would seem to meet the respondent's aim to be fair and reasonable in prioritising applications for the non-priority list. This called into question the respondent's submission that the current policy was necessary to achieve its aim. The Tribunal was critical of the respondent's decision to decline to elaborate at the hearing and held that it was not clear how, without any evidence to substantiate this claim, or without testing any other criteria, the respondent could say that such criteria would not be objectively justified. The Tribunal concluded that the respondent's policy was legitimate but that they had not proven that the current policy of allocating priority in accordance with the date of application was necessary. The Tribunal held that the complainant had proven that the priority given to applicants, based on date of application, put foreign adopted children at a particular disadvantage compared to Irish-born children in the care and custody of their biological parents; and the respondent had not proved this criteria was objectively justified by a legitimate aim or was appropriate and necessary. The Tribunal upheld the complaint of indirect discrimination on grounds of race.

In terms of redress, the Equality Tribunal ordered that: (1) the respondent immediately offer a place to the complainant's daughter; (2) the respondent review its admission policy to ensure that it does not indirectly discriminate against people on grounds of race, contrary to s 3(2)(h) of the Act; and (3) the respondent pays to the complainant the sum of €3,000 to compensate her for the effects of the discrimination experienced by her.

Gender—access to services

[5.46] *Carroll v Gruaig Barbers[113]—Equality Tribunal—Equal Status Acts 2000 to 2015, s 5(2)—discrimination on grounds of gender—refusal of barber shop to provide haircut to a female where traditional service provided catered for men*

The complainant asserted that she was discriminated against by the respondent when she was refused a haircut due to the fact that she was a woman.

The complainant claimed that on 24 May 2013, she went to the respondent barber shop and asked a female barber for 'an undercut' (to shave the side of her head). The complainant submitted that the barber informed her that she could not provide this service to her as she was female. The complainant asserted that she had her hair cut there previously and that she informed the female barber of this fact; however the barber stated that she was not allowed to cut women's hair and that she would get into trouble if

---

113. *Carroll v Gruaig Barbers* DEC–S/2015/005.

her boss saw her doing this on camera. The complainant also submitted that the respondent advised her that they could not cut her hair because of insurance reasons.

The respondent submitted that they operated their business as a barber shop and that this was a service provided to male customers. They submitted that their staff members were not trained or qualified as hairdressers and were specifically employed to cut men's hair and for the services provided in a men's barber shop. The respondent further stated that the premises and business is insured as a barber shop with insurance specifically covering the cutting of men's hair and that the premises were leased from the owners of the shopping centre for specific use as a barber shop. The respondent submitted that the service provided by the barber shop is a service of aesthetic, cosmetic or similar nature which is provided for in s 5(2) of the Acts and therefore can be provided exclusively to the male gender.

The question before the Equality Tribunal was whether or not the respondent discriminated against the complainant on grounds of gender in their refusal to provide her with a haircut. In reaching a decision, the Equality Tribunal had to consider s 3(2) and (2)(a) of the Equal Status Acts.

The complainant submitted that she was refused a service by the respondent and that this refusal was due to the fact that she is female. The respondent did not deny that the complainant was refused a service and agreed that this refusal was due to her gender. The Tribunal was satisfied that the complainant had established sufficient corroborating evidence to support a case of discrimination on the grounds of gender, which the respondent was required to rebut.

The Tribunal noted the respondent's evidence that, to their knowledge, no woman had ever had a haircut in their shop. The respondent denied that the complainant had ever had a haircut in their premises. The respondent further advised the Tribunal that it had interviewed all staff members in relation to the matter and that all staff members, including the female barber who had refused to cut the complainant's hair, had denied ever cutting her hair previously. The respondent stated that all of its staff members are trained as barbers and spend about 15 to 20 minutes on each haircut and that, as barbers, they would not be able to cut women's hair.

Furthermore, the respondent advised that under the terms of its lease it is only permitted to provide a 'barber shop service' and that it is a condition of its lease agreement that the premises is only allowed to be used as a 'barber shop, to include retail sale of ancillary products and the provision of hot shaves'. The respondent added that when it had bought the lease for the premises in 2011, it had initially wished to include ladies haircuts but was not permitted to do so under the terms of its lease as there was a well-known women's hairdresser already situated in another premises within the shopping centre. The respondent advised the Tribunal that any inquiries or requests it received in relation to women's haircuts were directed by them to the women's hairdressers in the shopping centre. The respondent advised the hearing that it is insured as a barber shop and that it has no insurance to cover women's hairdressing.

The respondent submitted that the exemption under s 5(2) of the Acts applies to it. This section allows differences in treatment of persons on gender grounds in relation to services of an aesthetic, cosmetic or similar nature, where the services require physical contact between the service provider and the recipient. The respondent submitted that it fell into this category. Furthermore, the purpose of the legislation is not to eradicate all differences between men and women because it allows certain differences to continue and these are comprehended within the explicit exceptions provided for within the Acts.

The respondent advised the Tribunal that this was a traditional service catering for men only. They maintained that men availing of this service expect to be in the company of other men. The respondent informed the hearing that it did not wish to offend or discriminate against the complainant but stated that its service is that of a barber shop which caters to men and not to women. At the hearing, the respondent acknowledged that the complainant may have been embarrassed by the refusal of a haircut and apologised to the complainant for any embarrassment or disappointment caused. The respondent went on to state that it would like to offer the complainant something on the lines of free service to her son or boyfriend to make up for any upset.

The Tribunal was satisfied that the cumulative effect of the defences advanced by the respondent in this case both justified and explained the respondent's refusal to provide the complainant with a haircut. The Tribunal was satisfied that the respondent had rebutted the inference of discrimination raised by the complainant and that the respondent was constrained by the terms of its lease agreement and that it is entitled to rely on the exemption provided under s 5(2). The Tribunal was satisfied that the complainant was not discriminated against on grounds of gender in relation to this matter.

Parallel proceedings

[5.47] See *Culkin v Sligo County Council*[114] in **CH 18** where the complainant pursued a claim of discrimination with the Equality Tribunal while simultaneously pursuing a personal injuries claim in the High Court.

---

114. *Culkin v Sligo County Council* [2015] IEHC 46.

Chapter 6

EMPLOYMENT RELATED TORTS

BULLYING

[6.01] *Ruffley v Board of Management of St Anne's School[1]—Court of Appeal—Ryan P, Irvine and Finlay Geoghegan JJ—personal injuries arising from alleged bullying in workplace—analysis of definition of workplace bullying—meaning of 'repeated', 'inappropriate behaviour', and 'reasonably ... undermining .... dignity at work'*

This was an appeal from the judgment of the High Court delivered on 9 May 2014[2] in which the plaintiff was awarded damages in the sum of €255,276 on foot of a claim for damages for personal injuries arising out of claimed bullying in the course of her employment as a special needs assistant in the defendant's national school.[3] In summary, the plaintiff was, over a 12-month period, the subject of a flawed disciplinary process conducted by the school. She instituted personal injury proceedings alleging that she was bullied through the imposition on her of the flawed process. The defendant appealed. Three issues arose on the appeal, two of which were easily disposed of, namely: whether there was a basis in the pleadings and on the evidence for an award of €47,000 for future loss of earnings; and whether there was sufficient evidence of causation to connect any wrongdoing on the part of the school or its officers with the plaintiff's mental health issues. All three judges concluded that there was no basis in the pleadings or the evidence for an award in respect of future loss of earnings and all three concluded that there was adequate evidence of causation.

[6.02] The third ground of appeal, with which the judgments in the Court of Appeal were primarily concerned, was whether the conduct of the defendant school and its officers in the operation of a disciplinary process (which all of the judges found to be flawed) amounted to workplace bullying, having regard to the definition of workplace bullying set out in the Industrial Relations Act 1990 (Code of Practice Detailing Procedures for Addressing Bullying in the Workplace) Declaration Order 2002;[4] and

---

1. *Ruffley v The Board of Management of St Anne's School* [2015] IECA 287.
2. *Ruffley v The Board of Management of St Anne's School* [2014] IEHC 235.
3. See *Arthur Cox Employment Law Yearbook 2014* at [5.02] for a note on the High Court judgment. In summary, the facts were that the plaintiff was disciplined through the imposition on her of a severe warning for locking the door of a sensory room from the inside and failing to complete a monitoring form correctly. There was considerable interaction on the issues over a 12-month period, after which the plaintiff went on certified sick leave due to work-related stress.
4. Industrial Relations Act 1990 (Code of Practice Detailing Procedures for Addressing Bullying in the Workplace) Declaration Order 2002 (SI 17/2002). (contd .../)

having regard to previous decisions of the Irish Courts on that matter.[5] On this issue, the Court by majority (Ryan P and Irvine J) allowed the defendant's appeal. Finlay Geoghegan J, in a dissenting judgment, would have dismissed the appeal. In all three judgments the definition of workplace bullying contained in the statutory instrument was accepted and extensively analysed. In particular each of the judgments addresses the terms 'repeated', 'inappropriate behaviour' and 'reasonably ... undermining ... dignity at work'.

Repeated behaviour

[6.03] In addressing whether the behaviour complained of is 'repeated', important nuances and distinctions appear in the judgments. In the judgment of Ryan P the following passage appears:

> 66. Was the behaviour repeated? My understanding of the meaning of this term is that it is the same behaviour or class of behaviour that is offensive and amounts to bullying. Name calling or humiliating comments or practical jokes are examples. It is stretching the meaning of the word "repeated" much too far to regard a continuing process of discipline in pursuit of legitimate concerns, even if actually mistaken or unfair, as repeated behaviour.

[6.04] Irvine J addressed the matter as follows:

> 39. First, bullying can only be identified retrospectively, that is to say its first incidence only amounts to bullying by virtue of its repetition. Secondly, incidences of inappropriate conduct do not have to be of the same nature or character that constitute bullying. Different types of behaviour when directed to one person may constitute bullying ...

> 45. ... Implicit in the requirement that the inappropriate conduct be repeated is, I believe, the requirement that the incidents of inappropriate conduct are reasonably proximate to each other. Otherwise, the incidences may amount to no more than individual and isolated events even though they might have a common thread. It is not easy to define what the necessary proximity is, but significant breaks in behaviour must, in my opinion, reduce, the extent to which inappropriate behaviour has the ability to undermine the dignity of the individual in their workplace. In other words I don't accept that it necessarily follows that the same three events occurring within a period of one month and which might reasonably

---

4.   (contd) Workplace bullying is 'repeated inappropriate behaviour, direct or indirect, whether verbal, physical or otherwise, conducted by one or more persons against another or others, at the place of work and/or in the course of employment, which could reasonably be regarded as undermining the individual's right to dignity at work. An isolated incident of the behaviour described in this definition may be an affront to dignity at work but, as a once off incident, is not considered to be bullying'.

5.   *Quigley v Complex Tooling & Moulding Ltd* [2009] 1 IR 349; *Berber v Dunnes Stores Ltd* [2009] IESC 10; *Maher v Jabil Global Services Ltd* [2005] IEHC 130 and *Glynn v Minister for Justice, Equality and Law Reform and the Attorney General* [2014] IEHC 133.

be considered to amount to bullying would necessarily amount to bullying if they happen over a period of three years.

[6.05] Finlay Geoghegan J addressed the matter in the following terms:

> 20. ....The phrase "repeated inappropriate behaviour" in the definition must, it appears to me, be construed in the context of the last sentence in the definition, namely, "An isolated incident of the behaviour described in this definition may be an affront to dignity at work, but, as a once-off incident, it is not considered to be bullying". It therefore appears to me that "repeated" in the definition is being used for the purpose of connoting behaviour which is more than either an "isolated incident" or "once-off incident". A disciplinary process which continued over a number of months and, as this one did, consisted of several meetings and interactions between the plaintiff and the Principal and the Chairman of the Board, and the latter inter se, and with other members of the Board cannot, as a matter of principle be considered to be either an isolated incident or a once-off incident. Whether inappropriate behaviour which undermines dignity at work is to be considered as repeated for the purpose of the definition must depend on an assessment of all the facts.

Inappropriate behaviour

[6.06] With reference to the requirement that the behaviour complained of be 'inappropriate' if it is to constitute bullying, the matter was again dealt with differently in the judgments. In essence, what was at issue was whether the institution by the defendant school of a disciplinary process against the plaintiff was or could have been considered to be 'inappropriate' and accordingly as potentially constituting bullying, assuming that the other requirements of the definition were met.

[6.07] Ryan P, having accepted that the plaintiff was denied due process and that she had a real ground of complaint in that regard, concluded that, for the purpose of the definition, the defendant school had not acted inappropriately. He dealt with the matter in the following terms:

> 73. Overall, it seems to me that the required elements of a bullying case have not been established here. Accepting all the criticisms that were made by the trial judge of the process and of Ms Dempsey and of Mr Lynch and the Board, here was a process that was engaged in that emanated from serious concerns. It is not that they were just and reasonable in their conclusions. The judge, as I see it was entitled to come to the conclusion that the Board was quite wrong in its views. He was also justified in coming to the conclusion that Ms Dempsey arrived at a bizarre decision that there was fabrication. But he does not find that Ms Dempsey contrived this whole process for the purpose of getting at the plaintiff and neither did Mr Lynch nor was there any suggestion that he did so.[6] So in circumstances

---

6.   This sentence suggests that the absence of intent on the part of the alleged wrongdoer is relevant. In his overall conclusion at para 74, Ryan P made a number of observations that suggest that the motive, intentions and bona fides of the wrongdoer are relevant, including the following: (contd .../)

where the Principal of the school and the Chairman of the Board were entitled to be concerned about a matter and were entitled to investigate it but failed to investigate it and mistakenly therefore or wrongly implicated the plaintiff, not in a matter for which she might not be criticised, but in a manner whose degree was not of the level that the Board considered it had reached. They were not entitled to consider the matter at the level that they did. So my view is that does not amount to bullying in law.

[6.08] Irvine J addressed the matter in the following terms:

39. Thirdly, what amounts to inappropriate behaviour must be objectively determined by the court and the test does not centre upon the intention of the person or persons concerned in the alleged bullying. The fact that the test is objective is clear from the decision of Kearns P in *Glynn v The Minister for Justice, Equality and Law Reform*[7] ... where he observed that the following question should be asked in relation to a claim of bullying stating at para 52:

> "whether the behaviour complained of, by reference to an objective test, imports that degree of calibrated inappropriateness and repetition which differentiates bullying from workplace or occupational stress."

40. As to the nature of the conduct that may amount to bullying, I agree with the views expressed by Finlay Geoghegan J in her judgment that just because repetitive inappropriate behaviour which undermines the dignity of a person in their workplace occurs in the course of a disciplinary process, such conduct is not as a matter of principle protected from a potential finding that it amounted to bullying. Behaviour that can objectively be viewed as bullying enjoys no safe haven merely by reason of the fact that it may have taken place in the context of a disciplinary process ...

41. ... That said it is important to recognise, in the context of bullying that is alleged to have occurred in the course of a disciplinary process, the differences between conduct, decisions and sanctions which might from a legal or procedural perspective be unlawful or appear harsh and circumstances which, objectively assessed, may be considered to amount to repeated inappropriate conduct that undermines the dignity of the worker in their workplace.

---

6.   (contd)

      '(i)   The motive was child protection in a school devoted exclusively to children with Special Needs ...

      (vi) This was a disciplinary process, perhaps arising from a misunderstanding, but honestly pursued in the interests of the children.

      (vii) There was nothing in the process of investigation that constituted a sustained campaign maliciously pursued in order to intimidate or humiliate or denigrate the plaintiff ...

      (ix) At worst, this was a botched disciplinary process and not a case of repeated offensive behaviour intended to destroy the plaintiff's dignity at work ...'

7.   *Glynn v Minister for Justice, Equality and Law Reform and the Attorney General* [2014] IEHC 133.

42. Given that the test as to whether conduct amounts to bullying is an objective one, the threshold at which conduct may be considered inappropriate, as opposed to wrong, harsh, insensitive or misguided, cannot be decided in a vacuum and must be assessed in the context of all of the relevant circumstances ...

44. For the purpose of assessing whether the trial judge's finding that the plaintiff was subjected to inappropriate conduct amounting to workplace bullying for over a period of one year can be sustained, it is first necessary to analyse the conduct of the Board and Ms Dempsey over all of the relevant period for the purpose of assessing whether it can be objectively considered to have been inappropriate ...

46. As to what amounts to behaviour that may fall within the definition of 'inappropriate' that is not a straightforward question. For example, a body which acts outside its competence or jurisdiction or behaves in a fashion contrary to what might be expected might be described as acting inappropriately. However, it's difficult to see, save in exceptional circumstances, how such conduct might be considered inappropriate in the bullying sense. That type of conduct is highly unlikely to undermine the dignity of the worker in the workplace ....

59. As to the threshold at which conduct slips in to the inappropriate category, the context in which it occurs is clearly material. In this regard the form filling event followed closely in time the door-locking incident. Both incidents had the potential to affect the wellbeing of the same child who had significant intellectual difficulties. Thus I am satisfied that on any objective view of these facts Ms Dempsey's conduct in deciding to bring Ms Ruffley's conduct to the attention of the board of management fell substantially below the threshold at which that decision, which was after all no more than a referral of Ms Ruffley's conduct for the consideration of a higher authority, might be considered to amount to inappropriate behaviour.

60. Further, whilst not determinative of the matter, the plaintiff, even after she engaged the services of IMPACT, never sought to make the case that the decision of Ms Dempsey to refer her conduct to the board for its consideration was inappropriate or was one that impacted on her dignity in the workplace. From an objective perspective, I venture to suggest that there are few parents of children with disabilities who would consider the referral of these two events to the board for its opinion anything other than appropriate in the circumstances. It would be extremely difficult for a school to operate if a principal could be accused of inappropriate conduct merely because they sought to transfer responsibility for a decision on a teacher's conduct to the board of management rather than adjudicating upon it themselves ...

63. Insofar as Ms Ruffley was not advised of the precise misconduct that was to be considered by the Board and was afforded no opportunity of defending herself, clearly the conduct of the board offended the principles of natural justice. Those facts of themselves however, do not establish inappropriate conduct in the sense identified in *Quigley*.[8] That is not to say that she could not have sought to impugn the validity of the board's decision on that basis.

---

8. *Quigley v Complex Tooling & Moulding Ltd* [2009] 1 IR 349.

64. Insofar as the trial judge concluded that it was inappropriate for Ms Dempsey to have brought the issue concerning the locked door to the board without first conducting an inquiry into the conduct of other SNAs to ascertain whether they engaged in the same practice, here I part company with the reasoning with the trial judge and my colleague Finlay Geoghegan J. I do not accept that there is any valid basis upon which Ms Dempsey's conduct objectively assessed could be viewed as inappropriate just because she was aware of the fact that Ms Ruffley maintained that other SNAs locked the door and she had not before consulting the board carried out an inquiry among the other twenty five SNAs to ascertain if this was so …

89. The fact that the board was aware that the plaintiff was upset by the finding and sanction imposed in the first instance, cannot be relevant to a consideration as to whether any particular conduct on its part should thereafter be deemed inappropriate. The test is an objective one. If the determination was to be made by reference to the subjective response of the individual, any rebuke of a worker could potentially amount to bullying. Insofar as the trial judge clearly factored this consideration into his conclusion that the plaintiff was bullied at this stage of the process, I regret to say that he fell into error …

93. Undoubtedly the investigation of the plaintiff's conduct by the defendant in this case was far from acceptable. It cannot be doubted but that the board in dealing with the conduct of Ms Ruffley at first instance acted in breach of her rights to natural justice and fair procedures. She wasn't told the precise nature of the complaint it decided to investigate in November 2009, and neither was she afforded a hearing to enable her to defend her alleged misconduct. To make matters worse the same body that decided the case against her at first instance also decided the appeal which she lodged against this decision.

94. All of these facts afforded the plaintiff substantial grounds upon which she might have instituted plenary proceedings seeking a declaration as to the invalidity of both the original decision of the board and the decision which it made on the appeal. For whatever reason she chose to eschew such an approach in favour of an action for damages for breach of duty on the part of her employer in respect of bullying the workplace.

95. However the fact that the board may have conducted the investigative and disciplinary process in the hopelessly flawed manner last described does not bring its conduct anywhere close to meeting the definition of bullying as set out in *Quigley.* On the facts of this particular case, objectively ascertained, the defendant could not be considered guilty of the type of repetitive inappropriate conduct which undermined the plaintiff's right to dignity in the workplace for a period of over a year as was found by the trial judge.

[6.09] Finlay Geoghegan J noted that:

8. there is no separate tort of bullying or harassment (see *Kelly v Bon Secours Health System* [2012] IEHC 21; *Nyhan v Commissioner of An Garda Síochána* [2012] IEHC 229). The claim is a claim for damages for breach of the duty of care allegedly owed by the employer to the employee. Where the substance of the claim is an allegation of what is termed bullying or harassment, the causes of action and

necessary proofs on the part of a plaintiff may differ depending on whether the alleged perpetrator is simply a fellow employee or whether, as was the factual position in this claim, the conduct alleged to constitute the bullying was by the employer, in the sense of either the employer itself or its management.[9]

9. On the facts herein the conduct complained of by the plaintiff is conduct of the Principal of the school, Ms Dempsey, and the Board of Management ... which is the employer, and its chairman. It is a claim based upon an allegation of corporate bullying, as that term has been used by McMahon & Binchy in the above cited extract.[10]

[6.10] Finlay Geoghegan J dealt with the question of inappropriate behaviour in the following terms:

14. The only uncertainty in the submissions of the parties as to the proper approach of the court in determining whether the conduct of the defendant and Principal, as found by the trial judge, was 'inappropriate behaviour' within the meaning of the definition of workplace bullying was whether or not this should be objectively determined by the court, or whether the intent of the person concerned was relevant ...

16. I am of the view that ... not only must the question as to whether or not the inappropriate behaviour was such that it could reasonably be regarded as undermining the individual's right to dignity at work be objectively assessed, but the question as to whether the behaviour is inappropriate must also be objectively assessed. It does not appear to me that it could be either dependent on a subjective perception by the plaintiff or indeed dependent on the intent of the perpetrator. Such an approach would be inconsistent with objectively determining whether the inappropriate behaviour is such that it could reasonably be regarded as undermining the individual's right to dignity at work. If appropriateness or not of the behaviour is to be objectively determined, then the intent of the perpetrator becomes irrelevant.

17. Accordingly I have concluded that a Court must first assess whether the conduct or behaviour alleged is objectively to be considered as repeated inappropriate behaviour. If so, it must then determine objectively whether it is reasonably to be regarded as undermining the individual's right to dignity at work.

---

9.   Finlay Geoghegan J cited with approval a passage from McMahon and Binchy, *Law of Torts* (4th edn, Bloomsbury Professional, 2013) at para 18.80 which is in the following terms:
     [18.80] There is no distinctive tort of bullying or harassment. The question is to be resolved in the context of employers' liability, by asking whether the employers took reasonable care not to expose the plaintiff to the risk of injury from such conduct. The answer will depend in large part on what facts ought to have been known to the employer. Naturally, matters are different where the plaintiff's claim is that he or she is victim of 'corporate bullying', where the allegation is that the management of the enterprise is implicated in the bullying activity. Such claims have succeeded in some recent cases, and failed in others.
10. See extract from McMahon and Binchy, *Law of Torts* above.

18. It appears both difficult and probably dangerous to try and define at a level of principle what would meet the threshold of "inappropriate behaviour". Any assessment of what is "appropriate" or "inappropriate" behaviour in a workplace context must depend on the relationship and relative positions of the individuals and the full factual context.

Dignity at work

[6.11] On the requirement that the repeated inappropriate behaviour could 'reasonably be regarded as undermining the individual's right to dignity at work', the judgments also differ significantly.

[6.12] Ryan P dealt with the matter as follows:

67. There is also a difficulty considering what happened as undermining the plaintiff's right to dignity at work. It may have undermined the plaintiff's work, or even her right to work, but it cannot properly be regarded as undermining her dignity. It is easy to see how name-calling etc—what would be considered obvious examples of bullying—would and could be regarded as undermining the person's dignity at work. Obviously, the fact that it may be different from other examples of bullying does not exclude this behaviour but it seems legitimate to look at how the plaintiff's dignity was threatened.

[6.13] Irvine J dealt with this issue in the following terms:

47. As to what the right to dignity in the workplace means, it is submitted that such a right entitles a person to be treated with reasonable fairness in the eyes of others. I agree with that submission. I also accept that a person who contends that their dignity in the workplace was interfered with does not have to prove a diminution of their standing in the eyes of fellow workers albeit that proof of such a fact would clearly make their claim much easier to establish. Without such proof a plaintiff would have to rely upon their own evidence to prove that their dignity was adversely affected in the workplace and in this regard it is essential to remember that whether a breach of that right has occurred is a question that must be answered by reference to an objective standard and not by reference to the subjective effect that the conduct under scrutiny may have had on the individual concerned. Otherwise the same conduct visited upon two different individuals, one more sensitive than the other, might result in a finding that one but not the other had been bullied.

48. While it is highly likely that in the vast majority of bullying cases there will be a public aspect to the undermining of the dignity of the victim, I am nonetheless satisfied that bullying can take place within the private confines of the relationship between two workers.[11]

---

11.   At paras 56, 57 and 58 of his judgment, Ryan P, in considering whether certain events could constitute bullying, treats as relevant the lack of publication of the matters complained of to third parties or colleagues.

[6.14] Finlay Geoghegan J addressed this issue in the following terms:

14. … It was common case, in accordance with the authorities, that a court, in assessing whether the alleged repeated inappropriate behaviour was such that it "could reasonably be regarded as undermining the individual's right to dignity at work" must make that assessment objectively for the very reasons explained by Kearns P in *Glynn v The Minister for Justice, Equality and Law Reform & Ors* [2014] IEHC 133. In that judgment, Kearns P at p 24, having set out the definition of workplace bullying, stated:

> "This wording must be taken as requiring an objective test to determine if bullying has occurred. The test must, for reasons of common sense, also be an objective one given that any other would leave every defendant vulnerable to allegations of bullying based on purely subjective perceptions on the part of a plaintiff who might contend that straightforward situations at work or otherwise were construed by him/her as amounting to bullying."

15. The above followed a full quotation of the definition, including the reference to the "repeated inappropriate behaviour". Counsel for the defendant drew attention to an earlier comment by Kearns P at p 22 of his judgment in relation to bullying as being "conduct which is intended to reduce that person's self-worth". He suggested that this cast some doubt upon the question as to whether Kearns P intended that the question as to whether the relevant conduct constituted inappropriate behaviour for the purposes of definition also be objectively assessed. However, in the same judgment Kearns P at p 23, identified as the first question that must be asked in every bullying case, "… whether the behaviour complained of, by reference to an objective test, imports that degree of calibrated inappropriateness and repetition which differentiates bullying from workplace stress or occupational stress".

16. I am of the view that for the very reasons identified by Kearns P., not only must the question as to whether or not the inappropriate behaviour is such that it could reasonably be regarded as undermining the individual's right to dignity at work be objectively assessed, but the question as to whether the behaviour is inappropriate must also be objectively assessed. It does not appear to me that it could be either dependent upon a subjective perception by the plaintiff, or indeed dependent upon intent of the perpetrator. Such an approach would be inconsistent with objectively determining whether the inappropriate behaviour is such that it could reasonably be regarded as undermining the individual's right to dignity at work. If appropriateness or not of the behaviour is to be objectively determined, then the intent of the perpetrator becomes irrelevant.

17. Accordingly, I have concluded that a court must first assess whether the conduct or behaviour alleged is objectively to be considered as repeated inappropriate behaviour. If so it must then determine objectively whether it is reasonably to be regarded as undermining the individual's right to dignity at work …

22. There was some discussion in the course of oral submissions as to what were the essential elements of an employee's right to dignity at work. Counsel was unable to assist the Court with any authorities which have considered this issue in

the context of the definition of workplace bullying in the 2002 Order or otherwise. I am not aware of any consideration by a court which is of assistance. Again, it appears to me dangerous to attempt to provide a general definition of the elements which constitute a person's right to dignity at work. Rather the Court should look at this in the context of the facts of this appeal and in particular both the context in which the alleged inappropriate behaviour arose and the relationship between the plaintiff and the defendant and Principal of the school. Whereas on the facts of this case the Court is considering the right of the plaintiff as employee to dignity at work in a context of her treatment by the Principal of the school and the board of management in relation to a disciplinary process such right to dignity must include, it appears to me, a right to be treated with respect, fairly and not less favourably than other colleagues in a similar position. It must include a right not to be singled out for disciplinary treatment in relation to a practice which whilst not acceptable was engaged in by other similar colleagues. It is obvious that an employee must expect, in a situation where it is contended that his or her performance has been less than what is expected or required that she may be subjected to a disciplinary process. However, it appears to me that her right to dignity at work includes a right to be treated with respect and fairly in the above sense and not singled out unfairly from colleagues in a similar position in such disciplinary process …

64. In my view, it was open to the trial judge to make the findings made and he was correct in determining that there was repeated inappropriate behaviour by or on behalf of defendant, and objectively, it was behaviour which could reasonably be regarded as undermining the plaintiff's right to dignity at that work. As stated at the outset of this judgment, the right to dignity at work in the context of a potential disciplinary process includes a right to be treated with respect, fairly and not less favourable than colleagues in a similar position. Further, it must include a right not to be singled out for disciplinary treatment in relation to a practice, which whilst not acceptable, was engaged in by other similar colleagues. This was precisely the effect of the repeated inappropriate behaviour by the defendant both directly and through its Principal on the plaintiff having regard to the findings made by the trial judge.[12]

65. In reaching this conclusion, I fully recognise that the locking of the Sensory Room door was properly considered by the Board to be a serious child protection issue. However, the door was fitted with a lock; it was agreed that no instruction had been given to SNAs not to lock the door; the trial judge, held it was a common practice amongst SNAs to lock the door; also, that such contention was immediately made by the plaintiff to the Principal. He further held that the Principal, prior to presenting the matter immediately to the board of management on 23rd November, failed to conduct any inquiry amongst the other SNAs as to whether they did or did not have a practice of locking the Sensory Room door, but on 20th October, she considered it necessary to give a general direction to the SNAs not to lock the Sensory Room door. The presentation by the Principal to the Board of the issue as a disciplinary matter related to the plaintiff alone was, in my view, on all the facts held, objectively inappropriate behaviour. The inappropriate

---

12.   It was on this point that Finlay Geoghegan J differed from her colleagues with respect to the outcome.

behaviour was repeated in the pursuit by the Principal with the support of the Board, as recorded in the minutes of the meeting on 23rd November, of a severe disciplinary sanction against the plaintiff. The Board itself, in my view, was guilty of inappropriate behaviour in furnishing a letter in which they gave as the basis for the stage 4 warning being issued to the plaintiff to be "as a result of the investigation that was carried out at the request of the Board of management into an incident that on the 14th September, 2009 ..." when as held by the trial judge that was simply "not correct" as no such investigation was carried out. On the findings of the trial judge, the behaviour of the Principal during the meeting of 27th January 2010, with the plaintiff was inappropriate. Finally, there was, as determined by the judge, at a time when the Board were made aware of both the plaintiff's case and the fact that several other SNAs also occasionally locked the Sensory Room door, the rejection of the plaintiff's appeal without any meaningful consideration of the plaintiff's case and the subsequent failure and refusal by the Board in the autumn of 2010, when given a fresh opportunity to consider the merits of the plaintiffs' case at that late stage. The above repeated inappropriate behaviour is such that objectively it could reasonably be regarded as undermining the plaintiff's right to dignity at work.

66. Accordingly, I would dismiss the defendant's appeal against the conclusion reached on this issue by the trial judge.

[6.15] *Ruffley* confirms that an employee who suffers a recognisable psychiatric illness by reason of workplace bullying for which the employer is responsible will be entitled to damages for negligence. In that case it was clear that the actions complained of, those of the school principal and board of management, were the actions of the employer. No issue arose with regard to vicarious liability, as would arise if the putative wrongdoer was a peer, a non-employee or someone acting possibly without or beyond the authority of the employer.

Although each of the three components of workplace bullying was considered by the Court of Appeal in detail, a number of questions remain. They include: (a) the impact (if any) on each of the three components of a finding of improper motive (or intent or a lack of bona fides) on the part of the putative wrongdoer; and (b) the relevance to the second and third components of publication to others by the putative wrongdoer of the actions complained of as distinct from circumstances where others are not made aware of those actions. Finally, the dissenting judgment again makes clear the importance of consistency on the part of an employer in a disciplinary situation. See also in this context *The Governor and Company of the Bank of Ireland v Reilly*.[13]

See also *Stapleton v St Colman's (Claremorris) Credit Union Ltd*,[14] a High Court personal injuries action for occupational stress at **[18.02]**.

---

13. *The Governor and Company of the Bank of Ireland v Reilly* [2015] IEHC 241 and see **[27. 21]**.

14. *Stapleton v St Colman's (Claremorris) Credit Union Ltd* [2015] IEHC 510.

Chapter 7

EUROPEAN UNION LAW

POSTED WORKERS

[7.01] *Sähköalojen ammattiliitto ry v Elektrobudowa Spółka Akcyjna[1] —reference for preliminary ruling—CJEU—Treaty on the Functioning of the European Union, arts 56 and 57—Posted Workers Directive 96/71/EC, arts 3, 5 and 6[2]—workers in company in host Member State posted to carry out works in alternative Member State— minimum wage provided for by collective agreements of alternative Member State— locus standi of trade union with seat in alternative Member State—where Polish legislation[3] prohibits the assignment to third party of claims relating to pay*

Directive 96/71/EC obliges Member States of the EU to ensure that workers who are posted from one Member State to another Member State are entitled to certain minimum rights. The CJEU determined that the laws and agreements in respect of pay and conditions in the host Member State apply to posted workers and determined the allowances that constitute minimum rates of pay in the Directive.

The Finnish Courts requested a preliminary ruling over its interpretation of an issue arising in a case concerning SAR, a Finnish Trade Union, against ESA, an electric company established in Poland. SAR had claimed over €6,500,000 in minimum pay rates and allowances on behalf of Polish workers, employed by ESA and posted to ESA's branch in Finland, under various Finnish collective agreements.

The Finnish Court requested the CJEU to clarify whether SAR had the right to represent the workers, in direct contradiction of Polish law which prohibited the assignment of claims created by an employment relationship; and secondly, to clarify the relevant rates of minimum pay and other associated allowances such as day allowance, travel allowance and holiday allowance which must be paid.

The CJEU determined that SAR was entitled to bring the claims on behalf of the workers as Finnish law was applicable. The Directive prohibited the scenario whereby Polish workers, posted to Finland, were prevented from assigning wage claims to SAR because of a Polish law. Questions of minimum rates of pay were, according to the CJEU, to be governed by the relevant laws and agreements of the host Member State. The CJEU also considered elements of basic pay, such as basic hourly pay or guaranteed piecework pay, according to pay groups, holiday allowance, daily allowances, compensation for daily travelling time and reimbursement of accommodation costs. The CJEU noted that the Directive was implemented to create a climate of fair competition between national companies and companies posting workers to host Member States

---

1. *Sähköalojen ammattiliitto ry v Elektrobudowa Spółka Akcyjna* (Case C–396/13).
2. Directive 96/71/EC of the European Parliament and of the Council of 16 December 1996 concerning the posting of workers in the framework of the provision of services.
3. Polish Labour Code, Art 84.

from abroad, and also to ensure that minimum protections were available to all workers in a Member State, including those posted from another Member State. The CJEU noted that the Directive does not harmonise mandatory rules for minimum protection but does identify the laws of the host Member States to be applied. The CJEU referred to previous case law in which certain allowances and supplements were not viewed to be part of the minimum wage of the host Member State. The CJEU determined that the national courts must ultimately decide if the rules applied by a company to determine rates of pay in accordance with the laws of the host Member State are accessible and clear. The CJEU noted that the rules for calculating the minimum wage under any relevant collective agreements must be binding and transparent.

The CJEU concluded by clarifying a number of elements with regard to minimum rates of pay for posted workers including that the Directive does not preclude a calculation of the minimum wage for hourly work and/or for piecework which is based on the categorisation of employees into pay groups, as provided for by the relevant collective agreements of the host Member State; a daily allowance must be regarded as part of the minimum wage; compensation for daily travelling time, paid to workers on condition that their daily journey to and from their place of work is of more than one hour's duration, must be regarded as part of the minimum wage of posted workers (a matter for the national court to verify); coverage of the cost of posted workers' accommodation is not to be regarded as an element of their minimum wage; an allowance taking the form of meal vouchers provided to the posted workers is not to be regarded as part of the latter's minimum salary; and pay received by a posted worker for the minimum paid annual holidays corresponds to the minimum wage to which those workers are entitled during the applicable reference period.

See also decisions of the CJEU at **[8.06]**, **[19.02]**, **[19.03]**, **[23.19]**, **[23.20]**, **[23.21]** and **[26.01]**.

Chapter 8

FIXED-TERM WORKERS

ENTITLEMENT TO A CONTRACT OF INDEFINITE DURATION

[8.01] *Galway County Council v Canavan[1]—Labour Court—appeal from decision of Rights Commissioner—Protection of Employees (Fixed-Term Work) Act 2003—renewal of fixed-term contracts beyond statutory limit—objective justification—objective justification must be determined at commencement of disputed contract—inadequate link between public funding and specific nature of work performed—general/broad objective justification approach by employer is inconsistent with the 2003 Act and European case law*

This was an appeal by the respondent from a decision of the Rights Commissioner in which it was held that the complainant had acquired a contract of indefinite duration under s 9(2) of the 2003 Act. The complainant was employed by the respondent on a series of successive fixed-term contracts of employment commencing on 6 October 2005 as an engineer on capital works that were being undertaken in the respondent's Council area. On 1 July 2008, the respondent extended the complainant's fixed-term contract for a further period terminating on 31 December 2011. The respondent renewed the fixed-term contract again on 30 November 2010 until the relevant engineering works were substantially completed. The complainant was still employed by the respondent at the date of the hearing. The complainant stated that he had acquired a contract of indefinite duration under s 9(2) of the 2003 Act, on the renewal of his contract of employment on 1 July 2008 and that no sufficient objective justification for the renewal of his fixed term at that time existed. The respondent stated that the work he was employed to undertake was routine civil engineering work. He acknowledged that the funding for the work originated from a public capital programme but argued that capital engineering works were part of the ongoing functions of the respondent and that the sources or nature of a funding programme are not objective justifications for not providing him with a contract of indefinite duration. The respondent stated that capital projects were each discretely funded from the public capital programme and were not part of fixed and permanent needs. The respondent stated that when specific capital works were completed, the requirement for the services of the complainant would also cease. The respondent argued that the complainant was given a contract of employment for the expected duration of the capital works and when the completion date of the capital works was delayed, the respondent extended the complainant's contract until the relevant works would complete. The respondent stated that the complainant's employment was closely linked to the specific nature of the capital works and as a result, met the objective justification test required for renewing a fixed-term contract.

---

1. *Galway County Council v Canavan* FTD1513.

The Court referred to the components of 'objective justification' as set out by the CJEU in *Bilka-Kaufhaus GmbH v Weber von Hartz*[2] where the CJEU held that the test of objective justification is that the measure relied on must meet a 'real need' and must be 'appropriate' and 'necessary' for that purpose. The Court also referred to *Angelidaki & Ors v Organismos Nomarkhiaki Aftondiikisi Rethimnis and Dimos Geropotamou*[3] in which the CJEU referred to the concept of 'objective reasons' provided by previous European case law as referring to precise and concrete circumstances characterising a given activity, which are therefore capable, in that particular context, of justifying the use of successive fixed-term employment contracts. Such circumstances may result, in particular, from the specific nature of the tasks for the performance of which such contracts have been concluded and from the inherent characteristics of those tasks or, as the case may be, from pursuit of a legitimate social-policy objective of a Member State. The Court also referred to the decision in *Russell v Mount Temple Comprehensive School*[4] as a clear authority for the proposition that the existence of objective grounds justifying the renewal of a fixed-term contract is to be determined at the commencement of the specific contract in question.

The respondent contended that all posts in the local authority sector associated with capital projects are temporary by their definition. The Court did not however accept that such a broad approach could be consistent with the tests set out in the 2003 Act or by the CJEU. The Court stated that no legitimate objective of the employer could be met by such a blanket approach. The Court also stated that the respondent had failed to clarify how the use of fixed-term contracts of employment was appropriate and necessary for that purpose. The Court stated that in circumstances where the local authority was the medium through which successive engineering capital projects were carried out, it was difficult to determine how the use of successive fixed-term contracts of employment could be appropriate and necessary for the purpose of completing any one of the capital projects. The respondent relied on the nature of the funding for capital projects in support of the contention that it was legitimate to rely on the use of successive fixed-term contracts of employment. The Court stated that this was not determinative of the matter. The Court stated that the test was more extensive than funding alone and more specific than the general proposition as outlined by the respondent. The Court stated that if it accepted that funding was a factor that justified the use of successive fixed-term contracts of employment, it must then consider whether the activity being funded is such that it justifies the use of successive fixed-term contracts of employment. The Court found that the respondent carried out engineering capital projects on an ongoing basis and that the funding for those projects came from the same source as the funding of the other work of local authorities raised locally. The Court found that there was no distinguishing feature in the source and origin of the funding of capital projects that justified the different treatment of staff employed on those projects as compared to staff employed on other non-capital projects.

---

2. *Bilka-Kaufhaus GmbH v Weber von Hartz* (Case 170/84) ECR 1607.
3. *Angelidaki & Ors v Organismos Nomarkhiaki Aftondiikisi Rethimnis and Dimos Geropotamou* (Joined Cases C–378/07 to C–380/07), [2009] ECR 1–3071.
4. *Russell v Mount Temple Comprehensive School* [2009] IEHC 533 (per Hanna J).

The Court stated that no evidence had been presented that a legitimate social policy objective applied such as would justify the use of successive fixed-term contracts of employment beyond the statutory time limit. The Court found that nothing in the inherent characteristics of the tasks involved in the projects that gave rise to the successive fixed-term contract of employment warranted their continuation beyond the statutory limit. The Court held that the respondent had not advanced objective grounds for the use of successive fixed-term contracts beyond the statutory time limit set and found that the complainant was entitled to a contract of indefinite duration. The Court found that there was no merit in the provision of a financial award in this case.

[8.02] *O'Doherty v UCD[5]—Labour Court—appeal from decision of Rights Commissioner—Protection of Employees (Fixed-Term Work) Act 2003, s 15(1)— whether complainant entitled to contract of indefinite duration—whether participation in research careers framework an objective ground*

The complainant was first employed by the respondent in May 2009 as a postdoctoral researcher in the School of Agriculture, Food and Veterinary Medicine under to a fixed-term contract to expire on 30 October 2010 and was assigned to the 'markers of stress and aging in Bovine Oocyte' project. This was followed by a fixed-term contract from 1 December 2010 until 30 November 2012 as a postdoctoral fellow (level 1) assigned to the 'reproductive biology research cluster' project. The complainant was furnished with a further fixed-term contract which commenced on 1 December 2012 until 30 November 2013 as a postdoctoral fellow (level 2); again assigning him to the 'reproductive biology research cluster' project. When the latter contract expired it was not renewed. The complainant was paid a redundancy payment and issued with a P45. It was noted by the Labour Court that the complainant had subsequently been employed by the respondent's school of medicine and medical science; however that contract had no bearing on this case.

It was asserted by the complainant that, as the aggregate duration of his contracts of employment exceeded four years, he accrued an entitlement to a contract of indefinite duration on his third contract, ie 1 December 2012. He submitted that there were no objective grounds to justify his ongoing temporary employment and challenged the alleged objective grounds advanced by the respondent for the renewal when there was, and is, a clear need for his ongoing employment. It was submitted on behalf of the respondent that a key function of the respondent in common with other universities was to engage in and encourage research and to provide research opportunities for successive groups of postgraduate and post doctorate researchers. This was an object and function of the respondent under ss 12 and 13 of the Universities Act 1997. It was submitted that if a university was to make research opportunities available, it must be permitted to progress successive cohorts of students and researchers through the available research roles. It would be impossible to do this if universities were forced to employ those involved in research on projects of indefinite duration following the completion or discontinuation of the research project in which the student researcher or researcher was engaged.

---

5.   *O'Doherty v UCD* FTD159.

The respondent had developed a Research Careers Framework (RCF) for the purpose of achieving the objective of employing persons for research projects to adequately train and develop the postdoctoral researchers to progress to a role in academia, or often in the private commercial sector. It was submitted by the respondent that it was understood and recognised that the role of a postdoctoral researcher was not a career but was a training and development opportunity, which facilitated development and growth for those who participate. Evidence was submitted that the RCF was a research career structure with clear role definition as follows: the postdoctoral fellow was an on-the-job training role that lasted between four and six years and was divided into three phases PD1, PD2 and research fellow, which was a non-tenurable early-stage academic role providing the opportunity to pursue a specific project typically funded by the fellow. The respondent submitted that the PD1 and PD2 roles train and develop the researcher to progress to the position of research fellow which is generally the final stepping stone for the researcher before entering the formal academic structure or a highly specialised research role in industry.

In this case, the complainant worked from May 2009 until November 2010 as a postdoctoral researcher (pre-postdoctoral training programme mapped to PD1). He worked as a PD1 from December 2010 for a period of 24 months. In December 2012 his employment was extended for a period of 12 months when he worked as a PD2. On 30 November 2013 the complainant was deemed to have completed his PD2 training and his contract expired and was not renewed. The complainant was furnished with written contracts of employment, each of which specified the objective grounds underlying the fixed-term nature of the contract.

It was submitted that the complainant was not entitled to a contract of indefinite duration at the time asserted by him, as he was employed as a PD2 under the RCF. This provided him with formalised training and development opportunities to adequately prepare him for enduring roles, both in academia and also in the commercial sector, where highly qualified, skilled and trained graduates with PhDs and postgraduate training were highly marketable. These were put forward by the respondent as the objective ground underpinning the renewal of the complainant's employment on a fixed-term basis. It was submitted that these constituted legitimate objective grounds and there was no less onerous manner in which these objectives could be achieved. The respondent accepted that the complainant's fixed-term contracts exceeded four years; however, this was to enable him to fully engage and complete PD1 and PD2 of the RCF.

The complainant disputed the respondent's assertions regarding the RCF and suggested that it was not a career-enhancing framework; but a device to denigrate the job of being a researcher which was retrofitted to cases to justify the denial of rights by the respondent. The complainant contended that it could not be a legitimate objective of the employer to provide world-class research by means of temporary, insecure employment. He queried the length of training as provided for by the RCF (6–10 years) in addition to the time taken to achieve a doctorate and disputed that such a cumulative training period of 12–19 years could be 'legitimate', 'appropriate or necessary'.

Reference was made by the respondent to the leading judgment of the CJEU in *Adeneler & Ors v Ellinikos Organismos Galaktos,*[6] which is an authority on what

---

6.   *Adeneler & Ors v Ellinikos Organismos Galaktos* (Case C–212/04).

constitutes objective grounds justifying successive renewals of fixed-term contracts. Two further Labour Court cases were cited by the respondent in support of its position. In *University College Cork v O'Riordan*[7] the Labour Court held:

> that the Court accepts that it is an entirely legitimate objective of the [University] to use fixed-term contracts to provide graduates with access to research opportunities and that they are entirely appropriate and necessary for that purpose.

In *University College Dublin v O'Mahony*[8] the Court held that:

> it would seem that if, in reality, a university has a properly structured scheme in place whereby graduates are provided with post-doctoral training or development opportunities, and that certain research work is reserved to participants in such programmes, the use of fixed-term contracts for the duration of the scheme would be unobjectionable.

It was submitted by the respondent that the Labour Court's view on postdoctoral training and development as expressed in these two cases should be adopted in the present case by upholding the RCF as a legitimate objective ground.

The Court considered evidence given to the Court by senior academics in the School of Agriculture and Food Science on behalf of the respondent and by the complainant himself. The Labour Court recited the relevant statutory provisions in ss 7, 8 and 9 of the 2003 Act. The Labour Court noted there was a wealth of authority in the jurisprudence of the CJEU on how the concept of objective justification should be applied. However, in *Adeneler*,[9] the CJEU had made it clear that the grounds relied on must be objectively justified by reference to the work actually performed and the circumstances under which it is performed. The Court noted the distinction drawn by the CJEU in *Adeneler* and also in *Kiriaki*[10] between work undertaken for the purpose of meeting the fixed and permanent needs of the employer and work for the purpose of meeting some temporary transient need. While work in the former category should normally be undertaken on permanent contracts of employment, temporary or fixed-term contracts would normally be suitable for work in the latter categories.

In this case the Court noted that the respondent's reliance on s 9(4) was grounded on the premise that the complainant's third contract was for the purpose of completing a PD2 role as provided for within its RCF, which was a structured research skills and career development programme for postdoctoral researchers. The complainant did not accept that he was employed on foot of such a programme but asserted instead that he was employed as one of the respondent's fixed and permanent research needs.

The Court noted that whether or not the complainant was in fact on such a structured programme was a question of fact which could only be established by evidence. The Court noted that the respondent had submitted extensive documentation outlining details of the research careers framework. The Labour Court noted that the respondent had initiated the research careers project in January 2008, to begin the process of

---

7. *University College Cork v O'Riordan* FTD1116.
8. *University College Dublin v O'Mahony* FTD1234.
9. *Adeneler & Ors v Ellinikos Organismos Galaktos* (Case C–212/04).
10. *Angelidaki & Ors v Organismos Nomarkhiaki Aftodiikisi Rethimnis and Dimos Geropotamou* (Case C–380/07).

implementing a clear career path to enable the development of research capability and transferable skills for the postdoctoral community within the respondent. The framework for this project was implemented over a period of two years.

Having considered the submissions of the parties along with the witness evidence, the Court noted that the complainant's fixed-term contract from 1 December 2012 stated it was a training and development role, which would be completed within the period of the contract. He was assigned to a specific programme of research under the supervision of a principal investigator, which was limited in duration to the 30 November 2013. The contract stated that the objective justification relied upon was to provide postdoctoral research training opportunities of limited duration. The contract stated:

> this will allow for progression over many years, of large numbers of postdoctoral trainees through the postdoctoral training programme providing intergenerational training in the methods and practice of research and scholarship. The objective grounds for the issue of this fixed-term contract rather than a permanent contract is in keeping with the forgoing objectives of the University. The contract aligns to the UCD Postdoctoral Research Fellow—Level 2 within Postdoctoral training programmes. It is intended that you will be assigned to reproductive biology research cluster project and it is intended that the project will end on the 30 November 2013. Should that project end prior to that date UCD reserves the right to terminate your employment with UCD by giving not less than one months' notice in writing.

The contract stated that the complainant should actively and fully engage in the career and skills development process which supported the training and developmental nature of the role. Documentation was submitted to the Labour Court by the respondent outlining the UCD research skills and career development programme which came under the auspices of the RCF. It established a structured and supportive skills and early career development model for postdoctoral research fellows level 1 and 2 at UCD and gave access to opportunities targeted towards developing their skills and career requirements. Documentation was also submitted to the Court listing an extensive list of professional courses/workshops geared towards postdoctoral researchers which were run by the respondent between November 2010 and January 2014. By the date of the claim the respondent had organised over 120 of these courses and workshops covering four development areas, research, research management, personal and professional excellence, teaching, learning and mentoring and innovation and transferable skills.

The Court noted that it must be careful to satisfy itself that the complainant was in fact not used to meet the fixed and permanent needs of the respondent in terms of the employment of research staff. The Labour Court noted the decision of the CJEU in *Samohano v University Pompu Fabra*[11] where the Court held that:

> the renewal of the successive fixed-term employment contracts issue was actually intended to cover temporary needs and that roles such as those at issue in the main proceedings were not in fact used to meet fixed and permanent needs in terms of employment of teaching staff.

---

11.   *Samohano v University Pompu Fabra* (Case C–190/32).

The Labour Court concluded that the purpose of the respondent's RCF was to enhance the research skills and career development of postdoctoral researchers and was a genuine requirement of the university. The conclusion of fixed-term contracts in those circumstances can be justified on objective grounds, notwithstanding that the work to which the contract relates forms part of the employer's fixed and permanent needs.

Based on the witness evidence coupled with the extensive documentation furnished to the Court on the respondent's RCF, the Labour Court was satisfied that the complainant was engaged on a structural postdoctoral development programme designed to enhance his research skills and career prospects. The Court based its conclusion on the following facts:

- The renewal of the complainant's contract of employment on 1 December 2012 stated that it was a training and development role and that the training would be completed within the period of the contract.

- The respondent had a formal scheme in place whereby postdoctoral research fellows levels 1 and 2 are provided with postdoctoral training and development opportunities and certain research work is assigned to participants in the programme.

- The contract stated that it was a condition of the complainant's employment that he should actively and fully engage in the career and skills development process supporting the training and development nature of this role.

- The purpose of the contract was in line with the respondent's objective to provide the complainant with a postdoctoral research training opportunity and it supplied him with details of his principal investigator.

- It was clear, from the contents of the complainant's application letter for the research fellow position which he applied for in September 2013, that the skills referred to in evidence were indeed acquired by the complainant during his employment as a postdoctoral researcher.

- It was not disputed that the complainant obtained opportunities, skills and recognition as part of the postdoctoral development programme.

- As part of the career and skills development process the respondent organised numerous courses and workshops designed to enhance the complainant's research skills and career prospects which the complainant chose not to attend.

- The complainant's contract of renewal in December 2012 was in accordance with the respondent's RCF objective of ensuring that the time taken to develop necessary skills after completion of his PhD was in line with the typical length of time, ie four years, for those in the sciences.

- The complainant's employment in November 2013 expired in line with the terms of his fixed-term contract and he was made redundant.

- The Code of Conduct for the Recruitment of Researchers, published by the European Commission in 2005 and adopted by the respondent, states that institutions appointing postdoctoral researchers must provide clear rules and explicit guidelines for the recruitment of postdoctoral researchers and states:

> Postdoctoral status should be transitional with the primary purpose of providing additional professional and development opportunities for a research career in the context of long term career prospects.

The Labour Court concluded that the statement of objective grounds in the complainant's renewed contract of employment referring to the provision of intergenerational training for postdoctoral trainees discloses a justification based on objective and transparent criteria, as envisaged by the CJEU in that it identified a legitimate aim which the respondent was seeking to pursue and offered an explanation why he was not being offered a contract of indefinite duration.

These grounds relied upon by the respondent were communicated to the complainant at the time and accordingly it was apt to infer that they were in the contemplation of the respondent at the material time. The Court believed that such an inference was just and equitable in the circumstances. The Court noted *UCD v O'Mahony*[12] where the Court held that:

> It would seem that if, in reality, a university has a properly structured scheme in place whereby graduates are provided with postdoctoral training or development opportunities and that certain research work is reserved to participants in such a programme, the use of fixed-term contracts for the duration of the scheme would be unobjectionable.

In this case, the Court was satisfied that the respondent had in place such a scheme and therefore the Court accepted that the renewal of the complainant's fixed-term contract for a period of one year was appropriate to achieve the objective pursued and was necessary for that purpose. The Court concluded that s 9(3) of the Act did not apply to the renewal and the complaint was not well founded. The decision of the Rights Commissioner was affirmed and the appeal was disallowed.

[8.03] *University of Limerick v Haverty*[13]*—Labour Court—appeal from decision of Rights Commissioner—Protection of Employees (Fixed-Term Work) Act 2003, s 9—successive fixed-term contracts—entitlement to contract of indefinite duration—whether objective grounds existed justifying renewal of complainant's fixed-term contracts—whether specified purpose contract fulfilled real, fixed and permanent need of respondent or whether need could be said to be temporary and transient*

The complainant appealed the decision of a Rights Commissioner that objective conditions existed justifying the renewal of his fixed-term contracts by the respondent, who had declined to issue him with a contract of indefinite duration.

The complainant was employed with the respondent on a series of fixed-term contracts, the first of which commenced on 1 December 2008 (the first contract). The first contract was a specified purpose contract, the specified purpose of which was work

---

12.   *UCD v O'Mahony* FTD1234.
13.   *University of Limerick v Haverty* FTD158.

on a particular project in the role of a postdoctoral researcher in process chemistry in the respondent's Department of Chemical and Environmental Studies. The complainant resigned from the first contract on 30 September 2009, two months ahead of when it had been envisaged that it would terminate. The complainant proceeded to apply for the position of Senior Research Fellow with the respondent, which position had been externally advertised on the terms of a specified purpose contract. He was successful in his application and commenced this specified purpose contract (the second contract) on 1 October 2009. The specific purpose of the second contract was stated to be work on a European project entitled 'Hydrolysis of Lignocellulosic Waste' (the European Project). The second contract was due to expire on 31 December 2012. However, due to additional funding secured from the European Union, it was extended until 31 March 2013 (the third contract). The complainant's employment with the respondent terminated on 31 March 2013 accordingly.

A preliminary issue arose as to whether the complainant's continuity of service was broken when he resigned from the first contract in 2009. The Labour Court sought additional information from both the complainant and the respondent on this issue. It was held that the complainant's continuity of service had not been broken in the circumstances.

The complainant submitted that he became entitled to a contract of indefinite duration at the time of the expiration of the second contract on 31 December 2012, at which point he had been employed on two specific-purpose contracts for a term in excess of four years. The complainant continued to work after 31 December 2012, having been informed that his contract was being extended until 31 March 2013. The complainant submitted that there had been no objective grounds to justify the renewal of the complainant's employment on a temporary basis. The respondent denied that the complainant was entitled to a contract of indefinite duration. It was submitted by the respondent that the complainant had been engaged for a specific purpose, ie completion of specific work on the European Project, which had been scheduled to conclude at the end of 2012. The only reason that the complainant's contract was extended until 31 March 2013 was the provision of extra funding from the European Union. This additional funding was provided to the respondent when it transpired that another university participant of the European Project was unable to complete certain elements of the European Project that had originally been assigned to it. The respondent was asked to take on this work, which was essential for the completion of the European Project, and was provided with additional funding in relation to same. This important work was allocated to the complainant, due to his specialist skill and knowledge.

The respondent argued that the complainant had at all times been aware that the European Project was due to finish on 31 December 2012 and that the additional funding extended it until 31 March 2013 only. It was further argued that the complainant had been aware of the terms upon which he was engaged, ie the specific purpose of the second contract.

It was submitted by the respondent that objective grounds existed which justified the renewal of the complainant's contract on a temporary basis. By way of background, the respondent explained the way in which international multi-participant projects operate in universities. A university research group generally participates in a project by working on a specific aspect of that project in respect of which they have particular expertise. A specific skill set and knowledge level was required for the role the complainant occupied on the terms of the second contract. The respondent stressed the importance of being able to engage employees with the relevant competencies to constitute a 'match' for each project.

The respondent relied on the Labour Court's decision in *National University of Ireland v Buckley*,[14] which also related to a third-party-funded research project in a university environment. The university in that case agreed to host the complainant for the purposes of the completion of a third-party-funded research project. The complainant was employed on a succession of fixed-term contracts for this purpose. The complainant claimed an entitlement to a contract of indefinite duration after the expiration of four years. The complainant's contract contained a clause which stated that the renewal of her employment on a temporary basis was justified by the fact that further temporary work had become available and that funding was available to support her work. The Court concluded that this provision was clear that further fixed-term work, and not a contract of indefinite duration, was being offered. It held that, as the complainant had signed the contract agreeing to the objective reasons for its renewal on a fixed-term basis, it was not open to her to resile subsequently from this position. Therefore she was not entitled to a contract of indefinite duration.

The respondent also addressed the requirement to determine the validity of objective grounds. The three-tier test for objective discrimination in indirect gender discrimination cases formulated by the CJEU in *Bilka-Kaufhaus GmbH v Weber von Hartz*[15] was cited. It was submitted that the respondent satisfied each limb of that test. Firstly, the respondent had a real need to employ a senior research fellow for the purposes of the European Project. Secondly, the issuing of a specific-purpose contract (and not a contract of indefinite duration) was entirely appropriate in circumstances where the European Project was originally scheduled to run for a period of 42 months, and had only been funded by the European Commission up to this point. Thirdly, the issuing of a specific-purpose contract to the complainant was necessary, ie there were no other means by which the respondent's objective could have been achieved.

The respondent referred to *Adeneler & Ors v Ellinikos Organismos Galaktos*[16] and *Kucuk v Land Nordrhein-Westfalen*.[17] In *Adeneler* the CJEU held that the concept of 'objective reasons' had to be understood to mean the precise and concrete circumstances characterising a given activity, which were therefore capable in that particular context of justifying the use of successive fixed-term employment contracts. With regard to *Kucuk*, the CJEU held that the Framework Agreement did not lay down a general obligation on Member States to provide for the conversion of fixed-term contracts into contracts of indefinite duration.

The Labour Court considered that the relevant statutory provisions were to be found in ss 7, 8 and 9 of the 2003 Act. It further noted that, as the Act was enacted to transpose

---

14.   *National University of Ireland v Buckley* FTD092.
15.   *Bilka-Kaufhaus GmbH v Weber von Hartz* (Case C–170/84).
16.   *Adeneler & Ors v Ellinikos Organismos Galaktos* (Case C–212/04).
17.   *Kucuk v Land Nordrhein-Westfalen* [2012] IRLR 697; ECJ (Case C–586/10).

the Framework Agreement into domestic law, its provisions must be interpreted and applied so as to achieve the objective pursued by the Framework Agreement. It was considered that the Framework Agreement served a dual purpose. Its first objective was to improve the quality of fixed-term work by applying the principle of equal treatment to fixed-term workers. Secondly, it was intended to provide a framework for the prevention of abuse arising from the successive use of fixed-term employment contracts.

It was noted by the Labour Court that cl 5 of the Framework Agreement was not directed at limiting the use of fixed-term contracts *per se*. Rather, it was intended to prevent the abuse of successive fixed-term contracts. What exactly constitutes abuse was left to the Member States to decide. As ss 8 and 9 of the Act were intended to give effect to cl 5 of the Framework Agreement, they must be interpreted and applied so as to achieve the objective pursued by the Framework Agreement.

Section 9(3) of the Act was considered by the Labour Court to be of particular relevance in this case. It was noted that Laffoy J had, in *Minister for Finance v McArdle*,[18] quoted with approval a passage from the determination of the Labour Court in which the effects of s 9(3) of the Act were considered. Laffoy J held s 9(3) rendered void *ab initio* the term of the contract which purported to provide for its expiry by the effluxion of time or the occurrence of a specified event. The offending term would be severed from the rest of the contract by operation of law, altering its character to one of indefinite duration.

The Labour Court considered that s 9(4) of the Act takes effect at the commencement of the impugned contract, as per Hanna J in *Russell v Mount Temple Comprehensive School*,[19] and that this could have the effect of transmuting a fixed-term contract to one of indefinite duration before the expiry of the duration referred to in either s 9(1) or 9(2). In relation to s 9(4) it was considered that, as the provision allows derogation from what is an important social right derived from European Union law, it must be construed and applied strictly. It was therefore for the party relying on the statutory defence to prove the facts necessary to make out that defence.

The Labour Court held that in this case it was clear from the second contract that it was a specified purpose contract for the purpose of working on the European Project. The grant agreement for the European Project outlined that it was expected to complete in 42 months. It was further held that the job description provided to the complainant in relation to the second contract was clear that the contract was for a specified purpose only. It was also clear from the complainant's application letter that when he applied for the second contract in 2009 he was fully aware of the nature of the role for which he was applying and that it was for a specified purpose only. The Labour Court concluded that, as in *Buckley*,[20] it was satisfied that the complainant at all times understood the nature of his contractual relationship with the respondent. He was at all times aware that it was never intended that the research position would be available indefinitely. The Labour Court further noted that while it must be satisfied that objective grounds exist justifying

18. *Minister for Finance v McArdle* [2007] 18 ELR 165.
19. *Russell v Mount Temple Comprehensive School* [2009] IEHC 533.
20. *National University of Ireland v Buckley* FTD092.

the successive renewal of fixed-term contracts, there was no dispute that this contract was a stand-alone contract.

Importantly, the Labour Court held that it must determine whether the work for which the complainant was employed pursuant to the second contract should be properly classified as coming within the fixed and permanent needs of the respondent, or whether it was part of a purely temporary or transient need. It held that it was clear that the European Project was a stand-alone project rather than forming part of a continuum of similar projects which could be regarded as meeting the respondent's permanent needs.

Accordingly, the Labour Court was satisfied that the objective grounds advanced by the respondent as constituting the grounds relied upon at the time the second contract was entered into met the three-tier test for objective justification formulated in *Bilka-Kaufhaus*. Employing the complainant for his specialist skills and expertise on a specified purpose contract to undertake and complete the European Project (which was temporary in nature) met the precise and concrete circumstances of the respondent to complete the specific nature of the task at the time and was not for the purposes of meeting the fixed and permanent needs of the respondent. As was the case in *Buckley*, the complainant, having applied for and accepted a contract agreeing to the objective reasons for its renewal on a fixed-term basis, cannot resile from this position and seek a contract of indefinite duration.

For the sake of completeness, the Labour Court also examined the renewal of the complainant's fixed-term contract from 1 January 2013 for a period of three months, ie the third contract. It was held that this renewal was justified by objective grounds. The respondent had a real need to retain the complainant, with his specialist skill and knowledge, to undertake the remaining work on the European Project, ie the project for which he was employed.

The Labour Court observed that the respondent's employment came to an end in circumstances amounting to a redundancy. He became entitled to a redundancy lump sum in March 2013 and remains so entitled.

The Court concluded that there were objective grounds justifying the renewal of the complainant's employment for a fixed-term on both 1 October 2009 and 1 January 2013. Accordingly s 9(3) of the Act did not apply to those renewals. The decision of the Rights Commissioner was upheld.

[8.04] *Health Service Executive v Doherty[21]—High Court—Noonan J—appeal on point of law from determination of Labour Court—Protection of Employees (Fixed-Term Work) Act 2003, ss 8(4), 9(4) and 15(6)—entitlement to contract of indefinite duration—whether appellant successfully demonstrated objective grounds justifying renewal of respondent's fixed-term contract—extent of High Court's jurisdiction—High Court has no authority to interfere with findings of fact*

The respondent consultant anaesthetist was employed continuously by the appellant on a series of fixed-term contracts over a five-year period from 9 June 2008 until 31 May 2013. The respondent argued that she was entitled to a contract of indefinite duration, as

---

21.   *Health Service Executive v Doherty* [2015] IEHC 611.

the appellant had failed to provide her with a written statement of the objective grounds justifying the renewal of her fixed-term contracts for a period in excess of four years. This is required by s 9 of the Protection of Employees (Fixed-Term Work) Act 2003 (the 2003 Act).

Although the claim was rejected by a Rights Commissioner on the basis that there had been no breach of s 9 of the 2003 Act, the Labour Court determined that the respondent was entitled to a contract of indefinite duration and that her employment with the appellant should be reinstated by operation of law. This case was the appellant's appeal to the High Court on a point of law under s 15(6) of the 2003 Act.

Noonan J laid out the pertinent facts in this matter as follows. The specified purpose of the respondent's original fixed-term contract was the filling of another consultant anaesthetist's post during her period of special leave. When this other consultant anaesthetist resigned, the specified purpose of the respondent's subsequent fixed-term contracts became the replacement of the consultant anaesthetist. Two of these fixed-term contracts stated that the respondent was not being offered a contract of indefinite duration as the appellant was proceeding to fill the post through the Public Appointments Service, as required in relation to all permanent employment consultant posts in the HSE.

In its determination, the Labour Court had noted that, in order to make out a defence under s 9(4) of the 2003 Act, the employer must prove each and every element of the defence and must show that objective grounds existed justifying the renewal of the fixed-term contract. Furthermore, it accepted the proposition that the filling of a vacant consultant position in a public hospital was a legitimate need of the appellant and reliance on open competition in order to secure the best available candidate was an appropriate way to achieve that end. The Labour Court held in the respondent's favour on the basis of an offer letter from the appellant to the respondent dated 15 February 2013 (the first February letter), which it held created a contract of indefinite duration. The first February letter partially sought to cover the period from 1 April 2012 to 31 May 2013, ie most of the time which it sought to cover had already elapsed. The Labour Court held that this letter triggered s 9 of the Act, which automatically converted the respondent's contract into a contract of indefinite duration when the appellant failed to meet the 2003 Act's requirement to show objective grounds justifying the renewal of a fixed-term contract.

The Labour Court's reasoning was threefold. Firstly, the first February letter was silent as to the filling of the permanent consultant post. It also did not provide that the respondent's position would be terminated upon that position being filled. Secondly, even if the letter had done so, it purported to cover a period of employment of which part had already elapsed and therefore the notice of the objective grounds would not have come before the renewal, as is required by the 2003 Act. Thirdly, the subsequent offer letter from the appellant to the respondent dated 19 February 2013 (the second February letter), which provided that the respondent's fixed-term post would expire when the position was permanently filled, never came into force as there was no evidence that the respondent had accepted it. The Labour Court considered that a contract of indefinite duration had already been in effect since the first February letter.

The appellant's case was that the Labour Court had erred in law in arriving at its determination. The appellant submitted that the first February letter was issued as a mistake and instead should have been issued as a cover letter to the second February letter. The appellant relied on *HSE v Sallam*[22] in arguing that the Labour Court had erred in effectively ignoring the course of dealing between the parties, in addition to previous correspondence which demonstrated clearly the continuing objective justification for the renewal of the respondent's fixed-term contract. The appellant submitted that this objective justification was 'on all fours' with one previously accepted as coming within the meaning of s 9(4) of the 2003 Act in *HSE v Umar*,[23] ie the need for temporary cover pending the appointment of a permanent consultant to the post. The appellant argued that the Labour Court had erred in confining its consideration to the first February letter, which had been issued by mistake. It argued that the Labour Court failed to take into account the subsequent second February letter.

The respondent's case was that none of the alleged errors of law cited by the appellant was in fact an error of law. Instead, they were findings of fact with which the High Court could not interfere on appeal. Section 15(6) of the Act was relied on by the respondent in this regard. In particular, the respondent argued that the Labour Court's determination that the respondent's contract was governed by the terms of the first February letter was a finding of fact which could not be disturbed in a statutory appeal of this nature.

In relation to the appellant's submission that the issuing of the first February letter was a mistake and that it was intended to be a cover letter to the second February letter, Noonan J held that this was not an argument that could be considered by the High Court. The reason for this was that it was based on evidence that had never been put to the Labour Court.

Next Noonan J considered the extent of the High Court's jurisdiction to interfere with the determination of the Labour Court on a point of fact or a point of law. He commented that 'this Court is confined to considering points of law only and whether an identifiable error of law was made by the Labour Court in reaching its determination'.

Noonan J referred to the established rule that the High Court must have regard to the doctrine of curial deference when considering appeals from the decisions of expert administrative tribunals and quasi-judicial bodies as set out by Hamilton CJ in *Henry Denny & Sons (Ireland) Ltd v Minister for Social Welfare*.[24] Noonan J noted that this meant he could not revisit findings of fact made by the Labour Court, unless they could be shown to have been unsupported by any evidence or to be irrational or unreasonable in light of the evidence before the High Court. The judge cited *Ryanair Ltd v Flynn*,[25] *Earagail Eisc Teoranta v Doherty & Ors*[26] and *Mulcahy v Minister for Justice Equality*

---

22.   *HSE v Sallam* [2014] IEHC 298.
23.   *HSE v Umar* [2011] IEHC 146.
24.   *Henry Denny & Sons (Ireland) Ltd v Minister for Social Welfare* [1998] 1 IR 34.
25.   *Ryanair Ltd v Flynn* [2000] 3 IR 240.
26.   *Earagail Eisc Teoranta v Doherty & Ors* [2015] IEHC 347.

and Law Reform & Anor[27] as cases in recent years which have upheld this principle of curial deference.[28]

The judge then focused on applying the principle of curial deference to the facts of the present case. Noonan J commented that the central feature of the Labour Court's determination was that the respondent's contractual relationship was governed by the first February letter and not by the second February letter. In making this determination, Noonan J considered that the Labour Court had expressly recognised that the existence of objective grounds justifying the renewal of a fixed-term contract was to be judged at the commencement of the impugned contract, in accordance with the High Court decision in *Russell v Mount Temple Comprehensive School.*[29] Noonan J noted the appellant's contention that the evidence put before the Labour Court was all in its favour on this point and that this evidence should have led to a finding in its favour. On the other hand, Noonan J took account of the evidence of the respondent that her role was not tied to the filling of the permanent vacancy created by the resignation of the other consultant anaesthetist, in particular on account of the fact that she carried out some different functions. In this way the respondent argued that the objective ground relied upon by the appellant was not in reality the true ground underlying the successive renewals of her contract. On the basis of this evidence Noonan J held that it could not be said that there was no basis upon which the Labour Court could have come to the conclusion that it did. Noonan J opined that the Labour Court could have accepted the respondent's submission as stated above. The Labour Court may then have drawn an inference under s 8(4) of the Act that the failure to state objective grounds was consistent with the fact that there were none, having regard to all the evidence. It may have considered that the second February letter represented a change of heart on behalf of the appellant. It may therefore have concluded, upon consideration of the evidence as a whole, that the appellant had failed to discharge its burden to prove each and every element of the defence under s 9(4) of the Act. It could not be said that this conclusion was unsustainable on the evidence, nor was it one which no reasonable person could have reached.

Noonan J considered that this approach was consistent with the views of Baker J in *Sallam.* That case, which involved facts similar to the present one (including appeal to the High Court on a point of law), was decided on the basis of the Labour Court's finding that the specified purpose had not been stated before the relevant contract had been entered into. Accordingly the Labour Court had drawn an inference that reasons 'were not in contemplation of the respondent at the material times'. The High Court in *Sallam* held that this was a finding of fact with which it could not interfere.

While Noonan J acknowledged that 'significant factual similarities' existed between this case and *HSE v Umar*, he concluded that the decision in *Umar* was of little assistance to the appellant in the present appeal, as that case involved an 'erroneous and impermissible attempt' by the Labour Court to amend statute.

---

27. *Mulcahy v Minister for Justice Equality and Law Reform & Anor* [2002] 13 ELR 12.
28. For further discussion on the doctrine of curial deference, see **CH 33**.
29. *Russell v Mount Temple Comprehensive School* [2009] IEHC 533.

Noonan J held that he was satisfied that the determination of the Labour Court in this case, that the respondent's contract was governed by the terms of the first February letter, was a finding of fact with which he could not interfere. He held that the Labour Court had correctly considered that the onus rested upon the appellant to make out each and every element of the defence provided for in s 9(4) of the Act that there were objective grounds justifying the renewal of the respondent's fixed-term contract. The Labour Court had been of the view that the appellant had failed to discharge this onus. This was a finding of fact which the High Court held it had no authority to interfere with. The appellant's appeal was accordingly refused.

TERMS OF A CONTRACT OF INDEFINITE DURATION

[8.05] *Kerry County Council v Walsh & Ors[30]—Labour Court—appeal from decision of Rights Commissioner—Protection of Employees (Fixed-Term Work) Act 2003— where complainants were entitled to contracts of indefinite duration—what are the applicable terms in a contract of indefinite duration[31]*

The Labour Court noted that originally there was an issue between the parties as to the employment status of the complainants and whether or not they had *locus standi* to bring proceedings under the 2003 Act. The respondent had contended that the complainants were not fixed-term employees within the statutory meaning as they were permanent seasonal workers. The complainants contended they were fixed-term employees at all material times. A case management conference was convened by the Labour Court to clarify points of contention in the case. At that stage, the Court noted that the question of the complainants' *locus standi* and entitlement to a contract of indefinite duration was no longer an issue and that it had been accepted by the respondent that all of the complainants were entitled to contracts of indefinite duration. The Court noted that the overriding issue between the parties related to the terms of contracts of indefinite duration to which the complainants were entitled and also the quantum of compensation.

The Labour Court noted that the complainants were employed by the respondent on seasonal contracts and were placed on a panel from which workers were drawn from time to time to augment the respondent's full-time staff. The duration of each assignment was determined by the work requirements of the respondent but historically the panels had a predetermined life span and on the expiry of this they were reconstituted. Each period of employment was treated as a period of fixed-term employment and the period of inactivity between such periods was regarded by the parties as a period of layoff since the complainants' placement on the panel created a

---

30. *Kerry County Council v Walsh & Ors* FTD154.
31. The complainants instituted separate individual claims which were heard together by a Rights Commissioner and seven separate decisions were issued. As the issues in all seven claims were identical, they were conjoined by the Labour Court for the purpose of this appeal.

realistic expectation that they would be later recalled when the need for further assignment arose. Thus the Court noted that the continuity of the complainants' employment was preserved as per the First Schedule of the Minimum Notice and Terms of Employment Acts 1973 to 2005.

In the claims before the Rights Commissioner, the complainants had contended that they were entitled to contracts of indefinite duration which provided them with permanent full-time employment. This claim was modified and subsequently, before the Labour Court, the complainants contended an entitlement to contracts of indefinite duration that specified the duration of the employment that they would be offered each year. The respondent contended that the contracts of indefinite duration to which the complainants were entitled should correspond in every respect (except in relation to tenure) to the fixed-term contracts from which they were derived, that is, they should provide the complainants with employment as permanent seasonal workers whose hours and duration of each assignment would be dictated by the respondent's work requirements and the necessity to augment its full-time staff.

The Labour Court noted the starting point for considering the form and content of a contract of indefinite duration that comes into being by operation of s 9(3) of the 2003 Act was defined in the judgment of Laffoy J in the *Minister for Finance v McArdle*,[32] where Laffoy J held that:

> … the expression of contract of indefinite duration should be understood in contra distinction to a contract of definite or a fixed-term contract. The terms and conditions of a contract of indefinite duration which comes into being by operation of s 9(3) must therefore be the same as those in the fixed-term contract from which it is derived, as modified by s 6, in all respects other than its fixed duration. Obviously these terms will vary from one employment to another and every case will be decided mainly on its own facts …

The Labour Court noted that the central finding in that case was that where a fixed-term contract is transmuted to one of indefinite duration by operation of law, the resulting contract has the same terms as that from which it is derived, save in respect of tenure. The Court noted that the decision of Laffoy J in *McArdle* had already been applied by the Labour Court in *Beary v Revenue Commissioners*.[33] The Court also noted the decision of the High Court in *Holland v Athlone Institute of Technology*[34] where Hogan J pointed out that finding that an employee acquired a contract of indefinite duration by operation of law does not place such an employee in a superior position to that of an ordinary employee whose status as the holder of a contract of indefinite duration was never in doubt.

The Court noted that at all material times the complainants' employment with the respondent was for a season and in that regard they were required to work less hours than a comparable full-time employee when measured over a period of up to 12 months. Hence, the contracts of indefinite duration that came into being, by operation of s 9(3)

32. *Minister for Finance v McArdle* [2007] 18 ELR 165.
33. *Beary v Revenue Commissioners* [2001] 22 ELR 137.
34. *Holland v Athlone Institute of Technology* [2012] 23 ELR 1.

of the 2003 Act, were seasonal in nature. Those contracts did not entitle the complainants to any fixed or predetermined amount of work in any year. Rather the employment to which they were contractually entitled was determined entirely by the exigencies of the respondent's requirements to augment the work of its full-time staff. If, as was contended by the complainants, the only type of contract of indefinite duration to which they could become entitled by operation of law was one that provided them with an entitlement to a fixed or defined period of employment in each year, this would amount to a significantly superior contractual arrangement than that which was provided by the contracts from which they were derived.

The Court held that if the complainants were correct in their assertion that any contract of indefinite duration must provide them with definite periods of employment each year there would appear to be clear objective grounds for not providing them with such a contract and this conclusion arose from the basis of their employment, which was to meet the intermittent or seasonal needs of the respondent, the duration of which was incapable of precise ascertainment. The Court held that, based on the authorities, the outcome contended for by the complainants was not sustainable in law. It followed that the respondent was not obliged to provide the complainants with the contractual entitlement to any definitively prescribed number of hours or periods of employment. The only entitlement that they could claim under the 2003 Act was to such hours of work and such assignments as were determined on the same basis as the fixed-term contracts under which they were employed at the time the claims were initiated. The Labour Court referred to the CJEU judgment in *Huet v Universite de Bretagne Occidentale*[35] where the CJEU held that the contract of indefinite duration must be in identical terms to the principal clauses set out in the previous contract from which they derived, unless there are grounds for not doing so; and must not be accompanied by material amendments to the clauses of the previous contract in a way that is overall unfavourable to the person concerned, when the subject matter of that person's tasks and the nature of his functions remain unchanged.

The only practical advantage that could accrue to the complainants by reason of the statutorily acquired status as permanent employees of the respondent was that they would remain on the panel for an indefinite duration at their current ranking, without the need to periodically reapply for inclusion on the panel.

The Court noted that the complainants had also alleged contraventions of ss 6 and 10 of the 2003 Act. These were, in the Court's view, overlapping claims as they each related to the filling of certain permanent posts by the respondent. The complainants contended that the respondent confirmed eligibility to apply for posts to permanent employees thus denying the complainants the opportunity to obtain permanent full-time employment. The complainants contended that this contravened ss 6 and 10 of the Act. The Court noted that the same set of facts could not be relied upon to maintain separate claims under two distinct provisions of the Act; however the Court was prepared to consider the claims made in the alternative. The particular claims related to incidences where the

---

35.   *Huet v Universite de Bretagne Occidentale* (Case C–251/11).

respondent advertised for different permanent posts that had become vacant. It was claimed that the competition for these posts was confined to two permanent employees of the respondent. As some of the vacancies post-dated the reference of the claims to the Rights Commissioner, they were not considered by the Court. The only incidents that were within the time limit related to the posts of tar depot operator and refuse collection driver. The union put in evidence copies of the advertisements published by the respondent for the vacancies. They were clearly addressed to permanent drivers only.

The Court noted s 10(1) of the Act which obliges an employer to inform fixed-term employees of permanent vacancies and noted that this subsection contained the concomitant obligation to allow fixed-term employees to apply for such a vacancy. The Court concluded that the advertisement in question purported to exclude fixed-term workers for consideration for the vacancy, which was a clear contravention of s 10(1). The respondent accepted that the advertisements for both positions were restricted to permanent workers. It was also alleged that the respondent was in breach of s 10(3) of the Act as the complainants were denied access to appropriate training opportunities to enhance their career prospects and specific reference was made to IT training opportunities that had been made available to permanent members of staff during the six-month reference period before the date of claims; this was not disputed by the respondent.

The Court noted that it had been accepted by all the parties that, at the material time, the complainants were regarded as fixed-term employees and thus the effect of the advertisements was to exclude them from applying for the posts which was a contravention of s 10(1) of the Act. The Court held that it was unnecessary to consider if these circumstances constituted a contravention of s 6, as the Court concluded that the contravention in relation to the filling of a permanent vacancy should be dealt with by application of s 10(1) of the Act. The Court further found that as the complainants were denied access to the IT training provided to permanent workers, the claims under s 10(3) were also well founded.

The Court concluded that the complaints under s 9 were well founded and that the complainants' fixed-term contracts of employment were transmuted by operation of s 9(3) of the Act to contracts of indefinite duration. The Court required the respondent to comply with the Act by recognising the permanent seasonal nature of the complainants' employment. The Court determined the respondent was in breach of s 10 and required the respondent to ensure that all permanent vacancies are advertised and open to fixed-term employees and further to ensure that training opportunities are made available to fixed-term employees in the future. The Court ordered the respondent to pay the sum of €5,000 to each of the seven complainants for the breaches. The respondent's cross-appeal failed.

CJEU DECISION

[8.06] *European Commission v Grand Duchy of Luxembourg*[36]*—CJEU— Framework Agreement on Fixed-Term Work—prevention of abusive use of successive fixed-term contracts—objective justification for renewal in domestic legislation—whether legislation providing for recurring successive fixed-term contracts in respect of occasional workers in entertainment arts constituted an exception to requirement for objective reasons*

This case came before the CJEU on the grounds that Luxembourg had not fulfilled its obligations to prevent the abusive use of successive fixed-term contracts in accordance with European law. Clause 5 of the Framework Agreement on Fixed-Term Work (Annex to Council Directive 1999/70/EC)[37] requires Member States, in circumstances where no equivalent statutory measures exist to prevent abuse, to provide objective reasons capable of justifying the renewal of contracts; or to determine the maximum total duration of a series of successive fixed-term employment contracts; or to limit the number of times that those contracts may be renewed.

Luxembourg law generally provided that the duration of fixed-term contracts could not, in respect of the same employee, exceed 24 months, inclusive of renewals. However, a separate provision of Luxembourg legislation provided that fixed-term contracts for occasional workers in the entertainment arts industry could be renewed more than twice, even for a total duration of more than 24 months, without giving rise to a contract of indefinite duration. The Commission argued that in these circumstances, Luxembourg law did not require the provision of objective reasons that would prevent the abusive use of successive fixed-term contracts. The Commission asserted that Luxembourg had not complied with its obligations to provide for 'objective justification' and as a result, applicable occasional workers were susceptible to abuse by way of successive fixed-term contracts with no maximum limitation on duration. Luxembourg argued that such workers were more likely to participate in individual projects limited by time and, as such, the temporary recruitment requirements of employers in this area sufficed as an 'objective reason' to justify the renewal of fixed-term contracts.

The CJEU found that Luxembourg's domestic law made no provision for requiring justification via an 'objective reason' for the renewal of successive fixed-term contracts in respect of occasional workers in the entertainment arts industry. The CJEU found that Luxembourg had not specified how its domestic law required such workers in the entertainment arts to engage in professional activities on a temporary basis. Employers in that industry were therefore in a position to provide successive fixed-term contracts to workers in order to meet lasting and permanent staffing needs as well as temporary staffing needs. The Court found that even if Luxembourg law did pursue its stated objective, to provide occasional workers in the entertainment arts industry with a degree of flexibility by enabling employment on the basis of recurring fixed-term contracts, this

---

36. *European Commission v Grand Duchy of Luxembourg* (Case C–238/14).
37. Directive 1999/70/EC of 28 June 1999 concerning the framework agreement on fixed-term work concluded by ETUC, UNICE and CEEP.

objective did not 'prove the existence of precise and concrete circumstances characterising the activity of such workers in the entertainment arts'. Luxembourg did not therefore provide justification for the use of successive fixed-term contracts in these circumstances. The CJEU found that Luxembourg had failed to fulfil its obligations to prevent the abuse of successive fixed-term contracts in the entertainment arts industry on the grounds that the specific Luxembourg law did not require justification by reference to an objective reason in the case of such workers.

Chapter 9

FREEDOM OF INFORMATION

WHAT BODIES ARE NOW SUBJECT TO FOI?

[9.01] The Freedom of Information Act 2014 (the Act) was enacted on 14 October 2014 and provides for the extension of FOI to all public bodies, subject to some exemptions, and to all bodies significantly funded by the State. Public bodies being brought within the ambit of FOI for the first time became subject to the law from 14 April 2015 (although, this period could be extended by the Minister by order under the Act, subject to a business case being made to the Minister). An order[1] was made by the Minister to delay the commencement of the Act for the following entities:

1. An Garda Síochána;

2. Gaslink Independent System Operator;

3. Eirgrid plc;

4. ESB Networks Limited; and

5. Iarnród Éireann.

This meant that these bodies became subject to the Act on 14 October 2015, rather than on the standard commencement date for new FOI bodies.

The Act applies retrospectively from 21 April 2008 in the case of an entity that, prior to enactment of the 2014 Act, was not a public body within the meaning of the previous Act.

Section 6 of the Act contains a generic definition enabling FOI to apply to all public bodies; hence as new public bodies are established they will automatically be subject to the terms of the Act, unless specifically exempt in whole or in part by Schedule 1 of the Act or by order of the Minister for Public Expenditure.

The Act also allows for the application of FOI to non-public bodies which are in receipt of significant funding from the State.

Exemptions are provided for certain bodies so as not to affect their ability to perform their core functions, including An Garda Síochána, the National Treasury Management Agency Group, the Central Bank of Ireland, etc.

NEW CODE OF PRACTICE

[9.02] To support the 2014 Act, a Code of Practice was published by the Central Policy Unit in December 2014. The Code draws on proposals made by two expert groups on

---

1.   Freedom of Information Act 2014 (Commencement Date for Certain Bodies) Order 2015 (SI 103/2015).

FOI, comprising a broad and varied range of representatives. The Code is intended to assist all public bodies, including those that are subject to FOI for the first time under the 2014 Act.

Chapter 10
HEALTH AND SAFETY

TRAINING

[10.01] *Meus v Dunnes Stores[1]—High Court—Barr J—Safety, Health and Welfare at Work Act 2005—personal injury—whether plaintiff had received adequate training for her position as store assistant—failure of employer to train its employees—failure to provide training comparable to real-life work—failure to confirm that plaintiff, a Polish national, understood training procedures—failure to follow up on induction training—damages for pain and suffering into the future— special damages*

The plaintiff worked as a shop assistant in the defendant's shop premises in Newbridge, Co Kildare. Each day the plaintiff was required to carry a number of large boxes containing suitcases of varying sizes from the storeroom to the shop floor. On the day of the incident, the subject of the proceedings, the plaintiff was required to fetch a number of boxes that were stacked high above her head and carry them to the shop floor. In order to do so, the plaintiff had to knock the boxes off the top of the pile and let them fall to the ground. The plaintiff used a trolley to transport the boxes, which were allegedly large and heavy, and consequently suffered an injury while loading the second trolley. The plaintiff injured her back when lifting one of the boxes to the level of her thigh and raising it to her right knee to give the box an additional lift, which would allow her to place the box onto the top shelf of the trolley. The plaintiff informed the court that she had encountered great difficulty lifting the box due to its size and weight. She stated that, in order to do so, it was necessary to bend over the box keeping her knees straight and her back bent.

Barr J highlighted that the extent of the training the plaintiff had received was a key issue in the proceedings for the purposes of determining liability. The plaintiff had signed a training card upon completion of her induction training at the time she joined the defendant's employment in August 2006. The card was effectively a record of the training and support provided by the defendant and received by the plaintiff during her induction period. The training card contained a table that indicated the date the plaintiff received each form of training, the type and the method of training and the identity of each trainer. Columns were included on the training card indicating each of the training modules undertaken to enable both the trainers and the employees to insert their signature upon completion of same. The types of training provided were stated to be training on induction, alcohol sales, hygiene levels, chemical training, health and safety and manual handling. The column for the trainers' signatures was blank for the most part, with the exception of health and safety and manual handling training, which had been signed. In the final column of the training card relating to the day of the plaintiff's induction, there appeared six signatures of the plaintiff in respect of each of the training

---

1.   *Meus v Dunnes Stores* [2014] IEHC 639.

modules. The plaintiff noted that these were her signatures but she denied receiving all of the training as indicated on the training card. In particular, the plaintiff noted that she did not receive any training in alcohol sales and further denied ever receiving any health and safety or manual handling training. She alleged that the only form of training she received on her first day was a tour of the shop but noted that she had received an employee handbook and a work uniform. The plaintiff informed the Court that she had been told by the defendant to provide her signature on the training record and that she did as she was told.

The defendant disputed the contention that the plaintiff was made to sign the card, despite not having received each of the training modules. The trainer in question gave evidence in the proceedings on behalf of the defendant and recalled giving training on the date in question to a group of new employees that included the plaintiff. The trainer noted that he had provided a physical demonstration to the employees with regard to lifting techniques and recalled using a box of A4 paper for the purpose of this demonstration. The trainer further noted that he had provided training on the crouch and lift technique. The trainer further stated that he had shown the group a slideshow dealing with manual handling, followed by a viewing of two DVDs on the subject of health and safety procedures, including one on the manual handling of loads. The plaintiff informed the Court that she had never viewed these DVDs. Under cross-examination, the trainer failed to explain the absence of the other trainer's signatures. He noted that he had signed the training card in respect of the training actually provided by him on 22 August 2006. It was noted that the plaintiff had been furnished with an employee handbook but submitted that she had difficulty reading and understanding the handbook due to her poor level of English. The trainer noted that when he had given instructions with regard to training techniques, he did not confirm with each new employee that they had understood him or understood the content of the slideshow and DVD presentations. The trainer also noted that the storeroom in which the plaintiff suffered the injury was smaller than the room in which the new employees were provided with health and safety training. Engineer's photos of the storeroom were presented to the trainer on examination. The trainer noted that the storeroom was in a congested state in the photos provided and concluded that there might have been a large delivery earlier on the day that the engineer inspected the storeroom and took the photos. The trainer also accepted that after the new employees had received their induction training, he had not checked with the plaintiff to see whether she was performing the work in accordance with the training received and, in particular, whether she was adopting the correct lifting technique. The trainer accepted that he had never followed up with any of the employees after the date of the induction training.

A consultant engineer gave evidence in the proceedings on behalf of the plaintiff and outlined the statutory provisions that he deemed applicable in the circumstances of the proceedings. The engineer noted that the defendant had drawn up a safety statement in accordance with the Safety, Health and Welfare at Work Act 2005 but had not performed a risk assessment on the work the plaintiff performed, which included carrying large and heavy boxes from the storeroom to the shop floor. In the order for discovery, the defendant was directed to produce a risk statement but this section had been returned with the words 'none such'. While a safety statement did exist and was presented to the

Court, it was accepted that the absence of a risk assessment reduced the overall value of the safety statement. The safety statement in this case was of a generic nature as no specific risk assessment had been carried out.

Barr J found that liability in these proceedings rested with the defendant. Barr J found the plaintiff to be a truthful witness and accepted her evidence that she did not receive adequate training in respect of the roles and duties connected to her employment, despite the defendant disputing the allegation that the plaintiff did not receive any manual handling training on the day of her induction. Barr J noted that in the event such training was provided to the plaintiff, it would have been inadequate and incomparable to the work the plaintiff would perform on the shop floor in real time. Further, no attempt was made to inquire whether the plaintiff, a Polish national, understood the content of the instructions allegedly provided to her in relation to the training. It was also noted that the plaintiff received no follow-up training; nor had her lifting techniques been monitored or assessed by a trainer on any future date. No risk assessment had been carried out in relation to the plaintiff's lifting duties on the shop floor or in the storeroom. Barr J noted that if a risk assessment had been carried out, the risk that the plaintiff could suffer back injury would have been evident. Barr J also found that the plaintiff could not be faulted for failing to seek assistance with regard to her lifting techniques or functions. The plaintiff noted in evidence that the shop floor was a very busy working environment and as such, it would have been difficult to request and obtain assistance from any of her colleagues during the hours of work. The defendant was in breach of reg 10 of the Safety, Health and Welfare at Work (General Application) Regulations 1993 and in breach of its duties at common law. The defendant was also in breach of s 10 of the Safety, Health and Welfare at Work Act 2005 having not provided instruction, training and supervision to its employees in relation to the their safety, health and welfare at work. The defendant also breached regs 13 and 28 of the 1993 Regulations, having not provided adequate training specifically in relation to the manual handling of loads by employees and further having not taken appropriate organisational measures to reduce the risk involved in the manual handling of such loads.

Barr J then examined the *quantum* of damages to be awarded to the plaintiff in the circumstances and referred to the treatment received by the plaintiff as a result of her injury. Barr J noted that the plaintiff had returned to Poland to attend an 'important hospital visit' but had not indicated to the defendant that she had suffered an injury at this time. The plaintiff received 'conservative treatment' in Poland before returning to Ireland. Upon her return, the plaintiff did not feel capable of working with the defendant anymore and commenced to work part time in a hotel in Newbridge. The plaintiff attended an orthopaedic surgeon on 24 September 2008. The primary clinical diagnosis was of acute lumbar trauma, particularly acute disc prolapse, which was stated to be entirely consistent with the biomechanics of the injury the plaintiff had described. As the clinical signs and symptoms suggested that there had been structural damage to the lumbar spine, the long-term prognosis at that time remained extremely guarded. In addition to lower back symptoms, there existed an associated right sciatic pain and persistent limitation of the right straight leg raise test with a positive sciatic stretch sign, which remained present for over six years after the initial injury. The surgeon concurred with the view of an orthopaedic specialist in Poland whom the plaintiff had visited that any further significant improvement in the plaintiff's condition was unlikely in the circumstances. He further noted that this was a reasonable explanation for the symptoms the plaintiff had incurred and was a justification for the treatment that the plaintiff had received in Poland. The surgeon noted that the plaintiff constantly expected pain and anticipated its onset upon certain movements and that she would attempt to avoid movements that caused such pain. The plaintiff noted that she was unable to perform a number of activities such as sports and, in particular, running; she had been advised to participate in swimming and walking, however her ability to swim was limited due to the pain she encountered. The plaintiff received substantial treatment in Poland and attended a rehabilitation clinic twice each week during the period of August to December in 2013.

The plaintiff was also examined by the defendant's doctor, who was of the opinion that any lingering complaints could be satisfactorily treated and fully resolved by way of a programme of exercises designed to manipulate the plaintiff's lumbo-sacral facet joints in tandem with the strengthening of her abdominal/para-spinal muscles. Such a programme would involve a daily commitment of 20–30 minute exercises and could be usefully supplemented by swimming. On the basis of these measures and in tandem with the adoption of good posture, the defendant's doctor noted that there was every reason to believe that the plaintiff's injury had the potential to fully settle over a period of 6–9 months. The defendant's doctor noted that it was extremely unlikely that the incident at work described by the plaintiff had resulted in the onset of disc degeneration.

Barr J was satisfied that the plaintiff had suffered a significant injury to her lower back which adversely affected her in both her work and social aspects of her life and that, in accordance with the surgeon's opinion, the plaintiff's level of chronic disability was likely to persist for the foreseeable future. Despite the conflict between the evidence of the parties' medical experts, Barr J favoured the evidence of the surgeon on behalf of the plaintiff. Barr J awarded the plaintiff general damages of €60,000, general damages for pain and suffering into the future of €20,000 and agreed special damages of €5,255 resulting in a total award of €85,255.

[10.02] *Gillane v Focus Ireland Ltd[2]—High Court—Murphy J—Safety Health and Welfare at Work Act 2005, s 19—Safety Health and Welfare at Work (General Application) Regulations 2007 (SI 299/2007)—health and safety—whether negligence and breach of statutory duty in configuration of plaintiff's workstation— personal injuries*

The plaintiff was employed as a housing support worker since 2003. She was initially based in an office designated for that purpose with other colleagues. From 2005–2007 she was seconded for a two-year period as a tenancy support worker based in a different office designated for that purpose. When this assignment ended, she was reassigned to the housing support unit. To accommodate her return, an extra desk was installed in the housing support unit office as the person who had replaced the plaintiff during her secondment was still in situ.

---

2.   *Gillane v Focus Ireland Ltd* [2015] IEHC 478.

Evidence was given about the close proximity of the plaintiff's desk to a boiler and to two radiators. The room's heating was controlled by the occupants who could adjust the temperature by means of a dial on the boiler beside the plaintiff's desk. The plaintiff gave evidence that she suffered from sinusitis and that, as she was sitting beside one of the radiators, she found the level of heating in the room to be oppressive and troubling. She responded to this by opening a window beside her workstation.

At the end of January 2008, the employee who had replaced the plaintiff on her secondment finished her contract and left the office resulting in four workstations but three people based in the office. The plaintiff remained at her workstation for a further six weeks but moved to another station in March. A routine assessment form was completed by all employees in March 2008 relating to their workplace. The Court noted various responses by the plaintiff in the assessment whereby she highlighted a number of concerns about her workstation and detailed physical symptoms that she was suffering which had caused her to go to a chiropractor and massage therapist. The Court noted that this was the first complaint the plaintiff had made about her workstation. On receipt of this complaint, the workstations were immediately reconfigured.

Murphy J was satisfied that no risk assessment was carried out before the decision was taken to place the plaintiff's workstation against the wall adjacent to a radiator and window. The Court held that it was entirely foreseeable that the person sitting at that workstation would be exposed to far greater levels of heat than those further back in the room. The Court further noted that, in order to provide sufficient heat for the whole room, it was likely that the person sitting directly adjacent to the radiator would experience excessive levels of heat and it was entirely foreseeable that that person would open the nearest window to alleviate the problem. The Court noted the evidence that the placement of a pedestal file cabinet under the desk was such that when using the visual display unit the plaintiff had to, on occasion, adopt a crooked position.

Murphy J was satisfied that, had a proper risk assessment been done as required by s 19 of the Safety Health and Welfare At Work Act 2005, the plaintiff's workstation would not have been oriented in this manner. The Court was further satisfied that the temperature for the plaintiff was not maintained as is required by reg 7 of the Safety Health and Welfare at Work (General Application) Regulations 2007.[3] Murphy J concluded that the *ad hoc* arrangement apparently arrived at by the defendant to accommodate the plaintiff in the housing support work unit was negligent and in breach of statutory duty and failed to have adequate regard for the safety and wellbeing of the plaintiff.

The Court then moved on to consider causation, ie, whether or not that negligence or breach of duty, including the breach of statutory duty, had caused the condition of which the plaintiff complained. Murphy J noted that the plaintiff was suffering from a chronic inflammatory condition which, when active, caused pain in her left trapezius and sternocleidomastoid muscles. The Court noted that, prior to the events giving rise to these proceedings, the plaintiff did not suffer from this condition; however, she did suffer from sinusitis, which is an inflammatory condition and can be an exacerbating factor in neck pain, according to the evidence of a consultant rheumatologist. The Court

---

3.   Safety Health and Welfare at Work (General Application) Regulations 2007 (SI 299/2007).

heard evidence from three medical practitioners and noted that, when viewing the evidence as a whole, the plaintiff's reporting in this case was not consistent. Although the Court did not consider there to be any deliberate falsification on the plaintiff's part, Murphy J said it gave her cause to pause when the plaintiff's doctors' opinions were based significantly on the accuracy of her reporting. The Court then highlighted a number of inconsistencies in the plaintiff's evidence as against accounts given by the varying medical experts.

The Court noted that, throughout the period from December 2007 to March 2008, the plaintiff had made no complaint to anyone about sitting in a draught or having to adopt an awkward posture at her desk, despite weekly meetings in which health and safety relating to clients and staff were the first items of the agenda. While the plaintiff did experience pain in her neck and shoulders during that period she made no connection between that pain and her workstation.

As the plaintiff's reporting was inconsistent in terms of the onset of her symptoms, ie no complaints were made by her as to the unsuitability of the work station in the three-month period during which she was assigned to it; the plaintiff only made a connection between her workstation and her condition on consulting a chiropractor who was not willing to give evidence to the Court; and an independent psychological assessment recommended by both medics had not been conducted, the Court had difficulty concluding that, as a matter of probability, the workstation was the cause of the plaintiff's condition. At most, Murphy J held that defects in the plaintiff's workstation were merely a contributory factor in the onset of her condition and had no causative role in the perpetuation of it.

Notwithstanding the plaintiff's confused reporting as to the sequence of events which the Court conceded was not surprising given the circumstances and the lapse of time and which confusion was not due to any dishonesty on the part of the plaintiff, the fact was that, for a period of three months, she was assigned to a work station that was defective and, during this time, she developed symptoms from which she had not previously suffered.

In reaching its conclusion that the plaintiff's workstation was a factor in the onset of her condition, the Court attached particular weight to the fact that, prior to her assignment to that station, the plaintiff had no history of inflammation of the type from which she now suffers. The Court held it was appropriate to compensate the plaintiff for the pain and suffering from which she suffered immediately following the onset of her symptoms, but not for her ongoing pain and suffering. The Court held that, in the particular circumstances of the case, it was appropriate to compensate the plaintiff for one year post onset of this condition to reflect the role of the defendant's negligence in its onset. The appropriate level of general damages was calculated to be €15,000, having regard to the significantly painful and debilitating nature of the plaintiff's condition during that period. The Court noted that while special damages were agreed at €4,000, having regard to its finding that the defendant was liable only for the first year of the pain and suffering attributable to the condition the Court proposed to reduce this to €1,000.

PERSONAL PROTECTIVE EQUIPMENT

[10.03] *Besenyei v Rosderra Irish Meats Group Ltd and Rosderra Meats Group[4]—Employment Appeals Tribunal—Unfair Dismissals Acts 1977 to 2007 as amended—preliminary issue—whether the EAT has jurisdiction to hear claim where it is not lodged within six months of dismissal—claimant dismissed summarily—whether date of dismissal for purpose of Act the date on which such notice would have expired—health and safety—refusal of claimant to wear safety equipment*

The claimant was employed in the respondent's meat processing plant from June 2005 until his dismissal in May 2013. Evidence was given that the claimant had received a progressive number of disciplinary warnings, including a verbal warning, a final written warning and a two-day suspension without pay prior to his dismissal. A decision to dismiss the claimant was appealed by him but the original decision to dismiss was upheld.

There appear to have been a number of issues considered in reaching the decision to dismiss but the primary reason was asserted to be the claimant's persistent refusal to wear a protective glove to comply with health and safety best practice when instructed to do so. The respondent submitted that the claimant had been given every opportunity to improve his behaviour but failed to do so and therefore left the respondent with no option but to dismiss him. The claimant admitted that he did not wish to wear the particular glove as it caused him pain in his elbow; however it was noted that no formal grievance had been lodged in this regard nor was any medical evidence put forward by him to the respondent.

The claimant gave evidence that he did not need to wear this glove as he was experienced and had not used it for the last 19 years. The claimant contended that the decision to dismiss was disproportionate.

The EAT firstly dealt with the preliminary issue as to whether the claim was in time given that the claimant's last day in work was 30 May 2013 and his claim was not filed until 19 December 2013. The EAT noted that the claimant's statutory notice entitlement was four weeks under the Minimum Notice and Terms of Employment Acts. The EAT held itself satisfied that the date of dismissal, for the purpose of jurisdiction in this case, was the date in which this notice would have expired if given. This was not affected by the fact that the claimant had not submitted a Minimum Notice Act claim.

The EAT declared it had jurisdiction to hear the claim. The EAT noted the principal reason for the dismissal was the claimant's refusal to wear the arm-length safety glove designed for use by boners on the respondent's production line. The EAT noted that production operations of this nature carry a high level of risk and thus compliance with health and safety regulations is paramount. Not only must risk assessments be carried out and health and safety measures implemented but they must be reviewed on an on-going basis. All employees also have obligations for their own safety. The EAT held it was unacceptable in circumstances where a properly conducted risk assessment had led to the introduction of a safety measure, that an employee should arbitrarily decide not to

---

4.   *Besenyei v Rosderra Irish Meats Group Ltd and Rosderra Meats Grou*p UD37/2014.

comply with the measure. The EAT noted that the claimant had no reason for so doing and even when faced with the prospect of dismissal, had refused to resile from his position. The EAT agreed that the respondent had been left with no option but to dismiss the claimant and thus no unfair dismissal had occurred.

RIGHT TO WORK IN A SAFE ENVIRONMENT

[10.04] *Hanlon v Smurfit Kappa Ireland Ltd t/a Smurfit Kappa Dublin[5]— Employment Appeals Tribunal—Unfair Dismissals Acts 1977 to 2015 as amended— unfair dismissal—health and safety—serious misconduct—where altercation took place on factory floor over trade union matter—claimant already had written warning over verbal aggression—fair procedures—right of employees to work in safe environment*

The claimant was employed as a general operative in the respondent's dispatch area. It appears that the claimant and his brother, who was also employed by the respondent, approached a fellow employee and senior shop steward at a machine where the shop steward worked and an altercation occurred over a union matter resulting in a strong verbal confrontation. The respondent's management conducted a fact-finding investigation into the incident. Investigation meetings took place with both the claimant and his brother separately to hear their version of events. They were both represented by their trade unions. Both individuals arrived with prepared statements to the meeting and the investigators took further statements. The respondent's quality manager conducted a formal investigation which proceeded on the basis that it was a company investigation of an incident rather than an investigation of a complaint against an employee. Further investigative meetings took place with the relevant parties.

The investigation found that a serious argument had occurred which was inappropriate in the workplace and which centred largely on trade union business. It was clear to the investigators that the shop steward had attempted to disengage from the argument on a number of occasions but both the claimant and his brother continued to engage. It was noted however that no formal written complaints from any of the parties were received. Formal disciplinary action proceeded against the claimant. He was informed that his employment was being terminated as a result. The respondent's evidence was that the claimant had been involved in a similar verbal altercation with the same individual in the past and was advised in writing by his manager that this type of behaviour was unacceptable and that any further incidents would result in disciplinary action. It was noted that the claimant had been issued with a written warning in November 2012 for serious misconduct, following an incident where he was inappropriately aggressive towards his managers. The incident in May 2013 was the third incident over a 12-month period.

The respondent submitted that it had a duty of care to all employees and that dismissal was the appropriate sanction in the circumstances. An appeal took place and upheld the findings of serious misconduct. The claimant's evidence was that he and his

---

5. *Hanlon v Smurfit Kappa Ireland Ltd t/a Smurfit Kappa Dublin* UD388/2014.

brother had a number of issues about certain workplace events and that they stopped at the individual's workstation to say hello and touch base with him and to confirm a number of trade union issues. Their evidence was that they were subjected to a tirade of abuse and that they did not walk away immediately as they wanted to enquire why they were greeted in such a way. The claimant however admitted that his conduct was unacceptable in the workplace and that this was an unsavoury incident. The claimant's evidence was that he was available for work until October/November 2014 and then secured alternative work at a significantly lower salary.

The EAT concluded that the dismissal of the claimant was fair. It was noted that the claimant, unlike his brother, had a written warning on file for verbal aggression and that this provided the valid and distinguishing factor in their treatment by the respondent employer, in justifying the fact that the claimant's brother was not dismissed as a result this incident. The EAT noted that while the respondent's procedures were not as clear in relation to the stages of the investigation as they might have been, the claimant was properly represented, adequately notified and provided with fair procedures at every stage. The EAT noted that the claimant and his brother had finished their shifts and were free to leave while the shop steward was working and had to stay at the machine he was working on. The consistent evidence showed that the shop steward repeatedly asked the claimant and his brother to go away, even walking physically away from them at one stage; however the claimant and his brother insisted on confronting the individual and the incident became abusive.

The EAT held that it was unfortunate that the claimant and his brother were insistent on the escalation of a conflict on the factory floor. The EAT noted that all employees had the right to work in a safe environment and that employers must do their best to ensure that right. In circumstances where employees are working in an industrial environment with heavy machinery operating at great speeds, the EAT held that it was within the band of reasonable responses for an employer to terminate the employment of an employee who had finished work, who had a warning on file and who refused to disengage with an employee at work when an abusive incident resulted. The claim was not upheld.

Penalisation

[10.05] *Katherine Gordon & Co Ltd v Crowley O'Toole[6]—Labour Court—appeal from a decision of a Rights Commissioner—Safety, Health and Welfare at Work Act 2005, s 27—penalisation—complaint or representation to the Health and Safety Authority not an operative factor in respondent's decision to dismiss—employer's obligation to discharge the burden and to prove no operative factor between dismissal and act protected from penalisation—delay of decision to dismiss for reasonable period of time*

This case concerned an appeal by the complainant under s 29(1) of the Safety, Health and Welfare at Work Act 2005. The Rights Commissioner found that the complainant

---

6.   *Katherine Gordon & Co Ltd v Crowley O'Toole* HSD155.

had not been penalised, within the meaning of the Act, for making a complaint about a workplace accident to bodies external to the respondent. The respondent operated a small accountancy practice out of an office in Cork. The complainant was employed as an accounting technician since 5 February 2013. The complainant suffered an industrial accident in her place of work on 25 November 2013. She reported the accident to the respondent on 6 December 2013. The complainant also reported the accident to the Health and Safety Authority on that same day. The Authority wrote to the respondent regarding the accident on 11 December 2013. On 13 December 2013, the complainant was dismissed from her employment.

The complainant stated that she was acting in compliance with the statutory provisions of the Safety, Health and Welfare at Work Act 2005 by reporting the accident and was protected from penalisation under s 27 upon doing so. She submitted that she was subsequently dismissed from her employment without cause. She rejected the respondent's assertion she had been underperforming. She stated that she had never been notified of any performance issues and that no evidence of underperformance had been provided to the Court. She stated that her dismissal was a consequence of her reporting the accident to the Health and Safety Authority and that this amounted to penalisation under s 27 of the 2005 Act.

The respondent informed the Court that the complainant had been underperforming for a period of time. The respondent noted that it had received a number of complaints regarding the complainant's performance. In one instance, a client had complained that his affairs had been handled in an un-professional manner and in another instance, a client had complained of the quality of work the complainant had undertaken. The respondent stated that the complainant had been spoken to on a number of occasions regarding her work and that she was aware her employment was at risk if there was no improvement. The respondent could not produce the complainant's personnel file notes to the Court. The respondent stated that the decision to dismiss the complainant was made on Friday 22 November 2013 and that the complainant was to be informed on Monday 25 November. The respondent noted the concern that the complainant would gain protection/entitlements under the Unfair Dismissals Act 1977 and this was taken into account when making the decision. On the day the respondent had intended to dismiss the complainant, the complainant had an accident at work. The complainant went on sick leave on 25 November after the decision had been made to dismiss her from her employment. The complainant submitted an occupational injuries form for completion by the respondent on 2 December 2013. The respondent reverted, confirming the position in writing to the complainant, by letter dated 9 December 2013. On the same day, the respondent also wrote to the complainant asking her to attend a nominated company doctor and requested that the complainant attend a meeting at the office. The respondent met with the complainant on 13 December, at which point the complainant was dismissed.

The Court considered s 27 of the 2005 Act, which refers to a prohibition on penalisation of an employee in various circumstances, including the making of a complaint to the Health and Safety Authority. The Court referred to the case of *Toni and*

Guy Blackrock Ltd v O'Neill[7] in which the Court considered the circumstances in which an infringement of s 27 may occur and stated that

> it is necessary for a claimant to establish that the determent of which he or she complains was imposed for having committed one of the acts protected by subsection 3. Thus the detriment giving rise to the complaint must have been incurred because of, or in retaliation for, the Claimant having committed a protected act. This suggested that where there is more than one causal factor in the chain of events leading to the detriment complained of the commission of a protected act must be an operative cause in the sense that "but for" the Claimant having committed the protected act he or she would not have suffered the detriment. This involves a consideration of the motive or reasons which influenced the decision maker in imposing the impugned determent.

The Court in this case confirmed that the burden lies with the respondent to show that the protected actions were not an operative factor in the respondent's decision to dismiss. The Court noted that the respondent attempted to discharge that burden by way of giving evidence to the Court in relation to the complainant's performance issues and by notifying the complainant of her shortcomings and making her aware that her employment was at risk. It was the respondent's position that the protected action taken by the complainant could not have influenced the decision to dismiss as the decision was made prior to the complainant's protected action. The Court stated that the complainant did not give evidence to the Court to rebut the respondent's assertions. The Court found the witness giving evidence on behalf of the respondent was a convincing, credible and honest person who gave evidence clearly and concisely. The Court found that the respondent did, in all probability, previously inform the complainant of her underperformance and that her employment was at risk and noted that the complainant did not deny this nor offer any evidence to the contrary. The Court also found credible the respondent's evidence that she decided to dismiss the complainant on 22 November 2013 and intended communicating the decision on 25 November 2013. The Court found that the respondent communicated the decision after a reasonable time had passed after the accident. The Court also found that it was reasonable in the circumstances for the respondent to have the complainant attend a company doctor.

The Court found that the respondent proved sufficiently that the protected actions undertaken by the complainant were not an operative factor in the respondent's decision to dismiss the complainant on 25 November 2013 and that the communication of the decision to dismiss had been deferred until after the complainant had dealt with the workplace accident. The Court found that there was no connection between the protected acts undertaken and the detriment suffered by the complainant. The appeal was dismissed and the decision of the Rights Commissioner was affirmed.

---

7.   *Toni and Guy Blackrock Ltd v O'Neill* HSD095.

Chapter 11

HUMAN RIGHTS

[11.01] *Boyraz v Turkey[1]—European Court of Human Rights—European Convention on Human Rights, arts 6, 8 and 14—discrimination on basis of gender—whether requirements for security officers to be male and have completed military service pursued a legitimate aim—fairness of proceedings—excessive length of proceedings before national courts*

This was an application under art 14 (prohibition of discrimination) of the European Convention on Human Rights (the Convention) in conjunction with art 8 of the Convention (right to respect for private and family life) and art 6(1) of the Convention (right to a fair hearing within a reasonable time).

The applicant in this case was a Turkish national, living in Turkey. In 1999 she passed an exam to become a public servant. She was subsequently informed that she had been appointed to the post of security officer in a branch of a state-run electricity company, Tedas. However, on 5 July 2000, the applicant was told that she would not be appointed to this post. She was informed that she did not fulfil the requirements for the post in that she was not male and had not completed military service. The applicant appealed against this decision on 18 September 2000 and, on 27 February 2001, the Ankara Administrative Court (the Administrative Court) ruled in her favour. Subsequently, Tedas offered the applicant a contract and the applicant commenced her duties on 11 July 2001.

The Administrative Court's decision was overturned by the Twelfth Division of the Supreme Administrative Court (the Supreme Court) on 31 March 2003. It held that the respondent's decision to revoke the applicant's appointment had been lawful. In coming to this decision, the Supreme Court noted that the requirements for the post of security officer were necessary given the nature of the post and were in the public interest. The applicant was dismissed from her post on 17 March 2004, having worked as a security officer with Tedas for almost three years. She lodged a petition and a request for rectification with the Supreme Court, both of which were refused. The Administrative Court also dismissed the applicant's case on 21 February 2006, taking account of the Supreme Court's decision. The applicant appealed but her request for rectification was ultimately dismissed on 17 September 2008.

Before the European Court of Human Rights (the ECHR), the applicant alleged that the findings of the national courts amounted to gender discrimination in contravention of art 14 of the Convention. The applicant also maintained that she had to wait an excessive length of time for her case to be heard in the national courts and that there had been unfairness in the administrative proceedings to dismiss her, contrary to art 6 of the Convention. In particular, she alleged that the Administrative Courts had delivered conflicting decisions in identical cases. The respondent maintained that the applicant's claims under arts 8 and 14 of the Convention were ill-founded, as the case at hand

---

1. *Boyraz v Turkey* Application No 61960/08.

concerned a right which was not secured by the Convention, namely the right to recruitment as a public servant. The ECHR agreed that the civil service had deliberately been omitted from the Convention. However, this was considered to be a moot point by the ECHR as the applicant had been assigned the post of security officer on a contractual basis. The issue in this case was held to be the applicant's dismissal on the basis of her gender. The ECHR noted that it had consistently determined that a civil servant was entitled to make a complaint in relation to his/her dismissal, if that dismissal was in violation of one of his/her rights under the Convention.

The ECHR held that the applicant's dismissal on the sole ground of her gender constituted an interference with her right to respect for her private life. In coming to this conclusion the ECHR considered the consequences of the applicant's dismissal for her family and her ability to practice a profession which corresponded with her qualifications. The ECHR therefore held that art 14 of the Convention was applicable, considered in conjunction with art 8 of the Convention. The Convention stated that the margin of appreciation afforded to Member States in assessing whether a difference in treatment was justified was narrower where such difference was based on gender. It was held that very weighty reasons would have to be established before such a difference in treatment could be considered compatible with the Convention. The ECHR stated that the respondent's decision to consider the applicant unsuitable for the post of security officer in the circumstances constituted a clear difference of treatment on grounds of gender. The ECHR noted that the Administrative Court had considered women unable to undertake responsibilities such as night work in rural areas or using physical force/ firearms in case of attack. The ECHR criticised the Supreme Court for not assessing these considerations. This was particularly the case in circumstances where the Supreme Administrative Court's General Assembly of Administrative Proceedings had only recently held that there was no issue with appointing women security officers in a case very similar to that of the applicant. The ECHR rejected the idea that the night work and occasional requirement to use firearms/physical force justified a difference in treatment of men and women. Further, it was held that the applicant's dismissal had not been on account of her failure to assume these duties. The ECHR concluded that the difference in treatment to which the applicant had been subject was not in pursuance of a legitimate aim and that it amounted to discrimination on grounds of gender. A violation of both art 8 and art 14 of the Convention had taken place.

In relation to the applicant's claim under art 6(1) of the Convention, the ECHR agreed that the length of her proceedings, which lasted eight years for two levels of jurisdiction, had been excessive. In relation to the fairness of the proceedings, the ECHR noted that the Supreme Court had simply endorsed the Administrative Court's judgment of 21 February 2006 in relation to the applicant's submissions on a case in which a different conclusion was reached in almost identical circumstances. The ECHR held that in normal circumstances this technique of reasoning was acceptable by an appellate court. However, it failed to satisfy the requirements in the applicant's case, as the General Assembly of Administrative Proceedings Divisions had given a decision in conflict with the Administrative Court's judgment. It was held that the Supreme Court had failed to satisfy its duty to provide adequate reasoning for its decisions, contrary to art 6(1) of the Convention.

The ECHR ordered the respondent to pay the applicant €10,000 in respect of non-pecuniary damage. One of the judges expressed a dissenting opinion from the ECHR's majority decision in relation to arts 8 and 14 of the Convention.

Chapter 12

IMMIGRATION

CASE LAW

[12.01] *Ali v Minister for Jobs, Enterprise and Innovation[1]—High Court—Employment Permits Acts 2003 to 2014—judicial review—whether Minister applying non-statutory criteria for determining acceptability of employment permit application ultra vires the legislation*

This case concerned an application before Noonan J for an order of *certiorari* quashing the decision of the Minister for Jobs, Enterprise and Innovation (the Minister) to refuse to grant an employment permit to the applicant and an application for other declaratory reliefs, including in respect of the Minister's criteria for granting and refusing employment permits.

The applicant was resident in Ireland under a student visa with a Stamp 2. Having secured an offer of employment as a sales support assistant with an annual salary of €18,000, he applied on three occasions for an employment permit under the Employment Permit Acts 2003 to 2014 as amended (the Acts). On each occasion, his application was refused.

In its refusal letter to the applicant, the Department of Jobs, Enterprise and Innovation (the Department) stated that the Minister is required to consider the extent to which a decision to grant a permit would be consistent with the government's economic policy and whether the granting of the permit would be in the public interest in terms of protecting the labour market.

The letter continued to set out the specific reasons for the refusal, which are summarised below:

- The role of 'sales support assistant' was ineligible for an employment permit, as there was already a sufficient supply of labour in the labour market for the filling of such roles.

- The remuneration for the role was below the applicable threshold for qualifying for a general employment permit (ie €30,000 per annum). Remuneration is a key indicator of the skills and experience required for a job and assists the Minister in determining the necessity for employing a foreign national. Granting the permit to the applicant would not be in the public interest or in line with the economic policy of the government, and would be contrary to ss 12(1)(d) and 12(1)(f) of the 2006 Act, as the annual remuneration of the applicant was not of the required level.

During the course of the hearing, the respondent referred to the government's economic policy and the Action Plan for Jobs 2014. It also referred to the criteria published on the

---

1. *Ali v Minister for Jobs, Enterprise and Innovation* [2015] IEHC 219.

Department's website in relation to the granting of an employment permit, which states that the Minister will consider, *inter alia*, the following when deciding whether to grant a work permit:

- A full description of the proposed employment.

- The employment named is not in an excluded job category under the ineligible categories of employment for employment permits.

- Information in respect of the qualifications and skills or experience that are required for the employment.

- Annual remuneration (generally above €30,000). The Department considers applications on an exceptional basis with remuneration lower than €30,000.

The respondent also referred to the Department's 'Ineligible Categories of Employment for Employment Permits' which sets out a list of categories that are considered to be ineligible for employment permits. This list includes the category of 'sales staff', which, the respondent submitted, would include the applicant's prospective role of sales support assistant.

The applicant asserted that the criteria adopted by the Minister for refusing an employment permit application were *ultra vires* the powers conferred on him by the Acts, and that the criteria were an attempt to circumvent s 14 of the Acts, which provides for the making of regulations on the granting or refusing of employment permit applications based on certain requirements. It was argued that s 14 of the Acts requires any such regulations, if made by the Minister, to be laid before both Houses of the Oireachtas, and that by imposing the non-statutory criteria, the Minister had 'avoided the legislative scrutiny mandated by the statute', which was *ultra vires*.

In support of this contention the applicant referred to Articles 15.2.1° and 15.2.2° of the Constitution, which place the sole and exclusive power of making laws for the State in the Oireachtas. The applicant also referred to the Supreme Court decision in *O'Neill v Minister for Agriculture and Food*.[2] In that case, it was held that the Minister for Agriculture's attempt to adopt a non-statutory scheme for the grant of licences under the Livestock (Artificial Insemination) Act 1947, which provided for the making of regulations for the establishment of such a scheme, was *ultra vires* the 1947 Act.

In response, the respondent referred to ss 11 and 12 of the Acts which mandate the Minister to have regard to certain matters when considering whether to grant or refuse a permit application, including the government's economic policy. The respondent submitted that the Acts authorise the Minister to refuse to grant a permit if, *inter alia*, to do so would be inconsistent with the government's economic policy or the public interest. The respondent further submitted that the Acts do not place an obligation on the Minister to make regulations governing the criteria for refusing or granting employment permits, and that the Minister has discretion in this regard.

The respondent argued that the Minister, in having regard to economic policy as he is obliged to do in considering an application for an employment permit, must be entitled

---

2.   *O'Neill v Minister for Agriculture and Food* [1998] 1 IR 539.

to consider matters of the type referred to in s 14 that may be the subject matter of regulations. The respondent stated that a situation where the Minister was not permitted to consider the items set out in s 14 of the Act, despite being obliged to consider the government's economic policy, could not have been the intention of the legislature.

In delivering his judgment, Noonan J distinguished the present case from *O'Neill*. In *O'Neill*, Noonan J described the scheme proposed by the Minister of Agriculture as being so radical in qualifying limited numbers of persons and disqualifying others who may have been equally competent from engaging in the business of artificial insemination, the Oireachtas, in using general words, could not have contemplated such far reaching intrusion on the rights of citizens and thus, the scheme was *ultra vires* the Act of 1947.

This was distinct from the Minister's criteria in this case. Noonan J described the Acts as comprehensively providing a framework for the granting of employment permits, including detailed provisions concerning the matters to which the Minister must and may have regard in deciding to grant or refuse an employment permit, which may be the subject matter of regulations. Noonan J held that the Acts clearly empower the Minister to grant employment permits whether or not regulations are made under s 14 and to refuse to grant an employment permit if, in his opinion, the granting of the permit would be manifestly inconsistent with the government's economic policy or public interest (ie, protection of the labour market). By way of example, Noonan J opined that it would be difficult to see how the need to protect the labour market could be addressed if the Minister were to be precluded from having regard to relevant categories of employment and remuneration levels.

Noonan J referred to *Crawford (Inspector of Taxes) v Centime Ltd*[3] in which Clarke J considered the adoption of guidelines by bodies when discharging their statutory functions. Noonan J agreed with Clarke J in holding that where a statutory discretionary power is conferred on a decision maker, those potentially affected by the power benefit from guidelines of how the decision maker's discretion shall generally be exercised. In this case, s 12 of the Acts clearly allows the Minister to refuse a permit application on finding that it would be either inconsistent with the government's economic policy or not in the public interest; however, these criteria, Noonan J opined, were, in and of themselves, 'rather sterile and uninformative reasons' for refusing a permit application, and reliance on those reasons only would leave unsuccessful applicants in the dark as to why their applications had failed. Noonan J stated that this type of response would likely be open to a reasons-based judicial review challenge.

Noonan J stated that in his view, there was a clear benefit to be derived from the publication of guidelines or criteria in relation to the granting or refusing of employment permits. There was no basis to infer that the legislature intended that the Minister could not take account of the matters specified in s 14 in assessing applications for employment permits in the absence of making regulations.

The application was dismissed.

---

3.   *Crawford (Inspector of Taxes) v Centime Ltd* [2006] IR 106.

[12.02] *Hussein v The Labour Court and Mohammad Younis (Notice Party)[4]—* *Supreme Court—appeal from High Court—judicial review—Organisation of Working Time Act 1997, s 28 as amended by Protection of Employees (Fixed-Term Work) Act 2003, s 19—National Minimum Wage Act 2000, s 31—work permit*

This case originated with an application by the notice party, a Pakistani national, to the Labour Relations Commission against the applicant under the Terms of Employment (Information) Acts 1994 to 2012, the National Minimum Wage Act 2000 and the Organisation of Working Time Act 1997. The notice party was not authorised to work in Ireland during the relevant period and did not have an employment permit. Notwithstanding this, the Rights Commissioner and the Labour Court on appeal determined that the notice party's statutory rights had been breached and awarded him €92,632.

The applicant brought judicial review proceedings against the respondent, arguing that as the notice party was never authorised to work in Ireland and did not have an employment permit, therefore he could not avail of statutory protections afforded to employees in Ireland. Hogan J held in favour of the applicant, and set aside the decisions of the Rights Commissioner and the Labour Court.[5]

However, the Supreme Court found that the trial judge had erred in his perception of the Labour Court determination insofar as it involved an examination of the Rights Commissioner's decision on its merits or its correctness of law, in circumstances where the decision of the Rights Commissioner was not the subject of the judicial review application. Therefore, the order of the High Court was limited to setting aside the two decisions of the Labour Court. The judgment of the Supreme Court was delivered by Murray J who found that it was not open to the trial judge, in judicial review, to make a new finding of fact on the merits of a case of this nature for the purpose of deciding whether the original decision was right or wrong. The original decision of the Rights Commissioner could not have been set aside and therefore still stood.

Murray J then considered that the notice party had submitted to the High Court that there was no actual finding of fact by the Rights Commissioner that the notice party had been working for the applicant without a work permit. Murray J found that, before the notice party could be denied his remedies before the Rights Commissioner on the grounds that his employment was illegal, the fact that he did not have a work permit would have to have been established and a finding to that effect made. There was no such finding. Murray J then undertook a review of the functions of the Labour Court. The jurisdiction and function of the Labour Court is confined to determining that a decision of the Rights Commissioner has been made and that the decision has not been carried out by the employer. In these circumstances, the Labour Court had no option but to decide the way it did. The Labour Court is not and cannot be concerned with whether the evidence before the Rights Commissioner supported the decision or whether it was the correct decision. It is only concerned with whether a decision has been made. Therefore, Murray J found that the Labour Court acted pursuant to, and in accordance

---

4.   *Hussein v The Labour Court and Mohammad Younis (Notice Party)* [2015] IESC 58.

5.   See also *Arthur Cox Employment Law Yearbook 2014* at [11.15] and [11.16].

with, its jurisdiction. Since the Labour Court acted properly, there was no basis to set aside its two decisions by way of judicial review. The judgment of the High Court referred to the decision of the Labour Court as 'upholding' the Rights Commissioner decision. However, Murray J found that it was manifestly not the Labour Court's function to uphold or refuse to uphold the merits of a decision of the Rights Commissioner, nor did it purport to do so.

Murray J concluded that judicial review proceedings are not, in any sense, an appeal from the decision in question. Judicial review is concerned with reviewing whether the decision maker has acted within his or her powers and in accordance with those powers. On the facts, there was no basis for suggesting that the applicant was entitled to have the decisions of the Labour Court set aside.

LEGISLATIVE DEVELOPMENTS

Employment Permits (Amendment) Regulations 2015

[12.03] The Employment Permits (Amendment) Regulations 2015[6] (the Regulations) commenced on 1 September 2015 and introduced changes to the existing Regulations to address skills shortages in a number of industries.

The Regulations expanded the occupations eligible for employment permits to include the following occupations formerly on the Ineligible Occupations List:

- telecommunications engineers;

- IT engineers;

- chiropractors who are members of the Chiropractic Association of Ireland;

- mobility instructors for the visually impaired; and

- meat boners.

The Regulations have re-categorised a number of medical-sector roles, namely, radiation therapists, orthotists and prosthetists as highly-skilled occupations; while healthcare practice managers, senior social services managers and directors have been removed from the Highly Skilled Occupations List.

The Regulations have also made some additions to ineligible categories for employment permits in areas where there is evidence that no shortages exist in the Irish labour market including:

- betting shop managers;

- graphic design managers;

- library managers;

- plant hire managers;

---

6.   Employment Permits (Amendment) Regulations 2015 (SI 349/2014).

- production managers;

- property, housing and estate managers; and

- dispensing opticians.

P30s

[12.04] The time allowed for submitting a P30 to Revenue in support of an employment permit application has been extended from two months to three months of the date of the permit application.

Passports

[12.05] The requirement that passports of permit applicants for renewal be valid for a period of 12 months prior to the date of application has been significantly reduced to three months. Importantly, the 12-month validity requirement still applies for first-time applicants

New forms

[12.06] The Regulations have prescribed new standard employment permit application forms for the grant and renewal of employment permits, forms notifying dismissal by reason of redundancy and change of name, and forms submitting decisions for review. There are no changes to the Trusted Partner Registration forms and Trusted Partner Employment Permit application forms.

Specific categories of employment

[12.07] The Regulations include specific changes to the applications for employment permits for chefs, occupational therapists, speech and language therapists and dieticians, the latter of whom are now required to register with CORU.

Employment Permits (Amendment) (No 2) Regulations 2015[7]

[12.08] These regulations provide that the minimum hourly and annual rates of remuneration for employments for which a Dependant/Partner/Spouse Employment Permit, a Reactivation or Exchange Employment Permit, a Sport/Cultural Employment Permit or an Internship Employment Permit is granted must be in accordance with the national minimum wage and/or applicable employment regulation orders for contract cleaning and/or security.

---

7.   Employment Permits (Amendment) (No 2) Regulations 2015 (SI 602/2015).

Immigration Act 2004 (Visas) (Amendment) Order 2015

[12.09] The Immigration Act 2004 (Visas) (Amendment) Order 2015[8] has amended the Immigration Act 2004 (Visas) Order 2014[9] to exempt Ethiopians authorised to travel between Ethiopia and Canada or the US from the requirement to be in possession of a valid Irish transit visa when passing through an Irish port.

Employment Permits (Trusted Partner) Regulations 2015[10]

[12.10] The Trusted Partner Initiative was launched on 12 May 2015, introducing a new form of registration available to certain employers to streamline the employment permit application process and easing the administrative burden involved in hiring non-EEA nationals.

The initiative facilitates a faster turnaround and reduced supporting document requirements for 'Trusted Partners' when making employment permit applications by removing the requirement that employers replicate the same employer/connected person information in respect of each application made.

Any person who makes an offer of employment, employers, connected persons and EEA contractors who are registered with the Revenue Commissioners and/or the Companies Registration Office may apply to the Department for 'Trusted Partner' status. Importantly, any employer that has been convicted of an offence under the Employment Permits Acts 2003 to 2014 or the Immigration Act 2004 as amended will be excluded from the Trusted Partner scheme for a period of five years from the date of conviction.

If Trusted Partner status is awarded, the employer is granted a unique Trusted Partner reference number which enables the Trusted Partner to use simplified application forms for a two-year period. Trusted Partner status must be renewed thereafter.

The initiative extends to all employment permit types except in the case of Contract for Services Employment Permits where it facilitates EEA contractors only.

Forms for applying for registration under the Trusted Partner Initiative are available on the Employment Permits section of the Department's website. The website also contains the streamlined forms to be completed by Trusted Partners, once their Trusted Partner status is confirmed. As part of the application the employer is required to make certain declarations. Non-compliance with declarations stated may result in the employer having its Trusted Partner status removed. There is no fee for making an application under the initiative. The processing time for applications is two to five working days.

There is no recourse to appeal if an application under the initiative is refused, which means it is imperative that applications are completed correctly in the first instance and that all relevant information is accurate.

---

8. Immigration Act 2004 (Visas) (Amendment) Order 2015 (SI 175/2015).
9. Immigration Act 2004 (Visas) Order 2014 (SI 473/2014).
10. Employment Permits (Trusted Partner) Regulations 2015 (SI 172/2015).

Revised immigration registration arrangements for holders of critical skills employment permits or green card employment permits

[12.11] Revised immigration registration arrangements for holders of a Critical Skills Employment Permit or a Green Card Employment Permit and associated immigration registration cards (GNIB cards) have been introduced with effect from 1 April 2015.

The revised procedure provides that, to apply for a Stamp 4, Green Card and Critical Skills Employment Permit holders are now required to obtain confirmation of employment by the Department. Permit holders must complete an application form and submit same to the Department six weeks before the expiry of their existing permit, accompanied by:

- confirmation of current employment;

- a letter from their employer, dated within the last three months confirming the permit holder's employment and job title;

- confirmation of remuneration paid;

- copies of three recent payslips within the last four months;

- copies of P60s issued for each year covering the duration of the permit; and

- documentary evidence of payments in respect of health insurance, if applicable.

Provided the Department is satisfied the permit holder is in compliance with the terms of his/her existing employment permit, a letter of confirmation will be issued to the permit holder to support his/her request for a Stamp 4.

This letter of confirmation is only required for the initial transition from employment permit to Stamp 4 permission and does not extend to parties already holding Stamp 4 permission.

The letter of confirmation should be brought to the Garda National Immigration Bureau with the following documents:

- current valid passport;

- Garda Certificate of Registration (GNIB card); and

- existing employment permit.

Once granted, the Stamp 4 immigration permission is valid for two years and must be renewed thereafter.

Chapter 13

INDUSTRIAL RELATIONS

INDUSTRIAL RELATIONS (AMENDMENT) ACT 2015

[13.01] The Industrial Relations (Amendment) Act 2015 was enacted on 22 July 2015 and came into force on 1 August 2015.

The Act makes provision for three main areas, namely:

(i) it creates a new regime for registered employment agreements ('REAs');

(ii) it makes provision for sectoral employment orders ('SEOs'); and

(iii) it adjusts the Labour Court's jurisdiction to make legally binding determinations affecting non-union employees, created by the Industrial Relations (Amendment) Act 2001.

Registered Employment Agreements

[13.02] The previous statutory regime governing REAs (Pt III of the Industrial Relations Act 1946) was declared to be unconstitutional by the Supreme Court in 2013,[1] and the 2015 Act accordingly creates an entirely new regime for REAs.

[13.03] An employment agreement (EA) is an agreement made between a trade union(s) of workers and an employer(s) (or a trade union(s) of employers), relating to the remuneration or conditions of employment of workers of any class, type or group, that is binding only on the parties to the agreement. An EA becomes an REA when it is registered in the Labour Court's Register of Employment Agreements.[2]

[13.04] Any party to an EA may apply to the Labour Court to have the EA registered, and the Labour Court must register the EA if the statutory conditions are satisfied. Those conditions[3] are:

• all the union(s) and the employer(s) party to EA agree that the EA should be registered;

• the EA is expressed to apply to all the workers of a particular class, type or group and their employers party to the EA;

---

1. *McGowan & Ors v The Labour Court & Anor* [2013] IESC 21. See the *Arthur Cox Employment Law Yearbook 2013* at [17.02].
2. Industrial Relations (Amendment) Act 2015, s 7.
3. Industrial Relations (Amendment) Act 2015, s 8.

- the trade union(s) party to the EA are substantially representative of the workers in the class, type or group to which the EA is expressed to apply;

- it is normal and desirable practice or expedient to have a separate REA for these workers in that class, type or group;

- registration of the EA is likely to promote harmonious relations between the workers and their employer(s) and the avoidance of industrial unrest;

- the EA provides that, if a trade dispute occurs between the workers and the employer(s) party to the EA, industrial action or a lock-out shall not take place until the dispute has been submitted to negotiation in the manner specified in the EA;

- the EA must specify the circumstances in which a party or parties may terminate the EA; and

- the EA must be in a form suitable for registration.

[13.05] The REA itself must specify the circumstances in which a party may terminate it. In addition, a party to an REA may apply to the Labour Court to have it cancelled or have its terms varied, either by agreement of all parties or, failing agreement, following a dispute resolution process and the involvement of the WRC.[4]

[13.06] A party to an REA may apply to the Labour Court for an interpretation of the REA or its application to any person, and the civil courts must have regard to any such interpretation if a dispute regarding an REA comes before them and may refer an REA to the Labour Court for interpretation.[5]

[13.07] In 2013, the previous REA regime (contained in Pt III of the Industrial Relations Act 1946) was struck down by the Supreme Court in *McGowan & Ors v Labour Court & Anor*[6] because an REA under the 1946 Act could bind employers who were not party to it. Accordingly the REA regime represented an impermissible exercise of the legislative power of the State which is reserved to the Oireachtas. Under the 2015 Act, REAs will be legally binding only on employers and unions who are party to them and on relevant employees of those employers. If there is a desire to bind non-party employers the persons concerned will need to seek an SEO.

[13.08] Any REA will apply to every employer of the class, type or group to which it is expressed to apply and to their workers party to the REA. If the contract of employment of an employee to whom an REA relates provides for a lower rate of remuneration, or

---

4. Industrial Relations (Amendment) Act 2015, ss 9 and 10.
5. Industrial Relations (Amendment) Act 2015, s 12. Note that this may ground an application for an interlocutory injunction to restrain a strike or picket. See *Dublin Airport Authority plc v SIPTU and Ryanair Ltd v SIPTU* [2014] IEHC 644, *Arthur Cox Employment Law Yearbook 2014* at [12.10].
6. *McGowan & Ors v Labour Court & Anor* [2013] IESC 21.

less favourable conditions than those set out in that REA, the more favourable REA provisions will be substituted for the equivalent provisions in the contract of employment.[7]

[13.09] The Act requires employers to whom an REA applies to keep employment records at the place of work to show compliance with the REA. These records must be kept for at least three years from the date of their making and an employer who fails to comply with this provision shall be guilty of an offence. A worker in respect of whom an infringement took place may present a complaint to a WRC Adjudication Officer, from whose decision there is an appeal to the Labour Court. The Adjudication Officer may direct compliance and award compensation of up to two years of remuneration.[8]

Sectoral Employment Orders (SEOs)

[13.10] SEOs are orders made by the Minister for Jobs, Enterprise and Innovation on the recommendation of the Labour Court and approved by resolution of both Houses of the Oireachtas, which set out the minimum rates of remuneration and the minimum pension and sick pay entitlements of workers of a particular class, type or group within a specified economic sector. They are similar to REAs but their application is not confined to employees of the employer(s) party to them and their scope is confined to pay, sick pay and pensions.

[13.11] The SEO regime partially replaces the previous REA regime that was declared unconstitutional. SEOs will apply to all workers and employers within the relevant sector but the crucial difference is that they will be contained in a Ministerial order approved by both Houses of the Oireachtas, as opposed to an agreement between private parties registered by the Labour Court.

[13.12] A trade union of workers who substantially represent workers of a particular class, type or group in an economic sector or a trade union of employers may apply to the Labour Court to have the Court review the remuneration and sick pay and pension entitlements of workers of that class, type or group within that sector.[9] A number of statutory conditions must be satisfied before the Court will engage in such a review. If the Labour Court deems it appropriate after carrying out its review, the Court can make a recommendation to the Minister with regard to rates of pay, sick pay and pension schemes in that sector, and in so doing it must have regard to certain matters[10] and it

---

7.   Industrial Relations (Amendment) Act 2015, s 11.
8.   Industrial Relations (Amendment) Act 2015, ss 22 and 23.
9.   Industrial Relations (Amendment) Act 2015, s 14.
10. Those conditions, which are set out in Industrial Relations (Amendment) Act 2015, s 14(2), in summary are:
     (i) where the request is made by a trade union of workers or jointly with a trade union of workers, the trade union of workers must be substantially representative of the workers of the particular class, type or group in the economic sector concerned; and
          (contd .../)

must be satisfied with regard to certain matters.[11] If the Minister is satisfied that the Labour Court has complied with the Act, the Minister must then make the SEO.[12]

---

10. (contd)
    (ii) where the request is made by a trade union or an organisation of employers or jointly with a trade union or an organisation of employers, the trade union or organisation concerned must be substantially representative of the employers of the workers concerned.

11. Those matters, which are set out in Industrial Relations (Amendment) Act 2015, s 16(2), in summary are:
    (a) the potential impact on levels of employment and unemployment in the identified economic sector concerned;
    (b) the terms of any relevant national agreement relating to pay and conditions for the time being in existence;
    (c) the potential impact on competitiveness in the economic sector concerned;
    (d) the general level of remuneration in other economic sectors in which workers of the same class, type or group are employed;
    (e) that the sectoral employment order shall be binding on all workers and employers in the economic sector concerned.

12. Those matters, which are set out in Industrial Relations (Amendment) Act 2015, ss 15 and 16(4), in summary are:
    (i)   the trade union of workers must be substantially representative of the workers of the particular class, type or group in the economic sector concerned, and in satisfying itself in that regard, the Court must take into consideration the number of workers in that class, type or group represented by the trade union of workers;
    (ii) where the request is made by a trade union or organisation of employers (or jointly with a trade union or organisation of employers), the trade union or organisation concerned must be substantially representative of the employers in the particular class, type or group in the economic sector concerned, and in satisfying itself in that regard, the Court must take into consideration the number of workers employed in the particular class, type or group in the economic sector concerned by employers represented by the trade union or organisation of employers concerned;
    (iii) the request must be expressed to apply to all workers of the particular class, type or group and their employers in the economic sector concerned;
    (iv) it must be a normal and desirable practice, or expedient, to have separate terms and conditions relating to remuneration, sick pay schemes or pension schemes in respect of workers of the particular class, type or group in the economic sector concerned;
    (v)   any recommendation must be likely to promote harmonious relations between workers of the particular class, type or group and their employers in the economic sector concerned;
    (vi) the making of the recommendation must promote harmonious relations between workers and employers and assist in the avoidance of industrial unrest in the economic sector concerned; and
    (vii) the making of the recommendation must be reasonably necessary to:
        (a) promote and preserve high standards of training and qualifications; and
        (b) ensure fair and sustainable rates of remuneration,
    in the economic sector concerned.

[13.13] The SEO regime has a number of safeguards for employers as follows:

(a) before the Labour Court can examine an economic sector, it must publish notice of the intended examination and hear representations from any interested parties from that sector;

(b) prior to making a recommendation for an SEO, the Labour Court must consider its effect on employment and competitiveness levels within the sector; and

(c) an employer may apply for an exemption from a specified SEO, although such exemptions are subject to onerous statutory controls.[13]

[13.14] An SEO will apply to every worker of the class, type or group in the economic sector to which it is expressed to apply and to their employers. If the contract of employment of a worker to whom an SEO relates provides for a lower rate of remuneration or less beneficial sick pay or pension entitlements than those set out in that SEO, the more favourable SEO provisions will be substituted for the equivalent provisions in the contract of employment.[14] In addition, an employer must not penalise an employee for relying on their rights in relation to the SEO system.[15]

[13.15] The Act requires employers to whom an SEO applies to keep employment records at the place of work to show compliance with the SEO. These records must be kept for at least three years from the date of their making and an employee who fails to do so shall be guilty of an offence.[16] A failure on the part of an employer to comply with the terms of an SEO can be the subject of a complaint to an Adjudication Officer (and an appeal to the Labour Court) and result in an award of up to two years of remuneration together with an order directing the employer to comply with its obligations thereunder.[17]

The Labour Court and non-union employees

[13.16] The Industrial Relations (Amendment) Act 2001 created a regime enabling the Labour Court to make non-legally binding recommendations and thereafter legally binding determinations with regard to disputes regarding terms and conditions of employment and dispute resolution and disciplinary procedures affecting employees for whom their employer does not engage in collective bargaining negotiations, but the Labour Court could not thereby impose collective bargaining on such an employer. The 2015 Act amends the regime created by the 2001 Act (as previously amended by the 2004 Act).

---

13. Industrial Relations (Amendment) Act 2015, ss 15, 16 and 17.
14. Industrial Relations (Amendment) Act 2015, s 19.
15. Industrial Relations (Amendment) Act 2015, s 20.
16. Industrial Relations (Amendment) Act 2015, s 22.
17. Industrial Relations (Amendment) Act 2015, s 23.

[13.17] In *Ryanair Ltd v The Labour Court*[18] the Supreme Court considered the meaning to be given to the term 'collective bargaining' in the 2001 Act and concluded that in a non-union company collective bargaining did not have to take the same form and adopt the provisions as would apply in collective bargaining with a trade union, and that the term should be given its 'ordinary dictionary meaning'. Following the *Ryanair* decision, the 2001 Act fell into disuse and the 2015 Act includes amendments designed to make the 2001 Act regime more attractive to trade unions such that it might again be used by unions to intervene in support of their members in non-union employments or sectors. There are also provisions which compel the Labour Court to adopt a wider perspective in considering whether to make such a recommendation or determination.

[13.18] The 2015 Act changes the 2001 Act regime by:

  (i)   defining the term 'collective bargaining', with particular reference to non-union companies and employees;[19]

  (ii) providing for a wider range of factors that the Labour Court must take into account in making its recommendations and determinations;[20]

  (iii) disapplying the regime where the number of union members party to the dispute is insignificant;[21]

  (iv) restricting the making of multiple applications to the Court in respect of the same categories of employees;[22] and

  (vi) extending the jurisdiction of the Circuit Court to grant injunctions to protect employees who may have been dismissed by reason of an application made to the Labour Court under the 2001 Act.[23]

[13.19] The Act defines collective bargaining as voluntary engagements or negotiations between any employer or employer's organisation on the one hand and a trade union of workers or an excepted body on the other hand, with the objective of seeking agreement regarding the working conditions or terms of employment or non-employment of workers.[24] The definition requires that there be more than consultation or the exchange of information. The purpose of the exercise must be to seek agreement on working conditions and terms of employment or non-employment.

[13.20] An excepted body, for the purpose of the Act, is a body that is independent and not under the domination and control of an employer or trade union of employers, all the

---

18.   *Ryanair Ltd v The Labour Court* [2007] IESC 6.
19.   Industrial Relations (Amendment) Act 2015, s 27.
20.   Industrial Relations (Amendment) Act 2015, s 28(b).
21.   Industrial Relations (Amendment) Act 2015, s 28(b).
22.   Industrial Relations (Amendment) Act 2015, s 28(b).
23.   Industrial Relations (Amendment) Act 2015, s 34.
24.   Industrial Relations (Amendment) Act 2015, s 27.

members of which body are employed by the employer and which carries on engagements or negotiations with the object of reaching agreement regarding the wages or other conditions of employment of its own members but of no other employers.[25] The 2015 Act seeks to restrict the circumstances in which an employee forum or works council can be considered to be an excepted body and thereby allow an employer to defeat an application to the Labour Court under the 2001 Act on jurisdictional grounds. There are a number of factors which the Labour Court must consider in deciding whether an arrangement should be considered to be an exempted body. An employer that asserts that it has engaged in collective bargaining with an excepted body will bear the burden of proving this. The 2015 Act provides criteria which the Labour Court must take into account in making a decision on this jurisdictional issue, as follows:

(i)   how employees are elected to the elected body;

(ii) how often the elected body holds elections;

(iii) whether, and to what extent, the employer has funded or resourced the elected body beyond minimum logistical support; and

(iv) how long the elected body has existed and whether the employer had previously engaged in collective bargaining with that body.[26]

[13.21] The Act does not impose any obligation on employers to engage in collective bargaining. However, the Act, by amending the 2001 Act, does broaden the circumstances in which workers, whose employers refuse to engage in collective bargaining, can have relevant disputes addressed.

[13.22] The conditions, with reference to a trade dispute relating to terms and conditions of employment and dispute resolution and disciplinary procedures that must be satisfied before the Labour Court can intervene, are that:

(a) The employer does not engage in collective bargaining as a matter of practice and any internal dispute resolution procedures used have failed to resolve the dispute;

(b) The employer has failed to observe a provision, either entirely or in good faith, of the Code of Practice on Voluntary Dispute Resolution. This failure must not have been because of the actions of the trade union or the employees; and

(c) The trade union or employees did not have recourse to industrial action after the dispute in question was referred to the Workplace Relations Commission in accordance with the provisions of the Code.[27]

---

25.   Industrial Relations (Amendment) Act 2015, s 27.
26.   Industrial Relations (Amendment) Act 2015, s 28.
27.   Industrial Relations (Amendment) Act 2001, s 2 (as amended).

[13.23] The number of workers party to the dispute must not be insignificant unless exceptional and compelling circumstances for investigating the dispute exist. In determining this, the Court must have regard to the total numbers employed by the employer in the grade, group or category to which the dispute relates and, if it establishes the numbers are not insignificant, the Court will then consider the total numbers of employees employed by the employer and involved in any related group, grade or category. The Act provides that a trade union may establish the numbers by way of a statutory declaration but an employer can then ask the Labour Court to examine the accuracy of the contents of this statutory declaration.[28]

What factors must the Labour Court take into account where the jurisdictional issues are satisfied?

[13.24] Any review of the remuneration or terms or conditions of employment of workers must relate to same in their totality. This will involve the Labour Court comparing the situations of the workers involved with similar workers employed in similar employments. This may include workers of an associated company outside the State. Regard may be had to the comparability of skills, responsibilities, and physical and mental effort required to perform the work involved. The Labour Court must consider the effect of any determination it might make on the maintenance of employment and the long term sustainability of the business involved.[29]

How are multiple claims dealt with?

[13.25] In general, the Labour Court will not consider an investigation where one was carried out within the previous 18 months.[30]

What protections are there for a worker who participates in such an investigation by the Labour Court?

[13.26] The Act provides that if a worker is dismissed by reason of their participation in the process, this will constitute unfair dismissal and such a worker may apply to the Circuit Court for interim relief pending the determination of a claim for unfair dismissal.[31]

[13.27] Employers who engage in collective bargaining with one or more trade unions will not be affected by the non-union provisions of the 2015 Act in respect of workers for whom a union is recognised for collective bargaining purposes. For non-union employers who engage with an employee forum or staff representative group, it will be

---

28.   Industrial Relations (Amendment) Act 2015, s 29.
29.   Industrial Relations (Amendment) Act 2015, s 30.
30.   Industrial Relations (Amendment) Act 2015, s 28.
31.   Industrial Relations (Amendment) Act 2015, s 34.

necessary to assess whether or not this employee forum or staff representative group constitutes an excepted body for the purposes of the Act and whether an employer would be able to prove that in accordance with the criteria given. Otherwise that employer will be vulnerable to a claim under the 2001 Act and a consequential Labour Court determination.

DISPUTE RESOLUTION CLAUSES IN COLLECTIVE AGREEMENTS

[13.28] *ACC Loan Management Ltd v A Worker*[32]*—Labour Court—Industrial Relations Acts 1946 to 2015—collective agreement—entitlement to redundancy payment—dispute resolution clause in collective agreement must be adhered to*

This case was referred to the Labour Court in accordance with s 20(1) of the Industrial Relations Act 1969. The worker agreed to be bound by the Court's recommendation. The nature of the case was a dispute between the respondent company and the worker in relation to a severance package. The worker maintained that senior management in the company informed him that his position in the respondent would cease and advised him to seek alternative employment. The worker also stated that he had not received the appropriate severance payment in accordance with a collective agreement concluded between the respondent, SIPTU and Unite in March 2014 (the Agreement). Management of the respondent contended that, as the worker could have been given a suitable role within the company, a severance payment would have been inappropriate.

The Labour Court considered that the dispute related to both the interpretation of the Agreement and its application. It noted that the Agreement made provision for dealing with disputes of this nature. Under the heading 'Introduction' the Agreement provided that any dispute regarding the interpretation or implementation of the Agreement would be referred to a facilitator. The Labour Court considered it clear that the parties themselves, in concluding the Agreement, had made provision for the way in which disputes concerning its interpretation and application should be processed. This provision made no mention of a reference to the Court under s 20(1) of the Industrial Relations Act 1969. It was held that where parties to a collective agreement have made express provision for resolving disputes by way of such a collective agreement, they were bound by what they agreed. Accordingly the Court recommended that the parties adhere to the Agreement and that the subject matter of the dispute before it be referred to the facilitator for guidance in accordance with the Agreement.

---

32.   *ACC Loan Management Ltd v A Worker* LCR 20902.

INTRODUCTION OF A GPS VEHICLE MANAGEMENT SYSTEM

[13.29] *UPC Ireland v Unite Services Industrial Professional Technical Union[33]—Labour Court—Industrial Relations Acts 1946 to 2015, s 26(1)—dispute concerning installation of GPS vehicle management system into company fleet*

This dispute concerned the proposed installation of a GPS vehicle management system into the UPC transport fleet. In the Labour Court the union argued that there was no need for a GPS system and that such a system was a form of 'big brother'. The union stated that there was a mistrust of management and that its main concern was the privacy of its members.

UPC submitted that the system would allow the company to make speedy decisions which would significantly improve the management of its fleet. It stated that any concerns had been addressed comprehensively and that the system was a commercial necessity for the purpose of managing the vehicles. It further stated that staff privacy would be respected.

In its recommendation, the Labour Court found that UPC was entitled to introduce GPS devices into its fleet for the express purpose of obtaining real-time information of its deployment and to assist with the efficient allocation of resources. It further found that workers are entitled to privacy and autonomy in the performance of their work and most particularly in the conduct of their personal lives.

The Court noted the commitment made by UPC that the system would not be used for any purpose other than that set out above; nor would the system be used to track or record details of the staff's personal use of company vehicles other than to record distances travelled and to protect against theft of, and other risks to, the vehicles.

The Court recommended that the union agree to the introduction of the GPS devices on a pilot basis for a period of 12 months. It further recommended that UPC and the union establish a committee of four (two from each side) to meet in the first three months after the devices' introduction and thereafter quarterly to monitor the deployment and use of the devices during the trial period. It stated that any issues which could not be resolved by the monitoring committee or that remain outstanding at the end of the trial period should be referred back to the Labour Court for a definitive recommendation.

TRADE UNION RECOGNITION

[13.30] *Mount Tabor Care Centre & Nursing Home v Unite[34]—Labour Court—Industrial Relations Acts 1946 to 2015—Industrial Relations Act 1969, s 20(1)—dispute concerning recognition of union by employer*

This case concerned a claim by the trade union Unite that the employer refused to recognise it for collective negotiations on pay and conditions.

---

33. *UPC v Unite Services Industrial Professional Technical Union* LCR20938.
34. *Mount Tabor Care Centre & Nursing Home and Unite* LCR 20987.

The union submitted that, as a result of the lack of meaningful engagement afforded to it by the respondent employer regarding terms and conditions issues, 20 of the workers employed by the respondent joined Unite in the latter part of 2014. Unite stated that it wrote to management in December 2014 regarding union recognition but that the respondent avoided all of its approaches. The respondent did not attend the hearing.

The Labour Court recommended that the respondent recognise Unite for collective bargaining and industrial relations purposes in respect of its employee members. The Court stated that the parties should meet at an early date for the purpose of concluding a collective agreement governing procedural and other matters relating to the implementation of the Court's recommendation.

ACTING UP

[13.31] *HSE West v A Worker*[35]*—Labour Court—Industrial Relations Acts 1946 to 2015—Industrial Relations Act 1969, s 20(1)—acting-up entitlements—dispute concerning application for regularisation under HSE HR Circular 017/2013*

This case concerned a dispute between the HSE and a worker relating to acting in a senior role. The worker contended that she had been acting in a Grade VII post since 2010 but continued to be paid at her substantive Grade IV rate of pay. She sought to be regularised in the Grade VII post and retrospectively be paid any allowances that should have applied to the period she spent acting up. The HSE contended that the worker applied to be regularised but was unsuccessful on the basis that she did not meet the eligibility criteria set out in HSE HR Circular 017/2013.

The Court noted that the worker had been requested to perform Grade VII duties on an acting-up basis in 2010 due to the retirement of the incumbent and that she had been carrying out those duties since then, while continuing to be paid at the lower grade, without an acting up allowance. The Court reviewed the terms of HSE HR Circular 017/2013 and noted that no appeals process was provided for whereby unsuccessful applicants for regularisation could appeal decisions internally.

The Court stated it was of the view that as the claimant had been carrying on the role of a higher grade since 2010, without additional remuneration, and as she continued to carry out that role, she should be paid the appropriate acting-up allowance retrospective to the date she commenced that acting-up role and made a recommendation to that effect. The Court similarly recommended that the claimant's position be regularised under HSE HR Circular 017/2013.

Finally, the Court stated that the HSE should adhere to its well-established procedure for resolving disputes and therefore such matters as encompassed by this claim should not come before the Court under s 20(1) of the Industrial Relations Act 1969.

---

35. *HSE West v A Worker* LCR21002.

PROMOTION

[13.32] *IBM Ireland v A Worker*[36]*—Labour Court—Industrial Relations Acts 1946 to 2015, s 20(1)—whether claimant unfairly overlooked for promotion—where claimant ineligible to apply for internal roles as position in scope for transfer within part of business—inordinate delay in dealing with grievance*

The claimant contended that he was purposely misled to believe he was in the running for a promotional post and further maintained that he was deliberately held back in his position and was prohibited from applying for other roles for the benefit of the respondent company. He raised an internal grievance which was not resolved after a period of more than 14 months.

The respondent denied that the claimant was unfairly overlooked for promotion. The claimant was ineligible to apply for internal roles as his position was in scope for a transfer. The respondent maintained that the grievance was dealt with in accordance with its internal procedures.

The Labour Court noted the claimant's disappointment at being excluded from consideration for a promotional position because his current role was in scope for a transfer with part of the business. The Court held that the respondent did not act improperly or unfairly in taking that factor into consideration in making the appointment at issue. However, the Court concluded that there was an inordinate and unjustified delay in addressing the grievance raised by the claimant through the internal procedures.

The Court noted that the claimant's sense of grievance at what occurred could have been addressed, and possibly assuaged, had the internal procedures operated within a reasonable timeframe. The Labour Court concluded that the failure to deal with the claimant's grievance should be acknowledged and the respondent should pay the claimant compensation in the amount of €2,000 for the effects of this shortcoming.

DEMOTION

[13.33] *Keelings Logistics Solutions v A Worker*[37]*—Labour Court—appeal from recommendation of Rights Commissioner—Industrial Relations Acts 1946 to 2015, s 13(9)—whether demotion of claimant lawful*

The claimant was employed as a warehouse team manager but was demoted from his position to general operative level following a failed health and safety audit for which he was held responsible. It was admitted by the claimant that he had left his position to attend a meeting that he believed would take approximately 20 minutes, however, due to circumstances beyond his control, he was absent for significantly longer. While the claimant accepted responsibility for his actions and understood that some sanction had to be imposed, he felt that given his employment record, the decision taken by management to demote him was very harsh, unwarranted and unnecessary. It was

---

36. *IBM Ireland v A Worker* LCR 21019.
37. *Keelings Logistics Solutions v A Worker* AD1516.

submitted by the respondent that the claimant was an experienced manager who should not have left his position on the morning of an audit and should not have signed off on the 'safe and legal book' to say he had carried out certain checks when he later admitted he had asked another colleague to do so.

It was further submitted by the respondent that the claimant's negligent conduct on the day not only failed the onsite audit but could have caused a very serious injury or fatality.

In the hearing before the Rights Commissioner, it was noted that the claimant was aware that an audit was to take place. The audit failed as a result of damaged racking pallets and this was not in dispute. The Rights Commissioner further noted that the claimant had made an error of judgment and had misprioritised his role by attending the meeting on the day. However, given his employment record, the Rights Commissioner recommended that the respondent consider reviewing the case in one year's time from the date of the demotion.

The Labour Court noted that the trade union had appealed this recommendation and was seeking reinstatement of the claimant to the position of warehouse team manager with effect from December 2014 at which time he had completed one year of the sanction. It was submitted by the union that, by demoting the claimant to the general operative, the respondent had imposed a sanction in perpetuity which, in all of the circumstances, was excessive, unnecessary and unwarranted, particularly taking account of the claimant's previous exemplary record. The respondent submitted that the breach of duties by the claimant was deemed to come within the realm of gross misconduct and accordingly warranted a severe disciplinary sanction. The Labour Court concluded that the sanction should be reconsidered and was of the view that a demotion in perpetuity was excessive in the circumstances. The Court recommended the claimant be reinstated in his role as warehouse team manager with effect from the date of the Labour Court decision.

PERFORMANCE MANAGEMENT

[13.34] *Matheson Solicitors v A Worker*[38]*—Labour Court—Industrial Relations Acts 1946 to 2015, s 20(1) —introduction of new performance management system— refusal to fully engage with new system—whether new system requirements were excessive, unfair and inappropriate*

This dispute arose from the introduction of a new method of employee assessment called the 'Legal Personal Assistant Programme'. The claimant employee objected to the new system on the basis that its requirements and the sanctions associated with any perceived underperformance were excessive and inappropriate. The claimant noted that if a staff member was unsuccessful in any of the required proficiency tests, remedial action was taken and a threat of disciplinary action existed where the required standards were not achieved. It was asserted by the claimant that the system was completely unfair and inappropriate. It was submitted by the respondent that the system had been accepted by

---

38.   *Matheson Solicitors v A Worker* LCR20931.

the vast majority of staff and its aim was to design, maintain and achieve reasonable proficiency in the use of a number of computer software packages routinely used in the performance of duties. The respondent noted that the programme had been successful and that a majority of legal personal assistants had complied with it and were certified as obtaining the required level of competencies in their job functions. The assessment process was designed to inform the respondent and employees of the skill level of an employee and what, if any, additional training was required to assist the employee in meeting the required standards. The respondent asserted that it must retain the right to manage its business and to ensure that its staff were sufficiently skilled to carry out their duties.

The Labour Court accepted that the new system was designed to ensure that the skills and competencies of legal personal assistants were kept up to date and that they were trained to a consistent standard in the use of software packages required for their job function. The Court also accepted that certain employees required more advanced skills, depending on the needs of their roles. The Labour Court held it was satisfied that such training requirements came within the realm of normal ongoing change and did not alter an employee's conditions of employment. The Labour Court noted that it was possible to seek an exemption from the programme depending on the personal and medical circumstances of an individual employee. The Court concluded that unless such an exemption applied to the claimant, the requirement for training and upskilling applied equally to her as it did to all other legal personal assistants. The Court recommended that the claimant be given every support opportunity and assistance, without a threat of disciplinary sanction, to undertake the training necessary to meet the required standard prior to the next assessment date.

REASSIGNMENT OF EMPLOYEES

[13.35] *HSE West v A Worker*[39]*—Labour Court—appeal from recommendation of Rights Commissioner—Industrial Relations Acts 1946 to 2015, s 13(9)—validity of decision to reassign employee to different position—deterioration in working relationship*

The claimant was appointed as a coordinator of critical incident response, but asserted that he had been gradually managed out of this position since 2007, culminating in his redeployment as a bereavement councillor in 2013. The claimant sought reinstatement as coordinator and the payment of travelling expenses in accordance with HSE policy. It was submitted by the respondent that the claimant's relationship with his colleagues had deteriorated to the point that it was adversely affecting their work and thus the decision to reassign him was made following numerous meetings and much correspondence. It was submitted by the respondent that the claimant had been reassigned to a position that was within the grade, salary and work appropriate to him.

The Labour Court noted that it was being invited to recommend the range of duties that ought to be assigned to the claimant by his employer and that while the claimant

---

39.   *HSE West v A Worker* AD1518.

clearly had bona fide views on how his particular skills ought to be deployed by the respondent, the prerogative to assign work within an employee's terms and conditions of employment rests with the employer. The Labour Court held it could not substitute its opinion on what is appropriate for that of the employer, except where there is manifest unfairness in the manner in which the employer exercises its prerogative. The Court noted that the respondent had decided to utilise the claimant's skills in a manner it considered appropriate, having regard to the prevailing circumstances. This decision did not contravene any provision of the claimant's contract of employment nor did it contravene any collective agreement applicable to him.

With regard to the claim for travel expenses, the Labour Court agreed with the submissions made by the claimant that expenses should be paid in accordance with established regulations and varied the Rights Commissioner recommendation in this regard.

ELIMINATION OF NIGHT SHIFT

[13.36] *Kerry Women's Refuge & Support Services v Services Industrial Professional Technical Union (SIPTU)[40]—Labour Court—Industrial Relations Act 1990, s 26(1)—elimination of night shift—reduction in work hours*

This dispute concerned the elimination of the night shift in Kerry Women's Refuge & Support Services which it was claimed by SIPTU resulted in a 50 per cent reduction in the hours of work for three members of staff. The Labour Court heard that, as a result of severe cuts in funding, it was deemed necessary by management in the company to curtail its services from midnight to 9 am. This resulted in a reduction in hours of the workers affected, reducing their hours from an average of 42 hours per week to an average of 21 hours per week. SIPTU sought to reverse the action taken or at least to provide the workers with a minimum of 31 hours per week.

This dispute was the subject of a conciliation conference under the auspices of the Labour Relations Commission. As agreement was not reached; the dispute was accordingly referred to the Labour Court under s 26(1) of the Industrial Relations Act 1990.

SIPTU submitted the following arguments:

(a) the company eliminated the night shift in November 2014 and the three workers in question had their hours cut from 42 to 21 hours per week;

(b) the reduction in hours applied only to the three workers concerned, who were also the longest-serving workers with 14, 17 and 18 years' service respectively; and

(c) the proposal by management to resolve the matter was based on the payment of an on-call allowance, relief cover and attendance at weekly meetings which were not acceptable to the workers.

---

40. *Kerry Women's Refuge & Support Services v Services Industrial Professional Technical Union* LCR21042.

The company submitted the following arguments:

(a) the company relied predominantly on State funding and donations and fundraising to deliver its services, and overall income had dropped significantly since 2010;

(b) the withdrawal of the Rent Supplement Payment reduced funding by 7 per cent, and the company anticipated a further reduction in funding from TUSLA of 3.5 per cent; and

(c) the company sought the elimination of the midnight to 9 am cover Monday to Sunday to replace it with an on-call arrangement, relief cover and attendance at weekly meetings to replace some of the hours lost.

The Labour Court stated that it was of the view that the parties should engage in further discussions to include and take account of the proposals made by management of the company on 7 January 2015 (incorporating its previous proposals made on 26 November 2014). The Labour Court stated that, with agreed modifications to these proposals, and with the extra hours provided since 1 July 2015 for relief cover, efforts should be made to try to achieve the minimum 31 hours aspired to by SIPTU. The Labour Court recommended that the discussions should be completed within a period of three months from the date of the Recommendation. The Labour Court also stated that when agreement was reached on new arrangements for the workers concerned, they should be reviewed after 12 months of operation.

TRANSFER AND REDISTRIBUTION OF WORK

[13.37] *An Post v CPSU*[41]*—Labour Court—Industrial Relations Acts 1946 to 2015, s 26(1)—whether transfer and redistribution of work to employees based in Sligo legitimate in circumstance where respondent in a position to offer voluntary redundancies to employees located in Dublin*

This matter was the subject of a conciliation conference from which emerged a proposal recommended for acceptance by both parties. The proposal was subsequently rejected by the trade union and the matter was referred to the Labour Court in accordance with s 26(1).

The union asserted that the transfer of work from back office operations in the GPO in Dublin to four members of staff located in Sligo created a precedent whereby work could be transferred at any point in time. The union further contended that its members were working under a threat that they may be redeployed to an alternative location at any time and asserted that this type of transfer undermined and suppressed the positions of workers based in central operations. It was asserted by the respondent employer that there was an urgent business need to transfer work to Sligo in order to avoid a staffing surplus. This occurred in a work area where there were employees actively seeking voluntary redundancies. The release of four employees and the transfer of work to Sligo would save the respondent a significant amount of money per annum.

---

41.   *An Post v CPSU* LCR 20929.

The Labour Court was unable to identify any disadvantage to the workers who were party to the dispute as a consequence of the respondent's proposal being implemented. The Court noted that all the evidence pointed in the opposite direction as this transfer would facilitate those who wished to avail of the voluntary severance scheme and on whose behalf the trade union had already made a representation. In those circumstances, the Labour Court recommended that the respondent's proposal be accepted. The Court noted that insofar as this dispute related to the demarcation of work between different union groups, the Court maintained its long-held position that such matters should not be addressed in its recommendations but should be dealt with by other established machinery.

Injunctions

[13.38] See also *University College Cork v Services Industrial Professional Technical Union and Irish Federation of University Teachers*[42] at [14.01] where the defendant unions were calling upon union members to engage in picketing at the main campus of the university in circumstances where union members employed at the main campus had not participated in the secret ballot.

Judicial review

[13.39] See also *Mulally & Ors v The Labour Court and Waterford County Council (Notice Party)* at [16.01].[43]

---

42. *University College Cork v SIPTU and IFUT* [2015] IEHC 282.

43. *Mullally & Ors v The Labour Court and Waterford County Council (Notice Party)* [2015] IEHC 351.

Chapter 14

INJUNCTIONS

RESTRAINING PICKETING

[14.01] *University College Cork v Services Industrial Professional Technical Union and Irish Federation of University Teachers[1]—High Court—Gilligan J—Industrial Relations Act 1990, ss 11(1), 14(2)(a), 19(1)—injunctive relief restraining defendant unions from engaging in industrial action on main campus of plaintiff university—watching, besetting, picketing and interfering—whether defendant unions calling upon union members to engage in picketing at main campus in circumstances where union members employed at main campus had not participated in the secret ballot—definition of 'engaging' in industrial action—serious issue to be determined—balance of convenience—damages not an adequate remedy*

The plaintiff is a university situated at a substantial campus in Cork City (the main campus). The plaintiff has a significant research institute, referred to as the Tyndall National Institute (Tyndall), which is part of the university but located approximately one kilometre away from the main campus. Tyndall specialises in the research and development of information and communication technologies. The defendant unions (SIPTU and IFUT) had, for a considerable period of time prior to the commencement of the proceedings, been involved in a trade dispute with the plaintiff in which the unions were seeking pay increases on behalf of their members in Tyndall.

On 22 April 2015, as a consequence of the ongoing pay dispute, the unions notified the plaintiff in writing of their intention to picket at the entrances to the 'employment' of the plaintiff on specified days in April and May 2015. The plaintiff wrote to the unions requesting further clarification of the term 'employment' and sought an undertaking that the proposed pickets would be confined solely to the entrances to Tyndall and that no pickets would be placed at any of the entrances to the main campus. The following day, the unions notified the plaintiff that they were withdrawing the notice of industrial action on the basis of the plaintiff's request for further clarification. Later that same day, the unions formally notified the plaintiff of their intention to picket the plaintiff's premises on various future dates and at a number of locations, including the picketing of six of the 12 entrances to the main campus from 7 am to 5.30 pm on Wednesday 13 May 2015 (ie the following week). The plaintiff's solicitors wrote to the unions on 30 April 2015 expressing concerns that university examinations scheduled for that day would be disrupted and querying the lawfulness, under the Industrial Relations Act 1990, of the proposed industrial action in which all union members were being called upon to engage but where only members employed at Tyndall had participated in the secret ballot.

On 1 May 2015, SIPTU responded stating that further communications issued to its members, including those employed at the main campus, were merely requests for

---

1. *University College Cork v SIPTU and IFUT* [2015] IEHC 282.

support and solidarity and that members employed at the main campus had not been called upon or encouraged to withdraw their labour on 13 May 2015. In circumstances where they refused to withdraw the notification of industrial action at the main campus, the plaintiff commenced proceedings against the unions seeking two interlocutory injunctions including: (a) an injunction restraining the unions from watching and/or besetting and/or picketing any of the plaintiff's premises other than the Tyndall premises; and (b) an injunction restraining the unions from interfering with access and/or egress to any of the plaintiff's main campus premises. The second defendant, IFUT, did not enter an appearance and was not represented in the injunction proceedings.

Gilligan J, in his judgment, noted the pertinent provisions of the 1990 Act, including: s 11(1), which provides for the general right of one or more persons to attend at an employer's premises for the purposes of engaging in peaceful communication and/or persuasion; s 14(2)(a), which provides that a trade union may only engage in industrial action after conducting a secret ballot, where the entitlement to vote is afforded to all union members, whom it is reasonable, at the time of the ballot for the union concerned to believe will be called upon to engage in the strike or other proposed industrial action; and s 19(1), which prohibits employers from obtaining an injunction against trade unions in respect of proposed industrial actions in circumstances where the secret ballot and associated industrial action requirements have been adhered to by the trade union.

The plaintiff contended that the proposed industrial action was unlawful under s 14(2)(a) as the unions had not conducted a ballot of all persons whom it was reasonable, at the time of the ballot, for the unions to believe would be called upon to engage in the proposed industrial action, namely the members of the unions employed at the main campus. The unions had conducted a secret ballot of their respective members in Tyndall only, seeking support for the taking of industrial action against the plaintiff; and, by a substantial majority, the members at Tyndall voted in favour of engaging in industrial action. However, the secret ballot was limited solely to union members employed in Tyndall and no ballot was taken in respect of the wider union membership throughout the university and consequently excluded the majority of the unions' members who were employed at the main campus. Subsequent to the holding of the secret ballot, communications from the unions to their members called for the 'escalation' of the picketing to include the main campus and called upon all members, including those employed at the main campus, to engage in the industrial action. The plaintiff asserted that, in respect of the pickets which were to be placed at the main campus, the unions failed to comply with their obligations in respect of the secret ballot under the 1990 Act and, as a result, forfeited the protections against injunctive relief taken by employers available to the unions under s 19(1) of the 1990 Act. The plaintiff asserted that, unless restrained by the Court, unlawful industrial action would occur. The plaintiff did not seek interlocutory relief in respect of the picketing at the Tyndall premises.

The plaintiff contended that a serious issue had been raised as to whether or not s 14(2)(a) had been complied with and that it was a matter for the unions to convince the Court that the legal requirements of the secret ballot under the 1990 Act had been adhered to and that the proposed industrial action was lawful. The unions contended that the escalation of the industrial action to include the picketing at the main campus was lawful as the members at the main campus were merely being asked to support the members who had voted in the secret ballot, for example, by way of providing refreshments to the picketers or by the sounding of car horns as motorists passed by the pickets, but that they had not been called upon to physically engage in the picketing at the entrances to the main campus.

In his judgment, Gilligan J noted that the members of the unions who were employed at the main campus had not participated in the secret ballot and that this wider group of members had now been called upon to engage in the industrial action on the main campus. Gilligan J also noted the significance of the fact that, in respect of the secret ballot referring to the industrial action, the employment was described as 'UCC Tyndall' and the location of the ballot count was the Tyndall Institute. Gilligan J further observed that, in respect of its application for interlocutory relief, the plaintiff only had to raise a serious issue to be tried by the Court as to the validity of the secret ballot and the lawfulness of the proposed industrial action in accordance with s 14(2)(a) of the 1990 Act. Gilligan J reviewed the correspondence issued by the unions to their members and to the plaintiff in order to ascertain the intentions of the unions upon conducting the secret ballot and subsequently, upon giving notice to the plaintiff of their intention to picket on the main campus. Gilligan J noted that the initial notification of industrial action by the unions did not make it clear that pickets would be placed at the main campus and that such clarification was only received upon request by the plaintiff. Gilligan J further noted that the communications from the unions to its members notifying them of the intention to escalate the picketing to the main campus did not request nor encourage members employed at the main campus to pass the picket. Gilligan J noted that the Court must take into account the circumstances where the secret ballot was conducted before it appeared there was any proposal to picket the main campus or to seek support from the members employed at the main campus. Gilligan J stated that, in reaching his decision, he was influenced by the specific terminology used by the unions by way of written correspondence to their members. Gilligan J referred to and relied upon the relevant and applicable legal principles in respect of the lawfulness of secret ballots and resulting industrial action as cited by him in *Dublin Airport Authority plc & Anor v Services Industrial Professional Technical Union.*[2]

Gilligan J determined that the plaintiff had raised a serious issue to be determined with regard to s 14(2)(a) as to whether members of the unions employed at the main campus, who did not participate in the secret ballot, were subsequently being called upon to engage in the picketing at the main campus. Gilligan J was satisfied that the hurdle of establishing whether a serious question to be determined had been passed by the plaintiff and that the *Campus Oil*[3] principles applied. Gilligan J further stated that in circumstances where student examinations might be affected, damages would not be an adequate remedy and further, that the balance of convenience favoured the granting of the relief sought. Gilligan J granted interlocutory injunctions: (i) restraining the unions from watching, besetting and/or picketing any of the plaintiff's main campus premises,

---

2.   *Dublin Airport Authority plc & Anor v SIPTU* [2014] IEHC 644. See *Arthur Cox Employment Law Yearbook 2014* at [12.10].

3.   *Campus Oil Ltd & Ors v Minister for Industry and Energy (No 2)*[1983] IR 88.

other than the premises known as Tyndall; and (ii) restraining the defendants from interfering with access and/or egress to any of the plaintiff's main campus.

RESTRAINING REASSIGNMENT

[14.02] *Earley v The Health Service Executive[4]—High Court—Kennedy J— application for interlocutory injunction—seeking to restrain reassignment of plaintiff temporarily from her position—seeking to restrain appointment of another person to plaintiff's position—whether plaintiff established strong case—whether damages an adequate remedy—where balance of convenience lies*

The plaintiff, an area director of nursing for the Galway Roscommon Mental Health Service, commenced these proceedings seeking interlocutory relief to restrain the defendant from reassigning her temporarily from her position and to restrain the defendant from appointing another person to her position.

The plaintiff had been employed by the defendant since 1998 and was appointed to her current position in 2012. She had responsibility for more than 60 facilities across the counties of Galway and Roscommon. On 1 July 2015, she was advised in writing that she was to be temporarily re-assigned, without prejudice, as an area director of nursing in a specialised capacity to the programme management office of the National Mental Health Division of the HSE. The reassignment took effect from 6 July 2015, on which date a third party was appointed as acting area director of nursing. It was noted by the Court that this third party was only in this position pending the determination of these interlocutory proceedings. Kennedy J noted that there had been alleged incidents within the relevant area involving service users and that anonymous letters of complaint had been received by the defendant, some of which related to these incidents. The defendant contended that it had determined to carry out appropriate inquiries by reason of these matters. The proposed inquiries were threefold: a systems analysis; a full national review; and a screening process investigating the anonymous correspondence received. The five serious incidents involved a service user, and it was submitted by the defendant that a question had arisen as to whether the incidents were appropriately reported or escalated. Concerns had been expressed by the Mental Health Commission after the receipt of an anonymous complaint by the defendant, the Mental Health Commission, the Nursing and Midwifery Board and the Minister for Health. The defendant advised the Court that a decision had been taken to commence the inquiries, that the systems analysis review would take 12 weeks and that the screening process would take a matter of weeks; however the Court noted that no time was provided for the national review. The defendant maintained that on conclusion of these inquiries, it might be required to undertake other procedures, including appropriate procedures involving the potential discipline of staff members. Kennedy J noted that the plaintiff was not the subject of any disciplinary or trust in care process.

It was noted that the plaintiff's belief that she had been the focus of personal attacks from the Psychiatric Nurses Association (PNA) which she believed were the result of

---

4.   *Earley v The Health Service Executive* [2015] IEHC 520.

her role in implementing changes within the HSE. It was contended by the plaintiff that the true motivation behind her reassignment was for industrial relations considerations. The plaintiff asserted that her temporary reassignment was a breach of her contract of employment, and of fair procedures and without any lawful basis and she sought to restrain the defendant from proceeding.

The Court considered the timing of the alleged incident vis-à-vis the decision to reassign the plaintiff. It was noted by Kennedy J that the approach to the plaintiff by her line manager was before the final alleged incident and before the second and third anonymous letters. It was submitted that the decision to carry out the inquiries by the defendant was not based primarily on the receipt of the anonymous letter; the factual matrix leading to its decision to temporarily transfer the plaintiff was broader. It was submitted that the plaintiff had been initially requested to move to another position which she declined; thereafter she was instructed to take up the aforementioned position on a temporary basis. The defendant submitted that the plaintiff was not singled out in any way but that other steps had been taken or were being taken in respect of other senior personnel with responsibility for mental health services in Co Roscommon. The defendant asserted it was necessary and appropriate that certain interim measures were put in place so that the defendant could be assured that day-to-day care in management arrangements were appropriate. In her affidavit, the plaintiff averred that she had sought the reasons in writing for requesting her voluntary assignment and expressed a concern that she was being victimised for her efforts to implement reform. The plaintiff further averred that the first three incidents were investigated and risk assessed locally and that it was determined not to escalate them. Reference was made by the plaintiff to a letter from the clinical director for Co Roscommon with responsibility for a residential facility which was relevant to the alleged incident. In this letter it was confirmed that the decision had been taken by the clinical director to deal with the incidents locally and this was communicated to the line manager, and to the plaintiff's line manager in November 2014. It was further averred by the plaintiff that she reported the July incidents to her line manager on 29 July 2014. The High Court noted that the date of communication was significant as this information was known to the defendant as of November 2014; yet no request was made of the plaintiff until May 2015. It was further submitted that the incidents of March and June 2015 were reported and assessed by local managers and were being dealt with in accordance with HSE policy. Kennedy J noted that this claim was not contradicted by the defendant.

The Court considered the application of the principles established in *Maha Lingham v Health Service Executive.*[5] Kennedy J noted that as the plaintiff was seeking a mandatory order it was necessary for her to establish a strong case in order to obtain the relief sought. Kennedy J then considered what was meant by this test. It was asserted on behalf of the defendant that, in order to establish that the plaintiff had a strong case, she must satisfy the Court that she would succeed ultimately in securing a permanent injunction. It was further submitted that a strong case was not made out if the plaintiff simply satisfied the Court that there had been a breach of her contract of employment as

---

5.   *Maha Lingham v Health Service Executive* [2006] 17 ELR 140.

the grant of an interlocutory injunction in an employment case would have the effect of enforcing a contract of employment, which is extremely rare.

It was accepted by the plaintiff that she must establish that she had a strong likelihood of success but the remedy ultimately sought would be different than that sought at the interlocutory stage and that the facts of the case illustrated this. Kennedy J was satisfied by the merit of this argument.

Kennedy J noted that in *Maha Lingham*, the Supreme Court held that the plaintiff seeking an injunction had to show that he had a strong case that he was probably going to be successful at trial. She held that a plaintiff seeking interlocutory relief did not need to reach the kind of threshold advanced by counsel for the defendant; if so, it would be difficult to see how any application for an injunction could be successful at interlocutory stage. Kennedy J noted the statement of Fennelly J in *Maha Lingham*:

> ...in such a case it is necessary for the applicant to show at least that he has a strong case that he is likely to succeed at the hearing of the action.

Kennedy J concluded that in this case it was necessary for the plaintiff to show that she had a strong case that she was likely to succeed at the hearing of the action.

It was asserted by the plaintiff that the defendant had no legal basis to reassign her on a temporary basis. The plaintiff made reference to the reliance by the defendant on clause 4 of her contract of employment. This clause provided as follows:

> You will be employed in Galway and Roscommon Health Services. Your initial assignment will be to Galway and Roscommon Mental Health Services. You may be required to work in any service area within the vicinity as the need arises.

It was submitted by the plaintiff that this was a location clause and that applying the ordinary principles of the construction of contracts, this clause did not permit the reassignment in the manner in it which occurred in this case but was concerned with physical location only. The Court noted that it was decided that the plaintiff should remain in the same office albeit carrying out other duties. Reference was made also to the reliance by the defendant on s 22 of the Health Act 2004, which, it contended, provides an express statutory power to determine the duties of employees. The defendant also sought to rely on an implied power to manage its affairs in an appropriate manner. It was submitted on behalf of the plaintiff that the initial power to appoint staff and determine their duties subject to the terms and conditions of employment may be agreed once a person is appointed; it would undermine any contract of employment if the HSE could ignore the contract and fall back on the initial power of an appointment. It was further submitted on behalf of the plaintiff that if such an implied power existed as contended by the defendant it would radically alter the terms and conditions of employment.

Kennedy J noted that the principles governing interlocutory injunctions must be flexible and could not be applied rigidly, confirming *Wallace v The Irish Aviation Authority*.[6] Kennedy J summarised that she must assess whether the alteration in the terms of the plaintiff's employment was such as to render it a breach of her contract of

---

6. *Wallace v The Irish Aviation Authority* [2012] IEHC 178.

employment. Kennedy J held that she was satisfied, applying *Maha Lingham*, that the plaintiff had demonstrated that she had a strong case that was likely to succeed at the hearing of the action. The Court noted the plaintiff's position that there was no factual basis for the decision to reassign her temporarily and that the five incidents and the manner in which they were addressed could not support the defendant's position. Kennedy J noted the plaintiff's position that the motivation was to simply appease the Psychiatric Nurses Association (PNA). The Court noted that it should not seek to resolve contested issues of fact in an application for an interlocutory injunction and that it did not intend to make any findings of fact. However, the Court noted that these factors were relevant and undisputed. The Court noted that, in temporarily reassigning the plaintiff for an unspecified duration, it may be necessary to undertake other procedures to include the potential disciplining of staff members during this time. The Court noted that the reality for the plaintiff was that she found herself in a position where she could not respond to any allegations because she had not been suspended and might have found herself in a worse position.

As to whether damages would be an adequate remedy for the plaintiff it was submitted by the defendant that, in bringing these proceedings, the plaintiff had herself caused or contributed to her alleged loss of reputation. This was rejected by the High Court as Kennedy J stated that this argument ignored the damage to a person's reputation which may apply within the individual's profession or business where a person is suspended pending a disciplinary hearing or pending an enquiry such as in this case. Kennedy J held that this damage was compounded where it was a senior person who was being reassigned and effectively removed from her duties as the plaintiff had been in the present case. This may carry with it a dramatic loss of status within her profession and therefore the Court concluded that damages were not an adequate remedy.

With regard to the balance of convenience, the Court noted the defendant's objection to the application on the basis that the Courts could not be involved in the ongoing supervision of the employment relationship. However, the Court noted that this did not arise in this case as the plaintiff was not asking the Court to supervise the employment relations but was requesting that she be permitted to do her job in accordance with her contract of employment. Kennedy J noted that the plaintiff was in a managerial position and continued to manage facilities in Galway which did not appear to trouble the defendant. Kennedy J stated that she could conclude that there was no question of her competence and she noted that the plaintiff continued to be paid her salary and therefore the defendant would not be at any financial loss if she returned to her duties. As regards the potential tensions within the workplace, the Court noted that the letter voluntarily furnished by the clinical director assisted the Court in concluding that there was a good working relationship with the management.

The Court noted that the proposed inquiries might take time and noted that no timeframe had been given regarding the national review and thus the plaintiff would remain on temporary reassignment for an unknown and therefore uncertain duration. It was noted that the plaintiff continued to work from the same office and had the same personal assistant. Kennedy J concluded that the balance of convenience favoured the plaintiff and the plaintiff would therefore succeed on the application. The interlocutory injunction was granted.

[14.03] *Earley v Health Service Executive[7]—High Court—O'Connor J—plaintiff seeking declaration that decision of defendant to reassign plaintiff was unlawful— plaintiff challenged decision and rationale for her temporary reassignment—whether bad faith, conspiracy or failure to recognise rights of plaintiff had been established— whether plaintiff had been denied natural justice—where defendant had breached contract of employment by reassigning plaintiff—whether defendant entitled to reassign plaintiff in order to facilitate a national review and analysis of a crisis within its services—protection of vulnerable service users*

Following the granting of the interlocutory injunction referred to at [14.02] the case came on for plenary hearing and the plaintiff sought a declaration that the decision of the defendant to temporarily reassign her from her role to an allegedly lesser role was unlawful. The plaintiff further submitted that the Court could have faith in the defendant as a statutory body to act in accordance with the granting of such a declaration.[8] The defendant argued that, despite the plaintiff not being subjected to an investigation or disciplinary process, her transfer was necessary while a review was being conducted into allegations of sexual abuse within the defendant's mental health facilities in Roscommon.

O'Connor J noted that the Mental Health Commission had expressed urgent and grave concerns regarding the welfare of some service users and the Nursing and Midwifery Board of Ireland had informed the defendant that An Garda Síochána had been alerted to the withholding of information in respect of offences against children and vulnerable persons. Mr Gloster, a then interim chief officer of the defendant in the Galway/Mayo/Roscommon area, had formed a 'reasonable, bona fide and honestly held opinion' that the mental health services in Roscommon required a special review to provide the necessary assurances and comfort required by both the defendant and the Mental Health Commission. O'Connor J also noted that the plaintiff was entitled to care, patience and understanding from the defendant at all stages of the process. O'Connor J further stated that the plaintiff:

> was effectively jeopardising the provision of mental health services in order to thwart what she feared was going to be a permanent reassignment without her perceived right to due process.

It was also noted that the plaintiff had no excuse for having 'consciously ignored' her temporary replacement's authority. The plaintiff had ignored her failure to obtain an interlocutory injunction preventing her temporary transfer and had not fully cooperated when she did ultimately obtain an injunction to reinstate her to her previous role. It was further emphasised that a Mental Health Commission interim report submitted to the Court and entitled 'Review of the quality, safety and governance of services within the Roscommon area' dated 22 October 2015 had stated 'that Mental Health Services for

---

7.   *Earley v Health Service Executive* [2015] IEHC 841.
8.   *McNamara v Health Service Executive* [2009] IEHC 418.

the people of Roscommon are dysfunctional and carry unnecessary risk'. Each of these elements resulted in O'Connor J concluding that while parties have a constitutional right to litigate disputes:

> this Court takes the opportunity to exhort all professionals in the future to recognise that the most vulnerable in society ... have rights which they ... and the courts ought not allow to be affected by the litigation process if at all possible.

The decision, the subject of the complaint, was the defendant's decision to temporarily reassign the plaintiff from her role as area director of nursing in the Galway/Roscommon mental health service to area director of nursing in a specialised capacity in the programme management office of the national mental health division. The plaintiff argued that her reassignment was motivated to appease the Psychiatric Nurses Association and was reliant on anonymous complaints regarding alleged wrongdoings. The plaintiff submitted that she had suffered reputational damage due to the temporary reassignment which linked her to the allegations of a cover-up of sexual abuse. O'Connor J next addressed each element of the plaintiff's arguments.

O'Connor J found that the plaintiff's terms of employment remained precisely the same. Her reassigned temporary role had the equivalent grade status and level of remuneration as her original role, save that she would no longer have an operational role. Further, the plaintiff could carry out her role from her existing office with her existing secretary and, as such, was not carrying out a fundamentally different job. O'Connor J noted that the plaintiff's contract obliged her to work 'in any service area' and that she was contractually obliged to 'undertake duties appropriate to her position'. O'Connor J concluded that neither the plaintiff nor a union representing her grade could veto a temporary reassignment on the basis of her contractual entitlements.

The plaintiff submitted that the defendant's 'Trust in Care Policy', which applied to health service employers in respect of upholding the dignity and welfare of patients/clients and the procedure for managing allegations of abuse against staff members, should have been applied to her circumstances. O'Connor J found that this policy was not applicable as the defendant had not made any allegation of a cover up against the plaintiff. O'Connor J also noted that the plaintiff's argument would have failed in any event due to the defendant's screening of the complaints which found that there was no prima facie complaint against the plaintiff; and the policy which allowed the defendant to take whatever protective measures were necessary for the welfare of patients at risk.

O'Connor J rejected the plaintiff's argument that she had been denied natural justice, noting that it would be 'an extraordinary state of affairs if an employer when requiring employees to do a similar job on a temporary basis must have a form of process akin to a disciplinary or suspending process'. O'Connor J noted that the plaintiff had been afforded an opportunity to engage but had not taken it and further stated that although the plaintiff was under no obligation to seek redress under the grievance procedure, her constant assertion of being deprived of natural justice did not sit with her decision to refrain from implementing the grievance procedure. O'Connor J commented that another employee who had been temporarily reassigned for the same reasons as the plaintiff had voluntarily agreed to the reassignment. This employee had utilised the grievance procedure to submit her complaint as opposed to the court system.

The plaintiff failed to establish loss of reputation or status on the basis of her reassignment. No evidence of damage had been submitted to the Court. O'Connor J stated that the plaintiff 'appear[ed] rather precious and melodramatic about the effect of her status as a result of the impugned decision'.

O'Connor J found Mr Gloster, witness for the defendant, to be supportive of the plaintiff throughout the process. O'Connor J felt that Mr Gloster had handled the concerns of the Mental Health Commission, the public, the staff, the unions and the external review group in a professional way. O'Connor J concluded that the defendant's decision to reassign the plaintiff had not been made in bad faith but rather to allow for the review and analysis of a crisis situation which the plaintiff failed to prove did not exist. O'Connor J noted that the defendant's actions had been taken in the best interests of the vulnerable service users involved. O'Connor J concluded that no evidence of bad faith, conspiracy or failure to recognise the rights of the plaintiff had been established.

The plaintiff's application failed. O'Connor J stated that a number of factors contributed to this decision, including the interpretation of the employment contract; the defiance of the plaintiff, the unchallenged evidence of Mr Gloster; and the entirely novel point of law raised by the plaintiff on the obligation to organise services contrary to what the defendant had concluded was the best approach in a crisis. O'Connor J concluded that the granting of the declaration as sought by the plaintiff would have risked exacerbating the crisis.

RESTRAINING DISMISSAL

[14.04] *Boyle v An Post*[9]*—High Court—Barrett J—fair procedures—mandatory injunctions—reinstatement—bias*

The plaintiff had worked as a postman with the defendant but was dismissed after he allegedly re-posted mail due for delivery. The defendant carried out an investigation and disciplinary process against, the plaintiff. The plaintiff claimed that the defendant did not adhere to fair procedures and that he was therefore unlawfully dismissed. The plaintiff sought interlocutory injunctions:

- reinstating him to his position with the defendant; or

- compelling the payment of his salary pending determination of the wrongful dismissal proceedings; or

- preventing the defendant dismissing him, save in accordance with fair procedures; and

- restraining the defendant from appointing a replacement for him other than temporarily.

---

9.   *Boyle v An Post* [2015] IEHC 589.

Barrett J noted that the substantive matter, namely the defendant's adherence or not to fair procedures (rather than perfect procedures, which is not required of any employer) in its decision to dismiss the plaintiff, was outside the scope of this application.

Barrett J noted that the plaintiff ultimately claimed that the defendant's letter dated 16 December 2014 which initiated the disciplinary process against him evidenced bias; that the defendant failed to keep him updated; that the defendant failed to consider any other reason why the post might have been reposted; and that he understood from his union that he would not be dismissed for re-posting. The defendant disputed these claims arguing that the plaintiff had been dismissed on notice; that it was concluded the plaintiff was responsible for the substantial quantities of re-posted mail; that damages were an adequate remedy; and the plaintiff, by his own admission, did not have the means to meet an undertaking as to damages; and the EAT was the appropriate venue for the claim.

Barrett J reviewed the precedents[10] for granting an injunction against an employer, which required the plaintiff to show 'that he is likely to succeed at the hearing of the action'. Barrett J adopted a dictum of Barrington J in the Supreme Court[11] that the terms 'natural and constitutional justice are broad terms and what the justice of a particular case will require will vary with the circumstances of the case'. Barrett J cited a previous case involving the defendant,[12] in which case Mr Rowland, an independent contractor, advanced similar arguments to those of the plaintiff. Murphy J there held that Mr Rowland had, in similar circumstances to the present case, been given sufficient detail to enable him 'reply'.

Barrett J then examined the defendant's letter of December 2014 in which, the plaintiff claimed, that the defendant, while offering him the opportunity to furnish an explanation, showed pre-judgment and bias against him. Barrett J noted that the mere fact of invocation of a disciplinary process against an employee displayed an element of pre-judgment of the employee's behaviour and also that 'one-letter does not a process make' so the Court would look to the entirety of the process, rather than the letter in isolation.

Barrett J then cited Murphy J again in *Rowland* that there was no issue with a disciplinary hearing directed by 'a neutral third party'. Barrett J noted that the word neutral may not be appropriate as the very act of an employee dismissing another employee of a common employer is not 'impartial', a meaning commonly attributed to the word 'neutral'. The only party who might approach the task in a spirit of neutrality would be an outside third party, and such an appointment was not required by the law (though even such an outsider may not be viewed as neutral as they are paid by the employer). The law therefore required that company employees or officers investigating and making decisions regarding dismissal, or determining appeals should approach the task 'with an appropriate level of objective detachment' which cannot be achieved 'without complete prior non-involvement', especially in small or medium enterprises, though it would be 'preferable' in a large organisation such as the defendant that any

10. *Maha Lingham v Health Service Executive* [2006] 17 ELR 140.
11. *Mooney v An Post* [1998] 4 IR 288.
12. *Rowland v An Post* [2011] IEHC 272.

appeal be heard by an executive without involvement of the HR department who could not therefore be seen as holding a vested interest. Barrett J then noted that the plaintiff had failed to highlight any 'substantive evidence' of bias against him and had therefore failed the *Maha Lingham* test of a strong case that is likely to succeed.

While the defendant submitted that the plaintiff should have brought his claim before the EAT, Barrett J noted that the plaintiff was entitled to bring what was an 'arguable claim' of wrongful dismissal before the Court and seek related reliefs. Notwithstanding the foregoing, the Court found that the plaintiff had failed to establish that he had a strong case that was likely to succeed at the hearing of the action.

Barrett J concluded that he did not believe damages were an adequate remedy if the plaintiff's action were to succeed; however the balance of convenience on the whole favoured the defendant, and for that reason the Court did not grant the injunctive reliefs sought by the plaintiff.

Chapter 15

INSOLVENCY

CAN AN EMPLOYMENT AWARD BE PAID FROM THE INSOLVENCY PAYMENTS SCHEME?

[15.01] *Glegola v Minister for Social Protection Ireland and Attorney General[1]—High Court—Hedigan J—judicial review—EU Directive 2008/94/EC—insolvency—whether applicant entitled to receive award in respect of unfair dismissal and arrears of remuneration from Insolvency Payments Scheme—whether employer company placed in liquidation or whether it continued to trade*

In these judicial review proceedings, the applicant sought an order of *mandamus* requiring the respondent to pay to her the amount of €16,818.75, being the measure of an award made to her against her former employer by a Rights Commissioner in respect of unfair dismissal, holiday and arrears of pay. The High Court noted that the Rights Commissioner had further found that the employer company had not been placed in liquidation and continued to trade. The applicant sought the award, either by way of direct implementation of art 3 of Directive 2008/94/EC[2] (the Directive) or in the alternative by way of so called *Francovich* damages, because the State had failed adequately to transpose the Directive. The applicant also sought a declaration that the State was in breach of the Directive in so far as it required the appointment of a liquidator or receiver before the employer was deemed insolvent under the Protection of Employees (Employers' Insolvency) Acts 1984 to 2012.

The applicant asserted that under the Directive she had a right to receive the amount of her award from the Insolvency Payments Scheme (the Scheme). It was for this reason she brought a petition to seek to restore the employer company to the register, as it had been previously removed due to the non-furnishing of accounts. In the same petition she had also sought the appointment of a liquidator, an order winding up the company or, in the alternative, a declaration pursuant to s 251 of the Companies Act 1990. In the petition, the Court made the declaration that the principal reason for the company not being wound up was the insufficiency of its assets. The applicant argued that this declaration was sufficient to entitle her to payment from the Scheme and in the alternative the State had failed to implement the Directive and she was entitled to the equivalent in damages to the amount awarded, so called *Francovich* damages.

It was asserted on behalf of the respondent that the applicant had failed to meet the requirements of art 2(1) of the Directive, in that she had not established that a request had been made for 'the opening of collective proceedings based on the insolvency of the employer' nor that the competent authority had established that her employer's business

---

1. *Glegola v Minister for Social Protection, Ireland and Attorney General* [2015] IEHC 428.
2. Council Directive 2008/94/EC on the Protection of Employees in the event of the Insolvency of their Employer.

had 'definitely closed down'. It was asserted therefore that the applicant did not have *locus standi* to maintain her claim. The respondent further asserted that the applicant was out of time with reference to the Protection of Employees (Employers' Insolvency) Acts 1984 to 2012.

The respondent denied that the declaration of the Court pursuant to the applicant's s 251 petition could entitle the applicant to the benefit of the Scheme given the provisions of the 1984 Act. It was accepted by the respondent that the 1984 Act was the implementing provision of the Directive and that the Directive referred to the insolvency law of Member States and did not harmonise the concept of insolvency. It was submitted on behalf of the respondent that s 4 of the 1984 Act provided for insolvency 'within the meaning of s 285 of the Companies Act 1963'. This meant the winding up of the company.

It was noted by the High Court that the respondent was arguing that the employer company had not been wound up and therefore was not insolvent and furthermore it had not been established that the applicant employer's 'undertaking or business had been definitively closed down'. The Court noted that the applicant had made the case to both the Rights Commissioner and the High Court that the business was in fact continuing.

Hedigan J noted that the first question to be determined was whether the applicant had brought herself within art 2 of the Directive because this was the point of departure for her claim upon the Scheme or in *Francovich* damages. He restated the provisions of art 2 of the Directive and noted that in *Mustafa*[3] the CJEU considered whether or not an employer's business had to be terminated before the guarantee institution's liability to pay had accrued. The High Court concluded that the key questions were:

— whether there had been an opening of collective proceedings provided for in art 2; and

— whether it had been established that the applicant's employer's business or undertaking had definitely closed down.

The Court noted that the employer company had been struck off the company register in October 2013 for failure to file accounts. The applicant had subsequently presented a petition to the High Court seeking orders *inter alia* to restore the company to the register pursuant to s 12(b)(3) of the Companies Act 1982. The applicant's grounding affidavit had confirmed she was not seeking to wind up the company, but reserved the right to make such an application should it be necessary. The High Court concluded that no application was made for the opening of collective proceedings based on the insolvency of the employer.

The recommendation of the Rights Commissioner recorded that the applicant did not accept that a redundancy situation had existed and that the company was not placed in liquidation and that it continued to trade. The recommendation recorded that there were plenty of opportunities for the applicant to be re-engaged and retrained. The High Court concluded that it was not established, as required by art 2.1(b), that the employer

---

3.   *Mustafa v Durektur na Fond 'Garontirani Vzemania na Rabotnitsite I Sluzhitelite' Kam Natsionalnia Osiguritelen Institut* (Case C–247/12).

undertaking or business had been definitely closed down. The High Court noted that the applicant had maintained during her Rights Commissioner case that the employer was continuing to trade notwithstanding a letter from the company's solicitor that it had ceased trading. The letter claiming the employer company had ceased trading was plainly not accepted by the applicant or the Rights Commissioner.

Hedigan J concluded that the requirements of art 2.1 of the Directive had not been met in regard to these two crucial matters. He held that they were *sine qua non* to an entitlement to claim upon the Scheme and therefore the application was to fail at the first hurdle. In the result, none of the other questions raised in the proceedings arose. The relief sought was refused.

Chapter 16

JUDICIAL REVIEW

RECOMMENDATIONS OF THE LABOUR COURT

[16.01] *Mullally, Power, Burns, Doyle and the Psychiatric Nurses Association (Irish Fire and Emergency Services Association) v The Labour Court and Waterford County Council (Notice Party)[1]—High Court—judicial review—certiorari—Industrial Relations Act 1946, s 68—Industrial Relations Act 1969, s 20(1)—failure to investigate trade dispute—constitutional rights—fair procedures*

The applicants had requested that the Labour Court investigate a trade union dispute under s 20(1) of the Industrial Relations Act 1969 (the Act). The applicants wished to have a trade union that was not a member of the Irish Congress of Trade Unions recognised for negotiation purposes. Their employer, Waterford County Council, said that they could not give such recognition as the trade union was not recognised nationally for negotiation purposes.

The Labour Court, in its recommendation, found that the employer already had well-established arrangements for collective bargaining with trade unions. The Labour Court found that while the applicants had an acknowledged right to be members of whatever organisation they chose, the exercise of that right could not be held to imply a concomitant obligation on the employer to negotiate with their chosen organisation. The applicants sought further review of the Labour Court's recommendation by which they were bound under s 20.

The High Court considered the issue of *res judicata,* which would preclude the applicants from applying for relief from the High Court. The Court found that the recommendation of the Labour Court, at most, amounted to a binding resolution of disputes for industrial relations purposes. The Act did not invest the Labour Court with the quality of legal finality and the Labour Court was not intended to create legally justiciable rights. The Labour Court recommendation, therefore, did not create *res judicata.*

The High Court then considered whether the remedy of prohibition lay in respect of the powers exercisable by the Labour Court by virtue of s 67 of the Act. This section provides that the Labour Court, having investigated a trade dispute, shall make a recommendation setting forth its opinion on the merits of the dispute and the terms on which it should be settled. The Act does not provide any machinery for enforcing the recommendation against the party bound by it and it does not provide for the taking of any consequential action by a superior authority. The High Court found that it is well established that prohibition may issue to any body which had the duty to act judicially

---

1. *Mullally, Power, Burns, Doyle and the Psychiatric Nurses Association (Irish Fire and Emergency Services Association) v The Labour Court and Waterford County Council (Notice Party)* [2015] IEHC 351.

and which, on consideration of facts and circumstances, has power by its determination, within its jurisdiction, to impose liability or to affect rights.

The Court found that this last point did not arise in the present case because the Act contains no provision to enable any superior authority to translate a recommendation of the Labour Court made under s 68 of the Act into an award binding on the parties nor does the Act permit of any sanction in the event of non-acceptance of the recommendation. The High Court found that the Labour Court closely resembles a court of law, though it cannot, by its recommendations, impose liabilities or affect rights.

However, this does not mean that a citizen has no redress in the event of the Labour Court attempting to exceed its statutory powers by invoking s 67 of the Act. The appropriate remedy would be an injunction to restrain the Labour Court. The High Court found that this remedy was not open to the applicant in the present matter as the Court had already held that the investigation complained of was not *ultra vires* the Labour Court.

The Court concluded that the Labour Court was not finally determining any issues of law or fact. The investigation was not an adjudicative process and created no *res judicata*. The Court held that the Labour Court's recommendation had strictly no legal effect and did not give rise to justiciable rights such as would permit the applicants to seek judicial review.

DECISION OF AN ACADEMIC INSTITUTION

[16.02] *Fassi v Dublin City University²—High Court—application for judicial review—Noonan J—certiorari—whether sufficient public element in relationship between PhD student and university to render decision to prohibit student progressing academic studies amenable to judicial review—whether decision of academic supervisory panel invalid where panel not properly constituted in accordance with its own internal regulations—whether decision of academic supervisory panel to review a student's academic progress after seven months premature—student's conduct disruptive and unacceptable*

The applicant was pursuing a PhD project at the International Centre for Neurotherapeutics (ICNT) of the respondent. The applicant was under the supervision of both a principal supervisor and an assistant supervisor. The applicant encountered numerous difficulties with the project from the outset. In December 2012, the applicant travelled to France to receive additional training in specific laboratory techniques that he was lacking, the cost of which was paid by ICNT. In February 2013, the applicant made an official complaint to the respondent with regard to the level of supervision and training that he had received during the project. The complaint was unsuccessful. In April 2013, the applicant noted that he had been informed by a representative of the

---

2.   *Fassi v Dublin City University* [2015] IEHC 38.

respondent that he would be dismissed from the project for reasons of poor performance. The applicant was provided with the opportunity to withdraw voluntarily from the project and in doing so, would receive an academic reference from the respondent. The applicant rejected the offer to withdraw voluntarily and submitted further formal complaints, one of which included a complaint to the HR department that he had been victimised.

On 2 May 2013, the principal and assistant supervisors signed a report entitled *Dublin City University Postgraduate Research Studies Annual Progress Report* (PGR2) which analysed the applicant's academic performance over the course of his first seven months on the project. The report noted that daily tasks that were assigned to the applicant proved to be a serious challenge and that the applicant's level of English was below an acceptable standard, despite suggestions from his supervisors that he should undertake English learning courses. The report also provided that, in addition to the applicant's poor performance, he had engaged in numerous confrontations with members of staff of the ICNT and that his behaviour was unacceptable and disruptive. The report further found that the applicant had not maintained satisfactory progress, was unsuitable to continue the PhD project with ICNT and that his registration for the next academic year should not be renewed. The applicant appealed the decision to the Graduate Research Studies Board (the board) of the respondent on the grounds that the respondent did not adhere to art 1.1.6 of its own regulations. These regulations required that all candidates must have a supervisory panel comprising of his supervisors and another independent member of academic staff, such panel to be established within three months of a student's registration on a project. The applicant also appealed on the grounds that there was a material administrative error in the assessment of his performance. The applicant further appealed on the grounds that his review period should have been conducted over a full academic year and that a seven-month review period was not a sufficient period of time to assess the applicant's performance. The board ultimately found that the applicant had not been provided with a properly constituted supervisory panel but that this was not material to the applicant's appeal as it did not contribute to his negative assessment regarding his progress. The board also found that the review period of seven months was adequate in the circumstances and that it did provide the supervisors with a sufficient opportunity to assess the suitability of the applicant with regard to the project. For these reasons, the applicant's appeal of the PGR2 decision to the board failed. The applicant subsequently complained to the Ombudsman in November 2013 and further submitted a claim to the EAT in January 2014. Neither of these complaints was successful.

The applicant applied for a judicial review seeking orders of *certiorari* quashing both the decision contained in the PGR2 in May and the decision of the board in October to remove the applicant from the project. The first ground of the appeal was that the decision based on the PGR2 was invalid as the supervisory panel had not been properly constituted in accordance with its own regulations. The second ground of appeal was that the PGR2 had been conducted prematurely, prior to the completion of a full academic year by the applicant. A third ground, relating to the failure to allow the applicant an oral hearing, was abandoned. The respondent submitted that its decisions were not amenable to judicial review as the matters at issue were solely within the sphere of private law and further that the issues alleged by the applicant in the pleadings had already been adjudicated upon and decided by the board and, consequently, could not be revisited. The respondent acknowledged that the supervisory team had not been properly constituted in accordance with its own regulations but noted that this issue had already been dealt with by the board and could also not be revisited.

In determining the respondent's first submission (that the matters at issue were solely within the sphere of private law), Noonan J relied on previous authorities including *Rajah v The Royal College of Surgeons*,[3] *Quinn v The Honourable Society of King's Inns*[4] and *Zhang v Athlone Institute of Technology*[5] which suggested that a body that derives its jurisdiction from contract or otherwise from the consent of its members will not be amenable to judicial review. Noonan J noted that it was still necessary to determine whether there existed a sufficient public element to the relationship to confer jurisdiction on the Court. Noonan J stated that it was clear that the relationship between the parties was governed by a contract whether express or implied. Noonan J found no reason to depart from previous authorities where the legal relationship between applicant student and respondent university were of a similar nature and the Courts in those instances had no jurisdiction to hear a judicial review of the respective universities' decision. Noonan J determined that there was not a sufficiently public element to the relationship between the applicant and respondent to warrant intervention by the Court. Even if it was the case that the decisions under attack were reviewable, Noonan J confirmed that he was satisfied that the two issues raised by the applicant were dealt with by the board, within its jurisdiction. Noonan J further confirmed that the decisions of educational institutions are not reviewable where they relate solely to matters of academic judgment. Noonan J also found that the applicant's challenge to the PGR2 was effectively a challenge to the supervisors' academic judgment and could not succeed. Noonan J further noted that the issues relating to the composition of the supervisory panel was not material to the judgment of the supervisors who had conducted the review and presented the report and was not fatal to the outcome of the PGR2 as alleged by the applicant. Noonan J agreed with the decision of the board on this issue. Noonan J found that the issues of sufficient academic progress and the adequacy of timing to review the applicant's progress were entirely a matter for the supervisory team and the board, both of which had sufficient knowledge and evidence of the applicant's ability and performance with regard to the academic project. Noonan J was satisfied that the issues raised by the applicant had been dealt with adequately and sufficiently by the board, both at the applicant's request and within the board's jurisdiction. The application and relief sought by the applicant were refused.

---

3.   *Rajah v The Royal College of Surgeons* [1994] 1 IR 384.
4.   *Quinn v The Honourable Society of King's Inns* [2004] 4 IR 344.
5.   *Zhang v Athlone Institute of Technology* [2013] IEHC 390.

DECISION OF THE INJURIES BOARD

[16.03] *Noel Recruitment (Ireland) Ltd v The Personal Injuries Assessment Board and Issak, otherwise known as Chapwanya (Notice Party)*⁶*—High Court—Kearns P—Personal Injuries Assessment Board Acts 2003 to 2007—judicial review— whether applicant entitled to an order of certiorari—where two separate authorisations granted by respondent to notice party arising from same workplace accident*

A workplace accident was alleged to have taken place and the notice party claimed he was injured while lifting bags of potatoes in a warehouse in October 2009. Using the name Michael Chapwanya, the notice party made an application to the respondent for an assessment of damages under s 11 of the Personal Injuries Assessment Board Acts 2003 to 2007 (the Acts). The applicant was named as the respondent employer in the first application as was Keelings Limited. The applicant was notified of the first application by the respondent in October 2010 and, as it did not respond, it was deemed to have consented to an assessment under s 14 of the Acts. Kearns P noted that no proceedings were subsequently issued by the notice party on foot of this authorisation, and furthermore, any potential proceedings were now statute barred under the Statute of Limitations 1957 as amended by s 50 of the Acts.

In March 2011, the notice party, using the name Moro Issak, made a second application for an assessment of damages under s 11 of the Acts, in respect of the same October 2009 accident. The applicant was again named as the respondent in the second application, as was Keelings Limited. Additionally, however, Tesco Ireland Limited was named as a respondent in this second application. On receipt of the notification of the second application, the applicant confirmed to the respondent that it did not consent to the assessment of this matter. In July 2011, the applicant was informed of the decision to authorise the proceedings by the notice party against the applicant notwithstanding that the purported authorisation was in respect of the same accident, the subject matter of the first authorisation, and the fact that both authorisations carried the same reference number. Kearns P concluded that it was beyond dispute that the respondent entertained two applications for the assessment of damages brought by the same person, in respect of the same accident, and in respect of which the respondent had issued two successive authorisations.

The Court noted that the applicant had now been served with a personal injury summons brought by the notice party as plaintiff, and on foot of the second authorisation issued by the respondent.

The Court considered the statutory framework and noted that the date of issue of an authorisation had significant implications for the time period within which proceedings must commence. Kearns P noted that s 50 of the Acts provided that the period of time beginning on the making of an application under s 11 and ending six months from the date of issue of an authorisation shall be disregarded for the purposes of the statutory

---

6. *Noel Recruitment (Ireland) Ltd v The Personal Injuries Assessment Board and Issak, otherwise known as Chapwanya (Notice Party)* [2015] IEHC 20.

time periods for bringing a personal injuries claim. On behalf of the applicant it was submitted that a statutory body, having been granted power to determine a particular question or application, exhausts its power once it determines that question and will be prevented from reconsidering or redetermining that application by virtue of the doctrine of *functus officio*.

The Court noted that as a result of the application made by the notice party to the respondent in October 2011 and the authorisation which issued on July 2013, the notice party had a period of approximately six and a half months thereafter to commence proceedings against the first and third respondents. It was submitted by the notice party that, having regard to the constitutional right of access to the Court, the terms of the Acts must be narrowly construed, and given that the Acts contained no express prohibition on the issuing of a second authorisation, they must be construed as permitting the respondent to do so. Kearns P said he was satisfied that no restriction on the constitutional right of access to the Court had arisen in this case.

The Court concluded that the first authorisation granted to the notice party specifically authorised the bringing of a personal injuries claim before the Courts. That right is not one exercisable forever in all circumstances, not least because of the existence of the Statute of Limitations 1957 as amended (the Statute), the constitutionality of which was not challenged in this case.

The Court also noted s 46 of the Acts which enable the respondent to make rules concerning the procedure to be followed in relation to the making of applications under s 11 of the Acts. Regard was had to s 46(3), which was relied upon by the notice party to assert that the respondent may amend an authorisation or grant an additional authorisation, in circumstances where a genuine oversight or mistake had occurred. Kearns P was satisfied that there was no evidence of any genuine oversight or ignorance of all the facts relating to the matter in this case; nor was there any suggestion that the notice party was not of sound mind or lacked the capacity to bring forward a claim.

Kearns P held he was satisfied that the statutory scheme governing the respondent did not expressly or implicitly permit the respondent to consider a second application against the same defendant in respect of the same accident, once an authorisation in respect of that accident had issued. The Acts do not purport to extend periods fixed for bringing claims under the Statute, save as expressly provided for by the Acts. There cannot otherwise be a rolling back of the Statute. Kearns P contemplated a scenario whereby time limits prescribed by the Statute could be indefinitely deferred by repeated applications to the respondent, and Kearns P held that this is the very antithesis of the speedy resolution to claims which the respondent was set up to bring about. The order sought was granted.

DECISION TO REMOVE A SCHOOL CHAPLAIN

[16.04] *Conroy v Board of Management of Gorey Community School[7]—High Court—Baker J—judicial review—order of certiorari to quash decision made by respondent to remove applicant from his position as chaplain of school—other restrictions placed on applicant with regards to his interaction with students*

The applicant, a Catholic Priest, was nominated 21 years ago to be the chaplain of Gorey Community School. While he was contractually a chaplain, his role evolved to include both pastoral and teaching duties in the school.

A former pupil made an allegation against the applicant, that he had had a sexual relationship with her in 2006 and 2007. The applicant was placed on administrative leave while this allegation was investigated both by the respondent and, following mandatory reporting, by the HSE. The allegations were denied in full by the applicant. The HSE determined that the complaint was not within its remit because the complainant was not under the relevant age of consent. The principal was, however, advised by the HSE that the allegations were very serious in nature and the respondent's board of management (the board) duly conducted its own investigation and enquiries. The applicant was advised of the specific complaint against him, following which a disciplinary hearing was convened in October 2012. The applicant was legally represented at this hearing. It was subsequently found by the respondent that there was no sexual impropriety on the part of the applicant. The Court noted that the letter conveying this decision in December 2012 did state that the respondent believed that certain aspects of the applicant's conduct were inappropriate; however, no further details were provided.

Following this finding, the applicant underwent a risk assessment, a process which took a number of months. The assessor was asked whether the applicant posed any risk to students of the school and concluded in the report that the applicant was low risk. The recommendations of the risk assessment report were that the applicant should not engage in counselling pupils in the school, that he should refer students seeking pastoral care to the school chaplain, that he should not have any lead role in group activities and that he should not participate in any trips with students. The applicant subsequently sought to be restored to his teaching duties with the school. He applied and became registered with the Teaching Council in September 2013 on a conditional basis. Following confirmation of this, the respondent informed him by letter of October 2013 that he could return to the school as a religious education teacher, subject to certain conditions and recommendations as per the risk assessment report.

In this application for judicial review, it was asserted by the applicant that by its letter of October 2013, the respondent in effect had removed him as chaplain of the school and in so doing had acted *ultra vires* and in breach of fair procedures. The applicant further asserted that the conditions imposed by the respondent were harsh, arbitrary, unreasonable and disproportionate. In a preliminary objection to this matter, the respondent asserted that these matters were not matters of public law and it denied

---

7. *Conroy v Board of Management of Gorey Community School* [2015] IEHC 103.

that there was any breach of fair procedures and natural justice. It was further submitted that the applicant was seeking to quash, by way of judicial review, the decision of the respondent made in October 2012 and that the applicant was out of time in this regard.

The Court firstly considered when the applicant was removed as chaplain. The respondent asserted that if such a decision was made, it was done 11 months earlier, following the disciplinary hearing in October 2012, and was communicated in December 2012. The Court noted that neither the letter of December 2012 nor that of October 2013 expressly removed the applicant as chaplain of the school but the Court noted that the October 2013 letter, offering the reinstatement of the applicant as a teacher of religious education, had the practical effect that he was offered a return to the school as teacher, and not as chaplain. The Court also concluded that the December 2012 letter contained an implicit dismissal of the applicant from his role as chaplain of the school as it referred to a possible return to the school as a religious education teacher. The Court accepted that, while it could be fairly said that there was no express removal of the applicant from the role, it was clear that the purpose of the risk assessment referred to in the December 2012 letter was not to restore the applicant as chaplain, but rather to consider whether he might possibly return to the school as a religious education teacher.

The Court concluded that the applicant was dismissed as chaplain by the letter of December 2012 and thus he was out of time to seek review of that decision. The Court noted that no reason had been advanced to support an extension of time, and as the applicant had engaged fully with the process commenced after the letter of December 2012, he had accepted the process to the extent that it would disentitle him to seek an extension.

The Court then considered whether the decision was amenable to judicial review and considered the deed of trust by which the school chaplain was designated as a member of staff of the school, notwithstanding that the initial nomination of him as chaplain may come through a religious authority. The Court concluded it could not be doubted that the chaplain was appointed by the respondent and was employed as a full-time member of staff which must mean that he was employed by the school. The Court held that the chaplain was a member of staff properly characterised as 'other staff of the school' and under s 24(3) of the Education Act 1998 and that a suspension and dismissal of him by the respondent must be done in accordance with the procedures 'agreed from time to time between the Minister, the patron, recognised school management organisations and any recognised trade union and staff association representing teachers or other staff as appropriate'.

The Court noted the judgment of O'Malley J in *Kelly v Board of Management of St Josephs National School*.[8] Baker J stated that she was adopting the analysis of O'Malley J and, in particular, noted that the combination of the provisions of the trust deed and the statutory provision had the effect of incorporating the procedures from the Act into any disciplinary process engaged by the school. Baker J noted O'Malley J's view that the public law element arose from the interconnection between the Minister in

---

8.   *Kelly v Board of Management of St Josephs National School* [2013] IEHC 392.

a public role and the mandatory nature of the statutory disciplinary procedures for teaching staff, following the publication of the Ministerial Circular 60/2009.

Baker J went on to consider the involvement of the Minister with the role of chaplain. The Court noted that the board of management had the power to appoint a chaplain, subject only to the fact that the chaplain must be nominated by the relevant religious authority. The Minister has no role in the selection criteria, appointment or dismissal. The Court concluded that the appointment of a chaplain is one which the respondent could exercise without the approval of the Minister; although the chaplain is a full-time member of staff and is to be paid, by the Minister, a salary equivalent to that of a teacher in the school.

The Court contrasted this with the role of the Minister overseeing the general organisation and curriculum of the school and also the role of the Minister in the provision of teachers of religious education, who are appointed by a selection committee and whose appointment is subject to formal approval by the Minister. No such provisions applied to the appointment of a chaplain and the chaplain was not deemed to be a teacher of religious education. The appointment of the role of the chaplain, the selection of the chaplain and the position in the curriculum do not have any Ministerial involvement. The role of chaplain is not subject to any covenant with the Minister and is not identified in the context of the community and education purpose. The role of the chaplain can be seen as residual and religious rather than a community role and thus, the Court concluded that there was no public law element in the appointment and dismissal of a chaplain.

The Court further confirmed that the fact that the State paid the salary of the chaplain did not import a sufficient public law element. Baker J concluded that the decision to remove the applicant as chaplain was taken in October 2012 (and communicated in December 2012), and that the applicant was out of time to bring an application for judicial review. Baker J further held that the applicant could not avail of the remedy of judicial review with regards to the removal of him as chaplain, as that removal arose from the wholly private contract between the parties and did not arise from any covenant with the Minister or from any statutory provisions or public law purpose, by which the Minister performed a role of protector of the community or public interest.

The High Court then considered the letter of October 2013 which proposed a return by the applicant to the school as a teacher of religious education, subject to his written acceptance of, and adherence to, certain conditions. The applicant sought an order of *certiorari* quashing the decision to impose these conditions as having been imposed in breach of fair procedures or outside the powers of the board. The Court concluded that what was being proposed was that the applicant would take a different role and that he would thereby become a teacher, subject to a different regime that prevailed with regards to teachers. The Court confirmed that if the applicant was to be characterised as a teacher then he was entitled to the benefit of the new mandatory scheme 'Towards 2016 Revised Procedures for Suspension and Dismissal of Teachers'. The Court concluded that that document applied and that the decision of the respondent was thus amenable to judicial review as an element of public law was present through the application of the circular. The Court further concluded that the conditions imposed on the return to work were disciplinary sanctions because the respondent could not have it both ways. It could not employ the applicant as a teacher of religious education *de novo*, as to do so would have required it to engage in the recruitment process provided under its articles of management and under legislation. The respondent changed the terms and conditions of the applicant's role as an employee of the school and Baker J characterised some of the conditions in the changed role as disciplinary in nature.

Baker J then considered the argument made by the applicant that the conditions were made in breach of fair procedures. The Court noted that the letter of December 2012 suggested that the respondent would consider a possible return of the applicant to the school, dependant firstly on a risk assessment and also then subject to certain conditions applying to any such appointment. The Court concluded that the applicant was fully informed before the disciplinary hearing of the matter and that he knew of, and was given full opportunity with representation to address, the nature of the complaint. The Court did not find any breach of fair procedures in this regard. Baker J then further considered the nature of the conditions imposed and specifically the argument made that they were arbitrary, disproportionate, and irrational and should be struck down. She noted that certain of the conditions did not give rise to any difficulty, namely a restriction on the applicant acting as a counsellor in circumstances where he did not have a counselling qualification and adherence to current child protection policies and garda vetting requirements which the Court found to be reasonable and not in any sense discriminatory or irrational. In relation to the further requirement that any students seeking pastoral care be referred to the chaplain and those with more personal problems be referred to the guidance counsellor, the Court concluded that neither could be regarded as a function of a teacher in religious education and thus could not be objected to.

The Court then considered the particular conditions that the applicant would have no contact with students outside of school without the consent of the principal, and that the applicant must continue to see his personal counsellor on a regular basis. The Court rejected the argument made by the applicant that these were harsh, arbitrary, unreasonable and disproportionate. The Court concluded that these conditions arose directly from the conduct of the applicant that led to the findings of inappropriate behaviour, all of which related to his conduct during a school trip abroad and his conduct with the complainant outside of school hours. The alteration of his position was done in a way that imposed conditions upon him which related to his behaviour outside of school. The Court further noted that the applicant had been granted a limited registration with the Teaching Council as a teacher and his registration contained certain stipulations which mirrored those contained in the requirements of the respondent. The respondent could not have reinstated or redeployed the applicant as a teacher and ignored the conditional nature of his registration, thus the Court held that the sanctions and conditions were not arbitrary, irrational or unduly harsh. The Court concluded that the decision to remove the applicant as chaplain was not one that was amenable to judicial review but the decision to employ the applicant as a teacher of religion in the school was one with a sufficient public law element to attract review. The Court noted the cooperation of the applicant with the risk assessment and held that there was no denial of his rights to fair procedures or constitutional justice in the process and that the conditions imposed were not harsh, arbitrary, disproportionate or irrational and were not ultra vires. The relief was refused.

See also *Ali v Minister for Jobs, Enterprise and Innovation* at [**12.01**],[9] *Hussein v The Labour Court and Mohammad Younis (Notice Party)*[10] at [**12.02**] and *Hosford v Minister for Social Protection*[11] at [**22.08**].

---

9.   *Ali v Minister for Jobs, Enterprise and Innovation* [2015] IEHC 219.

10.   *Hussein v The Labour Court and Mohammad Younis (Notice Party)* [2015] IESC 58.

11.   *Hosford v Minister for Social Protection* [2015] IEHC 59.

Chapter 17

LEGISLATION

SELECTED ACTS

Workplace Relations Act 2015 (No 16 of 2015)

[17.01] See CH 31.

Industrial Relations (Amendment) Act 2015 (No 27 of 2015)

[17.02] See CH 13.

Children and Family Relationships Act 2015 (No 9 of 2015)

[17.03] This Act was signed into law on 6 April 2015. It should be noted that the Act requires multiple commencement orders to be brought into force, of which only one, in respect of Pt 10 of the Act,[1] has been published at the time of print.

The principal objective of the Act is to update Irish laws on parentage, custody, access, maintenance and adoption. It specifically addresses the issue of the parentage and guardianship of children born through donor-assisted human reproduction procedures.

The Act amends a number of employment statutes as follows:

Adoption

[17.04] Civil partners and cohabiting couples who have lived together for three years will now be entitled to adopt jointly. Previously, while a single individual, regardless of their sexual orientation, was entitled to apply for an adoption order, only married couples were eligible to adopt jointly.

Section 177 of the Act amends the Adoptive Leave Act 1995 and provides that civil partners and cohabiting couples will be eligible for the same entitlement to adoptive leave which is provided under the Adoptive Leave Act 1995, ie, 24 weeks of adoptive leave and up to 16 weeks of additional leave.

One member of a same sex or cohabiting couple, the qualifying adopter, will become eligible for adoptive leave but the choice will be that of the couple.

The circumstances entitling an adoptive father to adoptive leave, where the adoptive mother has died, will also apply to civil partners or cohabitants where the qualifying adopter has died.

---

1. Child and Family Relationships Act 2015 (Part 10) (Commencement) Order 2015 (SI 263/ 2015).

It should be noted that this new, inclusive definition of 'adopting parent' is now incorporated into both the Redundancy Payments Acts 1967 to 2014 and the Unfair Dismissals Acts 1977 to 2015.

Maternity leave

[17.05] Similarly the Maternity Protection Act 1994 is amended by s 176 of the new Act to allow the parental leave and other safeguards currently provided for an employed father of a child to be extended to the 'other parent' of a child born as a result of donor-assisted human reproduction procedure.

Protective leave currently includes the father's entitlement to leave where the mother dies during the period of maternity leave; the other parent will now refer to the husband, civil partner or cohabitant of the mother.

Parental leave

[17.06] Section 178 of the Act takes account of the wider categories of persons who can be considered a parent in extending the entitlements and protections afforded by the Parental Leave Acts 1998 and 2006.

The definition of 'relevant parent' is now amended to include the parent, the adoptive parent or the adopting parent in respect of the child. By way of example in the case of a same-sex female couple, the rights currently held by fathers to parental leave will be extended to the second female partner.

National Minimum Wage (Low Pay Commission) Act 2015 (No 22 of 2015)

[17.07] The main purpose of the Act is to amend the National Minimum Wage Act 2000 to provide for the establishment of the Low Pay Commission on a statutory basis to advise the Minister of Jobs, Enterprise and Innovation on setting a national minimum wage. The function of the Low Pay Commission will be to examine and make recommendations to the Minister on the national minimum wage on an annual basis with a view to ensuring that the national minimum wage is adjusted incrementally over time, having regard to change in earnings, productivity, overall competitiveness and the likely impact any adjustment will have on employment and unemployment levels.

The Act also makes amendments to the Workplace Relations Act 2015.

Gender Recognition Act 2015 (No 25 of 2015)

[17.08] This Act provides for recognition of change of gender and provides for gender recognition certificates. Section 13(1) of the Act provides that a gender recognition certificate shall specify the date on which it issues and the following in relation to the person to whom it issues: (a) the person's forename and surname; (b) the person's date of birth; and (c) the person's gender.

Section 18(1) of the Act states that where a gender recognition certificate is issued to a person, the person's gender shall, from the date of that issue, become for all purposes, the preferred gender so that if the preferred gender is the male gender, the person's sex becomes that of a man and if it is the female gender, the person's sex becomes that of a woman.

It should be noted that s 18(4) provides that a person holding a gender recognition certificate shall not be required to produce it as proof of gender or identity for any purpose save as required by law. However, said person may produce the certificate if he or she so chooses. The Act further provides that the person to whom a gender recognition certificate is issued may subsequently request that the particulars relating to the recognition of the gender of the person are entered into the register of gender recognition to be maintained by the Ard–Chláraitheoir.

Thirty-Fourth Amendment of the Constitution (Marriage Equality) Act 2015

[17.09] This Act amends Article 41 of the Constitution and provides that marriage may be contracted by two persons without distinction as to their sex.

Marriage Act 2015 (No 35 of 2015)

[17.10] The purpose of the Marriage Act is to enact legislative provisions to enable couples to marry without distinction as to their sex and to deal with relationship matters. The Act will implement the constitutional obligation in Article 41.4 of the Constitution following the approval of the constitutional amendment in a referendum of the Irish People on 22 May 2015.

Financial Emergency Measures in the Public Interest Act 2015 (No 39 of 2015)

[17.11] This Act proposes to amend the previous five Financial Emergency Measures in the Public Interest (FEMPI) Acts which were enacted between 2009 and 2013 and begins a partial and phased restoration of the salary reductions made by them, as agreed by the Government and trade unions representing public servants in the Lansdowne Road Agreement. This Act also makes provision for the partial restoration of pension reductions to public servants.

Equality (Miscellaneous Provisions) Act 2015 (No 43 of 2015)

[17.12] See CH 5.

SELECTED STATUTORY INSTRUMENTS

Local Government Act 2001 (Part 15) Regulations 2015 (SI 29/2015)

[17.13] These Regulations revoke the Local Government Act 2001 (Part 15) Regulations 2004 (SI 770/2004). The 2001 Regulations prescribed the classes of local authority employees to whom the provisions of Pt 15 of the Local Government Act 2001 apply. Part 15 of the 2001 Act sets out an ethical framework for the local government service. The 2015 Regulations prescribe an annual declaration form to be furnished by relevant employees and members of local authorities which includes an undertaking to have regard to the relevant Code of Conduct, which they declare they have read and understood.

Industrial Relations (Amendment) Act 2015 (Commencement) Order 2015 (SI 329/2015)

[17.14] This Statutory Instrument appoints 1 August 2015 as the day on which the Industrial Relations (Amendment) Act 2015 came into effect.

Workplace Relations Act 2015 (Commencement) Order 2015 (SI 338/ 2015)

[17.15] This Statutory Instrument appoints 1 August 2015 as the day on which certain provisions of the Workplace Relations Act 2015 shall come into effect.

National Minimum Wage (Low Paid Commission) Act 2015 (Section 20) (Commencement) Order 2015 (SI 340/2015)

[17.16] This Statutory Instrument appoints 1 August 2015 as the day on which s 20(1)(b) of the National Minimum Wage (Low Paid Commission) Act 2015 came into effect.

Organisation of Working Time (Non-application of Certain Provisions to Persons Performing Mobile Road Transport Activities) Regulations 2015 (SI 342/2015)

[17.17] The purpose of this Statutory Instrument made under ss 3, 7, and 25 of the Organisation of Working Time Act 1997 is to clarify the law regarding organisation of working time and mobile transport workers. It removes mobile transport workers from the scope of certain provisions of the 1997 Act.

Industrial Relations Act 1969 (Section 3A) Order 2015 (SI 344/2015)

[17.18] This Statutory Instrument prescribes certain functions of the Labour Court for the purpose of s 3A of the Industrial Relations Act 1969 as inserted by s 78 of the Workplace Relations Act 2015.

Employment Permits (Amendment) Regulations 2015 (SI 349/2015)

[17.19] See CH 12.

Employment Permits (Trusted Partner) Regulations 2015 (SI 172/2015)

[17.20] See CH 12.

Public Service Management (Sick Leave) (Amendment) Regulations 2015 (SI 384/2015)

[17.21] This Statutory Instrument amends the existing regulations with regards to pregnancy-related illness and sick leave.

Industrial Relations Act 1976 (Section 8) Order 2015 (SI 385/2015)

[17.22] This Statutory Instrument provides for a new division of the Labour Court.

Workplace Relations Act 2015 (Commencement) (No 2) Order 2015 (SI 410/2015)

[17.23] This Statutory Instrument confirms 1 October 2015 as the effective date for most other provisions of the Workplace Relations Act.

Workplace Relations Act 2015 (Establishment Day) Order 2015 (SI 412/2015)

[17.24] This Statutory Instruments confirms 1 October 2015 as the establishment day for the purposes of the Workplace Relations Act 2015.

Labour Relations Commission (Dissolution Day) Order 2015 (SI 413/2015)

[17.25] This Statutory Instrument appoints 1 October 2015 as the dissolution day of the Labour Relations Commission for the purposes of Pt 5 of the Workplace Relations Act 2015.

Workplace Relations Act 2015 (Fixed Payment Notice) Regulations 2015 (SI 419/2015)

[17.26] This Statutory Instrument prescribes the form of fixed payment notices in lieu of prosecution, if appropriate, and the amount of the fixed payment in each case for certain alleged offences.

National Minimum Wage Order 2015 (SI 442/2015)

[17.27] This Statutory Instrument provides that the national minimum hourly wage shall be €9.15 with effect from 1 January 2016.

Protected Disclosures Act 2014 (Disclosure to Prescribed Persons) Order 2015 (SI 448/2015)

[17.28] This Statutory Instrument amends the Protected Disclosures Act 2014 (Section 7(2)) Order 2014 (SI 339/2014) which prescribes persons to whom a protected disclosure may be made under s 7(2) of the Protected Disclosures Act 2014.

Industrial Relations Act 1990 (Code of Practice on Protected Disclosures Act 2014) (Declaration) Order 2015 (SI 464/2015)

[17.29] This Statutory Instrument sets out a Code of Practice on the Protected Disclosures Act 2014 to help employers, workers and their representatives understand the law in relation to the disclosure of information regarding wrongdoing in the workplace and how to deal with the disclosure of such information.

Industrial Relations Act 1990 (Code of Practice on Victimisation) (Declaration) Order 2015 (SI 463/2015)

[17.30] This Statutory Instrument sets out an updated Code of Practice on victimisation arising from an employee's membership or activity on behalf of a trade union; from a manager discharging his/her managerial functions; or from other employees.

Workplace Relations Act 2015 (Fees) Regulations 2015 (SI 536/2015)

[17.31] See CH 31 at [31.13].

Employments Permits (Amendment) (No 2) Regulations (SI 602/2015)

[17.32] See CH 12.

SELECTED BILLS

Universities (Development and Innovation) (Amendment) Bill 2015 (No 4 of 2015)

[17.33] This is a Private Members Bill introduced by Senators Sean D Barrett, Fergal Quinn and David Norris. It proposes to amend the Universities Act 1997; to develop the operation of the universities; to encourage education, innovation, research and scholarship in the universities; and to make provisions for related matters.

Thirty-Fourth Amendment of the Constitution (Age of Eligibility for Election to the Office of President) Bill 2015 (No 6 of 2015)

[17.34] This Bill was presented by the Minister for Environment, Community and Local Government and proposed to amend art 12 of the Constitution to provide that every citizen that has reached the age of 21 years is eligible for election to the office of President. This was defeated in a Referendum which took place on 22 May 2015.

Public Services in Procurement (Social Value) Bill 2015 (No 7 of 2015)

[17.35] This Private Members Bill was introduced by Senators Daragh O'Brien, Diarmuid Wilson, Mark McSharry and Thomas Byrne and proposes to require public bodies to have regard to economic, social and environmental wellbeing in connection with public service contracts for related matters.

Industrial Relations (Members of the Garda Síochána and the Defence Forces) Bill 2015 (No 9 of 2015)

[17.36] This is a Private Members Bill introduced by Deputy Michael McNamara to provide for the right of representative associations, established under the Garda Síochána Act 2005, the Garda Síochána Act 1924 and the Defence (Amendment) Act 1990, to carry on negotiations for the fixing of pay or other conditions of employment of their members and to join the national umbrella organisation for employees. The Bill proposes to remove the prohibition of the right to strike by members of An Garda Síochána and clarifies that a member of An Garda Síochána, who becomes a party, or applies to become a party, to an insolvency arrangement, shall not be deemed to be failing wilfully and without good and sufficient cause to pay a lawful debt in such circumstances as to be liable to affect his or her ability to discharge the duty of a member.

Companies (Amendment) Bill 2015 (No 10 of 2015)

[17.37] This Private Members Bill introduced by Deputy Peadar Tóibín proposes to amend s 224 of the Companies Act 2014, to hold a company officer or officers, acting on behalf of a corporate body, personally liable where a breach of employment law is committed.

Public Health (Regulation of Electronic Cigarettes and Protection of Children) Bill 2015 (No 17 of 2015)

[17.38] This Bill was introduced by Senators Averil Power, John Crown and Mark Daly. The Bill proposes to provide for the prohibition of the consumption of electronic cigarettes in public service vehicles and places of work. The Bill further proposes the registration of persons engaged in the business of selling electronic cigarettes by retail. The Bill provides for the prohibition of advertising of electronic cigarettes; a prohibition on sponsorship by manufacturers and importers of electronic cigarettes; and prohibitions on certain marketing practices in relation to electronic cigarettes. It also provides for the standardised packaging of electronic cigarettes; for the prohibition of the sale of electronic cigarettes to those under 18 years; for the prohibition of the consumption of electronic cigarettes in vehicles where persons under 18 years are present; and for the insertion of childproof caps on liquid nicotine bottles.

Migrant and Regularisation Bill 2015 (No 19 of 2015)

[17.39] This Private Members Bill, introduced by Deputy Niall Collins, provides for the establishment of a scheme to enable certain foreign nationals, whose presence within the State is other than in accordance with the permission granted by the Minister, to apply for a known permission to remain within the State.

Office of Fiscal Prosecution Bill 2015 (No 34 of 2015)

[17.40] This Bill, introduced by Deputy Michael McNamara, provides for the establishment of the Office of Fiscal Prosecution to provide for the investigation and prosecution by the new office of certain offences; to enable proceedings relating to such cases to be taken expeditiously; to provide for criminal and civil enforcement; and to provide for matters incidental upon the establishment of the office. The offences in the Bill relate to banking, investment of funds and other financial activities, company law, money laundering and financial terrorism, theft and fraud, bribery and corruption, competition and consumer protection and crime relating to the raising and collection of taxes and duties.

Education (Admission to Schools) Bill 2015 (No 35 of 2015)

[17.41] This Bill is introduced by the Minister for Education and Skills and requires that a school recognised in accordance with s 10 of the Education Act 1998 should prepare and publish an admission policy. Such policy shall include a statement that the school shall not discriminate in its admission policy on specified grounds.

Public Electronic Communications Networks (Improper Use) Bill 2015 (No 36 of 2015)

[17.42] This Private Members Bill was introduced by Deputy Pat Rabbitte and provides for certain offences in connection with the improper use of public electronic communications networks. Section 13(1) of the Bill provides that it is an offence for a person to send or cause to be sent, by means of a public electronic communications network, a message or other matter that is grossly offensive or is indecent, obscene or menacing for the purpose of causing annoyance, inconvenience or needless anxiety to another; to send or cause to be sent by means of a public electronic communications network, a message that the sender knows to be false, or for the purpose of causing annoyance, inconvenience or needless anxiety to another; and to persistently and without reasonable cause make use of a public electronic communications network.

Harmful and Malicious Electronic Communications Bill 2015 (No 37 of 2015)

[17.43] This is a Private Members Bill introduced by Senators Lorraine Higgins, Ivana Bacik and John Whelan to protect against and mitigate harm caused to individuals by all or any digital communications and to provide such individuals with a means of redress for any such offending behaviour directed at them.

Employment Equality (Amendment) Bill 2015 (No 55 of 2015)

[17.44] This Private Members Bill was introduced by Deputies Ruth Coppinger, Joe Higgins and Paul Murphy and provides for equality for employees of education, medical and other services under the direction of religious organisations. The Bill provides that no religious organisation or body under the direction or control of a religious organisation may give less favourable treatment on grounds of gender, marital status, family status, sexual orientation, religion, age, membership of the Traveller Community, disability grounds or on grounds of race to employees, or perspective employees, in services that it operates, including education or medical institutions.

Parental Leave (Amendment) Bill 2015 (No 61 of 2015)

[17.45] This Private Members Bill introduced by Deputy Peadar Tóibín proposes to amend the existing parental leave legislation by introducing paid bereavement leave for employees. The Bill provides that bereavement leave shall not exceed three days in any period of 12 consecutive months or five days in any period of 36 consecutive months. The draft provisions are similar in terms of scope to the current *force majeure* provisions in the Act.

Education (Welfare) (Amendment) Bill 2015 (No 63 of 2015)

[17.46] This Private Members Bill introduced by Senator Mary Moran provides for an increase in the school leaving age to 17.

Banded Hours Contract Bill 2015 (No 73 of 2015)

[17.47] This Private Members Bill introduced by Deputy Peadar Tóibín provides for banded hour contracts, ie the right for a worker to request increased hours and a corresponding obligation on an employer to consider such a request. The Bill permits a refusal only on objectively justified grounds and places an obligation on an employer to provide information to workers on overall working hours available in the employment.

Education (Amendment) Bill 2015 (No 97 of 2015)

[17.48] This Bill, introduced by Deputy Jim Daly, proposes to establish an Ombudsman for Education to provide an appeal mechanism for decisions of Boards of Education concerning decisions of teachers and grievances against schools, and provides for the investigation and reporting by the Ombudsman for Education of various matters.

The Longer Healthy Living Bill 2015 (No 81 of 2015)

[17.49] This Bill was introduced by Senators John Crown, Sean D Barrett and Averil Power. This Bill insures that all those employees of the Department of Health and all those employed by bodies directly funded by the Department of Health may, if they wish, postpone their retirement where they would otherwise have been forced to retire at a particular age that is stipulated in their employment contract. This is subject to their continuing capacity to fulfil the duties of their employment in a safe fashion. Note the Bill provides that any individual who attains mandatory retirement age within two years of the commencement of the enactment of this Bill may apply to the Minister to have their employment re-initiated under the same terms and conditions that were available to them if they retired as a result of attaining that age.

Equality In Education Bill 2015 (No 114 of 2015)

[17.50] This Private Members Bill was introduced by Jonathan O Brien TD. The purpose of the Bill is to reform and update the law which currently allows religious ethos institutions providing education to discriminate against children in admitting them to schools based on their religion. The Bill amends the Equal Status Acts 2000 to 2015 to give effect to the principle that no child should be given preferential access to a publically funded school on the basis of their religion.

Equal Participation in Schools Bill 2015 (No 115 of 2015)

[17.51] This Bill was introduced by Deputies Ruth Coppinger, Joe Higgins and Paul Murphy TD and proposes to end religious discrimination in admission to primary and post-primary educational establishments and to provide for full participation of pupils of all faiths and none in non-primary and post-primary educational establishments.

Technological Universities Bill 2015 (No 121 of 2015)

[17.52] The principal purpose of this Bill is to provide for the establishment of technological universities a new type of higher education institution to be formed through the consolidation and merger of existing institutes of technology. The Bill also provides for the revision of the governance arrangements of the Dublin Institute of Technology and the institutes of technology under the Dublin Institute of Technology Act 1992 and the Regional Technical Colleges Act 1992 respectfully.

Industrial Relations (Blacklists) Bill 2015 (No 128 of 2015)

[17.53] This Bill was introduced by Deputy Peadar Tóbín and proposes to make it unlawful to compile, use, sell or supply blacklists containing details of people who are or have been, trade union members or who are taking part, or have taken part, in trade union activities or an industrial action where such blacklists may be used by employers to discriminate, in relation to recruitment or the treatment of existing workers, and the Bill provides for sanctions where such unlawful actions as detailed occur.

Chapter 18

LITIGATION

DUTY TO GIVE REASONS FOR A DECISION

[18.01] *Bank of Ireland Mortgage Bank v Heron and Heron[1]—Court of Appeal— appeal from order of High Court by O'Hanlon J—failure of High Court to give reasons for its decision*

The plaintiff maintained its entitlement to summary judgment and submitted that the defendants had failed to demonstrate they had a real or bona fide defence to the claim. The defendants submitted that they had raised sufficient matters to justify the case being adjourned to a plenary hearing.

The High Court had decided that the matter should go to plenary hearing and the defendants appealed to the Court of Appeal.

The Court of Appeal noted that the trial judge did not give any reasons to support her decision, which was not a satisfactory situation, from the point of view of either the parties or the Court of Appeal, as any decision made by a judge in an application for summary judgment has significant repercussions for the parties to the litigation.

A plaintiff whose claim is remitted to plenary hearing may encounter substantial delay in their efforts to recover the sums claimed as well as additional costs in bringing the action to a full trial. On the other hand, if a judgment is granted against a defendant, the consequences may be very serious as the defendant is denied the opportunity of a full trial due to a failure to reach the low threshold of proof of an arguable defence.

The Court of Appeal held that a failure on the part of a judge to give reasons for his or her decision means that the parties to the litigation cannot make an informed decision as to whether the order maybe successfully be challenged on appeal or not.

The Court of Appeal noted that the Superior Courts have repeatedly held that administrative bodies making judicial or quasi-judicial decisions must give reasons for their decisions. The Court of Appeal stated that, given the requirement on administrative bodies to give reasons for decisions, no lesser standard could be required of courts exercising judicial functions. The Court noted the decision of McCarthy J in *Foley v Murphy*[2] which referred to the judgment of Henry LJ in *Flannery v Halifax Estate Agencies Ltd*[3] where Henry LJ set out the importance of the duty to give reasons and noted that this duty is a function of due process and therefore of justice. That case was

---

1. *Bank of Ireland Mortgage Bank v Heron and Heron* [2015] IECA 66.
2. *Foley v Murphy* [2008] 1 IR 619.
3. *Flannery v Halifax Estate Agencies Ltd* [2000] 1 WLR 377.

cited with approval by Phillips MR in *English v Emery Reimbold and Strick Ltd*[4] who stated:

> The essential requirement is that the terms of the judgment should enable the parties and any appellate tribunal readily to analyse the reasoning that was essential to the judge's decision.

The Court of Appeal noted that the majority of judgments in the High Court are delivered *ex tempore* and that such judgments could not be expected to include anything like the same degree of detail or be as discursive as might be expected in a reserved judgment. However, even an *ex tempore* judgment must comply with the essential requirement identified by Lord Phillips, namely that it should enable the parties in any appellate tribunal readily to analyse the reasoning that was essential to the judge's decision. The Court of Appeal noted its sympathy to the predicament of High Court judges when faced with a lengthy motion list every week; however judges cannot be relieved of their obligations to set out briefly the principal reasons underlying decisions on that account. If they are unable to deliver a judgment because of the complexity of the facts or legal issues then judgment should be reserved. It is never sufficient to merely announce a decision without giving any reasons for it.

The Court of Appeal then went on to consider the substantive issue and noted its satisfaction that the defendants did not meet even the low threshold required to justify the case being adjourned to plenary hearing. The High Court judge had erred in her decision and therefore the Court allowed the appeal and entered judgment in favour of the plaintiff.

STATUTE OF LIMITATIONS

[18.02] *Stapleton v St Colmans (Claremorris) Credit Union Ltd[5]—High Court— Barrett J—personal injuries claim—whether personal injuries proceedings for alleged work-related stress could be struck out as being statute barred under Statutes of Limitation Acts 1957 to 2000 as amended*

The plaintiff was informed at a social occasion that an allegation of workplace bullying was made against her by a colleague at the defendant Credit Union. Thereafter, the plaintiff was considerably unhappy at work as she perceived there to be an ongoing and unresolved vilification of her good name. She was absent from work on stress-related sick leave between February and September 2012. She was dismissed from employment in September 2012 and a subsequent unfair dismissals claim[6] was successful and resulted in a reinstatement order. The plaintiff made an application to the Injuries Board on 24 March 2014 and an authorisation to bring the High Court proceedings issued on 26 March 2014. Barrett J noted that this occurred two years and eight months after the plaintiff had first attended her medical doctor for treatment of alleged work-related

---

4.   *English v Emery Reimbold and Strick Ltd* [2002] 1 WLR 2409.

5.   *Stapleton v St Colmans (Claremorris) Credit Union Ltd* [2015] IEHC 510.

6.   *Stapleton v St Colman's (Claremorris) Credit Union Ltd* UD 1776/2012.

stress, and two years and one month after she was diagnosed with a significant related ailment.

The defendant asserted that the proceedings were commenced out of time and noted that in the personal injuries summons it had been alleged that workplace vilification commenced against the plaintiff in June 2011, causing her to attend her doctor for work-related stress symptoms in August 2011. The defendant contended that there was no doubt that the plaintiff knew at the latest by 1 February 2012, when she was certified as unfit to work due to stress-related illness, that the injury itself had been significant and that the injury was attributable in all or part to the impugned acts or omissions of her employer.

The defendant submitted that under s 2 of the Statute of Limitations (Amendment) Act 1991, the plaintiff ought to have commenced her personal injury action within two years of 1 February 2012, given the two-year time limitation on personal injuries actions.

The plaintiff asserted that, in her application form to the Injuries Board, she identified the date of injury as being 18 September 2012, when she was dismissed from her employment, which resulted in her stress-related injury. Barrett J noted that by 18 September 2012 the date on which the plaintiff was dismissed from her employment, she had suffered the alleged personal injuries on which the indorsement of claim was focused. The High Court noted that, while there was reference in the indorsement of claim to the fact that the plaintiff had attended work on 18 September and was dismissed, a fair reading of the indorsement was that the injuries, for which compensation was being sought, were sustained in the previous year with emphasis on the summer of 2011.

The High Court noted that the plaintiff's difficulty was that, on her own account of the facts, she had the knowledge necessary to commence the proceedings at the latest on 1 February 2012. The High Court noted its sympathy for the plaintiff; however Barrett J referred to the Oireachtas decision that personal injuries proceedings must be commenced within a relatively short time of the injuries occurring. The plaintiff had acquired knowledge of the injuries at issue on 1 February 2012 at the latest, yet her application for authorisation to proceed with the proceedings was not made to the Injuries Board until the end of March 2014.

The High Court acceded to the application of the defendant that the proceedings be struck out as being statute barred, having been commenced outside the two-year time frame.

[18.03] *Culkin v Sligo County Council[7]—High Court—Kearns P—Employment Equality Acts 1998 and 2015, s 101(2)(a)—litigation—personal injury proceedings— rule in Henderson v Henderson—whether proceedings should be struck out as an abuse of process or duplication of plaintiff's equality claim against defendant*

The plaintiff was employed by the defendant county council in various capacities over a period of 39 years. It was asserted that he experienced difficulties in the course of

---

7.   *Culkin v Sligo County Council* [2015] IEHC 46.

employment to include bullying and harassment which left him suffering a number of psychological and physiological symptoms. It was accepted that in September 2009 the plaintiff made a complaint to the Equality Tribunal under the Employment Equality Acts 1998 to 2015. In his complaint form EE1 he stated that he was subject to discriminatory treatment in relation to 'access to employment, promotion regrading, training, conditions of employment, discriminatory dismissal, and victimisatory dismissal'. The plaintiff further alleged that, having completed a degree in 2005, he repeatedly applied for a number of engineering positions only to be deemed not qualified for promotion. His evidence was that he was continuously frustrated in his attempts to obtain engineering experience within the defendant because of his age and his disability, which he contended was induced by historic bullying and harassment.

In addition to his equality complaint, an authorisation from the Injuries Board was obtained to commence High Court proceedings in November 2010. His personal injuries summons issued on 2 February 2011.

It was noted by the High Court that the plaintiff's case before the Tribunal was heard over four days. A preliminary submission was made to the Tribunal on behalf of the defendant expressing the view that the matters before the Tribunal were the same as those in the High Court and that the plaintiff was precluded from pursuing both claims. It was noted by the Court that, at that point, the plaintiff requested that the Tribunal continue to hear the case.

The High Court noted the procedure for making a complaint to the Tribunal was governed by s 77(1) of the Employment Equality Acts 1998 to 2015. It was submitted by the defendant that the plaintiff's complaint to the Tribunal was almost identical to the complaints raised by him in his personal injuries proceedings. Reliance was placed on s 101 of the Acts which related to alternative avenues of redress.

Reliance was placed by the defendant on the High Court decision of Hedigan J in *Cunningham v Intel Ireland Ltd.*[8] It was submitted that the facts of *Cunningham* were identical to the present case and the decision of Hedigan J in relation to s 101(2), combined with the well-established rule in *Henderson v Henderson,*[9] both of which are designed to prevent the duplication of proceedings, made it clear that the plaintiff must elect to proceed either with the Tribunal proceedings or the High Court proceedings but could not pursue both. The plaintiff was given an opportunity to make a fully informed decision as to which set of proceedings he wished to pursue. It was further noted by the defendant that even after issuing his September 2009 complaint, the plaintiff could have opted to pursue personal injuries proceedings as long as he did so before an investigation of the equality complaint commenced under s 79 of the Acts.

It was further submitted by the defendant that the Labour Court had a wider discretion than the High Court in respect of awarding medical damages and there was no question therefore of the plaintiff's rights to a remedy being curtailed. It was submitted that the plaintiff's personal injuries proceedings should be dismissed.

The plaintiff submitted that rather than precluding a common law case based on the broad underlying facts, s 101(2)(a) exists to preclude cases which are already covered

8.   *Cunningham v Intel Ireland Ltd* [2013] IEHC 207.
9.   *Henderson v Henderson* (1843) 3 Hare 100, (1843) 67 ER 313.

and have been pursued under s 77(1) of the Acts. It was further suggested that *Cunningham* was distinguishable on the facts as the plaintiff was a litigant in person and therefore the decision of Hedigan J, while correct in relation to the facts and arguments advanced, was *per incuriam*.

Kearns P noted that the rule in *Henderson v Henderson* was well established and was frequently applied as part of the policy of the Courts to avoid double litigation of the same issues. It was noted that the plaintiff had issued a complaint before the Tribunal in September 2009 and his EEI complaint form contained the detail of the nature of the bullying to which he was allegedly subjected. The preliminary submissions made by the defendant were that the option of pursuing the Tribunal complaint or his common law claim was made clear to the plaintiff and he opted to pursue the remedy before the Tribunal. Kearns P held himself satisfied that the plaintiff was now estopped from resiling from this position, having had his claim rejected by the Tribunal.

The High Court held that to allow the plaintiff to proceed with his common law claim would be to breach the rule in *Henderson v Henderson* and in view of Kearns P would also fail to give effect to the intention of s 101(2)(a) of the Acts. Kearns P also considered the submissions of the plaintiff that the Court should depart from the decision in *Cunningham* on the basis that the plaintiff in that case was a lay litigant. The High Court, however, noted that the fact that a lay litigant was involved in those proceedings made it more likely to have caused the deciding judge to take even greater care in examining the submissions and his decision. It was noted by Kearns P that it had not been suggested that the decision of Hedigan J was in any way deficient or wrongly decided. The Court noted that the facts of *Cunningham* were closely related to the present application and Kearns P held himself not satisfied that a substantial reason to depart from that decision had been raised.

The High Court concluded that the matters complained of in the plaintiff's common law and Equality Tribunal proceedings both dated from the time a new supervisor was appointed and arose from the very same alleged incidences of mistreatment. The rule in *Henderson v Henderson* coupled with the provisions of s 101(2)(a) required that where there is such a considerable degree of overlap, the plaintiff should be precluded from pursuing his High Court proceedings. The Court noted that the plaintiff's right of appeal from the Equality Tribunal to the Labour Court remained and his right to an effective remedy was therefore unaffected. The personal injuries claim was dismissed.

WANT OF PROSECUTION

[18.04] *McLoughlin v Garvey[10]—Court of Appeal—Mahon J—appeal from decision of High Court to strike out plaintiff's proceedings for want of prosecution— inexcusable and inordinate delay—whether delay excusable in circumstances where plaintiff's son suffers from serious and debilitating medical condition—plaintiff has cared for her son to the exclusion of other activities and interests in her life*

These proceedings concern allegations of sexual abuse made by the plaintiff against her defendant brother relating to alleged incidents starting in 1976. The plaintiff commenced proceedings in the High Court by plenary summons in March 2006, approximately 28 years after the alleged abuse had ceased. She alleged that she was physically assaulted and falsely imprisoned by the defendant and was raped and repeatedly sexually assaulted by him over a period of four years. These allegations were denied in full. The Court of Appeal noted that pleadings had exchanged without undue delay until March 2007, the date of delivery of the defence. Discovery was furnished by the plaintiff in April 2008 and then nothing occurred for approximately 18 months, whereupon in October 2009 the plaintiff served a notice of intention to proceed. Two and a half years later a second notice of intention to proceed was served by the plaintiff, representing a period of approximately four years since the completion of discovery.

The defendant brought a motion in April 2012 seeking to have the plaintiff's claim dismissed for want of prosecution. This was heard by the High Court in July 2012 and Hogan J decided to strike out the proceedings because of inexcusable and inordinate delay. This case before the Court of Appeal concerned the parties' appeal and cross-appeal against the High Court order.

It was noted by Mahon J that the plaintiff had acknowledged the delay was inordinate and thereby that aspect of her appeal had been withdrawn. Mahon J noted that the plaintiff's son suffered from congenital hydrocephalus and had progressive medical issues, including epileptic seizures, which required neurological surgery in June 2012. The Court of Appeal noted that the plaintiff had devoted a great deal of her time and energy to looking after her son, and that this had significantly occupied her mind and time to the exclusion of many other activities and interests in her life. Mahon J noted that the issue for the Court was whether the extent of the care of the plaintiff's son was so significant as to justify a delay of approximately four years up to the date of service of the notice of motion seeking dismissal for want of prosecution.

Mahon J noted that the plaintiff's appeal was pursued on the grounds that the delay was excusable and that the balance of justice required that the claim not be dismissed. The Court noted that the jurisdiction of the Court of Appeal had recently been considered by the Court of Appeal in *Collins v Minister for Justice, Equality and Law Reform & Ors.*[11] In that case the Court considered previous decisions of the Supreme Court which had indicated that a High Court decision should only be interfered with where an error of principle was disclosed. The Court of Appeal held that, while it will

---

10. *McLoughlin v Garvey* [2015] IECA 80.

11. *Collins v Minister for Justice, Equality and Law Reform & Ors* [2015] IECA 27.

give great weight to the views of a trial judge, it retains the jurisdiction to exercise its discretion in a different manner, if appropriate, untrammelled by any *a priori* rule that would restrict the scope of the appeal to interfere with the decision of the High Court. Mahon J summarised the three-stage test for the consideration of applications to dismiss for want of prosecution as identified by Hamilton CJ in *Primor plc v Stokes Kennedy Crowley,*[12] that is: (i) whether the delay has been inordinate; (ii) if so, whether the delay is inexcusable; and (iii) even if the delay has been inordinate and inexcusable, the Court must nonetheless consider the balance of justice.

Mahon J held that in applying that test, the question was whether the delay of approximately four years between the plaintiff's affidavit of discovery in April 2008 and the filing of the notice of intention to proceed in March 2012, with due regard to the fact that the subject matter of the proceedings concerned events which took place 25 years previously, was excusable.

The Court noted the severity of the plaintiff's son's medical condition and that his deterioration between the years of 2008 and 2012 was confirmed in medical reports before the Court. In the medical report, the doctor expressed strong views as to the impact of the plaintiff's son's condition on the plaintiff's ability to apply her mind to the legal proceedings during the four-year period. Mahon J held that, in the particular circumstances of this case, the very serious medical condition of the plaintiff's son and more particularly the extent to which that medical condition deteriorated in 2008, provided a satisfactory explanation for the four-year delay between 2008 and 2012 and therefore the period of the delay was excusable.

Mahon J noted, however, that there must be a balance between delay which is permissible and had occurred for good reason and the effect of that delay on the defendant and his anxiety to bring proceedings against him to a conclusion, especially proceedings which involved allegations of serious sexual misconduct. Mahon J also referenced the requirements of Art 34.1 of the Constitution and art 6.1 of the Convention for the Protection of Human Rights and Fundamental Freedoms that there be an expeditious conclusion of legal proceedings. There is also the guarantee to citizens of the right to protect their good name in Art 43.2 of the Constitution. This was of particular relevance to the defendant, who was facing allegations of serious criminal and sexual misconduct which, if upheld, would result in grave reputational damage. Mahon J held that because he had found the delay to be excusable, it was not necessary for him to consider the balance of justice argument; however, he held that even if the delay were inexcusable, he would have considered that the balance of justice favoured the continuance of the proceedings.

The Court noted the concerns of the defendant as to the delay in prosecution and the prejudicial effect of this delay on the defendant's ability to defend the proceedings. Mahon J noted that, even if the proceedings were prosecuted with reasonable haste after their commencement, a period of close to 30 years would have passed since the matters complained of occurred before trial of the action might reasonably have taken place. Fading memories were always going to be a feature of this case. Mahon J held that the position was always going to be that a jury would be forced to choose between two

---

12. *Primor plc v Stokes Kennedy Crowley* [1996] 2 IR 459.

different narratives. This fact did not alter due to any delay on the part of the plaintiff after the commencement of the proceedings. It was also a feature in this case that the evidence of the plaintiff and the defendant's father would be particularly relevant. Although while the High Court had noted the plaintiff's father was in advancing years, Mahon J concluded that he was still in his 70s and it had not been suggested that he suffered from any particular cognitive difficulty or that his memory of events had deteriorated in any measurable or accelerated manner in recent years. Mahon J held that it was imperative that the case proceed to trial without further delay.

FRIVOLOUS AND VEXATIOUS CLAIMS

[18.05] *Harvey v The Courts Service & Ors[13]—High Court—O'Connor J—Unfair Dismissals Acts 1977 to 2015—Rules of the Superior Courts, Ord 19—lay litigant— compliance with court procedures and rules—particulars of statement of claim— submission of causes of action not included in statement of claim—frivolous and vexatious claims—rights and responsibilities in commencing legal proceedings— inherent jurisdiction to strike out proceedings where no reasonable cause of action exists*

This case concerned an application by the defendants to have proceedings struck out on the basis that the plaintiff had not complied with the Rules of the Superior Courts and that the proceedings were frivolous and vexatious. The plaintiff was a lay litigant and described himself as having been a civil servant within the Courts Service and, more particularly, a service officer from June 2000 to 4 May, 2007, at which point he was suspended. He was dismissed with effect from 5 September 2008. The plaintiff subsequently lodged an unfair dismissals claim with the EAT. The first defendant was identified as the 'Employer's full legal name' on the EAT form submitted by the plaintiff. The plaintiff listed each of the other defendants as officers or employees of the first defendant and stated that the defendants had engaged in detrimental wrongdoing against the plaintiff by unlawfully dismissing him. In the High Court proceedings the plaintiff, in his replying affidavit of July 2015, alleged that the EAT acted in an overtly corrupt manner at the hearing of his claim in 2011. He informed the Court that he had issued separate proceedings against the EAT.

The plaintiff issued a plenary summons on 4 February 2010 and subsequently renewed it on February 2011, July 2011, January 2012 and July 2012. The endorsement of claim sought reliefs only as against the second to seventh defendants. The plaintiff issued an amended statement of claim on 20 July 2015 in which the first defendant was referred to as the plaintiff's 'employer or under the aegis of the Department of Justice and Equality'.

---

13. *Harvey v The Courts Service & Ors* [2015] IEHC 680.

The defendants brought an application seeking a number of reliefs from the High Court including:

(i) an order under s 15(2) of the Unfair Dismissals Act 1977 striking out the plaintiff's claim on the grounds that the plaintiff was barred from recovering damages at common law for wrongful dismissal after having previously proceeded by way of a claim to the EAT;

(ii) an order under Ord 19(28) of the Rules of the Superior Courts striking out the plaintiff's claim on the grounds that there was no reasonable cause of action or that the claims were 'frivolous or vexatious';

(iii) an order under Ord 19(27) of the RSC striking out those matters in the plaintiff's statement of claim which were unnecessary and scandalous and which were designed to prejudice or embarrass the defendants;

(iv) an order striking out the plaintiff's action on the basis that the plaintiff's action was:

(a) unsustainable;

(b) bound to fail; and

(c) was frivolous and/or vexatious under the inherent jurisdiction of the Court.

The defendants submitted that the plaintiff opted to proceed with his claim regarding his dismissal by way of application to the EAT and, in doing so, triggered the operation of s 15(2) of the Unfair Dismissals Acts 1977 to 2015 (the Acts), which provides that where a recommendation has been made by a Rights Commissioner in respect of a claim by an employee for redress under that Act, or the hearing of a claim by the EAT has commenced, the employee shall not be entitled to recover damages at common law for wrongful dismissal in respect of the dismissal concerned.

The Court rejected the plaintiff's submission at the hearing that only the original statutory provision under the Unfair Dismissals Act 1977 could be relied upon. The Court noted that it cannot change the legislation and the Court is obliged to uphold the law as it is enacted by the Oireachtas. The High Court referred to various cases[14] that have established that a claim at common law for wrongful dismissal is prohibited where s 15 applies. The Court also rejected the plaintiff's submission that s 15(2) of the Acts should not apply as the plaintiff had never been provided with his terms and conditions of employment. The Court noted that the first defendant had not admitted that the plaintiff had not been provided with his terms and conditions of employment. The legislation provides that the plaintiff has no right to recover damages at common law for wrongful dismissal once the EAT has commenced hearing his claim and the Court found that the plaintiff's argument in this regard failed. The Court noted that this was a matter that was not justiciable between the plaintiff and the defendants in this case. The

---

14. *Parsons v Iarnród Éireann* [1997] 2 IR 523; *Nolan v Emo Oil Services Ltd* [2009] 20 ELR 122; *Cunningham v Intel Ireland Ltd* [2013] IEHC 207; and *Culkin v Sligo County Council* [2015] IEHC 46.

plaintiff's grievance with the EAT was not a matter to be determined in these proceedings. The plaintiff informed the Court that he had issued separate proceedings against the EAT.

The defendants submitted that that the plaintiff's amended statement of claim had no proper regard for Ord 19(3) of the RSC which requires 'in a summary form a statement of the material facts' and not the evidence by which the facts are to be proved. The Court stated that the amended statement of claim was in fact an attack on the defendants and was not a summary form of the material facts, as required by Ord 19(3), and stated that this would inform the Court's decision in respect of the defendant's application. The plaintiff submitted that he should not be disadvantaged due to his status as lay litigant. The Court rejected this and noted that the Court cannot differentiate between those who have legal representation and those who represent themselves but noted that the administration of justice can be improved by adhering to practice directions which facilitate the hearing of such applications. The Court noted that the defendants had complied with Practice Direction 54 which relates to proceedings involving a litigant without legal representation and an 'information sheet' had been filed and served on behalf of the defendants. In relation to the amended statement of claim, the Court noted that the plaintiff had failed to comply with the laws and rules of the Court required to enable him prosecute his claims.

During the course of the hearing, the plaintiff further alleged that he had been the subject of assault and defamation by one or more of the defendants and that the first defendant was vicariously liable in these circumstances. He submitted that these claims should be considered by the Court in this application. The Court noted that the endorsement of claim in the plenary summons did not seek reliefs against the first defendant and further, it included no reference to assault or defamation. The Court noted that the law requires that such serious allegations are particularised and further that statutory requirements are adhered to. The Court stated that the plaintiff ignored or was oblivious to these statutory requirements. The Court further noted that a claim for alleged defamation is governed by the Defamation Act 2009, which has a limitation period of one year that may be extended up to two years, if the case requires, and that claims for damages for personal injury from assault or negligence must be processed through the Injuries Board and then comply with the Civil Liability and Courts Act 2004. The Court referred to these statutory requirements in order that the plaintiff would understand the impediments he would have to overcome in order to prosecute any of the claims submitted at the hearing.

The Court also noted that neither the plenary summons nor the amended statement of claim referred to damages for assault or defamation. The Court stated that it could not import particulars into the proceedings at this late stage. The plaintiff had already been provided with the opportunity to amend his original statement of claim. The Court noted that the plaintiff had the right to bring a claim but that such rights carry responsibilities. In this case the plaintiff had the duty to deliver a statement of claim in accordance with the Rules of the Superior Courts. The Court rejected the plaintiff's attempt to seek damages for assault or defamation in these proceedings. The Court further noted that the plaintiff had made very serious allegations in the amended statement of claim. The Court noted that the plaintiff referred to contrived or false complaints without clarifying the specific words used, the identity of the individual(s) making the statements or when they were stated. The Court stated that the plaintiff had made serious allegations against fellow citizens and that while the plaintiff contended that he had been denied justice, he appeared to be unaware of the rights of others.

The Court accepted that Ord 19(28) of the Rules of the Superior Court, which provides that any pleading may be struck out on the grounds that it discloses no reasonable cause of action, was an appropriate rule to be considered in this case. The Court noted that it has an inherent jurisdiction to strike out proceedings where it is clear that the plaintiff's claim cannot succeed on the facts accepted or put forward by the plaintiff. The plaintiff also submitted that there may be a claim for 'tortious' interference with his right to a livelihood in addition to a claim for wrongful dismissal. The Court could not understand how the plaintiff's claims arising from his dismissal could now be cast into another cause of action called tortious interference with the right to a livelihood. The Court noted that the plaintiff had not, in any of his pleadings, referred to any tort or common law cause of action. The Court found that the plaintiff's case failed on the basis that it was clear the plaintiff's claim could not succeed. The Court found that the defendants had established that the plaintiff's claims in these proceedings were bound to fail even if the plaintiff's allegations in the amended statement of claim or those sought to be elaborated upon by him at the hearing of this motion were proven by the plaintiff at trial. The Court further noted that allowing the proceedings to progress any further would not afford any tangible benefit to the plaintiff. The Court also clarified that it did not have the inquisitorial powers sought by the plaintiff and that the administration of justice in the courts is adversarial, except where the Oireachtas otherwise provides. The Court did not have the right to set up an enquiry into the plaintiff's long series of complaints about his employment and dismissal. The High Court struck out the plaintiff's claims as against the defendants.

Chapter 19

PART-TIME WORK

PENSION RIGHTS

[19.01] *Minister for Education and Science v The Labour Court (respondent), Boyle and the Committee of Management of Hillside Park Pre-School (Notice Parties)[1]— High Court—O'Malley J—Protection of Employees (Part-Time Work) Act 2001— judicial review—certiorari—application to quash determination of Labour Court that the first notice party is an employee of the Minister within meaning of 2001 Act— whether notice party treated less favourably than full-time comparator in relation to pension rights*

Ms Boyle (the claimant) was employed as a teacher in a grant-aided pre-school for children of Travellers for over 20 years until the school closed in 2011. The grant amounted to 98 per cent of the salary payable to a primary school teacher and was paid to the management committee of the pre-school in respect of the claimant's salary; she was the only teacher in the school and worked 15 hours per week.

In 2009, the claimant took a claim to the Rights Commissioner Service under the 2001 Act, claiming she was less favourably treated than full-time workers by not being admitted to the National Teachers Superannuation Scheme. The claimant named each of the chairpersons of the management committee and the Department of Education and Science as being her employer. The chosen comparator was a national school teacher who worked in an early start unit in a primary school. The High Court noted that the pre-school had closed before the complaint was dealt with and that the claimant was paid redundancy by the Minister. The Rights Commissioner concluded that the Department of Education and Science was neither the employer of the claimant within the meaning of s 3(1) of the Act nor an associate employer within the meaning of s 7(5) of the Act but made no findings in respect of the management committee. This was appealed by the claimant to the Labour Court.

The Labour Court followed the judgment of Dunne J in *Catholic University School v Dooley.*[2] The Labour Court held that it must conclude that the Minister was to be regarded as the claimant's employer for the purposes of the claim. The Labour Court found that the comparator and the claimant were both employed by the Minister and that, while not engaged in the same work, they were engaged in work of equal value. In terms of redress, the Labour Court noted the order sought by the claimant directing the Minister to enter her into the Superannuation Scheme with effect from 1992; however the Court determined that this was not possible. Firstly the 2001 Act was not enacted until 2001 and the claimant could not have accrued any entitlement under the Act prior

---

1. *Minister for Education and Science v Labour Court (respondent), and Boyle and Committee of Management of Hillside Park Pre-School (Notice Parties)* [2015] IEHC 429.
2. *Catholic University School v Dooley* [2010] IEHC 496.

to its enactment, and secondly no complaint could be entertained unless it was made within six months of the date of the alleged contravention. The Labour Court held itself limited to making an order directing the Minister to enter the claimant into the Superannuation Scheme with effect from 21 September 2008, being six months before the date the claimant initiated her claim. The Labour Court awarded the claimant €10,000 compensation for the general effects of the discrimination suffered by the claimant.

In the judicial review proceedings before the High Court the Minister sought an order of *certiorari* in respect of the determination of the Labour Court asserting that the Labour Court had acted unfairly and *ultra vires* the 2001 Act; had erred in law in determining that the claimant and her comparator were employees of the Minister; had erred in law in directing the Minister to enter the claimant into the Superannuation Scheme where she did not satisfy the statutory requirements; and in making an award of compensation.

It was noted by the High Court that the management committee did not participate in the appeal. It was further noted that the claimant was a qualified secondary teacher rather than a primary school teacher. It was stated that she was employed by the school's Board of Management but that the Department paid 98 per cent of her salary by way of a grant to the Board. It was noted that all part-time teachers (learning support and resource teachers) in primary schools had been paid by the grant system until 2009 while the part-time teachers in special schools had been paid under the same system until January 2011. In 2011, by way of circular, the grant system was altered to direct payment to the teachers.

It was noted that the claimant commenced employment in 1992 and was paid a part-time hourly rate and thereafter she applied, and was accepted, to a special scheme open to part-time teachers who were wholly or mainly dependant for their livelihood on their earnings from part-time teaching and whose employment history met certain criteria. The claimant joined the scheme and her salary was set at the first point of the scale, with an allowance for her degree and her HDip. She was advised that she would remain on that point because she was not a fully qualified national school teacher. She subsequently obtained a Master's Degree and this was substituted for a previous qualification allowance, entitling her to an increase in pay. The High Court noted that further to a circular in 2000, which allowed secondary school teachers who teach in primary schools in a temporary or substitute capacity to be paid at the rate applicable to qualified national teachers, the claimant was placed on the second point and thereafter an incremental scale was applied to her.

O'Malley J noted that following the Financial Emergency Measures in the Public Interest (No 2) Act 2009, the claimant's salary was reduced on the same basis as that of national school teachers. It was maintained by the claimant, before the Labour Court, that the Minister must be deemed under the 2001 Act to be her employer because he was the person liable to pay her wages. In terms of redress, the claimant sought an order deeming her to be a member of the Superannuation Scheme with effect from the date of commencement in 1992 of her employment as an eligible part-time teacher. It was submitted on behalf of the Minister that the claimant was not his employee and that she had entered the contract with, and worked under a contract of employment for, the management committee. It was asserted that the pre-school was controlled and operated by the management committee and that the Minister had no involvement whatsoever with either the running of the school or the claimant's employment. The High Court noted the findings of the Labour Court that while the management of the school was vested in the management committee and the claimant was under the day-to-day control of that body in discharge of her duties, it was clear that the management committee exercised no control over the remuneration and other conditions attaching to her employment and that these were exclusively controlled by the Minister.

O'Malley J considered the judgments in both *Dooley* and *O'Keefe v Hickey*[3] in the Supreme Court. She noted that the State does not, and did not in the past, hand over funds to schools to do with as they wish. It sets the rules according to which the State pays the salaries of teachers, where they are not paid out of privately sourced funds. O'Malley J noted that salaries will not be paid by the Department unless the teacher chosen by the management has the qualification required by the Department and unless the allocation of posts by the Department to the school permits appointments to be made. O'Malley J noted that rates of pay, including allowances for qualifications, posts and responsibilities and so on, are negotiated by the Department in a collective bargaining process under the auspices of a statutory body, the Teaching Council, rather than being set by individual school management bodies negotiating with individual teachers. O'Malley J concluded that the Department carries out, in respect of State-funded teachers, the role normally carried out by an employer with regard to the payment of employees. The High Court noted the concession by the State that in respect of State-funded teachers, it is to be considered their employer for the purpose of the Payment of Wages Act 1991. The Court noted that this position was confirmed by of the Education Act 1998 as amended, s 24 of which provides for the powers of the Minister in relation to teachers' pay. O'Malley J noted that this was one of the results of the unique tripartite arrangement in education in Ireland. In relation to teachers whose salaries are paid by the State, the role of the employer is uniquely split; part of it is borne by the management of an individual school and part by the Department of Education. The former has the right to hire, discipline, dismiss and generally direct a teacher in the day-to-day running of the school. The Department on the other hand sets the rules about and pays the salaries. It thereby takes on what would normally be the rights of an employer in relation to pay. It followed, in the view of O'Malley J, that the Department carried the legal duties of an employer associated with pay. The High Court noted that to hold otherwise would be to impose on school management bodies legal responsibility where they have no legal powers.

The argument that it is open to individual schools to give better salaries or pension provisions, if they wished, did not deal with a primary liability to pay what is lawfully due. O'Malley J noted that the decision in *Dooley*, which was followed by Hedigan J in *Blackrock College v Brown*,[4] was entirely consistent with both the authorities and the factual situation of State-funded teachers. O'Malley J noted that over the years the Department has administered its functions with consciousness of its responsibilities and

---

3.   *O'Keefe v Hickey* [2009] 2 IR 302.
4.   *Blackrock College v Brown* [2013] IEHC 607.

that the 2008 circular was a good example. It clearly stated that the Department was to phase-in direct payment of salaries to part-time teachers in order to ensure compliance with the 2001 Act.

The Court noted that it was true that the claimant was not employed in a school 'recognised' under the Education Act 1998; however the Court noted that there was no legislation or other rule of law to prevent the Minister from entering into the kind of arrangement by which the claimant was employed. The Court noted the submission made by the Minister that the claimant had no entitlement to a pension because she was not a national school teacher and that the pension scheme was limited to national school teachers. O'Malley J held that this was a matter that goes to the appropriateness of the remedy rather than the claimant's substantive rights under the Act. O'Malley J held that if it was accepted by the High Court that, for the purposes of the 2001 Act, the claimant must be deemed to be employed by the Minster, then the claimant had to demonstrate that she had been treated less favourably than full-time employees who were doing comparable work within the definition of the Act. The High Court noted that the Labour Court had found in the claimant's favour and this aspect of that finding was not challenged in the judicial review proceedings.

The Court considered the Minister's complaint about how the redress was awarded by the Labour Court. The Court noted that the powers of the Labour Court under s 16 of the 2001 Act are to direct the employer to comply with s 9, ie to cease treating a part-time employee less favourably than a comparable full-time employee and/or to direct the payment of compensation. O'Malley J held that she did not think the jurisdiction of the Labour Court to direct compliance with the terms of the Act could encompass ordering the Minister to admit the claimant into a particular scheme, the terms of which set out qualifying conditions including a requirement to pay contributions. This, in the view of the High Court, went beyond ordering an employer to cease discrimination and comply with the Act and was *ultra vires*.

O'Malley J concluded that the loss suffered by the claimant in these circumstances was more appropriately dealt with by way of compensation. She noted that the power to award compensation was not limited under the 2001 Act to established special damages and therefore she concluded that the Labour Court did not act irrationally or unlawfully in awarding €10,000 to the claimant for discrimination. However, the Court remitted the matter to the Labour Court for re-consideration on the question of compensation, to take into account the findings of the High Court as to the invalidity of the direction to admit the claimant to the Superannuation Scheme.

O'Malley J concluded that publicly-funded school teachers must be deemed for the purpose of the 2001 Act to be employed by the Minister for Education. The Labour Court correctly found that the claimant in this case, although not a national school teacher or teacher in a recognised school, was employed on the same basis as such teachers. The claimant was found to be treated less favourably than full-time teachers doing comparable work and therefore was entitled to redress under the 2001 Act. However, the Labour Court was not empowered to order that she be admitted to the National Teachers Superannuation Scheme and thus the matter was remitted to the Labour Court for consideration on the question of compensation.

PRO RATA TEMPORIS

[19.02] *Österreichischer Gewerkschaftsbund v Verband Österreichischer Banken und Bankiers*[5]—*Court of Justice of the European Union—reference for preliminary ruling—social policy—Framework Agreement on Part-Time Work—principle of non-discrimination—collective agreement providing for dependent child allowance—calculation of allowance paid to part-time workers in accordance with principle of pro rata temporis*

This was a request for a preliminary ruling from Austria under art 267 of the TFEU.[6]

The request arose in the context of proceedings between the Austrian Trade Union Federation (Österreichischer Gewerkschaftsbund) (OG) and the Austrian Association of Banks and Bankers (Verband Österreichischer Banken und Bankiers) (the VÖBB). The proceedings concerned a dependent child allowance paid on the basis of a collective agreement applicable to bank staff and bankers (the Collective Agreement). Clause 4 of the Framework Agreement on Part-Time Work provides that part-time workers shall not be treated less favourably than comparable full-time workers purely on the basis that they work part time, unless the different treatment is justified on objective grounds (cl 4(1)). Where appropriate, the principle of *pro rata temporis* applies (cl 4(2)). This principle of non-discrimination is echoed in Austrian national law. The Collective Agreement provided that both household allowances and dependent child allowances were granted as social benefits. In relation to the calculation of these social benefits, the Collective Agreement provided that the household allowance for part-time workers was to be calculated on a *pro-rata* basis, dependent on the number of hours actually worked (para 21(2) of the Collective Agreement). Dependant child allowance was to be calculated in the same way for part-time workers (para 22 of the Collective Agreement).

OG, in its capacity as the competent body for the employees in the Austrian banking sector, lodged an application against the VÖBB, in its capacity as the competent body representing employers in the Austrian banking sector. The application was for a declaration under the special procedure provided for in para 54(2) of the Law on Labour and Social Courts.[7] Effectively what was being sought was a declaration from the Austrian Supreme Court that part-time workers who fall within the scope of the Collective Agreement are entitled to payment of the full amount of the dependent child allowance provided for in para 22(1) of that Collective Agreement, as opposed to an amount calculated *pro rata* on the number of hours worked.

---

5. *Österreichischer Gewerkschaftsbund v Verband Österreichischer Banken und Bankiers* (Case C–476/12).

6. It concerned the interpretation of cl 4 of the Framework Agreement on Part-Time Work concluded on 6 June 1997 (the 'Framework Agreement on Part-Time Work'), which is annexed to Council Directive 97/81/EC of 15 December 1997 concerning the Framework Agreement on Part-Time Work, as amended by Council Directive 98/23/EC of 7 April 1998. The interpretation of art 28 of the Charter of Fundamental Rights of the European Union was also relevant.

7. Arbeits-und Sozialgerichtsgesetz, BGBl. Nr 104/1985.

The Austrian Supreme Court expressed doubts as to the application of the principle *pro rata temporis* in the case. As a result, the Austrian Supreme Court decided to stay the proceedings before it and to refer the questions below to the Court for a preliminary ruling:

(1) Is the principle of *pro rata temporis* under Clause 4.2 of the Framework Agreement on Part-Time Work to be applied to a child allowance provided for in a collective agreement—such allowance being a social benefit provided by the employer in order to meet part of the parents' expenses for the maintenance of the child in respect of whom the allowance is obtained—on the basis of the (appropriate) nature of that benefit?

(2) If the answer to Question 1 is in the negative, is Clause 4.1 of the Framework Agreement on Part Time Work to be interpreted as meaning that the disadvantage suffered by part-time workers, due to the reduction in their entitlement to dependent child allowance in proportion with their working time, is—having regard to the social partners' wide discretion in the determination of a particular social and economic policy objective and of the measures capable of achieving it—objectively justified on the basis that a prohibition of a proportionate grant:

(a) makes part-time work in the form of parental part-time working and/or minor activity during a period of parental leave more difficult or impossible; and/or

(b) leads to distortion of competition on account of the greater financial burden placed on employers who employ a larger number of part-time workers, and to a lesser willingness on the part of employers to take on part-time workers; and/or

(c) leads to more favourable treatment of part-time workers who have additional part-time work and multiple entitlement to a benefit—such as a dependent child allowance—under a collective agreement; and/or

(d) leads to more favourable treatment of part-time workers, because they have more free time than full-time workers and thus have better childcare options available to them?

(3) If the answer to Question 1 and Question 2 is in the negative, is Article 28 of the Charter of Fundamental Rights of the European Union to be interpreted as meaning that where, in a system of employment law in which substantial elements of minimum employment standards are established in accordance with the agreed social policy assessments of specially selected and qualified parties to a collective agreement, a point of detail in a collective agreement (albeit a point that breaches the EU law principle of non-discrimination)—in this case, the proportionate grant of child allowance in the case of part-time working—is invalid (according to national practice), the penalty of invalidity extends to all the provisions of the collective agreement relating to that area (in this case, child allowance)?

In relation to question 1 above, the Court noted that the Austrian Court was essentially asking if cl 4.2 of the Framework Agreement on Part-Time Work must be interpreted to the effect that the principle *pro rata temporis* applies to the calculation of the amount of a dependent child allowance paid by the employer of a part-time worker pursuant to the Collective Agreement. The Court observed that the dependent child allowance at issue was not a benefit provided for by law and discharged by the State. On the contrary, it was paid by the employer under the Collective Agreement. The allowance had been negotiated by the contracting parties for the benefit of workers with dependent children. From this the Court concluded that the allowance could not be treated as a 'social security benefit', within the meaning of Regulation (EC) No 883/2004 of 29 April 2004 on the coordination of social security systems.[8] This was so, despite the fact that it pursued objectives similar to those of certain benefits provided for by that Regulation.

The Court further observed that OG and VÖBB were in agreement that the allowance constituted 'pay' to the employee. The Court cited *Krüger*[9] in support of its contention that the legal nature of the consideration is not important for the purposes of the application of art 157 TFEU, provided that it is granted in respect of the employment. It considered that since the dependent child allowance constituted part of a worker's pay, it had to be determined by the terms of the employment relationship agreed between the employer and the employee. The Court stated that it followed that if the employee is employed part-time in accordance with the terms of the employment relationship, it must be held that the calculation of the dependent child allowance in accordance with the principle of *pro rata temporis* was objectively justified, within the meaning of cl 4.1 of the Framework Agreement on Part-Time Work and within the meaning of cl 4.2 thereof. *Heimann and Toltschin*[10] were cited by analogy. The Court noted that on the one hand, it must be observed that the nature of the benefit at issue in the main proceedings could not preclude the application of cl 4.2 of the Framework Agreement on Part-Time Work. This was the case because the dependent child allowance was a divisible benefit. The case of *Bruno & Ors*[11] was cited by analogy. On the other hand, it was noted by the Court that it had already applied the principle of *pro rata temporis* to other benefits payable by the employer and related to a part-time employment relationship. For example, the Court had held that EU law did not preclude a retirement pension being calculated *pro rata temporis* in the case of part-time employment,[12] nor did it preclude paid annual leave from being calculated in accordance with the same principle.[13] It was held that in those cases, taking account of the reduced working time as compared with that of a full-time worker constituted an objective criterion allowing a proportionate reduction of the rights of the workers concerned. The Court concluded, having regard to all of the foregoing considerations, the answer to the

8.   OJ 2004 L 166, p 1.

9.   *Krüger Kreiskrankenhaus Ebersberg* (Case C–281/97), para 16.

10.   *Heimann and Toltschin v Kaiser* (Cases C–229/11 and C–230/11), para 34 and the case law cited.

11.   *Instituto nazionale della previdenza sociale (INPS) v Bruno & Ors* (Cases C–395/08 and C–396/08), para 34.

12.   *Schönheit v Stadt Frankfurt am Main* and *Becker v Land Hessen* (Cases C–4/02 and C–5/02), paras 90 and 91.

13.   *Zentralbetriebsrat der Landeskrankenhäuser Tirols* (Case C–486/08), EU:C:2010:215, para 33, and *Heimann and Toltschin*, EU:C:2012:693, para 36.

first question referred is that cl 4.2 of the Framework Agreement on Part-Time Work must be interpreted as meaning that the principle *pro rata temporis* applied to the calculation of the amount of a dependent child allowance paid by an employer to a part-time worker pursuant to a collective agreement such as that in issue. As a result of this conclusion, there was no need to address the other questions referred by the Austrian Court.

It was held that the decision on costs was a matter for the national court, as these proceedings were merely a step in the action pending before it. Costs incurred in submitting observations to the Court, other than the costs of the parties, were held not to be recoverable.

ANNUAL LEAVE AND THE PRINCIPLE OF PRO RATA TEMPORIS

[19.03] *Greenfield v The Care Bureau[14]—CJEU—reference for preliminary ruling on interpretation of Framework Agreement on Part-Time Work, cl 4.2, as amended by Council Directive 98/23/EC and Directive 2003/88/EC, art 7[15]—less favourable treatment—application of principle of pro rata temporis*

The claimant was employed by the respondent under a contract of employment in which it was stipulated that her working hours and days differed from week to week. Her remuneration for any week varied according to the number of days or hours worked/ performed. Under both UK law and her contract of employment, the claimant was entitled to 5.6 weeks of annual leave per year, which leave year began on 15 June. The claimant left employment with the respondent in May 2013. It was not disputed that she took seven days of paid leave during the final leave year. She had worked for a total of 1729.5 hours and took a total of 62.84 hours of paid leave, of which seven days of paid leave were taken in July 2012. During the 12-week period immediately preceding that holiday, the claimant's work pattern was one day of work per week.

From August 2012 onwards, the claimant began to work a pattern of 12 days on and 2 days off, taken as alternate weekends. That pattern amounted to an average of 41.4 hours of work per week. The respondent specified that all the claimant's hours, to include overtime, would be used in the calculation of her entitlements to paid annual leave. In November 2012, the claimant requested a week of paid leave; but she was informed that as a result of the holiday taken by her in July 2012, she had exhausted her entitlement to paid annual leave. Her entitlement to paid leave was calculated at the date on which the leave was taken, based on the working pattern for the 12-week period prior to the leave. Since the claimant had taken her leave at a time when her work pattern was one day per week, she had taken the equivalent of seven weeks of paid leave and accordingly had exhausted her entitlement to paid annual leave.

---

14. *Greenfield v The Care Bureau* (Case C–219/14).
15. Directive 2003/88/EC of the European Parliament and of the Council of 4 November 2003 concerning certain aspects of the organisation of working time OJ 2003 L 299, p 9

The claimant however asserted an entitlement to an allowance in lieu of paid leave not taken and brought proceedings against her employer in the employment tribunal which initially allowed her claim. There followed a period of uncertainty, during which time the decision was appealed to the UKEAT and then revoked by the employment tribunal, which decided instead to make the within reference to the CJEU. The claimant had argued before the employment tribunal that national law, read in conjunction with EU law, requires that annual leave already accrued and taken should be retroactively recalculated and adjusted following an increase in working hours, for example following a move from part-time to full-time work, so it has to be proportional to the new number of working hours and not the hours worked at the time the leave was taken. The respondent maintained that EU Law does not provide for a new calculation and that therefore Member States are not required to make such an adjustment under national law.

The CJEU concluded that the first and third questions should be considered together as they essentially asked whether cl 4.2 of the Framework Agreement on Part-Time Work and art 7 of the Directive 2003/88 on the Organisation of Working Time must be interpreted so that, in the event of an increase in the number of hours of work performed by a worker, Member States are obliged to provide, or are prohibited from providing, that the entitlement to paid annual leave already accrued, and possibly taken, must be re-calculated, if necessary, retroactively according to the worker's new work pattern. Furthermore, if a recalculation must be performed, whether that relates only to the period during which the working time of the worker has increased or to the whole leave year.

The CJEU emphasised the right of every worker to paid annual leave as a particularly important principle of EU social law, from which there can be no derogation. Furthermore, it noted from its own case law that the right to paid annual leave may not be interpreted restrictively. The CJEU noted that the purpose of entitlement to paid annual leave is to enable the worker to rest from carrying out the work he is required to do under his contract of employment. The CJEU held that consequently the entitlement to paid annual leave accrues, and must be calculated, with regard to the work patterns specified in the contract. The entitlement to minimum paid annual leave within the meaning of Directive 2003/88 must be calculated by reference to the days, hours, and or fractions of days and hours worked and specified on the contract of employment. The Court referenced its settled case law that the taking of annual leave at a period after the period during which the entitlement to leave has been accumulated had no connection to the time worked by the worker during that later period. The CJEU also noted that it had previously held that a change, and in particular a reduction, when moving from full-time to part-time employment, could not reduce the right to annual leave that the worker had accumulated during the period of full-time employment. It therefore followed with regard to the accrued entitlement to paid annual leave that it is necessary to distinguish periods during which the worker worked according to different working patterns; the number of units of annual leave accumulated in relation to the number of units worked is to be calculated for each period separately. The conclusion was not affected by the application of the *pro rata temporis* principle laid down in cl 4.2 of the Framework Agreement on Part-Time Work. The Court noted that, while it is the case that the application of that principle is appropriate for the grant of annual leave for a period of part-time employment since for such a period the reduction of the right to annual leave in comparison to that granted for a period of full-time employment is justified on objective grounds, the fact remains that the principle cannot be applied 'ex post' to a right to annual leave accumulated during a period of full-time work.

The Court noted that there was no requirement to make a new calculation of annual leave already accumulated where a worker increased the number of hours worked. Neither did it preclude the Member States adopting provisions more favourable to workers in making a new calculation. The distinction that should be made between different work patterns in relation to the accumulation of the entitlement to be paid annual leave had, however, no effect on the exercise of accrued rights. The same conclusion applied where the leave is not taken during the period in which it is accrued, in which the worker worked part-time, but during a later period in which he worked full-time. The Court concluded that, in the situation at issue, EU law therefore required a new calculation of rights to paid annual leave to be performed only for the period of work during which the worker increased the number of hours worked. The units of paid annual leave already taken during the period of part-time work which exceeded the right to paid annual leave accumulated during that period must be deducted from the rights newly accumulated, during the period when the worker increased the number of hours worked.

The CJEU concluded that the answers to the first and third questions posed was that cl 4.2 of the Framework Agreement on Part-Time Work and art 7 of the Directive must be interpreted as meaning that in the event of an increase in the number of hours worked by a worker, Member States were not obliged to provide that the entitlement to paid annual leave already accrued, and possibly taken, must be re-calculated retroactively accordingly to that worker's new work pattern. A new calculation must, however, be performed for the period by which the working time increased.

The CJEU was asked whether the calculation of the entitlement to paid leave is to be performed according to different principles, depending on whether what is being determined is an allowance in lieu of paid annual leave not taken where the employment relationship is terminated, or the outstanding annual leave entitlement where the employment relationship continues. The CJEU concluded that cl 4.2 and the Directive must be interpreted as meaning that the calculation of the entitlement to paid annual leave is to be performed according to the same principles in either situation.

Chapter 20

PENSIONS

BUDGET 2016

[20.01] Budget 2016 was announced on 13 October 2015 and the implementing Finance Bill was published on 22 October 2015. Together, they contained a number of pensions-related initiatives.

Pension levy

[20.02] The 0.15 per cent levy on pension fund assets introduced for 2014 and 2015 will be abolished at the end of 2015.

USC exemption on employer PRSA contributions

[20.03] The Finance Bill implementing Budget 2016 provides for an exemption for employees from USC on employer contributions to a PRSA, to bring the USC treatment of such contributions in line with employer contributions to occupational pension schemes.

Benefits for pensioners increase

[20.04] The State pension (contributory) will increase by €3 per week to €233.30 per week for recipients aged 66 and over with effect from 8 January 2016. The non-contributory pension and widow's pension will be subject to similar weekly increases.

Concerns in relation to sustainability

[20.05] Budget 2016 has introduced a 'tapered PRSI credit' with a maximum level of €12 per week to alleviate the 'step effect' across a range of incomes. The combination of this reduction in PRSI together with the increase in State pension gives cause for concern in relation to the long term sustainability of the State pension. Without the €50+ billion which might have been in the National Pensions Reserve Fund (NPRF) at this stage to provide the medium-term financial backing, concerns will continue as to the sustainability of an unchanged State pension for future retirees.

Public servants to benefit also

[20.06] A Bill has been introduced to partially unwind elements of the Financial Emergency Measures in the Public Interest (FEMPI) legislation in line with the

343

Lansdowne Road Agreement (May 2015). This will result in increases in both the pay and pension entitlements of public servants.

While the Budget has set out the financial impact of these improvements in pay for public servants, it is not clear whether the projections also reflect the increase in the unfunded pension liability which will result due to the retrospective nature of public service pensions design.

LEGISLATIVE UPDATES – IRELAND

Occupational Pension Scheme Regulations

[20.07] The Regulations enacted in January 2015[1] amend the Occupational Pension Scheme (Sections 50 and 50B) Regulations 2014[2] to extend the notification, submission and appeal provisions regarding benefit reductions to include groups representing the interests of pensioners and deferred scheme members. A representative group's members must comprise at least 50 per cent of the group they represent, which is seen by some as almost unworkable in practice.

Revaluation Regulations

[20.08] These Regulations[3] enacted in January 2015 determine that there will be a 0.2 per cent increase in the revaluation of preserved benefits for 2014.

LEGISLATIVE UPDATES – UNITED KINGDOM

Qualified Recognised Overseas Pension Schemes (QROPS)

[20.09] With effect from 6 April 2015, the conditions for a scheme to be a QROPS have changed as specified by Her Majesty's Revenue and Customs (HMRC) in the UK. In addition to the existing conditions, a scheme must now satisfy the 'Pension Age Test'. The Pension Age Test requires that benefits deriving from funds which received UK tax relief must not be paid to a member before age 55. If your scheme is a QROPS, you will have received communication from HMRC in this regard. They require that all registered QROPS confirm to them in writing that they meet this requirement. This can be done by showing either that: (a) Irish legislative requirements or (b) the rules of the scheme do not permit payment of UK member benefits before age 55.

Irish occupational pension schemes are allowed to provide benefits on early retirement from the age of 50. Therefore, the first method of satisfying the Pension Age

---

1.   Occupational Pension Schemes (Sections 50 and 50B) (Amendment) Regulations 2015 (SI 24/2015).
2.   Occupational Pension Scheme (Sections 50 and 50B) Regulations 2014 (SI 392/2014).
3.   Occupational Pension Schemes (Revaluation) Regulations 2015 (SI 42/2015).

Test cannot be met (ie, that the law of the country prohibits the payment of benefits before age 55 unless the member is retiring due to ill-health).

The second method of satisfying the Pension Age Test requires a review of scheme rules. If the rules prohibit the payment of pension (including by early retirement) before age 55 whether generally or specifically in the case of UK members, then the test will be met. If neither of the methods can be used to satisfy the test then employers and trustees have two options:

(i)   amend the provisions to prohibit the payment of benefits before age 55 in respect of UK members; or

(ii) cease to be a QROPS. If the scheme is no longer a QROPS this will not affect members who have already transferred UK tax relieved funds into the scheme and who are in receipt of benefits (even if they retired before age 55).

However, as a consequence of ceasing to be a QROPS:

(a)   the scheme will no longer be able to accept new transfers into the scheme from the UK without the member paying a UK tax charge of approximately 55 per cent on the transfer; and

(b)   HMRC have recently confirmed that members who have received a UK transfer in and who subsequently transfer out or retire before age 55 may be subject to a UK tax charge (this will depend on whether they are tax resident at the time of transfer out/retirement or were UK tax resident in the five years before the transfer out/retirement).

LEGISLATIVE UPDATES – EUROPE

European Market Infrastructure Regulation (EMIR)[4]

[20.10] EMIR is an EU Regulation which affects schemes using derivatives (including those which use them solely for hedging through their custodian). These regulations require certain over-the-counter (OTC) derivatives contracts to be cleared centrally. Pension schemes were given a three-year exemption from the OTC central clearing requirement, which was due to expire in August of this year, due to the need to provide significant amounts of cash collateral in order to meet margin calls – an inefficient way of holding assets. However, the European Commission has acknowledged the difficulties the EMIR regime causes for pension scheme trustees and has extended the exemption by a further two years to 15 August 2017.

Trustees should continue to work with advisors to ensure their compliance with the full EMIR regime when the exemption period ends.

---

4.   European Market Infrastructure Regulation (EMIR) Regulation 648/2012/EU.

PENSIONS AUTHORITY, GUIDANCE AND MODEL DOCUMENTS

Codes of governance for defined contribution schemes

[20.11] The Pensions Authority (the Authority) published for consultation proposed codes of governance for defined contribution (DC) schemes (the Codes) which are to be read in conjunction with the Authority's Trustee Handbook. The aim of the Codes is to provide practical guidance for DC trustees to ensure appropriate decisions are made. The Codes will not be a statement of law but will set out the standards expected of trustees. The Authority sought submissions on the proposed Codes (the closing date for consultation was 16 June 2015).

There are 12 proposed Codes contained in the guidance issued by the Authority.

The topics covered include:

(a) **Establish a governance plan of action and trustee meetings:** set out steps, timescales, ownership of tasks, service level agreements and report and monitor. Hold trustee meetings regularly with minuted outcomes – the number will depend on scheme size.

(b) **Risk management:** establish a risk management framework (including a risk register and risk controls) to identify, evaluate and manage the risks that are critical to the scheme and which have significant impact on the scheme's ability to provide reasonable member benefits.

(c) **Keep records and report scheme information:** ensure records are accurate, complete and up-to-date bearing in mind data protection legislation. Ensure the Authority's online register of schemes (ISIS) contains accurate and up-to-date information.

(d) **Investment:** ensure proper investment of scheme assets and that investment powers are exercised in the best interests of the members.

(e) **Member communications:** ensure these are accurate and clear.

(f) **Communicate costs and value for money:** ensure all costs and charges borne by members are clearly disclosed to them and that they are reasonable, competitive and provide value for money.

The current intention is that trustees will be required to submit an annual compliance return to the Authority in which they will confirm compliance with the Codes. This will first require the enactment of relevant legislation.

Financial management guidelines for defined benefit schemes

[20.12] On 22 May 2015 the Authority published guidelines for the financial management of defined benefit schemes (the Guidelines). The Guidelines set out the Authority's view on good practice for trustees to follow in order to understand and manage their funding and investment. The purpose of the Guidelines is to identify threats to the ability of the scheme to meet its liabilities and to allow the trustees to consider what they should do in response.

The Guidelines cover four areas:

(a) **Data about the scheme that the trustees should have available to them**: this includes scheme asset values, investment return and allocations, scheme liabilities and costs.

(b) **Governance practices relevant to financial management**: this includes holding regular trustee meetings, appropriate and permitted delegation, engaging advisers, service level agreements, using SIPPs and understanding scheme contribution provisions.

(c) **Processes that the trustees should follow**: including review of investment strategy, contribution and funding adequacy, investment manager performance and scheme costs and using risk matrices.

(d) **Analysis that the trustees should undertake in order to arrive at decisions**: the two questions the trustees should ask themselves in this regard are:

(i) are the scheme contributions adequate to provide the benefits of the scheme in the short and long term?

(ii) what is the risk that the benefits cannot be paid?

Trustees should ensure that they have access to adequate actuarial and investment advice. However, the responsibility for the scheme always rests with the trustees, who should therefore ensure that they understand the advice they receive and the decisions they, as trustees, are required to take.

Where in the guidance it is stated that action should be taken, this refers to recommended good practice. The Guidelines supplement the Authority's Trustee Handbook and do not set out all of the trustees' compliance obligations.

Prescribed s 50 guidance

[20.13] The Authority published prescribed guidance in relation to a s 50 application by the trustees of a scheme. The guidance is prescribed by the Minister under the Occupational Pension Schemes (Funding Standard) Regulations 1993 to 2013. The purpose of the guidance is to set out the manner in which trustees may make an application to the Authority for a direction under s 50 and the requirements to be met by the trustees in relation to any such application. The guidance requires that, prior to the making of an application, the trustees must undertake a comprehensive review of the scheme covering a number of bases which are detailed in the guidance. One of the key directions of the guidance is the requirement to notify members, people in receipt of benefits under the scheme, any authorised trade unions representing members or any representative group, of the information specified in the guidance. The guidance also states that it is a matter for the trustees to ensure that their application is submitted in good time, in advance of any deadline of the obligations of trustees under s 49 to submit a funding proposal.

Amendments to Pensions Authority Guidance Notes

[20.14] In November 2015 the Authority updated the Guidance Notes relating to the Pensions Provisions of the Family Law Act 1995, the Family Law (Divorce) Act 1996 and the Civil Partnership and Certain Rights and Obligations of Cohabitants Act 2010. Paragraph 222 of the Guidance Notes refers to circumstances whereby a transfer payment is being made in respect of a scheme member who has left service. The revisions to the Guidance Notes clarify that, where no independent benefit has been established for the non-member spouse, the transfer payment which is made in respect of this member should only relate to the amount of benefit to which the member is entitled pursuant to the pension adjustment order in place on the scheme benefit. The designated benefit of the non-member spouse does not transfer.

UPDATED REVENUE PENSIONS MANUAL

[20.15] The Revenue Commissioners updated several chapters of the Pensions Manual (the Manual) throughout 2015 to reflect the changes made by the Finance Act 2014 and amendments to the Taxes Consolidation Act 1997. In particular the following practices have been updated:

(1) the treatment of retirement arrangements which are the subject of a pension adjustment order;

(2) the withdrawal of up to 4 per cent of the value of an Approved Minimum Retirement Fund (AMRF) to the AMRF owner which will be liable to tax in the same manner as distributions from an ARF;

(3) the annual rate of imputed distribution from Approved Retirement Funds (ARFs) and vested Personal Retirement Savings Accounts has been reduced from 5 per cent to 4 per cent in certain circumstances; and

(4) individuals are now to be considered separately in respect of determinations to consider whether they satisfy the trivial 'once-off pension' options where benefits are payable under a pension arrangement in respect of which a PAO applies.

CASE LAW

Ireland

[20.16] *Lett v Earagail Eisc Teoranta[5]—Labour Court—Employment Equality Acts 1998 to 2015—discrimination on grounds of age—compulsory retirement—fixing and promulgation of retirement policy—promulgation of employee handbook—employment contract implied terms—incorporation of pension scheme terms in employment contract*

In this case, the Labour Court considered appeals by both the complainant and the respondent against a decision of the Equality Tribunal[6] where the complainant had been awarded €24,000 in relation to an age discrimination complaint following compulsory retirement.

In the original complaint, the complainant (Mr Lett) claimed he was forced to retire at age 66 and had his hours reduced from five days a week to three days a week for the month immediately prior to his forced retirement. The complainant had argued age discrimination in relation to the change in his hours and his dismissal. After examining the facts, the Tribunal was satisfied that the complainant did not receive a copy of the respondent's handbook with his contract, which meant that he might not have been aware that the respondent's mandatory age of retirement was 65. The complainant refused to retire at 65 and the respondent informed the complainant that he would be allowed to continue until age 66 so that he could qualify for the old age pension. Twenty-eight days prior to his 66th birthday his hours were reduced to three days a week.

The Tribunal found that the complainant had established a prima facie case of age discrimination. While the respondent put forward a number of objective justifications for this discrimination, the Tribunal rejected these arguments. In doing so it took into account the fact that the employer offered no evidence to show that the complainant's ability to perform his duties had been in any way diminished due to his age. It also noted that the role of the complainant had not been filled after he left, which led the Tribunal to question if it had been necessary for him to retire. The Tribunal characterised the respondent's approach to retirement as 'one size fits all' and stated that, in this case, the approach was not objectively justified.

Before the Labour Court, the focus was principally on whether or not the respondent's policy on retirement was incorporated in the complainant's contract of employment in circumstances where the contract made no specific provision in that regard.

No authority was opened to the Court for the proposition that the mere existence of a retirement policy, in and of itself, could attract immunity against liability for a unilateral termination of employment on grounds of age.

In the course of its determination, the Court considered that the complainant was a member (and trustee) of a pension scheme of which the respondent was the principal

---

5.   *Lett v Earagail Eisc Teoranta* EDA1513.
6.   See *Arthur Cox Employment Law Yearbook 2014* at [4.20] for case summary.

employer, and the Court accepted that the terms of a pension scheme may be relied upon as either implying a term as to retirement or by incorporating the terms of the scheme into an employment contract. The pension scheme in this case provided than an employee may retire at any age between the age of 60 and 75 but the Court was of the view that this did not preclude the employer from fixing a retirement age within that range. The respondent argued that retirement age was fixed at 65 on publication of the employee handbook containing its policy on retirement.

The Court accepted that, in principle, a policy on retirement could take effect as a contractual term if it is promulgated in such a manner that those to whom it applies either knew, or ought to have known, of its existence. On the evidence in this case, however, the Court accepted that the complainant neither had sight of, nor knew of, the employee handbook which included the respondent's policy on retirement. The Court also found on the evidence that the retirement policy was not so well known and acquiesced to as to attract contractual status by application of the 'custom and practice' or 'officious bystander' tests.

The Court held that the respondent had not fixed a retirement age in respect of the complainant and, as a result, the respondent's appeal against the Tribunal's finding that the complainant was dismissed because of his age was not allowed. As no evidence was adduced to counter the position of the respondent that the complainant's working week prior to termination had been reduced because of the trading and financial circumstances of the respondent, the respondent's appeal against the Tribunal's finding that this constituted age discrimination was allowed. The complainant's appeal against the quantum of the Tribunal's award was not allowed.

There continues to be an unhelpful ambiguity regarding the approach to compulsory retirement in the employment context and the clear exemption from age discrimination in the context of a default normal pension age under s 72(1)(d) of the Pensions Act 1990 (without a requirement for objective justification).

Employer's liability to contribute to scheme in wind up

[20.17] *Holloway & Ors v Damianus BV & Ors*[7]*—Court of Appeal—whether trustees entitled to make contribution demand in excess of the statutory minimum funding standard in circumstances where scheme solvent on the statutory minimum funding standard basis*

The Court of Appeal affirmed the High Court's judgment in the *Omega Pharma*[8] case requiring the employers to make contributions to the employees' defined benefit pension scheme in excess of the statutory minimum funding standard in circumstances where the scheme was being wound up.

There were two key issues in the High Court case, which were appealed by the employers to the Court of Appeal. The first related to when the employers' contribution liability terminated. The Court of Appeal upheld the High Court decision in finding that

---

7. *Holloway & Ors v Damianus BV & Ors* [2015] IECA 19.

8. *Holloway & Ors v Damianus BV & Ors* [2014] IEHC 383.

the parties had agreed three months' notice in accordance with the notice provisions in the trust deed.

The second issue was whether the trustees were entitled to make a contribution demand in excess of the statutory minimum funding standard in circumstances where the scheme was solvent on the statutory minimum funding standard basis.

In the High Court, the employers had argued that there was no justification for the contribution demand, given that the scheme was solvent on the minimum funding standard basis and that the employers' obligation had therefore been satisfied. This argument was rejected by the High Court, which concluded that the trustees had come to a reasonable decision as to the amount of the contribution demand in the absence of any engagement by the employers.

In the Court of Appeal, the employers conceded that the statutory minimum funding standard was not sufficient to 'support the Fund in order to provide the benefits under the Scheme'. The second issue was therefore not argued before the Court of Appeal. Accordingly, the Court of Appeal found that the contribution demand which the trustees had sought was the 'shortfall' for the purposes of the scheme and that the trustees were entitled to recover this shortfall.

FEMPI Acts

[20.18] *Minister for Public Expenditure and Reform v Pensions Ombudsman and Farrell (Notice Party)[9]—High Court—Noonan J—appeal against determination by Pensions Ombudsman—Pensions Acts 1990 to 2014, s 140—jurisdiction of Pensions Ombudsman*

The High Court has dismissed an appeal by the Minister for Public Expenditure and Reform against a determination by the Pensions Ombudsman regarding a complaint made by the notice party. Noonan J stated that the Pensions Ombudsman (the Ombudsman) had 'strayed well outside his jurisdiction' in making the determination.

The notice party was a retired employee of the National Treasury Management Agency (the NTMA). In 1996, Mr Farrell transferred the entire proceeds of his private pension fund to the NTMA pension scheme (the NTMA Scheme). From January 2011, further to the introduction of the measures contained in the Financial Emergency Measures in the Public Interest Act 2010 (the FEMPI Act) his pension was subject to the reductions imposed by the Public Service Pension Reduction (PSPR). Of his entire pension entitlement from the NTMA Scheme, 62.7 per cent was the result of Mr Farrell's own private funding. Mr Farrell argued that applying the FEMPI Act to the entirety of his pension entitlement would result in the State making a profit at his own expense. Mr Farrell lodged a complaint with the Minister for Finance in the first instance and subsequently with the Minister for Public Expenditure and Reform (the Minister). Later Mr Farrell wrote to the Ombudsman requesting that he examine the case. The Ombudsman issued his final determination which directed that the FEMPI

---

9.   *Minister for Public Expenditure and Reform v Pensions Ombudsman and Farrell (Notice Party)* [2015] IEHC 183.

Act would only apply to the portion of Mr Farrell's pension entitlement which was funded directly by the State. The Minister appealed this determination under the Pensions Act 1990 to 2014 (the Pension Acts). Primarily, the Minister argued that the Ombudsman's determination was made without jurisdiction.

In refusing the appeal, Noonan J, held that a certain lack of formality was a recognised feature of investigations such as those by the Ombudsman. It should have been noted by the Minister that the commencement of an investigation by the Ombudsman indicated that the Ombudsman believed he had jurisdiction on the matter. The judge rejected the submission by the appellants that they had not previously taken issue with the jurisdiction of the Ombudsman because they were unaware he had begun an investigation. Noonan J indicated that the extent of the communication between the Minister and the Ombudsman ought to have been sufficient notice that an investigation by the Ombudsman had begun.

Noonan J noted that the Ombudsman was not entitled to review the Minister's refusal to grant the exemption from the FEMPI Act or to substitute his decision on the facts of the case for that of the Minister.

Disability discrimination

[20.19] *Sheils v Boliden Tara Mines and the Tara Mines Pension Scheme[10]— Equality Tribunal—Pensions Acts 1990 to 2011, s 81—res judicata*

This case concerned a claim of discrimination on grounds of disability under s 81 of the Pensions Acts 1990 to 2011 (as they were then cited) in relation to the respondent's occupational pension scheme. The Equality Tribunal held that it did not have jurisdiction to hear the case as the matter had previously been decided by the Supreme Court in 2010 in *Boliden Tara Mines Ltd v Cosgrove & Ors*[11] in which Hardiman J delivered judgment on 21 December 2010.

Nevertheless, the Equality Tribunal did call a joint hearing in April 2015 and gave the complainant the opportunity to make oral statements in response to the explanations the Tribunal provided for the case being outside of the its jurisdiction.

The Equality Tribunal noted that the issue of discrimination under the Pensions Acts, while raised in the defendant's pleadings, was not pursued by his legal representatives in oral proceedings and therefore decided against him. On this basis, he concluded that the matter was *res judicata*. He noted that only an express statement by Hardiman J, in his written judgment, that the discrimination complaint be remitted back to the Equality Tribunal, would permit him to investigate the matter, and there was no such statement.

It was emphasised that a decision of the Supreme Court is binding on all lower courts and tribunals and that such matters cannot be re-litigated.

---

10.   *Sheils v Boliden Tara Mines and the Tara Mines Pension Scheme* PEN/2014/001, DEC–P2015–003.

11.   *Boliden Tara Mines Ltd v Cosgrove & Ors* [2010] IESC 62.

Sexual orientation/civil partner discrimination

[20.20] *A Retired Civil Servant and his Civil Partner v A Government Department, Ireland and the AG[12]—Equality Tribunal—Pensions Acts 1990 to 2014—entitlement of civil partner to benefit from retired partner's pension scheme benefits*

This case concerned a claim brought by a retired civil servant and his civil partner that either or both of them were discriminated against by the respondents on the grounds of sexual orientation contrary to the Pensions Acts.

Mr A (the complainant) was a retired civil servant who was employed in the Civil Service from 1974 until 1 June 1995. On his appointment as an 'established male officer' in 1974, Mr A became a member of the Civil Service Widows' and Children's Contributory Pension Scheme (referred to as the Original Scheme). That scheme provided for a refund of contributions paid if the member was single at the time of his retirement.

In September 1984 a new pension scheme (referred to as the Revised Scheme) was established. This was open to male and female 'established officers' and provided benefits for various categories of dependants excluded from the Original Scheme including spouses married after retirement and children born after retirement. The Revised Scheme did not provide for any refund of contributions paid if the member was single at the time of retirement. On 13 June 1984 Mr A exercised his right to opt out of this scheme.

On 1 June 1995 Mr A retired. As he was a member of the Original Scheme and was single at the time of his retirement he was entitled to a full refund of his contributions. Mr A and his partner, Mr B, entered into a civil partnership in 2010, which was recognised in this jurisdiction from January 2011.

In January 2011, Mr B wrote to the respondent, enquiring as to whether he was entitled to any benefit under his civil partner's pension scheme. Ongoing correspondence ensued, which included appeals by the complainants to the Minister of that Department. Mr A was advised that his partner had no entitlement to any benefit under the provisions of the Original Scheme. In July 2013 the Minister advised Mr A and Mr B that he had decided to uphold the original decision that Mr A should not be allowed to revisit the decision he exercised in 1984 not to join the Revised Scheme.

The complainants stated that 'civil servants who had remained in the "Original Scheme" were excluded from a civil partner benefit because of their spousal choice in 1984'. The complainants contended that this placed Mr A at a particular disadvantage compared to heterosexuals in the Civil Service, all of whom had been given options of benefiting a spouse while he had no opportunity to benefit a civil partner.

Furthermore, it was submitted by the complainant that he was less favourably treated than a heterosexual comparator following the enactment of the Civil Partnership and Certain Rights and Obligations of Cohabitants Act 2010 in contravention of judgments of the Court of Justice of the European Union (CJEU). The Tribunal noted that the

---

12. *A Retired Civil Servant and his Civil Partner v A Government Department, Ireland and the AG* PEN/2013/014, DEC–P2015–002.

CJEU had outlined in the judgments referred to that a finding of discrimination on the grounds of sexual orientation requires that the situations in question be comparable in the light of the benefit concerned. The complainant stated that when civil partnership was introduced in Ireland in 2011 under the Civil Partnership Act 2010, spousal pensions for civil partners were introduced for members of the Revised Scheme. The complainant contended that this put him at a particular disadvantage compared to heterosexuals in the Civil Service, all of whom had been given options of benefiting a spouse while he had been given no such opportunity of benefitting his civil partner. The Tribunal noted that the complainant was incorrect in his implication that civil servants who remained in the Original Scheme were excluded from benefits for surviving civil partners.

The Tribunal also noted that from the evidence of the respondents, which was not disputed by the complainant, the individuals in the cases referenced by the complainant were married at the time they each had opted out of the Revised Scheme. Consequently, as married people, they would not be entitled to a refund of contributions on retirement. Unlike the complainant, who received a full refund of his contributions to the Original Scheme on his retirement, these individuals were not entitled to or received no such refund. As such, the Tribunal was not satisfied that the circumstances were comparable.

In concluding, the Tribunal found, under s 77A of the Employment Equality Acts, that the complainant had no reasonable chance of succeeding and ultimately found the complainants' claims to be frivolous, vexatious and misconceived and therefore all claims were dismissed.

Changes to pensionable salary

[20.21] *Durkin v The Pension Ombudsman & Anor[13]—High Court—appeal against determination of Pensions Ombudsman—Pensions Acts 1990 to 2014, s 140—consent to changes in pension plan*

This was a decision of the High Court on an appeal brought by a former member of the SIAC Construction Ltd Non-Contributory Pension and Death Benefits Plan (the Plan), against a final determination of the Pensions Ombudsman (the Ombudsman). The Ombudsman held that the appellant had provided valid consent to the changes implemented to the Plan and that the changes made were not subject to the preservation requirements of the Pensions Acts 1990 to 2014 (the Acts).

The appellant was employed by SIAC Construction Ltd (the Company) from November 1990 to January 2012. In March 2008, the Company sought to limit its exposure to pension liabilities by capping the salary level at which pensions were to be assessed. This was achieved by the execution of a deed of amendment. The changes to salary introduced by that deed required the 'receipt by the Trustees of the prior written consent of the Member'.

In April 2012, the appellant had issued a complaint to the Trustees under the internal dispute resolution procedure in the plan. The appellant complained that the document

---

13. *Durkin v The Pension Ombudsman & Anor* [2015] IEHC 566.

provided to him, which illustrated his options on leaving service, was incorrect. He argued that valid consent had not been obtained to the change in the method of calculation of his pensionable salary. Secondly, he contended that the effect of the deed of amendment should have been made on a 'phased-in' basis under the preservation requirements of the Acts. The Trustees dismissed the complaint in a determination issued on 25 July 2013. The appellant then appealed the Trustees' determination to the Ombudsman.

While the Ombudsman was critical of the process used to obtain the consent of the appellant, stating that it was not in keeping with best practice, he did not attribute this to any negligent or fraudulent intent. The Ombudsman was satisfied that the appellant had understood and consented to the changes. Furthermore, the Ombudsman agreed with the legal advice previously received by the Trustees that the changes made by the deed of amendment did not contravene the preservation requirements and therefore were not required to be phased-in. The appellant appealed the determination of the Ombudsman to the High Court under s 140 of the Acts.

The Court held that the appellant was not entitled to a *de novo* appeal. The Court found that the appellant was only entitled to an appeal of the decision of the Pensions Ombudsman where there had been 'serious and significant error or a series of such errors'. He was not entitled to challenge the determination of the Ombudsman on its merits. The Court had not been persuaded by the appellant that 'the Ombudsman could not reasonably have come to his conclusions based on the facts before him'. On the second point of appeal, the Court deferred to the Ombudsman's expertise in the area (as permitted by the decision in *Ulster Bank Investment Funds Ltd v Financial Services Ombudsman*).[14] As a result, the Court found that the placing of a limit on pensionable salary to which consent was obtained did not alter the definition of pensionable salary and did not amount to a change in the basis of calculation of long service benefit. Accordingly the preservation requirements of the Acts did not apply.

See also *The Minister for Education & Skills & Anor v The Pensions Ombudsman & Anor*[15] at **[22.11]**.

UK

Duty of good faith; consequences of breach

[20.22] *IBM United Kingdom Holdings Ltd v Dalgleish*[16]*—High Court of England and Wales—remedies available to members following breach of its duty of good faith by employer*

The High Court of England and Wales issued its ruling on the remedies available to members in relation to the judgment it previously issued against IBM,[17] finding that

---

14.   *Ulster Bank Investment Funds Ltd v Financial Services Ombudsman* [2006] IEHC 323.

15.   *The Minister for Education & Anor v The Pensions Ombudsman & Anor* [2015] IEHC 792.

16.   *IBM United Kingdom Holdings Ltd v Dalgleish* [2015] EQHC 389 (Ch).

17.   *IBM United Kingdom Holdings Ltd v Dalgleish* [2014] EWHC 980 (Ch).

IBM had breached its duty of good faith towards those members when introducing pension changes.

The ruling on remedies is over 180 pages long and deals with a number of clarifications and issues, many of which are very specific to the facts of the case. However, two significant points emerge. They are that, taking account of the overriding finding of IBM not having acted in good faith:

- The notices issued by IBM to cease future accrual on a defined benefit (DB) basis were found to be 'voidable'. Affected members could therefore choose to have their benefits treated as if DB accrual continued (losing the proceeds of the replacement defined contribution arrangement) or to keep the replacement defined contribution benefits.

- The members' agreement that salary increases would not be pensionable was unenforceable. Affected members were contractually entitled to retain such increases. As a result, the trustees of the DB scheme were required to treat them as pensionable in accordance with the rules of the scheme.

It is important to note that the remedies judgment does not prevent either of the above methods being used by employers in the future. However, in the particular circumstances of the IBM case, IBM was found to have breached its duty of good faith and accordingly the two methods could not be validly used by it.

Following the IBM case, if employers seek to close their pension scheme to future accrual, the manner in which this can be achieved will need to be carefully considered and appropriate legal advice taken. There would be significant financial consequences for employers if it were found that the scheme closure was unenforceable and the members were treated as remaining in pensionable service.

Personal liability of trustees

[20.23] *Bridge Trustees Ltd[18]—Deputy Pensions Ombudsman—trustees personally liable for payments made in breach of trust*

This was a decision of the Deputy Pensions Ombudsman (the Ombudsman) in the UK handed down on 31 March 2015, which held two trustees personally liable for payments made in breach of trust. The Ombudsman held that the two trustees were not protected by the exoneration and indemnity provisions in the Scheme Trust Deed and Rules and ordered a payment of £193,000.

The indemnity clause granted protection to the trustees but did not extend to cases of fraud or 'deliberate disregard of the interests of the beneficiaries' by the trustees. Two of the trustees were directors of Pilkington's Tiles Ltd (Pilkington). On 24 December 2009, Capita, the scheme administrator, transferred excess DC contributions to Pilkington's bank account (the Transfer).

The Trustees concerned subsequently agreed to the company's request for a loan of £205,000 to pay the 2008 Pension Protection Fund (PPF) levy, which it otherwise could

---

18. *Bridge Trustees Ltd* PO–763.

not afford. The Trustees concerned did not mention the Transfer to the other two trustees. The Trustees authorised further payments of excess employer contributions from the scheme to Pilkington's of £5,819.68, therefore, transferring a total of £193,010.93 from the scheme to Pilkington's over a three-month period.

Pilkington's entered administration in June 2010. Bridge Trustees Ltd were appointed trustees and, subsequently, made a complaint to the Pensions Ombudsman that the Trustees concerned contravened rule 5.6 of the scheme rules in relation to excess contributions and failed to act in the members' best interests.

The Trustees concerned admitted that they had authorised the repayment to Pilkington, but claimed that Capita advised them that the excess contributions must be repaid under the rules of the scheme.

Rule 5.6 of the scheme provided that excess employer DC contributions, resulting from early leavers whose benefits had not vested, should be held in a general reserve and applied by the trustees:

> as the principal employer shall from time to time direct to pay the costs and expenses of the scheme and/or to reduce the amount of the contributions which would otherwise be required from the employers ...

The Ombudsman upheld the complaint against the Trustees concerned and confirmed that in no circumstances could rule 5.6 be interpreted to allow payment from the scheme's general reserve back to Pilkington.

The Ombudsman also found that, on the balance of probabilities, the scheme administrator would not have advised the Trustees concerned to repay the excess employer contributions to Pilkington. The Ombudsman found it critical to this conclusion that Capita provided administration, but not consultancy, services to the trustees. In any event, the Ombudsman found that the Trustees concerned could not be excused by simply relying on any such advice; rather, trustees should consider the reasonableness of any advice and challenge it if necessary. Furthermore, the Ombudsman found that the Trustees concerned should have considered seeking legal and tax advice, which they had not.

The Ombudsman found the Trustees concerned to be in breach of trust in authorising the payment in contravention of the scheme rules. In addition, they had failed to inform their fellow trustees of the repayment, which was relevant to the decision to make a loan to Pilkington's to pay the PPF levy. The Ombudsman reasoned that if the other two trustees had been aware of the repayment, they might have concluded that the loan was not reasonable or prudent.

The Ombudsman concluded that the Trustees were more interested in the company's position than protecting the interests of the members of the scheme. The Ombudsman found the actions of the Trustees concerned to be a conscious decision on their part which amounted to a deliberate disregard of the interests of members. The Ombudsman emphasised that this conclusion turned on the fact that the initial transfer in December 2009 to Pilkington was more than had been transferred by Capita to the scheme, which showed that the Trustees were more interested in returning the money to the company than the interests of the members. The Trustees concerned could not, therefore, enjoy the protection of the indemnity and exoneration clause and were directed to reimburse the scheme for the total excess employer DC contributions payments to the company of £193,010.93 plus interest together with any tax charges and late payment charges.

This case illustrates the potential personal liability of pension trustees. It also illustrates the dangers of trustees relying solely on indemnity and exoneration clauses for protection. Trustee liability insurance can provide further protection against personal liability – and will typically cover defence costs as well. However, whether insurance could have protected the Trustees on the specific facts of this case would depend on the precise wording of the policy. Policies typically exclude actions where there is a personal benefit to the insured in carrying out the wrongful act or if there has been an intentional breach of a provision or law. The Ombudsman found that there was no evidence of the Trustees gaining personally by the repayment. However, the Ombudsman's finding of a 'conscious wrongdoing' and a 'deliberate disregard of the interest of the members' is such that a pension trustee insurance policy (and we have no knowledge that there was any such policy) might not provide cover.

Meaning of accrued benefits

[20.24] *Sterling Insurance Trustees Ltd v Sterling Insurance Group Ltd*[19]*—High Court of England and Wales—Pensions Act 1995, s 67—meaning of phrase 'accrual due'*

The case concerned the meaning of the phrase 'benefits accrued due in respect of any member up to [the date of the amendment]' in a restriction on a power of amendment that prohibited amendments that substantially reduce in aggregate the value of such benefits. An amendment had been made which terminated the accrual of final salary benefits and did so in a way that broke the link between past service benefits and future salary increases. The question was whether the breaking of the final salary link was valid or ineffective as contrary to the restriction on the amendment power.

The Court accepted the parties' agreed position (subject to a reservation by the employer of the right to argue the contrary on appeal) that the meaning of the word 'accrued' in this context, when it is the only word used to describe the benefits, is such that it includes the final salary link, following *In re Courage Group's Pension Schemes*[20] and *Briggs & Ors v Gleeds & Ors*.[21] It was also common ground that the meaning of the word 'due' when used on its own, was to refer to benefits already payable, thus not including the final salary link. The question was what the meaning of the composite phrase 'accrued due' was in this context.

The judge (Nugee J) rejected the employer's argument that the phrase 'accrued due' meant 'become due' and thus referred to benefits already due to be paid. He held that it should be interpreted as meaning 'accrued for', recognising that this was not giving the phrase the meaning it commonly has among lawyers, which is indeed in the sense of 'fallen due'.

---

19.   *Sterling Insurance Trustees Ltd v Sterling Insurance Group Ltd* (CD 3 July 2015).
20.   *In re Courage Group's Pension Schemes* [1987] 1 WLR 495.
21.   *Briggs & Ors v Gleeds & Ors* [2014] EWHC 1178 (Ch).

The judge reached his result by applying the process of 'correction by construction' discussed in *Chartbrook Ltd v Persimmon Homes & Ors*,[22] and was satisfied that 'something must have gone wrong with the language' of the clause, principally, but not only, by reason of the fact that the protection accorded to members under the employer's interpretation of the phrase would have been less than that already conferred by s 67 of the Pensions Act 1995, which was in force at the date the deed containing the amendment power was executed.

The judge granted leave to appeal, recognising that the question of construction was a difficult one in relation to which the Court of Appeal might take a different view, and also expressed the view that it would be desirable for the Court of Appeal to consider the decision in *In re Courage* regarding the meaning of the phrase 'secured' benefits, and consequently the meaning of 'accrued' benefits adopted in *Briggs v Gleeds* in reliance on *In re Courage*.

Europe

Data protection; transfer of data overseas

[20.25] *Schrems v Data Protection Commissioner*[23]*—CJEU—Directive 95/46/EC— pensions aspects of ECJ ruling on EU–US 'Safe Harbor' arrangement*

On 6 October 2015 the CJEU handed down its preliminary ruling to the Irish High Court that Commission Decision 2000/520/EC (the Decision) in relation to the transfer of data from Facebook Ireland to servers in the USA where it was processed, known as the EU–US 'Safe Harbor' framework, was invalid.[24]

The Decision stressed that the right to protection of personal data is 'guaranteed' by the Charter of Fundamental Rights of the European Union (the Charter) and that the Data Protection Directive and the roles of the national supervisory authorities in protecting this right are to be applied in light of the Charter.

There are two main consequences for occupational pension schemes:

(a) EU Schemes that transfer data to the US

Pension schemes based in the EU that transfer members' personal data to the US will need to establish a replacement system of adequate protection if they currently rely on the Safe Harbor framework. This may affect schemes that exchange member data with US parent companies or where administration for group company pension arrangements is managed from a US-based subsidiary.

(b) Third-party administrators that hold scheme data in the US

Where a pension scheme uses third-party administrators based in the US it would be prudent for scheme trustees to confirm with such administrators whether there has been any transfer of personal data, supplied by the scheme or the employer,

---

22.   *Chartbrook Ltd v Persimmon Homes & Ors* [2009] UKHL 38.

23.   *Schrems v Data Protection Commissioner* (Case C–362/14).

24.   See **Ch 4** Data Protection at **[4.01]**.

to the US relying on the Safe Harbor framework. In such a case, the administration agreement appointing the third-party administrator may have to be revisited and updated accordingly.

MISCELLANEOUS
VAT and pension funds

[20.26] The Revenue Commissioner's VAT Manual has been updated to set out the VAT treatment applying to pension funds following decisions of the Court of Justice of the European Union (CJEU) in *Wheels*,[25] *ATP*[26] and *PPG*.[27]

(a) VAT treatment of management services supplied to pension funds

[20.27] The CJEU ruled that defined contribution occupational pension schemes may be treated as 'special investment funds' within the meaning of art 135.1(g) of Council Directive 2006/112/EC where certain conditions are met. The Revenue Commissioners have indicated their acceptance, as a consequence of that decision, that a defined contribution scheme (within the meaning of the Pensions Act 1990) is regarded as a specified fund. Accordingly, the management of such schemes us exempt from VAT. One-member arrangements do not come within the scope of the exemption. (See Part 05.71 of the VAT Manual.)

The CJEU ruled that a defined benefit scheme could not be regarded as a special investment fund within the meaning of art 135.1(g) of Council Directive 2006/112/EC. Consequently, fund managers should continue to charge VAT on services supplied to defined benefit pension schemes. (See Part 05.72 of the VAT Manual.)

(b) VAT deductibility in respect of pension fund costs

[20.28] The CJEU provided clarity on an employer's entitlement to deductibility in the setting up and management of a pension fund for its employees. (See Part 05.73 of the VAT Manual.)

Universal retirement savings group

[20.29] In February 2015, the Minister for Social Protection announced the establishment of a Universal Retirement Savings Group to 'develop a roadmap and timeline' for the introduction of a new universal pension scheme that will be mandatory

---

25.   *Wheels Common Investment Fund Trustees Ltd & Ors v Commissioners for HM's Revenue and Customs* (Case C–424/11).

26.   *ATP PensionService A/S v Skatteministeriet* (Case C–464/12).

27.   *PPG Holdings BV cs te Hoogezand v Inspecteur van de Belastingdienst/Noord/kantoor Groningen* (Case C–26/12).

for employees. The Minister noted that just half of workers in Ireland have a pension other than the State pension and workers in the private sector are less likely to have a private pension. The Minister did not indicate when the new universal pension scheme would be introduced.

This announcement is consistent with the OECD report, *Review of the Irish Pension System*, which was published in April 2013. The OECD report considered that the main policy goal of reforming the Irish pension system should be to improve the adequacy of pensions and suggested the introduction of compulsory pension scheme membership (which was favoured over the auto-enrolment system introduced in the UK or additional tax relief or other incentives for pension savings). The report did not detail costings or contribution structures.

Extension of retirement grace period for public sector pensions

[20.30] The Minister for Public Expenditure and Reform secured approval to extend – to June 2016 – the 'grace period' within which public servants can retire under the terms and conditions which they held prior to the pay reductions which were made under the Financial Emergency Measures in the Public Interest Act 2014.

The number of civil servants who retired in 2013 was less than anticipated due to the extension of the 'grace period' resulting in savings to the Exchequer under the superannuation and retired allowances vote of €36 million.

Pensions Council

[20.31] In February 2015, the Minister for Social Protection announced the membership of the Pensions Council, the body created in March 2014 to operate as a pensions advisory panel and report to the Minister for Social Protection on matters of pensions policy.

The Social Welfare and Pensions (Miscellaneous) Act 2013 had restructured the Pensions Board and split its functions into two distinct elements. With effect from 7 March 2014, the Pensions Board was renamed the Pensions Authority and its CEO, Brendan Kennedy, was given the title of Pensions Regulator.

The role of the Pensions Authority is confined to regulatory matters. The policy functions of the old Pensions Board were transferred to the new Pensions Council. The work of the Pensions Council includes the representation and protection of the interests of the consumer. Its first task was to review and advise on the implementation of the recommendations contained in the *Report on Pension Changes in Ireland*, published in 2012 by the Department of Social Protection. Among the issues highlighted by that report was the transparency and reasonableness of pension charges. The Minister has stated that the Pensions Council would 'monitor the implementation of recommendations in the Report on Pension Changes to tackle excessive fees' and advise on the requirement for further action.

Pension schemes with 'double insolvency' in government PIP Scheme

[20.32] The government's Pensions Insolvency Payments Scheme (PIPS) was established in 2010 to provide for double insolvency situations where both the pension scheme and the principal employer were insolvent. PIPS involves the government taking the assets in insolvent pension schemes and committing to paying annuities to the pensioners in return. This was considered a more cost-effective alternative than buying annuities from private providers that charged profit margins, which was previously the case for such schemes. The government was able to reduce the cost as it does not require a profit margin, although it is still cost-neutral for the Exchequer.

The €178 million settlement in December 2014 in relation to the Waterford Crystal pension scheme was made in respect of active and deferred members. It is for this reason that only members of the Waterford Crystal pension scheme who were pensioners at the time of the double insolvency in 2009 and whose pension entitlements were fully protected are members of the PIPS. The reasoning behind including these members in the PIPS is to lower the cost of looking after the pensioners, which frees up a small amount of resources for the active and deferred members.

When responding to whether the Waterford Crystal settlement would set a precedent for other pension schemes, the Department for Social Protection stated that the Waterford Crystal settlement 'will inform' other claims. However, it is worth noting that the combined deficit of just over €100 million of the Waterford Crystal schemes dwarfs any other schemes affected by double insolvency.

To apply to PIPS, a pension scheme's trustees must first apply to the Pensions Authority to be eligible under PIPS. Once certified, the scheme must apply to the Minister for Finance to participate in the scheme. If the Minister approves the application and the trustees accept the offer and quote from the Minister, arrangements can then be made to pay the assets to the Exchequer and to set up annuity payments to pensioners.

As of January 2015, 11 schemes had applied for PIPS since the scheme was introduced in May 2010. Of these schemes, all have been approved by the Pensions Authority, nine have been approved by the Minister and are in payment, one has applied and is in the approval process and the other has not yet applied to the Minister. The Waterford Crystal schemes had been in payment under PIPS before the settlement in December 2014 in respect of the active and deferred members.

Lump sums from Waterford Crystal settlement increased by €4m as a result of mediation

[20.33] The Labour Relations Commission, which chaired the original settlement negotiations in December 2014, chaired a mediation process which concluded in March 2015, resulting in the service of former workers involved being calculated from years and months of permanent company service, rather than service in the pension scheme.

The reasoning for this was due to the inconsistency in the eligibility criteria for entering members into the pension schemes. The effect of this measure was to increase the total cost of the lump sum portion of the settlement from €41 million to €45 million, bringing the total cost of the settlement to €182 million. The balance of €137 million is to fund the ongoing pension payments for the former workers concerned.

As a result of the mediation, members are to be paid €1,200 per member per year (calculated by years and months of permanent company service) to compensate for the stress and delay in bringing cases to resolve the matter to the Irish and European courts.

The ongoing pension payments remain unchanged from the December settlement specifically those with pensions under €12,000 will get 90 per cent of their pension; those with pensions between €12,000 and €24,000 will get 90 per cent of €12,000, plus 67 per cent of remaining benefit between €12,001 and €24,000; and workers with pensions in excess of €24,000 will receive 90 per cent of €12,000, 67 per cent of benefit between €12,001 and €24,000 and 50 per cent of any remaining benefit above €24,000.

Pensions Authority note on pension transfers outside the State

[20.34] On 11 August 2015 the Pensions Authority published a note on transfers of pension savings from occupational pension schemes and Personal Retirement Savings Accounts (PRSAs) to other arrangements established outside the State. The note sets out the risks members and contributors should consider before making such a transfer and outlines for trustees and PRSA providers the circumstances in which such a transfer can be made.

Chapter 21

PROTECTIVE LEAVE

ENTITLEMENT TO PAID MATERNITY LEAVE

[21.01] *A Worker v Cork Association for Autism*[1]*—Labour Court—Industrial Relations Acts 1946 to 2015, s 20(1)—voluntary organisation under Health Act 2004, s 39—entitlement to paid maternity leave—withdrawal of paid maternity leave without agreement—contractual entitlement to paid maternity leave benefit*

The claimant was employed by the respondent, a voluntary organisation funded under s 39 of the Health Act 2004, for over 12 years. The claimant sought to avail of the maternity leave payment scheme in November 2013 as she was expecting to give birth in April 2014. However, she was informed that the scheme was not available anymore. In accordance with the Financial Emergency Measures in the Public Interest Act 2009, support grants were cut and cost-saving measures were introduced by the respondent in order to increase the efficiency of the organisation. The respondent sought to end the payment of salary increments to staff, but after discussions with the unions this proposal was withdrawn. The respondent subsequently made a unilateral decision to suspend paid maternity leave.

The claimant brought a claim seeking an entitlement to apply for and avail of the maternity leave payment scheme. The claimant noted that the decision to cease maternity leave payment was taken without any consultation or agreement with the claimant's union. The claimant further noted that the respondent effectively introduced a cost-saving measure that targeted and impacted only the female members of staff of child-bearing age and had no impact on any other type of worker in the organisation.

The respondent noted that it had carried out an organisational review in 2011, the results of which were that it would be unable to meet its financial commitments in late 2012. On this basis, all employees were given 12 months' notice that paid maternity leave would be suspended from January 2013 onwards. The respondent noted its intention that paid maternity leave would be reintroduced for employees if the organisation's finances were to substantially recover.

The Labour Court accepted that the respondent was faced with severe financial difficulties which required significant action to ensure its future viability. The Labour Court also noted that the claimant's contractual terms of employment included a provision for a paid maternity leave benefit. The Labour Court accepted that the claimant's conditions of employment entitled her to be paid for the period of her maternity leave incurred in 2014. The Labour Court recommended that the claimant be entitled to payment for that period of maternity leave.

---

1. *A Worker v Cork Association for Autism* CD/14/231, LCR20906.

ACCESS TO MATERNITY/ADOPTIVE BENEFITS IN SURROGACY ARRANGEMENTS

[21.02] *G v The Department of Social Protection*[2]*—High Court—O'Malley J— appeal of decision of Circuit Court—Equal Status Acts 2000 to 2015— discrimination—maternity benefit/adoptive benefit—genetic mother—surrogacy arrangement—medical condition*

In 2006, while pregnant, the appellant was diagnosed with cervical cancer and had to undergo a hysterectomy as a result of which she was unable to support a pregnancy. The appellant and her husband subsequently entered into a surrogacy arrangement in a foreign jurisdiction, with a surrogate who gave birth to a baby in January 2011. The appellant and her husband were the registered parents of the child under the law of the state in question while the surrogate mother was not identified on the child's birth certificate. Previous to the birth of the child the appellant made enquiries of the respondent about maternity benefits but was informed that under current legislation she would have no statutory right to maternity leave and as a result no statutory entitlement to maternity benefits. An application to the appellant's employer for special leave from her employment equivalent to that available for adoptive leave after the birth of the child was successful. Her employer was willing to grant the leave. However, it could not offer her paid maternity leave and told her that she would have to seek payment from the Department of Social Protection directly.

The Equality Authority wrote on the appellant's behalf to the respondent requesting it to use its discretion to give a payment for leave comparable to that of a working adoptive mother. It was acknowledged the type of leave granted by the appellant's employer had no statutory basis in either the adoption or maternity protection legislation. Payment was sought on the basis that it was available to every other working mother who had a child either naturally or through adoption. The respondent replied setting out the qualification conditions for adoptive benefit and maternity benefit. To make a payment outside the statutory framework would, according to the respondent be ultra *vires*. In June 2011 the Equality Authority, on behalf of the appellant, filed the complaint before the Equality Tribunal.

The appellant's complaint to the Equality Tribunal alleged unlawful discrimination on grounds of disability to include a failure to provide reasonable accommodation, and on grounds of family status and gender contrary to s 5(1) of the Equal Status Acts 2000 to 2015 (the Acts). The case in relation to the appellant's disability was based on the fact that, by reason of her medical condition, she could not have a family by natural means. The Tribunal considered the provisions of ss 2(1) and 3 of the Acts and noted that the appellant's medical condition was a disability within the meaning of s 2 of the Acts.

In relation to family status she argued without prejudice to her contention that as a matter of law she was the mother of the child that she was at least in the position of being in *loco parentis* but was being treated differently from other women responsible

---

2.   *G v The Department of Social Protection* [2015] IEHC 419.

for newborns or children. The gender complaint was that her situation was such as could only arise in respect of a woman.

The Equality Tribunal ultimately dismissed the appellant's complaint. The Tribunal noted that the Irish legal system operates a default legal assumption that the person giving birth to a child is the child's legal mother and that there is no legal recognition of surrogacy in this jurisdiction. It was clear that this was a matter that raised a number of complex issues which the legislature should consider in due course. The Tribunal went on to find that in deciding, as a matter of policy, to establish a special scheme for maternity and adoptive leave the Oireachtas necessarily had to define the scope and limits of its application. The Tribunal held that the definitions currently contained in the statutes did not recognise the situation that the appellant found herself in and in such circumstances the respondent had no option but to turn down her application.

The High Court noted that the appeal hearing before the Circuit Court appeared to have been conducted on the same basis as before the Tribunal and that the decision of Lindsay J in the Circuit Court affirmed the finding of the Equality Tribunal. The Circuit Court ultimately found that the appellant had not been treated less favourably within the meaning of the Acts and that any action by the respondent by way of a special provision would be outside the scope of the Acts and would accordingly be *ultra vires*. O'Malley J noted that under s 28(3) of the Acts any appeal to the High Court was on a point of law only. The points of law raised on behalf of the appellant were that the Circuit Court had erred in law in concluding that because there was no legislative regulation of surrogacy in Ireland the appellant's complaint did not come within the scope of the Acts; and that the Circuit Court had erred in law in concluding:

— that because surrogacy had not been envisaged when the Acts became law, the appellant's complaint did not come within the scope of the Acts;

— that the appellant had not been less favourably treated within the meaning of the Acts; and

— that the taking of any action by the respondent by way of special provision would be beyond the defined scope of the Acts and consequently *ultra vires* the power of the respondent.

O'Malley J considered the detail of submissions made by the parties. She held that the first question to be addressed was whether or not the provisions of the Acts were capable of being applied to surrogacy-related issues. In this regard, O'Malley J agreed with the appellant that the Acts are intended to cover a broad range of human life and activity and that it is for all purposes to reduce the social wrong of discrimination based on improper considerations. O'Malley J held that the Circuit Court fell into error in holding that the Acts could not be relied upon in relation to novel factual situations not familiar to the legislature at the time of enactment. O'Malley J then went on to consider what was the proper definition of the service provided by the respondent. O'Malley J held that to limit the service to the operation of the statutory code of benefits and allowances as asserted by the respondent was too restrictive as it took no account of the fact that the respondent also administered a large number of non-statutory payment schemes. O'Malley J concluded that the service provided by the respondent was the administration or operation of the statutory code and of other non-statutory payment schemes. It was noted by the High Court that the statutory provisions at issue in this case related solely to mothers whether natural or adoptive. O'Malley J noted that it was clear in light of the judgment of the Supreme Court in *MR*[3] that the appellant could not claim the status of mother under Irish law. O'Malley J noted that while this was a source of great distress to the appellant, pending introduction by the Oireachtas of legislation dealing with this situation, it was not for the Courts to attempt to resolve the complex questions that need to be addressed.

O'Malley J held that it followed that the appellant could not, for the purpose of a claim of discrimination, choose to compare herself directly with the two categories of mother recognised under Irish law, ie, mothers who have given birth and mothers who have adopted. Both of these categories are entitled to social welfare payments that, in the applicable qualification conditions, relate directly to the legal status of motherhood. The appellant did not have that status. If she did, the Court held it would be likely that she would have a strong case based on constitutional grounds. It was noted by the Court that the appellant maintained that her case did not depend on the status of motherhood and that she was also a person who was in *loco parentis* of a child and therefore she was discriminated against because she had not been pregnant. She also asserted that she was discriminated against on grounds of disability and gender.

O'Malley J concluded that the claim of gender discrimination would not be tenable while noting that it was true that the appellant's medical condition was one that could only affect a woman. However, the Court held that since no man can qualify for either maternity leave or adoptive leave payments in any circumstances, the appellant had not been treated less favourably than any man is or would be if he had a child through a surrogacy arrangement or otherwise. O'Malley J held that, on the face of it, the appellant had certainly been discriminated against because she did not bear her child. The appellant suggested that this was a discriminatory exclusion from the social welfare legislation within the terms of the Acts and that the refusal of the respondent to grant her an equivalent non-statutory payment was a matter entitling her to compensation. O'Malley J held that the difficultly she had with this argument lay in the fact that the payment from which the appellant said that she had been excluded, for discriminatory reasons, was one that was created by statute. A claim to be legally entitled to compensation necessarily involves a claim that one has been subjected to a legal wrong but in this particular incident such a wrong can only be established on the assumption that one statute can be held to be legally deficient by reference to another, ie by reference to the Acts. O'Malley J concluded that she could not see how the appellant could maintain a claim of unlawful discrimination without saying, in effect, that the Social Welfare Act discriminated against her unlawfully. O'Malley J held it was not open to a Court to make a finding of unlawfulness in one statute on the basis of the policy of the other. There had been no assessment of the constitutionality of the choices made in the social welfare code which should be the only legitimate basis for such a finding. O'Malley J held that the word 'provision' in s 3(1)(c) could not be interpreted as including a statutory provision which would have the effect of elevating the Acts to all

---

3.   *MR & Ors v An T-Ard Chláraitheoir and the Attorney General* [2014] IESC 60.

but constitutional level; permitting the legitimacy of all other legislation to be assessed by reference to it.

O'Malley J held that she was not persuaded by the respondent's argument that a non-statutory scheme to make provision for women in the appellant's position would be *ultra vires*. The existence of a broad range of non-statutory schemes demonstrated that the respondent frequently used such schemes as a flexible alternative or supplement to primary legislation, presumably on the basis of public policy objective and assessment. However O'Malley J held it was not open to a Court to hold that the respondent was derelict in not legislating for or not creating a scheme in this instance, without holding that the policy choices embodied in the primary legislation were legally deficient. The appellant argued that the Acts had envisaged an order of compensation if discrimination was established, even if the respondent had no legal power to remove or ameliorate the discrimination complaint by way of making a non-statutory payment. O'Malley J held that this raised the problem of whether the Acts could be relied upon in this fashion to find there was discrimination contrary to the Acts embodied in other legislation. In the view of the Court it could not. The Court noted that it was easy to understand why the appellant felt she had been treated badly; why the Tribunal referred to the case as raising compelling considerations; and why the learned Circuit Court judge accepted that the respondent's decision might have seemed unfair and unjust. However, the High Court noted that there was, as yet, no legislation governing the complex issues that arise in the context of surrogate births. The Court's view was that the Acts could not be used to fill the gap and therefore the appeal must be dismissed.

Chapter 22

PUBLIC SERVANTS

SUMMARY DISMISSAL FROM AN GARDA SÍOCHÁNA

[22.01] *McEnery v Commissioner of An Garda Síochána[1]—High Court—Kearns P— judicial review—Garda Síochána (Discipline) Regulations 2007, regs 5 and 39— summary dismissal from An Garda Síochána—applicant convicted of assault on member of public—whether criminal conviction justifies summary dismissal—fair procedures—whether reasons for dismissal provided*

The applicant sought to challenge her summary dismissal by the Commissioner. The reason given for the applicant's dismissal was that she had breached the garda disciplinary code by assaulting a member of the public.

The applicant sought an order of *certiorari* quashing the decision to dismiss her. She also sought an injunction by way of application for judicial review, restraining the respondent from dismissing her pursuant to reg 39 of the Garda Síochána (Discipline) Regulations 2007 as amended (the Regulations). The applicant further sought an order of prohibition restraining the respondent from dismissing her. Lastly she sought a declaration that the respondent had acted *ultra vires* in dismissing her under the Regulations and/or in breach of natural justice.

The applicant had been a sergeant in An Garda Síochána. In 2011 she was sent forward for trial by jury on a charge of assault causing harm contrary to s 3 of the Non-Fatal Offences against the Person Act 1997 (the Act). Although she was acquitted under s 3 of the Act, she was convicted of assault under s 2 of the Act. She was given a sentence of four months' imprisonment, suspended for six months on the condition of good behaviour and that she enter into an oral bond in the sum of €200 to keep the peace. Her conviction was upheld on appeal by the Court of Criminal Appeal. On 24 December 2012 the applicant received a notice from the Commissioner under reg 39 of the Regulations (the Notice). The Notice conveyed the Commissioner's intention to dismiss the applicant, subject to obtaining the consent of the Minister for Justice and Equality. The stated grounds for the dismissal were that the applicant had committed a breach of discipline. The Notice stated that the Commissioner considered the breach to be of such gravity that the holding of an inquiry would not affect his decision to dismiss her. The applicant was invited to advance reasons against the proposed dismissal. The applicant made a submission to the Commissioner on 20 February 2013, outlining the reasons why she should not be dismissed. By way of letter dated 25 March 2013 the Commissioner informed the applicant that he was not convinced by the reasons set out in her submission and that he would be seeking the requisite consent from the Minister for Justice and Equality to dismiss her.

---

1. *McEnery v Commissioner of an Garda Síochána* [2014] IEHC 545.

Kearns P considered the Regulations under which the applicant was dismissed. He noted that criminal conduct constituted a breach of discipline under the Regulations. He considered in particular reg 39 of the Regulations, which sets out the summary dismissal procedure for members of An Garda Síochána. He noted that the Commissioner could not be in any doubt as to the material facts while exercising the power to summarily dismiss. In addition, the Commissioner must be of the opinion that the breach of discipline is of such gravity that it merits dismissal and that the holding of an inquiry would not affect his or her decision in the matter. Finally Kearns P noted that the dismissal must be consented to by the Minister for Justice and Equality, and the individual garda must be given the opportunity to submit reasons against his or her dismissal. He noted that these provisions had been adhered to in the present case.

The applicant submitted that, notwithstanding the Regulations, the fact of a criminal conviction in the absence of other reasons could not constitute grounds for summary dismissal. Secondly, it was the applicant's contention that the fact of such a conviction did not absolve the respondent from the duty to conduct its own inquiry into the applicant's conduct. Thirdly, it was maintained that the respondent had failed to provide adequate or sufficient reasons to dismiss the applicant and that such failure constituted a breach of fair procedures and natural justice. *Mallak v Minister for Justice, Equality and Law Reform*[2] and *Rawson v Minister for Defence*[3] were cited in support of this contention. Fourthly, the applicant submitted that the respondent acted in an unreasonable and disproportionate manner in failing to have regard to the nature, circumstances and context of the applicant's breach of discipline. Fifthly, the applicant accused the respondent of failing to distinguish her case from those of other members of An Garda Síochána who were spared the ultimate sanction of dismissal.

The respondent's case was that the applicant's summary dismissal fell squarely within the scope of reg 39 of the Regulations. It was submitted that there was no doubt as to the material facts of the case and that the applicant could not re-open her conviction. The respondent maintained that the applicant had been made fully aware of the reasons for her dismissal and that she had been given the opportunity to make submissions in relation thereto. It was strongly denied that there was any lack of fair procedures in this case. Finally, the respondent stated that the duty to give reasons for dismissal must be seen in context, and that in this case there was no 'tangled web of facts to be unravelled'.

It was considered beyond doubt by Kearns P that reg 39 of the Regulations afforded the Commissioner the necessary powers to dismiss the applicant summarily. It was noted that the applicant could not re-open her conviction. Kearns P held that it was a well-established concept that it is not for the courts to decide what amounts to conduct sufficient to warrant the summary dismissal of a member of An Garda Síochána. He cited *Galvin v Commissioner of An Garda Síochána & Ors*[4] and *Stroker v Doherty*[5] in

---

2.   *Mallak v Minister for Justice, Equality and Law Reform* [2012] IESC 59.
3.   *Rawson v Minister for Defence* [2012] IESC 26.
4.   *Galvin v Commissioner of An Garda Síochána & Ors* [2011] IEHC 486.
5.   *Stroker v Doherty* [1991] 1 IR 23.

this regard. Kearns P cited *State (Jordan) v Commissioner of An Garda Síochána*[6] and stated that although the existence of a summary power of dismissal was considered to be 'unusual and exceptional', it was necessary in some circumstances. He noted that a conviction of assault on a member of the public would appear to fall into this category.

Kearns P noted that the applicant's main ground of complaint was that the Commissioner acted in breach of fair procedures and constitutional justice in that he relied solely on the conviction and failed to have regard to other considerations, such as a sanction less severe than dismissal. The applicant stated that there were other members of An Garda Síochána who had been acquitted of assault causing harm contrary to s 3 of the Act and convicted instead of an offence under s 2 of the Act. These employees had not been dismissed. Kearns P considered the circumstances of the four members of An Garda Síochána (including the applicant) who had been convicted of assault in the last five years. He noted that two members of An Garda Síochána who had been convicted of s 3 assault had resigned their posts. Another member of An Garda Síochána was convicted, like the applicant, of s 2 assault and sentenced to a three-month custodial sentence. Kearns P considered the fact that this conviction and sentence were under appeal and subject to an investigation pursuant to s 102(4) of the Garda Síochána Act 2005. As a result, no decision as to disciplinary action had yet been taken in that case. Kearns P concluded that the applicant had failed to establish a factual basis for holding that her treatment had been discriminatory or disproportionate in comparison with any other case.

In relation to the applicant's point that a lesser penalty did not appear to have been considered by the Commissioner, Kearns P placed emphasis on the fact that the applicant had been invited to make submissions on the proposal to dismiss her. These submissions had been considered by the Commissioner in arriving at his final decision to dismiss the applicant. Therefore, it was held that the Commissioner's ultimate decision could not be said to fail an irrationality test as is understood in the context of judicial review. In considering whether applicant's argument that the Commissioner failed to justify his decision to dismiss with adequate reasons, Kearns P held that the reasons had been clearly set out in the Notice.

Kearns P accepted that decision-makers must achieve fairness by giving adequate reasons so as to leave the party affected in no doubt as to the considerations underpinning the decision to dismiss. The President held that this was emphasised in two Supreme Court decisions cited by the applicant. However, Kearns P stated that the extent of this obligation must be viewed in context. He proceeded to distinguish *EMI Records (Ireland) Ltd v The Data Protection Commissioner*[7] on the basis that there could have been no reasonable doubt in the applicant's mind as to what the reasons for her dismissal were. He distinguished *Kelly v The Commissioner of An Garda Síochána*[8] on the same ground. Also, unlike *Kelly*, the Kearns P held there was no material dispute of fact in the present case.

The application for relief was refused.

---

6.   *State (Jordan) v Commissioner of An Garda Síochána* [1987] ILRM 107.

7.   *EMI Records (Ireland) Ltd v The Data Protection Commissioner* [2013] IESC 34.

8.   *Kelly v The Commissioner of An Garda Síochána* [2013] IESC 47.

[22.02] *McEnery v Commissioner of An Garda Síochána*[9]—*Court of Appeal—Kelly J—judicial review—Garda Síochána (Discipline) Regulations 2007, reg 39—policing law—appellant challenged summary dismissal from An Garda Síochána—appellant convicted of assaulting member of public—whether criminal conviction justifies summary dismissal—fair procedures—whether breach of discipline and material facts were both considered*

This was an appeal against the judgment of Kearns P in the High Court in which he had refused to grant *certiorari* to the appellant, a sergeant in An Garda Síochána, of a decision of the Commissioner of An Garda Síochána (the Commissioner) to dismiss her summarily. The reason given for the appellant's dismissal was that she had breached the garda disciplinary code by assaulting a member of the public.

The facts of the case are set out in **para [22.01]** above.

The appellant contended in the present appeal that the Notice of the Commissioner (conveying the Commissioner's intention to dismiss the appellant) conflated two distinct statutory requirements (ie the breach of the Regulations and the facts upon which the breach was based). The appellant did not seek to deny that the conduct which gave rise to the conviction breached the Regulations but merely that she was entitled to have taken into consideration the material facts or conduct which gave rise to the conviction. This would involve a consideration by the Commissioner of the transcript of her Circuit Court hearing and of evidence adduced by her of her own character and circumstances. The Commissioner argued that fair procedures were in fact followed and the appellant was given an opportunity to make submissions pursuant to the Regulations.

Kelly J first commented on the nature of the power to summarily dismiss contained in reg 39 of the Regulations. First, it is an exceptional power. Second, it can only be used in 'very limited circumstances'. The Regulations deal with the procedures for garda discipline in significant detail and provide for the establishment of a board of inquiry and appeal in most circumstances. Third, its exercise is not subject to the unfair dismissals legislation. The only limit on its use is the requirement that the Minister for Justice consent to the decision; and the Regulations do not require any particular information to be given to the Minister nor do they provide for a garda such as the appellant to make representations to the Minister. Thus, judicial review is the only recourse open to a garda such as the appellant to challenge the decision. In light of all these aspects of the power, Kelly J noted that:

> the Courts on judicial review ought to be astute to ensure that the power is exercised properly and in accordance with law.

The judge stated that, on the plain wording of reg 39 of the Regulations, the Commissioner must not be in any doubt as to:

(i)   the material facts;

(ii) whether the relevant breach of discipline is of such gravity that both '*the facts and the breach merit dismissal*' (Kelly J's emphasis); and

(iii) whether the holding of an inquiry could not affect his or her decision.

---

9.   *McEnery v Commissioner of an Garda Síochána* [2015] IECA 217.

Kelly J considered that the key element of these criteria was that they expressly distinguished between the material facts and the breach of discipline.

Kelly J concluded that, having analysed the Notice sent by the Commissioner in the instant case, the Commissioner had indeed conflated two matters upon which he needed to be satisfied pursuant to the Regulations. The Commissioner had only considered the conviction (or criminal conduct) which constituted the breach of discipline and failed to consider the material facts which were extraneous to the relevant breach but nevertheless material. Kelly J noted that, by doing this, the Commissioner had 'blinkered himself from a consideration of the material facts' and this meant that the statutory power to summarily dismiss had not been exercised lawfully.

The appeal was allowed on the above basis and an order for *certiorari* granted quashing the Commissioner's decision. However, the Court stated that this would not preclude the Commissioner from subsequently taking whatever lawful steps he deemed appropriate concerning the appellant, provided that these were in compliance with the Regulations.

PUBLIC SERVICE AGREEMENT/PROHIBITION ON REDUNDANCY

[22.03] *Trinity College Dublin v Irish Federation of University Teachers[10]—Labour Court—Industrial Relations Acts 1946 to 2015, s 26(1)—whether redundancy of claimant was in breach of Public Service Agreement, cl 1.6*

The claimant worked on a variety of projects with a variety of funding support. It was asserted on his behalf by his trade union that the respondent had failed to offer the claimant alternative available work prior to his redundancy and in so doing had acted in breach of a Public Service Agreement. It was submitted by the respondent that it had a long established exit mechanism which predated the Public Service Agreement and hundreds of employees had been made redundant using this exit mechanism. The Labour Court concluded that the college's decision to make the claimant redundant was not consistent with clause 1.6 of the Public Service Agreement and accordingly found that the claimant's employment was continuous and recommended that it be treated as such.

---

10.   *Trinity College Dublin v Irish Federation of University Teachers* LCR 20962.

SCOPE OF FINANCIAL EMERGENCY MEASURES IN THE PUBLIC INTEREST ACTS

[22.04] *Nic Bhrádaig v Employment Appeals Tribunal and Mount Anville Secondary School, Minister for Expenditure and Reform and Minister for Education and Skills (Notice Parties)[11]—High Court —appeal from decision of EAT on point of law— Baker J—Payment of Wages Act 1991—Financial Emergency Measures in the Public Interest (No 2) Act 2009—whether employee in fee-paying private school is a public servant[12]*

This was a statutory appeal on a point of law brought in respect of a decision of the EAT concerning the applicability of the Financial Emergency Measures in the Public Interest (No 2) Act 2009 to the appellant. The appellant, an employee of Mount Anville Secondary School, was unsuccessful in her claim before a Rights Commissioner who determined that she was a public servant within the meaning of the legislation and that pay reductions under the 2009 Act may be lawfully made. This was affirmed by a majority decision of the EAT.

The appellant claimed that she was not a public servant within the meaning of the 2009 Act and that the reductions to her salary were not lawfully made. The High Court held that the definition of a 'public service body' includes two elements:

> ... the body must be in whole or in part funded whether directly or indirectly from Exchequer funds, and a public service pension scheme must exist or apply or be one that may be made in respect of that body.

The Court noted that the Exchequer did not pay the salary of the appellant but the school did receive Exchequer funding both directly and indirectly. The appellant argued that she was not paid from State resources and she had no State-funded pension. The notice parties submitted that the 2009 Act applies to all public services bodies and to the staff employed by those bodies even if the salaries of these staff are not paid by the Exchequer. The Court held that the language of the statute is clear and the ordinary and plain meaning of the expression 'wholly or partly funded directly or indirectly' meant that the first part of the test was satisfied.

The Court then addressed the second part of the test. The appellant did not have an entitlement to an occupational State pension arising from her employment. The appellant also pointed to the fact that in some schools secretaries' salaries are paid by the Department of Education and Skills and they enjoy better terms and conditions of employment. However, Mount Anville Secondary School falls into the definition of a 'secondary school' within the meaning of SI 435/2009.[13] It is a school in which Exchequer funds pay for the remuneration of the teachers and it was noted that certain

---

11. *Nic Bhrádaig v Employment Appeals Tribunal and Mount Anville Secondary School, Minister for Expenditure and Reform and Minister for Education and Skills (Notice Parties)* [2015] IEHC 305.

12. See *Arthur Cox Employment Law Yearbook 2014* at [21.10] for the EAT decision.

13. The Secondary Community and Comprehensive School Teacher's Pension Scheme 2009 (SI 435/2009).

staff members do avail of such a pension. The Court held that while the State might pay the salaries of teachers, they are employed by the individual school in which they work. The Court found that the appellant was wrong to characterise the State as the employer of the teachers in Mount Anville and to argue, by that premise, that only she and other persons whose salaries are paid from school funds are employed by the school. The Court found that the legislation was sufficiently drafted to include, within the test, a body where a public pension scheme is available to some but not all members of staff.

Finally, the appellant argued that as the purpose of the legislation was to improve public finances, this purpose was not achieved by the reduction in her salary. She submitted that any saving by the school of the percentage by which her salary had been reduced, did not have the effect that the amount saved was returned to the Exchequer. The Court did not accept this submission; it found that the legislation is unambiguous and therefore it was unnecessary to look to the purpose of the legislation as an interpretive tool. Accordingly, it was held that although the appellant was correct in her assertion that the school did not benefit from the reduction in her salary, the legislation does define her as a person to whom the statutory reduction must be applied and she was, for the purpose of this Act alone, 'a public servant'.

The Court rejected the appeal and affirmed the decision of the EAT.

PAY PARITY IN A UNIVERSITY

[22.05] *National University of Ireland, Galway v A Worker[14]—Labour Court—appeal from recommendation of Rights Commissioner—Industrial Relations Acts 1946 to 2015, s 13(9)—Industrial Relations Act 1969—whether role of university fellow analogous to that of university lecturer—appropriate rate of pay to be paid to claimant following her appointment to lecturer (below the bar) grade*

The claimant was employed as a lecturer (below the bar) and on commencement of employment her pay was subject to a 10 per cent reduction, as applicable to new entrants to the public service. Management applied the lower rate of pay to the claimant on the basis that it was an entry grade and was not analogous to a previous experience within the public service. This was strongly contested by her trade union on the basis that the claimant was previously employed as a university fellow and the two roles were submitted to be analogous/comparable.

The respondent's management did not accept that the roles of university fellow and lecturer (below the bar) are analogous. This claim arose in the context of a circular letter from the Department of Finance dated 21 December 2010 which dealt with the application of a decision of Government, of 2 December, which provided for a salary reduction of 10 per cent for new entrants to the public service. The relevant part of the letter provided that the reduction should not be applied to those recruited to an analogous grade/role as that which he or she held previously in the public service.

---

14. *National University of Ireland Galway v A Worker* AD1529.

The Labour Court considered the content of the roles performed by the claimant while employed as a Fellow and that of her current role and held it was clear that the essential characteristics of both roles were broadly the same. The Labour Court was satisfied that both roles were analogous and thus the claimant should properly have been placed on the pre-January 2011 scale with effect from the date of her appointment. The Labour Court held that any necessary consequential adjustment to the claimant's incremental placing should be made so as to reflect the position she would have been in, had she been placed on the pre-January 2011 scale on her appointment to a current position. The appeal was allowed.

[22.06] *University College Cork v A Worker[15]—Labour Court—appeal from recommendation of Rights Commissioner—Industrial Relations Acts 1946 to 2015, s 13(9)—classification of claimant as new entrant on returning to public service— whether role of dental nurse and registered general nurse analogous in nature*

The claimant alleged she had been placed on an incorrect salary scale having returned to the public service after previous service. The claimant asserted that her previous work experience in the public service as a dental nurse should be taken into consideration for the purpose of establishing her correct rate of pay. The claimant further asserted that she was incorrectly classified as a new entrant when she returned to the public service after completing training to become a registered general nurse. The claimant asserted that she had suffered financial loss as a consequence of being placed on the incorrect salary scale.

It was submitted by the respondent that the roles of dental nurse and registered general nurse were by no means analogous in nature and that the classification of the claimant as a new entrant was proper and that she had been appropriately remunerated at all times. It was further submitted that this claim was cost-increasing and was thus prohibited under the terms of the Public Services Agreement.

The Labour Court noted that the core issue for consideration was whether the positions of dental nurse and registered general nurse were analogous for the purpose of Department of Finance Circular, dated 21 December 2010, on the application of a 10 per cent reduction in pay rates to entry grades for the public service. The Labour Court considered the submissions made and held it was clear that there were substantial differences between both positions in terms of duties, qualification and salary and thus the positions could not be classified as being analogous within the meaning of the Circular. The Union's claim could not succeed, thus the appeal was disallowed and the Rights Commissioner recommendation was affirmed.

---

15.   *University College Cork v A Worker* AD1540.

BANK TIME

[22.07] *Dublin City Council v SIPTU & Anor[16]—Labour Court—Industrial Relations Acts 1946 to 2015, s 26(1)—whether proposal to end bank time could be unilaterally withdrawn by respondent*

This case concerned the proposed withdrawal of 'bank time'. It was submitted by the trade union that bank time cannot unilaterally be withdrawn by management. Bank time was introduced at a time when salary payments were to be made by electronic fund transfer instead of traditional methods of payment and had become an established condition of employment. It was submitted by the respondent that the provision of bank time was unnecessary and inappropriate given the wide range of banking services available to customers. Bank time has been withdrawn throughout the public service without the payment of compensation.

The Labour Court concluded that there had been significant material changes in banking services and practices since bank time was first introduced, and in these circumstances it was not unreasonable for the respondent to seek this cessation of that concession. The Labour Court noted that all parties accepted that the original intention was that bank time would be taken during working hours and consequently its elimination could not be fairly characterised as involving an extension of the working week for those affected by the proposals.

The Labour Court accepted that there was no longer any justification for the continuance of this practice and that it should be discontinued. The Court recommended that the parties should engage in discussions in relation to the preferred mode of restoring the working time involved having regard to the imperative of maintaining a consistent approach.

TRANSFER OF A PUBLIC SERVANT

[22.08] *Hosford v Minister for Social Protection[17]—High Court—Noonan J— judicial review—whether transfer of applicant, a higher executive officer in the Department of Social Protection, from one position to another was ultra vires and unlawful—where conduct of applicant led to his transfer*

The applicant worked in the Scope section of the Department of Social Protection from August 2009. The function of the Scope section was to determine the employment status of individuals for the purposes of their PRSI liabilities and entitlements under the relevant social welfare legislation. The applicant was also appointed as a deciding officer under s 299 of the Social Welfare Consolidation Act 2005.

An issue arose regarding the appropriate classification of individuals who worked in companies of which they were directors and shareholders, and particularly the

---

16.   *Dublin City Council v SIPTU & Anor* LCR 20950.
17.   *Hosford v Minister for Social Protection* [2015] IEHC 59.

classification of these individuals as self-employed for PRSI purposes, depending on the nature of their shareholding and other factors.

Noonan J noted that the applicant had developed a very definite view of the law which he continued to apply without regard to any policy consideration. Noonan J further noted that the applicant had made allegations to supervisors and external parties that the Department's policy was unlawful. This issue became a source of considerable conflict and friction between the applicant and his superiors within the Department. The Court noted that the applicant viewed himself as a whistleblower and had complained unsuccessfully to the Ombudsman. He also had disclosed confidential material and privileged legal advice to outside parties, including the Ombudsman, the Revenue Commissioners and his legal advisors. In correspondence to the Department, the applicant noted his intention to make a protected disclosure to a range of bodies under the then draft legislation on protected disclosures.

The Court noted that considerable time and effort was devoted within the Department to dealing with lengthy correspondence from the applicant and it was noted that meetings were frequently disrupted where the applicant was involved.

The respondent, in its replying affidavit, set out in detail the numerous difficulties that it had encountered with the applicant in relation to his duties within the Scope section. It was alleged by the respondent that the applicant had refused to follow the instructions of his line managers and a number of examples were given in this regard. In September 2013 the principal officer of the Scope section requested that human resources reassign the applicant in the interest of the smooth running of the section. Later that month the applicant was advised that he was being reassigned to a new initiative called People Point. The applicant was advised that notwithstanding he was a good worker and had initiated a number of improvements within the section, he was being reassigned due to his difficulty in accepting management decisions and carrying out management instructions as directed. In the view of the respondent, the People Point project was a shared human resources facility for the entire civil service, and was a very important high-profile project for the Department. The applicant did not agree. The Court noted that the applicant's pay and conditions and promotional prospects were entirely unaffected by his reassignment. No disciplinary action was taken against him, and Noonan J noted the respondent's view was that the new role was not a demotion. In June 2014, the applicant transferred again to what he himself described as a 'key' position in the facilities management finance unit. The Court noted that no complaint had been made within proceedings about this subsequent reassignment.

Noonan J noted that the applicant's claim could be narrowed to the sole contention that his reassignment to People Point was invalid because it was made by the respondent *mala fides* for improper motives. The applicant identified the purpose was to discipline him for upholding the law and 'to prevent him from interfering further in the perpetuation of unlawful policies' by the respondent. The applicant further alleged that the transfer amounted to a public rebuke and humiliation of him, was defamatory and had caused great damage to his reputation and standing.

The respondent submitted that it had the right to transfer officers within the Department at its absolute discretion. It was noted that this was a statutory right and had been accepted by the applicant in his contractual documentation, which stated as follows: 'I am prepared if appointed to the post of higher executive officer in the Department of Social Welfare, to perform any duties which may be assigned to me from time to time by direction of the Minister of Social Welfare appropriate to my new appointment.' It was alleged that this transfer was a purely administrative action which did not engage any rights the applicant may enjoy under the Constitution or European Convention of Human Rights. It was submitted by the respondent that the merits of the transfer were not a matter for the Court, which could not act as an appellate tribunal from the decision of the respondent. It was further submitted by the respondent that the transfer complained of had now expired and that there had been no complaint about the applicant's current position and thus his claim was moot. It was further noted that the applicant had tendered no evidence about having suffered any financial or other loss. Finally, it was submitted by the respondent that the applicant was seeking to use his transfer as a platform to ventilate his views on the law relating to proprietary directors and attempting to cause embarrassment to the respondent, which was, in the view of the respondent, a clear abuse of process.

Noonan J noted the acceptance by the applicant that he was and remained liable to transfer at the sole discretion of the respondent. The Court noted that it could not be realistically suggested that every decision to reassign a civil servant engaged the full panoply of constitutional and Convention rights, and that the party affected must be afforded fair procedures including, for example, the right to make submissions or be given reasons, as this would be absurd.

The Court further noted that there was a range of decisions in the context of employment that may be taken, which are merely administrative or managerial in nature, and do not give rise to rights amenable to judicial review. The Court however noted that the position may be different where the decision complained of is disciplinary in nature and involves the imposition of a penalty or dismissal. In this case, the applicant had made a number of very serious allegations against the respondent which were notably unsupported by any evidence, other than his own opinion. The Court further noted the significant conflict of evidence on both sides which could not be resolved by the Court in the absence of cross-examination. The onus of proving his case rested on the applicant, and Noonan J held that he had not discharged the onus of establishing any factual basis upon which the Court could interfere with the respondent's decision. The Court further noted that there was no evidence that the applicant had suffered any detriment whatsoever and although it had been suggested by the applicant that his standing and reputation had been damaged, the only evidence of this was the applicant's own belief. This was inconsistent with subsequent events which have led to the reassignment of the applicant to a highly responsible position which he himself described as being key. The Court noted that, given the subsequent transfer of the applicant about which he made no complaint, the proceedings were effectively moot.

The Court described the applicant as being on a crusade. The Court noted that it had been invited to make determinations regarding the status of proprietary directors for PRSI purposes and that a number of lengthy submissions had been made by the applicant in this regard. Noonan J concluded that the applicant had sought to abuse the process of the Court to ventilate matters of no relevance to the proceedings. The application was dismissed.

See also *Minister for Education, and Science v The Labour Court, Boyle and the Committee of Management of Hillside Park Pre-School (Notice Parties)* discussed at **Ch 19** para **[19.01]**. For more judicial review decisions, see **Ch 16**.

ON-CALL RATES

[22.09] *St Vincent's University Hospital v Irish Nurses' and Midwives' Organisation (INMO)[18]—Labour Court—Industrial Relations Act 1990, s 26(1)—locally agreed enhanced on-call rates—Public Sector Agreement 2010 to 2014—agreed compensation formula*

This dispute concerned a claim by the INMO on behalf of three anaesthetic nurses in the liver transplant unit of the respondent hospital for the restoration of locally agreed enhanced on-call rates. The issue of the removal of the enhanced on-call rates, which were paid over and above the nationally agreed theatre rates, was previously the subject of a Labour Court Recommendation[19] where the Court recommended the following:

> The Court understands from the parties that plans are underway to increase the number of Theatre Nurses capable of providing the Liver Transplant Service and this will facilitate standardisation of on-call arrangements. Therefore, the Court recommends that the existing on-call arrangement should be retained until such time as the frequency of on-call arrangements for the staff of the Liver Transplant Service are standardised with similar Theatre Nursing grades.

Improvements were made to the frequency of on-call arrangements and the enhanced rates ceased to be paid with effect from 1 October 2012. In line with the Public Sector Agreement 2010–2014, agreed compensation was paid to each of the claimants for the loss of higher earnings. However, the INMO was dissatisfied with the level of frequency of on-call. In September 2014, the situation deteriorated due to a number of retirements, resulting in the level of on-call arrangements increasing again for the claimants. As a result the INMO submitted a claim to the Labour Court for the restoration of the enhanced rates from 14 September 2014. It submitted that the level of frequency was affected by management's failure to include relief cover to take account of annual leave and other forms of leave, the liability of the claimants to be on the general theatre on-call roster and their liability to be rostered for night duty. The INMO submitted that it was only fair and just that the nurses be paid the fair and appropriate rate for the extreme inconvenience related to on-call work in the national liver transplant unit. The INMO also stated that it would only be by restoring the rates that the nurses would have any chance to have a normal working and family life by having more colleagues incentivised to provide the life-saving and essential public service provided in the liver transplant unit.

---

18.   *St Vincent's University Hospital v Irish Nurses' and Midwives' Organisation* CD/15/186, LCR21049.

19.   Labour Court Recommendation No 20347.

The respondent stated that a realignment took place with effect from 1 October 2012 to bring about an on-call commitment of an average of six to seven days' on-call over a 10-week period, with no more than a one-in-six on-call commitment. However, as a result of retirements, resignations and the facilitation of leave of absence, the on-call commitment increased. Management stated that, since 2012, all nursing staff who participated in the on-call after-hours arrangements for the liver transplant service were paid in line with the national on-call rates applicable to theatre nurses. The respondent further stated that plans were put in place to improve the participation level as early as possible subject to available nurses, training and transplant activity. The respondent stated that since 1 June 2015, the respondent had reached a one-in-six rota; that by October 2015 it would reach a one-in-eight rota, and by January 2016 it would achieve a one-in-nine rota.

The dispute was not resolved at local level and was the subject of a conciliation conference in the Labour Relations Commission at which agreement was not reached. The dispute was accordingly referred to the Labour Court in accordance with s 26(1) of the Industrial Relations Act 1990.

The Labour Court stated that it did not find merit in re-introducing the enhanced on-call rates as sought by the INMO. The Court noted that the reduced numbers of employees available for on-call within the unit, which resulted in a deterioration of the on-call arrangement in September 2014, was an issue which was being actively addressed by management and continuing efforts were being made to improve the situation even further.

The Court recommended that management's plans to improve the frequency of on-call commitments should include taking account of relief cover for employees' leave arrangements and for the claimants' liability to be available for the general theatre on-call roster. The Court did not see any reason to take account of night-duty rosters in this regard.

The Court recommended that the on-call arrangements should be reviewed in May 2016 to ascertain their effectiveness.

REVISED ANNUAL LEAVE ARRANGEMENTS

[22.10] *Royal Irish Academy of Music v Services Industrial Professional Technical Union (SIPTU)[20]—Labour Court—Industrial Relations Act 1990, s 26(1)— Department of Education and Skills Circular—revised annual leave arrangements*

This dispute concerned the implementation by the Royal Irish Academy of Music (RIAM) of a Circular from the Department of Education and Skills on Revised Annual Leave Arrangements for Staff Employed by Universities and Colleges, which SIPTU submitted did not apply to the RIAM and, if it did, had been applied incorrectly.

---

20. *Royal Irish Academy of Music v Services Industrial Professional Technical Union* CD/15/187, Recommendation No LCR21048.

This dispute was the subject of a Conciliation Conference in the Labour Relations Commission, but as agreement was not reached, the dispute was referred to the Labour Court in accordance with s 26(1) of the Industrial Relations Act 1990.

SIPTU submitted the following arguments at the Labour Court hearing:

In 2009 the RIAM sought to engage with SIPTU regarding the introduction of annualised hours for administrative staff. Prior to agreement being reached, the RIAM sought the approval of the Department of Education and Skills, but the Department indicated that it had no role in the matter and it was a matter for the governors of RIAM to appoint staff and agree their terms and conditions of employment (including vacations).

In February 2014, workers in the RIAM received an email advising them that their leave was to be capped. It also set out the method of calculation of the compensation days and the specific dates on which compensation days were to be taken. In all other institutions where this cap was applied discussions had taken place.

Workers in the sector covered by the Circular could access flexi-time and time-in-lieu as a means to ensure that any additional time worked was compensated.

The RIAM submitted the following arguments at the Labour Court hearing:

• The RIAM is a public sector body and it operates under the direction of the Department of Education and Skills. It is obliged to adhere to the requirements of the Public Service Agreement and the requirements of its funding body. This includes the application of the Circular in line with the Labour Court's previous Recommendation.[21]

• The RIAM is obliged to apply the Circular and to achieve the harmonisation envisaged. In relation to the method by which the Circular was applied, the RIAM adhered to its own established practice.

It was the practice that management decided on the dates of closing and re-opening and that annual leave periods were then notified to staff.

The Labour Court noted that it was clear that the employees associated with the claim were aligned for the purposes of pay and some conditions of employment with corresponding grades in the Education Sector. The Labour Court concluded that they were, therefore, encompassed by the outcome of negotiations between the State as an employer and the Public Service Unions affiliated to the Public Services Committee of ICTU. The Circular in issue in the case set out the terms of an agreement concluded between Public Service Management and the Public Services Committee of ICTU. The Labour Court held that in those circumstances it was not unreasonable that the terms of the Circular be applied to those associated with this claim. The Court recommended that the position in that regard be accepted.

It was noted that workers in corresponding grades in comparable employments have access to time off in lieu of overtime and to flexi-time. The Labour Court stated that there was no good reason in principle as to why similar arrangements should not apply to the staff of the RIAM. The Court recommended that negotiations should take place

---

21.   Labour Court Recommendation LCR20679

between the parties on the introduction of such arrangements. The Court did not recommend any change in the established arrangements for the times at which annual leave was allocated.

POWER OF MINISTERS TO RESTRICT PENSION PAYMENTS TO A RETIRED PUBLIC SERVANT

[22.11] *The Minister for Education & Skills & Anor v The Pensions Ombudsman & Anor[22]—High Court—Baker J—Financial Measures (Miscellaneous Provisions) Act 2009—Pensions Act 1990—Pensions Ombudsman—jurisdiction—discretion*

This was an appeal by the Ministers for Public Expenditure and Reform and Education and Skills against a decision of the Pensions Ombudsman that the Ministers could not restrict pension payments to Mr Gleeson who had retired, per an agreement reached with his employers, at 60.

Mr Gleeson had worked as Secretary of Trinity College Dublin (TCD) and was entitled to a pension under the relevant pension scheme which was established in April 1972. The normal retirement age under the scheme was 65 years. Rules associated with the scheme, which were amended in May 1986, granted the trustees of the scheme the power to augment, 'with the consent of the Employer', the benefits to which a person would be entitled under the scheme. In 2002, due to a funding shortfall, the trustees decided that augmentation would no longer be permitted unless it would be cost neutral to the scheme. By 2009, the scheme and its assets (€279 million) had to be transferred to the National Pensions Reserve Fund (NPRF) because of its significant deficit (liabilities were calculated at €595 million). The discretion to 'augment' any pension now rested with the Ministers.

In 2005, Mr Gleeson's role changed from Secretary of TCD to Director of Strategic Initiatives, and, as part of the reorganisation, he reached an agreement with the then Provost that he would be entitled to retire on full pension on his 60th birthday. On the basis of this agreement, €544,000 was transferred by instalments to ensure that this was cost neutral to the scheme. Mr Gleeson retired in July 2011 (at age 60) and received full pension (€92,153 per annum) between August and November of that year.

TCD argued the decision to 'augment' Mr Gleeson's pension had been made in 2005, prior to the scheme's transfer to the NPRF but TCD was ordered to adjust his pension and recoup the payments already made in excess of an early retirement sum of €71,674. Mr Gleeson appealed this determination of the Ministers to the Higher Education Authority, which delivered its decision rejecting his appeal in July 2012. Mr Gleeson then appealed to the Pensions Ombudsman, who determined that the trustees had made the relevant decision in 2005 and allowed his appeal in June 2014. The respondents argued that the Ombudsman had erred in law and that, having found 'maladministration' in TCD's decision-making in 2005, still found in Mr Gleeson's favour.

---

22. *The Minister for Education & Skills & Anor v The Pensions Ombudsman & Anor* [2015] IEHC 792.

Baker J noted that the High Court's role in hearing a statutory appeal is to determine whether the decision as a whole contained serious and significant errors and questions of fact were not open to appeal. The respondents argued that the Ombudsman misinterpreted the rules of the scheme and further, that the Ombudsman had found that the trustees had invalidly exercised their discretion to augment Mr Gleeson's pension. Mr Gleeson argued that he did not retire early but retired at the date established by his 2005 contract.

The respondents argued that the Ombudsman had no statutory jurisdiction to adjudicate on the issue of breach of contract but Baker J noted that the Ombudsman was granted a wide jurisdiction to interpret contractual terms[23] and could therefore make a determination on the pension arrangements reached in 2005.

Baker J noted the evidence presented to the Ombudsman, including submissions from the current Provost and the head of HR at TCD, to the effect that the 2005 contract had the approval of all necessary persons. The Ombudsman had criticised poor corporate governance which meant evidence surrounding the 2005 contract was incomplete and it was unclear whether the contract was ever approved by the Trinity Board, although it was 'conceivable even probable' that management had a free hand regarding the reorganisation at the time. Baker J considered there was 'ample' evidence that Mr Gleeson had not retired early and the Ombudsman did not err in so finding.

Citing Kelly J in *Murray v The Trustees and Administrators of the Irish Airlines (General Employees) Superannuation Scheme*,[24] Baker J noted that the Pensions Act 1990 is 'a self-contained statutory code' which grants the Ombudsman a wide jurisdiction to achieve a result that he 'considers necessary or expedient for the satisfaction of the complaint or the resolution of the dispute'. The Ombudsman exercised his powers to determine that Mr Gleeson did not retire early and any effort by the respondents to exercise their discretion was 'impermissible and oppressive'.

The appeal therefore failed.

See also **Ch 20** on **Pensions**.

INTERVIEW PROCESS – ASSOCIATE PROFESSOR

[22.12] *Trinity College Dublin v A Worker*[25]—*Labour Court—appeal from recommendation of Rights Commissioner—Industrial Relations Acts 1946 to 2015—Industrial Relations Act 1969, s 13(9)—assessment criteria for interview process—due process*

This case concerned the interview process for the position of associate professor in Trinity College Dublin (Trinity). The union, IFUT, argued that management of Trinity had failed to comply with due process in the selection procedures when Trinity had changed the assessment criteria given to candidates on the day of interview.

---

23.   *Willis & Ors v The Pensions Ombudsman* [2013] IEHC 352.
24.   *Murray v The Trustees and Administrators of the Irish Airlines (General Employees) Superannuation Scheme* [2007] IEHC 27.
25.   *Trinity College Dublin v A Worker* AD1552.

Trinity argued that all candidates were assessed by the interview panel using the same and correct selection criteria at interview.

The case initially came before a Rights Commissioner who found that the claimant had not presented a valid complaint. The Rights Commissioner acknowledged the importance of the position of associate professorship, which does not come up very often and therefore would be of immense importance to potential candidates. However, the Rights Commissioner found that the overarching principles of adhering to Trinity's policies and procedures were complied with. The Rights Commissioner noted that it was acknowledged openly that incorrect information was initially issued to the potential candidates but it was stressed that these were not the criteria utilised by the appointments board, but rather the correct procedure, which was indicated to all the assessors as appropriate and correct for the appointment process. The Rights Commissioner appreciated the confusion that may have ensued as a result of this error and stated that Trinity could have been more proactive in the dissemination of the appropriate information immediately following the interview process and should have organised a more formal debrief and feedback session.

However, on the premise that the claimant was seeking retroactively to be appointed to the same level of post, the Rights Commissioner found that this was not a valid request. In particular, the Rights Commissioner stated that:

1.   It is not within my remit to make appointments for open and competitive selection processes.

2.   That even considering natural justice and fairness in a candidate process there can only be 1 'winner'.

It is my recommendation therefore that, as regrettable to the individual claimant that the outcome of the process was not her own appointment, that she accepts that the process was indeed fair and reasonable.

The claimant appealed the Rights Commissioner's Recommendation to the Labour Court in accordance with s 13(9) of the Industrial Relations Act 1969.

Before the Labour Court, the claimant argued that, had she been graded as per the criteria given to the candidates, she would have received a score which would have deemed her appointable to the position. The union argued on the claimant's behalf that she had suffered considerable professional damage to her reputation both within and outside the College and amongst professional colleagues as well as enduring a high level of physical and emotional distress.

It was accepted by Trinity that the same particulars of marking criteria were mistakenly furnished to all three candidates who attended for interview for the post. However, Trinity further submitted that the appointment procedures for associate professor(s) were fully adhered to and the correct marking scheme was applied to all candidates in determining who would be offered the position. All three candidates were interviewed and assessed by a five-person academic interview panel, which included two external assessors. The panel applied the correct selection criteria for associate professor in the scoring of all candidates on the day of interview.

The Labour Court concurred with the findings and recommendation of the Rights Commissioner and upheld that recommendation. The Labour Court did not uphold the claim for a compensatory award in this case.

Furthermore, the Labour Court recommended that Trinity should review aspects of its selection process to:

(i)   ensure consistency and transparency with regard to the assessment of candidates in terms of the criteria to be applied in respect of the post on offer;

(ii)   ensure consistency and transparency with regard to the points/percentage threshold applicable to determine whether or not candidates are successful at interview; and

(iii)   ensure that appropriate wording is used to declare that a candidate is deemed eligible for the position applied for. Words such as 'appointable and unappointable' should cease to be used due to the possible negative connotations associated with the latter.

Chapter 23

REDUNDANCY

EXISTENCE OF A GENUINE REDUNDANCY

[23.01] *Quinn (Junior) v Quinn Insurance Ltd[1]—Employment Appeals Tribunal— Unfair Dismissals Acts 1977 to 2015—Redundancy Payments Acts 1967 to 2014— when a redundancy is regarded as genuine—impersonal nature of redundancy— reasonableness of employer considered*

The claimant held the position of head of claims for Quinn Insurance before he was made redundant by the Court-appointed joint administrators. The administrators were appointed in March 2010 in order to ascertain whether any part of the business could be re-opened and to resize the business before the process of selling the business began. The administrators divided the position of head of claims into two separate positions. The claimant was not considered for either of these positions. The claimant was asked not to attend any more senior management meetings and his access to the IT system was disabled. An important meeting described as a 'reintegration meeting' was held in June 2011 during which the claimant was offered a number of lower paid positions. The claimant suggested that this was only a 'tick the box exercise' to which the administrator replied that 'we could end up in court someday'. The claimant was then made redundant in August 2011.

The EAT was asked to consider whether the claimant's redundancy was a 'genuine' redundancy. The EAT noted that redundancy must be for reasons not related to the employee concerned. The 1967 Act highlights a number of areas where redundancy arises. These include where the employer intends to cease carrying on the business for which the employee is hired, where the requirement of an employee to carry out a particular kind of work for an employer has ceased and where the employer intends to carry on his business with fewer employees.

Given the claimant's previous experience as head of claims, the EAT felt that there were other positions for which the claimant could have been considered. The head of claims position was split in two. The EAT felt that the claimant would have been able to do either of these jobs. The EAT accepted that as far back as April 2010 the claimant had been excluded from meetings. The administrators had not made any attempt to discuss the selection criteria for redundancy with the claimant and had not allowed him to submit any alternatives to redundancy.

A major question for the EAT in determining whether the redundancy was genuine was whether the administrators had acted reasonably. Under s 5 of the Unfair Dismissals (Amendment) Act 1993, the reasonableness of an employer's conduct is an essential factor in the context of all dismissals. The EAT held that the dismissal lacked the impersonality necessary for it to be reasonable and was therefore not a genuine

---

1. *Quinn (Junior) v Quinn Insurance Ltd* UD2415/2011.

redundancy. The EAT concluded that the administrators could not show a redundancy situation existed and that the claimant had been dismissed under a cloak of redundancy. The EAT considered *JVC Europe Ltd v Jerome Panisi*[2] where the High Court held that redundancy cannot be used to 'weed out' employees that are regarded as less competent. To disguise a dismissal as a redundancy is unlawful. The EAT held that the dismissal was a total disregard for the claimant's employment rights when viewed against the background of antagonistic relations between the parties. The EAT awarded the claimant compensation of €95,000.

[23.02] *Melia v M & J Gleeson & Company*[3]—*Employment Appeals Tribunal— appeal from decision of Rights Commissioner—Unfair Dismissals Acts 1977 to 2015—redundancy—dismissal—whether loss of contract by respondent a genuine reason for redundancy—whether claimant had asked to be made redundant—lack of evidence produced by respondent*

The claimant was employed as a lorry driver with the respondent haulage company from 13 June 2005 until his dismissal, by reason of redundancy, on 23 December 2011. For some time before being made redundant, the claimant had been reduced to a three-day working week. The respondent explained that one of its largest clients had informed them that they would no longer be engaging their services. In anticipation of this, the respondent saw fit to make a number of drivers redundant. The principle of last in, first out (LIFO) was used to compile a list of those to be made redundant. The claimant was not included on this list. However, it was decided that the claimant would now be required to drive a rigid truck, as opposed to the articulated lorry that he had been driving. There was to be no change to his terms and conditions of employment, except for the fact that he could no longer bring the truck home with him.

The respondent gave evidence that one week after this change was implemented, the claimant approached the manager and requested to be made redundant. He had indicated that the new arrangement was not suitable for him. The claimant was made redundant as per his request and the last person on the LIFO list escaped redundancy. It transpired, the respondent did not lose the contract immediately, as anticipated, rather it continued for approximately another eight months. The respondent made a decision to contract this work out to another company. This company employed some of the respondent's former drivers. The claimant was not one of those engaged by the other company. The respondent stated their belief that the claimant did not want this job as he had already secured himself employment elsewhere. It was the claimant's case that he never requested to be made redundant. He agreed that he had changed from driving an articulated lorry to a rigid truck one week prior to being made redundant. However, he denied that he had told his manager that he did not want to continue with that new arrangement. The claimant stated that he had only discovered after his dismissal that another driver with less service than him had been kept on by the respondent.

---

2.   *JVC Europe Ltd v Jerome Panisi* [2012] 23 ELR 70.

3.   *Melia v M & J Gleeson & Company* UD1569/2012.

The claimant disputed the existence of a genuine redundancy situation at the time of his dismissal. In the alternative, if a genuine reason for redundancy was held to exist, he maintained that he had been unfairly selected for redundancy. The claimant informed the EAT that he had been employed elsewhere from January 2012 to May 2012 on a part time casual basis and earned an average of €200 per week.

The EAT indicated that it was satisfied that the future loss of the large contract necessitated redundancies at some stage in the respondent. However, it was not convinced that the loss of this contract was imminent in December 2011 and doubted that there was a requirement for redundancies at that time. It was noted that the respondent failed to call any independent witnesses or to produce any documentation in support of its version of events in relation to the loss of the contract or of the circumstances in which services continued to be provided until the autumn of 2012. Similarly no documentary evidence or independent witnesses were presented in relation to the arrangement entered into with an independent haulier from December 2011. The EAT further considered that some of the evidence of the respondent's witnesses surrounding this particular issue was unreliable. Further, the EAT had been informed that it had become necessary to re-engage drivers as employees in September 2012 due to the acquisition of additional work from an important customer of the respondent. It was noted that no documentation in support of this had been furnished to the EAT. In relation to the circumstances in which the claimant left his employment, the claimant stated that he was told that there was no more work available and that he had accepted this in good faith. On the other hand the respondent maintained that the claimant had opted for voluntary redundancy because he had not been comfortable with proposed changes in work practices. The EAT held that, on balance, the claimant's evidence was to be preferred, as it was not considered credible that he would have voluntarily forfeited a job paying him a gross salary of €695 per week for one that paid approximately one third of that figure.

The EAT concluded that the respondent failed to discharge the burden of proof to satisfy it that the termination of the claimant's employment was a genuine redundancy, involving a fair selection process. Accordingly the EAT held that the claimant was unfairly dismissed and awarded the claimant €20,000 in addition to the redundancy payment already received by the claimant.

[23.03] *McDonald v Computer Placement Ltd[4]—Employment Appeals Tribunal— Unfair Dismissals Acts 1977 to 2015—whether genuine redundancy situation existed—whether alternatives to redundancy considered by respondent—whether consultation process had taken place with claimant*

The claimant was employed as a health and safety consultant in a company which formed part of a group acquired by the respondent in 2009. The respondent offered a range of staffing, recruitment, management and outsourcing services. The claimant maintained that he received insufficient notice of his redundancy from the respondent and that no alternatives to redundancy were offered to him.

---

4.   *McDonald v Computer Placement Ltd* UD1551/2012.

Evidence was given on behalf of the respondent that there was a reduced requirement for health and safety consultancy within the sector. A human resources and organisational review was undertaken, which concluded that the cost associated with delivery of the health and safety service had surpassed the revenue it generated. The figures being generated did not meet budget targets and the provision of the consultancy services showed a loss of €18,000 for the period from October 2011 to March 2012. The claimant was asked to produce a business plan for the future. The plan produced by the claimant was not considered by the respondent to demonstrate how the consultancy business could be brought into profitability. Following the human resources and organisational review the respondent restructured the company. Self-employed contractors were engaged to deliver health and safety consultancy services on a 'needs basis'. The claimant was informed that there would be work available to him as a self-employed consultant if he wished to avail of same.

The respondent had lost its largest consultancy customer in September 2011. It was making a loss and the *status quo* could not be maintained. The board conferred authority on the managing director to take whatever action he saw fit to address the issues with the consultancy aspect of the business. In May 2012, the managing director met with the claimant to inform him of the company's decision to engage self-employed contractors to deliver health and safety consultancy services on a 'needs basis'. He informed the claimant that his position was at risk of redundancy. In June 2012, the claimant received a letter informing him that his employment was being terminated by way of redundancy. The EAT was informed that there was no reason why the claimant could not have provided a consultancy service to the respondent on a self-employed basis after his redundancy.

The claimant was given his statutory redundancy entitlement. The other consultancy manager employed by the respondent was also made redundant in June 2012. Both consultancy managers were earning €50,000 per annum before they were made redundant and neither manager had been replaced at the time of hearing. The EAT was told that the focus of the respondent is now on training, and career management and consultancy work now account for only 3.9 per cent of turnover.

The claimant gave evidence that his salary had been increased to €54,000 in 2007. He told the EAT that, although it was a challenging business environment, he had secured earnings of €44,000 for the respondent in 2011 by way of his training work. He stated that he had never been made aware of any difficulty with the figures he provided to the respondent. The claimant stated that the meeting in May 2012 had been described to him as a 'quick chat' and said that it had been very informal. From the meeting he deduced that he was likely to be placed on a three-day week or to take a reduction in pay. He stated that he would have been happy with either of those outcomes. The clamant gave evidence that he had been stunned that he was made redundant and that no alternatives other than redundancy had been put to him.

The EAT was satisfied that the claimant had been consulted in relation to the potential redundancy situation. He had prepared a business plan in order for the respondent to assess the viability of the business going forward. The EAT noted the fact that the consultancy part of the business now only accounted for 3.9 per cent of annual turnover. It held that the respondent was only obliged to offer the claimant an alternative position if another position existed for which the claimant was qualified. As no such position existed in the respondent, there was no obligation on the respondent in this regard. The EAT noted that it had been open to the claimant to apply for a position as an independent contractor, but he had failed to do so. The EAT concluded that a genuine redundancy situation existed and that the claimant was fairly selected for redundancy. The claim of unfair dismissal failed.

[23.04] *Meekel v Delmec Engineering Ltd[5]—Employment Appeals Tribunal—appeal from decision of Rights Commissioner—Unfair Dismissals Acts 1977 to 2015— Payment of Wages Act 1991—redundancy procedure—oral agreement—entitlement to commission—failure to indicate redundancy as reason for termination— redundancy not effected in reasonable manner—failure to implement procedures— decrease of compensation award on appeal due to claimant's contribution— mitigation of loss—whether commission included in claimant's remuneration for purposes of compensation*

The claims arose by way of an appeal from a Rights Commissioner decision to award compensation of €60,000 to the claimant for unfair dismissal and to make no award under the Payment of Wages Act 1991. The respondent appealed the recommendation under the Unfair Dismissals Acts 1977 to 2015 as amended and the claimant appealed the recommendation under the Payment of Wages Act 1991.

The claimant commenced employment as a business development manager with the respondent on 1 September 2010 under a written contract of employment. The claimant was hired to manage international sales as the respondent's business had substantially decreased due to the recession. The promotion of international business was viewed by management at the time as a way of securing the respondent's future. The claimant's role involved liaising with governmental organisations in various countries in relation to setting up local companies, registration and hiring of local staff. The claimant's contract of employment provided that he would be paid an annual salary of €50,000 plus 5 per cent commission on all paid invoices for international sales. During the first year, on foot of paid invoices, the claimant earned commission of approximately €12,393.

In September 2011, six people were let go from the respondent and a number of staff were put on short-time work. In the same period, the claimant was promoted to the position of manager of international business. An issue arose in relation to the negotiation of this second management contract around April 2012. An annual salary of €64,000 and commission paid at the rate of 10 per cent on profits from international sales was the subject of negotiation between the parties. The claimant noted at the hearing that negotiations regarding this agreement had been ongoing, that the agreement had not been finalised and that it had never been reduced to writing at any stage. In any event, the claimant did not receive any commission on foot of his new position or this second agreement as no profits in the relevant sector were made during that particular time period. The claimant and the respondent sought to negotiate a third agreement to enable the claimant to earn commission in circumstances where international sales were

---

5.   *Meekel v Delmec Engineering Ltd* UD653/2013, PW265/2013.

not sufficient in this respect. The parties failed to reach an agreement on a third contract, which was to provide that commission would be paid at the rate of 10 per cent on the combined profits from the Irish market and international sales. The claimant had informed management that the terms of the third contract were not acceptable as the agreement provided that commission was contingent on matters outside of the claimant's control. The respondent continued to experience cash-flow problems in March 2012. Significant delays were incurred in international operations and many international contracts were running behind time. In an effort to control this, the respondent appointed new managers for both the Irish and international operations. While the claimant accepted that new management was required and had been assigned to assist with reducing the significant level of delays, the claimant was not satisfied with the new arrangement as a new manager was now signing off on international operations. The claimant felt that he was being manoeuvred out of his position with the respondent. In June 2012, the respondent's CEO met with the rest of the management team and together examined the roles within the organisation and devised a series of cutbacks.

The claimant attended a meeting with management on 14 August 2012. The claimant noted that the issue of redundancy was not discussed at this meeting but that the claimant was requested to hand over his customer list and company mobile phone to management. He requested and was furnished with a reference. On that same day and after the meeting, the CEO informed the claimant by telephone that due to the respondent's financial difficulties, the claimant's contract would be terminated. The claimant received a letter later that day confirming his termination citing financial difficulties and stating that 'the company is not in a financial position to continue as was previous'. The claimant and four other members of staff were made redundant at that time and other employees had their salaries reduced by 10 per cent. The CEO and his wife took no salary for a period of time. The claimant disputed the need to make his position redundant. He noted that after his employment was terminated, a new employee had been hired by the respondent and was referred to on the respondent's website as a sales representative. The CEO, under cross-examination, confirmed that the respondent had employed a new employee in December 2012 but that the employee had ceased to be a salaried employee within six months of his commencement. The claimant noted that he was unaware of other employees being made redundant, put on short time or being subjected to pay cuts.

The EAT accepted that the respondent was suffering financial difficulties during the period in question and significant cost cutting measures were required. The respondent was entitled to do so by way of redundancies, or putting staff on short time or making salary cuts. The EAT did not accept that the termination of the claimant's employment was mainly and wholly by reason of redundancy. The EAT found that the termination of the claimant's employment was mainly attributable to the failure of the claimant and the respondent to conclude a revised agreement with regard to the calculation of the claimant's commission. The EAT based this finding on the fact that the letter of termination received by the claimant did not refer explicitly to redundancy but stated that his termination was on the basis that 'unfortunately the company is not in a financial position to continue as was previous'. This wording suggested to the EAT that the termination may have come about because of a failure to replace the previous agreement on the calculation of commission. The EAT noted that even if a genuine need to make the claimant redundant existed, the redundancy was not effected in a reasonable manner given the absolute failure on the part of the respondent to follow the necessary procedures, fair or otherwise. The EAT upheld the decision of the Rights Commissioner, but varied the award of compensation from €60,000 to €35,000. In calculating the award, the EAT took account of the respondent's annual salary (€50,000) and had regard to the fact that the claimant secured alternative employment six months after the termination of his employment. The EAT found that commission formed part of the claimant's remuneration and wages and relied on the definition of remuneration in s 7(3) of the Unfair Dismissals Act 1977 and the definition of wages in s 1 of the Payment of Wages Act 1991. The EAT also upheld the decision of the Rights Commissioner that the claim under the Payment of Wages Act 1991 failed due to the difficulties in attempting to reconcile the financial information provided by each of the parties before the EAT and further, due to the uncertainty of the legality of the commission contract.

FAIR PROCEDURES

[23.05] *Kerrigan v Smurfit Kappa Ireland Ltd, c/o Smurfit Kappa Group*[6]*— Employment Appeals Tribunal—Unfair Dismissals Acts 1977 to 2015—redundancy selection procedure—enforcement of post-termination provisions—whether claimant entitled to bring claim after having signed a waiver in full settlement of any future claims—whether employee required to have informed consent to ensure validity of executed waiver—fair procedures—whether a 'last in, first out' policy had to be explicitly communicated to claimant or whether claimant's prior knowledge of common practice would suffice*

This case concerned the enforceability of a duly signed waiver and the payment by the respondent in full and final settlement of all claims arising from the termination of an employment contract for the reason of redundancy.

In 2008, the respondent's business decreased significantly and a number of smaller plants, including the respondent's plant in Cork, lost up to 50 per cent of their business. As a result, a series of redundancies took place. The respondent closed its Waterford plant where 30 employees were made redundant and all remaining business was transferred to the Cork plant. A large customer of the Cork plant took away its business and the Cork plant was rationalised from its three eight-hour daily shifts (five days a week) to one daily shift each day. As a result, the Cork plant was unable to perform all manufacturing activities. This resulted in the transfer of work to the Dublin and Lurgan plants on the basis of their technical capabilities. The work that remained in Cork was mostly regional work, suited to a single-shift plant operation. Over the period, 110 to 120 employees (compromising 80 per cent of its workforce) in the Cork plant were made redundant. The next and final stage of the restructuring concerned the restructuring of the sales development executives, one of whom was the claimant. It was noted that the sales development team was the last team to be restructured as the

---

6. *Kerrigan v Smurfit Kappa Ireland Ltd, c/o Smurfit Kappa Group* UD1921/2011.

respondent wanted to keep its customers reassured and fully serviced. The role of a sales development executive was to manage the key accounts in his area and develop new business. Three sales development executives, including the claimant, reported to the Cork office, each one responsible for a defined area. One was based in Cork, one in Galway and the claimant was based in Waterford with responsibility for accounts in Waterford and the surrounding South East area. Management conducted a review in the middle of 2010 with regard to where the account orders were being manufactured and how best to manage this from a sales perspective. The review confirmed the need for redundancies in the sales structure.

In September 2010, the claimant, who worked in the Waterford office, was called to a meeting with the general manager and the regional sales manager. The claimant was informed that the sales team was being restructured and that his position would be made redundant with immediate effect. The selection of the claimant for redundancy was based on the percentage sales volumes of the three sales development executives reporting to the Cork office. The respondent noted that the decision to implement redundancies was based on objective criteria at all stages. The claimant was aggrieved and was subsequently invited to attend a further meeting. At that meeting, the claimant refused to sign the Form RP50 on the basis that the date of termination and monetary calculations contained on the form were incorrect.

The claimant also refused to sign a waiver, which he had allegedly partially read, on the basis that it was also incorrect. The claimant noted that he was told that if he did not sign the waiver, he would not be entitled to receive the *ex gratia* element of his severance payment. The claimant alleged that the general manager did not read through the waiver with him at any stage. At a subsequent meeting, the claimant did read the waiver in full and signed both it and the Form RP50. The waiver provided that the claimant would accept the sum of €25,280.76 gross, in full and final settlement of all claims arising out of his employment or the termination thereof. The waiver explicitly stated that 'all claims' would include claims under relevant employment legislation. The waiver also provided a clause to the effect that the claimant had read and understood the terms prior to execution. The respondent noted that the claimant had played an active role in negotiating the settlement figure but did accept that the claimant had not been advised to seek independent advice prior to signing the waiver. Due to the commercial sensitivity of the redundancies and the proximity of the relationships between the sales employees and their customers, the contracts of employment were terminated 'pretty much immediately'. Last in, first out (LIFO) was applied on a site-by-site basis; however, the claimant was the only sales development executive and employee in the Waterford area at the time.

The claimant disputed his selection for redundancy but accepted that each sales development executive had a defined geographical area. A number of Dublin sales development executives were entitled by the respondent to keep their customers in Cork and Waterford and continue to work in this area. When work was serviced out to Dublin and Lurgan in 2009, the claimant followed the work and travelled to those plants at least once every month and reported to managers in Dublin, Cork and Lurgan. The claimant was expected by the respondent to sell products for all three plants. The claimant noted that he was expected to optimise on both volume and value and achieve high margins.

The claimant noted that he could not understand the reason for the timing of his redundancy as only a few days before the decision was taken he was provided with a company car. The claimant alleged that he had not been consulted on the decision to make him redundant and that voluntary redundancy, pay decreases or the prospect of alternative positions had not been considered nor communicated to the claimant at any stage by the respondent. The claimant also asserted that the entire pool of sales executives should have been considered for redundancy. The claimant noted that his contract of employment provided for one month's notice of termination of his employment. Notice could be waived and/or payment in lieu of notice could be accepted by mutual agreement. The claimant did not agree to waive his notice and wanted to work out his notice but unlike the employees in the previous redundancies, he was not allowed to work out his notice.

The respondent contended that there existed sufficient grounds for a redundancy situation. It was noted that high sales volume did not equate to high sales value and that the sales in Cork were of a higher sales value. It was further contended that fewer of the Cork-based sales development executive's customers were affected by the changes than were customers of the claimant and another sales development executive. The products that the Cork based sales development executive dealt with were more suited to Cork and the service requirements of the Cork customers were better facilitated. It was noted that the respondent decided to retain the Cork sales development executive in Cork, to transfer the Galway sales executive to Lurgan and to make the claimant redundant. The Dublin and Lurgan plants could absorb the management of the claimant's customer accounts and could service customer needs for the products transferred within their existing resources. The remainder of the claimant's accounts were absorbed by the Cork plant. It was noted that a decision was reached on 11 August 2010 to the effect that the claimant's position would be made redundant and that this decision was explained to the claimant at the meeting on 8 September 2010. It was noted that the claimant's performance was never in issue. No other vacancy existed with the respondent as 140 redundancies had taken place. The respondent denied the claimant's assertion that the Cork sales development executive, who had less service with the respondent, remained in employment during the redundancy periods as his father was a significant customer of the respondent. The respondent contended that the EAT had no jurisdiction to hear the claim as the claimant had signed a waiver and accepted payment in full and final settlement of all claims arising *inter alia* from the termination of his employment.

The EAT dealt with the issue of its jurisdiction to hear the claim in circumstances where a waiver or release had been executed by the claimant in full and final settlement of all claims. The EAT noted that despite the fact that a claim under the Unfair Dismissals Acts 1977 to 2015 was specifically excluded by the waiver, the respondent was not entitled to deny the EAT jurisdiction in circumstances where the applicant had not been advised in writing to take appropriate advice as to his employment and legal rights. The EAT further noted that in a traumatic situation for an employee such as a redundancy it is vital that he be advised to seek appropriate advice. The parties agreed that the claimant received no such advice. The EAT found that it had jurisdiction to hear the appeal.

The EAT accepted the claimant's evidence that he had only been provided with a part of the page of the policy 'Compulsory Redundancy/Restructuring Terms', and that he had not been provided with the page stating that LIFO would apply. However, the EAT noted that it had been common practice for redundancies to occur and that in such situations, the respondent had always applied the LIFO process on a site by site basis. The EAT noted that the selection of the claimant for redundancy was not unfair.

The EAT found that there was a lack of fair, or any, procedures with regard to the dismissal of the claimant and that this case was an appropriate case to exercise the discretion conferred on the EAT by s 6(7) of the Unfair Dismissals Act 1977 as substituted by s 5(b) of the Unfair Dismissals (Amendment) Act 1993 and have regard to the reasonableness, or otherwise, of the conduct (whether by act or omission) of the employer in relation to the dismissal. The EAT found that the respondent's failure to apply fair procedures in the circumstances was unreasonable and found the dismissal unfair on this basis. The appeal succeeded and the EAT awarded the claimant compensation of €10,000, in addition to a sum equivalent in amount to his redundancy lump sum and *ex gratia* payment.

VOLUNTARY REDUNDANCY/*EX-GRATIA* REDUNDANCY

[23.06] *Business Mobile Security Ltd t/a Senaca Group v A Worker*[7]*—Labour Court—appeal from recommendation of Rights Commissioner—Industrial Relations Acts 1946 to 2015—application for voluntary redundancy—obligation on employer to communicate with and assist employee with voluntary redundancy process—ability to avail of voluntary redundancy after passing of application deadline*

This case concerns an employer's refusal to accept an application for voluntary redundancy from the claimant in circumstances where the deadline for the application had passed. The claimant claimed that upon being notified of the redundancy situation, he had informed management of his intention to apply for voluntary redundancy. The claimant had not received the relevant application documentation as he was absent on annual leave and as a result, he missed the deadline for application. The respondent contended that the claimant was fully aware of the closing date for applications before leaving for holidays and that the closing date had passed before his return. The respondent, in support of its wish to accommodate all employees, noted that the scheme was in fact over-subscribed, but that all applications received in time were facilitated. The Rights Commissioner had recommended that the respondent pay the claimant compensation of €9,000.

The respondent noted that the claimant was fully aware of the closing date for applications for the voluntary redundancy scheme on offer and that the respondent and the claimant had communicated on the issue while the claimant was on holiday. The respondent noted that management could not accept the claimant's application where the claimant had not submitted his written application on time. The claimant noted he did not view the email instructing him to confirm his intention to formally apply for his

---

7.   *Business Mobile Security Ltd t/a Senaca Group v A Worker* AD151.

redundancy until he had returned from holiday at which point the date for receipt of applications had passed. The claimant submitted that confirmation of his intention to apply for voluntary redundancy and the previous expression of interest should have been sufficient for him to have been considered by the respondent for voluntary redundancy despite having missed the deadline.

The Labour Court found that both the respondent and claimant were equally responsible for the dispute which was the subject of the appeal. On this basis, the Court found that both parties should equally share the cost of the dispute. In that context the Court determined that the €9,000 recommended by the Rights Commissioner be replaced by the sum of €6,934.91, which equates to 50 per cent of the redundancy payment the claimant would have received, had he submitted an application for voluntary redundancy within the time limits set by the respondent.

[23.07] *Ages and Stages Crèche Dundalk v SIPTU[8]—Labour Court—Industrial Relations Acts 1946 to 2015, s 26(1)—claim for ex gratia redundancy payments—financial difficulties—public funds*

The respondent crèche closed in August 2014 due to financial difficulties and its workers were made redundant receiving only their statutory entitlements. The SIPTU claim for enhanced redundancy terms was rejected by the respondent for financial reasons. The parties failed to reach agreement at a Labour Relations Commission Conciliation Conference and the dispute was referred to the Labour Court.

The Court recommended accepting the Union's claim for an *ex gratia* severance payment of three weeks' pay per year of service, in addition to the workers' statutory redundancy entitlements. The Court noted that the respondent could not meet the cost of this recommendation, but also noted that a number of public agencies had funded the respondent and these agencies 'would be in a position to meet the cost of this claim'. The Court recommended that the respondent approach each of these public agencies to source funding to meet the redundancy costs.

CONDUCT OF AN EMPLOYEE DURING A REDUNDANCY PROCESS

[23.08] *McDonnell v Barclays Insurance Dublin t/a Barclays Assurance Dublin Ltd, Barclays Insurance t/a Barclays Assurance Dublin Ltd and Barclays Insurance Ltd t/a Barclays Assurance Dublin[9]—Employment Appeals Tribunal—Unfair Dismissals Acts 1977 to 2015—redundancy while claimant on sick leave—whether contractual entitlement to income protection—lack of engagement by claimant*

The claimant was employed as a product manager with the respondent company, which is in the business of providing financial services, in particular underwriting income

---

8. *Ages and Stages Crèche Dundalk v SIPTU* LCR 21017.
9. *McDonnell v Barclays Insurance Dublin t/a Barclays Assurance Dublin Ltd, Barclays Insurance t/a Barclays Assurance Dublin Ltd and Barclays Insurance Ltd t/a Barclays Assurance Dublin Ltd* UD 799/2013.

protection, since April 2010. The respondent's parent company had been downsizing the Dublin office over the course of the 24 months immediately preceding the claimant's dismissal. Redundancies had taken place which reduced the headcount in the respondent's organisation from 40 in 2011 to 27 in 2014. The claimant was made redundant in December 2012, along with three other colleagues.

The claimant went on sick leave in November 2011 and remained on sick leave until he was made redundant. A viral infection led to the claimant developing liver problems. A HR executive in the respondent communicated extensively with the claimant regarding the discontinuance of his sick pay and an application to the income continuance scheme. The application for the income continuance scheme was to be completed in part by the respondent, in part by the claimant and in part by the claimant's doctor. When the claimant had been on six months' paid sick leave, the respondent contacted the claimant in respect of the application for income continuance as per the respondent's sick pay policy. The respondent had filled in its part of the application form and sent it to the claimant, along with a required GP form and consent for medical information. Part of the income assessment process also included a visit from a claims assessor to the claimant's home and this was explained by the respondent to the claimant. The claimant, however, raised issue with the need for a visit by a claims assessor. Extensive communication followed between the HR executive and the claimant. The claimant refused to deal with the insurance company which underwrote the income protection scheme and maintained that it was the respondent's responsibility to deal with the insurance company. The claimant argued that the respondent was contractually obliged to provide him with income protection and that the contract for income protection was between the respondent and the insurance company. Accordingly, since there was no contractual relationship between the claimant and the insurance company, it was the respondent's obligation to complete the claimant's application for income protection. The HR executive repeatedly explained that the respondent could not fill out the claimant's part of the form on his behalf, nor could the respondent fill out the part of the application form that was to be filled out by the claimant's doctor.

The claimant initiated the grievance procedure. He complained that the medical information being sought by the third party insurance company was far in excess of what the respondent sought at the commencement of his employment and he was contractually entitled to the income continuance. In evidence, the claimant contended that he had never refused to sign the salary protection application form and that he had merely wanted the respondent to confirm that it was the owner of the policy and therefore responsibility rested with the respondent. This was the crux of the matter for the claimant. In addition the claimant had sought a copy of the policy document since May 2012 but did not receive it until October 2012, due to a misunderstanding on the part of the respondent.

The redundancy process involving the claimant commenced on 10 September 2012. All staff members were briefed and, as the claimant was absent on sick leave, he was contacted by telephone by the head of operations who informed him that his role was at risk of redundancy. The claimant received formal notification and information on the redundancy and consultation process by post. The claimant's sick leave was not considered as part of the redundancy selection process and the claimant was invited to consider alternative roles that were available within the organisation. The claimant expressed an interest in two other roles; maternity cover for production manager role and a data analyst role. Both of these roles were different to the role occupied by the claimant.

The head of operations contacted the claimant on 2 October 2012 to inform him that his role would be made redundant on 22 October 2012. The claimant was informed of his right to appeal. He was also informed that two others had expressed an interest in the data analyst role and that he should confirm if he was applying for it and that there would be an interview process. The claimant was invited to attend an interview for the data analyst role on 19 October 2012. The claimant replied that he was unfit for interview and contended again that he was entitled to income continuance.

The two other applicants for the data analyst role turned it down and therefore the claimant was offered the position without having interviewed for it. A new contract for this role was sent to the claimant. The claimant was offered the same salary and his service was preserved. However, the respondent's pension policy had changed from a defined benefit to a defined contribution scheme for all new entrants from 1 January 2012 and this change was reflected in the new contract. The change in pension benefits became an issue for the claimant. The offer of the data analyst role was made subject to the claimant accepting and signing terms and conditions of the new contract. The claimant then contended that no new contract was required. The respondent informed the claimant that his old position was redundant and that he should return the new contract for the data analyst role (signed by him) by 8 November 2012 or the respondent would conclude that he had refused the alternative position and his redundancy would proceed.

On 22 November 2012 the head of operations informed the claimant that his employment would terminate on 22 December 2012. The claimant indicated that he would appeal through the grievance procedure; however he was initially told that it would be dealt with through the appeals procedure. The managing director decided to deal with the claimant's issues through the grievance procedure as other issues arose at the appeal.

The claimant's specific grievances related to: his role being redundant, the withdrawal of the data analyst role, the terms and conditions of the new role (specifically the worsening of pension entitlements) and the income protection scheme. The claimant contended that he should have been on the income protection scheme by the time that the redundancy consultation period occurred and that the data analyst role should have been held open for him until he returned from sick leave. The managing director listened to all the claimant's grievances at the grievance meeting, at which the claimant declined representation, and afterwards investigated all of them. The managing director gave evidence that he was concerned because he believed that if the grievances were substantiated they were very serious. The managing director reviewed the claimant's file, correspondence, the income protection policy, the respondent's handbook and the claimant's contract of employment.

The managing director found that the communication in regard to the withdrawal of the data analyst role was very clear. The role was withdrawn because the new contract had not been signed by the claimant even though he was given many opportunities and extensions to sign. The claimant believed that his contract could be amended to suit the new position but the managing director believed that it was the right of the respondent, not the claimant, to change the contract. Regarding the income protection scheme, the managing director felt that it was clear that there was a policy in place with a third party company and, as such, there would be claim forms to be filled in. The claimant worked for the respondent in the insurance business. The claimant had a health insurance policy through the respondent which required him to claim directly from the third-party insurance company. The managing director was satisfied that the claimant was clearly informed that he had to fill in the forms. He was satisfied that the correspondence from the respondent was very fair and that the income protection scheme was not initiated because the claimant did not fill in the forms. The claimant's grievances were not upheld.

The EAT found that none of the tasks being asked of the claimant in respect of the income continuance application was particularly onerous nor was there anything untoward in the assumption that the claimant was the person best placed to provide the details required for the application. In addition, the EAT stated that it must attribute to the claimant a better understanding of insurance than many people, given he had actually worked in the industry.

The claimant's lack of engagement during this period of time was neither condoned nor understood by the EAT which held that the correspondence demonstrated an almost wilful refusal to engage with, and understand, the true need to facilitate a claim. While the correspondence also discloses a growing frustration within the respondent, there can be no doubt that its personnel were anxious to get this matter dealt with expeditiously and successfully.

The EAT noted that the insurance policy forms were never completed and an application for indemnification was never made. The EAT found that it could not know whether the claim would have been successful and equally it could not know what the respondent would have done had it been unsuccessful. The EAT stated:

> Suffice to say that the employer appeared to this division of the Tribunal to have acted with fairness despite the frustrating attitude of the claimant. It is further noted that the claimant was on two-thirds of his basic salary up to the date of his dismissal.

The EAT found the claimant's reasoning to have been clouded and, at times, obdurate. The EAT also found that allegations of discrimination by the claimant were ill-founded and inflammatory. While the engagement between the parties on the issue of income protection had no real bearing on the eventual termination of the employment, it was regrettable that there was an exceptional delay in getting the policy document to the claimant.

The EAT accepted that the claimant would have been disappointed that the defined benefit pension plan was being replaced by a defined contribution plan and it was understandable that he sought to preserve the terms and conditions of his previously-held contract of employment, wherein the defined benefit plan was articulated. The EAT noted that this change was being effected for all employees.

The EAT accepted that the claimant's position was made redundant. The EAT found that, arising out of that redundancy, the contract of employment attaching to that job was also made redundant and the claimant had no entitlement to insist that his old contract of employment together with its terms and conditions could transfer seamlessly to the new position. The new position of data analyst was created in a post-restructuring and redundancy era. Employees had the choice to take their redundancy or look for one of the newly-created positions. The fact that the terms attaching to the new positions were less attractive is not relevant as the position is taken subject to these openly acknowledged terms. The claimant had the choice and, in the end, his actions led to him refusing the position and being made redundant.

The EAT noted that the claimant was given numerous opportunities to prevent the redundancy confirmation arising and that the respondent was effectively forced to make a stand at the end of a protracted period of prevarication and obfuscation.

The EAT found that there was no unfair dismissal. The EAT further noted that the ongoing interaction between the parties after the redundancy had no bearing on the lawfulness of the termination of employment.

SELECTION FOR REDUNDANCY

[23.09] *Dolan v Bruscar Bhearna Teoranta t/a Barna Waste[10]—Employment Appeals Tribunal—Unfair Dismissals Acts 1977 to 2015—unfair dismissal—redundancy— failure to act in fair and reasonable manner—failure to apply selection criteria or last in first out rule*

The claimant was employed by the respondent company in sales and marketing. The respondent gave evidence that the claimant was a good employee and he worked hard and completed his tasks satisfactorily. The business of the respondent was profitable in the 2000's and was expanding into the areas of recycling and composting. However, the recession resulted in financial difficulties and the business went into examinership in April 2013. As a consequence of this, cost-cutting measures were introduced which included redundancies and pay cuts. The respondent decided to cut the number of employees in sales and marketing from 13 to 3 and this included the claimant. The HR manager wrote to all 13 sales employees on 29 August 2013 telling them their positions would be redundant from 25 October 2013 and invited anyone interested to apply for one of the three customer service representative posts. The customer service representative post required a C1 driving licence. The claimant did not have a C1 driving licence. The respondent gave evidence that if the claimant had expressed interest in the new position he would have been given time to undertake the necessary training and to take the test for a C1 driving licence. The claimant was not informed of this.

The claimant gave evidence that he thought he had asked the respondent about the last in first out rule. He also gave evidence that he thought that he would be kept on. The claimant did not apply for one of the customer service representative posts because he did not have a C1 licence and nobody had told him the time would be extended. Only

---

10.   *Dolan v Bruscar Bhearna Teoranta t/a Barna Waste* UD762/2014.

one of the 13 relevant employees applied for the new post and that candidate was interviewed, found suitable and appointed. The financial controller of the respondent accepted in evidence the respondent did have a selection process for redundancy but that no selection procedure or selection matrix were applied.

The EAT acknowledged that, in order to enable the business to survive, costs had to be cut. The EAT accepted that the respondent was faced with serious financial difficulties and needed to take action to address the situation. The EAT found however that there was an onus on the respondent to act in a reasonable and fair manner. In this regard, the respondent's Employee Handbook provided for the use of a 'selection matrix' or last in first out in the event of a redundancy situation arising. The respondent did not use either.

The EAT found that a redundancy situation existed, however the three new positions were similar to the point of being almost identical with the 13 existing roles that were being made redundant. Accordingly the EAT found that it would have been appropriate for the respondent to have used a selection procedure to decide who would be made redundant and which employees would be retained in the three remaining roles.

The EAT found that the respondent's failure to use any selection procedure, either as outlined in the Employee Handbook or other suitable procedure, rendered the termination of the claimant's employment unfair. The claimant was awarded compensation of €7,500.

[23.10] *Coad v Eurobase Ltd[11]—Employment Appeals Tribunal—Unfair Dismissals Acts 1977 to 2015—redundancy—unfair selection for redundancy—selection criteria for redundancy—need to retain skills basis—whether fair procedures were followed in making claimant redundant—whether alternatives to redundancy considered— onus on claimant to mitigate his loss*

The claimant commenced work as a machine operator with the respondent in August 2011 and was made redundant in June 2013. Although it was accepted that there was a need for redundancy, the claimant alleged that he was unfairly selected. The respondent disputed this allegation and stated that selection was carried out on a need to retain skills basis.

The electronics manager gave evidence that, due to the loss of a major customer, there was a downturn in the respondent's business. The loss of this customer affected the surface mount machine area where the claimant worked, rather than the soldering area. In order for an employee to work in the soldering area, FÁS certification was needed and this involved a 10-week training course and was only available to people who had been unemployed for a certain period. The claimant did not have this certification. Furthermore, he did not do soldering work and worked on the less skilled end of the machine line, rather than the end which required setting up the programme. The respondent could not afford the cost of training current employees, such as the claimant, to get FÁS soldering certification as the cost was prohibitive (approximately €60,000).

---

11.   *Coad v Eurobase Ltd* UD1138/2013.

Staff members were informed at meetings in June 2013 of the difficulties. On 14 June 2013, the electronics manager wrote to the claimant informing him that staff in the surface mount machine area would be reduced following assessment by matrix. The claimant was also informed that the staff would be retained on a need to retain skills basis. On 19 June 2013 the claimant was informed that he was being made redundant as and from 28 June 2013.

The electronics manager gave evidence that she considered alternatives such as short time, but that this would not work due to skill requirements. Out of the six employees on the machine line, two had been made redundant. In cross-examination it was put to the electronics manager that two employees who had commenced with the respondent in April 2013 were retained over the claimant. She explained that this was because both of these employees had the certification for soldering. It was put to her that the claimant could and did do soldering. The electronics manager's response was that if he did it was minimal. It was further put to her that the claimant could and did work at both ends of the machine line. In response she said that once the line was set up, even if the other person on the more skilled end of the line took a break, the line could continue without input from the claimant. Finally, it was put to the electronics manager in cross-examination that soldering had not been included on the matrix.

The managing director and founder of the respondent company reiterated the electronics manager's evidence and stressed the difficult situation the respondent found itself in and its efforts to ensure the survival of the respondent.

The claimant stated he was a qualified electrician and had been self-employed prior to commencing work with the respondent. He maintained that he could and did work on both ends of the machine line, for example when an operator was on a break or was off for some reason. He said he could solder and did do some soldering in the respondent company. The claimant disputed that the respondent had considered all available options. He said that some of the people on the machine line could do soldering and could have been moved to the soldering area instead of hiring two new people in April 2013 and letting two employees go. The claimant maintained that he had not been permitted to see the matrix assessment for other employees and stated that there had been no mention of an appeal regarding the decision to make him redundant.

During cross examination the claimant accepted that the two employees taken on in April had different qualifications and could carry out soldering, but he stressed that he could do it too. It was put to the claimant that he did discuss the decision to make him redundant with the managing director, and that he asked her to let him remain on until he had the two years' service in order to claim redundancy, as this would enable him to access the back-to-education allowance scheme. The claimant stated that he decided to go back to education only because his job was finishing and that he would have taken a job if one was available. He gave evidence of his loss and his efforts to mitigate same. He notified the EAT that he had gone back to education in September 2014 to study electrical engineering.

It was accepted by all parties and by the EAT that the respondent needed to effect a redundancy due to a downturn in its business. Regarding the selection process, the EAT found that due to the fact that 'last in first out' was not applied, the claimant (with service of almost two years) was selected for redundancy and two employees who had only about two month's service were retained. This was because the redundancies were made on a need to retain skills basis and these two employees had completed a 10-week soldering course with FÁS and received the necessary certification. The EAT concluded that the respondent did not adequately or at all consider alternatives to redundancy, such as moving one or two of the machine line operators with soldering skills to the soldering area instead of retaining the two FÁS trained employees. The EAT considered that had they done so, there would have been no need to make the claimant redundant. The EAT further found that the procedures used in effecting the redundancies were rushed. However, it did not believe that the respondent had acted in bad faith, but rather acted in the immediacy of the situation it found itself in.

In the circumstances, the EAT concluded that the claimant was unfairly selected for redundancy and was not afforded adequate procedures, therefore the claimant was unfairly dismissed and the claim succeeded. The EAT awarded the claimant compensation of €4,400. In calculating the level of compensation the EAT took into consideration the efforts of the claimant to mitigate his losses and found that these efforts did not meet the standard set by the EAT in *Sheehan v Continental Administration Co Ltd*[12] that:

> a claimant who finds himself out of work should employ a reasonable amount of
> time each weekday in seeking work. It is not enough to inform agencies that you
> are available for work nor merely to post an application to various companies
> seeking work ... The time that a claimant finds on his hands is not his own, unless
> he chooses it to be, but rather to be profitably employed in seeking to mitigate his
> loss.[13]

[23.11] *Cranitch v Matflo Engineering Ltd*[14]*—Employment Appeals Tribunal— Unfair Dismissals Acts 1977 to 2015—redundancy—whether claimant validly made redundant and whether fairly selected—consideration of selection criteria*

The claimant worked for the respondent's engineering and fabrication business from January 1989, originally as a steel fabricator but was later promoted to the position of foreman of the workshop. The respondent had a core staff of ten working in the workshop, as well as two directors working in the business. Evidence was that the business began to decline in 2009, and in 2010 workers were put on a three-day week for 13 weeks; but the business continued to operate on a five day per week basis. The situation deteriorated in 2011 and three-day weeks were introduced on two separate occasions. The respondent's evidence was that in 2012 the business was barely surviving and the employees were again put on short time as the business was in survival mode and was accumulating debt.

After a period of 20 weeks sick leave, the claimant returned to work in October 2012 and sought a three-day week. A week later employees were put on a three-day week and there was mention of voluntary redundancies. The employees were informed the

---

12.   *Sheehan v Continental Administration Co Ltd* UD858/1999.
13.   *Sheehan v Continental Administration Co Ltd* UD858/1999.
14.   *Cranitch v Matflo Engineering Ltd* UD1368/2013.

business was quiet and that they were being made redundant. The respondent's evidence was that voluntary redundancy was offered to staff in October 2012 and, while the claimant enquired about it, he lost interest because it was only on a statutory redundancy basis. As no-one availed of the offer, the only option open to the respondent was to make six of the ten workforce redundant.

Redundancy selection was based on the future needs of the business and the four best workers with essential skills to meet orders were retained. The respondent conceded that last in first out was not applied. Evidence to the EAT was that the four employees retained had the skills required to keep the business viable as follows: employee A owned a computerised plasma cutting machine which the respondent purchased from him and he was the only employee who could work the machine; employee B was the only spray painter in the business; employee C was a leading steel fabricator in the business and did all the work for one of the major customers; and employee D was also a senior steel fabricator and, like the claimant, he was with the respondent from commencement but he was not a foreman.

The claimant was the workshop foreman and due to the reduction in number of employees in the workshop, a foreman was no longer required and this position was therefore selected for redundancy. The respondent's evidence was that the claimant was a valued employee with long service. Although the respondent did consider retraining him, due to the precarious financial situation of the respondent there was no time to retrain him and risk losing remaining customers.

On 1 November 2012, the respondent's managing director met with those being made redundant to inform them of who was being retained and why. The managing director met with the claimant in his office for this purpose. A letter to the claimant stated that his redundancy would be effected on 31 December 2012 and detailed the amount of his redundancy payment. The claimant queried why he had been selected for redundancy as he had trained one of the employees being retained but he did not receive a satisfactory response. He was never told why he was selected for redundancy. On 6 November, the claimant approached the managing director in an aggressive manner about his redundancy and an altercation ensued. Thereafter, the managing director told the claimant that he was not required to work out his notice and handed him a letter to this effect, enclosing a cheque equivalent to eight weeks of wages.

The claimant accepted the business could operate without a foreman and that the position was genuinely made redundant but he asserted there had been no prior consultation and no notice of redundancy and that he was not told what criteria was used to select him. The claimant maintained he was capable of taking up all remaining positions with the exception of operating the plasma machine.

The EAT held that a genuine redundancy situation did exist and that the claimant's position of foreman, which was a unique position in the respondent, was made redundant. The EAT noted that more than 50 per cent of the employees were made redundant and those best suited to business requirements were retained in employment. The reasons for retention in employment were explained to the claimant and the other employees who were made redundant. The claimant was made aware why he was selected for redundancy. The EAT held that the claimant's dismissal did not come within the circumstances set out in s 6(3) of the Unfair Dismissals Acts which would render the dismissal for redundancy unfair. While under s 6(4)(c) redundancy is a fair reason for dismissal, s 6(7) provides, in determining whether a dismissal is unfair, the EAT may have regard where it considers it appropriate 'to the reasonableness or otherwise of the conduct (whether by act or omission) of the employer in relation to the dismissal'.

The EAT, in exercising this discretion held that it did not find that the respondent had acted unreasonably in failing to engage in a consultation process. In circumstances where the business was in serious decline, short time was implemented on more than one occasion voluntary redundancies were sought and more than half the workforce was made redundant. The EAT held that the dismissal was not unfair and that the claim failed.

[23.12] *O'Connor v Cove Brewers Ltd t/a Cove Bar*[15]*—Employment Appeals Tribunal—Unfair Dismissals Acts 1977 to 2015—redundancy—unfair dismissal— unfair selection for redundancy in circumstances where no prior consultation with claimant and no alternatives considered*

The claimant worked as a kitchen porter for the respondent bar, commencing employment in June 2011. Her duties entailed washing up and cleaning the kitchen area. She also assisted the chef in preparing vegetables and making sandwiches. The respondent runs a bar and serves bar food, operating seven days a week. Four to five staff work in the kitchen and two to three staff are bartenders. Due to a downturn in business, the directors of the business decided that staff hours were to be reduced. Evidence was given that it was an ongoing process to cut back staff hours over a period of three to four months. The respondent's position was that the claimant worked efficiently as a kitchen porter and her role entailed washing up and cleaning in the kitchen area. The respondent's evidence was that the claimant never prepared or served during her tenure. In October 2013, a new kitchen assistant was employed by the respondent whose role entailed helping out with the cooking of food and cleaning up.

In December 2013, the claimant was informed that she was being let go as the kitchen was under pressure and their hours were being cut. There was not enough work for a second kitchen porter and the existing kitchen porter had longer service than the claimant. The claimant's position was that when the new kitchen assistant was employed she showed her how to use the dishwasher and explained washer duties as the kitchen porter. The claimant was taken aback on hearing of her redundancy and was upset, as she had not seen it coming. The claimant had been unable to secure alternative employment since her employment came to an end.

The EAT concluded that the respondent had failed to meet the onus on it to demonstrate that the claimant had been fairly dismissed. The EAT accepted the respondent needed to re-organise its business to meet financial challenges but the EAT was not satisfied that due regard was had to potential alternatives that may have been available to the respondent, short of dismissing the claimant. The EAT noted there was no prior consultation with the claimant and no opportunity was given to her to make any observations or suggestions around her dismissal. The position was simply presented as

---

15. *O'Connor v Cove Brewers Ltd t/a Cove Bar* UD464/2014.

a fait accompli. The EAT noted that no evidence as to any alternatives was presented. The EAT also noted that in a relatively short period before the claimant's dismissal a new employee was taken on. While this new employee had the title of kitchen assistant, as opposed to the claimant's title of kitchen porter, her arrival clearly saw her take over duties of both the claimant and of a fellow colleague. The EAT concluded that the introduction of this new employee and the consequent reduction of the claimant's hours had led to a situation where her services were no longer required. The EAT held that there was something intrinsically unfair in the claimant's selection for redundancy in the particular set of circumstances. The EAT upheld the claim of unfair dismissal and awarded the claimant compensation of €6,000.

[23.13] *Morris v Callan Tansey Solicitors[16]—Employment Appeals Tribunal—Unfair Dismissals Acts 1977 to 2015—unfair selection for redundancy—objective selection criteria—availability of positions in alternative work locations*

The claimant commenced employment with the respondent law firm as a legal secretary in July 1980, and worked in a full time capacity until 1995. Thereafter, with the agreement of the respondent, she worked part time until the termination of her employment by reason of redundancy in July 2013. The respondent had offices in Sligo Town and in Boyle, Co Roscommon, and the claimant worked her entire career in the Boyle office.

The managing partner of the respondent gave evidence that in April/May 2013 the firm employed three partners, two solicitors, and eight support staff (including the claimant) in the Boyle office. Due to the economic downturn from 2008 onwards, the partners were obliged to make decisions in relation to personnel to maintain the practice's long-term security. There was a decrease in private client work, conveyancing, probate, and District Court litigation. The partners reviewed the cost base and resources and it was in that context that the positions of secretarial staff had to be reviewed.

Evidence was given that on 1 May 2013, the three partners met separately with the claimant, and another secretary and indicated to them that their positions were under threat and it was possible that they would be made redundant. The claimant gave evidence that she enquired at this meeting if there were any other options available and the managing partner said that there were not and that the decision was made. The claimant gave evidence that she was not offered the opportunity of having representation at the meeting and was in shock after it. She told the EAT that no attendance notes were taken at the meeting and she was never provided with any selection criteria. She was never informed of any means by which she could appeal the decision and was offered no alternative to redundancy. The claimant told the EAT that she was the longest-serving member of staff and had been given no warning whatsoever of her redundancy.

Three full-time positions subsequently became available in the Sligo office. The partners met with the secretaries again (including the claimant) and offered them alternative positions in the Sligo office. The claimant informed the partners by email that she would not be accepting the proposal. The claimant gave evidence to the EAT

---

16. *Morris v Callan Tansey Solicitors* UD143/2014.

that she believed that the firm was 'covering their tracks' by making such an offer, as the Sligo office was 48 km from her home. The claimant stated that it was not feasible for her to accept this offer of a full-time position due to her domestic circumstances. It was subsequently confirmed to the claimant that her employment would terminate due to redundancy, and the claimant was paid her statutory redundancy entitlement, her notice entitlement and outstanding holidays. The claimant's position was not replaced in the firm.

The respondent accepted that no indication was given to the claimant prior to the meeting of 1 May 2013 that her position was at risk of redundancy and there was no selection criteria provided to the claimant. The respondent confirmed that the firm did not seek voluntary redundancies. The managing partner confirmed that another secretary was also made redundant and that the firm did not apply a policy of last in first out (LIFO).

The EAT noted that no meaningful consultation took place between the respondent and the claimant. The respondent failed to give advance warning of the nature of the meeting of 1 May 2013 when the claimant was informed that the decision to make her redundant had been made. The claimant was not afforded an appeal procedure. Furthermore, she was not offered the opportunity of having representation at the aforementioned meeting and at the follow-up meeting on 24 May 2013. There were no written notes or memos of the meetings. There was no attempt to secure a voluntary redundancy. No consideration was given to an alternative to redundancy, such as a pay cut or reduced hours and the respondent did not consider a LIFO policy. The EAT noted that the offer to the claimant of a full-time position in the Sligo office was not a viable option due to her domestic situation, Sligo being 48km from the claimant's home.

The EAT held that the respondent acted unreasonably in failing to apply objective criteria to the selection of the claimant for redundancy. The EAT found that the claimant was unfairly selected for redundancy and was unfairly dismissed accordingly. The EAT awarded the claimant the sum of €12,765.06 under the Acts and noted that this award was separate and distinct from any redundancy payment already paid to the claimant.

[23.14] *MacEvilly v KOD/Lyons Solicitors[17]—Employment Appeals Tribunal— Unfair Dismissals Acts 1977 to 2015—redundancy—unfair selection for redundancy in circumstances where merger of two solicitor firms—whether selection criteria unfair and loaded against claimant*

The claimant was a criminal law solicitor employed by the respondent, having previously transferred to that entity under the transfer of undertakings legislation[18] from a firm known as TL & Co Ltd, following a merger with KOD Solicitors. The claimant joined the practice of TL & Co Ltd in 2001 and worked as a solicitor in the criminal courts. Following the death of the firm's principal solicitor, another colleague took over the practice and worked alongside the claimant for a number of years. It was accepted

---

17. *MacEvilly v KOD/Lyons Solicitors* UD805/2013.
18. European Communities (Protection of Employees on Transfer of Undertakings) Regulations 2003.

that the claimant had built up considerable expertise with the bulk of her work being in the criminal courts, particularly in the District Court at Blanchardstown. A decision was taken to merge the practice with another criminal law practice, KOD Solicitors. By mid-2010 a process of due diligence was under way and the claimant's evidence to the EAT was that she became aware in January 2011 of a rumour that the practice was being taken over. The claimant's evidence was that this was not something she was expecting and she previously had an understanding that she could achieve partnership in the current practice. The claimant's evidence was that she had no knowledge what the merger would mean for her, or indeed any of her colleagues, and in fact, the formal merger was not announced until August 2011.

The EAT noted that all of the employees involved in a merger of this sort could have expected a process of rationalisation; as between the two workplaces there was staff of nearly 50 people. Undoubtedly the support staff, such as secretarial and administrative staff, would be expected to be anxious. Additionally the EAT held that professional staff would have needed to assess where they stood. For example, the claimant knew, or ought to have known, that one of the partners in KOD/Lyons Solicitors was on permanent assignment to the courthouse in Blanchardstown where the claimant worked most days. The EAT noted that this fact must have occurred to the claimant. Furthermore the EAT accepted that the claimant could not consider herself to have been insulated from the commercial realities around her as she had taken a 10 per cent drop in salary in 2010 and there had also been a redundancy in her firm. In addition, the enormous reduction in criminal legal aid fees would have been well known to her.

The EAT noted that, following the announcement of the merger, there followed a long period of inactivity and the process of merging took considerably longer than anyone expected. Following the merger, the merger team made a decision that some redundancies would have to be made. The EAT noted that there were eleven solicitors in the new entity of which five were partners. This left a pool of six solicitors whose jobs were in focus.

The EAT heard considerable evidence as to the composition of the selection pool and noted that ultimately three solicitors were exempt from the selection pool on the grounds that their jobs were distinct and unique within the framework of the practice. One worked in the civil courts, one handled immigration and the other specialised in the area of social welfare.

A decision was taken to reduce the selection pool to three persons, the claimant and two other solicitors. The EAT noted that, extraordinarily, length of service was not a consideration and instead each of the three solicitors was assessed on what they proposed to bring into the practice rather than what they had achieved in the past. In October 2012, the claimant was invited to a meeting with three partners at which time she was told she was in a pool being considered for redundancy. The claimant's evidence to the EAT was that she was utterly shocked at this fact. No indication had been given to her that the merger might jeopardise her position as a solicitor of eleven years standing and the EAT noted that, in the years preceding the merger, there had been discussions about partnership opportunities for the claimant within her existing firm. The Tribunal noted that, while the claimant probably recognised that the merger would diminish her chances of becoming a partner, she clearly had no expectation that her services, loyalty and hard work would be discarded.

The EAT recognised that the merger was always going to be difficult and there was an inevitability that long-standing employees would feel themselves personally slighted. The EAT accepted that the claimant had been informed, but hadn't understood the significance of the fact that one of her colleagues, who had less service than her but who was part of the merger team, had been made a partner. This colleague was junior to the claimant and had been made a partner ahead of her; and while this, of itself, may not be hugely relevant, in this case it was relevant, as the partnership immediately excluded this colleague from being in the selection pool with the claimant. In addition, one of the other persons within the selection pool appeared on the firm website to have been appointed to head of the circuit criminal court practice, a position which the claimant believed she could, with her experience, have been easily trained up for. The claimant's evidence was that it appeared as if there was a concerted effort to protect others, thereby leaving her exposed. The EAT noted the most obvious difficultly for the claimant was the fact that among the KOD Solicitors there was a partner who exclusively handled the criminal and District Court in Blanchardstown where the claimant herself had carried out a significant portion of her practice. The EAT held it was obvious that this clear duplication of roles would be unnecessary into the future and if the partner was not willing to diversify, then the claimant should have realised this would cause her difficulty. The EAT also noted that her employer knew from the time of the initiation of their merger that this situation was untenable and encouragement should have been given, and provision made, to encourage the claimant to diversify.

As a consequence of her employer's failure to look at the claimant's current role, the EAT held that partners had, in effect, painted the claimant into a corner which created an inevitability of redundancy for her, and her alone. The EAT concluded that from a starting point in 2010 up to the end of 2012, the claimant's usefulness to the firm had been wound down. The EAT accepted on balance that the selection process was not fair, as the claimant arrived at the process with no warning and was competing against colleagues who had been actively encouraged to diversify their practices when the claimant was given no hint that diversification could create a protective shield around her. The criteria of 'additional value' and diversification into other areas was unfair in circumstances where the claimant was given one day to show how this had been, and would be, achieved, albeit further time was ultimately granted. In addition, certain solicitors were ring-fenced for exclusion in a manner which appeared to the EAT to be unfair. The EAT accepted that the redundancy selection process was unfair and could be perceived to have been loaded against the claimant. The claimant's dismissal was unfair and the failure to have an appeals procedure further compounded this unfairness. The EAT took into account the genuine effort made by the claimant to get on with her career and awarded her compensation of €80,000 making a deduction for a redundancy payment of €14,388 which had already been paid to her.

ENTITLEMENT TO REDUNDANCY PAYMENT

[23.15] *Ruane v Bridie Lyons t/a C Lyons Tractor Sales*[19]*—Employment Appeals Tribunal—appeal from decision of Rights Commissioner—Redundancy Payments Acts 1967 to 2014—entitlement to redundancy payment—reinstatement after successful appeal—failure of employer to communicate status of employee—failure to make claimant redundant due to period of suspension*

The claimant commenced employment with the respondent, a small family-run business, in June 1990. The respondent issued the claimant with written terms and conditions in 2012, which he refused to sign for various reasons. The statement of terms stated the claimant's position to be that of stores manager; but, the claimant also had a sales role. By the middle of 2011, the respondent had lost its agency business of selling tractors. In November 2011, the claimant's employment was terminated on the grounds of alleged misconduct. The claimant appealed the decision to dismiss him.

In December 2011, the claimant received a letter from the independent investigator who had heard his appeal informing him that the decision to terminate his employment had been overturned and that he would be reinstated in his original position effective from the date he was dismissed. However, he was simultaneously suspended without pay pending the outcome of a referral of the incident to An Garda Síochána.

The respondent maintained that the claimant remained on suspension and had not been dismissed at any point. In evidence, the claimant stated that the respondent had made all of its employees redundant by the end of December 2011. The claimant provided photographic evidence that there had been a sign on the respondent's premises since late December 2011 stating that the premises was closed for business. The claimant stated that he had received no communication from the respondent since late 2011. In February 2012, the claimant commenced employment with another employer.

The respondent informed the EAT that in 2011, it conducted a review of each aspect of the business. The respondent stated that it had been advised to keep the stores/parts section of the business open as it remained the only profitable part of the business. The claimant was employed in this part of the business. The owners accepted this advice and permanently shut down the other parts of the business in December 2011. A number of office staff and workshop employees were made redundant at this time. The respondent stated that the stores part of the business where the claimant was employed, remained open and in business. The respondent informed the EAT that the 'closed' sign on the gates of the premises had only been placed on the premises' gates for the period of the 2011 Christmas holidays. The respondent, in evidence, stated that the sign had been removed in January 2012, as part of the business was still running. The claimant had been suspended without pay from his position of stores manager at this time, pending the outcome of the disciplinary matter. The respondent informed the EAT that it had hired another employee to assist with the claimant's duties while the claimant remained on suspension. That new employee subsequently left the business in May 2012 when he secured alternative employment. He was not replaced and the respondent's owners

---

19. *Ruane v Bridie Lyons t/a C Lyons Tractor Sales* RP159/2012, MN174/2012.

continued to carry out the original employees' duties until the stores part of the business closed in December 2012. The respondent contended that the claimant continued to be an employee and had remained on a period of suspension at all times. The respondent stated that the claimant was never dismissed, had not been made redundant and was never issued with a P45. The respondent stated that the claimant had secured employment with an alternative employer in early 2012 during his period of suspension while still engaged as an employee of the respondent. The claimant maintained that his employment ceased with the respondent prior to the end of January 2012 and that he was entitled to a redundancy payment.

The EAT noted the conflict of evidence between the parties. The EAT was satisfied that the respondent's business was winding down from late 2011 and that the respondent ultimately ceased trading on 21 December 2012. All of the remaining staff had previously been made redundant with the exception of the claimant, who was reinstated as a result of an internal appeals process, effective from his date of dismissal of 8 November 2011. The EAT noted that the claimant had not been dismissed by the respondent at any point but did note that if the claimant had not been on a period of suspension, he would have been made redundant as the stores manager position no longer existed. The EAT found that the claimant's claim for redundancy succeeded despite he not having been dismissed or made redundant. The EAT awarded the claimant a lump sum payment under the Redundancy Payments Acts 1967 to 2014. The claim under the Minimum Notice and Terms of Employment Acts 1973 to 2005 failed as no evidence had been presented by the claimant in this regard.

OFFERS OF ALTERNATIVE EMPLOYMENT

[23.16] *Essalhi-Ferenc v Fitzers Holdings Ltd[20]—Employment Appeals Tribunal— Redundancy Payments Acts 1967 to 2014—whether claimant unreasonably refused suitable alternative employment—whether entitled to redundancy payment*

The claimant worked mainly as a waitress in one of the respondent's restaurants but she also worked manager shifts for which she was paid extra. Following the cessation of business at her restaurant, the claimant was offered a post which was considered to be sufficiently near to her former location; although it was conceded that it was not possible to offer her a post at the respondent's restaurant nearest to that where she previously worked. The claimant maintained that the alternative post offered was not suitable in terms of its location and the terms and conditions associated with it. Before the EAT, detailed testimony was proffered, maps were studied and the availability of public transport was detailed as were shift times. The EAT considered child-minding arrangements and noted that the claimant was not enthused at being asked whether she could have cycled to the new location. It was also noted that there was no mention of any examination by the claimant of the possibility of her getting a lift to and from work. Evidence was given for the respondent that the claimant could have had as many manager shifts at the new location as had been offered to her in the past.

---

20.   *Essalhi-Ferenc v Fitzers Holdings Ltd* RP94/2014.

The EAT was satisfied that the holding company of the respondent group assumed responsibility for the closure of the respondent's business without objection from the claimant. The closure arose as a direct result of a failure to resolve a difficulty between the respondent and its landlord. The EAT noted that when the issue with the landlord presented itself it was immediately relayed to the staff of the respondent, including the claimant, and efforts were made to provide staff with alternatives.

The EAT considered whether a suitable alternative had been offered to the claimant and whether she had unreasonably refused it. The EAT noted the location of the claimant's proposed new employment and compared it with her former location. The EAT accepted that a moderate increase in travel time and probable moderate additional expense would have arisen for her. The EAT also examined the written commitment given by the respondent to the claimant, undertaking to preserve the same terms and conditions that were present in her former employment in the new position. The EAT found and determined that: (a) the refusal of the claimant to accept the position offered to her because of its location was, in the circumstances, unreasonable; and (b) the concerns of the claimant in respect of the proposed full implementation of the terms and conditions of her previous employment in her new position were not well founded.

The EAT determined that the respondent had provided a suitable alternative employment to the claimant which she had unreasonably refused and thus she was not entitled to a redundancy payment as claimed.

[23.17] *McBride v Ladbroke (Ireland) Ltd*[21]*—Employment Appeals Tribunal—appeal from decision of Rights Commissioner—Redundancy Payments Acts 1967 to 2014— offer of alternative employment affecting entitlement to statutory redundancy payment*

This case was an appeal of a Rights Commissioner decision in which it was held that the claimant was not entitled to a payment under the Redundancy Payments Acts 1969 to 2014.

The claimant was employed as a customer service advisor in one of the respondent's shops in Cork from 25 April 2007 to 31 August 2014. The claimant, along with other staff members, was invited to attend a group meeting on 12 August 2014 where they were informed that the store that they were working in would close on 19 August 2014. The employees were provided with an information pack containing, inter alia, an options/preference form for completion to indicate their preference for redundancy or redeployment to a suitable alternative role. Individual meetings were subsequently held with the affected employees.

The EAT noted that there was a conflict in evidence between what the respondent and claimant said occurred at this meeting.

The claimant asserted that his role was made redundant on 12 August 2014 and that the respondent informed him that there would be no redeployment opportunities for him. The claimant submitted that, on that basis, he initially informed the respondent that he wished to avail of a redundancy package.

---

21.   *McBride v Ladbroke (Ireland) Ltd* RP788/2014.

The respondent's evidence was that this meeting commenced the 30-day consultation period, which would result either in redundancy or redeployment for the employees concerned. The respondent asserted that the employees were advised that if redundancies were to be confirmed, it would not be implementing redundancies until after the consultation period. The respondent further asserted that, in response to a subsequent query, it confirmed that if an employee secured alternative employment during the consultation period it would waive the requirement to following notice.

On 20 August 2014, the claimant contacted HR in the respondent to enquire about the possibility of alternative employment with the respondent. HR advised the claimant that he would be notified of any available opportunities in the following days.

On 22 August 2014, the claimant wrote to the respondent to inform it that he had found alternative employment and was giving one week's notice.

The respondent wrote to the claimant on 26 August to offer him an alternative role. As this offer came within the 30-day consultation period, the respondent stated that the claimant's role was therefore never made redundant. The claimant gave evidence that he resigned, as he understood his role with the respondent was redundant from 12 August 2014, and that he was entitled to a redundancy payment from the respondent.

The respondent gave evidence that it was clearly communicated to employees that the redundancies would not be implemented during the consultation period, and that the claimant was the only individual to believe that his redundancy took effect from 12 August 2014. In actual fact all, bar one, of the employees involved in the process were offered suitable alternative employment, as opposed to redundancy.

The EAT reviewed the letter provided to employees following the meeting of 12 August 2014, which read:

> As discussed at our meeting we have now commenced a 30 day consultation period at the end of which a redundancy payment or offer of redeployment to a suitable alternative position will be made to you.

On a review of the above, and the oral evidence, the EAT held that it preferred the respondent's evidence, and that the claimant was not made redundant on 12 August 2014. It held that the claimant turned down the offer of redeployment because he had already accepted an offer of employment from another employer, not because the role offered was not a suitable alternative. The claimant's appeal was rejected.

TERMINATION OF EMPLOYMENT AT THE END OF AN APPRENTICESHIP

[23.18] *Toomey v Hemblestan Ltd t/a Dungarvan Nissan*[22]—*Employment Appeals Tribunal—Redundancy Payments Acts 1967 to 2014—Minimum Notice and Terms of Employment Acts 1973 to 2005—termination of employment due to end of apprenticeship—casual employment after apprenticeship*

The claimant gave evidence that he commenced his training as an apprentice mechanic with the respondent in November 2008 and completed his apprenticeship in November 2012. Two weeks prior to the completion of the apprenticeship, the claimant received a written notice from the respondent that his employment would terminate by reason of the end of his apprenticeship.

The claimant said he subsequently received a telephone call from the respondent on 11 December 2012 to come in and was asked to look at a vehicle. He received a letter in June 2013 stating that his employment had resumed on 19 December 2012. On 5 July 2013 he was told that there was no work for him and he finished on 13 July 2013.

The claimant submitted that because his employment had been resumed, he was in employment for more than one month after the end of his apprenticeship and was entitled to a redundancy payment and pay in lieu of notice for the statutory notice period applicable to a period of employment from November 2008 to July 2013.

JF, a director for the respondent, told the EAT that in 2008 things became very difficult in the motor trade industry as a result of the recession but he nonetheless did his best to keep the claimant on so that he could finish his apprenticeship. At the end of the apprenticeship, and after serving the appropriate written notice on the claimant on 16 November 2012, JF let the claimant go, having given him his P45. JF stated that he had only taken the claimant back some weeks later to cover for another mechanic who was out on sick leave. The work was casual until 2 January 2013, when the claimant was put back on the payroll. He let the claimant go on 12 July 2013 after serving one week's notice because he had no work for him.

The EAT made a finding that the claimant's employment was terminated on 30 November 2012 by reason of the end of his apprenticeship and in accordance with s 7(4) of the Redundancy Payments Acts 1967 to 2014 he was not entitled to a redundancy payment.

Section 7(4) of the 1967 Act provides as follows:

> Notwithstanding any other provision of this Act where an employee who has been serving a period of apprenticeship training with an employer under an apprenticeship agreement is dismissed within one month after the end of that period, that employee shall not, by reason of that dismissal, be entitled to redundancy payment.

---

22. *Toomey v Hemblestan Ltd t/a Dungarvan Nissan* RP1071/2013, MN779/2013.

The EAT then considered whether the claimant was entitled to the benefit of s 9(2) of the Acts, which provides the following:

> (2) An employee shall not be taken for the purposes of this Part to be dismissed by his employer if his contract of employment is renewed, or he is re-engaged by the same employer under a new contract of employment, and—
>
> (a)   in a case where the provisions of the contract as renewed or of the new contract as to the capacity and place in which he is employed, and as to the other terms and conditions of his employment, do not differ from the corresponding provisions of the previous contract, the renewal or re-engagement takes effect immediately on the ending of his employment under the previous contract, or
>
> (b)   in any other case, the renewal or re-engagement is in pursuance of an offer in writing made by his employer before the ending of his employment under the previous contract, and takes effect either immediately on the ending of that employment or after an interval of not more than four weeks thereafter.

The EAT held that in respect of s 9(2)(a), any renewal or re-engagement of the claimant by the respondent did not take effect immediately on the ending of the claimant's previous contract: the previous contract ended on 30 November 2012 and the new contract commenced on 11 December 2012. The EAT stated that it was satisfied that the ending of one contract and the commencement of the other was not arranged by the respondent to frustrate any employment rights of the claimant. The EAT held that in respect of s 9(2)(b), the offer in writing to resume employment was not made by the respondent before the ending of the previous employment. Accordingly the claim under the Acts failed.

The EAT held that the claim under the Minimum Notice and Terms of Employment Acts 1973 to 2005 failed as the claimant was given his statutory entitlement of one week's notice.

COLLECTIVE REDUNDANCY

[23.19] *Lyttle & Ors v Bluebird UK Bidco 2 Ltd[23]—request for preliminary rulings from CJEU from Northern Ireland, Spain and UK Court of Appeal—Opinion of Advocate General Wahl—collective redundancies—exact scope of concept of 'establishment' referred to in art 1(a)(ii) of Directive 98/59/EC[24]—whether fixed-term contracts that have expired should be taken into account for numerical thresholds?*

As these three distinct cases raise the same question they were dealt with together by Advocate General Wahl notwithstanding that they were not formally joined. In essence

---

23.   *Lyttle & Ors v Bluebird UK Bidco 2 Ltd* (Case C–182/13); *Canas v Nexea Gestion Documental SA, Fondo de Garantia Salarial* (Case C–392/13); and *Union of Shop, Distributive and Allied Workers, Wilson v WW Realisation 1 Ltd & Ors* (Case C–80/14).

24.   Council Directive 98/59/EC on the Approximation of the Laws of Member States Relating to Collective Redundancies.

the CJEU was asked to determine the exact scope of the concept of 'establishment' referred to in the Directive.

The factual background to each claim is that each of the claimants was made compulsorily redundant as part of mass redundancies at specific points in time. In each case, no collective consultation took place. In the *Lyttle* case, the respondent owned a retail clothing business Bonmarché. As part of a redundancy programme, there was significant reduction in both the numbers of clothing stores and employees across the UK and Northern Ireland. The claimants formed part of a group of 19 employees in Northern Ireland, who were made redundant during the spring of 2012. The claimants each worked at a different store and, as each store had fewer than 20 employees, the redundancy process did not include any collective consultation.

The other UK referral concerned the retail businesses of Woolworths and Ethel Austin, see [23.20]. On becoming insolvent they went into administration and thousands of employees in the UK were dismissed. The representative trade union sought protective awards against the employers because of their failure to consult employees about the proposed redundancies. Approximately 4,500 workers were denied a protective award on the basis that they had worked at stores with fewer than 20 workers, each store being regarded as a separate establishment.

The third referral arose from a collective redundancy situation in Spain, see [23.21].

Article 1(a) of the Directive permits Members States to define the threshold for consultation as either:

(i) where the number of redundancies is either, over a period of 30 days:

- at least 10 in establishments normally employing more than 20 and less than 100 workers;

- at least 10% of the number of workers in establishments normally employing at least 100 but less than 300 employees;

- at least 30 in establishments normally employing 300 workers or more; or

(ii) where the number of redundancies is, over a period of 90 days, at least 20, whatever the number of workers normally employed in the establishments in question.

Two of the three referrals in this case arose in the context of the implementing UK legislation[25] which provides that: 'where an employer is proposing to dismiss as redundant 20 or more employees at one establishment within a period of 90 days or less, the employer shall consult about the dismissals ...'

The issues raised by the referring courts were essentially the same: (i) does 'establishment' have the same meaning in art 1(1)(a)(ii) as in art 1(1)(a)(i)? If not, can an establishment be constituted by an organisational sub-unit of an undertaking which consists of, or includes, more than one local economic unit?

---

25.   Trade Union and Labour Relations (Consolidation) Act 1992, s 188(1).

(ii) Does the phrase in art 1(1)(a)(ii) refer to the number of dismissals across all the employer's establishments or does it instead refer to 20 in any particular establishment or to 20 overall?

The Advocate General noted that under Directive 98/59 the definition of collective redundancies was split into two parts, and noted that the CJEU had, in *Rockfon*,[26] already interpreted the concept of establishment in relation to art 1(a)(i) as 'the unit to which the workers were made redundant or assigned to carry out their duties'.

The Advocate General noted that in *Rockfon*, the CJEU held that an establishment is the local employment, and the CJEU did not find it appropriate to equate the concept at issue with 'an undertaking'. The Advocate General noted that one of the lessons to be learned from *Rockfon* is that the Court did not pay any heed to the way in which the employer-entity was structured, but focused instead on the local employment unit.

The Advocate General opined that, in his view, the concept of 'establishment' as referred to in art 1(1)(a)(ii) of Directive 98/59 has the same meaning as under art 1(1)(a)(i) of the Directive. The concept must be construed in the same way in both sections of art 1(1)(a). That concept denoted the unit to which the workers made redundant were assigned to carry out their duties, and this is for the national court to determine. The Advocate General noted that it was for the referring courts to determine how exactly the local employment unit is constituted in each situation and this was a factual matter. The Advocate General opined that it was not necessary for the entity to have legal, economic, financial, administrative or technological autonomy to be regarded as an establishment.

The Advocate General noted that this did not preclude Member States from enacting implementing rules on the basis of that concept which, without lowering the level of minimum protection, were more favourable to the worker.

Finally, the Advocate General addressed a specific question raised by the referring Spanish Court, namely whether fixed-term contracts that expire should be taken into account as Directive-relevant dismissals for the purposes of calculating thresholds in art 1(1)(a) of the Directive. The Advocate General found that all collective redundancies effective under contracts of employment concluded for limited periods of time or for specific tasks are excluded from the scope of the Directive, save where such redundancies take place prior to the date of expiry of such contracts or before their completion. It is irrelevant whether the grounds for termination of such contracts are the same. This did not preclude Member States from enacting rules which, without lowering the level of minimum protection, are more favourable to workers.

In its judgment in *Lyttle*, the CJEU held that the term 'establishment' in art 1(1)(a)(ii) of the Directive must be interpreted in the same way as the term in art 1(1)(a)(i) of that Directive. Thus art 1(1)(a)(ii) does not preclude national legislation that lays down an obligation to inform and consult workers in the event of a dismissal, within 90 days, of at least 20 workers from a particular establishment and not where the aggregate number of dismissals across all of the establishments or across some of the establishments of an undertaking over the same period reaches or exceeds the threshold of 20 workers.

---

26.   *Rockfon A/S v Specialarbejderforbundet I Danmark* (Case C–449/93).

[23.20] *Union of Shop, Distributive and Allied Workers (USDAW), Wilson v WW Realisation, No 1 Ltd in Liquidation, Ethel Austin Ltd and Secretary for State for Business, Innovation and Skills[27]—'Woolworths Case'—request for preliminary ruling from CJEU—UK Court of Appeal—collective redundancies—exact scope of concept of 'establishment' referred to in art 1(a)(ii) of Directive 98/59/EC*

In this case, the CJEU considered the relevant provisions of the Trade Union and Labour Relations (Consolidation) Act 1992 (TULRCA) which implemented the United Kingdom's obligations under Directive 98/59/EC.[28] The CJEU noted s 188(1) of the TULRCA which provides that 'where an employer proposes to dismiss as redundant 20 or more employees at one establishment within a period of 90 days or less, the employer shall consult about the dismissals of all the persons who are appropriate representatives of any of the employees who may be affected by the proposed dismissals or maybe affected by measures taken in connection with these dismissals'.

The TULRCA provides that where an employer fails to comply with the requirements of consultation a complaint can be presented and if upheld, a protective award eg an amount by way of compensation may be ordered. Where a protected award is made every employee of a description to which the award relates is in principle entitled to be paid remuneration by his employer for the protected period.

The CJEU then considered the factual background which was that Woolworths and Ethel Austin were high street retailers with stores operating throughout the UK. When they became insolvent and subsequently went into administration this resulted in the dismissal of thousands of employees across the United Kingdom on grounds of redundancy. USDAW in its capacity as a representative trade union, brought claims before employment tribunals in Liverpool and London against those two companies on behalf of several thousand of its members, who as former employees of those companies were dismissed on grounds of redundancy.

Mrs Wilson was an employee of Woolworths and was the USDAW representative on a national employee forum created by Woolworths to deal with various issues to include consultation prior to collective redundancy. She and her union sought the protective awards against the employers in favour of the dismissed employees on the grounds that prior to the adoption of the redundancy programmes, the consultation procedure provided for in TULRCA had not been followed. The CJEU noted under the Employment Rights Act 1996[29] if protective awards were made against an employer but they were not in a position to satisfy them, an employee could then require the Secretary of State for Business to pay and he would be required to pay that award up to the statutory maximum as arrears of pay.

In two separate decisions, the employment tribunals in Liverpool and London made protective awards in favour of a number of employees dismissed by Woolworths and

---

27. *Union of Shop, Distributive and Allied Workers (USDAW), Wilson v WW Realisation, No 1 Ltd in Liquidation, Ethel Austin Ltd and Secretary for State for Business, Innovation and Skills* (Case C–80/14).

28. Directive 98/59/EC on the approximation of the laws of the Member States on Collective Redundancies

29. Employment Rights Act 1996, s 182.

Ethel Austin. However approximately 4,500 former employees were denied a protective award on grounds that they had worked at stores with fewer than 20 employees and that each store was to be regarded as a separate establishment.

On appeal the UK EAT held that a reading of TULCRA compatible with the Directive required the deletion of the words 'at one establishment' pursuant to the obligation placed on a national court[30] to interpret its national law in light of the wording and purpose of the directive concerned. The UK EAT also held that USDAW and Mrs Wilson could rely on the direct effect of rights under the Directive on the ground that the Secretary of State for Business was a party to the case, and that he was responsible for paying the protective awards to the employees. This was appealed to the Court of Appeal of England and Wales by the Secretary of State for Business.

The Court of Appeal of England and Wales (Civil Division) decided to stay proceedings and refer the following questions to the CJEU for preliminary ruling.

1.   In article 1(1)(a)(ii) of Directive 98/59, does the phrase "at least 20" refer to the number of dismissals across all of the employer's establishments in which dismissals are effected within a 90 day period, or does it refer to the number of dismissals in each individual establishment? If article 1(1)(a)(ii) of that Directive refers to the number of dismissals in each individual establishment, what is the meaning of "establishment"? In particular should "establishment" be construed to mean the whole of the relevant retail business being a single economic business unit or such part of the business as is contemplating making redundancies, rather than to a unit to which a worker is assigned their duties, such as each individual store.

2.   In circumstances where an employee claims a protective award against a private employer can the Member State concerned rely on or plead the fact that the Directive 98/59 does not give rise to directly effective rights against the employer in circumstances where a) the private employer would, but for the failure of the Member State to properly implement the Directive have been liable to pay a protective award to the employee because of the failure of that employee to consult in accordance with the Directive; and b) that that employer being insolvent in the event that a protective award is made against the employer and it not satisfied by that employer and an application is made to the member state, that member state will itself be liable to pay any such protective award to the employee under domestic legislation that implements directive 2008/94, subject to any of the limitation of liability imposed on the member states guarantee institution pursuant to art 4 of that Directive.

In its request for preliminary ruling, the Court of Appeal stated that USDAW and Mrs Wilson had submitted that the concept of a collective redundancy in art 1(1)(a)(ii) of the Directive[31] was not limited to a situation in which at least 20 employees in each establishment are made redundant over a period of 90 days but encompasses a situation on which at least 20 employees of the same employer are made redundant over a period of 90 days whatever the number of workers at the establishment in question that is to say

---

30.   *Marleasing* (Case C–106/89).
31.   Directive 98/59/EC.

the establishments at which the redundancies are made. In the alternative USDAW and Mrs Wilson submitted that even if the provision of Directive is to be read as is referring to at least 20 workers to be made redundant at each establishment, the term 'establishment' was to be construed as consisting of the whole of the retail businesses operated by Woolworths and Ethel Austin respectfully. It was submitted that it was the retail business as a whole that was an economic business unit. USDAW and Mrs Wilson further submitted that as a Secretary for State for Business was liable for payment of protective awards pursuant to Directive 2008/94,[32] they contended that they were entitled to rely on the effects of Directive 98/59 on the principle of vertical direct effect which applied to that Directive.

The CJEU summarised that by its first question the referring Court was asking in essence whether the term 'establishment' is to be interpreted in the same way as the term 'establishment' in art 1(1)(a)(ii) of that Directive and secondly whether art 1(1)(a)(ii) of Directive 98/59 is to be interpreted as precluding national legislation that lays down an obligation to inform and consult workers in the event of their dismissal, within a 90 day period, of at least 20 workers from a particular establishment of a undertaking and not where the aggregate number of dismissals across all of the establishments or across some of the establishments in an undertaking over the same period reaches or exceeds the threshold of 20 workers.

The CJEU noted that the United Kingdom had opted for the threshold for its application set out in art 1(1)(a)(ii) of the Directive. Under applicable national law where an employer is proposing to shed at least 20 jobs at an establishment within a period of 90 days it was required to comply with the procedure for informing and consulting workers in connection with that proposal. The CJEU stated that in accordance with case law of the Court the term 'establishment' which is not defined in the Directive is a term of EU Law and could not be defined by reference to the laws of Member States. It must, on that basis, be interpreted in an autonomous and uniform manner in the EU legal order. The CJEU noted that it had already interpreted that the term 'establishment' or 'establishments' in art 1(1)(a) of Directive 98/59 and referred to its judgment in *Rockfon*.[33] The CJEU noted that it had been decided in that case that the term 'establishment' in art 1(1)(a) of Directive must be interpreted as designating, depending on the circumstances, the unit to which the workers made redundant are assigned to carry out their duties. It is not essential in order for there to be an 'establishment' that the unit in question is endowed with the management that can independently effect collective redundancy.

The CJEU further referred to its judgment in *Athinaiki Chartopoiia*[34] where it further clarified the term 'establishment' by holding that for the purpose of the application of Directive 98/59, an establishment in the context of an undertaking may consist of distinct entity, having certain degree of permanence and stability, which is assigned to perform one or more given tasks and has a workforce, technical means and a certain

---

32. Directive 2008/94/EC on the protection of employees in the event of the insolvency of their employer.
33. *Rockfon A/S v Specialarbejderforbundet I Danmark* (Case C–449/93).
34. *Athinaiki Chartopoiia* (Case C–270/05).

organisational structure allowing for the accomplishment of those tasks. The CJEU held this case law was applicable to the present case and that the meaning of the terms 'establishment' or 'establishments' in art 1(1)(a)(i) of Directive of 98/59 is the same of that of terms 'establishment' or 'establishments' in art 1(1)(a)(ii) of that Directive. The CJEU further held that art 1(1)(a)(ii) of Directive 98/59 must be interpreted as not precluding national legislation that lays down an obligation to inform and consult workers in the event of the dismissal, within a period of 90 days of at least 20 workers from a particular establishment of an undertaking and not with the aggregate number of dismissals across all of the establishments or across some of the establishments in an undertaking over the same period reaches or excludes the threshold of 20 workers. The CJEU confirmed that as the law of the United Kingdom was not incompatible with Directive 98/59, there was no need to reply to the second question.

[23.21] *Canas v Nexea Gestion Documental SA, Fondo de Garantia Salarial[35]— CJEU—Directive 98/59/EC[36]—preliminary ruling—social policy—collective redundancy—meaning of 'establishment' and 'undertaking'—undertaking as reference unit for collective redundancy—expiry of contracts for limited period of time or specific tasks—method of calculating number of workers for purposes of collective redundancy*

This case concerned a request for a preliminary ruling in relation to the interpretation of Council Directive 98/59/EC regarding national laws on collective redundancies. The Directive provides that where an employer is contemplating collective redundancies, he must ensure to commence consultations with the workers representatives in sufficient time to allow for an agreement to be reached. Under the terms of the Directive, a 'collective redundancy' is defined as a dismissal effected by an employer for one or more reasons not related to the individual workers concerned where the number of redundancies is, over a period of 90 days, at least 20, regardless of the number of workers normally employed in the establishments in question. Where a redundancy qualifies as a collective redundancy, an employer must adhere to a consultation process with the workers' representatives in good time with a view to reaching an agreement.

The claimant was employed by Nexea Gestion Documental SA, a company engaged in providing hybrid mail services and an entity within the Correos commercial group. In July 2012, Nexea had two establishments in Madrid and Barcelona, employing 164 and 20 employees respectively. Between October and November 2012, three fixed-term employment contracts expired in Madrid and two expired in the Barcelona. In December 2012, less than 90 days later, 13 more employees in Barcelona (including the claimant) were dismissed on economic grounds. Before the Social Court in Barcelona, the claimant contested his dismissal on the grounds that Nexea had fraudulently circumvented the application of the procedure relating to collective redundancies, a mandatory requirement under the Directive. Spanish redundancy legislation provides

35.   *Canas v Nexea Gestion Documental SA, Fondo de Garantia Salarial* (Case C–392/13).
36.   Directive 98/59/EC of 20 July 1998 on the approximation of the laws of the Member States relating to Collective Redundancies.

that redundancies are deemed to be collective redundancies where contracts of employment are terminated on economic, technical or organisational grounds and where over a period of 90 days, such termination affects at least 10 per cent of the workers in undertakings employing between 100 and 300 workers. The Social Court in Barcelona stated that if the five contracts of employment that ended between October and November 2012 were included in the number of dismissals effected in December 2012, a collective redundancy situation would arise in accordance with Spanish legislation. The Social Court in Barcelona asked the CJEU to consider whether the Directive precludes Spanish legislation from defining 'collective redundancies' by reference to an undertaking (ie Nexea including Madrid and Barcelona) and not an establishment (ie the establishment in Barcelona only) as the single reference. The CJEU was also required to consider whether account has to be taken of individual employment contracts limited to certain time periods or specific tasks that terminate on the expiry of that time or task for the purposes of a collective redundancy. Finally, the CJEU was asked to consider whether, when considering the existence of a collective redundancy situation effected under contracts of employment limited by time or completion of a specific task, it is necessary for the cause of the collective redundancies to derive from the same collective contractual framework for the same duration or task.

The CJEU restated that where an undertaking includes several entities, it is the entity to which the workers made redundant are assigned to carry out their duties that constitutes the establishment for the purposes of the Directive, as confirmed in *Union of Shop, Distributive and Allied Workers (USDAW) and Wilson v WW Realisation 1 Ltd & Ors*.[37] The CJEU found that any national legislation that provides for the undertaking and not the establishment as the sole reference in relation to a collective redundancy situation is contrary to the Directive where the effect of the application of that criterion precludes the information and consultation process provided for by the Directive, where the terminations would have been considered 'collective redundancies' if the establishment has been used as the reference. Replacing the term 'establishment' with 'undertaking' can be regarded as favourable to workers only if the employees' protections under the Directive are retained. Having said this, the CJEU noted, in the case before it, that the number of terminations did not reach the applicable threshold under Spanish legislation at the level of the undertaking (Nexea). As the establishment in Barcelona employed no more than 20 workers during the applicable period, the threshold provided for under the Directive was not reached either. The Directive did not apply in this case.

Finally, in considering the question of whether terminations of contracts concluded for limited periods of time or specific tasks should be taken into consideration, the CJEU confirmed that such contracts are excluded from the scope of the Directive. The wording and scheme of the Directive provide that such contracts terminate pursuant to their clauses or pursuant to applicable law and not at the impetus of the employing entity. Terminations of such contracts should therefore not be taken into account when determining whether a collective redundancy situation exists. The CJEU further held

---

37.   *Union of Shop, Distributive and Allied Workers (USDAW) and Wilson v WW Realisation 1 Ltd & Ors* (Case C–80/14). See [23.20].

that it is not necessary for the cause of such collective redundancies to derive from the same collective contractual framework for the same duration or the same task. The CJEU noted that the Directive has one qualitative criterion and that is that the cause of the dismissal must not be related to the individual workers concerned. The CJEU noted that to introduce additional requirements would restrict the scope of the Directive and potentially undercut the objective of the Directive to offer protection to workers in the event of collective redundancies.

Chapter 24

TAXATION RELATING TO EMPLOYMENT

EXPENSES OF NON-EXECUTIVE DIRECTORS

[24.01] Section 6 of the Finance Act 2015 inserts s 195B into the Taxes Consolidation Act 1997 (TCA). The new section provides that payments made by a company to or on behalf of a non-Irish resident, non-executive director relating to vouched travel and subsistence expenses are exempt from income tax when calculating that director's Irish income tax liability. This exemption only applies if the expenses are incurred solely for the purpose of the attendance by the director, in his or her capacity as a director, at a meeting relating to the conduct of the affairs of the company.

This legislative change effectively replaces the position set out by Revenue in *eBrief No 61/14* in 2014.

EMPLOYMENT AND INVESTMENT INCENTIVE (EII) SCHEME

[24.02] The EII allows an individual investor to obtain income tax relief on investments in small and medium sized trading companies. The use of the funds must contribute directly to the maintenance or creation of employment in the company. The Finance Act 2014 introduced amendments to the tax regime for income tax relief for investments made in these companies. The introduction of the amendments was subject to a Ministerial Order which could not be commenced until EU clearance was obtained. As EU clearance has since been obtained, the Finance Minister appointed 13 October 2015 as the effective date of the commencement of these amendments and those measures will apply in respect of shares in qualifying companies issued on or after that date, subject to additional conditions introduced by the Finance Act 2015.

Section 18 of the Finance Act 2015 amends Pt 16 of the TCA. The following changes have been implemented:

(i)   companies operating nursing homes can now raise funding to enlarge their capacity and to extend the nursing home or residential care units associated with that nursing home;

(ii) a qualifying company must now meet the conditions of paras 5 and 6 of art 21 of Commission Regulation (EU) 651/2014 of 17 June 2014;

(iii) the definition of a qualifying employee now requires employment for at least 30 hours a week and an employment capable of lasting at least 12 months; and

(iv) the employment test for qualification of relief now requires that there be a difference in the total emoluments paid before investment and after investment of at least the emolument of one qualifying employee.

Covered below in greater detail, Revenue stated in *eBrief No 107/15* that as the relief now operates under EU State Aid rules, companies that were qualifying companies for the relief prior to 13 October 2015 may now be excluded, on account of the conditions imposed by art 21 of Commission Regulation (EU) 651/2014 of 17 June 2014. Any company or potential investor in a company that had received outline approval for the relief from Revenue prior to 13 October 2015 but had not raised relevant funding by that date must now consider, before issuing shares, whether or not it is a qualifying company under the amended relief. In addition, Revenue announced in *eBrief No 114/15* that a FAQ guide had been prepared to assist with questions relating to the EII scheme. This guide can be accessed in Revenue's Tax and Duty Manual at Part 16.00.08.[1]

EU State Aid rules consideration

[24.03] In order to comply with the EU State Aid rules, paras 5 and 6 of art 21 of Commission Regulation (EU) 651/2014 should be considered:

5. Eligible undertakings shall be undertakings which at the time of the initial risk finance investment are unlisted SMEs and fulfil at least one of the following conditions:

(a)   They have not been operating in any market;

(b)   They have been operating in any market for less than 7 years following their first commercial sale;

(c)   They require an initial risk finance investment which, based on a business plan prepared in view of entering a new product or geographical market, is higher than 50% of their average annual turnover in the preceding 5 years.

6. The risk finance aid may also cover follow-on investments made in eligible undertakings, including after the 7 year period mentioned in paragraph 5(b), if the following cumulative conditions are fulfilled:

(a)   The total amount of risk finance mentioned in paragraph 9 is not exceeded;

(b)   The possibility of follow-on investments was foreseen in the original business plan;

(c)   The undertaking receiving follow-on investments has not become linked, within the meaning of Article 3(3) of Annex I with another undertaking other than the financial intermediary or the independent private investor providing risk finance under the measure, unless the new entity fulfils the conditions of the SME definition.

---

1.   ww.revenue.ie/en/about/foi/s16/income-tax-capital-gains-tax-corporation-tax/part-16/16-00-08.pdf.

UNIVERSAL SOCIAL CHARGE

[24.04] Section 2 of the Finance Act 2015 amends Pt 18D of the TCA by setting out revised band thresholds and tax rates. The net effect is that all employees should see a reduction in their USC charge, and an increased number of employees should fall into the exempt category of USC.

Section 2 of the Finance Act 2015 also provides for an exemption from an employee USC charge in respect of employer contributions to a PRSA, in line with the existing exemption for employer contributions to occupational pension schemes.

USC Thresholds

2015		2016	
Exempt category	**Rate**	**Exempt category**	**Rate**
Total income below €12,012.00	exempt	Total income below €13,000.00	exempt
Where USC is payable		**Where USC is payable**	
Income up to €12,012.00	1.5%	Income up to €12,012.00	1%
Income from €12,012.01 to €17,576.00	3.5%	Income from €12,012.01 to €17,576.00	3%
Income from €17,576.01 to €70,044.00	7%	Income from €17,576.01 to €70,044.00	5.5%
Income above €70,044.00	8%	Income above €70,044.00	8%

PAY RELATED SOCIAL INSURANCE

[24.05] Section 10 of the Social Welfare and Pensions Act 2015 amends s 13 of the Social Welfare Consolidation Act 2005 and introduces two changes to PRSI for the benefit of lower income workers and their employers.

Section 10(1)(a) of the Social Welfare and Pensions Act 2015 amends s 13(2)(b) of the Social Welfare Consolidation Act 2005 and moves Class A employees whose earnings are between €352.01 and €424 per week onto a tapered PRSI weekly credit system. The maximum relief that can be claimed per week is limited to €12.

The relief is calculated using the following formula:

$$\text{Relief} = 12 - 1/6*(A - 352.01)$$

Where:

A   is the employee's reckonable income.

This relief allows lower income workers to make a graduated step up to the full 4 per cent Class A PRSI tax rate. Currently a worker earning €352 a week pays no Class A employee's PRSI while a worker earning €352.01 pays €14.08 in PRSI a week. Using the formula above, this worker would now be entitled to a €12 PRSI credit per week, reducing the employee PRSI charge to €2.08. The value of the credit falls as income increases until at €424 no PRSI credit is available.

Section 10(1)(b) of the Social Welfare and Pensions Act 2015 amends s 13(2)(d) of the Social Welfare Consolidation Act 2005 and expands the lower 8.5 per cent Class A rate of employer PRSI to weekly earnings of up to €376 (increased from €356).

SMALL BENEFITS EXEMPTION

[24.06] Section 11 of the Finance Act 2015 inserts s 112B into the TCA. The new section places onto a statutory footing the previous concessional 'Small Benefits Exemption' granted by Revenue in respect of employee vouchers. Whereas previously Revenue had allowed a voucher/gift card to the value of €250 to be given to employees once per year the new statutory provision increases the limit to €500, subject to the following conditions:

(i)   the voucher is not part of a salary sacrifice arrangement;

(ii) the voucher cannot be redeemed for cash; and

(iii) not more than one voucher can be given to an employee in a year of assessment.

Where s 112B relief applies, the voucher will not be treated as a perquisite and PAYE, USC or PRSI will not be charged.

TERMINATION PAYMENTS

[24.07] Section 5 of the Finance Act 2015 amends s 192A(1) of the TCA. It expands the list of 'relevant authorities' by substituting the following for s 192A(1)(b) of the TCA:

(b)   the Director of the Equality Tribunal,

(ba) an adjudication officer of the Workplace Relations Commission,

(bb) the Workplace Relations Commission,

(bc) the District Court.

Section 192A of the TCA provides for an exemption from income tax in respect of certain awards or settlements made in accordance with a recommendation, decision or determination by a relevant authority for the infringement of an employee's rights or entitlements or an employer's obligations under employment legislation. A payment made under a settlement agreement arrived at under a mediation process is treated as if it had been made in accordance with such a recommendation, decision or determination of a relevant authority.

SUBSISTENCE EXPENSES
Changes made to civil service distance requirements and rates

[24.08] *eBrief No 63/15* reports that following an agreed recommendation made by the General Council under the scheme of conciliation and arbitration for the Civil Service

(General Council Report 1531 refers), changes were made to the Civil Service distance requirements and rates with effect from 1 July 2015.

Changes include:

(a) where previously two classes of rates existed, there is now a new single class of overnight allowance which covers a period of up to 24 hours from the time of departure, as well as any further period not exceeding five hours, and which will only be payable free of tax in respect of an absence which is necessarily spent overnight at least 100km away from the employee's home and normal place of work; and

(b) where previously two classes of rates existed, there is now a new single class of day allowance, which applies to a continuous absence of five hours or more, and which will only be payable free of tax where the absence is not at a place within 8km (as opposed to 5km from 5 March 2009 to 30 June 2015) of the employee's home or normal place of work.

The following schedule lists the newly agreed and previous rates:

Class	Overnight Allowances			Day Allowances	
	Normal rate	Reduced rate	Detention rate	10 hours or more	5 hours but less than 10 hours
From 1 July 2015					
	€125	€112.50	€62.50	€33.61	€14.01
Previously from 5 March 2009 to 30 June 2015					
Class A	€108.99	€100.48	€54.48	€33.61	€13.71
Class B	€107.69	€92.11	€53.87	€33.61	€13.71

SHARE RETURNS

Electronic Form RSS1

[24.09] In *eBrief No 24/15* Revenue sets out companies' obligations to provide information in relation to the grant, assignment or release of rights or the allotment of shares, or the transfer of any asset under rights granted in accordance with s 128(11) of the TCA.

Following the enactment of the Finance Act 2014, such information must be delivered in an electronic format approved by the Revenue Commissioners, not later than 31 March in the year of assessment following the year in which any such event takes place. The law provides for both civil penalties and criminal sanctions for failure to make a return, the making of a false return, or facilitating the making of a false return.

Form RSS1 is available on the Revenue website in a spreadsheet format, tailored to capture the relevant information and is easy and quick to complete and submit.

VAT TREATMENT: EMPLOYMENT AGENCY

[24.10] In *eBrief No 04/15* Revenue updates Chapter 5 of the VAT Manual with its current position on the VAT treatment of employment agencies and home care services.

Revenue states that the status of agency staff who are sourced, placed or made available by employment agencies is a matter of fact determined on the basis of contracts and/or the actual working and other arrangements that may exist from time to time between the staff, the agency and the company, firm, body or other entity in which the staff work, referred to below for convenience as the 'organisation'.

In accordance with s 37(1) of the VAT Consolidation Act 2010, as amended, VAT is chargeable on the full consideration which the agency becomes entitled to receive in respect of or in relation to the supply of agency staff to the organisation, including all taxes, commissions, costs and charges whatsoever but not including VAT chargeable in respect of the supply. The relevant rate of VAT is the standard rate in force at the time of the supply (currently 23 per cent).

If an agency is acting as principal in the supply of staff to organisations, the 'full consideration' which the agency becomes entitled to receive in respect of, or in relation to, the supply includes such monies as commissions, fees, wages, employers' PRSI, holiday pay, sick pay and other monies due under the Organisation of Working Time Act 1997.

On the other hand, if an agency is acting as agent in the supply of staff to organisations, the 'full consideration' would normally exclude such monies as wages, employers' PRSI, holiday pay, sick pay and other monies due under the Organisation of Working Time Act 1997. The VAT treatment does not affect the position in relation to the operation of PAYE/PRSI.

PAYE EXCLUSION ORDERS

Non-Irish resident employees

[24.11] *eBrief No 03/15* sets out Revenue's position on non-Irish resident employees who are recruited abroad and exercise all duties abroad. Revenue considers that such an employee does not need to apply for a PPS number nor does the employer need to apply for an Exclusion Order where the employee:

(i)   is not resident in Ireland for tax purposes;

(ii)   has been recruited abroad;

(iii)   carries out all the duties of employment abroad;

(iv)   is not a director of the employer; and

(v)   is outside the charge to tax in Ireland.

Paragraph 5.1A has been added to the Revenue's PAYE Exclusion Orders Manual to reflect this position.

UK DECISIONS

[24.12] *James H Donald (Darvel) Ltd v HMRC²—Upper Tribunal—national insurance contributions (NIC) avoidance scheme failed*

The Upper Tribunal has ruled that a tax and national insurance contributions (NIC) avoidance scheme under which employees gave up salary in return for a broadly equivalent payment in the form of dividends failed. Applying the reasoning of the Court of Appeal in *HMRC v PA Holdings Ltd³* and upholding the (unreported) decision of the First-Tier Tribunal, the Tribunal determined that, focusing on substance and not form, the receipts were employment income and not dividend income.

[24.13] *Reed Employment plc v HMRC⁴—Court of Appeal—agency workers—travel expenses—non-taxable*

The Court of Appeal rejected an appeal brought by Reed Employment Plc against an Upper Tribunal decision. Reed had sought to make non-taxable payments in respect of travel expenses to its employees who worked as agency workers with a proportionate reduction in gross salary. Tax and NIC savings were mostly kept by Reed. The Court of Appeal agreed with HMRC's argument that the payments were made as part of overall wages and, as a result, should have been subject to tax and NIC.

[24.14] *A v HMRC⁵—First-Tier Tribunal—whether settlement under compromise agreement relating to discrimination claim taxable as earnings*

The First-Tier Tribunal found that a settlement under a compromise agreement relating to a discrimination claim was not taxable as earnings from employment. The issue was the treatment of a £600,000 payment Mr A had received when leaving. Mr A contended that the payment was not employment income, as it was compensation in relation to a threatened race discrimination claim for his unfair treatment in receiving low or no bonuses over several years and no salary increases. HMRC argued that the payment was chargeable as earnings from employment because it was designed to make good shortfalls in salary and bonus. The First-Tier Tribunal noted that the test was whether a payment was a reward for services past, present or future and ultimately held that the payment did not amount to 'earnings' under s 62 of the Income Tax (Earnings and Pensions) Act 2003.

2.   *James H Donald (Darvel) Ltd v HMRC* [2015] UKUT 514 (TCC).
3.   *HMRC v PA Holdings Ltd* [2011] EWCA Civ 1414.
4.   *Reed Employment plc v HMRC* [2015] EWCA Civ 805.
5.   *A v HMRC* [2015] UKFFT 89 (TC).

Chapter 25

TEMPORARY AGENCY WORK

[25.01] *Paul Doyle Hire Services Ltd v Furlong[1]—Labour Court—appeal from decision of Rights Commissioner—Protection of Employees (Temporary Agency Work) Act 2012—extension of time due to reasonable cause—basic working and employment conditions—whether higher rates of subsistence pay and pay in respect of travelling time received by agency worker could be offset against arrears of wages owed to him—definition of pay*

The claimant was employed by the respondent as an agency worker from 25 June 2012 to 22 April 2014. He was paid €9 per hour while working as a helper on a refuse truck and €11.50 per hour while working as a driver. At all material times, he was assigned to work for Greenstar, a waste collection company. The claimant contended that the rate of pay he received was less than that paid to direct employees of Greenstar engaged in like work. However, he accepted he received travelling time and subsistence at a higher rate than that of Greenstar employees.

The claimant alleged that under a collective agreement in force between Greenstar and SIPTU, the rate of pay for a helper was €9.15 per hour and €12.50 per hour for a driver. The claimant therefore contended that he was entitled to the difference between the rate of pay received and that provided for in the collective agreement for the duration of his assignment to Greenstar. The respondent accepted that the collective agreement in place between Greenstar and SIPTU provided for the rates of pay alleged by the claimant and that the claimant was underpaid relative to rates of pay paid by Greenstar to comparable direct hires. However, the respondent submitted the claimant could only recover the difference in pay in respect of the six-month period prior to the referral of his original complaint to the Rights Commissioner Service. The respondent also submitted that, in considering any arrears of pay to which the claimant may be entitled, account should be taken of the fact that the claimant received travelling time and subsistence pay at a higher rate than that paid by Greenstar to its direct employees.

The Labour Court firstly considered whether the claim was confined to the difference in pay in respect of the six-month period prior to the referral of his original complaint to the Rights Commissioner Service or whether the relevant time period should be extended, as argued by the claimant, on the grounds of reasonable cause. The claimant did not attend the hearing before the Labour Court but his trade union representative explained that the claim had not been pursued at an earlier stage as Greenstar's business was, at that time, being sold and the union decided not to initiate the claim until after the Greenstar business had been sold. The Court noted that the test for determining whether the time limit for lodgement of a claim can be extended for reasonable cause imposes a 'relatively low threshold of reasonableness on an applicant for an extension of time'. The Court however stated that there is 'some limitation on the range of issues which can be taken into account in considering such an application'. The

---

1.   *Paul Doyle Hire Services Ltd v Furlong* AWD1512.

Court referred to the High Court judgment in *O'Donnell v Dun Laoghaire Corporation*[2] in which the High Court emphasised that a reason relied on for an extension of time must excuse the delay on an objective standard.

The Court did not accept that the reason submitted by the claimant's representative for not advancing the claim sooner was explained or justified and, therefore, refused the extension of time application. Accordingly, the Court held that the claimant was confined to recovering the difference in pay in respect of the six-month period prior to the referral of his complaint only.

The Court then considered the respondent's contention that, as the claimant was in receipt of a higher rate of subsistence payments and travelling time relative to that applicable to direct employees of Greenstar, these additional payments should be off-set against any arrears due to the claimant by reason of having been paid a lower hourly rate. The Court examined the definition of pay set out in the 2012 Act and noted that it did not refer to subsistence payments or travelling time. The Court stated that, in circumstances where the Oireachtas had not provided that the totality of an agency worker's remuneration should be taken account of when determining compliance with the 2012 Act, it was not open to the Court to import such a provision into the Act. The Court therefore held that no form of set-off could be made or credit given against the amount due to the claimant by way of arrears of wages under the Act.

The Court also noted that an entitlement to meal allowances, sick pay and pension entitlements does not come within the statutory meaning of basic employment and working conditions and could not be provided for in awards under the 2012 Act.

The Court upheld the claimant's claim and amended the Rights Commissioner's decision in light of its findings.

[25.02] *Paul Doyle Hire Services Ltd v Stafford*[3]*—Labour Court—Protection of Employees (Temporary Agency Work) Act 2012—appeal from decision of Rights Commissioner—extension of time due to reasonable cause—basic working and employment conditions—whether higher rates of subsistence pay and pay in respect of travelling time received by agency worker could be offset against arrears of wages owed to him*

The facts were identical, in all material respects, to the claim referred to in *Paul Doyle Hire Services Ltd v Furlong*[4] at para [25.01] above. The only significant difference in the matters to be considered by the Court were the grounds for the claimant's application for an extension of time. The claimant, in direct evidence to the Court, confirmed that he was aware of the rates of pay paid to comparable direct employees of Greenstar but advised he was unaware of the grounds for a claim against the respondent until his union asked him to complete a referral form to the Rights Commissioner Service. The Court referred to the judgment of Laffoy J in *Minister for Finance v Civil and Public Services*

2. *O'Donnell v Dun Laoghaire Corporation* [1991] ILRM 301.
3. *Paul Doyle Hire Services Ltd v Stafford* AWD1513.
4. *Paul Doyle Hire Services Ltd v Furlong* AWD1512.

Union & Ors[5] as authority for the proposition that the absence of actual knowledge on the part of a claimant concerning his or her rights cannot be relied upon to excuse a failure to make a claim within the statutory time limit of six months.

The Court ultimately concluded that the reason advanced for the delay in initiating the claim was neither explained nor justified and, accordingly, the application for an extension of time was refused.

---

5. *Minister for Finance v Civil and Public Services Union & Ors* [2007] 18 ELR 36.

Chapter 26

TRANSFER OF UNDERTAKINGS

Intra-Group Transfer

[26.01] *Ferreira da Silva e Brito & Ors v Estado Portugues[1]—CJEU—Transfer of Undertakings, Directive 2001/23/EC[2]—request for preliminary ruling—where undertaking wound up by majority shareholder who subsequently took over certain services and assets—whether transfer occurs—whether Portuguese Supreme Court obliged to request preliminary hearing*

This request for a preliminary ruling arose from the winding up of Air Atlantis SA (AIA), a company which operated non-scheduled (charter) flights in the air transport sector in Portugal. The applicant and 96 others were employed by AIA and dismissed as part of a collective redundancy. Three months later the main shareholder in AIA, TAP began to operate at least some of the flights which AIA had previously been contracted to provide and it also operated a number of charter flights, a market in which it had previously not been active. In providing these services, TAP used some of the assets which AIA used for its activities to include four aeroplanes. TAP also assumed responsibility for the payment of charges under leasing contracts relating to these aircraft and took over certain office equipment which previously belonged to AIA and which it had used at its premises in Lisbon and Faro as well as other moveable property. In addition, TAP took on a number of former AIA employees.

The applicants challenged the collective redundancy before the Lisbon Labour Court from which they sought reinstatement within TAP and payment of remuneration. The claims were upheld in part; insofar as the Court ordered that the applicants be reinstated in the corresponding grades and be paid compensation. The Labour Tribunal in Lisbon found there was a transfer of a business at least in part; as the identity of the business had been retained and its activities had been continued, TAP having replaced the former employer in the contract of employment. The Court of Appeal set aside the order to reinstate the applicants and to pay compensation. The Court of Appeal took the view that the action against the collective redundancy was time barred. This ultimately led to a further appeal before the Supreme Court of Justice which held that the collective redundancy was not unlawful. The Supreme Court held that the fact that a commercial activity is merely continued was not sufficient to conclude that there had been a transfer of a business since the business must also retain its identity. In the present case, when TAP operated the flights in question over the course of the summer of 1993, it did not use an entity with the same identity as the entity previously belonging to AIA. In the view of the Portuguese Supreme Court a transfer of a business could not be said to have

---

1. *Ferreira da Silva e Brito & Ors v Estado Portugues* (Case C–160/14).
2. Directive 2001/23/EC on the approximation of the laws of the Member States relating to the safeguarding of employees' rights in the event of transfers of undertakings, businesses or parts of undertakings or businesses.

occurred since the two entities were not identical. The Supreme Court also concluded that there had not been a transfer of customers from AIA to TAP.

The applicants had requested that the Supreme Court make a reference for a preliminary ruling to the CJEU, however the Portuguese Supreme Court held that this was not necessary and referred to the fact that there was no material doubt as to the interpretation of the rules that would make a reference for preliminary ruling necessary. The Supreme Court further held that the CJEU had developed settled case law on the issue of interpretation of the rules relating to the transfer of business and the Directive such that the concepts were so clear that there was no need for a prior consultation of the CJEU. The applicants then brought an action for a declaration of non-contractual civil liability against the Portuguese State, claiming it should be ordered to pay damages for certain material losses they had sustained. In support of their actions they submitted that the judgment of the Supreme Court in Portugal was manifestly unlawful as it interpreted the concept of a transfer of a business within the meaning of Directive 2001/23/EC incorrectly and the Supreme Court failed to comply with its obligation to refer the appropriate questions concerning the interpretation of EU Law to the CJEU.

It was submitted by the Portuguese State that under art 13(2) of the RRCEE (Portuguese National Law) a claim for damages must be based on the prior setting aside, by the Court having jurisdiction, of the decision that caused a loss or damage. It was submitted that since the decision of the Supreme Court of Justice had not been set aside, the damages sought were not payable. In the circumstances, the Court of First Instance of Lisbon decided to stay the proceedings and to refer three questions to the CJEU for preliminary ruling.

The first question posed was whether art 1(1) of the Directive must be interpreted as meaning that the concept of the 'transfer of a business' encompasses a situation in which an undertaking active in the charter flights market is wound up by its majority shareholder, which is itself an air transport undertaking, and which then takes the place of the undertaking that has been wound up by: taking over aircraft leasing contracts and ongoing charter flight contracts; carrying on activities previously carried on by the undertaking that had been wound up; re-instating some employees that had been seconded to that undertaking and assigning them tasks identical to those previously performed; and taking over small items of equipment from the undertaking that has been wound up.

In considering this question the CJEU noted that the aim of the Directive was to ensure continuity of employment relationships within an economic entity, irrespective of any change of ownership. The decisive criterion in establishing the existence of a transfer is therefore the fact the entity in question retains its identity, as indicated *inter alia* by the fact that its operation is actually continued or resumed. The CJEU held it was necessary to consider all the facts characterising the transaction concerned, in particular, the type of undertaking or business concerned; whether or not its tangible assets such as buildings and movable property are transferred; the value of its intangible assets at the time of transfer; whether or not the majority of its employees are taken over by the new employer; whether or not its customers are transferred; the degree of similarity between the activities carried on before and after the transfer; and the period, if any, for which those activities were suspended.

The CJEU noted that these were merely single factors in the overall assessment. They could not be considered in isolation. The Court further pointed out that the degree of importance to be attached to each criterion will necessarily vary according to the activity carried on, and the production or operating methods employed in the undertaking business or part of a business. The CJEU held that the first question should be examined in light of its case law while account should be taken of the principal matters of fact set out by the National Court in the order for reference. With reference to the situation at issue, which concerned the air transport sector, the fact that the tangible assets are transferred must be regarded as a key factor for the purpose of determining whether there is a transfer of a business within the meaning of art 1(1) of the Directive. The CJEU noted that the order for reference indicated that TAP replaced AIA in the aircraft leasing contracts and actually used the aircraft concerned, which showed that it took over assets that were essential for pursuing the activity previously carried on by AIA. In addition, a certain amount of other equipment was also taken over. The CJEU noted that the fact that the entity whose assets and a part of whose staff were taken over was integrated into TAP's structure, without that entity retaining an autonomous organisational structure, was irrelevant for the purpose of applying art 1(1) of the Directive, since a link was preserved between the assets and staff transferred to TAP and the pursuit of activities previously carried on by the company that had been wound up. Against this background, it was immaterial that the assets concerned were used for operating scheduled flights as well as charter flights given the flights in issue were in any event transport operations and TAP honoured AIA's contractual obligations with regards to those charter flights. The CJEU referenced its judgment in *Klarenberg*[3] that what was relevant for the purpose of finding that the identity of the transfer of entity had been preserved was not the retention of the specific organisation imposed by the undertaking on the various elements of production which were transferred, but rather the retention of the functional link of interdependence and complementarity between those elements. This allowed the transferee to use them, even if they were integrated after the transfer in a new and different organisational structure.

The CJEU concluded that art 1(1) of the Directive must be interpreted as meaning that the concept of a transfer of a business does encompass the situation posed in the first question.

In its second question, the referring Court sought to ascertain whether in circumstances such as those at issue and because of the fact that lower Courts had given conflicting decisions concerning the interpretation of the concepts of a transfer of a business within the meaning of art 1(1) of the Directive, the third paragraph of art 267 TFEU must be construed as meaning that a Court or Tribunal against whose decisions there is no judicial remedy under national law is, in principle, obliged to refer the matter to the Court of Justice in order to obtain an interpretation of that concept. The CJEU noted that a Court or Tribunal against whose decisions there is no judicial remedy under national law is obliged, where a question of the EU law is raised before it, to comply with its obligation to bring the matter before the CJEU unless it is established that the question raised is irrelevant or that the provision of EU law concerned has already been

---

3. *Klarenberg v Ferrotron Technologies GmbH* (Case C–466/07).

interpreted by the Court and the correct application of EU law is so obvious as to leave no scope for any reasonable doubt.

The fact that other national Courts or Tribunals have given contradictory decisions is not a conclusive factor capable of triggering the obligations set out in the third paragraph of art 267 TFEU. However, the CJEU held that the question as to how the concept of a transfer of a business should be interpreted has given rise to a great deal of uncertainty on the part of many national Courts and Tribunals which, as a consequence, have found it necessary to make a reference to the CJEU. That uncertainty shows that not only are there difficulties of interpretation but also there is a risk of diversions in judicial decisions within the EU. It follows that in circumstances such as in this case, a national Court or Tribunal against whose decisions there is no judicial remedy under national law must comply with its obligation to make a reference to the Court in order to avert the risk of an incorrect interpretation of EU law.

In its third question, the referring Court sought to ascertain whether EU Law and the principles set down by the Court with regard to state liability for loss or damage caused to individuals as a result of an infringement of EU law by a Court or Tribunal against whose decisions there is no judicial remedy under national law, must be interpreted as precluding a provision of national law which requires, as a pre-condition, the setting aside of the decision given by that Court or Tribunal which caused the loss or damage, when such setting aside is in practice impossible. The CJEU concluded that a rule of national law such as the rule in art 13(2) of the RRCEE in Portugal may make it excessively difficult to obtain reparation for the loss or damage caused by infringement of EU law in question. The CJEU noted that the situation in which decisions of the Supreme Court of Justice in Portugal may be subject to review were extremely limited. The CJEU therefore held that the answer to the third question is that EU law and in particular the principles laid down by the CJEU regarding state liability for loss and damage caused to individuals as a result of an infringement of EU law by a Court or Tribunal against whose decisions there is no judicial remedy under national law, must be interpreted as precluding such a provision of a national law.

Application of 2003 Regulations to the Office of County Sheriff

[26.02] *Brady v McNamara[4]—Employment Appeals Tribunal—appeal from decision of Rights Commissioner—European Communities (Protection of Employees on Transfer of Undertakings) Regulations 2003—Unfair Dismissals Acts 1977 to 2015— Redundancy Payments Acts 1967 to 2014—preliminary issue—whether claimant's employment had transferred pursuant to 2003 Regulations—whether office of Sheriff an economic entity where held by a natural person—whether respondent in breach of reg 8—whether claimant made redundant for economic technical or organisational reasons— entitlement to redundancy payment*

The EAT decided, with the agreement of the parties, to determine as a preliminary issue whether the 2003 Regulations applied to the respondent and, if so, whether there was a

---

4.   *Brady v McNamara* TU36/2014.

relevant transfer. Following the determination on the preliminary issue the EAT would, if appropriate, proceed to hear the appeal and also to determine whether there had been a breach of the 2003 Regulations.

The claimant commenced employment as a court messenger with the then Sheriff for County Cork in July 1987 and his evidence was that his employment had transferred in 1995 to MOD, the former Sheriff for County Cork, under the 2003 Regulations. He had received what he described as a letter of undertaking from MOD informing him that his employment would further transfer in February 2013 to MOD's successor by virtue of the 2003 Regulations. The claimant's evidence was that he was led to believe that he would transfer to the new County Sheriff, ie the respondent, however, while some discussions did take place with the new County Sheriff, he received correspondence in April 2013 confirming that his employment with MOD had terminated in mid-February 2013 and that the new County Sheriff had no work for him. The question therefore arose as to whether the claimant's employment had transferred to the respondent as the new County Sheriff for Cork pursuant to the 2003 Regulations.

It was submitted by the respondent that the post of Cork County Sheriff could not be an economic entity as it is held by a natural person (entity) and, furthermore, that the post of Cork County Sheriff is a public administrative authority carrying out a public administrative function and, accordingly, is entitled to the exemption provided for in reg 3(5) of the 2003 Regulations. The EAT concluded that the respondent was an economic entity for the purpose of the 2003 Regulations and that there had been a relevant transfer for the purposes of the 2003 Regulations as regards recruitment at the Office of Sheriff:

> the Sheriff was the employer for the purpose of the 2003 Regulations, as 'employer' in those Regulations was defined as the person who under a contract of employment … is liable to pay the wages of the individual concerned in respect of the work or service concerned.

The EAT held that the Office of Sheriff is not precluded from being an economic entity by reason of the office being held by a natural person, as all economic entities will necessarily also be a natural or legal entity. For the purpose of the 2003 Regulations it does not matter whether the transferor or transferee is a legal or natural entity or whether they are private or public bodies. The 2003 Regulations apply to public and private undertakings engaged in economic activities, whether or not they are operating for gain.

The EAT observed that the functions of the employees of the respondent and the former County Sheriff are mainly the enforcement of judgments. The County Sheriff also arranges for the tendering of sale of goods, including seized vehicles. The EAT noted that the role of returning officer at elections is a function to be performed by the County Sheriff rather than by the respondent's employees and therefore this is not a duty of the employment relationship between the respondent, her predecessor and the employees. The EAT noted the provisions of the Courts Officers Act 1945, namely, that only the Sheriff or a person nominated by the Minster can carry out the role of returning officer at elections and held that this requirement to carry out this occasional function for the State when the need arises did not bring the Office of Sheriff as employer outside the ambit of the 2003 Regulations.

The statutory proofs put forward by the respondent in support of the assertion that the respondent was an administrative authority dealt in the main with the relationship between the respondent *qua* County Sheriff and the State rather than the relationship between the respondent as an employer and her employees.

Statutes have conferred the power on Sheriffs, such as the respondent, to enforce judgments passed to the Sheriff by the Courts or by the Revenue Commissioners. All such judgments are intended to result in the recovery of money with gain to the Office of the Sheriff. To that extent, the respondent is in the nature of a debt collection agency for the State, albeit such debt collection has to be carried out in accordance with the Enforcement of Court Orders Act 1926 and, with regards to Revenue warrants, in accordance with the Taxes Consolidation Act 1997. The EAT held that the functions of the Office of Sheriff constitute economic activity.

The EAT accepted that the functions of the respondent are administrative functions insofar as the enforcement of judgments is an executive function and is a public administrative function. The enforcement of judgments is not an administration of justice. The fact that the functions are administrative functions does not necessarily preclude such functions constituting economic activity; nor do they preclude the respondent from constituting an economic entity.[5]

The EAT noted the provisions of reg 3(2) of the 2003 Regulations and the definition of economic entity. The EAT found that the respondent's activities enforcing judgments passed to her was economic activity that was central and at least ancillary to an administrative entity. The EAT noted the decision of the CJEU in *Sanchez Hildago & Ors v Asociation de Servicious Aser and Socieded Cooperative Minerva*,[6] where, at para 34, the judgment said that the term 'economic entity' referred to an organised grouping of persons and of assets enabling an economic activity which pursues a specific objective to be exercised.

The EAT found that the respondent and her staff are such an organised grouping of persons and of assets, enabling an economic activity which pursues the specific objective of debt collection for the State. The EAT noted that in the exemption provided in reg 3(5) there is no statutory definition of what constitutes a public administrative authority. The EAT noted that case law had evolved which suggested that the scope of reg 3(5) excludes only a relatively limited range of situations involving the transfer of entities pursuing non-economic objectives within the public sector and this reflects the approach taken by the CJEU in *Henke. Henke* established that the reorganisation of the structure of public administration or the transfer of purely administrative functions does not constitute a transfer of an undertaking within the meaning of the Directive, and that activities of an economic nature are required in order for there to be a relevant transfer. In this case, the EAT found that there were activities of an economic nature, namely debt collection.

The EAT noted that the CJEU has subsequently confirmed the limited application of the *Henke* exception. The EAT stated that the exemption in reg 3(5) of the 2003

---

5.   *Henke v Gemeinde Schierke Verwaltungsgemeinschaft Brocken* (Case C–298/94).
6.   *Sanchez Hildago & Ors v Asociation de Servicious Aser and Socieded Cooperative Minerva* (Case C–173/1996).

Regulations is intended to apply to situations where, for example, the housing functions of borough councils are transferred to county councils and staff are transferred by legislation (Ministerial order or otherwise) on terms and conditions of employment similar to those previously enjoyed by them and that the exemption does not apply, and was not intended to apply, to situations whereby the exemption would operate to deprive employees of the protection of the Regulations, where no other protection exists, as would apply in the instant case.

In concluding that there was a relevant transfer for the purpose of the 2003 Regulations, the EAT noted that in *Spijkers*[7] the CJEU held at para 15 that there is a transfer of an undertaking or business or part of a business to another where the business in question retains its identity. In order to establish whether or not such a transfer takes place it is necessary to consider whether, having regard to all the facts characterising the transaction, the business is disposed of as a going concern as would be indicated, *inter alia*, by the fact that its operation is actually continued or resumed by the new employer with the same or similar activities. The EAT found in this case that the operation of the business of the former Sheriff of County Cork was either carried on or resumed by the respondent with the same activities, some of the assets and the same workforce.

The EAT noted the findings in *Suzen*[8] and accepted that the fact that the work or contract of the former County Sheriff for Cork transferred to the respondent did not, of itself, mean that there had been a relevant transfer. In this case, more than just the work or contract of the former County Sheriff of Cork had transferred – many of the employees transferred and tangible assets such as computers and the building would have transferred but for the unsuitability of its location for the respondent. Accordingly, the EAT found that there was a transfer of assets and the majority of workers from the former Sheriff of County Cork to the respondent, enabling an economic activity which pursued a specific objective (the enforcement of debt) to be exercised.

The EAT noted that in *Sanchez Hildago & Ors* the CJEU had said it was for a national court to determine whether a transfer had occurred in cases before it, and in doing so, the national court must consider the following:

- Whether there is an economic activity. In this case the EAT answered this in the affirmative.

- The mere fact that the service successively provided by the old and new undertaking, to which the services were contracted out or to whom the contract is awarded, is similar does not justify the conclusion that a transfer of such entity had incurred. The EAT noted that in this case there was more than the mere fact that a similar service was contracted out.

- Is it a stable economic entity? In this case the EAT held that it was. The EAT noted that while the entity might be sufficiently structured and autonomous, it will not necessarily have significant assets, material or immaterial. These assets are often reduced to the most basic where the activity is essentially based on

---

7.   *Spijkers v Gebroeders Benedik Abattoir CV* (Case C–24/1985).

8.   *Ayse Suzen v Zehnacker Gebaudereinigung GmbH Krankenhausservice* (Case C–13/95).

manpower. Thus an organised grouping of wage earners who are specifically and permanently assigned to a common task may, in the absence of other factors, amount to an economic entity. In this case, the EAT found that the employees of the transferor taken over by the respondent could, in the absence of other factors, amount to an economic entity but in any event the EAT found that there were other relevant factors such as the transfer of assets.

- Is the entity capable of maintaining its identity after it has been transferred? In this case the EAT found that the entity was capable and did retain its identity. The EAT concluded that there was a transfer of an economic entity which retained its identity for the purpose of reg 3 because the respondent and her predecessors in title had the same jurisdiction and powers which would lead to insignificant or no differences in their respective cultures and approach to work.[9] Although there was a new person running the operation, the economic entity retained its identity insofar as it had the same name, carried out the same work and had taken over a majority of the workforce of the former entity and some of the assets. Finally, the undertaking was transferred as a going concern insofar as the working process by the former County Sheriff of County Cork was handed back to the State to be continued by his successor in title even though expired summons or warrants may have needed to be renewed.

The EAT concluded that it would hear the substantive appeal.

[26.03] The substantive case came[10] before the EAT by way of a direct claim by the claimant under the Unfair Dismissals Acts and the Redundancy Payments Acts and by way of an appeal by the respondent against the decision of a Rights Commissioner under the 2003 Regulations. At the outset the claimant withdrew his claim under the Unfair Dismissals Acts and confirmed he was proceeding with this claim under the Redundancy Payment Acts. The EAT noted its hearing and findings on the preliminary issue.[11]

The claimant's evidence was that he had received what he described as a letter of undertaking from MOD informing him that his employment would transfer in February 2013 to MOD's successor by virtue of the 2003 Regulations. The claimant's evidence was that he was led to believe that he would be transferred to the new County Sheriff and at no time was it indicated to him that he might have difficulty with the change in employer. The claimant asserted that there was essentially no consultation with MOD, rather he was given the letter. However, the EAT noted that the relevant information could not have been provided in February 2013, as MOD did not know at that time who the successor was meant to be and would not have had the information necessary in order for him to assess whether a transfer would occur as this would depend on how his successor planned to run the Office of Sheriff. All he could have known at this point was that the contract was to be awarded to a successor.

---

9. *Law Society v Secretary of State for Justice & Anor* [2010] EWHC 352 [QB].
10. UD1323/2013, RP629/2013.
11. TU36/2014.

The claimant's evidence was that he did have some discussions with the respondent (MOD's successor) following which she wrote to him in April 2013 stating that his employment with MOD had terminated in mid-February 2013. He received a further letter in May 2013 from the respondent stating that his contract had come to an end on 13 February 2013 and that MOD had not consulted with her. He was informed by the respondent that she had no work for him. The claimant asserted that the respondent had discussed with him the difficulties of the job, taking account of his age and the difficulty in insuring him and he asserted that either the respondent or MOD was liable for a redundancy payment to him. He noted that MOD had given him his P45 in April 2013.

Evidence was given by the respondent that she applied for the position of Sheriff for County Cork pursuant to an advertisement. On or about 13 February 2013 she was informed by letter that she had been shortlisted for the appointment and shortly thereafter she was contacted by the Minister's Office stating the post was hers. The appointment was announced at Cabinet in February 2013 and she was appointed with effect from 1 March 2013. Files from MOD, the former Sheriff, were taken back by the Revenue Commissioner on 15 February 2013. The respondent had a 15-minute meeting with MOD on 28 February 2013 and this was her first contact with him. He was unable to provide her with contracts of employment for his staff and it was asserted that all she received from him was a list of names. The respondent's evidence was that the claimant worked part-time and that, in any event, she would not have had work for him until May 2013, when the revenue warrants were given to her. The respondent did not take over the premises used by MOD for the work of the County Sheriff, but she took some computers because she intended using the same IT services. She took a photocopier and took on about four members of the staff of the former County Sheriff. The respondent's position was that she had taken advice on being appointed County Sheriff and was advised that the 2003 Regulations did not apply. She conceded that she did have some discussions with the claimant regarding health and safety issues of doing the job, taking into account his age and the difficulties in obtaining insurance cover for him.

The respondent asserted that there was no failure to comply with reg 8 as she was never in a position to comply, due to the date of her appointment; also, before her appointment, she had no way of knowing that she would be the new Sheriff for County Cork. The respondent's position was that the claimant's contract had been terminated before she was appointed as County Sheriff and that she had not been provided either with a contract or contractual details of the employee by her predecessor.

The EAT noted reg 8 of the 2003 Regulations which requires that certain information be provided by the transferor to employees or their representatives, where reasonably practicable, no later than 30 days before the transfer is carried out. The EAT found that, by the time the State had appointed the respondent as Sheriff for County Cork, there was no opportunity for her to comply with reg 8, either within 30 days or otherwise, before any transfer of undertakings occurred. The EAT found that, on the facts of this case, it would be irrational or unreasonable to hold that there was a breach of reg 8 by the respondent and accordingly the appeal was allowed and the decision of the Rights Commissioner set aside.

The EAT noted the position under reg 13 of the 2006 Regulations (the UK equivalent of reg 8) where it was held in the UK in *Allen & Ors v Morrisons Facilities Services*

Ltd[12] that the relevant obligation owed to affected employees of the transferor is imposed on the transferor and that an order can only be made against a transferee if the tribunal finds the complaint against the transferor well founded and the transferor shows that the transferee failed to perform their obligations under reg 13(4). The UKEAT in that case went on to hold that there was no independent cause of action which could be pursued by the claimants against the transferees.

The EAT noted the findings of the Rights Commissioner that the respondent was responsible for termination of the claimant's contract of employment and that he had been made redundant in accordance with the 2003 Regulations and was entitled to redundancy payment. The EAT noted its findings in a prior case[13] that the claimant's contract had been terminated by the former Cork County Sheriff and that his claim for redundancy against the former Cork County Sheriff had succeeded. The EAT decided to allow the appeal under the 2003 Regulations and set aside this decision of the Rights Commissioner.

In allowing the appeal, the EAT held that MOD, the former Sheriff for County Cork, failed to pursue the issue of transferring the contracts across to the respondent and simply asserted to the employee that TUPE applied. The failure of MOD to furnish contractual details for the employee meant that the respondent was not in a position to ascertain whether the employee was subject to an express clause (oral or written) that he would be required to retire at 65 years of age, which, when he commenced in 1987, would have been the norm. In the absence of this, the EAT concluded that the retention of the claimant by MOD well beyond retirement age was not a contractual right or obligation that could transfer to the respondent.

The claimant's contract had terminated prior to the appointment of the respondent as County Sheriff of Cork and the claimant was claiming redundancy for a period ending prior to the appointment of the respondent. MOD failed to make any meaningful efforts to secure the transfer of the claimant to the respondent. MOD also failed to consider and discuss with the claimant that there could be difficulties in his continuing employment with any new County Sheriff in circumstances where the claimant was past what is considered normal retirement age, which could result in health and safety issues as well as difficulties in obtaining employer's liability insurance in respect of the claimant.

At the time that MOD asserted by letter to the claimant that he would be transferring to whoever was appointed as the new County Sheriff, all that could be said, with any certainty, was that there may be a transfer of undertaking as, if the respondent had only taken over the contract, no transfer of undertakings would have occurred. This assertion had the potential to act to the detriment of the claimant as he was led to believe that everything would be okay. The issuing of a P45 by MOD to the claimant in April 2013 indicated an acceptance by MOD that the claimant had not transferred to the respondent. The appeal was allowed.

---

12. *Allen & Ors v Morrisons Facilities Services Ltd* [2014] UKEAT/0298/13/DM.

13. *Brady v O'Driscoll* RP82/2014.

Collective agreements

[26.04] *Deveci & Ors v Scandinavian Airlines System Denmark-Norway-Sweden[14]—EFTA Court—Business Transfer Directive 2001/23/EC,[15] arts 3(1) and (3)—whether on cessation of collective agreement applicable to transferring employees, a transferee was permitted to apply its own collective agreement to the transferring employees which resulted in pay reductions*

This case arose from a referral by a Norwegian Court of Appeal to the EFTA Court as to whether the claimants were protected under the Business Transfer Directive. The transferor, Spirit Air Cargo Handling Norway AS, was wholly owned by a company belonging to the SAS Group. It was active in terminal operations and cargo handling. A decision was taken to transfer the business of Spirit Air Cargo Handling Norway AS to the transferee. This transfer of undertaking became effective on 1 March 2012. The transferee was a consortium, wholly owned by three Nordic limited liability companies who themselves were owned by a parent company SAS AB and part of the SAS group.

The Court noted that the transferee's employees and the claimants, ie the newly transferred employees, were represented by the same trade unions. The transferor and the transferee were bound by a number of collective agreements and were members of the same employer confederations on a national level and thus were bound by the same basic and nationwide collective agreements. However, those collective agreements were supplemented by third-tier special agreements on pay rates which differed between the transferee and the transferor.

In January 2012, the claimants' trade unions gave notice of termination of the nationwide collective agreements, the effective date of which was 31 March 2012. After the transfer took place on 1 March 2012, the transferee continued to pay the transferring employees in accordance with the rates stipulated in the special agreement for the transferor. However on 30 March 2012, the transferee informed the transferring employees they would be covered by the third-tier special agreement applying to the transferee and thus individual terms would be adjusted by 1 May 2012. As of that date, the employees in question were paid in accordance with special agreements that applied in the transferee's undertaking. The Court noted that under the current special agreement, the pay level in the transferee's undertaking was on average between 4 and 8 per cent lower than for corresponding employee categories in the transferor. The changes were made at an individual level in the magnitude of plus 3 per cent to minus 11.5 per cent. When the employees were assigned a grade in the applicable pay tables in the transferee's undertaking they were fully credited for their seniority and qualifications under the former employment relationship with the transferor. The claimants, 129

---

14. *Deveci & Ors v Scandinavian Airlines System Denmark-Norway-Sweden* (Case E–10/14).
15. Council Directive 2001/23/EC on the Approximation of the Laws of the Member States Relating to the Safeguarding of Employees' Rights in the Event of Transfers of Undertakings, Businesses or Parts of Undertakings or Businesses.

former employees of the transferor, did not accept the pay reduction which resulted from the transfer to the new collective agreement. They sought an order requiring the transferee to continue to apply the higher pay rates in accordance with the special agreement entered into by the transferor.

An initial judgment of the Norwegian District Court found in favour of the transferee which was appealed to the Court of Appeal. An advisory opinion from the EFTA Court was sought as to whether there was consistency with art 3(1) and (3) of Directive 2001/23. The first question was whether it was compatible with art 3(3) of the Directive that the conditions of the collective agreement in the transferee undertaking were applied to the employees covered by the transfer after the expiry of the collective agreement, even if this resulted in a pay reduction. In its third question, the referring Court asked whether the answer to question 1 depended on whether the reduction (in pay) was significant.

The EFTA Court assessed both of these questions together. The Court noted that the intention of the Directive was to achieve partial harmonisation and not to establish a uniform level of protection within its scope throughout the European Economic Area. The Directive aimed to ensure a fair balance between the interests of the transferred employees and of the transferee undertaking. Under art 3(3) of the Directive, the transferee shall continue to observe the terms and conditions agreed in a collective agreement on the same terms applicable to the transfer or under that agreement until the date of termination or expiry of the collective agreement, or the entry into force or application of another collective agreement. The Court held that if conditions of pay enjoyed by the transferring employees, under the previous collective agreement with the transferor, were replaced with conditions of pay laid down by the collective agreement in force with the transferee, but only after the expiry of the former agreement, the entitlement to a particular salary was not linked to the transfer but to the expiry of the collective agreements. The Court held that the Directive safeguards employees' rights and obligations in force on the date of transfer but was not intended to protect mere expectations as to rights and, therefore, hypothetical advantages flowing from future changes to collective agreements.

The issue of whether the application of new conditions results in a pay reduction and the scale of any reduction has no influence on the assessment under the Directive. The Court noted that art 3(3) of the Directive does not prescribe the application of a collective agreement but is related to its terms and conditions governing matters of pay. It followed that the rates of pay put in place by a collective agreement fell within the scope of art 3(3) of the Directive, whether or not those conditions were applicable to the persons concerned by virtue of the collective agreement or a national rule maintaining the effect of a collective agreement after its expiration. It was sufficient that such terms and conditions had been put in place by a collective agreement and effectively bound the transferor and the employees transferred.

The Court held that, in the interest of employees, a national rule may give continuing effects to a collective agreement in order to avoid a rupture of the framework governing the employment relationship, and the Court noted that this was the case in Norway. Therefore, it must be assessed whether such a rule complies with the main object of the Directive, ie to ensure a fair balance between the interest of the employees and those of the transferee. The Court noted the decision in *Alemo-Herron & Ors*[16] and reiterated that the transferee must be in a position to make adjustments and changes as necessary to carry on its operation. Since continued effects applicable after the expiration of a collective agreement limit the freedom of action of the transferee, such a national rule must be limited in its duration otherwise it would bind the transferee indefinitely. The Court held that the answer to the first and third questions must be that it is consistent with art 3(3) of the Directive if conditions of pay enjoyed by the transferring employees under the collective agreement with the transferor are replaced, in conformity with national law, by conditions of pay laid down by the collective agreement in force with the transferee after the expiry of the former collective agreements. A pay reduction, whether significant or otherwise, cannot influence this assessment.

However, where the national law provides for continuing effects in a situation such as the present, art 3(3) of the Directive has to be interpreted as meaning that the terms and conditions laid down in a collective agreement to which such continuing effects apply, constitute terms and conditions agreed in any collective agreement, so long as those employment relationships are not subject to a new collective agreement, or new individual agreements are not concluded with the employees concerned.

In its second question, the national Court asked the EFTA Court whether it was compatible with art 3(1) and (3) of the Directive that the conditions of the collective agreements in the transferee's undertaking are applied to the employees covered by the transfer even if this results in a pay reduction at a time when the collective agreement that applied to the transferor was still in force. The Court held that art 3(3) of the Directive does not prevent the transferee from applying to the transferring employees the terms and conditions laid down by the collective agreement in force, including those concerning pay, at the time of, or two months after, the transfer, if that collective agreement is made applicable in accordance with national law.

However art 3 of the Directive precluded the possibility that transferring employees suffer a substantial loss of income in comparison with their situation immediately prior to the transfer because the duration of their service with the transferor is not specifically taken into account when the starting salary position at the transferee is determined, and where the conditions for remuneration under the newly applicable collective agreement have regard to the length of service. In that determination the equivalent duration of service of those employees already in the service of the transferee must be taken into consideration. It was for the national court to examine whether the conditions of pay under the transferee's collective agreement take due account of length of service.

---

16. *Alemo-Herron & Ors v Parkwood Leisure Ltd* (Case C–426/11).

Responsibility for a disciplinary appeal process

[26.05] *Salmon v Castlebeck Care (Teesdale) Ltd (In Administration) & Anor[17]—UK Employment Appeal Tribunal—Transfer of Undertakings (Protection of Employment) Regulations 2006 (SI 2006/246), reg 4(3)—contracts of employment— terms of employment—appeals procedure—unfair dismissal—reason for dismissal— transfer of undertaking—effect of successful appeal—Rules of Procedure*

The claimant was employed by the first respondent and was summarily dismissed for alleged gross negligence. She appealed under the first respondent's disciplinary procedure. A few months later, the business of the first respondent transferred to the second respondent, Danshell Healthcare Ltd. The claimant's appeal was heard shortly after the transfer and the dismissal was deemed 'unsafe'. She received no express order of reinstatement, nor did she receive any clear and unequivocal indication that her contract had been revived.

The claimant brought unsuccessful unfair dismissal proceedings against both of the respondents. The case was rejected against the second respondent as it was held that Danshell Healthcare Ltd had never employed her and that her employment had not transferred to it under the 2006 Regulations[18] (TUPE).

The employment tribunal decided that, in addition to a successful appeal, there must be a decision to reinstate for TUPE to apply. The tribunal also noted that there had been no communication of the decision on the appeal.

The claimant appealed this. She submitted that the effect of her successful appeal had been to revive her contract of employment and, accordingly, she fell within reg 4 of TUPE as someone who had been employed immediately before the transfer with the effect that her employment had automatically transferred to Danshell Healthcare Ltd.

It was submitted on behalf of the claimant: firstly, that the employment tribunal erred in concluding that there had been no effective reinstatement of the contract as a result of what happened; and secondly, that it erred in holding that the outcome of the appeal needed to be communicated to be effective.

The respondents relied heavily on *G4S Justice Services (UK) Ltd v Anstey[19]* in their arguments. It was put forward that, as in that case, the contractual obligation to hear and determine appeals heard post-transfer against dismissals effected post-transfer lay with the transferor, notwithstanding the transfer. In the present proceedings, two employees of Danshell heard the appeal. The respondents contend that for this reason, the disciplinary appeal could not have been properly heard by Danshell and for that reason any decision made on appeal was without substance and effect. However, this argument had not been previously raised and was therefore rejected by the UK EAT in following *Glennie v Independent Magazines (UK) Ltd.[20]* It was found in that case that the UK EAT

---

17.   *Salmon v Castlebeck Care (Teesdale) Ltd (In Administration) & Anor* [2015] IRLR 189.
18.   Transfer of Undertakings (Protection of Employment) Regulations 2006 (SI 2006/246).
19.   *G4S Justice Services (UK) Ltd v Anstey* [2006] IRLR 588 EAT.
20.   *Glennie v Independent Magazines (UK) Ltd* [1999] IRLR 719.

had been in error in exercising its discretion to allow a new point to be heard for the first time on appeal to it from the employment tribunal.

On the issue of the effect of a successful appeal, the UK EAT noted that this was now an established area of law. *G4S* referred to and treated *Roberts v West Coast Trains Ltd*[21] as binding authority, which it was as to principle. *Roberts* unequivocally states that:

> The effect of the decision on appeal is to revive retrospectively the contract of employment terminated by the earlier decision to dismiss so as to treat the employee as if he had never been dismissed.

The UK EAT stated that, from its consideration of the case law, it had 'no hesitation' in thinking that the employment tribunal had erred in looking for a separate decision, consequent upon a successful appeal, that there should be 'reinstatement'. It was held therefore that a successful appeal automatically revives the contract.

The respondents further argued that there had been no clarity about whether there had been a successful appeal. They maintained that the words used by the employment judge conveyed only a recommendation of the panel and the proposed outcome and that there was uncertainty around them. The UK EAT followed the decision in *McMaster*[22] in making a ruling on this point. It stated that, as in that case, the use of the word 'recommended' or the word 'proposed' does not have the uncertainty to which the judge referred to; nor is it to be believed that the judge meant it in that sense. The judge referred repeatedly to the 'outcome' of the appeal and this is a word which does not admit uncertainty or a tentative decision.

As to the question of whether it was necessary to communicate the outcome of the successful appeal, the UK EAT took the view that, as the claimant's contract automatically revived following the successful appeal, there was no need for express communication.

It therefore followed that, as she was employed immediately prior to the transfer of the business from the first respondent to Danshell, her rights lay against Danshell and not against the first respondent.

The UK EAT concluded that the appeal should be allowed.

Dismissal

[26.06] *Ansari v Lodge Services Dublin Ltd & Albany House*[23]*—Employment Appeals Tribunal—Unfair Dismissals Acts 1977 to 2015—dispute whether transfer of undertakings occurred—dismissal based on mistaken belief that employee's employment had transferred*

The claimant was employed as a retail security officer from July 2008.

---

21. *Roberts v West Coast Trains Ltd* [2004] IRLR 788.
22. *McMaster v Antrim Borough Council* [2011] IRLR 235 NICA.
23. *Ansari v Lodge Services Dublin Ltd and Albany House* UD792/2014, MN403/2014.

It was the claimant's case that he was unfairly dismissed by the respondent company. The respondent denied dismissal and contended that the claimant's employment transferred to another undertaking in December 2013.

The claimant was based at a number of store locations throughout his employment but from June 2013 to November 2013 he was based at two locations in Limerick for Client A. In September 2013, Client A renegotiated its contract, resulting in the respondent's loss of the contract for the Limerick stores to another security provider. As a result, a number of the respondent's employees were due to transfer to the new security provider under the European Communities (Protection of Employees on Transfer of Undertakings) Regulations 2003 (the '2003 Regulations') with effect from 1 December 2013. The claimant was one of the employees due to transfer.

The respondent's managing director gave evidence that the respondent sent the claimant a letter dated 18 November 2013 advising him that he would transfer but that should there be suitable alternative employment within the respondent, it would be advertised and the claimant could apply for these roles.

This was contradicted by the claimant, who asserted that he had received no word from the respondent from November 2013 until January 2014, following his request to the respondent for his work roster, which the claimant asserted was 43 days after he had received any correspondence from the respondent.

The operations manager said that he spoke with the claimant on 2 December 2013 and reminded the claimant that his employment would transfer, and told him that there was no alternative work for the claimant with the respondent in the Limerick area.

The EAT heard that the respondent believed that the claimant's employment came to an end on 30 November 2013, but that after the claimant emailed the managing director in January 2014, the respondent understood that the claimant had not transferred to the new security provider, and sent him his P45.

There was a conflict in evidence between the claimant and the respondent in respect of whether the 2003 Regulations applied. The claimant asserted that the 2003 Regulations were not activated as only one of the respondent's employees transferred to the new security provider. The respondent stated that all, bar one, of its employees in that area transferred to Client A's security provider.

The operations manager gave evidence that when the proposed transfer was communicated to the affected employees, the claimant contacted him to express his discontent with the proposal, as it would potentially jeopardise his employment with his other employer. The operations manager gave evidence that he advised the claimant that he would only be required to work 20 hours per week, so his other employment should not be affected.

In his evidence, the claimant stated that he was not advised of the potential transfer by the respondent, and only heard of the proposals via other sources. The claimant submitted to the EAT that due to his seniority, he believed he would be retained as an employee.

The EAT held that if there was a transfer under the 2003 Regulations when the new security provider took over the services, the respondent would not have complied with the information and consultation requirements in the 2003 Regulations. Any purported communication to the claimant by the respondent was insufficient to meet the statutory criteria. It was noted that there was no documentary evidence to support any communication that a transfer occurred.

The EAT held that a transfer of undertaking did not take place and that the claimant was unfairly dismissed and was awarded €8,000 in compensation. The EAT held that, as the claimant was aware that the respondent lost its contract with its client in November 2013, he was on notice of the termination of his employment, and therefore his claim under the Minimum Notice and Terms of Employment Acts 1973 to 2005 was not upheld.

Chapter 27

UNFAIR DISMISSAL

PRELIMINARY ISSUES

Continuous service

[27.01] *Kearney v Seel Publishing Ltd (in liquidation) t/a North County Leader[1]—Employment Appeals Tribunal—Unfair Dismissals Acts 1977 to 2015—preliminary issue whether claimant had requisite service to bring claim—employment status—whether claimant an employee or self-employed contractor*

The claimant operated as a freelance journalist submitting photographs and articles for publication to the respondent who operated a weekly journal. The relationship between the parties commenced in July 2011, and in June 2012, the claimant was advised that the respondent would cease publishing temporarily. It was asserted by the respondent that this event terminated the relationship between the parties as a layoff situation existed. It was submitted by the respondent that the claimant did not have the 12 months of continuous service required to bring a claim and that the claim was lodged outside of the six-month limit set out in the legislation. It was further asserted that the claimant operated as a freelance journalist and photographer, was engaged under a contract for services and was thus not an employee. Evidence to support this was that the claimant had discretion to create a story idea, write an article and submit it to the news desk, which would then decide if it was to be published. The same process applied for photography, except in respect of the 'clubbers page' where the respondent decided which venue the photographer must attend. The claimant provided his own equipment, and if an article was published the claimant was paid per word. The manner of payment was supported by invoices. The respondent asserted that there were no guarantees that the work would be published and although the claimant was not excluded from submitting work to other publications, the respondent did acknowledge it got first refusal.

The claimant asserted that his relationship with the respondent did not end until August 2012 and accordingly he had 12 months of continuous service. To support this, he submitted confirmation from the Department of Social Protection, which deemed him to be employed under a contract of service; however it was noted by the EAT that this decision was under appeal by the respondent. The claimant asserted that he was an employee in so far as the respondent controlled where he attended when photographing for the publication and also he had no room to negotiate rates and was required to work in the respondent's offices to provide holiday cover for a period of seven days.

The EAT noted that a period of layoff does not terminate employment. Insofar as the claimant worked in the office providing holiday cover for seven days, he was employed by the respondent. The EAT applied three tests, control, integration and enterprise to

---

1. *Kearney v Seel Publishing Ltd (in liq) t/a North County Leader* UD258/2013.

decide if the claimant was an employee or self-employed. In relation to control, the EAT noted that the claimant was free to decide where he could go and what he should deal with. His role was not integrated into the business because there was a number of other freelancers who also chose what to do. The EAT concluded that on all three tests the claimant was self-employed and thus it had no jurisdiction to hear his unfair dismissals claim.

[27.02] *Kenyon v Macxchange Ltd t/a Compu B[2]—Employment Appeals Tribunal— Unfair Dismissals Acts 1977 to 2015, s 2(a)—unfair dismissal—preliminary issue— whether claimant had requisite one year of continuous service to bring claim— claimant's first contract of employment terminated—rehired one week later by same respondent*

This was a dispute about when the claimant's employment as business-to-business education manager commenced with the respondent. The respondent maintained the claimant commenced employment on 5 December 2011, although the claimant submitted his start date was 28 November 2011. The respondent sells Apple computer products with a staff of 80 employees.

On 26 November 2012, the claimant was called to a meeting in a coffee shop where his first employment contract was terminated. He was then rehired on 4 December 2012 under a second contract and was required to work from home and did not have involvement in the running of the respondent's shop as under the first contract. The claimant's evidence was that he was told that the respondent was not happy with his performance and that he was not meeting the required targets; although the claimant disputed that targets had been set for him. The claimant's evidence was that in 2012 his sales were in excess of €1,000,000. When he was informed that he was being dismissed and rehired, the claimant felt he had no option but to continue working for the respondent as he had a mortgage and a family to support. With the new arrangements in place, the claimant worked 40 per cent from home, 10 to 15 per cent in the store and the rest of the time on the road. The claimant denied he had been given a second contract of employment by the respondent and argued that his employment had been continuous. It was submitted by the respondent that, although the company did have documentation regarding targets, it was not available for the hearing. The respondent denied that the claimant had been dismissed and rehired so as to avoid him having one year's service. In response to a question from the EAT, the respondent stated that the difference between the contracts was that the claimant no longer managed staff and he had accepted the new work arrangement and contract. However, the respondent was unable to explain why the second contract was not signed by the claimant and why it had come from the respondent's headquarters. The EAT considered the evidence before it and found that the claimant had continuity of service with the respondent from the date of his commencement on 5 December 2011 until the termination of his employment on 31 July 2013.

---

2. *Kenyon v Macxchange Ltd t/a Compu B* UD132/2014.

Whether claim statute barred/exceptional circumstances

[27.03] *Ali Raza Khan v Deeal Retail Ltd[3]—Employment Appeals Tribunal—appeal from decision of Rights Commissioner—Unfair Dismissals Acts 1977 to 2015—preliminary issue—whether claim statute barred where workplace relations complaint form submitted one day outside statutory time—whether exceptional circumstances existed to allow an extension of statutory time limits—failure of claimant to produce medical evidence*

This was an appeal by the claimant of a decision of a Rights Commissioner who found that the claim was statute barred. The claimant's workplace relations complaint form was submitted to the Rights Commissioner service by fax on 20 March 2013 and by post on 21 March 2013. It stated that the claimant had received one week's notice of termination on 13 September 2012 and his employment ended on 20 September 2012. The Rights Commissioner found that he had no jurisdiction to hear the claim as the form was submitted one day outside the statutory time limits.

The respondent contended that the claimant's employment had ended on 13 September 2012 by reason of gross misconduct following an allegation of sexual assault by a junior colleague. It was contended by the respondent that, as a result, no notice period applied. The claimant contended that he had suffered from an epileptic episode and that the incident had occurred afterwards. He did not have any memory of this incident but did not dispute that it had occurred. The claimant's first argument was that he had engaged in correspondence with the respondent, the last of which exchanged on 30 October 2012 and that this process of appeal and correspondence delayed the date of dismissal. The EAT did not accept this, as the claimant clearly had the benefit of legal advice at the time of dismissal and the letter of dismissal had stated clearly that 13 September was the date of dismissal. The EAT noted that the appeal did not take place as the claimant did not attend.

It was contended by the claimant that he had been seeking medical treatment in his home country of Pakistan for a number of months and only arrived back to Ireland shortly before the six-month time limit to lodge a claim expired. The claimant contended that if the EAT found that the dismissal was not for misconduct, a notice period would apply which would bring the claimant within the statutory time limits. The EAT held that medical evidence must be supplied by the claimant in order to forward either or both of those arguments. The case was adjourned to allow the claimant time to produce medical evidence and, notwithstanding that the matter was put in for mention before the EAT on two separate occasions to see if medical evidence would be produced, no medical evidence was produced by the claimant. The EAT, in its determination, noted that it had given the claimant every opportunity to produce medical evidence to show that he was receiving treatment to allow an extension of the statutory time limits but this was not forthcoming. The EAT affirmed the original decision of the Rights Commissioner that the complaint was statute barred.

---

3. *Ali Raza Khan v Deeal Retail Ltd* UD1722/2013.

[27.04] *Cronin v Rigney Dolphin[4]—Employment Appeals Tribunal—appeal from decision of Rights Commissioner—Unfair Dismissals Acts 1977 to 2015—preliminary issue of timing of complaint being made—exceptional circumstances—reactive depression—medical evidence*

A preliminary issue arose in relation to the time limit for submitting the complaint under the Acts. The date of the dismissal was 23 July 2013, and the complaint was filed in February 2014, outside of the six-month period. The claimant asked the EAT to hold that there had been exceptional circumstances which led to the delay and requested that it extend the time limit.

The EAT heard evidence from the claimant's doctor, who informed the EAT that the claimant consulted him in January 2014 and that he was diagnosed with reactive depression and was prescribed medication. The claimant's doctor stated that he did not consider the claimant at the time to be capable of prosecuting a complaint under the Acts. There were however no medical records to this effect. Counsel for the respondent sought an adjournment to have the claimant medically examined. The EAT did not grant this application on the grounds that it did not believe that anything of evidential value could come from such an examination.

The evidence of the claimant was that he felt he was going nowhere; he was humiliated, embarrassed, had no confidence and had 'hit a wall'. The EAT noted that this seemed to be consistent with the claimant being symptomatic prior to the January 2014 diagnosis. The EAT accepted the evidence of the claimant's doctor that he was suffering from reactive depression which affected the claimant's ability to act in his own best interests and to file his claim under the Acts in a timely manner. The EAT noted that finding new work led to a lifting of the claimant's reactive depression and he appeared to have a renewed capacity to deal with and progress his claim under the Acts.

The EAT found that there were 'exceptional circumstances' within the meaning of the Acts and extended the time for the claimant's filing of his claim under the Acts.

[27.05] *Duffin v St James's Hospital[5]—Employment Appeals Tribunal—Unfair Dismissals Acts 1977 to 2015—unfair dismissal—time limits—failure by employee's solicitor to lodge complaint within time limits*

The respondent's representative submitted that the EAT had no jurisdiction to hear the claim because it was made outside the statutory time period. The claimant gave evidence that she had consulted her solicitor shortly after she was dismissed and left the matter in his hands.

The claimant was dismissed from her employment in June 2013. She engaged her solicitors in August 2012. They represented her at disciplinary meetings and wrote comprehensive letters on her behalf. The claimant's workplace relations form was filed in May 2014 almost one year after her dismissal. The T2 was filed in August 2014 and the claimant was served with a copy of that document on 14 August 2014. At para 1 of

---

4.   *Cronin v Rigney Dolphin* UD589/2015.
5.   *Duffin v St James's Hospital* UD924/2014.

that document it stated 'The claimant was out of time when she filed her claim'. Therefore the EAT found she was on notice of the preliminary issue from that date.

The EAT noted its jurisdiction to extend the six-month time limit up to 12 months if exceptional circumstances prevented the bringing of the claim in the first six months and referred to the case of *Byrne v Quigley*[6] where the EAT stated that 'exceptional' means something out of the ordinary and, at the very least, the circumstances must be unusual, probably quite unusual, but not necessarily highly unusual. The EAT noted that it was unfortunate that the claimant's solicitors were not present at the hearing, having been discharged on the morning of the hearing and therefore could not explain the circumstances in relation to the delay.

The EAT found no circumstances existed at the material time that prevented the claimant from filing her claim within time and therefore that the EAT had no jurisdiction to hear the claim.

Parallel claim for personal injuries

[27.06] *Neeson v John O'Rourke & Seán O'Rourke Chartered Accountants[7]— Employment Appeals Tribunal—Unfair Dismissals Acts 1977 to 2015, ss 15(3) and 8(2)—constructive dismissal—parallel claim for personal injuries initiated in Circuit Court—preliminary issues in relation to jurisdiction of EAT—claimant entitled to have her claim heard by EAT as hearing of her personal injuries claim had not yet commenced—preliminary issue in relation to making of complaint under Unfair Dismissals Acts 1977 to 2015 while claimant still in employment—employee engaged with employer for months after alleged date of termination—date of dismissal—claim not validly lodged as lodged prior to claimant's termination*

This was a claim for constructive dismissal. The claimant also lodged a personal injuries action for bullying and harassment at common law in the Circuit Court, relying upon the same set of events which had taken place in the course of her employment. The respondent raised two preliminary points with the EAT.

The respondent argued that the potential existed for overlapping issues between the present case and the one before the Circuit Court. Accordingly, the first preliminary point raised by the respondent was that the EAT should decline jurisdiction to hear the claim for constructive dismissal. In the alternative, the respondent sought to adjourn the hearing of the claim before the EAT pending the outcome of the claimant's personal injuries action in the Circuit Court.

In its determination of this preliminary issue, the EAT considered s 15(3) of the Acts (as substituted by s 10 of the Unfair Dismissals (Amendment) Act of 1993), which provides:

> Where the hearing by a Court of proceedings for damages at common law for wrongful dismissal of an employee has commenced, the employee shall not be

6. *Byrne v Quigley* [1995] ELR 205.
7. *Neeson v John O'Rourke & Seán O'Rourke Chartered Accountants* UD2049/2011.

entitled to redress under this Act in respect of the dismissal to which the proceedings relate.

The EAT noted that this subsection precluded redress under the Acts where the hearing by the court of a claim for damages for wrongful dismissal at common law had *commenced*. This 'new' subsection introduced by the 1993 Act, differed from the 'old' subsection which precluded redress under the Acts where a claim for damages for wrongful dismissal at common law had been *initiated* by or on behalf of the employee. The EAT noted that the hearing of the action before the Circuit Court had not commenced and held that, accordingly, it was not precluded from hearing the claim under the Acts.

In addition, the EAT placed emphasis on the traumatic effect and the long term consequences which dismissal can have on an employee in holding that the claimant was entitled to a finding as to the fairness or otherwise of her constructive dismissal claim. In this regard it was considered relevant that the Circuit Court can only make such a finding on an appeal from a determination of the EAT. Accordingly, the EAT refused the respondent's application and accepted that it had jurisdiction to hear the claim.

The second preliminary point made by the respondent was that the EAT did not have jurisdiction to hear the claim under the Acts as the claim had been lodged while the claimant was still in its employment. For the purposes of addressing this second preliminary issue, the EAT opted to take evidence on this matter in conjunction with evidence on the substantive case.

In order to determine whether the claimant's complaint was validly lodged before the EAT, the EAT first considered the date upon which dismissal could be said to have occurred. As this was a constructive dismissal claim, the question related to the date on which the claimant terminated her employment with the respondent. The EAT considered the evidence in relation to the claimant's submission of medical certificates to the respondent until March 2012 and the fact that she had been in receipt of illness benefit payments (which were only available to employees) from the Department of Social Protection until February 2012. It took note of the fact that the claimant did not at any time submit a letter of resignation to the respondent and considered the different dates upon which the claimant might be said to have terminated her employment. It held that it was clear that the claimant's employment with the respondent continued in existence beyond the date of termination as per her claim form, ie 26 April 2011. While the EAT attached some weight to the communication of 18 October 2011 wherein the claimant's legal representative indicated she was proceeding to issue unfair dismissal and personal injuries proceedings, it was ultimately satisfied that the claimant terminated her employment on 12/13 January 2012. It considered the entirety of the claimant's behaviour in reaching this conclusion.

The EAT then considered whether the constructive dismissal claim was validly lodged with it, so as to confer jurisdiction on it to hear and determine the claim.

The EAT considered s 8(2) of the Acts, which provides for the lodging of a claim 'within the period of 6 months beginning on the date of the relevant dismissal'. The EAT noted that this 'new' s 8(2), introduced by the Unfair Dismissals (Amendment) Act 1993, differed from the 'old' provision, which merely required the lodging of the claim 'within 6 months of the date of the relevant dismissal'. The EAT was of the view that this amendment demonstrated a manifest intention by the legislature to preclude claims being lodged before the dismissal date.

The EAT considered the recent High Court decision in *Brady v EAT*[8] in relation to the premature lodgement of a claim with the EAT. In *Brady* the employee had been made redundant on 16 December 2011. His claim was lodged with the EAT on 23 December 2011. The respondent argued that this was prior to the statutory date of dismissal when the statutory notice period was taken into account, ie 30 December 2011. Barrett J held in *Brady* that the lodgement of the claim on 23 December was valid. The EAT took note of para 8 of the High Court judgment in *Brady*, which made three main points:

- 'prescribed time periods are typically intended to thwart the tardy, not punish the prompt';

- a longstanding principle of equity provides that 'equity aids the vigilant, not the indolent'; and

- the practical issue of whether a person (in these circumstances the EAT) could be said not to have received notice within a prescribed period, 'if it had notice immediately prior to, at the commencement of, and throughout that period'. The High Court concluded that 'it would be absurd to hold that where the Employment Appeals Tribunal had notice of the claim at the commencement of, and throughout, the six month period that Mr Brady should be denied the opportunity to bring his claim because the EAT, through no fault of Mr Brady, may also have had notice of the claim immediately prior to the applicable six-month period'.

The EAT concluded, from a reading of *Brady*, that the wording of the old s 8(2) of the Acts had not been before the High Court and there had been no focus on the significance of the specific wording of the amending provision or on the intention behind it. The EAT stated that it had not had 'the benefit of any evidence on the debate surrounding this change and what mischief it was trying to cure'. However, the EAT placed considerable emphasis on the insertion of the words 'beginning on' in s 8(2). It held that, giving these words their natural and ordinary meaning, the amendment must be interpreted to mean that a claim must be lodged after the dismissal. Accordingly it determined that the claim was not validly before it, having been lodged prior to the dismissal. The EAT further stated that, in the event that it was mistaken in relation to the above conclusion, it would come to the same decision in reliance on para 9 of Barrett J's judgment, where he stated:

> Of course there will be some boundary in time and some circumstances in which an ostensibly premature notice will be found in fact to have been premature and thus not duly lodged within the appropriate time period for the purposes of s.8(2).

---

8.   *Brady v EAT and Bohemians Football Club* [2014] IEHC 302. See *Arthur Cox Employment Law Yearbook 2014* at [27.07].

In this regard the EAT found it noteworthy that the claim was lodged some 12 weeks before the date of dismissal. It was on this basis that the EAT distinguished the case in question from both *Brady* and *Matthews v Sandisk International Ltd*,[9] which Barrett J found supported his conclusions, wherein the claims were lodged one week and two and a half weeks respectively before the dates of dismissal. The EAT also highlighted other significant distinguishing factors in *Brady*, such as the fact that Mr Brady had been informed on 16 September that his dismissal was effective 'now'. This was considered in *Brady* to constitute a clear and unequivocal oral representation to him that his dismissal was effective immediately and in those circumstances it would be unfair and inequitable to hold that the dismissal occurred some two weeks later. Another finding in *Brady* was that the respondent had deprived the employee of the opportunity to cure the defect within the prescribed statutory time limit by failing to raise its objection on the jurisdictional issue in a timely manner in its defence. The EAT, having regard to the fact that this was a constructive dismissal case with relatively different facts to those before the High Court in *Brady*, concluded that the boundaries in time and circumstances referred to by Barrett J in *Brady* did not exist in this case.

Finally the EAT stated that there could be a danger in the lenient treatment of premature claims, as the system could become 'clogged up' with claims based on an employee's expectation that a dismissal might occur sometime in the future. Many of these claims would subsequently be withdrawn.

The EAT declined jurisdiction to determine the substantive case in circumstances where the claim had not been lodged in accordance with s 8(2) of the Acts.

AGENCY WORK – SECTION 13 OF THE UNFAIR DISMISSALS (AMENDMENT) ACT 1993

[27.07] *Dunphy v Industrial Temps Ltd t/a Industrial Temps & Anor*[10]—*Employment Appeals Tribunal—Unfair Dismissals Acts 1977 to 2015—Minimum Notice and Terms of Employment Acts 1973 to 2005—Unfair Dismissals (Amendment) Act 1993, s 13—dismissal of agency employee for gross misconduct—who was appropriate respondent*

A preliminary issue arose in this case as to who was the appropriate respondent. Respondent 1 operated as an employment agency who supplied the claimant (a haulage driver) and other drivers to respondent 2. Respondent 2 is a haulage company whose business in Ireland is focused on one multi-million Euro contract with a third company (the client company) who was not party to this case. There was no appearance or representation on behalf of respondent 1. Respondent 2 raised two preliminary issues: (a) that the claim was out of time; and (b) that the claimant was not its employee and was not dismissed by it. The EAT decided that exceptional circumstances existed and that the claim was not out of time.

---

9.   *Matthews v Sandisk International Ltd* UD331/2010.

10.   *Dunphy v Industrial Temps Ltd t/a Industrial Temps & Anor* UD718/2014, MN986/2012.

The claimant was a truck driver delivering goods to supermarket outlets belonging to the client company. He was employed though respondent 1, the recruitment agency and was on placement with respondent 2. He was employed from April 2009 until 12 May 2012 and was dismissed by letter dated 22 May 2013 as a result of an incident on 12 May 2012. On that day, the claimant completed a 13-hour shift and went to sign out at approximately 8pm. When he was stopped at security he offered his bag as usual to be searched; however the security guard asked the claimant to put his leg up so security could check his sock. It appears that the claimant reluctantly agreed to this search and was eventually given the go ahead to leave. The evidence was that the claimant had never been asked before to lift his trousers, and as a consequence, he rang respondent 1's recruitment manager to report the matter. His evidence was that the recruitment manager sympathised with him and told him it would not happen again. On 22 May he received a letter of dismissal from respondent 1 signed by the recruitment manager. He submitted an appeal but no appeal took place.

Evidence on behalf of respondent 2 from its transport manager was that he was contacted directly by an employee who was onsite during the incident in question. The relevant security guard had made a complaint against the claimant and an investigation was under way. It had been alleged that the claimant was verbally abusive and aggressive and that he had made a racial reference. The relevant transport manager reviewed the CCTV footage of the incident with the representative of the employment agency. The agency was given a copy of the CCTV footage and they said they would investigate the matter. They did not engage further with the transport manager in relation to the matter.

It was submitted that the client company's view was that the claimant's refusal to comply with a search was, in itself, gross misconduct and when he was reminded of the policy he allegedly became aggressive and verbally abusive and asked the security guard (of Asian origin) where he was from. The security guard took offence to this and believed that if he were Irish he would not have been asked this. The second respondent's evidence was that as a result of the client company's withdrawal of the claimant's site invitation, they had no work to offer the claimant. It was further submitted that respondent 2 had no involvement in the dismissal of the claimant and was unaware of it until the claim was submitted to the EAT by the claimant.

The EAT held that it was satisfied that although the claimant was recruited through an agency, the correct respondent for the purpose of the unfair dismissal legislation, as per s 13 of the Unfair Dismissals (Amendment) Act 1993, was respondent 2. The claim against respondent 1, the employment agency, was dismissed.

The EAT held that the respondent 2 should have been aware of the legislation and its responsibilities towards agency workers. The EAT considered the sanction of dismissal to be excessive. It noted that the claimant could be seen at the end of the CCTV footage to have shown his socks as requested. The EAT concluded that the claimant's question to security about where he was from was an attempt to mollify the situation and was not a racist comment. The claimant was never given an opportunity to be heard, as no investigation meeting or disciplinary procedures were instigated. The EAT upheld the claim of unfair dismissal and awarded the claimant compensation of €23,000. He was also awarded notice of two weeks' pay under the Minimum Notice and Terms of Employment Acts 1973 to 2005.

[27.08] *Granaghan v DSV Solutions Ltd[11]—Employment Appeals Tribunal—Unfair Dismissals Acts 1977 to 2015—Unfair Dismissals (Amendment) Act 1993, s 13—end user is employer—substitution of respondent as employer—expiry of time period*

The matter came before the EAT on foot of a workplace relations complaint form filed with the EAT on 11 September 2013. The form claimed unfair dismissal against the employer known as Grafton Recruitment, a well-known recruitment agency. The form detailed the work address as being DSV Packaging. The claimant stated that he was dismissed on 7 May 2013 by an individual from Grafton Recruitment.

The EAT was informed that this matter came before another division of the EAT some eight months previously when the claimant and Grafton Recruitment attended before the EAT for hearing. At that time, representatives for Grafton Recruitment successfully argued that Grafton Recruitment should be released from those proceedings in light of s 13 of the Unfair Dismissals (Amendment) Act 1993, which section provides that an individual agency worker shall be deemed an employee of the end user under a contract of employment for the purposes of liability for an unfair dismissal claim under the Acts.

The EAT was informed that Grafton Recruitment successfully argued that, for the purpose of the Unfair Dismissal legislation only, DSV Packaging should have been considered as the correct employer in circumstances where the claimant had been placed by Grafton Recruitment in the DSV packaging plant since February 2012. The outcome of that previous EAT case was that Grafton Recruitment was released and DSV Packaging was invited to attend the EAT at an adjourned date (the within proceedings).

DSV Packaging contended that it was only put on notice of its having any role in the proceedings some 18 months after the termination of the claimant's employment (and on foot of whatever communication emanated from the EAT of the initial hearing after the claimant's complaint against Grafton Recruitment). It was put to the EAT that the time limits for bringing proceedings against a proposed employer had long since expired and it was not permissible for the EAT to direct a new workplace relations complaint form to issue. It was further submitted that the previous division of the EAT would not have had this power either as the 12 months (allowed under the legislation) had expired when Grafton Recruitment and the claimant had appeared before that division in November 2014.

Ultimately, the claimant requested that the EAT exercise its power to give leave to the claimant to institute proceedings against a 'proposed respondent' where, due to inadvertence, a named respondent has been incorrectly identified in some material particular. This power lies in s 39 of the Organisation of Working Time Act 1997.

The claimant invited the EAT to follow the reasoning of Hogan J in *O'Higgins v University College Dublin and The Labour Court[12]* wherein the judge found that it would be grossly disproportionate to disallow the claim by reason of a technical error (ie name the two directors instead of the limited company). The EAT was asked to revisit

---

11.   *Granaghan v DSV Solutions Ltd* UD1249/2013.

12.   *O'Higgins v University College Dublin and The Labour Court* [2014] 25 ELR 1.

the initial workplace relations complaint form and correct the misstatement contained therein whereby DSV Packaging should have been named as the employer.

DSV Packaging argued that such a correction would go way beyond the powers of the EAT in such circumstances. It contended that, the letter sent by the claimant, dated 10 July 2013, in the immediate aftermath of the termination of the employment demonstrates that the claimant and/or his legal advisers knew or ought to have known that the claimant was an employee of either Grafton Recruitment or DSV Packaging and that faced with this uncertainty it was reckless of them to proceed against one party only (Grafton Recruitment).

The EAT accepted that any ordinary reading of the workplace relations complaint form which issued on 11 September 2013 disclosed an intention to nominate Grafton Recruitment as the employer for the purpose of the Unfair Dismissals legislation, and that the fact that the name of DSV Packaging appeared on the form at all was purely incidental and intended only to provide a place of work. The EAT found that it could not, under s 39, replace one proposed employer with another, as such correction would go well beyond the EAT's power to correct a material particular which appeared by reason of inadvertence.

The EAT declined jurisdiction against the notice party for the claim under the Unfair Dismissals Acts 1977 to 2015.

Involvement of third parties

[27.09] *Kelly v Kelco Services Ltd[13]—Employment Appeals Tribunal—Unfair Dismissals Acts 1977 to 2015—Minimum Notice and Terms of Employment Acts 1973 to 2005—whether claimant unfairly dismissed following incident in client institution where claimant asked not to return to premises because of complaint received— whether this behaviour constituted gross misconduct— whether alternative disciplinary measure considered*

The claimant was employed by the respondent as a plumber and was based with the respondent's client, a medical institution, three days a week. A complaint was received from a female because of an incident that occurred involving the claimant. As a result, the institution wrote to the respondent to confirm that the claimant was not permitted to return to the premises. The claimant, a male plumber, was required to repair a water tap in the female bathrooms. An explanation was given by the claimant that he called out through the door that he was going inside the female bathroom and that while he did hear a voice calling back he presumed that that voice had come from another part of the building and did not emanate from the bathroom. The claimant entered the bathroom and came upon the complainant who was exiting a cubicle.

The EAT considered the evidence provided by the respondent and the claimant and also a letter submitted by the complainant with regard to the incident. The EAT noted that there was a serious error of judgment on the part of the claimant and he should have known that his behaviour was inappropriate and ill-advised. Once it became apparent

---

13.   *Kelly v Kelco Services Ltd* UD638/2014, MN298/2014.

that there was someone using the bathroom facilities, the onus was on him to exit himself from the situation. The EAT noted that the event caused a co-worker to feel belittled and vulnerable and the fact that the client institution had requested that the claimant not return to the workplace left his employer, the respondent, in a difficult position. It was noted that the respondent had conducted an investigation and disciplinary process and while a sincere attempt had been made at this for a small organisation, it was noted that the original complainant was never talked to or interviewed and the statement provided by her was well after the fact. It was also noted that certain aspects of the complainant's statement went beyond the complaint she was making.

The EAT noted the conflict in evidence and concluded that the claimant's actions did lack sensitivity and that once the complaint had been made about him, his position within the client institution became precarious as he was only ever on a contract for service basis and therefore his services were dispensable. However, the EAT determined that the respondent could not reasonably have concluded on the basis of the evidence before it that his behaviour constituted gross misconduct, and accordingly the decision to dismiss him on this basis was unfair. The EAT found that it was possible that a less draconian disciplinary measure could have been imposed but accepted that the respondent may not have had alternative employment for the claimant at his salary level. The EAT therefore found that the claimant's position, had he been retained, would have been on remuneration far below that enjoyed by him before the incident.

The claim for unfair dismissal was upheld and, in contemplating redress, the EAT took account of the fact that a plumber with 43 years of experience was not in a position to find work on a casual or other basis and therefore awarded compensation of €6,000 under the Act. His claim under the Minimum Notice and Terms of Employments Act succeeded and he was awarded €3,702, being six weeks of gross pay in lieu of notice.

EXPIRY OF A FIXED-TERM CONTRACT

[27.10] *Simpson v Applus Car Testing Service Ltd t/a National Car Testing Services Ltd*[14]—*Employment Appeals Tribunal—Unfair Dismissals Acts 1977 to 2015—fixed-term contract—whether expiry of fixed-term contract is an unfair dismissal—whether business subject to seasonal downturns—whether objective commercial reason to dismiss claimant—dismissal on performance grounds*

The claimant was employed on a series of fixed-term contracts with the respondent and on the conclusion of the last contract, he was dismissed. The EAT noted that the conclusion of employment on the expiry of a fixed-term contract is a dismissal. However, whether it was an unfair dismissal depended on the circumstances of the case. If the fixed-term contract is in writing, signed by both parties and excludes the Unfair Dismissals legislation and further is a genuine fixed-term arrangement, no claim for

---

14. *Simpson v Applus Car Testing Service Ltd t/a National Car Testing Services Ltd* UD72/2013.

unfair dismissal arises. The onus is on the employer to prove that the contract was a genuine fixed-term arrangement and the dismissal was not unfair.

It was the respondent's position that the work was seasonal and that it did not require the claimant to work the latter half of the year due to business downturn at that time. The claimant's case was that there was no justifiable and objective reason for the succession of fixed-term contracts. He stated that the respondent had a growing business and that he was, in fact, very busy at the time he was dismissed and that there were no further reductions of staff after his termination.

The EAT was not convinced by the evidence proffered by the respondent to show the business was subject to seasonal downturns. The evidence instead appeared to show growth at the latter half of the year.

The EAT concluded that there was no objective commercial reason for the claimant to be dismissed. The EAT found that the claimant had a legitimate expectation that he would be made permanent and that the pattern of fixed-term employees being made permanent supported this view.

The EAT was of the opinion that the claimant was dismissed on performance grounds and not because of the expiration of his contract. The EAT concluded that fixed-term contracts were not dictated by demand for employees but were being used as a performance tool. Employees who did not achieve or exceed target faced the non-renewal of their contract. The end of his employment was not determined by objective considerations but by an assessment of his performance. Where there are performance issues with an employee there are clear procedures that must be followed within a business, and an employee has fundamental rights that must be protected.

The EAT placed significance on the fact that the respondent had no interest in maintaining a line of communication with the claimant or in enquiring into his availability to return to the role, despite having trained him for it. This lent credence to the opinion of the EAT that the claimant was dismissed on performance grounds.

The EAT found that the claimant had been unfairly dismissed and he was awarded compensation of €15,000.

DISMISSALS ON GROUNDS OF PERFORMANCE OR CAPABILITY

[27.11] *Counter Products Marketing (Ireland) Ltd v Mulcahy*[15]*—Employment Appeals Tribunal—Unfair Dismissals Acts 1977 to 2015—dismissal for consistent failure to meet performance targets—failure to investigate grievance—unfair dismissal—claimant's repeated assertions that his circumstances were different to those of other managers disregarded without being satisfactorily investigated*

The claimant made a claim to the Rights Commissioner stating he was unfairly dismissed. Having heard the evidence, the Rights Commissioner determined the employee was unfairly dismissed and awarded the sum of €10,000. The respondent employer appealed the determination to the EAT.

---

15. *Counter Products Marketing (Ireland) Ltd v Mulcahy* UD1419/2013.

The claimant was employed as a sales manager with responsibility for ensuring his team of sales representatives achieved their monthly target. The respondent operated a performance management policy to address any under-performance of the sales managers.

A disciplinary meeting was held on 29 March 2012 to address the alleged failing of the claimant to meet set performance targets for 9 January 2012 to 20 January 2012 and 20 February to 2 March 2012. At the conclusion of the meeting the client service manager decided a sanction of verbal warning should apply. The claimant appealed the verbal warning but the sanction was upheld on appeal.

Following from this, there was a failure on the part of the claimant to reach the designated targets set for May 2012. A further disciplinary meeting was convened on 6 July 2012 where once again under performance was addressed with the claimant. The claimant raised the fact that he had previously requested staff workshops in his April review but the client service manager did not recollect receiving such a request. The claimant was issued with a first written warning but lodged an appeal against that sanction which was successful.

A further disciplinary meeting was convened with the claimant on 27 September 2012 for once again failing to meet targets for a four-week period from 30 July 2012 to 3 September 2012. The claimant was sanctioned with a first written warning following this meeting. During cross-examination a representative of the respondent accepted that the claimant had raised a number of ongoing issues with his sales team at this meeting including an issue with a member of his team and the fact that his team was the only unionised team. The respondent contended that it had no knowledge that the claimant's team was on a work to rule.

A further disciplinary meeting was held with the claimant on 20 November 2012, again for failing to meet targets. It was decided that the claimant should be issued with a final written warning; however, due to an administrative error this was recorded as a first written warning. The claimant appealed the sanction which he thought was a first written warning but the appeal was unsuccessful.

The client service manager gave evidence. He gave a detailed explanation of how performance targets were set for sales representatives and their managers. The client service manager told the EAT that all targets were achievable and varying circumstances during each target period (for example depleted staffing levels) were taken into account. All managers were given an initial two-week training session. However each area had different requirements and challenges and therefore the training given in each area varied.

The client service manager was present for the last two months of the claimant's employment and was his manager during that time. The performance targets in the claimant's area were 14 per cent compared to other areas in the country. The client service manager told the EAT that he could not understand this as the claimant had the same challenges as managers in other areas.

The client service manager met with the claimant on 5 March 2013 to discuss his performance review from 28 January 2013 to 28 February 2013 and the claimant's failure to meet the targets which had been set for him. The claimant did not avail of the right to have representation present at the meeting.

At this meeting the client service manager listed the one-to-one training the claimant had received from him, a training session the claimant's team had over two days in early February, a mini workshop that had been set up and meetings the claimant had attended during this time. The claimant replied that the 15 sales that had been lost were due to the fault of the 'leads' issue and the main line telecommunications operator. The claimant also raised the issue of a formal grievance he had made that had not been heard or dealt with in accordance with company procedure. Following this meeting a decision to dismiss the claimant was imposed. The client service manager stated that all other options were considered.

In cross-examination the client service manager said he had only been involved in one disciplinary procedure. When put to him, he told the EAT that allowances in the claimant's targets in respect of the staff headcount had been taken into account. The claimant had never mentioned to him that his staff were on a work to rule and no official notification of same had been received from the union. No other managers had been dismissed for under performance. The client service manager explained that where once there were seven sales managers employed there were now six.

The Human Resource generalist gave evidence. His first involvement in this matter was on 14 January 2013 when he emailed the claimant to invite him to a disciplinary meeting on 16 January 2013. The following day, 15 January 2013, the claimant submitted a detailed grievance relating to training, client operational issues and a disciplinary meeting he had attended on 11 January 2013.

On 16 January 2013 the claimant, the Human Resource generalist, the client sales manager and another colleague as note taker attended the meeting to discuss the failure of the claimant to meet his set targets from 26 November 2012 to 4 January 2013. The Human Resource generalist's notes of the meeting were opened to the EAT. A sanction of final written warning was imposed and would remain on the employee's file for a period of 12 months. The claimant was also informed that any further sanctions could lead to his dismissal. The claimant did not appeal the sanction.

The disciplinary meeting held on 5 March 2013 resulted in the claimant's dismissal. The Human Resource generalist told the EAT that demotion or suspension were not options and the decision to dismiss the claimant was 'not taken lightly'. The claimant was not replaced and his duties were divided between two existing regional sales managers.

The EAT noted that it was obliged to make an assessment based on that information and to determine if the employer had discharged the onus of satisfying the EAT that the dismissal was fair. The EAT noted that an element of the mutual relationship of trust between an employer and employee is that the former provides constructive support to an employee where this is sought and clearly needed. The EAT was not satisfied that this support was provided to the claimant either in the performance management process or independent of it.

The EAT stated that the level of investigation that it would have expected to see in advance of a decision to dismiss the claimant was absent on this occasion. The EAT was not convinced by the apparent trivialisation by the respondent of the issues raised by the claimant referable to the unionisation of his team and the backdrop to that development. This was an issue for the respondent as a whole and not just for the claimant, who was given no meaningful support. The EAT believed that the claimant and his team needed practical help and support which was not forthcoming. Dealing with the claimant seemed to ultimately be reduced to a statistical analysis outside of any meaningful contextualisation. The EAT noted that there was no fairness in this.

The EAT stated that it had no doubt but that the claimant was resolute in facing the challenges of his role and, indeed, may have overestimated his own ability to face those challenges without support; however, this did not in any way exonerate the respondent from identifying and acting on a clear need for practical help. The EAT held that the repeated rationale of the respondent that the same issues were faced by all managers, which position was adopted without any meaningful investigation into the challenges faced by the claimant and specifically related to him, was fundamentally flawed. The claimant's repeated assertions that his circumstances were different to those of other managers were disregarded without being satisfactorily investigated.

The EAT found that the presumption that the claimant's dismissal was unfair was not rebutted by the respondent. In measuring compensation, the EAT considered the claimant's period of employment and the fact that the employment subsequently secured by him was at a reduced salary. The claimant was awarded compensation in the sum of €30,000.

[27.12] *Noreika v The Printed Image Ltd[16]—Employment Appeals Tribunal—Unfair Dismissals Acts 1977 to 2015—dismissal following progressive set of disciplinary warnings arising from claimant's work performance, attitude, aggressive behaviour and conduct towards his work colleagues—procedural failings by respondent employer—lack of representation at disciplinary meetings—lack of opportunity to confront accusers—no right of appeal—contribution of claimant to his dismissal*

The claimant was employed as a general operative in the respondent's print and design company from July 2011. In 2012, issues arose regarding his work performance and attitude to co-workers, in particular to female co-workers. Initially the respondent dealt with issues of concern informally with the claimant's line manager, and the claimant appeared to have been moved a number of times within different departments in the workplace. However in June 2012, a formal complaint was made by a female work colleague regarding the claimant's behaviour in the canteen, which was witnessed by a number of other colleagues. Following an investigation the claimant was issued with a written warning with regards to his aggressive behaviour, foul language and rudeness to a colleague. He was informed that there should be an immediate improvement in his attitude to work and colleagues and he was advised that further infractions could lead to dismissal. Further evidence was given as to the claimant's continuing negative attitude and a further incident in September 2012 whereby he refused to carry out a task when requested to do so by his supervisor. A formal complaint regarding the complainant ensued and, following an investigation, he was issued with a final written warning for his actions in being rude and unhelpful to his supervisor when asked to carry out a task which was part of his duties.

---

16. *Noreika v The Printed Image Ltd* UD245/2013.

Evidence was given that the claimant did not seem to care when reprimanded. A further altercation took place in October 2012 with a delivery driver. However on this occasion the respondent supported the complainant in relation to that matter and accepted that the claimant was not at fault. The claimant asserted that he had received warnings from the respondent for no reason and that in each case he was only giving his opinion to work colleagues and supervisors and denied being disrespectful towards them. His evidence was that his difficulties began when he refused to work overtime as the respondent only paid a flat rate for overtime. There was a conflict of evidence as to whether the claimant was required to drive a forklift truck for which he had no licence. The claimant asserted that when he refused to drive the forklift he was put under pressure and yet the respondent would not facilitate him in obtaining a licence. The respondent asserted that the claimant did not have a licence to drive the forklift and was not required to do so. The claimant was absent on sick leave from November until December 2012 and on his return in January 2013 he made a verbal attack on a co-worker who had attempted to assist him.

In January 2013 the claimant refused to carry out a task, changing wheelie bins, when requested to do so by his supervisor and was immediately called to a meeting with the production director and the supervisor. The parties disputed whether the claimant was asked to carry out the task with immediate effect or whether this was something that could be done later on. The respondent had suggested that the claimant had refused to carry out the task but the claimant asserted that he had said he would do so later, which he did. In the opinion of the respondent, the claimant appeared careless and had a dismissive and negative attitude. As he had already received a verbal warning and two written warnings he was dismissed with immediate effect, asked to leave the premises immediately and was paid his notice entitlement.

Evidence to the EAT was that he did not leave the premises, as instructed, but went to the canteen and behaved in an intimidating manner towards the operations manager. The claimant asserted that on the day of his dismissal he wrote an account of what had happened but was told by the respondent he could not do so on company time. His evidence to the EAT was that his written account of events was taken from him and he was told that it would be put on his file. It had not been seen since. The claimant confirmed he had received one warning, which he had signed and another warning which he did not sign, as he felt he had done nothing wrong with regards to this second warning and had not shouted at his colleagues. The claimant received no notification of the meetings in relation to these warnings and he was not given any opportunity to hear witnesses to the alleged incidents. There was a dispute between the parties as to whether the claimant had previously sought to be dismissed so that he could obtain social welfare benefits.

The EAT concluded that it was not satisfied that the respondent had followed fair procedures in deciding to dismiss the claimant. There was no notice given to the claimant of disciplinary meetings and he was not given the opportunity to address his accusers. He was not afforded the opportunity to be represented at these meetings and was not informed of his right to appeal the decision to dismiss, therefore the EAT found that he had been unfairly dismissed. However, the EAT concluded that the claimant had contributed to a large degree to his dismissal and that he made no effort to mitigate his loss for the first six months post dismissal. He was awarded €2,500 compensation.

[27.13] *Corbett v Harvey Norman Trading (Ireland) Ltd[17]—Employment Appeals Tribunal—Unfair Dismissals Acts 1977 to 2015—dismissal for performance—where respondent engaged claimant in progressive series of warnings with regard to his poor performance*

The claimant was employed as a warehouse operative. His role was to receive goods that had been delivered, check and count them and to enter these goods into the stock management computer system and place pricing stickers on the stock. The respondent submitted that the claimant had disciplinary issues for poor performance with regards to the intake and registration of goods and, although he was offered help and counselling, he continued to make errors in the performance of his job. The evidence was that from January 2011, he received a written warning for poor performance which was followed by further counselling for poor performance in November 2012.

In February 2013 the claimant received a poor annual assessment and got additional training. In March 2013 he got a written warning for continued poor performance and in July 2013 he received a final written warning and a suspension of one week because of poor performance. On his return from suspension, difficulties again arose with regard to his performance in his role. The respondent stated that this was the 'final straw' and that a meeting was held with the claimant in August 2013 where it was decided that his employment should be terminated. He exercised his right of appeal; however the appeal hearing upheld the original decision to dismiss.

The claimant's position was that his job was extremely hard and busy and, while he conceded silly mistakes were made, they were never intentional. The claimant submitted that he was overworked and this was the reason for his apparent inability to perform adequately in his role.

The EAT concluded that the respondent had acted fairly and reasonably in the manner in which it approached the claimant's difficulties with the carrying out of his roles. The EAT was satisfied that the claimant had been afforded fair procedures leading to his dismissal and thus the claim for unjust dismissal was not upheld.

---

17.   *Corbett v Harvey Norman Trading (Ireland) Ltd* UD1626/2013.

[27.14] *Morrison v Tesco Ireland Ltd*[18]—*Employment Appeals Tribunal—Unfair Dismissals Acts 1977 to 2015—dismissal for failure to reach or maintain minimum work standard—minimum work standard agreed with trade union—whether claimant's injury impacted on his productivity—whether respondent aware of injury and its alleged impact on claimant's productivity—claimant's duty to raise relevant injury as health and safety issue—employee's responsibility to submit medical certificates—whether dismissal of claimant reasonable in circumstances where claimant unable to perform his job to requisite standard*

The claimant was dismissed from his position as a warehouse operative. The respondent maintained that the claimant was dismissed because he failed to reach or maintain the minimum work standard required of the respondent's employees.

The respondent's HR manager explained to the EAT that he worked in the Donabate centre, which opened in 2006. The claimant had originally worked for the respondent in Tallaght and was subsequently transferred to the Donabate distribution centre. The HR manager explained that the minimum productivity rate for the respondent's employees was set at 84pi, referable to the task of picking orders, ie placing goods onto receptacles to send to various stores. He stated that the vast majority of employees achieved a productivity rate of 100pi and a new employee after 6–8 weeks' training can obtain 81pi. He explained that if an employee's productivity rate was more than 84pi, there was no issue with his/her performance. If, on the other hand, an employee's productivity rate fell short of the minimum, it was common for the respondent to address this with the employee in an informal intervention. The employee's team manager would most likely discuss the matter with the employee to discover the reason for the poor performance and the possibility of re-training would be explored. This interaction was often on an informal and ongoing basis. If an employee continued to fall short of the requisite standard, a formal disciplinary process could be initiated, but not unless at least two informal interventions had been exhausted. The HR manager explained that the respondent did not wish to enter a disciplinary situation if it could be avoided; they wanted to take a 'pragmatic view'.

In cross-examination the HR manager agreed that there were guidelines for the maximum weight that a warehouse operative should lift. He stated that, as a general rule, nobody should lift anything above their shoulder. When it was put to him that the claimant was asked to lift goods that were at his head height, he replied that his colleagues would know more about the matter. The HR manager was also asked if he had been aware that the claimant had a back problem. He replied that he was aware that the respondent had referred the claimant to the company doctor, but he was not aware that it was because of his back. When it was put to him that the claimant had been absent from work from March 2010 to July 2010 with a back injury, the HR manager responded that this period of absence had predated his role, as he commenced his role in HR in July 2011. The HR manager was asked if he was aware that the claimant had been awarded €6,500 because of a back injury sustained at work and he replied that he was not.

---

18. *Morrison v Tesco Ireland Ltd* UD1470/2013.

In summary the respondent's position was that there was a 'Procedural and Operating Agreement' in place between the respondent and SIPTU since 2006 and that the claimant consistently fell below the required performance rate specified in this agreement. Furthermore, the respondent maintained that the disciplinary procedure contained within this agreement had been followed in reaching the decision to dismiss the claimant. Therefore, the respondent contended that the claimant had not been unfairly dismissed.

The claimant stated that his productivity had never been considered problematic when he worked in Tallaght; it only became an issue after he began work in the Donabate centre. Although he agreed that he consistently failed to reach the agreed minimum productivity rate of 84pi in the Donabate distribution centre, he attributed this to the fact that he was older than most of his colleagues and that he had suffered a back injury in 2010. He stated that he had applied for the alternative position of clerk within the respondent, which would not have involved as much lifting, however his application had been unsuccessful. This was the case despite the fact that he had previously carried out the task of clerk and occasionally continued to do so, after being rejected for the job. The claimant stated that other jobs would come up from time to time but he was usually unaware of these, as he would only be told about jobs which his manager recommended to him. He told the EAT that he never raised his back problems as a health and safety issue, but maintained that the respondent was aware of his condition.

In summary, the claimant's position was that he could not reach the minimum productivity rate despite his best efforts and that it was unreasonable of the respondent to dismiss him for this.

The EAT held that it was satisfied that the respondent acted reasonably and followed fair procedures in reaching its decision to dismiss the claimant. Although the claimant suffered a back injury in 2010, he never raised an issue thereafter in relation to health and safety. Furthermore, he did not provide medical evidence in respect of an ongoing back problem, nor did he request supports for his back. The EAT concluded that the claimant was unable to obtain the minimum standard set for his position and was thus was unable to perform the function for which he was employed. Therefore the claimant was not unfairly dismissed by the respondent and his claim failed.

DISMISSALS ON GROUNDS OF CAPACITY OR ILLNESS

[27.15] *Hayes v Boliden Tara Mines Ltd[19]—Employment Appeals Tribunal—Unfair Dismissals Acts 1977 to 2015—unfair dismissal—grounds of capability—claimant on long-term certified sick leave—whether claimant entitled to return to work on alternative/light duties—whether requirement on respondent to create alternative work to facilitate employee's return to work*

The claimant was employed as a miner in the respondent's underground lead mine. His duties were physical in nature and included blasting rock, driving and carving out the face of the mine. The role by its nature is hazardous given the environment. It was noted

---

19.   *Hayes v Boliden Tara Mines Ltd* UD1218/2014.

that the claimant was on certified sick leave from December 2009 to 30 June 2014, the date his employment was terminated. In June 2009, the claimant suffered a significant injury at work requiring extended absences. Although he returned to work in August 2009 for eight weeks, he was required to take a further six weeks leave until December 2009. At that stage he was certified by his GP as unfit for full duties as a result of the June 2009 accident. A long period of certified absence followed whereupon in March 2011 the claimant sought a return to work to carry out light duties. The respondent's position was that it was not in a position to offer alternative work at that point.

Evidence was given on behalf of the respondent that its alternative duty policy was available to employees following workplace accidents where, for a period of 10 days, they can avail of alternative duties. Thereafter, any extended course of alternative duty is subject to a review and/or is decided on a case-by-case basis.

The respondent's evidence was that the claimant had never been certified fit to return to work on full duties by either his own GP or the company doctor. It was further submitted that the only person that could certify him fit to return to work on some sort of long-term alternative duty was the company doctor but, even if this was done, it was submitted that there must still be a vacancy in this regard. It was further submitted that the respondent was not under an obligation to create a role for its employees in this situation.

The EAT noted that the meeting took place in December 2013 following assessment by the respondent's company doctor and a number of interactions between the parties. The meeting was adjourned at the request of the claimant's union representative and a further meeting took place in January 2014. At this meeting the claimant formally requested to return to work to perform alternative/light duties. It was agreed that the claimant would attend a company-nominated medical expert to assess his fitness to return to work. Two further medical assessments took place and the substantive medical report was received in March 2014. The conclusion reached by the relevant doctor was that the claimant was not fit to resume mining duties and was not fit for alternative work duties that required physical or manual handing tasks.

As there was no suitable alternative work for the claimant, the respondent had no option but to terminate his employment. The meeting took place in May 2014 when these findings were presented to the claimant. The letter issued on 6 May which terminated his employment with notice and offered him an opportunity to provide alternative medical opinion to that of the company doctor as to whether he was fit to return to work. This decision was not appealed by the claimant.

At the hearing the claimant suggested a number of alternative roles that he could have done, including the laundry rooms; however the respondent's evidence was that he had never been certified fit to return to either full duties or alternative duties and therefore could not be considered for such a role, especially one such as laundry which was a very physical job. The respondent's position was that a personal injuries claim taken by the claimant in relation to the June incident was not held against him and was not a factor in considering him for alternative duties. The claimant asserted that he was not aware of the 10-day 'alternative duty' policy at the time and felt that it was not imposed on employees. The claimant's evidence was that in July 2012 the company doctor had told him that he would certify him fit for alternative duties if HR agreed and he believed that the company was aware of this. It was confirmed that the claimant's own doctor had never certified him fit to return to full duties. The claimant confirmed that he did not seek any opinion other than the company doctor's in relation to his capacity and did not appeal the decision to dismiss on legal advice. His evidence was that he remained on an invalidity pension from the date of dismissal to the date of the hearing and had not yet been certified to return to work but hoped to be approved for partial capacity benefit imminently.

The EAT noted that it had to consider whether the decision to dismiss was fair and reasonable in all of the circumstances. It noted the statutory provisions set out in s 6(4) of the Acts. The EAT considered the nature of the work in the mine which was demanding physically and mentally. The EAT accepted that advancing the face of the mine was physical and hazardous in its nature and that most of the roles involved going down into the mine which the claimant would not or could not do. The EAT noted the evidence given that there was very little work available above ground that was not somewhat physical in nature or required some work underground.

The EAT concluded that the evidence before it on light and alternative duties seemed contradictory. On the one hand, the respondent's witness said that light duties were limited to 10 days but on the other hand it appeared that the company doctor could certify an employee fit to return to work on long-term light duties but only if there was a vacancy. While the evidence was not consistent for the purpose of the claim the EAT took it to mean a long-term role other than the claimant's original role. It was not clear to the EAT whether the search for alternative roles for the claimant was a retrospective exercise by the witness for the purpose of the claim or whether he was actually considered at the relevant time. In any event, the EAT accepted that the medical evidence showed that the claimant was never certified fit to return on full duties or on light alternative duties between December 2009 and June 2014. The EAT noted that the respondent had relied upon the reports from the company doctor in relation to the claimant and the claimant was given the opportunity to challenge the assessment but chose not to. The EAT further noted the inconsistency that the claimant was, on the one hand, seeking alternative light duties from the respondent but at the same time he did not have his own GP medically assess him on this basis or on whether he could return to work for full duty.

The EAT accepted that only the company doctor could formally certify him fit to return on alternative duties and the EAT also accepted that there was no obligation on an employer to create a role in terms of alternative work to facilitate an employee's return to work.

While the EAT regarded the procedure used to terminate the claimant's employment as unusual it did not in the circumstances render the dismissal unfair. It was noted that the claimant did not exercise his right of appeal. The EAT concluded that, although the respondent did not act perfectly, the decision was reasonable in all of the circumstances and therefore the claim failed.

[27.16] *Hoey v White Horse Insurance Ireland Ltd[20]—Employment Appeals Tribunal—Unfair Dismissals Acts 1977 to 2015—Minimum Notice and Terms of Employment Acts 1973 to 2005—incapacity-related or pregnancy-related dismissal—disentitlement to notice on basis of incapacity—employer's failure to consider medical advice when deciding to dismiss employee on grounds of incapacity*

The claimant was employed as a claims manager in the respondent until her dismissal, purportedly on grounds of incapacity, in August 2013. The claimant asserted that she was dismissed because of her pregnancy, which resulted in her inability to work during summer 2013.

The respondent submitted that the claimant's dismissal was due to her ongoing incapacity from September 2012 to August 2013, and that as the claimant was unfit for work at the time of her dismissal, she was not entitled to notice.

The parties' evidence was based on medical reports which made different findings in relation to the claimant's ability to return to work.

The EAT noted that s 6(4)(a) of the Acts requires it to determine if the dismissal results wholly or mainly from 'the capability, competence or qualifications of the employee for performing work of the kind which he was employed by the employer to do'.

The EAT referred to the decision of the High Court in *Bolger v Showerings (Ireland) Ltd[21]* which stated:

   (a)   for dismissal on grounds of incapacity to be deemed fair, the onus is on the employer to show that:

- It was the incapacity which was the reason for the dismissal;

- The reason was substantial;

- The employee received fair notice that the question of his dismissal for incapacity was being considered; and

- The employee was afforded an opportunity of being heard.

The EAT held that the dismissal was procedurally unfair. The respondent did not follow its own procedures and more importantly did not inform the claimant that her dismissal was being considered in advance of the teleconference on 30 July 2013.

The EAT was also critical of the respondent's disregard for the medical evidence provided to the claimant by the respondent.

The EAT awarded the claimant €20,000 in compensation and awarded €1,515.50, being the equivalent to two weeks of pay in lieu of notice.

20.   *Hoey v White Horse Insurance Ireland Ltd* UD1519/2013, MN118/2014. See also **[5.31]**.

21.   *Bolger v Showerings (Ireland) Ltd* [1990] ELR 184.

[27.17] *Ward v Coverall Courier Services Ltd[22]—Employment Appeals Tribunal— Unfair Dismissals Acts 1977 to 2015—unfair dismissal—workplace accident— certified sick leave—whether claimant fit to return to work—whether redundancy relevant—respondent should have had claimant assessed by its own medical practitioner*

The claimant had been employed as a courier with the respondent since 1988. His duties included the delivery of packages on behalf of clients of the respondent company. He was paid net weekly wages of €449.75, plus a weekly subsistence allowance of €100.00 per week. The claimant was the only employee of the respondent.

In August 2010 the claimant was involved in a workplace accident which rendered him unfit for work until November 2010. The claimant returned to work at that time, but in June/July 2012, the claimant was again absent from work on certified sick leave. The claimant was informed by the managing director of the respondent (MD) that a medical certificate certifying him fit to return to work would be required if he intended to resume his duties. It was not agreed how close to full health the claimant would have to be before the respondent would accept him back to work. The claimant attended a consultant orthopaedic surgeon on 19 March 2013. After the assessment the surgeon issued the claimant with a medical certificate which stated that there had been an approximate 70 to 75 per cent improvement in his condition and that, in the surgeon's opinion, the claimant was fit to return to work.

The EAT held that the medical evidence provided by the claimant to the respondent established that the claimant was fit to return to work. The respondent could have had the claimant medically examined by its own medical practitioner to verify this fact but failed to do so. It followed that without medical evidence to the contrary the respondent was not entitled to disregard the evidence of the claimant. The EAT concluded that the claimant was unfairly dismissed and awarded him the sum of €15,000.

[27.18] *Cunningham v Premco Distributors Ltd[23]—Employment Appeals Tribunal— Unfair Dismissals Acts 1977 to 2015—dispute in relation to fact of dismissal—duty on employer to make contact with employees in relation to provision of medical certificates*

The fact of dismissal in this case was in dispute. The respondent was a car parts distributor and the claimant worked as a store man for the respondent.

The EAT heard evidence from two witnesses, the claimant and a director of the respondent (JF). On 31 October 2013 a difficulty arose for the respondent when it discovered that the courier company it used could no longer provide it with a service. This caused a problem for the respondent, as products had to be delivered to customers the next day. JF requested a meeting with a business acquaintance (Mr F) who he thought could assist with finding a solution.

It transpired that Mr F visited the premises at some stage, requesting to see JF. Mr F had been told that JF was occupied at a meeting, so he left. JF asked who had told Mr F

---

22.   *Ward v Coverall Courier Services Ltd* UD1263/2013.
23.   *Cunningham v Premco Distributors Ltd* UD1666/2013.

that he was at a meeting, angry that Mr F had been misinformed. The claimant accepted that he had been the one to deliver the message. A verbal altercation ensued between JF and the claimant. The claimant left the premises. He maintained that he subsequently made contact with the respondent's warehouse manager, who told him that had JF told him and others that if the claimant was to return to the premises he was not to be allowed to gain entry.

On 1 November 2013, the claimant submitted a sick certificate. It was common case that this certificate covered the claimant's absence from work up until the beginning of December 2013. The claimant told the EAT that he had subsequently submitted a certificate to the effect that he was fit to return to work, a submission which was disputed by JF. No certificate of return to work was opened or provided to the EAT.

The EAT held that the claimant's case should succeed. The EAT held that no further sick certificates were submitted after the beginning of December. It considered that even if the claimant's fitness to return to work certificate was not received by the respondent, it was incumbent on JF as an employer to make an effort to contact the employee to clarify the situation, given that JF had stated that the claimant was not to return to work. In the absence of such efforts, the EAT found that the claimant was unfairly dismissed. The EAT determined that compensation in the amount of €42,640 was the appropriate remedy.

RETIREMENT

[27.19] *O'Connor v Beaufield Mews Ltd t/a Beaufield Mews Restaurant[24]— Employment Appeals Tribunal—Unfair Dismissals Acts 1977 to 2015—whether employee unfairly dismissed when his employment was terminated at the age of 65— respondent's retirement policy took effect at age 65—another employee of respondent had been allowed to work after turning 65—physical nature of role*

This case came before the EAT by way of an employee appealing the decision of a Rights Commissioner. The claimant had worked for the respondent for 30 years. Following a period of illness, he had been certified fit to return to work in June 2012. Shortly thereafter he received a letter from the respondent which indicated that, as he had reached the age of 65 in May 2012, his employment was terminated.

It was undisputed evidence that the claimant was not provided with a contract of employment until 2008 and that the claimant had never signed the contract. The claimant stated in evidence that he had never even read it. A director of the respondent company gave evidence that the claimant's contract of employment and the company handbook made specific reference to the retirement age of 65. It was stated that the respondent company had implemented this retirement policy with other employees and that the claimant had never disputed the term in his contract. The claimant argued that some months after his own employment had ended, another employee had reached the age of 65 and remained in employment with the respondent. The claimant maintained that he had been unfairly dismissed.

---

24. *O'Connor v Beaufield Mews Ltd t/a Beaufield Mews Restaurant* UD556/2013.

By majority, the EAT held that the dismissal was not unfair. It considered that the retirement policy of 65 years, which was clearly stated in the contract, was reasonable given the physical nature of the job. It was held that the retention of another employee after reaching 65 years of age was of no significance in this case. The role of this other employee was more of a supervisory role and the respondent relied upon this employee for certain specific duties, including locking up the premises. The appeal under the Unfair Dismissals Acts 1977 to 2015 therefore failed and the decision of the Rights Commissioner was upheld.

The dissenting opinion of the EAT stated that the respondent had to show that it had acted reasonably and within the law in dismissing the claimant. He placed particular emphasis on the fact that there had been no formal procedures in place for the claimant to appeal the decision to dismiss. On this basis alone, the dismissal was unfair.

AUTOMATICALLY UNFAIR DISMISSALS – PREGNANCY

[27.20] *O'Brien v Thomas Kiely t/a Thomas Kiely Catering[25]—Employment Appeals Tribunal—Unfair Dismissals Acts 1977 to 2015—dismissal as result of pregnancy— financial difficulties of respondent—hiring of employee in claimant's position one week after her dismissal*

The claimant first commenced employment on a casual basis in May 2012. When the respondent was successful in attaining a catering contract in two schools (in Newport and Nenagh), he contacted the claimant in July 2012 and offered her the position of a catering assistant in the Newport College. The claimant accepted the position and informed the respondent that she was pregnant. The respondent congratulated her. The claimant commenced employment in Newport College on 27 August 2012, but her employment was terminated a few weeks later on 14 September 2012. The claimant maintained that she was dismissed as a result of her pregnancy.

The respondent gave evidence that although the claimant had been hired as a catering assistant, it soon became apparent that it was not financially viable to employ both the claimant and a qualified chef in Newport College. He decided to terminate the claimant's employment. The reason she was chosen for termination instead of the qualified chef was that she had no experience of working in an industrial kitchen and did not have HACCP training. The respondent decided that he would run the premises in Newport College himself, while the qualified chef would move to the premises in Nenagh College. However, personal issues soon arose for the respondent and he stated that he had to hire a previous employee qualified to cover the Newport premises while he took time off. On cross-examination the respondent admitted that he had not informed the claimant that he had been awarded a three-year contract with the college.

The claimant agreed with the respondent's evidence insofar as he had congratulated her on her pregnancy and had said that the termination of her employment was for financial reasons. However, she argued that her dismissal could not have been solely on account of financial reasons because the respondent had hired another employee just

---

25. *O'Brien v Thomas Kiely t/a Thomas Kiely Catering* UD325/2013

one week after her dismissal. The EAT enquired as to whether the claimant had her HACCP qualification. She responded that she did have it, but that it had expired and she was waiting to be notified to attend a refresher course.

The EAT concluded that the respondent had adduced sufficient evidence to displace the statutory presumption set out in the Unfair Dismissals Acts 1977 to 2015 by the Maternity Protection Act 1994, that the claimant's employment was terminated by reason of her pregnancy. The EAT placed particular emphasis on the evidence of the respondent that he had informed the claimant early in her employment that the respondent's position was perilous, as evidenced by the bank statements he submitted to the EAT at the hearing. Accordingly, the EAT found that the claimant was not unfairly dismissed and her claim under the Unfair Dismissals Acts 1977 to 2015 failed.

DISMISSALS ON GROUNDS OF CONDUCT

Misuse of email/suspension

[27.21] *The Governor and Company of the Bank of Ireland v Reilly*[26]*—High Court— Noonan J—appeal from decision of Circuit Court—Unfair Dismissals Acts 1977 to 2015—material on work emails contrary to company email policy—suspension while investigation ongoing—reasonableness of employer's response—reinstatement*

A review of the claimant's work email took place in light of concerns that, in forwarding certain emails which contained inappropriate content and images, he may have breached the bank's email policy. The claimant was suspended by his immediate superior on the instructions from the respondent's head office. An investigation was conducted into his suspected breach of the email policy, with the investigator ultimately finding that the content of the emails he had sent could reasonably be regarded as pornographic, indecent, obscene, offensive, rude and generally distasteful. The claimant subsequently participated in a disciplinary process, the outcome of which was his dismissal by reason of gross misconduct. The claimant appealed internally and alleged that he had not been treated consistently with others who similarly had been found to have circulated inappropriate emails via their work email. His appeal was unsuccessful and, under the respondent's procedures, he had the right to appeal to an independent third party. His external appeal was also unsuccessful and, thereafter, he sought to challenge his dismissal by way of an unfair dismissal claim before the EAT, the outcome of which was appealed to the Circuit Court and ultimately to the High Court.

In the High Court, Noonan J, noted that, in defending an unfair dismissal claim, the onus is on the employer to establish that there were substantial grounds justifying the dismissal. Noonan J stated that while the Court may have regard to what it considers the reasonableness of the employer's conduct in relation to the dismissal, the Court may not substitute its own judgment as to whether the dismissal was reasonable for that of the employer. The correct test to be applied in adjudicating claims of this nature is to consider whether it was reasonable of the employer to dismiss the employee in the

---

26. *The Governor and Company of the Bank of Ireland v Reilly* [2015] IEHC 241.

circumstances. If no reasonable employer would have done so, then the dismissal would be unfair. The question is whether the employer's decision to dismiss was within the band of reasonableness.

The Court examined in detail the decision to suspend. Firstly, the Court stated that the decision to suspend an employee, whether paid or unpaid, 'is an extremely serious measure which can cause irreparable damage to [the employee's] reputation and standing' and noted that even a paid holding suspension 'can have the consequences of the kind mentioned'. Accordingly, a paid holding suspension should not be undertaken lightly and only after consideration of the necessity for the suspension. The Court accepted that a holding suspension would be justified if it were seen to be necessary:

(i)   to prevent a repetition of the conduct complained of and/or to prevent interference with evidence;

(ii) to protect persons at risk from such conduct; or

(iii) to protect the employer's own business and reputation where the conduct in issue is known by those doing business with the employer.

In other words, it should be to facilitate the proper conduct of an investigation and any consequent disciplinary process. However, in this case, given the claimant's work mailbox had been forensically copied at the outset of the investigation into his suspected misconduct, the Court found his suspension entirely unnecessary as he could not interfere with any evidence that might be pertinent to the investigation to be conducted.

The Court also examined the procedures employed in suspending the claimant. Noonan J noted with some concern that the manager who made the decision to suspend the claimant did so without seeing any of the email evidence that was the reason for the suspension, and further only suspended three of the five employees (one of whom was the claimant) who were all subject to an investigation in relation to alleged breaches of the employer's email policy. The employer argued that the claimant did not have an entitlement to natural justice or fair procedures at this early stage. This was rejected by the Court, with Noonan J stating that the least the claimant was entitled to was an explanation of the reason for his suspension. Noonan J concluded that the reason why only three of the five employees under investigation were suspended was due to the fact that the employer had formed the view that the contents of their mailboxes represented more serious misconduct than that of the two who were not suspended.

In considering the reasonableness of the respondent's decision to dismiss the claimant, the Court embarked on a detailed analysis of the inappropriate emails that had been circulated by the claimant, whether the respondent had an established 'zero-tolerance' policy in relation to the breach of its email policy, and whether the claimant's actions had any impact on the respondent. The Court accepted that the emails that the claimant had circulated were inappropriate and deserved the imposition of some disciplinary sanction. However, the Court noted that no one had complained about these emails and, therefore, it could be concluded that no one was offended by these emails. The Court further stated that the respondent had suffered no loss, damage or detriment whatsoever as a consequence of the claimant's misconduct. Against this, the Court assessed the impact of the dismissal on the claimant and concluded that his dismissal had had a catastrophic effect on him. The Court concluded that the respondent's conduct in dismissing the claimant could not, by any objective standard, be described as reasonable.

The Court noted that while the bank had paid 'lip service to procedures, it [was] clear there was only ever going to be one outcome'. The Court was particularly critical of the fact that the distribution list for the email which contained the image that had been classed by the respondent as the most serious of all, had never been presented to the claimant in the course of the disciplinary process, notwithstanding his repeated requests for same. The Court noted that this distribution list only became available after the claimant commenced proceedings and it then showed that the email had originated in the respondent's head office, from where it had been sent to a colleague of the claimant, who in turn forwarded it to his colleagues, who had also forwarded it in turn. The Court noted the inconsistency in treatment in circumstances where the actions of the colleague, who had evidently forwarded some of the same emails, were never investigated and further stated its view that the respondent had gone to considerable lengths to conceal the provenance of this distribution list.

The claimant sought reinstatement. While the Court accepted that account could be taken of the extent to which an employee contributed to their dismissal in considering whether the remedy of reinstatement was appropriate, the fact that an employee contributed to his dismissal did not automatically mean, as the respondent had argued, that reinstatement could not be ordered. The Court concluded that an award of compensation would fall short of providing adequate redress in this case, and that the only appropriate remedy was reinstatement. The claimant was granted reinstatement to the job he held prior to being dismissed in May 2009 on the same terms and conditions of employment and with his continuity preserved. The claimant was also entitled to back pay from the date of his dismissal.

Gross Misconduct

Physical altercations

[27.22] *Harris v Tesco Ireland Ltd*[27]—*Employment Appeals Tribunal—Unfair Dismissals Acts 1977 to 2015—unfair dismissal—claimant had physical altercation with customer outside respondent's premises—whether incident warranted dismissal—whether fair procedures followed*

This was an appeal by the claimant against a recommendation of the Rights Commissioner under the Unfair Dismissals Acts 1977 to 2015. The respondent also appealed the Rights Commissioner's recommendation of an award of €18,000 to the claimant. This case should be read in conjunction with *Tesco Ireland Ltd v Harris*,[28] which was heard at the same time.

The claimant was employed with the respondent as a security guard from 10 December 2001 until his dismissal on 7 April 2012. The claimant performed his duties in a number of locations, but on the date of the incident that led to his dismissal, he was

27. *Harris v Tesco Ireland Ltd* UD1661/2012.
28. *Tesco Ireland Ltd v Harris* UD1667/2012

working in a shopping centre in North County Dublin. On 12 March 2012 an incident occurred between the claimant and a customer outside the respondent's premises in the public area of the shopping centre.

An investigation meeting was held on 13 March 2012, which the claimant attended with his union representative. The Deputy Store Manager (DSM) was the investigating officer at this meeting and the personnel manager (PM) was the note-taker. The CCTV footage of the incident was viewed. The statements of both the claimant and a security guard who witnessed the incident (BA) were read out. On 20 March 2012, a second investigation meeting took place, at which the claimant was once more accompanied by his union representative. The investigation officer at this meeting was PM, as DSM was on leave. On 26 March 2012, a disciplinary hearing was held and DSM was once again the investigating officer. PM acted as note-taker. Once more the claimant attended with his union representative. On 30 March 2012, a letter of dismissal issued from DSM to the claimant. The claimant exercised his right to appeal but the decision to dismiss was upheld at an appeal hearing on 1 May 2012.

The claimant told the EAT that the customer had insulted him. This had caused the claimant to follow the customer off the respondent's premises. He admitted that he initiated physical contact with the customer. He caught the customer by the collar and the customer grabbed his shirt. They then separated and the claimant returned to the store. The claimant added that he had had previous problems with this particular customer, which he had never officially reported to management. The meeting concluded and the claimant was informed that the situation would be reviewed.

DSM gave evidence on behalf of the respondent. She explained that the claimant had been dismissed from his employment for breaching company policy and because he had admitted to initiating physical contact with the customer. BA also gave evidence on behalf of the respondent. He explained that he had followed the claimant out of the shopping centre after the customer. He heard the customer call the claimant a 'f*****g nut case'. When BA subsequently asked the claimant why the customer called him that name, the claimant replied that he had had problems with that particular customer before.

PM also gave evidence on behalf of the respondent. She stated that a similar incident had occurred between the claimant and a customer back in 2003. This prior incident had resulted in the claimant being issued with a written warning. The claimant's representative objected to the raising of this issue, as the warning should only have remained on the claimant's file for 12 months. In response PM said that she raised the former incident purely on account of the similarities it bore to the incident in this case. PM informed the EAT that neither she nor management was aware of any prior issues with the customer in question.

The majority decision of the EAT was that the sanction of dismissal was proportionate in the circumstances. Emphasis was placed on the fact that one of the functions of a security guard is to prevent the type of occurrence that formed the subject matter of the claimant's claim. The EAT held that the claimant had been unprovoked on the day in question. He had assaulted the customer of his own volition. The EAT noted that there was no evidence of the verbal abuse which the claimant alleged had taken place prior to the day of the incident in question. Furthermore, the claimant had not made any formal complaints to his line manager in relation thereto. The EAT addressed the procedural flaws raised by the claimant in relation to the disciplinary process. While the EAT found merit in some of the claimant's arguments in this regard, it was considered that the respondent's failings were not of such a degree so as to render the dismissal unfair.

One member of the EAT dissented, holding that the sanction of dismissal had been disproportionate. This opinion was based firstly on the fact that there were well-known staff issues with this particular customer, secondly on the fact that this particular incident was extreme, thirdly that the claimant's reaction had been out of character/spur of the moment; and fourthly in consideration of the claimant's age and his ability to obtain alternative employment. This dissenting member of the EAT noted the other options that had been open to the respondent, ie final written warning, suspension without pay, reduction in pay, relocation or alternative work in that or another store.

[27.23] *Cooper v Johnston Mooney & O'Brien Bakeries*[29]*—Employment Appeals Tribunal—Unfair Dismissals Acts 1977 to 2015—dismissal for gross misconduct— whether claimant had been unfairly dismissed as result of altercation with fellow employee*

The claimant was dismissed following an altercation with a fellow employee, AD. The EAT heard evidence from AD that, on the night in question, he had been holding an uncontrolled air hose when the claimant approached him and tried to take the hose. It was accepted by both parties that for health and safety reasons, the hose should not have been in use. AD told the EAT that a tug of war ensued and that he told the claimant that he would put the hose in a fellow employee's locker. He stated that the claimant would not allow him do this and pushed him against the wall. A manager then intervened and took the hose.

AD submitted that, as he was walking away, the claimant hit him and jumped on him. AD stated that he subsequently woke up on the ground after losing consciousness. AD accepted that he had called the claimant a bad boy and lazy during the altercation. Later on that evening, AD met with the claimant and asked him if he was happy after the incident and AD told the EAT that the claimant had responded by raising his two thumbs.

AD had provided a statement concerning the incidents, a copy of which was opened to the EAT, and he was subsequently issued with a final written warning and suspended for one week without pay following an investigation.

The EAT heard evidence that the respondent held an investigation into the incident and that both AD and the claimant were suspended pending the outcome. The matter subsequently progressed to a disciplinary hearing. At the hearing the claimant admitted that he grabbed AD by the neck. There was commonality in all the statements provided and there was no dispute that an assault had occurred.

The chair of the disciplinary hearing gave evidence that the claimant did not express a high level of remorse for his actions and did not apologise. He told the EAT that he

---

29. *Cooper v Johnston Mooney & O'Brien Bakeries* UD169/2014.

believed that the assault was at the upper end of the scale and this factor, coupled with the claimant's lack of remorse, satisfied him that dismissal was the appropriate sanction. The claimant was notified of the decision by letter and was given the opportunity to appeal the decision, which he did. The decision to dismiss the claimant was upheld on appeal.

The claimant told the EAT that he believed he was correct to challenge AD concerning the air hose but that he accepted that it was wrong to engage in a fight. He accepted that he 'flipped' and lost control in the first incident but he described his actions regarding the second incident as a 'controlled take down' to defend himself and did not accept that it was an assault.

The EAT noted that in *Allied Irish Banks v Purcell*[30] it was stated that: 'It is clear that it is not for the EAT or this court to ask whether it would dismiss in the circumstances or substitute its view for the employer's view, but to ask was it reasonably open to the respondent to make the decision it made rather than necessarily the one that the EAT or the court would have taken.'

The EAT found that the respondent had discharged the onus of proof and that the claimant had been fairly dismissed. The EAT stated that, while there may have been some provocation, the actions of the claimant were entirely unacceptable in a workplace situation and amounted to gross misconduct.

[27.24] *Kinsella v Securitas Security Services Ltd*[31] *and Lewental v Securitas Security Services Ltd*[32]—*Employment Appeals Tribunal—Unfair Dismissals Acts 1977 to 2015—fair procedures—dismissal for gross misconduct where alleged misuse of force by security officers*

The claimants were employed by the respondent as security officers. Both were dismissed for gross misconduct following two incidents of alleged misuse of force in the manner in which the claimants carried out two arrests.

The claimants received letters from the respondent's human resources manager which outlined the separate incidents and which enclosed the incident reports. They were both required to attend disciplinary meetings. Following the meetings, the claimants received letters informing them of the termination of their employment. Both claimants were given the right to appeal.

The claimants submitted that they had followed the procedures laid down by the respondents in their officer handbook. They also gave evidence that they had reported both incidents to their supervisor and had given him the incident reports to fax to the respondent's head office. Their supervisor had not been interviewed by the respondent in relation to the incidents when determining whether there had been gross misconduct. The claimants stated that they had been given no warning that there had been any issue with the manner in which they had carried out the arrests, prior to the receipt of the letters in relation to the disciplinary hearing.

---

30. *Allied Irish Banks v Purcell* [2012] 23 ELR 189.
31. *Kinsella v Securitas Security Services Ltd* UD1119/2012.
32. *Lewental v Securitas Security Services Ltd* UD1124/2012.

The EAT found that there was an absolute breach of procedures on the part of the respondent. The EAT was satisfied that reasonable force had been used during both incidents and that the claimants had been unfairly dismissed.

Breach of trust/dishonesty

[27.25] *Cullen v McGrath t/a The Bridgend Bar[33]—Employment Appeals Tribunal— Unfair Dismissals Acts 1977 to 2015—theft—disciplinary procedures lacking—not sufficiently unfair to warrant overturning dismissal*

The claimant, a barman in the public house owned by the respondent was dismissed following allegations of theft of stock and cash.

The EAT heard that the respondent began to notice stock losses and decided to begin monitoring the claimant who was predominately in charge of the bar during the week. The respondent employed a stock taker in 2012 who took stock every two months. The respondent gave evidence that the stock losses increased in early 2013, and thereafter the stock taker took stock weekly.

On 15 April 2013, the respondent was informed by the stock taker that the cumulative losses of stock had increased. The respondent gave evidence that he informed the claimant that there was €300 to €400 loss each week since January 2013 and asked him 'what do you think is happening?'. The respondent advised the claimant that An Garda Síochána may become involved in the matter. The claimant denied wrongdoing. The respondent explained the losses of that evening to the claimant, and noted that the claimant was responsible for the till that evening. The respondent then suspended the claimant with immediate effect.

A meeting was scheduled between the respondent and the claimant on 6 May 2013. During the course of the meeting, the respondent asked the claimant if he had anything to confess and went through the evidence of missing stock with the claimant again, including photographs of empty bottles which were not accounted for. The claimant again denied all wrongdoing. The respondent then terminated the claimant's employment at this meeting.

The claimant asserted that the respondent invited him to attend the bar for 'a chat' and did not inform him of the disciplinary nature of the meeting or advise him to bring a representative to the meeting. The claimant informed the EAT that he was shocked to be dismissed in these circumstances.

The EAT stated that the test in theft cases is: 'was the investigation into the alleged theft fair and did it lead to a reasonable belief by the employer that the employee was responsible for the theft.'

The EAT found that the stock take by the respondent was a fair investigation of the alleged theft. It further noted that the claimant had sole responsibility for the bar that night and yet he was unable to provide any explanation as to why the stock was missing either at the meetings with the respondent or on the date of the hearing before the EAT.

---

33. *Cullen v McGrath t/a The Bridgend Bar* UD1298/2013.

In dismissing the claim, the EAT noted that the respondent's disciplinary procedures were flawed but it held that in the circumstances, the procedures were not sufficiently unfair to undermine the overall fairness of the decision to dismiss.

[27.26] *Cottingham v Wine Street Bakeries t/a O'Hehirs Bakery[34]—Employment Appeals Tribunal—Unfair Dismissals Acts 1977 to 2015—removal of food items that were still in date—dismissal for alleged theft—whether fair procedures applied*

The claimant was employed as a sales assistant, and subsequently as a manager, in the respondent's shop. The manager reported the claimant to the operations manager for removing from the premises food packages containing breakfast food items and cooked chicken and ham contrary to the respondent's waste management policy. The waste management guidelines stated that any out-of-date stock was to be disposed of as it is not fit for human consumption. Members of staff were not permitted to remove this stock from the premises for that reason. In this case, the food items were checked and were confirmed to be in date and usable, although the claimant claimed they were out-of-date stock.

The operations manager checked the order level of the shop and found it to be consistent with the other shops. The operations manager then arranged to meet with the claimant. The claimant admitted to removing the items but maintained that they had been out of date. The operations manager then spent two hours speaking with the claimant who informed her that she was having personal problems. The claimant asked what she should do and the operation manager advised her that, if she resigned, no disciplinary action would be taken against her which could potentially affect her future employment prospects. A full investigation took place, followed by a disciplinary hearing, at which the claimant was accompanied. The claimant's position was that the products she removed were out of date and this was permitted. However, the respondent's position was that the removal of in-date stock which could have been sold was theft. The disciplinary decision maker particularly noted that the food was neatly packaged and left in the fridge to be removed, if it was out of date it would have contaminated the other food in the fridge. The claimant's actions were considered theft and this was compounded by her position as shop manager, a role of responsibility. She was dismissed and this was upheld on internal appeal.

The claimant in her evidence stated that she did not recall ever seeing a food safety manual or a waste management policy and that she knew of other staff who took out of date stock home. She also submitted that she had no prior notice of the initial meeting with the operation manager. The claimant said that she felt intimidated and threatened by the operation manager's manner.

The EAT dismissed the claim and found that the respondent acted reasonably in the circumstances. It also found that the procedures used by the respondent were fair and reasonable.

---

34.   *Cottingham v Wine Street Bakeries t/a O'Hehirs Bakery* UD211/2013.

[27.27] *Fogarty v Byrne t/a Gala Service Station[35]—Employment Appeals Tribunal— appeal from decision of Rights Commissioner—Unfair Dismissals Acts 1977 to 2015—dismissal for removal of food products—unfair procedures*

The claimant commenced employment in 2002 in the role of delicatessen manager. The respondent had a policy, which the claimant was aware of, that no food waste should be removed by employees with the exception that on Tuesday mornings the claimant was permitted to take waste bread product home to feed chickens.

A separate issue arose when the respondent became aware that customers were getting food at discounted rates at the delicatessen. The respondent met with all staff on this issue, including the claimant, informing them that this practice was not permitted. A notice was displayed to remind staff of this policy. No disciplinary action was taken at that time. However, on foot of this, the respondent had commenced monitoring CCTV of the deli counter.

On 5 July the respondent asked the claimant to a meeting, having observed her remove waste food from the deli area. He asked a number of questions which he had prepared and wrote down the claimant's responses. The claimant's representative produced the original note of the meeting held that day and there was conflicting evidence regarding the document which the respondent opened to the EAT as an accurate note of that meeting. The claimant confirmed that she was aware of the policy and explained that she had two dogs and had taken waste deli products home to feed them.

In a letter dated 10 July, the claimant was invited to attend a disciplinary meeting. The purpose of the meeting was to discuss two allegations namely alleged theft of company property and alleged breach of trust and confidence. The claimant's union representative was delayed and it was agreed to proceed with the meeting. The claimant explained that she had only taken food which would not sell and had been in the unit for a period of four to five hours. The respondent submitted that it was not possible to know if the food would sell. He took the decision to dismiss the employee on the grounds that trust was broken. He could no longer trust the employee to operate the tills and handle food products.

The EAT noted that there were no specific dates of alleged breaches of company policy given to the claimant in the investigative or disciplinary meetings. The respondent conducted the investigation, the disciplinary hearing, made the decision to dismiss and effectively thwarted union representation for the claimant by failing to delay or reschedule the disciplinary hearing. However, there was no similar urgency to progress the appeal of the claimant. This was further aggravated by the fact that there was no meaningful appeal offered to the claimant. These factors meant that the procedure was unfair. Additionally, in all of the circumstances, the decision to dismiss was a disproportionate sanction that no reasonable employer should have come to.

The EAT therefore found that the dismissal was unfair and awarded the claimant compensation of €19,500.

---

35.   *Fogarty v Byrne t/a Gala Service Station* UD453/2013, UD358/2013.

[27.28] *Byrne v St Pauls Garda Medical Aid Society*[36]*—Employment Appeals Tribunal—Unfair Dismissals Acts 1977 to 2015—dismissal for breach of trust and confidence*

The claimant was employed by the respondent in January 1998 with general office duties and responsibility for processing members' claims. The respondent provides health insurance for its members, including members of An Garda Síochána, student gardaí and retired members of the force. Employees are also members, including the claimant, who was employed in a claims assessor role.

In 2011, while the claimant was out on sick leave, the office manager found four folders of approximately 50 claims in the claimant's unlocked drawer and, on the top of each folder, she found a cheque which had expired. It was established that the four cheques were not processed or receipted. This was reported to the office manager. In January 2012, the Revenue Commissioners notified the respondent of an investigation into the claimant's tax affairs. All of the claimant's insurance claims were gathered by the office manager as a result. It was noted that on the form 'GMA' (Garda Medical Aid) was entirely Tippexed over and this was brought to the attention of the office manager. It was also noted that on the claimant's claim form, a handwritten note appeared stating 'please send bills to home address'. The respondent established an investigation committee to examine whether the claimant had breached its policy and procedures in that a number of circulars had issued which stated that no alternations or writing should appear on claim forms. A particular issue for the respondent was that it had moved to new office premises in 2008 and thus the claimant should have been aware of the four cheques as she would have moved them during the relocation process.

The EAT noted that the claimant was dismissed from the employment for gross misconduct following a finding that her behaviour destroyed the trust and confidence which an employer must have in its employees in order to retain them in employment. The EAT was satisfied that a full and independent enquiry was carried out in relation to the four allegations and that the respondent had given the claimant every opportunity to state her case and/or deny the allegations. The EAT noted that when giving evidence, the claimant did not deny she had left cheques in her desk drawer and did not deny writing 'please send bills to home address'. The EAT noted the terms of the circular whereby it was clear that forms such as the claimant's claim form should not have been written on. The EAT was satisfied that, despite the claimant's evidence that she didn't think anything of it and that it was done all the time, she did have knowledge of the circular and did knowingly write on the form. The EAT noted, however, that this allegation, in isolation, would not amount to gross misconduct.

The EAT noted that the claimant had not denied using Tippex on the claim form in any of her correspondence during the investigation process. All she had said was that she had nothing to add. The EAT concluded that that statement, coupled with the evidence that only the claimant could have something to gain from altering the document, led the EAT to conclude that she did alter the document. The EAT held that whether she gained anything by so doing was not relevant.

36.　*Byrne v St Pauls Garda Medical Aid Society* UD397/2013.

The EAT held that the claimant's inaction in relation to the cheques had a negative financial effect on the respondent. The EAT's view was that to leave cheques in a drawer for a period of four years was totally unacceptable and led to a breach of trust between the claimant and the respondent. The EAT held that, while not perfect, the investigation and disciplinary process were sufficient and that the claimant was afforded every opportunity to state her case, however, for her personal reasons, she chose not to. The EAT concluded that the respondent's finding that the claimant's actions had destroyed the trust and confidence they had in her was well-founded and further found that her dismissal was warranted and fair in all of the circumstances. Her claim failed.

[27.29] *Akinfaye v Tesco Ireland Ltd[37]—Employment Appeals Tribunal—Unfair Dismissals Acts 1977 to 2015—dismissal for breach of honesty and trust—whether claimant had been unfairly dismissed as result of her use of coupons in respondent's store—proportionality of sanction*

At the outset, the manager (JR) of the store where the claimant was employed explained to the EAT that the incidents in question related to the use of money-off coupons as payment for shopping purchased by the claimant while she was on maternity leave. Coupons had been used on four occasions for items that either had not been purchased or which were of a higher value. It was also submitted that the claimant had asked two staff members to assist her in putting the self-scan checkout into 'assist mode'.

The EAT stated that the case had some unusual factors in that the matters complained of, and which ultimately led to her dismissal, took place while the claimant had been interacting with the respondent as an ordinary customer while she was on maternity leave. It was noted that the EAT had not been invited to make any ruling in relation to the question of whether or not incidents which occurred during the claimant's pregnancy could be taken into account in a decision to dismiss. Nevertheless, the EAT stated that it was appropriate for the respondent to take these incidents into account as the claimant had indicated that she would be returning to work at the end of her maternity leave.

The EAT found that no evidence had been adduced to show that the respondent suffered any loss as a result of the claimant availing of coupons. The EAT stated that the respondent's attitude appeared to be that it went without saying that such loss must have been incurred. The EAT felt that a reasonable employer would have ascertained whether or not there was an actual loss in assessing any disciplinary action or sanction. Despite this, the EAT found that there was some misuse of coupons and that, as the claimant was at a management level, it was inappropriate for her to be acting in this manner. While no proof of financial loss had been given, the EAT held that there was potential for such loss and also for reputational damage to the respondent. It further held that such action by the claimant was a poor example for staff over whom she had supervisory responsibility.

The EAT held that the respondent was justified in taking disciplinary action but that the claimant's dismissal was not fair either substantively or procedurally. The EAT found

---

37.   *Akinfaye v Tesco Ireland Ltd* UD630/2012.

that compensation should be awarded to the claimant but that her substantial contribution to her own dismissal should also be taken into account. The claimant was awarded €10,000 compensation.

[27.30] *Kalinins v ISS Ireland Ltd t/a ISS Facility Services[38]—Employment Appeals Tribunal—Unfair Dismissals Acts 1977 to 2015—dismissal for covering for colleague who had left his work station*

The claimant, a security guard, was dismissed for allegedly covering for a colleague who had absented himself from his work station.

The claimant held a post of trust on the site of a major client and when the respondent's customer service manager visited the site on 23 May 2012, the claimant had said that his colleague, SG2, was in another part of the warehouse. When the respondent looked at CCTV footage it was concluded that SG2 had left early a number of times. On 23 May 2012, SG2 had left at 4.40am, rather than at 7.00am when his shift was due to end. It was concluded that the claimant had lied and he was dismissed.

The site in question had high-value products such as alcohol and household goods. Trucks would be signed in and out by the two-man security team and drivers and vehicle registrations were noted. It was essential to the respondent and its clients that there would be two security men on duty on the site, one to man a security hut and the other to carry out patrols. There was no security supervisor onsite and, as the respondent had products for major multiples, security guards had to check in hourly with the control room.

It was confirmed that a security man could leave 10 or 15 minutes before the end of a shift but only if a relieving security man from the next shift had arrived early. Otherwise there would be health and safety exposure and furthermore the respondent's client was being charged for two security men rather than one.

The customer services manager told the EAT that he did not believe that the claimant had seen him arrive on his auditing visit before 6 am on 23 May 2012 but the customer services manager said that, once the claimant had become aware of his arrival, the claimant had been busy on his mobile phone. The claimant finally admitted that SG2 had gone home early and he also stated that SG2 never left early prior to this incident.

The customer services manager confirmed that he was involved in the investigation process and the disciplinary process, and he also made the decision to dismiss the claimant. He stated that, as a manager, he was capable of making a judgment call. The claimant was not in a supervisory role and was the same level as SG2. Other sanctions were considered but dismissal was decided to be the only course of action.

The HR director told the EAT that he heard the claimant's appeal. He met the claimant on 20 July 2015. The claimant indicated to the HR director that he had made a mistake but felt maybe suspension rather than dismissal would be appropriate. After considering all aspects of the case, the HR director decided to uphold the decision of dismissal.

---

38.   *Kalinins v ISS Ireland Ltd t/a ISS Facility Services* UD1508/2012.

The claimant told the EAT that he made a mistake in covering for SG2, who was the same grade as himself. At the time, he felt he had a moral dilemma as SG2 had family issues. And he did not know what to do. The claimant felt that an appropriate punishment could have been suspension rather than dismissal and felt the sanction was disproportionate.

The EAT concluded that the case was fairly put by the respondent. The claimant had originally disputed the evidence but subsequently co-operated in full with the investigation, hearing and appeal. Under all the circumstances, the EAT found the dismissal fair due to the seriousness of the possible consequences of the claimant's actions.

Breach of cash-handling procedures

[27.31] *Oney v Persian Properties t/a O'Callaghan Hotels[39]—Employment Appeals Tribunal—Unfair Dismissals Acts 1977 to 2015—unfair dismissal—breach of cash-handling procedures*

The claimant commenced employment with the respondent hotel in July 2011 as a duty manager and had responsibility for both the bar float and safe float.

On 1 and 2 February 2014 a cash integrity audit was carried out by RM on behalf of the respondent. The claimant was on duty on 1 and 2 February. This report highlighted a number of alleged incidents which constituted an alleged breach of the cash-handling policy, void procedures and an allegation of theft on the part of the claimant.

Having regard to all the evidence throughout the course of this two-day hearing, in particular the expert evidence of RM, the EAT was satisfied that the claimant was systematically in breach of the respondent's cash-handling procedures on the night of 1 February 2014. It was noted, however, by the EAT that there were weaknesses in elements of the respondent's application of their own cash-handling procedures, however on balance the EAT was satisfied that the dismissal was fair and in those circumstances the claim under the Acts failed.

[27.32] *Pender v Woodies DIY Ltd t/a Woodies DIY and Garden Centres Arena[40]— Employment Appeals Tribunal—Unfair Dismissals Acts 1977 to 2015—unfair dismissal—breach of cash-handling procedures—dismissal not upheld on appeal— claimant moved to another role—was there in fact a dismissal—re-engagement*

The claimant was chief cashier at the respondent's Coolock Store for eight and a half years and was dismissed for breach of the respondent's cash-handling procedures.

The duty manager brought issues to the store manager's attention after a cashier told him she was uncomfortable with the way the claimant handled some refunds. The store manager then carried out an investigation. He gave evidence that when he looked at CCTV footage he found three examples of the claimant issuing refunds where no customer was present and no product was returned. Usually, when a customer requested

---

39. *Oney v Persian Properties t/a O'Callaghan Hotels* UD543/2014.
40. *Pender v Woodies DIY Ltd t/a Woodies DIY and Garden Centres Arena* UD460/2014.

a refund, the customer was asked to sign the receipt and write his/her address on it. In these cases the claimant signed off on the refunds. The store manager first spoke informally with the claimant about refunds but he was not satisfied with her answers. The store manager then spoke to the claimant formally and offered the claimant the opportunity to be accompanied at the meeting. The store manager suspended the claimant with pay while he investigated further.

The claimant was invited to a disciplinary hearing. The executive area manager ran the disciplinary process. The executive area manager gave evidence during the hearing. He said the claimant's role was pivotal; she was a go between managers and floor staff and she was responsible for looking after the cash. The executive area manager explained that cash was counted and recorded every day and anomalies were reported. It was common to have anomalies in a store that had up to a thousand transactions a day. An anomaly of up to €2 per till per day was allowed. If there was a larger anomaly it was recorded and the duty manager was informed and he in turn had a chat with the cashier.

At the disciplinary hearing, the claimant admitted to putting through two fictitious transactions. This action prevented the respondent from investigating cash shortfalls. The claimant had taken discarded receipts out of a bin and put them through as refunds. She signed the receipts with false names. She involved a junior staff member in processing one of the transactions. The issue came to light when the junior staff member spoke about it. Before the claimant went on holidays she was aware of a deficit of €30 in the tills and she covered this with her own money. The executive area manager struggled to understand this action.

The executive area manager considered lesser sanctions but decided to dismiss the claimant. The claimant appealed the decision to dismiss and the operations director dealt with the claimant's appeal of the decision to dismiss her. The executive manager gave evidence that he had looked at all the information and he asked the claimant if she was aware of the processes and found she was familiar with them. The claimant had processed refunds without a customer being present and as a result stock was recorded as being present when it was not. In 25 years of big box retail experience, the operations director stated that he had never seen this before. The executive manager was not satisfied with the claimant's explanation. However, he considered the sanction of dismissal as a bit high and he wanted to put her into an environment where she could be re-trained. The executive manager gave her a final written warning to ensure she did not falsify records again. She was offered a different position in a different location on the same salary. The claimant was not satisfied with this.

The EAT, concluded that the actions of the claimant were such that they indicated to the respondent that she was indulging in practices contrary to good procedures, which may or may not have been countenanced by the respondent's administration in previous years.

The EAT deemed the dismissal of the claimant in these circumstances to be somewhat harsh. By offering a different position, in a different location to the one the claimant held, without a reduction in salary, the respondent was in effect terminating her employment from the position she held.

In the circumstances, the EAT determined that the dismissal was unfair, in light of the expressed opinion of the person who conducted the appeal. The EAT gave consideration to the remedies available to it and found the most appropriate remedy in this case to be re-engagement in the same location from the date of the order.

Breach of confidentiality

[27.33] *Forder v AV Pound & Company Ltd[41]—Employment Appeals Tribunal— Unfair Dismissals Acts 1977 to 2015—unfair dismissal—contractual duty of confidentiality—non-solicitation clause—disclosure of confidential information to competitor during course of employment—whether employee's conduct might reasonably be considered to damage or constitute danger to employer's business— duty not to establish competing business—failure to follow reasonable management instructions—dismissal for sending emails containing company information to competitor—breach of employee's duty of fidelity*

The claimant commenced employment in the respondent's original company base in South Africa in 1981 and moved to Ireland in 2003 to take up employment with the respondent's new company in Ireland as a product manager. She was part of a three-person sales team. The respondent was one of a group of companies that acted as a broker to facilitate commercial contracts between suppliers and buyers of industrial chemical raw materials. The claimant's contract of employment with the respondent contained a confidentiality clause and a non-solicitation clause. The CEO took over the management of the Irish office in 2005/6 and shortly after informed the directors that he and the claimant were in a relationship. The CEO was also a director of another company, Multi Bulk, which was set up to invoice group companies for salaries. In 2007, the CEO bought out the other two directors of Multi Bulk, one of whom was a member of the claimant's three-person sales team. The claimant was later appointed as a director of Multi Bulk.

The relationship between the CEO and the other directors began to break down and the CEO's employment with the group terminated on 13 August 2008. By email dated 18 August 2008 to employees and the claimant, it was further confirmed that the decision to terminate was taken by the board after having received legal advice and that such termination was in order. An exit package of over €5.5 million was finalised in mid-February 2010 and the ex-CEO resigned as a director of the holding company with retrospective effect from January 2009 and an acting CEO was put in place. All employees were informed of the ex-CEO's resignation. The settlement, although payable over a five-year period, was paid by the end of November 2010.

The relationship between the claimant and members of her sales team also broke down. From January 2010 onwards, it was noted that the claimant felt isolated and excluded in the office and felt she did not receive the same level of bonus as others. She noted that she was overwhelmed and could not perform some of her functions as she was not receiving adequate information to fulfil her role. The claimant was absent on sick

41. *Forder v AV Pound & Company Ltd* UD927/2011, MN1057/2011, WT385/2011.

497

leave for three to four days in June and July and had held informal discussions with the group's HR manager during this period. In August 2010, following a period of stress related sick leave, the claimant outlined her concerns in an email. The claimant noted that she wanted to discuss her concerns informally but that her complaint was treated as a formal complaint, and a formal grievance meeting was held on 5 October 2010 at which her complaint was not upheld.

In September 2010, the claimant informed management that she was attending a trade fair in Dusseldorf in October with the ex-CEO. Management was concerned as a number of the respondent's suppliers would be at the trade fair and instructed the claimant in writing that she was not to represent the respondent at the trade fair. After the trade fair, management received information that the ex-CEO had approached a supplier of the respondent at the trade fair. Management was concerned that the claimant also engaged with suppliers at the trade fair and an examination of the claimant's work emails confirmed these concerns. At an investigation meeting on 2 December 2010 the claimant was questioned about her contact with suppliers or customers prior to attending the trade fair. The claimant indicated that the ex-CEO had been representing Multi Bulk at the trade fair and was entitled to do so, as it was still his private business. The claimant confirmed to the respondent at this meeting that she did not hold a position outside of the respondent company. The claimant was suspended at the meeting, pending further investigation, and she was asked to hand over all company property and passwords. The claimant immediately returned to her desk and deleted material from her blackberry and computer despite being requested again to leave the premises. The investigation findings were provided to the Board and the acting CEO was selected to conduct the disciplinary meeting. The claimant ignored all requests over the following months to provide passwords for her electronic company equipment.

At the disciplinary meeting, the claimant answered allegations that she was undertaking private work on company premises and during working hours without permission; holding a position with a competing company in direct conflict with her current position; taking part in activities which caused the respondent to lose faith in her integrity, and engaging in conduct which could be construed as being in breach of the respondent's core rules of confidentiality; as well as to serious breaches of the respondent's rules and procedures and failing to follow reasonable management instructions. Emails and documentation were put to the claimant that indicated that she was passing on potential business developments to the ex-CEO. It was further alleged that the claimant had been working in competition with the respondent while holding a position with a competing company and that the claimant had made blatant attempts to solicit one of the respondent's key suppliers and that Multi Bulk was to be the competing company. The claimant acknowledged that she had sent company information, including information on the supply of raw materials, customer pricing and transaction information and the respondent's quotations to her personal email account and contended that she was doing so to prove that she was being excluded at work. She further noted that she was sending such information to her personal account for safekeeping in case the work systems crashed. The acting CEO noted his belief that the claimant was storing information in order to compete with the respondent at a later date.

The EAT noted the non-solicitation and confidentiality clause contained within the claimant's contract of employment. The EAT referred to the test to be applied in cases of misconduct and the question of reasonableness. The EAT stated that it was necessary to ascertain whether the company genuinely believed that the employee conducted herself as alleged, had reasonable grounds to sustain that belief, and whether the penalty of dismissal was proportionate to the alleged misconduct. The EAT was satisfied that it was reasonable for the respondent to believe that the claimant was or was intending to compete, and /or was assisting the ex-CEO to compete with the respondent. The EAT referred to a number of emails that had been provided in evidence which showed a clear intention on the part of the claimant to compete with the respondent and the group. The EAT further noted that the ex-CEO had set up a meeting with a supplier of the respondent at the trade fair, the claimant accompanied the ex-CEO to the trade fair and, although instructed not to represent the respondent at the trade fair, made preliminary enquiries as to whether a supplier of the respondent would be present at the trade fair. As regards the allegation of competing, the EAT noted it was irrelevant whether the respondent had correctly identified the company which was to compete or was competing with the respondent. The EAT noted that it was reasonable for the acting CEO to believe that the claimant was transmitting confidential company marketing information including information on the costings of its raw materials, pricing and margins to the ex-CEO, her partner, contrary to the instruction and the interests of the respondent and the group. The claimant was in breach of her core contractual duty of confidentiality to the respondent; as she was in giving the ex-CEO the respondent's IP address. The EAT noted that it was irrelevant that in some instances the ex-CEO may have, through inadvertence and oversight on the part of senior personnel, received company information from another source or sources within the respondent or that the respondent's IP address was readily obtainable in any circumstances. The EAT ultimately found that that there existed grounds for the respondent's belief that the claimant was guilty of the allegations against her. The EAT found that the respondent did have a reasonable belief that the claimant was guilty of the alleged misconduct and that dismissal was not disproportionate in the circumstances. The EAT found that the allegations constituted a breach of an employee's duty of fidelity. This duty applies not only to establishing a competing business but also to the activities of an employee, which might reasonably be considered to damage or constitute a danger to the employer's business. The claim failed.

[27.34] *Anderson v O'Connor & O'Connor t/a OCPM Property Consultants[42]—Employment Appeals Tribunal—Unfair Dismissals Acts 1977 to 2015—Organisation of Working Time Act 1997—summary dismissal—removal of files—downloading of software—breach of fair procedures—covert recording of disciplinary meeting—breach of trust*

The claimant worked for the respondent company for five years but raised suspicion when he became interested in the respondent's accounts and began working outside normal working hours; for which he received no extra pay. The respondent stated that the claimant had solicited work from a caretaker on behalf of the respondent where it had been made clear to him that this caretaker was not to be contracted and the claimant had, the respondent claimed, incited that caretaker to falsify records.

The 'last straw' according to the respondent arose when the claimant downloaded the respondent's software. The respondent submitted that the claimant had access to records for over 2,900 clients and would have 'hit the ground running' on establishing his own business. The claimant was summarily dismissed. A recording of this meeting was made by the respondent without the claimant's knowledge and was played to the EAT.

The respondent, in evidence, had agreed that dismissal was a serious step but claimed he 'had no time for niceties' and that the claimant was 'guilty until proven innocent'. An employee gave evidence that she asked if the claimant had the respondent's permission to download the software and the claimant responded that he did. Another witness testified that there was no reason to take this information off the premises.

The claimant explained that he had known the managing director of the respondent prior to his employment and had not been given a contract on commencing his job. He claimed that he had never been instructed not to remove files from the office, nor was he given extra money for extra work and admitted engaging the caretaker despite been instructed not to do so.

The claimant stated that he was called to a meeting with the managing director of the respondent, whose tone he described as aggressive, on 24 April 2013 and was summarily dismissed. The claimant asserted that this occurred even though the managing director was aware that he had been unable to use the downloaded information (as it was not accepted by his computer), that he had a habit of taking work home with him and that there was nothing particularly sensitive about the files. He added that he had, at that time, no intention of leaving the respondent. He claimed that he was not given a right to reply to the allegations or appeal his dismissal. He later set up his own company.

The EAT concluded that both parties had acted inappropriately. The respondent's trust and confidence in the claimant had been 'misplaced, if not abused' and the claimant's attempts to usurp the respondent's business were 'disloyal and inappropriate'. The EAT also criticised the respondent's failure to follow fair and proper procedures on

---

42.   *Anderson v O'Connor & O'Connor t/a OCPM Property Consultants* UD954/2013, WT169/2015

termination of the claimant's employment. The EAT found that the claimant was unfairly dismissed but awarded no compensation.

Criminal convictions

[27.35] *O'Connell v An Post, General Post Office[43]—Employment Appeals Tribunal—Unfair Dismissal Acts 1977 to 2015—dismissal on grounds of theft and breach of trust where claimant pleaded guilty to 12 criminal counts—whether respondent made sufficient allowance for claimant's medical condition where claimant suffered from severe depression*

The claimant, a postman, was employed from January 1991 to September 2013 when he was dismissed on grounds of theft and breach of trust when he pleaded guilty to 12 criminal charges.

It was submitted that, at the time of the claimant's dismissal, the respondent had not made sufficient allowance for his medical condition. It was further suggested that the respondent's occupational support services had not properly fulfilled their duty of care in relation to the treatment of the claimant.

The respondent's decision makers acknowledged their awareness of the claimant's psychiatric circumstances, but they found that these had not mitigated his conduct. It emerged that the respondent's human resources personnel had explored the possibility of ill-health retirement for the claimant. However, it noted that the respondent's medical function had not found this appropriate.

The EAT held that this had been a personal tragedy for the claimant but that the dismissal had not been substantively or procedurally unfair. It was not established that the claimant was fit for work. The respondent did have a duty of care but was not the provider of primary care services and the respondent's procedures were not challenged to a grave extent. The EAT held that the claimant's own actions cost him his job. A dismissed person's personal circumstances can aggravate as well as mitigate his offence. Dismissal was the only appropriate sanction. While the EAT had empathy for the claimant, the respondent had to have regard to its own protection. The EAT noted the claimant had major issues in his personal life and had not concealed his circumstances entirely; he had recourse to an external entity and had lost his home. The EAT noted the claimant evinced willingness to take punishment for his crime but noted that he had appealed his criminal sentence. The EAT unanimously concluded that dismissal was within the range of responses available to the respondent in all of the circumstances of the claimant's conduct. Notwithstanding his efforts to have the EAT see his personal circumstances as more mitigating than aggravating, his claim failed.

---

43.   *O'Connell v An Post, General Post Office* UD47/2014.

Garda vetting

[27.36] Stynes v Cloverland Healthcare Ltd,[44] Keogh v Cloverland Healthcare Ltd[45]—Employment Appeals Tribunal—appeal from decision of Rights Commissioner—Unfair Dismissals Acts 1977 to 2015—unfair dismissals—Health Information Quality Authority (HIQA)—requirement to conduct garda vetting on current employees—discovery of pre-employment convictions—dismissal on return from maternity leave

Both of these cases contain almost identical facts and each claim was an appeal from a decision of the Rights Commissioner regarding the dismissal of the claimants, in circumstances where the respondent became aware of pre-employment convictions of both claimants.

The first claimant commenced work for the respondent as a laundry operative in 2007 and the second claimant as a care assistant in 2004. The respondent had no issues with the claimants' performance up to the date of their respective claims. During their employment with the respondent, HIQA published amended regulations for nursing homes which provided for an additional requirement for nursing home employees to engage in the garda vetting process. The garda vetting process subsequently revealed that both claimants had a number of convictions, all of which pre-dated their employment with the respondent. The first claimant was on maternity leave when the respondent contacted her in March 2012 informing her of the findings of the garda vetting process. On her return from maternity leave, the first claimant was requested to attend a meeting with the respondent on 14 September 2012 at which point she was informed that her employment would be terminated. The second claimant was also contacted while on maternity leave and was requested to attend a meeting the day after her return to work at which point she was informed that her employment with the respondent would be terminated.

The EAT noted in both cases that the respondent's business concerned the provision of care for vulnerable adults. The EAT further noted that the respondent had an obligation to balance the needs of the vulnerable adults with its duties and obligations to its employees. The EAT found that the respondent erred, in terminating the employment of both claimants, by failing to carry out a risk assessment to determine whether the claimants were capable of continuing in employment with the respondent in light of the findings of the garda vetting process. The respondent should also have had regard for the previous service records of the claimants. In the case of the first claimant, the EAT noted that the claimant's position as a laundry operative did not in fact require any contact with patients. The EAT found that the summary dismissal of the claimants amounted to an unfair dismissal under the Acts and awarded the claimants the sums of €21,120 and €20,064 respectively.

---

44.   *Stynes v Cloverland Healthcare Ltd* UD384/2013.
45.   *Keogh v Cloverland Healthcare Ltd* UD439/2013.

[27.37] *Donoghue v Dublin West Home Help Ltd*[46]—*Employment Appeals Tribunal—appeal from decision of Rights Commissioner—Unfair Dismissals Acts 1977 to 2015—unfair dismissal—garda vetting of employees—where claimant home help/carer failed to disclose convictions*

This was an appeal by the claimant against a decision of a Rights Commissioner who had found that she had been fairly dismissed. The claimant was employed as a home help/carer with the respondent since 2006. Garda vetting of new employees and existing employees of the respondent commenced in 2009 and 2010 respectively.

The respondent provided garda vetting forms to existing staff in 2010 and gave instructions to staff to complete the forms in full and in detail. The claimant did not return hers until September 2011. The garda vetting outcome was returned to the respondent in May 2012 and the claimant's form detailed 10 convictions which she had not disclosed. It was the claimant's evidence that she genuinely could not remember the details of the convictions she held, such as dates and relevant years. However, the claimant answered honestly on the form that she had received convictions and she outlined two offences that she could remember the details of. Despite her fears of losing her employment, the claimant listed all of the addresses at which she had resided in the knowledge that the vetting form would be returned with details of all of her convictions. The claimant outlined to the EAT that when the convictions occurred she was in a domestically violent situation and the actions associated with the convictions occurred under duress from her husband. At the time of the hearing she was divorced.

On 6 November 2012 the claimant confirmed in a meeting with her line manager that the convictions correctly related to her. The manager reported the matter to the respondent's board and a decision was taken to place the claimant on suspension pending an investigation. The manager was requested to conduct a risk assessment and the claimant was advised of this. In conducting the risk assessment the manager considered the vulnerability of the clients visited by the claimant. The risk assessment found that the claimant would not pose a risk if supervised; but she was entering clients' homes unsupervised. However, the manager felt that trust had broken down by virtue of the fact that the claimant did not disclose all of the convictions and she noted that three of the convictions were received during the tenure of the claimant's employment. The manager recommended that the claimant could not continue in employment with the respondent due to the nature of the work environment.

The manager's risk assessment was provided to the board. A member of the board gave evidence of a meeting conducted with the claimant in January 2013. At the meeting the claimant was informed that the non-disclosure of convictions would have to be considered. A further meeting on 4 February 2013 was held wherein the claimant outlined the circumstances around the convictions and reasons why she had not listed all of the convictions such as: not remembering dates; not enough space on the form; and that she had been upfront with the manager that more would be returned on the form than she had included.

---

46.   *Donoghue v Dublin West Home Help Ltd* UD691/2014.

Following this meeting the board member and a colleague considered all of the documentation, including the risk assessment, representations made by the claimant and written correspondence from a number of sources in support of the claimant. There was a particular concern surrounding the issue of non-disclosure on the part of the claimant and the respondent found it was not credible that the claimant did not remember the dates she received the three most recent convictions.

Cognisant of the claimant's role, other options were examined such as controls that could possibly be put in place, but the respondent gave evidence that these were not feasible from an expenditure point of view. In addition there were only few occasions when the respondent required two members of staff to work together. A decision was taken to dismiss the claimant due to the non-disclosure of the convictions. This decision was taken by the board member and a colleague but their findings were also discussed with the chairman of the board.

An appeal of the decision to dismiss was offered to, and accepted by, the claimant. An outside individual was sought by the board to conduct the appeal and a lecturer in human resource management was selected with the agreement of the union representing the claimant. This appeals officer did not give evidence to the EAT but the member of the board confirmed that she was present at the appeal and the decision to dismiss was upheld. During cross examination the board member confirmed that, as well as being present at the appeal, the claimant was also questioned by the appeals officer as part of the appeal process.

The EAT determined that the claimant was fairly dismissed. The EAT noted that it came to this conclusion reluctantly, but found that the respondent had acted reasonably in all the circumstances despite some procedural difficulties in relation to the appeal.

Unauthorised use of the internet

[27.38] *Dempsey v Righpur Ltd t/a Boru Stoves[47]—Employment Appeals Tribunal— Unfair Dismissals Acts 1977 to 2015—unauthorised use of internet on respondent's premises—whether process used to dismiss claimant fair and in accordance with natural procedures—right to receive notification of disciplinary hearing—right to be accompanied to disciplinary hearing—whether preparation of letter of dismissal prior to disciplinary hearing suggests foregone conclusion of dismissal*

This claim was initiated by the claimant following his summary dismissal on 6 December 2013 from his employment with the respondent. The claimant was employed with the respondent as a machine operator and forklift driver since 1 April 2011.

The incident which led to the claimant's dismissal occurred on 5 December 2013. The respondent stated that a few weeks prior to the incident the claimant and some other employees had been suspected of using the internet in one of the respondent's offices while at work. A general warning had been issued to all staff at that time in relation to the unauthorised use of the internet in the plant.

---

47.   *Dempsey v Righpur Ltd t/a Boru Stoves* UD204/2014.

On 5 December 2013, a director of the respondent (D) unexpectedly visited the respondent's plant during the night shift. D observed the claimant and another employee viewing a video clip of a football match, using social media, on a screen which was properly used for the operation of a machine. This screen had been blocked from accessing the internet because of the risk of contracting a virus and possibly shutting down production. D let them know he was there and they went about their business. D called the claimant to his office the following day. It was D's evidence that although the claimant admitted to using the internet more than once, he denied having altered the settings on the screen to allow access to the internet.

It was the respondent's position that the claimant had breached his contract of employment and caused a breakdown in trust to occur. The respondent called the claimant to a meeting. The claimant was not given an opportunity to bring representation to the meeting, nor was he informed that the meeting could result in his dismissal. At the end of the meeting the claimant was furnished with a pre-prepared letter of dismissal. He was not informed of his right to appeal the decision to dismiss him.

The claimant told the EAT that he had been called over to the screen by his colleague to view a football clip on the night in question. This clip lasted no more than one or two minutes. While he was watching the clip, D came up behind him. The claimant denied D's evidence that he had told D that he had used the internet this way in work a number of times previously. He maintained before the EAT that this was the first time he had used the internet in such a way. He further maintained that he had no part in showing the clip on the screen and that his colleague had admitted responsibility for this to D at the time they were caught.

The EAT concluded that the claimant was unfairly dismissed by the respondent. Emphasis was placed on the fact that the claimant was dismissed without fair procedures and contrary to natural justice. The meeting of 6 December 2013 was intended to be an investigation and disciplinary meeting, but the claimant was given no prior notification of this meeting, nor was he afforded the opportunity to be accompanied. Notably the EAT held that, as the letter of dismissal was prepared prior to the meeting, the decision to dismiss the claimant was a foregone conclusion. The claimant was awarded compensation of €17,500.

Social media

[27.39] *Brown v The Mountview/Blakestown/Hartstown/Huntstown Community Drugs Team Ltd t/a Adapt[48]—Employment Appeals Tribunal—Unfair Dismissals Acts 1977 to 2015—gross misconduct—allegedly unacceptable use of Facebook— whether claimant unfairly dismissed as result of posting photograph on his Facebook page—whether claimant should have been aware that he was exposing respondent to risk*

The respondent provides a range of services to people experiencing problems with drugs and/or alcohol. It also provides holistic services to vulnerable users who have been victims, and in some cases perpetrators, of gun crime. The claimant had been employed as a project worker with the respondent since January 2003.

In February 2014, the claimant's line manager (LM) became aware that the claimant had posted a staged photograph of himself on Facebook in which he was holding a gun to a 'victim's' head. The photograph could be viewed by any members of the public using Facebook, including service users of the respondent company. The claimant was absent from work on sick leave at the time when LM became aware of the photograph. Upon his return to work, the claimant was suspended on full pay and invited to a hearing. He was given the opportunity to be represented at this meeting. At the initial hearing, which took place on 9 April 2014, the claimant provided a detailed letter. LM told the EAT that the claimant appeared to consider the photograph to be a joke and that she found this attitude to be highly inappropriate.

The claimant was invited to a further hearing on 14 April 2014, conducted by LM and a member of the board and HR sub-group (M). The claimant was represented at this meeting. The claimant subsequently received a letter confirming the joint decision of LM and M to dismiss him for gross misconduct. The letter stated that the photograph undermined the respondent's professional integrity, was unacceptable and could not be tolerated. LM was of the view that if the photograph had been seen by the respondent's service users or their families, the reputation of the respondent's service would have been damaged. LM accepted that she had not received any complaints in relation to the photograph and that employees had not been provided with training regarding Facebook usage. She also gave evidence that there had been no serious issues regarding the claimant's work performance prior to the publication of the photograph. M testified that the manner of the photograph, and the fact that the claimant had posed for it, published it and thought it was a joke left her confidence in him completely broken. She confirmed to the EAT that she had been involved in the initial decision-making process along with LM.

The claimant exercised his right to appeal the decision by letter dated 22 April 2014 and an appeal hearing was conducted by a disciplinary appeals committee. LM was questioned as part of the appeals process but was not otherwise involved in the appeal. The acting chairperson of the board and a child protection officer (P) gave evidence that

---

48. *Brown v The Mountview/Blakestown/Hartstown/Huntstown Community Drugs Team Ltd t/a Adapt*, UD1447/2014.

he had been involved in the appeal hearing, along with a HR consultant. The claimant had been legally represented at the appeal hearing. P stated that he was incredibly disappointed that the claimant had posed for such a photograph, given the context of the work of the respondent. P stated that he believed the photograph ruined the credibility of their project and he said that the board could not condone it. He also accepted that no complaints had been received in relation to the photograph.

An issue of objective bias was raised by the claimant's legal representative in relation to the appeal hearing and a new appeals panel was subsequently convened. L, a director of the board, was part of the second appeals panel and she gave evidence before the EAT. L told the EAT that she found it hard to put into words the effect that the photograph would have on service users and their families if it was viewed by them. She said that her trust in the claimant was broken and the decision to dismiss the claimant was upheld.

The claimant told the EAT that his job involved meeting service users on a one-to-one basis. He said that prior to working for the respondent, he worked on a voluntary basis for two years working with the homeless. He gave evidence that he had no education and a history of drug addiction. He explained that while on holiday in Thailand in 2008 he visited an amusement park and posed for the photograph. He clarified that the photograph was staged, the gun was fake and the ammunition which he wore around his waist was false. He compared posing for the photograph to dressing up in a costume at Halloween. He said that he made no attempt to hide the photograph and explained that he had showed it, along with other photographs, to his work colleagues when he returned to work from Thailand in 2008.

The claimant said that he did not realise that the photograph was in the public domain as he had posted it on his private Facebook account and that he had removed it immediately when it was brought to his attention. He told the EAT that he now accepts that putting the photograph on Facebook was wrong and it could have been accessed and transmitted by other Facebook users but he said he was not aware of it at the time. The claimant said that he was never requested by anyone in the community to remove the photograph and he was never told that he had given the respondent a bad name. The claimant told the EAT that he had admitted to his actions immediately and cooperated with the investigation. He had not made any efforts to secure alternative employment since his dismissal and had become financially dependent on friends and family. He suffered a lot of ill health and was in receipt of illness benefit. He had been prescribed anti-depressants by his GP.

D, a colleague of the claimant, said that the claimant had shown her the photograph when he returned from Thailand. She said that she did not think a whole lot of it but she accepted that it might shock some people. D told the EAT that she had supported the claimant since his dismissal and she described him as being very down and very sad. The EAT also heard evidence from an addict who had been helped by the claimant, and the mother of an addict who had been counselled by the claimant, who told the EAT that the claimant had helped her family for 15 years. Both gave evidence that they knew the photograph was staged.

The EAT concluded that the dismissal of the claimant was disproportionate and unfair in the circumstances. However, it was accepted that the respondent had acted in good faith, having regard to the work which they did. The EAT listed the following as being particularly pertinent in the case:

— the photograph was allowed to remain on Facebook for circa two months before it was removed. The EAT held that the respondent could have made a greater effort to remove the photograph having regard to the possible and potential damage and shock attributed to it by the respondent;

— no complaint was made to the respondent concerning the incident;

— no complaint was made to the Gardaí or any other relevant body;

— the complainant's record prior to the incident was generally misconduct free;

— there was no apparent damage or harm sustained by the respondent arising directly from the incident; and

— evidence had been adduced that the claimant was a dedicated worker.

The EAT stated that, in the circumstances, a less severe sanction could have been imposed. However, the EAT also stated that the claimant had made a serious error of judgement and that he had contributed significantly to his own downfall. It was held that the claimant had been somewhat reckless and careless as to the possible dangers of Facebook, given the nature of his work. He exposed the respondent, its servants or agents, patients, victim's etc to considerable risk and danger of which he should have been aware.

The EAT noted s 6(7) of the Unfair Dismissals Act 1977 and also noted the sentiments expressed in *Mehigan v Dyflin Publications Ltd*[49] and in *Governor and Company of the Bank of Ireland v Reilly*[50] regarding the reasonableness of an employer's conduct in relation to dismissals.

The EAT ultimately found that the claimant had been unfairly dismissed, but having regard to the fact that he was not available for work as he was unwell and in receipt of disability allowance. It was held that he was to receive the minimum statutory compensation of four weeks' salary, which amounted to €3,230.

Use of iPad whilst driving

[27.40] *Purcell v Last Passive Ltd t/a Aircoach*[51]—*Employment Appeals Tribunal—appeal from decision of Rights Commissioner—Unfair Dismissals Acts 1977 to 2015—dismissal on grounds of gross misconduct for failing to abide by health and safety procedures—use of iPAD while driving coach*

The claimant was a driver for the Aircoach service provided by the respondent. The claimant began working with the respondent on 15 September 2008. The claimant had a good relationship with all of the staff and had an exemplary record.

---

49.   *Mehigan v Dyflin Publications Ltd* UD582/2001.

50.   *Governor and Company of the Bank of Ireland v Reilly* [2015] IEHC 241. See **[27.21]**.

51.   *Purcell v Last Passive Ltd t/a Aircoach* UD1223/2014, MN745/2013.

On 22 July 2013, the operations manager of the respondent company was informed of a third-party complaint that a driver had been observed using an electrical device while driving a vehicle on the M50 on 22 July 2013. This driver was identified as the claimant. CCTV footage of the incident showed the claimant had departed from Greystones and travelled north on the M50 towards Dublin airport where the depot is located. There were no passengers on board. Over a 40–45 minute period the claimant was seen to take out an iPad. During this period he removed one hand from the steering wheel. On two or three occasions the claimant had neither hand on the steering wheel. On one occasion the claimant held the iPad up to his ear. This happened while the claimant was driving at 100 kmph.

Employees of the respondent undertake a week of training which includes introduction to the respondent's policies in relation to the use of mobile and electronic devices. Prohibited electronic items include mobile phones, ear pieces, blue tooth, Satnavs, iPods and iPads. Employees refer to 'The Mobile Communication and Driving Policy' as the 'Mobile Phone Policy'. Twelve cameras are positioned in each vehicle.

The claimant was suspended with full pay pending an enquiry into the matter on 24 July 2013 via a telephone call from the operations manager. A preliminary investigation took place on 25 July 2013. The claimant was permitted to view the CCTV footage of the incident but the witness refused to provide him with details of the third party, who did not want to disclose their personal details. On 22 July 2013, the claimant had worked a 12-hour roster and claimed he was using the iPad to keep him alert and focused. The claimant said he was listening to an audio radio on the iPad as the coach radio was not working and there was wind coming from the door of the coach. The claimant felt that he had not been driving erratically and had been watching the mirrors constantly. He stated that he felt completely in control of the vehicle on the day. He also thought the respondent should have no issue as it was not a mobile phone he was using. When the meeting concluded the witness advised him to attend a disciplinary meeting scheduled for 29 July 2013. He was informed of his right to be accompanied by a union representative or a work colleague.

The witness chaired the disciplinary meeting. The claimant could not recall if he had read the 'Mobile Phone Policy'. The claimant saw no serious breach in safety policy and said he was fully in control of the vehicle. The operations manager explored various disciplinary options. As the claimant had put both himself and others in danger his employment was terminated and he was issued with a letter of the same date to that effect. The claimant was notified of his right to appeal within seven days.

The managing director of the respondent heard the appeal on 22 of August 2013. He was satisfied that the complaint from the third party was legitimate and the claimant had not been denied fair and natural justice. He stated that it was apparent from the CCTV footage that the claimant was significantly distracted when using the iPad, which amounted to a serious breach of health and safety procedures.

The EAT considered all the evidence and legal submissions and was satisfied that there existed substantial grounds to justify dismissal. Those grounds being that the claimant's actions constituted a serious safety risk and were in clear breach of the company policies. The EAT also concluded that the respondent had acted reasonably at all times and there was no denial of fair procedures or natural justice. Accordingly the appeal was dismissed. The claim under the Minimum Notice and Terms of Employment Acts 1973 to 2005 also failed.

Falling asleep at work

[27.41] *Malijs v Bloomfield Care Centre Ltd*[52]—*Employment Appeals Tribunal— appeal from decision of Rights Commissioner—Unfair Dismissals Acts 1977 to 2015—Terms of Employment (Information) Acts 1994 and 2012—gross misconduct—whether dismissal on grounds of gross misconduct fair in circumstances where appellant allowed to continue to work after the alleged incident of gross misconduct*

This was an appeal to the EAT by an employee of Rights Commissioner recommendations under the Unfair Dismissals Acts 1977 to 2015 and the Terms of Employment (Information) Acts 1994 and 2012.

The claimant was a care assistant working for the respondent psychiatric hospital/ nursing home. The claimant was dismissed by the respondent for falling asleep while caring for a patient on 18 May 2012. The respondent's assistant director gave evidence to the EAT. He explained that, on the night in question, the claimant had been caring for an acute patient who had a severe condition (Patient X). Patient X was extremely paranoid, psychotic and extremely unpredictable. There had been two serious violent incidents previously regarding Patient X. As he had a history of violence, against women in particular, he always required a male carer. As Patient X did not sleep at night, he had to be monitored with the same level of care for 24 hours every day.

The staff nurse on the night in question also gave evidence to the EAT. She explained that her responsibilities included making sure that the unit was staffed appropriately. When she called in to Patient X's room on 18 May 2012, she found the claimant asleep in the room. The claimant woke up after she called him twice. She reprimanded him for falling asleep and told him that if he was tired he should tell another member of staff and go to the nurse's station for a break. She notified the clinical nurse manager of the incident. Later, on the same night, the staff nurse stated that she once again discovered the claimant asleep in Patient X's room. Again she woke him and advised him to get someone to cover for him if he needed a break. The staff nurse told the EAT that an incident of the same nature had occurred on 3 June 2012, when the staff nurse once again found the claimant asleep on the job. These incidents prompted the staff nurse to file an adverse report with the respondent in relation to the claimant. The head of Human Resources in the respondent hospital met with the claimant on 25 June 2012. The claimant was represented by a member of SIPTU. After the meeting the claimant signed minutes of the meeting. The claimant was invited to further meetings in relation to this matter, some of which he declined to attend. When the EAT asked the staff nurse whether she had a difficult relationship with the claimant, she responded that she was not aware of any such difficulty.

---

52.   *Malijs v Bloomfield Care Centre Ltd* UD1164/2013, TE158/2013.

The EAT heard evidence from the respondent's deputy CEO and financial controller, who stated that he had reviewed all of the information regarding the matter and that he had been the person who decided that dismissal of the claimant was the appropriate sanction. The claimant was issued with a letter confirming his dismissal on 4 September 2012. The claimant appealed the respondent's decision to dismiss him, but the appeal was ultimately unsuccessful.

The claimant's evidence was that there had been no incidents with his employment from its commencement in 2007 until 2012. He described the layout of Patient X's room, explaining that there was one chair with a hard surface and no armrests and another more comfortable chair. The claimant stated that he never sat in the more comfortable chair. He stated that on 18 May 2012 he reported for his twelve hour shift. He explained that he had to have sight of Patient X at all times and it was for this purpose that he left the door open. The protocol for going on a break was that the claimant would seek permission from the staff nurse. The claimant stated that the respondent previously had a male staff nurse, who would give him breaks whenever he requested them. However, the staff nurse did not give him the breaks that he had asked of her. On the night in question the claimant stated that the staff nurse had called to Patient X's room and asked the claimant if he was asleep. He responded immediately by saying no. It was the claimant's evidence that the staff nurse had called to the room twice that night and that no one else called into the room. He said that the clinical nurse manager had spoken to him about the night in question a few days later and had told him that everything was going to be fine.

The claimant explained that on 3 June 2012, a similar situation occurred when the staff nurse had asked him from the doorway whether he was asleep. When she began to tell the claimant his duties he told her that he was aware of them. The staff nurse told him to make tea/coffee if he was tired and the claimant had decided not to argue with her. He made a cup of tea and returned directly to the room. The claimant told the EAT that he had a difficult relationship with the nurse from the time she started working for the respondent.

The EAT concluded that the claimant was unfairly dismissed and that his claim under the Acts should succeed. The EAT noted that the procedures that the respondent followed were far from ideal, placing particular emphasis on the fact that the claimant was allowed to continue working after an incident which the respondent considered to constitute gross misconduct. The EAT stated that it was for the respondent to evaluate the performance of an employee and that their action should be a reflection of their attitude to the conduct. In this case, the respondent had not deemed the claimant's conduct sufficiently serious to justify his dismissal at the time of the alleged actions and he continued his employment subsequent to the alleged events. The EAT concluded that the employer was not entitled to dismiss the claimant in these circumstances. However, the EAT took account of the fact that the claimant had contributed significantly to his dismissal and awarded him compensation of €4,000. The appeal under the Terms of Employment (Information) Acts 1994 and 2012 was not prosecuted.

[27.42] *Marshall v Conduit Enterprise Ltd*[53]—*Employment Appeals Tribunal—Unfair Dismissals Acts 1977 to 2015—call centre—emergency call answering services—falling asleep at work*

The respondent provides call centre facilities including the 999 emergency call answering service in Dublin, Navan and Ballyshannon.

A HR co-ordinator told the EAT that the claimant was based in a call centre answering emergency 999 calls. Calls were answered within a standard five-second duration but normally a call was answered within one second. Three weeks' training was provided and a shift pattern was worked.

The claimant was working a night shift 8 pm to 8 am on the night of 12 June 2013. The HR coordinator said that she received a telephone call from the front line manager to say the claimant had called him regarding an incident at approximately 7 am. PC, the lead operator, sent an email regarding the incident to the HR coordinator and the front line manager at 6.57 am.

The HR coordinator telephoned the claimant and asked what had happened. The claimant told the HR coordinator that she had fallen asleep, and that PC had woken her up, and she was upset/distressed. The HR co-ordinator told her to go home and ring her later. On 14 June 2013 notice of an investigative meeting was sent to the claimant, she was suspended on full pay and a meeting was arranged for Monday 17 June 2013. The claimant was also sent a copy of the email from PC and details of a call with a duration of 19.38 minutes. She was given the right to be represented. Notes of the meeting were read to the EAT. The claimant maintained that she did not willingly fall asleep. She sat away from colleagues on the night in question, everything was fine but it was very hot and she took an antihistamine at around 5 am. The next thing PC was shaking her shoulder. She also said that she was on other medication and her doctor advised her (after the event) of the consequences of taking the antihistamine. A final meeting was scheduled for 18 June. The claimant's employment was terminated due to a breach of trust and confidence.

PC gave sworn testimony and said that he was a lead operator and had been taking calls on the night in question. The claimant was on a 12-hour shift from 8 pm to 8 am. All was fine until 6.19 am when he saw the claimant had her eyes closed. He called her twice and then had to give her a nudge. The claimant was startled. He told her to get some fresh air. There was discussion with the front line manager. PC told the EAT that he had not been told that the claimant had been on medication at the time. He logged what he had observed. He had no contact with the claimant after that. When asked about the air conditioning, PC could not recall if it had been turned up or down at the time. PC said that he had worked with the claimant for some three years and said that he thought her to have been 'a brilliant operator'. He said that the claimant's line had been open for 19 minutes on the night in question and that this would cause concern. He was not really surprised that the claimant was dismissed. He felt sorry for her and he had gotten on well with her. There had been no previous issue.

---

53.   *Marshall v Conduit Enterprise Ltd* UD1293/2013.

The claimant in her sworn testimony said that in her three years with the respondent she had received very favourable recognition. She felt that she was good at her work and took it very seriously. Before her dismissal she had never had any disciplinary or corrective action against her. She was assessed continually and scored very highly. On the night in question the air conditioning was turned off. She suffered from hay fever. She had raised with the respondent the issue of the optimum temperature and the opening and closing of windows. The claimant was already on medication for other reasons. Eight hours into the material shift she took an antihistamine. She had been taking calls as normal. Then the lead operator was calling her and she came to. She was advised to get fresh air. She was in a panic that she had fainted. She had fainted once years previously. When asked why she had fainted as distinct from falling asleep, the claimant said that she had thought herself ill and had contacted a doctor. She had not felt safe to drive. She believed that what had happened had been due to the combination of medications that she had taken.

When told that she could have someone with her when meeting with the respondent, the claimant had wanted the front line manager but was told that the front line manager would be with the respondent side, She felt 'hamstrung' and did not know who else to bring. She had no experience of investigative meetings. The respondent said that she had fallen asleep. She denied to the EAT that she had admitted this. She said that it had been a health issue and said that the respondent should contact her doctor. This did not happen. The HR coordinator had accepted that it was all just because of medication taken.

When questioned by the EAT, the claimant said that she had passed out. She felt helpless and 'completely in the dark'. She had been told to go home and keep her mouth shut. When asked about sitting away from people, the claimant said that one could sit where one liked and that she had sat away from others to focus on her job but that she had fainted. When asked if any sanction other than dismissal had been discussed with her, the claimant said that she was just told that she was dismissed for gross misconduct.

Under cross-examination, the claimant said that she had worked many 12-hour shifts and had been in the last three hours of such a shift when she had fainted. She did not describe hay fever as an illness and had not considered it a health issue. The HR coordinator had spoken to her about the heating and the use of layers of clothing to address temperature issues.

It was put to the claimant that it was only to the EAT that she had described herself as having fainted. She said that she had had a loss of consciousness (due to a combination of medications) but denied having fallen asleep. She regretted not having received back-up more quickly.

The EAT decided by a majority that the claimant was unfairly dismissed. The EAT majority was not satisfied that the claimant had been guilty of a culpable act. While the EAT acknowledged that the breach was a serious one and one that could potentially result in an emergency call not being dealt with, the sanction of dismissal for gross misconduct of an employee who had been described as 'a brilliant operator' for a single incident, which was inadvertently caused, was disproportionate. The EAT also took into account the candour displayed by the claimant in dealing with the allegation. The EAT allowed the claim under the Acts and awarded the claimant the sum of €9,750.

Persistent absenteeism

[27.43] *Wall v Paul Doyle Hire Services Ltd*[54]—*Employment Appeals Tribunal— Unfair Dismissals Acts 1977 to 2015—unfair dismissal—persistent absenteeism— claimant's contribution to his own dismissal*

The claimant was employed by the respondent as a general operative from January 2012 until his dismissal in December 2013. Evidence was adduced by a director of the respondent and the claimant.

The director outlined in evidence the claimant's employment history which saw him receive a written warning by letter dated 1 October 2013. The warning was issued for absenteeism and failure to follow the respondent's reporting procedure and was to remain on the claimant's file for 12 months. The claimant's contract of employment stated that absences due to sickness or injury must be advised to the director no later than 8 am on the first day of the absence.

Subsequently, the claimant received a final written warning on 29 October 2013 for further unauthorised absence and failure to follow the respondent's absence reporting procedure. The final written warning was in place for 12 months on his file.

The claimant gave evidence to the EAT of the circumstances surrounding his non-attendance at work on those occasions.

The respondent wrote a letter dated 2 December 2013 inviting the claimant to attend a disciplinary meeting in relation to an alleged unauthorised absence from work on 2 December 2013 and alleged failure to follow the relevant reporting procedure for absences. The claimant had not reported his absence until 10.30 am. The letter asked the claimant to attend at 2 pm on that date, which was an error; the meeting was in fact scheduled for 4 December 2013. The claimant failed to appear for the meeting and it was rescheduled to 6 December 2013. At the disciplinary meeting the claimant outlined he was absent on 2 December as he had suffered chest pains throughout the night before falling asleep one and a half hours prior to starting work. As a result he did not report his absence from work until 10.30 am. He also attended the accident and emergency department of a hospital for nine hours on 2 December 2013 due to the chest pains.

The director of the respondent made the decision that dismissal was the appropriate sanction. A letter of dismissal of 8 December 2013 was sent to the claimant which stated that the claimant was dismissed for an unauthorised absence on 2 December against alleged background of absenteeism.

While the EAT found that there were certainly some issues around the claimant's attendance; the claimant had faced some significant challenges which, while he may have handled these poorly, entitled him to reasonable consideration from the respondent. In particular, the EAT held that the unauthorised absence on 2 December, given the background to that non-attendance would not, of itself, have warranted dismissal.

However, the EAT considered whether there was a history of absenteeism such as would have entitled the respondent to treat the non-attendance on 2 December as the 'final straw'. On balance, the EAT concluded that there had been absences that

---

54.   *Wall v Paul Doyle Hire Services Ltd* UD 458/2014.

presented challenges to the respondent and the running of its business and that, while the claimant had encountered some challenges that led to his non-attendances, the claimant might have done more to address the issue. The EAT found that the claimant did not seem to appreciate the need for clear communication with his employer when he could not attend.

The EAT concluded that the respondent should have been a little more considerate in its dealings with the claimant and specifically around the challenging circumstances that contributed to the claimant's absence on 2 December. The EAT was further of the opinion that, while an employer might have considered that some sanction was necessary, a reasonable employer would not have applied a sanction of outright dismissal on that occasion.

The EAT found that the claimant was unfairly dismissed. However, in awarding compensation, the EAT had regard to the claimant's own contribution to his ultimate dismissal. Accordingly, the EAT awarded the claimant €6,000 in compensation in respect of his unfair dismissal.

Breach of company procedures

[27.44] *Gould v ICTS Ireland Ltd and ICTS UK Ltd*[55]*—Employment Appeals Tribunal—Unfair Dismissals Acts 1977 to 2015—Minimum Notice and Terms of Employment Acts 1973 to 2005—Organisation of Working Time Act 1997—unfair dismissal—alleged gross misconduct where claimant who was employed to conduct security searches on an aircraft did not carry out security search in accordance with respondent's policy*

The respondent provides contract security services to airlines for transatlantic flights and employed the claimant to conduct security searches on the aircraft. The claimant was employed from 6 June 2010 until 31 August 2012 when he was dismissed. It was explained to the EAT that the respondent was subject to both the security guidelines of the Department of Transport and also the guidelines of the various airlines to which they were contracted. Extensive classroom and on-the-job training was provided to security staff with an annual exam and recurrent training. The respondent's evidence was that there was a specific protocol for searching an aircraft that is subject to inspection from the Department of Transport, of which the claimant was fully aware and had been trained in.

On 11 July 2012 the aircraft that the claimant was working on was subject to a Department of Transport inspection. The Department subsequently informed the airline, following the inspection, that the airline was not compliant with the search guidelines. The respondent was informed by the airline and the assistant station manager was asked to investigate. The inspection failure concerned the search of life vests and overhead bins. It was noted that there was no specific detail or staff named in the inspection results and that the assistant station manager did not have sight of the inspection detail before or during the investigation. However, the life vests in economy class and first

---

55. *Gould v ICTS Ireland Ltd and ICTS UK Ltd* UD301/2013, MN154/2013, WT38/2013.

class require a different search procedure and as a result, the assistant station manager was able to identify from the three rostered staff that the complaint concerned the claimant as he was responsible for economy class.

This was confirmed during the investigation meeting, which took place with the claimant in July 2012. A follow-up meeting took place with the claimant and another manager as the assistant station manager was unavailable. Meetings were held and statements were taken from other staff on board. It was noted by the EAT that the respondent's position was that officially the aircraft could only be searched after the cleaners had finished and left the aircraft; but, due to time constraints, the claimant said that the practice was for the cleaners to start at the back of the aircraft and the security search would start behind them when the area was sterile and the cleaners had moved forward. Thus the cleaning and security search is staggered but simultaneous. The EAT noted that extensive evidence was provided to it on the method and manner in which the searches took place. On instruction from the disciplinary officer, the assistant station manager interviewed 14 supervisors who unanimously said that it was not the practice to simultaneously conduct the security search with the cleaners still on board. The investigation concluded that the claimant had carried out the search but in the wrong sequential order, thereby invalidating the security search. He was subsequently suspended on 27 July 2012. He was advised that the allegations, if proven, could lead to dismissal.

A disciplinary meeting took place at which the original inspection report and all supporting documentation were considered. At this meeting the claimant had admitted that he searched the overhead bins before the cleaners had come on board and was aware this was contrary to procedure. He was not asked if he conducted a second search after the cleaners had left and the claimant did not say that he had conducted a second search. It was determined that the claimant had acted irresponsibly by not conducting the search after the cleaners had left the aircraft and this was held to be a gross misconduct that warranted dismissal. It was acknowledged that no lesser sanction was considered. In a subsequent appeal meeting the claimant openly admitted to searching the overhead bins first before the cleaners had finished and left the aircraft, which was contrary to search protocol. The decision to dismiss him was upheld and he was informed of this in writing. No lesser sanction was considered as the claimant's only explanation was that, although wrong, his search method was common practice. However no evidence was found to suggest that his method was common practice. It was noted by the respondent that at no point during the disciplinary process did the claimant say that he had completed a second search after the cleaners had left the aircraft.

Before the EAT, the claimant disputed ever admitting to doing the search the wrong way and said that he did conduct a subsequent search the way that everyone did and in fact completed a second search after the cleaners left, which the Department of Transport Inspectors did not witness. He had let the cleaners move ahead by six to eight seats and then followed them conducting the search in the sterile area behind them. After he completed his side of the aircraft he helped another staff member complete the right side. The claimant made reference to the fact that a certain document he had requested had never been received by him, nor had he received the minutes of the appeal meeting.

He further noted that, while on suspension, he was due to be on annual leave but as the suspension letter instructed him to be available at all times he did not take his holiday.

The EAT acknowledged that while there might have been minor procedural deficiencies in the disciplinary process, the claimant had failed to satisfy the EAT that he had conducted the search of the aircraft as per the statutory requirements of the respondent's procedure. Bearing in mind the nature and inherent responsibilities of the respondent and claimant to ensure the adequate safety of air passengers, the EAT held that higher standards than might otherwise be required must be adhered to in such circumstances. On balance, the EAT held that the claimant had been fairly dismissed and therefore his claim failed. The EAT was further satisfied that, as the claimant was required to be available during his suspension, he could not be on annual leave and thus he was awarded the sum of €1,380, being the equivalent of 10 days of annual leave under the 1997 Act.

[27.45] *Ijisonuwe v Aer Lingus Ltd[56]—Employment Appeals Tribunal—appeal from decision of Rights Commissioner—Unfair Dismissals Acts 1977 to 2015—breach of respondent's check-in and safety procedures—whether dismissal proportionate sanction—whether fair procedures applied*

The claimant was employed as a check-in agent with the respondent and was on duty on the morning in question to check in flights departing for the UK. The layout of the check-in areas corresponded with the baggage-sorting areas to ensure that passengers' baggage was loaded on the correct flights. According to the respondent's check-in procedures, it was generally not permitted to check in passengers at areas which did not correspond to their travel destination as this would cause issues in the baggage-sorting hall. During the hearing, evidence was given by the respondent and colleagues of the claimant that on 14 June 2010 a man entered the airport terminal apparently intending to travel to Nigeria via Amsterdam. This man who was accompanied by a woman and an infant was initially directed by the respondent's customer service agent to the relevant check-in area for the Amsterdam flight. However, the individual attended before the claimant to check-in for the flight instead.

It was agreed by both parties that the man was not in fact travelling and that only the woman and infant were passengers. However, it was alleged that the man attempted to check-in on behalf of the passengers and that the passengers were not present at the check-in desk during the process. This was a breach of the respondent's check-in and security procedures, as it meant the claimant could not perform the required identification checks for the passengers and also could not put the 'dangerous goods' questions to the passengers. The claimant disputed that the passengers were not at his desk and claimed that the woman was attending to the infant near his desk during the check-in process. However, he admitted that he dealt mostly with the man as the woman allegedly did not speak English. There were also issues regarding the claimant's failure to charge the correct amount of excess baggage fees to the passengers.

---

56.   *Ijisonuwe v Aer Lingus Ltd* UD27/2013.

However, the most significant allegation against the claimant was that he printed baggage security tags and boarding passes and handed these documents to the man (who was not the named passenger) without securing them to the baggage directly. According to the respondent, this represented a serious breach of its security procedures due to the potential consequences and was therefore considered to be an act of gross misconduct. It was not until the man attempted to load the baggage onto an unmanned baggage belt that he was discovered by the claimant's colleague. The colleague then directed the passengers to the correct check-in area for their intended destination and noticed that the man had baggage tags in his hands. The passengers were checked in according to correct procedures by another of the claimant's colleagues.

The incident was reported to the claimant's superiors and he was called to a meeting with the duty manager and the terminal manager to explain the incident. It was the respondent's position that during this meeting, the claimant admitted to breaching procedures and alleged that he stated 'please forgive me you only caught me once'. The claimant was suspended following this meeting and an investigation and disciplinary process ensued. The claimant was subsequently dismissed for gross misconduct due to his serious breaches of the respondent's check-in and safety procedures. The decision was upheld on appeal.

During the EAT hearing it was claimed that the respondent breached fair procedures in the disciplinary process as the claimant was not informed of the nature of the initial meeting with the terminal manager and therefore was not afforded the right to representation at this meeting. It was further claimed that the respondent did not provide adequate notification of the disciplinary meeting and that the claimant was not permitted to challenge the witness statements of the other employees during the disciplinary process. During the hearing the claimant also denied that he had admitted to breaches of procedures during the disciplinary process. It was put to the EAT that dismissal was a disproportionate sanction in light of the breaches of fair procedures and the claimant's rebuttal of the respondent's version of events.

The EAT determined unanimously that the claimant was in breach of the respondent's procedures, which it recognised are of paramount importance to the respondent, given the particular industry. The EAT was satisfied that the claimant had received all necessary and appropriate training in relation to the safety and check-in procedures, evidence of which was adduced during the hearing. The EAT noted that there were minor procedural proficiencies in the handling of the disciplinary process however, in all of the circumstances, it was satisfied that the dismissal did not amount to an unfair dismissal. Accordingly, the decision of the Rights Commissioner was upheld.

Lack of engagement

[27.46] *Finegan v PhoneWatch Ltd[57]—Circuit Court—Judge Linnane—appeal from decision of Employment Appeals Tribunal—Unfair Dismissals (Amendment) Act 1993, s 11—unfair dismissal for gross misconduct—introduction of new working rota—subsequent failure of appellant to attend work and consequent disciplinary process –refusal of claimant to engage in grievance or disciplinary procedure— failure to comply with reasonable requests to attend work as rostered*

The claimant's unfair dismissal claim before the EAT is set out in the *Arthur Cox Employment Yearbook 2014* – see [27.57]. This *de novo* appeal by the claimant to the Circuit Court was heard by Linnane J.

The claimant was dismissed for refusing to work, as rostered, on certain Saturday shifts – a requirement which the claimant submitted was not provided for in his contract of employment with the respondent. The EAT held that the dismissal was not unfair as the respondent's disciplinary procedure was fair and the respondent had made every attempt to avoid dismissal. It was noted that the claimant did not participate in the respondent's disciplinary or grievance procedure and that the respondent's request for the employee to work one Saturday out of nine was reasonable, having regard to customer demand.

The Court heard that the claimant was initially employed by the respondent as a field service engineer in 1993. The claimant subsequently advised the respondent that he no longer felt able to undertake the driving required for the field role, and the respondent transferred him to the customer sales team in May 2008. As part of this transfer, the respondent issued the claimant with a letter which expressly provided that his hours of work would be determined in accordance with the respondent's customer call rota. The rota had previously scheduled employees on the customer service team to work only Monday to Friday. In January 2011, due to an increase in customer demand, the respondent informed employees that they would be rostered for work in one out of every nine Saturdays.

The respondent submitted that the employees' written contracts of employment provided for Saturday work as part of normal working hours, with a day off *in lieu*, and the change to the rota had been agreed with the trade union. The claimant argued that the terms of his written contract of employment, which he had unilaterally altered by handwritten amendment, provided that he would only be required to work Monday to Friday, and that any work on Saturday would be paid at the overtime rate.

The Court heard undisputed evidence that the claimant failed to attend work when he was rostered for Saturdays in March, June and November 2010 and that the claimant had notified the respondent in advance of his non-attendance, stating that he would not work on a Saturday as this was not provided for in his written contract of employment.

The Court heard how the respondent referred the claimant to its grievance procedure to ventilate his issues regarding being rostered to work for certain Saturdays, and the

---

57. *Finegan v PhoneWatch Ltd* Circuit Court Record No 006752/14. Note: under appeal to High Court.

claimant was advised that he could continue to work these shifts under protest until the grievance was resolved. Linnane J noted, however, that while the claimant instigated a grievance against the respondent, he failed to see the grievance to conclusion and refused to work under protest, but rather, did not present for work when rostered on Saturdays.

The respondent brought the claimant through a progressive disciplinary process regarding his failure to present for work on the Saturdays that he was rostered. The respondent had issued the claimant with verbal warnings and written warnings and subsequently a final written warning. The disciplinary procedure culminated in the claimant's dismissal on grounds of gross misconduct – over a year and a half after the claimant's initial failure to report for work on Saturdays. The Court noted that, in line with the respondent's internal procedures, the claimant appealed his dismissal, and that the decision to dismiss him was upheld internally and also by the EAT.

The respondent gave evidence that during the course of the disciplinary process, the claimant failed to attend the disciplinary meetings scheduled and refused to engage with the respondent.

In her judgment, Linnane J referred to correspondence between the claimant and the respondent throughout the relevant period, and held that it was quite clear that the respondent had tried to facilitate the claimant regarding Saturday work (including offering him flexible working times) and had clearly warned the claimant that he could be dismissed if he failed to report for work as rostered. Linnane J held that, the respondent had reasonable grounds to dismiss the claimant. She held that the claimant had repeatedly failed to comply with the reasonable request of the respondent to attend work as rostered on one Saturday in nine. She held that the claimant acted unreasonably in failing to attend work as scheduled and also failing to participate in the disciplinary meetings with the respondent. Linnane J dismissed the appeal. Note this decision is under appeal to the High Court.

[27.47] *Kearns v Provident Personal Credit Ltd*[58]*—Employment Appeals Tribunal— Unfair Dismissal Acts 1977 to 2015—gross misconduct for alleged theft— unsubstantiated allegations—money-lending business*

The claimant was employed as an area manager with the respondent, a registered moneylender. The respondent's structure has a number of self-employed agents locally providing high interest loans and collecting weekly repayments under the agreed terms of the loans provided. Development managers are employed by the respondent and are responsible for overseeing the agents in the field. These managers reported to area managers, such as the claimant. It was noted by the EAT that in March 2013, the claimant was moved laterally to Wicklow following a disciplinary process which left him with a written warning on file. In his evidence, the claimant said he was satisfied with this move as he was retaining his position as area manager overseeing the work of four development managers who in turn oversaw up to 50 self-employed agents in the field. It was noted by the EAT that from time to time agents may require float cheques

---

58.   *Kearns v Provident Personal Credit Ltd* UD1652/2013.

up to the amount of €3,000 to facilitate loan requests sought by customers. It appears that the claimant began to have concerns about one of the agents within his territory, who was operating a very successful agency amounting to almost 40 per cent of the area's productivity. He had expressed real and serious concerns at the extent of the agency and the vulnerability of having such enormous sums of money being overseen by one individual.

In April 2013, the claimant escalated these concerns and sought the assistance of a divisional manager to oversee this agency, which request the EAT held was absolutely appropriate in the circumstances. A meeting took place between the claimant and the agent, in the presence of the claimant's relevant development manager, to discuss the issues and the EAT noted that there was a robust exchange of views at this meeting. Subsequently the relevant agent raised a formal complaint which was the subject of a formal investigation and proposed disciplinary hearing. It was noted, however, at the EAT that this disciplinary hearing did not take place because of a series of unusual events which led to the claimant's dismissal.

The EAT noted that the end of June was a significant date in the respondent's annual operation. There was a half-yearly stock take and bonuses and shareholder dividends were determined at this point in the calendar year. It was accepted in evidence that the claimant's area at this time was well below target and he wished to increase the figures. The claimant's evidence was that he knew the potential of the particular agent to generate a number of loans, but that he knew the agent was not minded to issue these loans and because of the pending disciplinary process between the two individuals he was not allowed to communicate with him. The EAT noted that the claimant's evidence was that his line manager was anxious that his area was so far behind target and he was directed to do whatever could be done to improve the figures. However, this appears to have been rejected by the relevant line manager. It is noted that the claimant maintained that he consistently acted under the direction of his line manager. He obtained €27,000, nine cheques for €3,000 each, withdrawn from the company account which was described by various witnesses as an unusual transaction. It was noted that the money was returned the very next day. The claimant's explanation for this was that he withdrew the money on the understanding from his line manager that this had been sanctioned as he was expected to step into the relevant agent's shoes and distribute loans to the individuals who had requested loans where the agent refused to grant same. The claimant's evidence was that he had a change of heart and, on advice from his wife, he decided not to interfere with the agency, not to obey the direction of his supervisor and simply to return the money.

The EAT noted that the unusual movement of money was noticed immediately by the respondent and the claimant was invited to attend a meeting regarding this issue. The EAT noted that, whether rightly or wrongly, the issue was rolled up with the previous complaint which had been raised by the agent against the claimant. There was a period of time when the claimant was unavailable to attend any meetings because of ill-health. The EAT noted that at the disciplinary meeting which took place in August 2013, the claimant said very little about the €27,000, other than to say he acted on the instructions of his line manager. The EAT noted in particular the fulsome and rational information and explanation given to the EAT in evidence was not given to the claimant's employer in the aftermath of the incident nor was it ever given, other than before the hearing of the EAT. The EAT noted that while ongoing correspondence was exchanged, the claimant did little to protect himself and simply created an aura of suspicion where one need not necessarily have applied. The claimant's supervisor simply denied that he had instructed the claimant to take out such a large amount of money and this was never challenged by the claimant. The EAT noted that the complaint initiated by the agent against the claimant was found to be unsubstantiated and the letter of dismissal which issued found the claimant's actions to have amounted to a theft and to have been unauthorised.

The EAT concluded that, the claimant's explanation was plausible, insofar as no other explanation was put to the EAT that made any sense. The EAT was critical of the claimant for having kept an obdurate silence on what his reasons were, other than to say that he was following the direction of his manager. The EAT was further critical of the claimant for failing and refusing to explain what had happened. The claimant's refusal to engage with the process in a sensible way left the respondent with no option other than to assume the worst and dismiss him for gross misconduct.

The EAT accepted that the respondent had acted reasonably insofar as they gave the claimant every opportunity to engage with the process of investigation. The EAT's view was that the claimant had become caught up with his own animosity towards the individual agent, which had little to do with the explanation for the €27,000 issue. The claimant could not expect the EAT to find the dismissal to have been unfair when, through his own actions, he was fully responsible for his employer reaching that decision. The claim therefore failed.

[27.48] *McNamara v Board of Management St Joseph's National School*[59]*— Employment Appeals Tribunal—Unfair Dismissals Acts 1977 to 2015—Minimum Notice and Terms of Employment Acts 1973 to 2005—sick leave—refusal to engage and cooperate with employer—dismissal wholly and completely justified in light of employee's conduct*

The claimant was employed by the respondent on 1 September 1997 as a primary school teacher. The claimant took carer's leave in 2007/2008 and a career break in 2008 and 2009, all with the consent of the respondent. In February 2009, the claimant wrote to the respondent informing them of her intention to return to the school when it re-opened in September. At that point, and because she was absent from the school for a period in excess of two years, the operating procedures applicable to boards of management required that the respondent refer the claimant for assessment to an occupational health service. Accordingly, the claimant was referred to an occupational health service, and while she indicated in a letter dated 24 June 2009 addressed to the respondent, that she was complying with the pre-employment procedure with that service, she failed to contact them to set up an appointment. However, prior to the claimant's letter of 24 June 2009, she wrote to the respondent on 26 May 2009, indicating her intention to apply for a further leave of absence for one year. The respondent replied informing her that the

---

59. *McNamara v Board of Management St Joseph's National School* UD846/2012.

only leave then available to her was unpaid certified sick leave which had to be approved by the board of management of the school.

On 28 August 2009, days before the school opened, the principal received a letter which was hand delivered to him in the school by a third party, informing him that the claimant would not be returning to school and was taking sick leave. The respondent then made an appointment with the occupational health service for the claimant to be assessed, but the claimant did not attend this appointment.

On 19 March 2010, the respondent wrote to the claimant informing her that her entitlement to salary while on sick leave would expire on 7 April 2010. Again, the respondent reminded her of the necessity of a medical referral, should she decide to return to work. The claimant then sought an 'unpaid leave of absence' but, at that point, the only option available to her was 'unpaid sick leave', which fact had been brought to her attention in a letter from the respondent dated 16 April 2010. The claimant did not respond to the letter from the respondent. The respondent then arranged a further appointment with the occupational health service on 15 June 2010, which the claimant did not attend. The claimant did attend the occupational health service in July 2009 and this report did consider her medically fit to resume her employment, but the claimant did not act on this report to resume her teaching duties.

The respondent received a further report from the occupational health service, dated 23 December 2010, stating that the claimant was unfit for work as a teacher, and this would remain so indefinitely. Further appointments were set up with the occupational health service but the claimant failed to attend them. The respondent made a further appointment with the occupational health service on 25 May 2011, prior to which they wrote to the claimant on the 13 May 2011, informing her of the appointment, in addition to informing her that the board of management was meeting on 16 June to consider her future employment with the school. She was invited to attend the meeting and bring a work colleague or union representative with her. The claimant did not attend the medical appointment, or meeting, nor did she reply to the letter.

The respondent again wrote to the claimant on 31 August 2011, informing her of their requirement to seek further medical advice on her prospect of recovery and return to work. An appointment was set up with the occupational health service for 7 September 2011, but the claimant, while replying to the letter, did not allude to the appointment, nor did she attend it. This was the fourth medical appointment that the claimant failed to attend since the April 2011.

The respondent again wrote to the claimant on 10 October 2011, informing her of its decision to hold a further meeting to discuss her future employment in the school, on 16 November 2011, and, again, the claimant was invited to attend, along with a work colleague or union representative. This letter clearly set out the serious repercussions attaching to her refusal to work with them. There was no reply to this letter and neither did the claimant attend the meeting.

The board of management met on 16 November 2011 and decided to terminate the claimant's contract of employment with them, which decision was based on the five medical reports from the occupational health service, dated between 30 November 2009 and 23 December 2010. This decision was communicated to the claimant in a registered letter dated 18 November 2011, and, as this letter was returned to the school, the respondent again wrote to the claimant on 25 January 2012, which letter was hand delivered to the claimant.

During the EAT hearing, the claimant's representatives made much of the fact that the board of management had written to the occupational health service supplying certain information which did not reflect well on the claimant and which could have influenced his report on her but the EAT was satisfied that this was unfounded. The doctor was clear in his evidence that the information supplied to him did not influence him in any way.

The claimant challenged the contents of the doctor's report but offered no evidence of any kind to refute any of the contents. The claimant also insisted that she did not receive several letters from the respondent or copies of some of the doctor's reports, but the EAT was satisfied that copies of all correspondence from all persons were sent to the claimant. The claimant further contended that she did not attend the medical appointments on the advices of her union, but letters from the claimant's union were contained in the booklet of documents handed into the EAT, which disproved same. Indeed, one of the letters clearly showed that the union had, at one point, urged her to attend a medical appointment.

The EAT found the evidence given by the claimant inconsistent and evasive. She appeared unable to answer a direct question satisfactorily, or at all, and at times, gave answers unconnected to the question asked. She contradicted herself to such an extent that the EAT were left with no choice but to approach all of her evidence with caution.

The EAT found the termination of the claimant's employment was not unfair and in the circumstances, was wholly and completely justified. The respondent did all in their power to help and assist the claimant, but the evidence clearly showed that the claimant refused to engage and co-operate with them. The medical reports on which the respondent relied and on which they based their decision to terminate the claimant's employment was the only evidence they had available to them, given that the claimant refused to co-operate with them in any way whatsoever, and they were entitled to rely on same, in the absence of any other evidence.

Drug and alcohol screening

[27.49] *Wojciechowski, Olszewski, Smiecinski v PRL Group*[60]*—Employment Appeals Tribunal—Unfair Dismissals Acts 1977 to 2015—drug and alcohol screening— random selection—employees' refusal to provide urine samples for testing—dismissal deemed to be unfair*

The three claimants who were Polish were employed as general operatives and drove forklift trucks and worked on the respondent's Dublin site. At the time of the claimants' employment, the respondent's safety statement provided (among other things) that: 'They will ensure that, while at work, if reasonably required by management, submit to

---

60.   *Wojciechowski, Olszewski, Smiecinski v PRL Group* UD1543/2013, UD1551/2013, UD1565/2013.

any appropriate, reasonable and proportionate tests by, or under the supervision of, a registered medical examiner.'

All of the respondent's documents were prepared in English. A Polish version of all documents was available on request. The Drug and Alcohol Policy in existence at the time of the employees' tenure stated: 'Testing—Any employee suspected of being under the influence of intoxicants or involved in a work-related accident may be subject to with-cause testing.'

Following a tip-off from a security officer, 38 employees, including the three claimants, were randomly selected to attend a medical practitioner to provide a urine specimen for drug screening in accordance with company requirements. The operations director together with the Group HR manager, met the second and third claimants on 4 June 2013 to inform them of the need to attend for drug screening, the importance attached to such screening, and that a doctor would provide a report of the screening afterwards. The Group HR manager read through the relevant material from the Drug and Alcohol Policy, the Employee Handbook, the Safety Statement and the relevant section of the Safety Health and Welfare at Work Act 2005 and explained that should they refuse to attend for drug screening they could face disciplinary action. The respondent provided a taxi to take the claimants to the general practitioner, Dr GM. The second and third claimants were referred to him for drug screening. Beforehand he spoke to them and explained the procedures. He read through the consent form. He was quite happy both claimants understood the procedures and knew beforehand what was involved in the drug screening. He did not see the need for a translator to be present. Both claimants refused to complete the consent form and said they were not proceeding with the drug test. He told them that he would inform the respondent accordingly. Dr GM telephoned the Group HR manager and told her that both claimants did not consent to drug screening that day.

Later that day, the operations director and the Group HR manager again met the second and third claimants. They offered another employee to act as a translator but both claimants declined that offer. The Group HR manager advised them that she spoke to Dr GM and that it was a very serious matter for the respondent. Because of their refusal to consent to drug testing they could be subjected to disciplinary action. The claimants were asked to attend a disciplinary meeting the next day, 5 June 2013.

The Group HR manager and the operations director met the claimants separately. The Group HR manager explained the seriousness of their refusal to attend for drug testing and asked them the reason for their refusal to consent to drug testing. Both claimants said 'I do not consent to drug testing'. Without a valid reason for their refusal, the Group HR manager said the respondent had no alternative but to summarily dismiss them without a valid reason/explanation. They were both offered a right of appeal to this decision within seven days. They did not appeal their dismissals. The Group HR manager explained that the depot was a seven-day operation and very busy. Health and safety was foremost in the respondent's mind. The Group HR manager was satisfied that the claimants had no issue in communicating in English. No alternative to dismissal was considered.

On 11 June 2013 the first claimant was asked to attend at the medical practitioner's surgery, to submit to drug screening. This claimant refused to attend at the surgery. Later that day the first claimant was instructed to attend a disciplinary hearing on 13 June 2013. The respondent considered what the claimant said at that meeting. By letter dated 13 June 2013, the first claimant was informed by the respondent that the bond of trust had irretrievably broken down and he was summarily dismissed. He was offered a right of appeal. He chose not to appeal the decision to dismiss him.

The EAT noted that there was no provision in the respondent's Drug and Alcohol Policy to select employees for 'random testing' but that the Policy has since been amended to include 'random testing'. The EAT further noted that while the Polish version of the Drug and Alcohol Policy was available, the claimants had not been furnished individually with a copy of the translated document.

The EAT determined that the claimants were unfairly dismissed; however, it considered that they contributed significantly to their own dismissals. In the circumstances, the EAT awarded the claimants €1,500 each under the Acts.

FAIR PROCEDURES

[27.50] *Frawley v Lionbridge International*[61]*—Employment Appeals Tribunal— Unfair Dismissals Acts 1977 to 2015—summary dismissal—provision of severance agreement to claimant—whether redundancy situation existed—lack of any procedures in effecting dismissal of claimant—claimant awarded €94,000 in compensation*

The claimant had been employed for 18 years with the respondent. She held a project managing role when she was dismissed on 8 November 2013. The claimant stated that there were no historical difficulties during her employment with the respondent. On 8 November 2013 the claimant returned from lunch to discover that she could not unlock her computer account. She was summoned to a meeting with her manager and the Human Resources manager and was informed that she was dismissed with immediate effect. She was handed an envelope and given 10 minutes to leave the building.

There had been no consultations with staff regarding redundancies within the respondent company. The envelope which had been given to the claimant at the meeting contained an offer of a sum referred to as a 'severance agreement'. It was stated that acceptance of this sum was on the proviso that the claimant must sign away her rights under the unfair dismissals legislation. Further, the agreement required the claimant to state that she had received legal advice, which she had not. The claimant did not accept the severance sum offered. When the claimant later queried if the sum being offered was by way of a redundancy payment she was told that 'the company is not going down the redundancy route on this occasion'. Within a month of her dismissal the respondent advertised the claimant's position on a 12-month contract basis. The option of moving to a 12-month contract had not been put to the claimant. The claimant subsequently discovered that 12 of the respondent's employees had been dismissed on the same date.

The respondent employer conceded that the claimant was unfairly dismissed from her employment. The respondent requested that the EAT find that compensation was the

---

61.   *Frawley v Lionbridge International* UD1627/2013.

appropriate remedy. The claimant confirmed that compensation was the only remedy she was seeking.

The EAT accepted that the claimant had been dismissed without any procedure at all, quite apart from any fair procedure. It was considered that the respondent had made a crude economic decision and terminated the claimant's employment without any regard for the claimant herself. The EAT noted that the respondent appeared to be motivated by a wish to replace the permanent employment of the claimant with an impermanent position in circumstances where a redundancy situation was not considered to have arisen. The EAT was satisfied that the claimant had made every reasonable effort to mitigate her loss. She had managed to secure work, but it was on a contract basis and on a lesser salary. Her current contract was soon to expire. She was also at the loss of pension contributions and health insurance premiums. In these circumstances, the EAT found that compensation in the amount of €94,000 was appropriate.

Improper influence on a decision-maker

[27.51] *Ramphal v Department for Transport[62]—UK Employment Appeal Tribunal—Judge Serota QC—unfair dismissal—alleged misconduct in relation to expenses and use of hire cars—decision maker received advice from human resources—improper influence on decision maker by human resources which led to change in outcome of investigation process and sanction imposed—entitlement of employee facing disciplinary charges—role of decision maker*

The claimant was employed by the respondent as an aviation security compliance inspector. An investigation commenced into possible misconduct by him in relation to his expenses and his use of hire cars. It was accepted that the manager conducting the investigation was inexperienced in disciplinary proceedings and thus, during the course of preparing his report and his decision in this matter, he received advice from the respondent's human resources department. The advice he was given was not limited to matters of law and procedure, but also concerned in the level of potential sanction, with a view to achieving consistency. The advice received also extended to issues of the claimant's credibility and the level of culpability.

At the employment tribunal, the employment judge dismissed the claim for unfair dismissal. The UK EAT noted the provisions of the respondent's disciplinary procedure that provided for investigation of allegations of misconduct and which set out how cases should be decided. The procedure made it clear that persons conducting investigations of disciplinary proceedings could consult human resources if they wished to do so at any stage of the proceedings. Certain documents required by the UK EAT were heavily redacted. The documentation did reveal however that there had been a number of revisions to the decision maker's report. The UK EAT also noted that legal advice was given but that communications between human resources, the legal department and the decision maker were not disclosed because of legal professional privilege.

---

62. *Ramphal v Department for Transport* UKEAT/0352/14/DA.

The claimant's duties involved overseeing transport and industry compliance with appropriate rules and requirements, to include open and covert inspections and meetings. As his territory extended across the UK he was required to spend a significant time on the road, for which he was entitled to receive subsistence. To facilitate travel he was entitled to a hire car and the related expenses would be paid by the respondent's credit card.

This case arose from a random audit of the claimant's transport and subsistence claim which resulted in a number of items requiring further examination. It was noted by the UK EAT that all of the claimant's expense claims had been signed off by his manager. The UK EAT noted that the main concerns seemed to be excessive petrol consumption and possible use of hire cars for personal reasons, which would constitute misuse. The investigator was appointed to carry out an investigation. His initial function was to determine if there was a case to answer. It was noted that, as he had not previously acted in disciplinary proceedings, he met with human resources, familiarised himself with the disciplinary procedure and noted the distinctions between misconduct, and gross misconduct and the appropriate penalties. He also received guidance as to the appropriate procedure. The claimant was advised of the disciplinary charge, which appeared to have been one of gross misconduct, and a disciplinary hearing took place. It was noted that the same person was appointed to carry out the disciplinary procedure as well as the investigation procedure.

The claimant was dismissed for gross misconduct. The UK EAT noted that from the time the investigation commenced until such time as the claimant was dismissed, there was significant interaction between the decision maker and human resources. The UK EAT set out in detail the extent of the communications between the parties to include a number of draft reports with revisions from all parties. The UK EAT noted that none of the draft reports were dated or marked and therefore it was not clear which report was prepared on which date.

However it was notable that after contact between the decision maker and human resources, there was a complete change of view of the decision maker's factual findings and his recommendations as to sanction. Favourable comments to the claimant were removed and replaced with critical comments, the overall view of culpability became one of gross negligence and the recommendation of sanction became summary dismissal for gross misconduct instead of a final written warning.

The UK EAT noted that the employment tribunal had identified the issues and noted the somewhat lax procedures in the absence of detailed guidelines in relation to expense claims. It was noted the majority of transactions for which the claimant claimed reimbursement were found by the tribunal to be compliant. While the employment judge did consider the issue of improper influence, he concluded that the decision maker had made a decision which was reasonably open to him and that the reason for the dismissal was misconduct, namely, the improper use of a corporate credit card on petrol and the hire car.

The key ground of appeal was that the employment judge had failed to apply the principles set out in *Chhabra v West London Mental Health NHS Trust*.[63] The claimant's

---

63.   *Chhabra v West London Mental Health NHS Trust* [2013] UKSC 80.

counsel drew attention to the process leading to the dismissal and the reshaping of the decision maker's view from a finding of no gross misconduct and a recommendation of a written warning to an eventual finding of gross misconduct and a recommendation of summary dismissal, which was ultimately implemented.

It was submitted that the employment judge had failed to consider adequately the effect of the intervention of human resources, which went beyond permissible assistance and which had actually expressed views on findings and had invited changes to both the assessment of the claimant's credibility and culpability and the appropriate penalty. The UK EAT accepted this and held that the advice given by human resources went significantly beyond advice limited to process and procedure. It was noted that the tribunal had failed to explain what it was, if not the advice from human resources, that led the decision maker to change his views; the advice apparently having been limited to the standard of culpability required for gross misconduct. No new evidence had come to light that might explain the change of heart of the decision maker.

The UK EAT concluded that the only authority relevant was that of *Chhabra*. In that case the judge held that while there would generally be:

> no impropriety in a case investigator seeking advice from an employer's human resources department for example on questions of procedure. I do not think it was illegitimate for an employer, through its human resources department or a similar function to assist a case investigator in the presentation of a report to ensure all matters have been addressed and to achieve clarity. In this case the report was altered in many ways that went beyond clarifying its conclusions. The amendment of the draft report by a member of the employer's management which occurred in this case was not within agreed procedure. The report had to be the product of the case investigator, it was not.

The UK EAT noted that these were carefully chosen words of a judge of the Supreme Court. The respondent asserted that it was an implied term that a report of an investigating officer for a disciplinary enquiry must be the product of the case investigator. This was not accepted by the UK EAT. The UK EAT further held that for the dismissal to be fair there had to be a fair investigation and dismissal procedure. If the integrity of a final decision to dismiss has been influenced by persons outside the procedure it was, in the opinion of the UK EAT, unfair but all the more so if the claimant had no knowledge of it.

The UK EAT noted that having originally found there was no dishonesty in his final report, the decision maker subsequently concluded that he could not accept the claimant's explanations of his accidental misuse of the credit card or explanations for the level of fuel consumption and therefore was guilty of gross misconduct, with a recommendation for dismissal. The UK EAT held that, had the employment judge been aware of the decision in *Chhabra* as it was accepted he was not, he would have wanted to investigate carefully the influence of human resources on the decision maker and to explain the reasoning behind the decision maker's dramatic change of view, after representations from human resources. This clearly went beyond giving advice on procedure and clarification and appeared to have led to the reshaping of the decision maker's views, carrying him on a journey from a conclusion that there was no gross misconduct with an appropriate sanction of written warning, to one of gross misconduct and a recommendation for, and then a decision of, summary dismissal.

The UK EAT held that it was disturbing to note the dramatic change in the decision maker's approach after the intervention by human resources. The UK EAT was critical of human resources involving themselves in issues of culpability which should have been reserved for the decision maker. The changes in the decision maker's findings were so striking that they gave rise to an inference of improper influence and thus the employment Judge should have given clear and cogent reasons for accepting that there was no such influence.

The UK EAT concluded that while an investigating officer was entitled to call for advice from human resources, human resources must be very careful to limit their advice essentially to questions of law, procedure and process and to avoid straying into areas of culpability; let alone advising on the appropriate sanction in relation to culpability. The advice went beyond addressing issues of consistency. The UK EAT further held that it was not for human resources to advise whether the finding should be one of simple misconduct or gross misconduct. The UK EAT held that an employee facing disciplinary charges in a dismissal procedure was entitled to assume that the decision would be taken by the appropriate officer, without having been lobbied by other parties as to the finding he should make as to culpability. He should be given notice of any changes in the case he has to meet so that he can deal with them and also be given notice of representations made by others to the dismissing officer that go beyond legal advice and advice on matters of processing procedure. The UK EAT noted that it was far from clear to what extent the claimant was aware of the changes made to the case against him as a result of the interventions from human resources.

The UK EAT held that the decision of unfair dismissal could not stand and the matter was remitted back to the employment judge for consideration on whether the influence of human resources was improper and if so whether it had a material effect on the ultimate decision to dismiss; both in respect of culpability and whether there was such influence on the decision that the claimant had been guilty of gross negligence and should be summarily dismissed.

Failure to disclose documents

[27.52] *Old v Palace Fields Primary Academy[64]—UK Employment Appeal Tribunal—appeal from decision of employment tribunal—Clark J—unfair dismissal—allegation of gross misconduct—procedural irregularity in disciplinary process—failure to disclose all materials to claimant*

The claimant had been working as a teacher in the respondent school for 21 years. Her attention was drawn to an incident of bullying on 2 July 2012. One of the pupils in her class had written 'fat b*****' across a photo of another pupil in the class who had special needs. The claimant's treatment of this bullying incident was in question. A teaching assistant employed by the respondent maintained that the claimant had

---

64.   *Old v Palace Fields Primary Academy* UKEAT/0085/14/BA.

enlarged the image and called several pupils over to see it. This version of events was strongly refuted by the claimant. An investigation was followed by disciplinary action. The respondent's disciplinary panel preferred the evidence of the teaching assistant and made the decision to dismiss the claimant for gross misconduct. The employment tribunal held that this was not an unfair dismissal, the reason for dismissal had been fair and there were no procedural shortcomings at play.

The UK EAT considered the claimant's argument that two witness statements given by children in her class, which were of potential assistance to her case, were not disclosed to her during the course of the investigation or the disciplinary process. Secondly, the UK EAT judge considered the claimant's evidence that minutes of two meetings between the claimant and the head teacher of the respondent had not been disclosed to the claimant, on the ground that they would not form part of the disciplinary panel's investigations. It transpired that these minutes were in fact considered by the disciplinary panel. The UK EAT held that such non-disclosure and reliance on material which an employee has not been afforded sight of would not necessarily render a dismissal unfair. However, such matters must be taken into account in deciding if a dismissal followed fair procedures. The claimant's appeal was allowed and the case was remitted to the employment tribunal to decide whether the dismissal was substantively or procedurally unfair. The UK EAT noted that all circumstances would have to be taken into account by the employment tribunal in coming to a decision on this matter, including the fact that after 21 years of service the claimant was potentially facing a career-destroying outcome.

Appeals

[27.53] *Murphy v DWG Refrigeration Wholesale Ltd[65]—Employment Appeals Tribunal—Unfair Dismissals Acts 1977 to 2015—Minimum Notice and Terms of Employment Acts 1973 to 2005—gross misconduct—falsification of expense receipts—defects with disciplinary process cured at appeal stage—employee fairly dismissed*

The claimant was employed by the respondent, and its predecessors, since 2004. Since about 2008 he had been a general manager. The respondent is an English company and the claimant had worked for its Irish branch. The claimant's role involved a lot of travelling around the country to meet customers and he was encouraged to entertain customers, in respect of which he was periodically reimbursed on submission of receipts.

The procedure for seeking reimbursement of expenses was that a spreadsheet would be compiled on a monthly basis by the claimant and submitted to a director for approval while the receipts were separately sent to the respondent's accounts department.

In October 2012, while one of the respondent's directors (AK) was in Dublin, he was given a number of receipts in respect of which reimbursement had been sought. When AK looked at the receipts, he noticed an anomaly between the receipts and the claim

---

65. *Murphy v DWG Refrigeration Wholesale Ltd* UD 215/2013, MN128/2013.

made by the claimant. A hole had been pierced in the receipt through the date, although the date did also appear at the bottom of the receipt. When the expenses claim was looked at it, it was noted that the claim had been for a breakfast meeting in Dublin on a particular Wednesday whereas the receipt was from a premises in Naas the following Saturday. The EAT was told that the claimant lives in County Kildare. On his return to England, AK checked through the other expenses claims made by the claimant in 2012 and noticed what he considered to be a significant number of anomalies. AK passed his findings to the HR department. The respondent decided that the matter was sufficiently serious to suspend the claimant on full pay pending a disciplinary hearing.

Criticism was made of AK in cross-examination to the effect that he was conflicted in his investigation because he had initially approved the claims for payment. However, the EAT did not accept that there was any conflict on AK's part nor was there any inappropriate conduct in the manner of his investigation. A disciplinary meeting was convened before the sales and marketing director, on 25 October 2012. The claimant was provided with a copy of AK's investigation report and with copies of the relevant expenses claim forms and receipts in advance of the disciplinary hearing. On foot of the hearing, a decision was taken to dismiss the claimant. It was suggested to the sales and marketing director in cross-examination that he was aware that the claimant had dyslexia and that his dyslexia accounted for the errors in claims. The sales and marketing director told the EAT that dyslexia could not account for the number of receipts that had been defaced. Further, an explanation of dyslexia does not appear to have been advanced in any way at the disciplinary hearing.

It was also suggested that the various customers should have been contacted to ascertain whether they had been entertained by the claimant at the relevant times. This was not done because the respondent considered this to be an internal matter and did not want its customers drawn into it. The EAT accepted that this was reasonable in the circumstances of this case where the damage to the receipts and the errors in the claims, both in time and place, were so manifest.

A subsequent appeal against dismissal was heard by the respondent's distribution director. The claimant submitted a letter of appeal which referred to a number of letters from customers. While the distribution director accepted as genuine the cases where there were letters from customers, he nonetheless decided to uphold the claimant's dismissal. The distribution director told the EAT that the claimant did not mention his dyslexia in the course of the hearing.

In his evidence to the EAT, the claimant had no real explanation why the dates and locations on many claims differed from the receipts. The claimant told the EAT that he had not damaged or changed any of the receipts. However, the EAT noted that it was of significance that the claimant had accepted in cross examination that he had decided to say little at the disciplinary hearing. During the EAT hearing, the claimant complained that he had not been allowed to contact customers and that he had not been allowed access to certain documents until the appeal. Further, he was required to travel to England for the appeal hearing. The EAT noted that in the circumstances it might have been better for the appeal to have been heard in Ireland but it was not satisfied that this amounted to an unfairness. The EAT did note that the procedure adopted in the disciplinary hearing where the claimant had not been allowed access to his documents was not satisfactory. However, the EAT was satisfied that it did not amount to an unfairness such as would render the dismissal unfair as the claimant had full access to documents and customers by the time of the appeal and the appeal was, in effect, a full re-hearing. Therefore, whatever unfairness there had been was cured by the appeal process.

The EAT was satisfied that there was sufficient evidence of misconduct such that a reasonable employer would have been justified in dismissing the claimant and it was not for the EAT to determine whether it would have come to a different conclusion on the facts. The EAT noted that it was required to be satisfied that there were sufficient grounds to allow a reasonable employer take the course that was taken. The EAT noted that, while there were defects in the disciplinary process, they were not of such a nature or magnitude to require a finding of procedural unfairness. Accordingly, the EAT dismissed the claimant's unfair dismissal claim and was satisfied that, in the circumstances of the misconduct in this case, the respondent was entitled to dismiss the claimant without notice. Accordingly the claim pursuant to the Minimum Notice and Terms of Employment Acts 1973 to 2005 was also dismissed.

Failure to advise of potential outcome of process

[27.54] *Fahavane Ltd v Flood*[66]*—Employment Appeals Tribunal—appeal from a decision of a Rights Commissioner—Unfair Dismissals Acts 1977 to 2015—dismissal for misconduct—breach of trust and confidence in employee—fair procedures— failure to furnish employee with findings of investigation conducted into his conduct—failure to conduct thorough investigation—failure to inform employee that his job was in jeopardy—insufficient degrees of separation between those deciding on dismissal and those determining appeal*

The claimant commenced employment with the respondent, who operated a small business in the security and audio-visual market, in February 2004. The claimant worked in the roles of sound engineer and alarm installation technician. The work of the respondent included the installation of social alarms in the homes of vulnerable elderly people on the instruction of Task, a community group. A staff purchase scheme was available to employees of the employer, whereby they could purchase discounted electronic goods on 'easy payment' terms.

On 6 July 2011, DA, one of the directors of the respondent, allocated a job in Cashel to the claimant. When DA subsequently reviewed the claimant's work sheet for 6 July 2011, he noticed that the claimant had not indicated a finish time in relation to the job in Cashel. This finish time was required in order to invoice the customer. When DA raised the matter with the claimant he inserted a finish time of 6 pm.

In August 2011, the respondent received an enquiry about a social alarm. He was surprised to discover there were none in stock. He mentioned this fact to the claimant. DA's suspicions were raised and he proceeded to make enquiries in relation to the social alarm which was supposed to be installed by the claimant in Cashel on 6 July 2011. As

---

66.   *Fahavane Ltd v Flood* UD1719/2013.

each alarm had a unique identification number, it was not difficult to track down. It transpired that an alarm had been installed in the home of NF, who had the same name as the claimant, on 6 July 2011.

The respondent commenced an investigation and enlisted the assistance of a HR consultant. The claimant was furnished with a copy of the respondent's Disciplinary and Grievance Procedure and invited to an investigatory meeting by letter dated 20 September 2011. On 3 October 2011 the investigatory meeting was conducted by the consultant and DA. Nobody from SIPTU was available to represent the claimant on the date set for the meeting, but the claimant confirmed that he was happy to proceed regardless. At the meeting the claimant confessed that on 6 July 2011 he had installed a social alarm in his parents' home in Dublin without the respondent's authorisation. By way of explanation he stated that he had asked someone in Task if he could install an alarm for his elderly parents and whether such an alarm could be given to him at special rate. It was confirmed that he could have an alarm at a reduced rate and Task suggested that the claimant take an alarm from the respondent's stock, as there were no other alarms available and Task would replace it. At the investigatory meeting the claimant accepted that this was wrong and he apologised for his conduct. He explained that he had not thought of it as inappropriate at the time. He accepted that he failed to confess to DA on two separate occasions, ie when DA mentioned to him that there were no alarms in stock and when DA queried the lack of a finish time on his work sheet for 6 July 2011. He confessed to having used the respondent's van for his trip to Dublin. He told the consultant and DA that he had topped up the van with €30 worth of diesel. At the time of the investigation the claimant had not taken steps to pay for the alarm in question.

A disciplinary meeting was scheduled for 10 October 2011. The claimant was encouraged to avail of his right of representation due to the seriousness of the allegations against him. At this point, although the claimant had been furnished with the minutes of the meeting which took place on 3 October, he had not been provided with any findings of the investigation which had taken place. The claimant apologised once again at the disciplinary meeting. The respondent stated that the claimant's actions in taking the alarm and installing it without authorisation and payment constituted a serious breach of trust. The claimant was informed that his employment was being terminated for gross misconduct. He was furnished with a letter of dismissal dated 10 October 2011, signed by DA. The letter made reference to the opportunities which had been open to the claimant to confess his actions to DA and of which he had failed to avail. DA also stated that the claimant had furnished no explanation for his actions.

The claimant availed of his internal right of appeal of the decision to dismiss him. The appeal was heard by DB and AL (of the same HR consultancy firm). The claimant put forward six grounds of appeal and was represented at the appeal hearing by his trade union representative. The respondent did not contest the claimant's evidence regarding his contact with Task. Nonetheless, the original decision to dismiss the claimant was upheld.

DA stated that trust in his employees was essential in the security business and in circumstances where their work caused them to enter the homes of vulnerable people. The HR consultant denied in cross examination that the letter of dismissal had been prepared prior to the disciplinary meeting and stated that, despite the date on the letter, it had been drafted and signed some two days after the disciplinary meeting. Although she accepted that no formal findings had been presented to the claimant following the investigation, she reminded the EAT that the claimant had accepted and apologised for his behaviour at the investigation meeting. The HR consultant also accepted that it had not been made clear to the claimant throughout the process that his job was in jeopardy. However, her evidence was that the case was dealt with in a fair and transparent manner and she was satisfied that the dismissal of the claimant was warranted in the circumstances.

The claimant told the EAT that he had believed the social alarms to be the property of Task community services, as opposed to belonging to the respondent. The respondent received commission from Task when an alarm was installed. The commission sheet given to the respondent notifies it of the location of a particular alarm. The claimant explained that on 6 July he had finished his work in Cashel at around 3 pm. He then drove to his parents' house in Dublin and installed the alarm. He then returned to Kerry, arriving around 11 pm. The reason he put 6 pm as the finish time on his work sheet was that this would have been the approximate time of his return had he not continued on to Dublin from Cashel. The claimant explained that he did not think he had done anything wrong, he believed that the alarm belonged to Task and he had Task's assurances that it would be replaced. It was only when he received an invitation to an investigatory meeting that he realised that the alarm box was the respondent's property that he was guilty of wrongdoing and that Task had not replaced the alarm he had taken from stock. He expected to get a 'telling off' or a warning. When there was no one from SIPTU available to represent him at the investigation meeting with the respondent he was willing to proceed regardless, as he had been unaware of the gravity of the situation.

In response to the question of why he had declined to confess his behaviour to DA the claimant explained that his relationship with DA had deteriorated in the year leading up to his dismissal for reasons related to proposed redundancies in July 2010. The claimant argued that DA had never gone so far as to ask him if he had removed or installed the alarm in question. The claimant reiterated that he was not informed that his job was in jeopardy before the disciplinary meeting on 10 October 2011, which resulted in his dismissal. This meeting was the first time on which his behaviour was classified as 'gross and serious misconduct'. The claimant confirmed to the EAT that he did not fully read the respondent's Disciplinary and Grievance Procedures. He declined to raise any objections to the notes and minutes of meetings, as he 'did not think anything of them and just signed them'.

The EAT held that there were a number of procedural flaws in the disciplinary procedures which had rendered the claimant's dismissal unfair. It was held that a full and fair investigation involves some exploration of the core facts established. Such exploration was found to be lacking in this case, in circumstances where no further enquiries were made following discovery at the investigation meeting that the claimant knew that the alarm was company property. The EAT noted that it was only at the EAT hearing that this was fully explored. Accordingly, the full facts, or their veracity, were not considered by the decision makers. The EAT took note of the fact that emphasis was placed by the decision makers on the fact the claimant had declined to avail of the opportunities 'to come clean' and confess his actions to DA. It was held that relying on an inference when there is an opportunity to put a direct question to an claimant was unfair.

The EAT held that the failure to advise the claimant that the disciplinary process could result in his dismissal was fatal. This had resulted in the claimant attending the disciplinary meeting without his trade union representative. While the respondent had made the claimant aware (both before the disciplinary meeting and at the commencement of the meeting) of his right to have his trade union representative present, the claimant proceeded without representation on the mistaken expectation that he would receive a 'telling off' or a warning. He had not been aware of the gravity of the situation in making his decision to be unrepresented at the meeting.

In relation to procedural issues, the EAT was not satisfied that there was sufficient independence between those deciding on the dismissal and those determining the appeal. Notwithstanding that the respondent was a small organisation, it was held that this offended against the principle that 'Not only must justice be done but it must be seen to be done'. In relation to the substantive side of the case the EAT accepted, on the balance of probabilities, that the claimant had been aware that the respondent was paid commission by Task.

The EAT concluded that the claimant's dismissal had been unfair and that the respondent's appeal must fail. The claimant's contribution to his dismissal was taken into account in awarding the claimant compensation in the sum of €15,000.

Lack of evidence

[27.55] *O'Halloran v Ballykisteen Hotel Ltd[67]—Employment Appeals Tribunal— Unfair Dismissals Acts 1977 to 2015—Minimum Notice and Terms of Employment Acts 1973 to 2005—unfair dismissal—allegation of interference with company property—whether claimant's actions constituted gross misconduct—no evidence of wrongdoing on behalf of claimant—claimant denied fair process*

The claimant worked as a restaurant manager in the respondent's hotel. He was dismissed on 9 March 2013, about seven years after he commenced his employment with the respondent. The dismissal was said to be on account of gross misconduct which was related to alleged interference with company property. In his evidence, the claimant explained that the allegation against him was that he had interfered with a security camera. He explained that, while on duty in the bar area of the hotel, he had noticed handprints on a wall. Upon investigation, he noted that a surveillance camera had been installed in proximity to where the handprints were. A few other employees were present at the time and also saw the camera. The claimant replaced the camera and discussed the matter with his deputy manager.

The claimant was subsequently asked to attend a meeting. He was informed that this meeting was disciplinary in nature and advised that he could have a witness present. He asked a nearby co-worker to accompany him. The claimant stated that the general

---

67.   *O'Halloran v Ballykisteen Hotel Ltd* UD625/2013, MN322/2013.

manager of the respondent had been present at the meeting, but had not spoken. The claimant had not been familiar with the person who was chairing the meeting, who said that the claimant knew why he was there. When the claimant protested that he did not, the interviewer asked him not to take him 'for a mug' and then introduced himself as an external security advisor. It was alleged that the claimant had purposefully sought to locate and interfere with surveillance cameras. The claimant resolutely denied this allegation. He was offered the choice between resigning or being dismissed. When he refused to resign, he was immediately furnished with a letter terminating his employment forthwith. The claimant told the EAT that he had managed to secure alternative employment six weeks later, thereby mitigating his losses.

The EAT held, that the claimant's dismissal was both unwarranted and grossly unfair. It was stated that the evidence before the EAT was indicative of no wrongdoing whatsoever on the claimant's part. The EAT questioned the motivation of the respondent in dismissing the claimant in the absence of wrongdoing. The EAT concluded that the claimant had been denied a process that would meet even minimum standards and that the claimant had been treated unfairly. The EAT stated that: 'the Company failed on almost every conceivable ground and showed a complete lack of respect for the claimant as an employee. Where was the fairness here or, indeed, the basis for any disciplinary action at all? Where was the investigation? At what point was the claimant given an opportunity to be heard and to defend himself? Where were the principles of Natural Justice adhered to?'

The EAT considered this to be a clear case of unfair dismissal, deserving of compensation. The EAT stated that the claimant's resolve in mitigating his losses was a credit to him. However, the EAT was bound to award him his actual losses only; accordingly, an award of €2,925 (this amount being equivalent to six weeks' gross pay at €487.50 per week) was made to the claimant. The EAT further held that the claimant was entitled to notice pay of €1,950 (this amount being equivalent to four weeks' gross pay at €487.50 per week).

Lack of impartial decision-makers

[27.56] *Young v Tower Brook Ltd t/a Castle Durrow House Hotel[68]—Employment Appeals Tribunal—Unfair Dismissals Acts 1977 to 2015—Minimum Notice and Terms of Employment Acts 1973 to 2005—unfair dismissal—where claimant did not participate in disciplinary process as he considered it to be unfair and to be in breach of principles of natural justice—dismissal for aggressive behaviour and failure to engage in process*

The claimant was employed since 2000 as a general labourer on the grounds of the respondent's country house hotel. It was common case that an altercation took place at nine o'clock on 4 June 2013, the morning after a wedding at the premises; where loud noise generated by the claimant and another employee who were moving bottles, beer kegs and rubbish attracted the attention of one of the respondent's directors. It was

---

68. *Young v Tower Brook Ltd t/a Castle Durrow House Hotel* UD1598/2013, MN783/2013.

asserted by the respondent that the claimant had previously been warned not to engage in any work that would disturb hotel guests before 10am. However, the claimant contended that moving rubbish from the night before was a priority so that guests would not see it and that he noted that the hotel room closest to where he was working had already been vacated. Evidence was given that there was an angry verbal exchange regarding this issue and it was asserted that the claimant had acted in a threatening manner and pushed the director onto a flower bed with a keg of beer. However, the claimant asserted that the director had pushed him in the chest and instructed him to stop working.

Later that day there was another contentious meeting between the parties. Further exchanges took place the following day with the financial controller of the respondent, who gave evidence that she was frightened of the claimant as he was behaving in an agitated manner.

The claimant asserted that management had failed to attend a meeting as arranged and whilst colourful language had been used between the parties, there had been no physical exchange. The claimant was then suspended with pay and two meetings were arranged for 10 June and 22 August, neither of which the claimant attended. The respondent proceeded to dismiss the claimant following a consultation between the directors. The EAT noted that the letter confirming the termination of the claimant's employment made reference to his alleged aggressive behaviour towards the managing director and financial controller of the company.

However, the EAT noted that the evidence before it indicated that the claimant was dismissed primarily due to his failure to engage with the disciplinary process. It was noted that the financial controller, who was involved in the discussions leading to the dismissal, was unable to advise the EAT as to why the claimant was dismissed. The evidence of the claimant was that he had not participated in the process conducted by the respondent as he considered it to be unfair and in breach of principles of natural justice and this was noted by the EAT.

The EAT held that procedurally it was entirely inappropriate that the disciplinary process was conducted by the company director and financial controller, essentially the two complainants against the claimant and, in the case of the director, the person who was the principal participant in the incident of 4 June. The EAT could not fault the claimant for failing to engage with such a fundamentally flawed process. It was further noted that the claimant had made it abundantly clear to the respondent why he would not engage; yet the respondent took no steps whatsoever to address these legitimate concerns. The EAT preferred the claimant's evidence as to the interactions that had occurred on 4 and 5 June and concluded that, on balance, there were no grounds to dismiss the claimant as a result of what occurred on those dates. The claim of unfair dismissal was well founded and the EAT awarded the claimant compensation of €30,000. He was further awarded €2,178 in lieu of six weeks minimum notice.

See also *Jones v Bulmers Ltd*[69] at **[27.87]**

---

69. *Jones v Bulmers Ltd* UD423/2014, UD587/2014.

Delay

[27.57] *Godsland v Applus Car Testing Ltd[70]—Employment Appeals Tribunal— Unfair Dismissals Acts 1977 to 2015—dismissal where claimant tested his own vehicle in breach of respondent's integrity guidelines and rules—delay of 12 months between incident and subsequent investigation—unfair process*

The claimant was employed initially as a vehicle inspector with the respondent who was engaged in national car testing. The claimant was promoted to team leader, a more senior role, which carried responsibility for sustaining the business. The claimant was furnished with a contract of employment, an employee handbook and the respondent's code of ethics policy. Evidence was given that the respondent is open to regular scrutiny and that significant external audits are completed regularly and that the claimant had been fully trained in his role. Evidence was also given as to the respondent's integrity guidelines which were in place to assist employees in navigating difficult situations. It was emphasised that the respondent's employees must avoid any situations where the interests of the respondent diverged from their own personal interest or those of persons with whom they are in close personal/business contact. For example if an employee had any history pertaining to a vehicle presented for a test, this must be disclosed. It was forbidden to test one's own vehicle or one belonging to a family member.

On 10 March 2012, when the claimant tested his own vehicle and paid for this test. The claimant maintained that he was never informed that testing his own vehicle could result in dismissal. It was noted that in February 2013 the claimant had lodged a complaint against an attempt to increase his hours. In June 2013 the claimant received an invitation from the regional manager to an investigative meeting concerning the testing of his own car. It was noted by the EAT that there was no explanation of how this matter had come to the respondent's attention or why the action was being taken now, more than one year after the incident. During this intervening time, the claimant had continued to work without issue. The meeting took place in July and the claimant accepted that he had reassigned his car to be tested by himself in an effort to get things started. In a second, subsequent investigative meeting the claimant described his behaviour as a lapse in judgment; however it was deemed to be serious misconduct by the respondent. A disciplinary meeting took place and concluded with the claimant being suspended with pay pending a final decision. The claimant was informed that his employment was terminated with effect from 27 September 2013 and he appealed this unsuccessfully.

The EAT noted that the facts were not in dispute and that the claimant, who was an experienced and long-standing employee of the respondent, tested his own car contrary to the respondent's integrity programme which clearly forbids this. It was further noted by the EAT that the claimant had accepted that he shouldn't have tested his own car, while maintaining he was never informed that this could result in his dismissal. The EAT held that it had to determine whether the action of the claimant was serious enough to justify dismissal and whether the respondent, in dismissing the claimant, had acted in a

---

70.   *Godsland v Applus Car Testing Ltd* UD1422/2013.

manner that was arbitrary, unfair or irrational. It was noted that the claimant's actions had the potential to embarrass the respondent and undermine its reputation if they came to the attention of the external auditors; hence the respondent had no option but to take serious issue with his action.

The EAT was critical of the fact that, for more than one year, the respondent had overlooked the claimant's action. The EAT concluded that this delay had undermined the ultimate decision to dismiss. It was noted the claimant had continued to work for the respondent and there had been no further issues. The EAT concluded that the delay in progressing the issue amounted to unfair process. The EAT concluded that the dismissal of the claimant was unfair and awarded him compensation of €35,000.

[27.58] *Dubrowski v Strathroy Dairy[71]—Employment Appeals Tribunal—Unfair Dismissals Acts 1977 to 2015—Minimum Notice and Terms of Employment Acts 1973 to 2005—unfair dismissal—delay in dismissing employee after alleged conduct—accident at work—separate personal injury proceedings—failure by employee to persistently mitigate his loss*

The respondent operated a milk distribution depot in which the claimant was employed as a truck driver from 6 February 2007 until he was dismissed on 2 February 2014. The claimant was involved in an accident at work on 23 August 2011 and was absent from work on sick leave thereafter until his dismissal. The claimant sued the respondent in relation to this accident and six other accidents prior to that date. These actions were all settled prior to a court hearing.

It was the claimant's position that the respondent had refused to allow him return to work, even though the company doctor certified him fit to return to work and that he was dismissed because he had sued the respondent in relation to the workplace accidents. The claimant had indicated he was unfit for the position that he had held and his GP had issued a letter to that effect. However the company doctor had issued a later medical report to say that the claimant was fully fit for the position he held. This medical report was commissioned by the company for action by the company in their deliberations on the claimant's future with the company. Therefore there were no medical grounds on which to terminate the claimant's employment.

The respondent denied that the claimant was dismissed because of his proceedings against the respondent and told the EAT that the claimant was dismissed because:

(1) the claimant had failed to report two accidents at work, one in January 2011 and the other on 18 August 2011; and

(2) there was no guarantee that the claimant would not have another accident at work and they were not happy that it was safe to take him back.

The EAT noted that in the replies to the High Court Notice for Further and Better Particulars dated 10 September 2012, the claimant had already supplied the respondent with the particulars of all the injuries sustained by the claimant and the dates of all the accidents. In the circumstances the respondent had knowledge of each of the accidents

71. *Dubrowski v Strathroy Dairy* (ROI) UD468/2014, MN196/2014.

at that time, even if they had not been reported when they actually occurred. The EAT determined that the respondent, in waiting a further 18 months, had dissipated the reasonableness of treating the claimant in the manner they did. In the circumstances the EAT found that the claimant should not have been sanctioned in such a manner.

The EAT found that the claimant was unfairly dismissed and that the most appropriate remedy was compensation. The EAT was not satisfied that the claimant sought to mitigate his loss and, in all the circumstances, awarded the claimant the sum of €10,000. The EAT also awarded the claimant €2,184 under the Minimum Notice and Terms of Employment Acts 1973 to 2005.

Trade union representation

[27.59] *Leigh v SpeedKing Couriers Ltd t/a Fastway Couriers (Midlands)[72]— Employment Appeals Tribunal—Unfair Dismissals Acts 1977 to 2015—Minimum Notice and Terms of Employment Acts 1973 to 2005—dismissal for gross misconduct—procedural failings on part of respondent employer—failure to allow trade union representation—overlaps between investigation and disciplinary process—lack of independent appeal—failure of respondent to adhere to proper process*

The claimant was involved in a serious incident where a banger was exploded in the workplace causing injury to a number of employees. The EAT noted that the claimant admitted responsibility from the outset but claimed that there had been nothing unlawful in his actions and that he had not appreciated the potential serious consequences of his actions. He was summoned to a fact-finding meeting in October 2013 and was advised of his right to bring a fellow employee but was not informed of his right to have representation. The respondent's view was that the precedent in the workplace was to afford an employee the opportunity of being accompanied by a work colleague or other witness. It was noted that the respondent's employee handbook was part of the employment contract and that handbook provided for a right to representation. The EAT noted that there was no suggestion in the handbook that there were any parameters as to the claimant's choice of representation and it was further noted that the respondent's grievance procedure provided for union representation. The EAT concluded that where it is expressly stated, in an employment handbook, in the context of a grievance procedure that a union representative may represent an employee, it followed, by extension, that a union representative may also represent an employee in the disciplinary process.

It was noted that there had been a previous incident involving a banger and a subsequent more serious incident and that both were taken into account when arriving at the decision to impose the disciplinary sanction of dismissal. The EAT concluded that the first incident was not adequately investigated by the respondent. The EAT noted that, subsequent to the fact-finding meeting, another employee in the workplace was

---

72. *Leigh v SpeedKing Couriers Ltd t/a Fastway Couriers (Midlands)* UD28/2014, MN484/2014.

interviewed and alleged that the claimant had encouraged him to throw a banger-baring frisbee in the direction of a number of workers. This version of events was the polar opposite of what the claimant had stated. The decision-maker had confirmed that all statements had been taken into account before arriving at a decision to dismiss. The EAT noted that this particular statement was never put to the claimant, nor was he afforded any opportunity to dispute the contents of the statement. The EAT noted that, in a case such as this, the importance of an employee being allowed to have his representative of choice present in accordance with his contractual entitlement could not be overstated. It was, however, noted that the claimant did have his chosen representative to assist him in seeking to have a lesser sanction than dismissal considered.

The EAT held that it was concerned at the overlaps between the investigative and disciplinary process and the dual roles of the respondent's management in particular. There was a clear failure to maintain a desirable separation between the investigative and disciplinary process. The respondent's evidence to the EAT was indicative of its belief that the admission by the claimant exonerated it from adhering to best practice in both the investigative and disciplinary processes. The EAT held, however, that there should have been no departure from best practice in the circumstances, even if the sanction was inevitable. Any fair consideration of the possibility of a sanction short of dismissal would have dictated that the claimant be given every reasonable opportunity to know the information being relied upon by the respondent and that he be afforded the opportunity to represent his position and to make fully informed representations.

The EAT held that significant aspects of the respondent's evidence were unreliable. It appears that minutes of a fact-finding meeting put forward by the respondent's witnesses as being originals were, in fact, amended subsequent to that meeting, which the EAT found to be extremely disturbing. The EAT noted that it had been informed that the appeal decision-maker was a person who was not previously involved in the process however, in that individual's evidence it was clear that the appeal decision-maker was the person who decided to dismiss the complainant. The EAT noted that the claimant had not been advised of the risk of dismissal prior to the fact-finding meeting. There was no evidence before the EAT that the claimant had received a written communication confirming it to be a disciplinary meeting; nor to advise him to be represented; nor to set out the issues that would be put to him. At the meeting he was given a letter of termination signed by the investigator, a person who the EAT concluded should not have a role at this stage of the meeting. With regard to the appeal, which took place on 31 October, the EAT noted the respondent's employee handbook stated that the appeal should be conducted by a member of management not previously connected with the process. The respondent sought to satisfy the EAT that the appeal decision-maker had no such previous involvement, however, the appeal decision-maker himself on his own evidence admitted that he had decided to dismiss the claimant as he felt that the appeal could only be put to him as most senior management. Again, the claimant was advised that he could only have a fellow employee present and was refused representation by his union representative.

The EAT concluded that a properly constituted appeal represented the claimant's final opportunity to make a case for mitigation. He had a contractual right to his representation of choice, which was refused to him on spurious grounds that the union representative had not given prior notice of her attendance and did not produce written consent of the claimant who was representing him. The respondent's position in this regard was held by the EAT to be completely disingenuous. The EAT held that the exclusion of the claimant's union representative, and the denial to him of his representative of choice, was unfair and a fundamental breach of his contractual entitlements. The EAT concluded that the failure to adhere to proper process in this matter constituted a fundamental breach of the claimant's contractual rights and a disregard of the principles of natural justice. The EAT considered the claimant to have been unfairly dismissed and awarded him €1,500 compensation and his notice entitlements.

Need to ensure claimant comprehends process

[27.60] *Perenc v Dunnes Stores[73]—Employment Appeals Tribunal—Unfair Dismissals Acts 1977 to 2015—dismissal for selling alcohol to a minor—test purchase by An Garda Síochána—procedural fairness—claimant's lack of comprehension of process—failure of employer to observe fair procedures during investigation and disciplinary processes*

In June 2013 the claimant, a Polish national, was dismissed from her employment with the respondent retailer, following an investigation and disciplinary process which had been initiated by reason of the claimant's breach of the employer's policy on the sale of alcohol to persons under the age of 18.

On 30 May 2013, the claimant sold one bottle of wine to a purchaser aged 16. This purchaser had been deployed by An Garda Síochána in a test purchase in an attempt to prevent underage people from purchasing alcohol. Immediately after the transaction, a member of An Garda Síochána made herself known to the claimant and informed her of the possibility of prosecution of her as well as her employer. The CCTV footage of this transaction was clear and showed that the sale was made without any hesitation by the claimant.

Employees of the respondent gave evidence that they receive comprehensive training in the policy and procedure for the sale of alcohol. It was accepted that the claimant, along with other members of staff, receive this specific training once and sometimes twice a year. Reminders of this policy are located within the workplace along with a double-prompt function in the till whenever someone attempts to buy alcohol.

The claimant had worked with the respondent for six and a half years. Evidence was given of her exemplary record and excellent overall performance. The member of An Garda Síochána gave evidence that the claimant was 'shocked' when she was formally cautioned.

Within an hour and a half, the claimant was brought into two meetings; the first lasting 25 minutes and the second lasting 15 minutes. Both meetings were investigatory in nature. Two more meetings were conducted the following day, 31 May 2013. These meetings were overseen by the store manager, who was accompanied by the HR

---

73. *Perenc v Dunnes Stores* UD1441/2013.

manager. As per the respondent's disciplinary and dismissal procedures, a third party also attended these meetings at the respondent's request.

By 5 June 2013 the matter entered the disciplinary stage and it was decided to terminate the claimant's employment for reasons of gross misconduct. The respondent afforded the claimant a right to appeal this decision, the outcome of which amounted to one line, stating: 'having considered all the matters, I find the sanction to be fair and I uphold the appeal'.

The EAT focused on the procedural fairness attaching to the termination of the employment. The EAT was keen to note that it was aware of the fact that the respondent was entitled to deal with this sort of misconduct with the utmost gravity, given the potential for prosecution. With regard to the third party accompanying the claimant, the EAT noted that this seemed to merely satisfy the respondent's dismissal disciplinary policies instead of offering an extra element of guidance and advice for the claimant. These third parties remained mute during the process. The EAT noted that there is a significant difference between an employee being accompanied to a disciplinary meeting and an employee having someone attending on their behalf.

The EAT focused on the claimant's difficulty with the English language and general comprehension of what was happening. In assessing the notes taken during the four meetings, the EAT found that the claimant said very little and was neither confident not articulate. The claimant merely agreed with everything being put forward to her without any evidence of her thoroughly understanding the severity of the consequences. As the claimant was a native of Poland, English was not her first language, which was evidenced by her repeated answers of 'I don't know how to say them' and 'I do not know the question, can you say it again'. Two letters were submitted to the investigator and the HR manager on 31 May regarding the claimant's concern for her lack of confidence with the English language. The one line appeal consideration by the respondent was deemed by the EAT to be a rubber-stamping exercise. The EAT did not doubt that the breach of the policy for the sale of alcohol was of such a serious nature that the possibility of the claimant keeping her job was slim; however this did not mean that the claimant could be treated in such a nature as to not be able to articulate her own plea in mitigation. The EAT concluded that although it accepted the situation was serious, the employer could not be allowed to deny the claimant her right to procedural fairness. The EAT awarded the claimant compensation of €16,000.

Appropriateness and proportionality of sanction of dismissal

[27.61] *Sadowska v Players Leisure Ltd t/a Players Leisure Ltd*[74]*—Employment Appeals Tribunal—Unfair Dismissals Acts 1977 to 2015—Minimum Notice and Terms of Employment Acts 1973 to 2005—gross misconduct—unauthorised borrowings from respondent's petty cash—zero-tolerance policy—proportionality of sanction of dismissal—whether alternatives to dismissal considered—claimant's length of service should have been taken into account by respondent when deciding on appropriate sanction*

The respondent operated an amusement arcade/casino. The claimant was employed as a senior cashier from 5 October 2005 until 8 August 2013, when she was dismissed for gross misconduct.

The EAT heard evidence from an operations manager for the respondent (DM) who had carried out the initial investigation into the incidents that led to the claimant's dismissal. DM gave evidence that on Monday 22 July 2013, the claimant told him that she had taken a total of €20 from the respondent's till between Saturday 20 July 2013 and Sunday 21 July 2013. She stated that she had used this money to pay for taxis home after her shifts in the early hours of the morning. The claimant had left two notes of this transaction at the time – one handwritten and one on the computer. She had not requested permission to take the money at the relevant time but instead had decided to inform DM on Monday 22 July. DM told the claimant that he would be investigating the matter fully, as he considered it to be very serious. Accordingly, DM carried out an investigation, consulted the staff handbook and consulted with the owner of the respondent. He concluded that the incident amounted to gross misconduct and referred it to the owner of the respondent for his consideration and possible disciplinary action. DM told the EAT that a practice used to prevail in and around 2008–2009, where the respondent would pay for an employee's taxi home if his/her shift ended at 6am. The respondent had felt that this practice was being abused, therefore it was discontinued. The practice, when in place, had been to submit receipts for reimbursement.

The owner of the respondent explained that DM carried out the day-to-day running of the business, but he checked the accounts weekly himself, with the assistance of another employee. He explained that cash sheets are posted into a safe at the end of each shift and are only referred to if a discrepancy arises in the computer records. The owner reiterated that the claimant had been dismissed for taking money from the float without permission. He stated his opinion that, if the claimant needed money, she should have contacted the duty manager in his onsite apartment, and he could have accessed petty cash if necessary. The owner described the working relationship that the claimant had with the respondent over the term of her employment, which had, in the past, been difficult. The claimant had lodged a claim against the respondent in relation to public holiday pay. She was awarded a sum of money by a Rights Commissioner further to this complaint. Furthermore, the claimant had been issued with a final written warning for photographing rosters and cash sheets in the respondent's cash office. A bullying

---

74. *Sadowska v Players Leisure Ltd t/a Players Leisure Ltd* UD1658/2013, MN707/2013.

complaint had been lodged against the claimant by a colleague, which was in the course of investigation when the colleague resigned. At the time of the incident in question, the respondent's management team were reporting that the claimant was causing a bad atmosphere in the workplace. The owner decided to uphold the claimant's dismissal on the basis that the respondent had zero tolerance for taking money from the float. If she required a taxi she should have phoned the duty manager.

The claimant, in her evidence, alleged that her duty manager started picking on her in April 2011. She stated that she had had to join a trade union for support. The claimant explained that on Saturday 20 July 2013 a festival had been on in Bray. At the end of her shift she was afraid to walk home as the streets were still busy. Her own personal card had expired. She accepted that she had taken €10 from the float and made a note of it on the cash sheet and computer. She found herself in the same situation of having no money the next day, so she took a further €10 from the float. On Monday 22 July she told DM what she had done and offered to pay the money back. The disciplinary procedure was not commenced until two weeks after she informed DM of her actions.

The EAT accepted that the claimant had been dismissed because she removed cash from the float without prior authorisation to pay for a taxi home on two successive nights, an action which the respondent believed warranted dismissal. In considering the proportionality of the sanction, the EAT placed emphasis on the fact that the claimant had worked for the respondent for over seven years and that the respondent had failed to consider an alternative sanction. The EAT held that it was not satisfied that the actions of the claimant amounted to gross misconduct. Accordingly, the dismissal of the claimant was found to be unfair. However, the EAT considered that the claimant had contributed to her own difficulty by not disclosing the matter to her manager at the earliest available opportunity, ie Sunday 21 July 2013. Accordingly the claimant was awarded compensation of €5,000. The claimant's claim under the Minimum Notice and Terms of Employment Acts 1973 to 2005 also succeeded and the claimant was awarded the sum of €1,760 (ie four weeks' pay).

[27.62] *Rafter v Connaught Gold Co-Op-Aurivo Co-Op Society Ltd t/a Aurivo Co-Operative Society Ltd[75]—Employment Appeals Tribunal—Unfair Dismissals Acts 1977 to 2015, s 6(4)(b)—fair procedures——proportionality of sanction—test of reasonableness—requirement to take into account employee's long and unblemished employment record—need for conclusive evidence of wrongdoing to justify dismissal for misconduct*

The claimant, was dismissed by the respondent which was engaged in the food industry. The respondent alleged that the claimant was dismissed for gross misconduct after he wrote a comment about a fellow employee on the top of a carton of milk. The EAT described the comment as having 'dark undertones'. The carton, which formed part of a multipack, was sent out to an agent for distribution.

---

75.   *Rafter v Connaught Gold Co-Op-Aurivo Co-Op Society Ltd t/a Aurivo Co-Operative Society Ltd* UD48/2014.

The respondent was made aware of the writing on the carton when its site manager received a call from a milk agent on 15 July. The pack was returned and the respondent was able to deduce that the carton had been produced on 9 July at 14.11 pm. There had been four employees on the work rota at that time.

The respondent raised the incident with staff at a meeting on 17 July. The site manager invited employees (including the claimant, who was in attendance) to approach him if they knew anything about the incident. The respondent engaged a graphologist to assess the handwriting of the four employees who had been on the rota at the relevant time. The graphologist's report concluded that the writing was that of the claimant. On 6 August the claimant was invited to a meeting with the respondent. He was invited to bring a representative. He denied any knowledge of the incident. He was presented with the report from the graphologist and advised of the seriousness of the allegation. The respondent suspended the claimant on full pay pending further investigation. The claimant gave the respondent permission to view CCTV footage of the day in question. The site manager's evidence was that the claimant could be seen in the vicinity of the milk machine at the time of the incident and he could be seen removing a carton from the run. He told the EAT that this had been for the purpose of conducting a quality check.

The claimant was dismissed at a meeting on 14 August. The respondent's decision to dismiss was confirmed by letter dated 16 August. The claimant appealed the decision to dismiss to the head of finance. The head of finance stated his satisfaction with the fairness of the procedures adopted by the respondent. He explained that, although he had considered a lesser sanction he believed the punishment was justified in circumstances where the reputation of the respondent's brand could have been damaged. He added that the claimant had been given adequate representation and in the circumstances he had considered it appropriate to uphold the sanction of dismissal.

The claimant denied involvement in the incident in question. In relation to the first meeting held with all employees, the claimant commented that it would have been difficult for anyone to confess responsibility for the incident because of the nature of the comment and the likely repercussions. In relation to the meeting held on 6 August the claimant told the EAT that he did not know what the meeting was about when he was invited to it. He stated that he had not been allowed to view his handwriting sample. He voiced his disagreement with the findings of the graphologist. In relation to the CCTV footage and the milk cartons, he argued that it was not possible to match up the carton in question because the production line took two or three minutes to fully revolve. He also mentioned the possibility that the carton in question could have come from the production line of the previous day. The claimant told the EAT that he did not agree with the sanction of dismissal because he had put his 'heart and soul into the company'. He further objected to the process employed on the basis that the investigation, disciplinary process and decision to dismiss were all carried out by the same person.

The EAT considered it clear that heavy reliance had been placed by the respondent on the CCTV footage and the report of the graphologist. However, the EAT held that the findings in both these matters were 'far from conclusive'. Upon viewing the CCTV footage, the EAT unanimously agreed that it did not contain the evidence as represented by the respondent.

The EAT cited s 6(4)(b) of the 1977 Act as justifying dismissals for reasons relating to 'conduct'. It was noted that, because no definition is attached to this term in the 1977 Act, every case must be decided with regard to the facts of that particular case. It was held that:

> ... an act, minor in one situation, can be gross misconduct in another situation. All
> will depend on such factors as the nature of the work of the employee, the
> "conduct" involved and the level of responsibility accorded to the employee.
> There are no hard and fast rules.

The EAT noted that its role in unfair dismissal cases is not to establish an objective standard but to ask whether the decision to dismiss comes within the band of reasonable responses an employer might take, having regard to the particular circumstances of the case.

> The test of reasonableness includes the nature and extent of the enquiry carried
> out by the employer prior to a decision to dismiss, and the conclusion arrived at by
> the employer on the basis of the information resulting from such enquiry.

The EAT noted that the respondent in this case had carried out a full and detailed investigation into the matter. It appeared to the EAT that the claimant was aware of all allegations and complaints against him. He was also given an opportunity to respond to same.

The EAT held that, once the investigation has been concluded, one must look at the reasonableness of the conclusion arrived at. It was noted that the test for 'reasonableness' had been established by the EAT in *Noritake (Ireland) Ltd v Kenna*,[76] as follows:

(1)   did the employer believe that the employee misconducted himself as alleged? If so,

(2)   did the company have reasonable grounds to sustain that belief? If so,

(3)   was the penalty of dismissal proportionate to the alleged misconduct?

The EAT determined that the answer to question 1 had to be in the affirmative, ie the respondent believed that the claimant had misconducted himself. However, the EAT considered that the reply to question 2 must be in the negative, in that while the respondent had some grounds to sustain its belief in the claimant's guilt, the evidence on which they based this belief was not conclusive. Finally, in relation to question 3, the EAT concluded that the dismissal was not proportionate to the alleged misconduct. The EAT commented:

> there was no danger to life or limb herein, nor do we accept that the Respondents
> name, reputation or product would have been as negatively impacted as suggested
> by the Respondent.

Emphasis was also placed on the claimant's strong, 'unblemished' and long employment history with the respondent (10 years service). It appeared to the EAT that no

---

76.   *Noritake (Ireland) Ltd v Kenna* UD 88/1983.

consideration whatsoever had been afforded to these matters, either in the initial investigation or the appeal hearing. Accordingly, the EAT held the dismissal of the claimant unfair and awarded him compensation of €25,000.

Custom and practice

[27.63] *Coady v Oxigen Environmental[77]—Employment Appeals Tribunal—Unfair Dismissals Acts 1977 to 2015—appeal from decision of Rights Commissioner— alleged gross misconduct—whether appellant's conduct could be excused on basis of custom and practice in respondent company—whether appellant received sufficient notice that custom and practice in question was to be discontinued—use of private investigator to prove alleged gross misconduct—whether lesser sanction would have been more appropriate in the circumstances*

This was an appeal by the claimant of a decision of a Rights Commissioner, who held that the claimant had not been unfairly dismissed.

The respondent operates a waste collection system. The claimant worked as a lorry driver with the respondent from 7 February 2011 until his dismissal on 24 December 2012. The claimant was dismissed for gross misconduct, specifically the lifting of waste from his own home without being a paying customer of the respondent. It was the claimant's contention that the free lifting of waste from his own home had been established as a perk of his job through custom and practice in the respondent. On this basis, he maintained that he had been unfairly dismissed. On the other hand, the respondent asserted that it was entitled to dismiss the claimant for what it considered to constitute gross misconduct.

The respondent first became suspicious that the claimant was having waste lifted from his home, without paying for same, on 12 November 2012. While checking on an injured colleague who was with the claimant in his collection vehicle, the operations manager noticed that the vehicle was close to the claimant's house, but the collection bins in the claimant's driveway were not displaying the respondent's label. The operations manager checked the respondent's system and confirmed that the claimant was not a customer of the respondent. The respondent hired a private investigator and surveillance was carried out on 21, 26 and 29 November and on 10 and 13 December 2012. At the hearing, the respondent presented a video of domestic waste being lifted from the claimant's house by one of the respondent's employees on 26 November 2012. The claimant confirmed that this was his house and that the domestic waste being lifted was his.

The operations manager explained to the EAT that a 25 per cent discounted waste collection service had been offered to those employees who were not customers of the respondent, and that the claimant was one of these employees. The discounted rate had been offered by way of a hand-delivered memo dated 25 October 2012. It was contended that this memo was proof that the claimant could not have been in any doubt that free collection was not an established custom and practice after 25 October 2012. It was the

---

77. *Coady v Oxigen Environmental* UD1048/2013.

operations manager's evidence that the claimant continued lifting his own domestic waste without being a paying customer after he was furnished with this memo, ie on 26 November 2012.

The operations manager met with the claimant on 14 December 2012 and handed him a letter notifying him of his suspension with pay. A disciplinary meeting was held on Friday 21 December 2012. This meeting was chaired by CD and attended by the claimant, a member of HR and a member of SIPTU, who accompanied the claimant. At this meeting the claimant confirmed that he had collected his own domestic waste using the respondent's service. He explained that the reason for his action was that he was told that it was a perk of the job. The claimant confirmed that he was not a customer of the respondent or of any other waste collection service. Following this meeting the claimant was dismissed for gross misconduct by way of letter dated 24 December 2012. He was advised of his right to appeal this decision, a right which he exercised on 31 December 2012. The appeal hearing was held on 10 January 2013 and was chaired by AD. In attendance at the appeal hearing were the claimant, the operations manager for the respondent's midland region, SIPTU representatives and the local shop steward. AD upheld the decision to dismiss the claimant on the grounds of misconduct, having considered all the relevant evidence. The outcome of the appeal was communicated to the claimant by way of letter dated 15 January 2013.

During cross-examination the operations manager was asked whether his domestic waste and that of another employee had been picked up for free. He stated that this was an entirely different situation. He explained that certain employees were given free collection for a limited time in order to facilitate the respondent's expansion into the routes where these employees lived. The respondent wanted to be seen in these areas with a view to attracting new customers. He clarified that he was a paying customer of the respondent at the time of the hearing. It was put to the operations manager that the claimant had not received the memo offering the staff discount. He denied this, stating that he delivered the letters himself in an envelope with the employees' payslips.

It was the claimant's evidence that he had been trained by an employee of the respondent when he commenced work with the respondent. This employee took him on the collection route in order to familiarise him with the route and its customers. He had explained to the claimant that the collection of the claimant's domestic waste was a 'perk of the job', established by custom and practice in the company. The claimant named other employees of the respondent, including the operations manager, who availed of the same 'perk'. The claimant further explained that employees who were not on routes serviced by the respondent brought their domestic waste to work in plastic bags and disposed of them in the waste collection vehicles. The claimant readily accepted that the domestic waste being lifted in the video made on 26 November 2012 was his domestic waste and that the collection vehicle in the video was his vehicle, and was driven by him.

In cross-examination the claimant maintained that he never received the memo dated 25 October 2012. He said that he would have remembered if the operations manager had given him that memo.

The EAT made the following findings in this case:

—   there was in fact a custom and practice of employees disposing of their own domestic waste by way of the respondent's collection system, despite the fact that they were not paying customers of the respondent;

—   the respondent was entitled to disavow this practice. Provided that the employees were unequivocally informed of same, the respondent was entitled thereafter to discipline those employees who carried on the discontinued practice;

—   the claimant in this case may not have been informed at all, but at least was not unequivocally informed, that the practice was to discontinue;

—   rather than expend monies on a private investigator, the respondent could have ensured that the employees were unequivocally informed that the practice was to discontinue and that the consequence of continuance would be the dismissal of the employee in question. The EAT was satisfied that a warning of this nature would have resulted in employee compliance; and

—   a lesser sanction than dismissal would have sufficed in the circumstances.

Accordingly, the claimant's appeal was upheld and the EAT set aside the earlier recommendation of the Rights Commissioner in this matter. The claimant was awarded compensation of €13,452 for unfair dismissal. In calculating the appropriate level of compensation, the EAT took into consideration the claimant's efforts to mitigate his losses, which it did not consider to meet the standard set out by the EAT in *Sheehan v Continental Administration Co Ltd*[78] that:

a claimant who finds himself out of work should employ a reasonable amount of time each weekday in seeking work. It is not enough to inform agencies that you are available for work nor merely to post an application to various companies seeking work ... The time that a claimant finds on his hands is not his own, unless he chooses it to be, but rather to be profitably employed in seeking to mitigate his loss.

[27.64] *Casserley and Foy v AGI Media Packaging (Dublin) Ltd*[79]*—Employment Appeals Tribunal—Unfair Dismissals Acts 1977 to 2015—Minimum Notice and Terms of Employment Acts 1973 to 2005—dismissal—whether claimants' conduct in going on an extended break without clocking out was gross misconduct—custom and practice—requirement that employer acts reasonably when taking decision to dismiss*

The claimants were employed in the respondent's printing company. Each of its printing presses had two persons allocated. Printer number 1 was the decision maker, which in this case was claimant 1 and printer number 2, namely claimant 2, assisted with the printing. Claimant 1 commenced employment with the respondent in 2003, claimant 2 commenced in 2001 and neither had any previous disciplinary issues.

---

78.   *Sheehan v Continental Administration Co Ltd* UD858/1999.

79.   *Casserley and Foy v AGI Media Packaging (Dublin) Ltd* UD520/2013, MN291/2013, UD521/2013, MN292/2013.

On 22 December 2012, the production manager arrived on site because of an outstanding production issue from the previous evening. When he arrived, he found the factory floor quiet and presumed the staff were taking their break in the canteen, as the claimants' 12-hour shift had started at 6am. As time went on, the only staff member who returned was the one who had taken his break in the canteen. In addition the production manager came across one of the claimants' mobile telephones. It was established that the claimants had used their access swipes to leave the building at 11.10am. The general manager was informed and the four employees (including the claimants) returned to the premises at 1.06. They explained that they had left the premises to buy lunch and had not brought their mobile phones with them: however their car became blocked by another vehicle, which had caused an unforeseen delay in their return. A proposed meeting with the production manager did not proceed and a decision was taken to cease production for the day. The four employees were advised that they were suspended until the incident was further investigated. The claimants made an approach later that day to meet with the production manager, however this was refused by the respondent who advised that a meeting would be organised for a later date. The EAT noted that the claimants offered to stay late to make up the time and to work for free to get the print jobs completed, but a decision had already been taken to cease production on the day in question. It was confirmed that when employees commenced their shift at 6am they were entitled to a break by 11am, at which time they had the option of a short break followed by a longer lunch break later or they could take a longer break of one hour at that time.

Individual investigation meetings were held on 8 January with the claimants, their union representatives and management. The respondent maintained that the situation had jeopardised customer relations with its main client, who accounted for 70 per cent to 80 per cent of their overall print packaging work. From the respondent's perspective it was imperative to satisfy this company's demands and it was decided to progress the matter to disciplinary stage. A letter inviting the claimants to disciplinary meetings referenced the serious allegation that they had clocked in for work and then left their working posts and the site without authorisation and without clocking out for a considerable period of time. A decision was taken to dismiss the claimants from employment and this was upheld on appeal.

The respondent maintained in evidence that, even on a Saturday, it was expected that permission would have been sought to leave the site from the production manager, who could be telephoned if he was not onsite. A company memo from 2008 stated that, for health and safety reasons, staff must clock in and clock out for their breaks and that disciplinary action would be taken if the memo was not adhered to.

Evidence was given that if staff remained on the premises for their breaks, they did not have to clock in or clock out but in order to leave the site, permission must be obtained. It was further submitted that a memo to this effect was issued to employees with their payslips.

The EAT noted that the disciplinary decision maker did not have the company's clock-in cards to know whether the employees left the premises on their breaks but stated that, in reaching the decision to dismiss, she and the other decision maker had spoken with the production manager who confirmed that employees telephoned him about everything, including permission to leave the premises. The EAT further noted that the company's disciplinary procedures defined gross misconduct as including a number of different matters, including the falsification of documents (especially time cards), absence from the employer's premises during working hours without prior permission and other offences of similar gravity. Evidence was given that delivery of packaging was due on 27 December and this date was a particular pressure point due to the service level agreement to deliver print packaging to their client in a particular time frame. It was conceded by the general manager that, when considering the appeal, he did not look at previous clock cards to consider whether there was a history of clocking out for breaks, but that he had taken advice on this matter from the production manager and other management regarding custom and practice. It was submitted that the employees of the respondent did not have a contract of employment and that other than the memo and custom and practice that existed, it was not cited elsewhere to employees that permission must be given to leave the premises for their break.

In reaching its determination, the EAT noted the following: the claimants had no contracts of employment, hence there was no provision that the employees had to clock out for breaks or get permission to do so; and no evidence was given to the EAT that the claimants were advised verbally that they would have to get permission to leave or clock out. According to the respondent, there was a notice put on the noticeboard in September 2012 that all staff members clock in and out on a daily basis to include breaks, however the claimants asserted that this was put up after they had left employment. Evidence was given by a former colleague of the respondent that employees never had to clock out for breaks. The EAT noted that the claimants had offered to work for free to finish off the printing, and the EAT considered it extraordinary that this offer was not accepted by the respondent.

The EAT was satisfied that it was custom and practice to go on a break during the washout process and the EAT determined that leaving the premises was not gross misconduct. The EAT concluded that the employees were acting in a completely reasonable and acceptable manner. They went on a legitimate break and it was high-handed to suspend them.

The respondent claimed that the memo about clocking in and out was put in the claimants' pay packets, however the EAT noted that the respondent did not offer any witness evidence from the person who was supposed to have put the notice into the claimants' wage packet. The claimants further denied they ever received such a notice.

The EAT noted the statutory obligation on employers to act reasonably in taking a decision to dismiss an employee on grounds of misconduct. The EAT concluded that the claimants had been unfairly dismissed and awarded the first claimant €75,000, together with his notice, and the second claimant was awarded €33,000, together with his notice.

CONSTRUCTIVE DISMISSAL

Unfair disciplinary process

[27.65] *Smith v RSA Insurance Ireland Ltd*[80]*—Employment Appeals Tribunal— Unfair Dismissals Acts 1977 to 2015—constructive dismissal—public suspension of CEO—where concerns arose in relation to claims reserves*

The claimant alleged that he was constructively dismissed as CEO of the respondent in November 2013 and complained primarily about three matters. Firstly, the public way in which he was suspended from employment by way of an announcement on RTE's six o'clock news; secondly, the content of a draft report sent to the Central Bank, which he alleged was outside the terms of reference of an investigation and constituted a personal character assassination; and thirdly the coupling of a difficulty with motor claims with a large claims reserve issue. It was submitted by the respondent that the claimant was the author of his own demise and resigned his employment to avoid engaging in a proposed investigation in relation to serious concerns the respondent had about the process of setting and the actual setting of large claim reserves. The respondent further alleged that serious concerns went unreported for a prolonged period of time because of the regime of fear, bullying and aggression visited on the claimant's fellow employees by him.

The EAT noted that the burden of proof in a constructive dismissal case is a very high one and lies with the claimant, who must show that his resignation was not voluntary. The EAT stated that the legal test to be applied is the 'and/or test'. Firstly, the EAT must look at the contract of employment and establish whether or not there has been a significant breach going to the root of the contract. The EAT noted the decision is *Western Excavating (ECC) Ltd v Sharp*[81] and held that if the employer is guilty of conduct which is a significant breach going to the root of the contract of employment or which shows the employer no longer intends to be bound by one or more of the essential terms of the contract, then the employee is entitled to treat himself as discharged from any further performance. If the EAT is not satisfied that the breach of contract has been proven it is obliged to consider the reasonableness test, ie whether an employer conducted himself or his affairs so unreasonably that the employee cannot not fairly be expected to put up with it any longer, then the employee is justified in leaving. The EAT noted that, when assessing this test, all of the circumstances of the case must be considered to establish whether or not it was reasonable for the claimant to terminate his contract of employment.

It was asserted by the respondent that, in addition to these tests, the EAT should consider the further test set out by Lord Denning in *British Leyland UK Law v Smith*[82] as to whether it was reasonable for the employer to dismiss the individual. However, the EAT did not agree that the *British Leyland* case could apply to constructive dismissal cases in Ireland. The EAT noted that the onus in relation to constructive dismissal lies with the claimant. The reasonableness of the claimant's decision to resign can only be

---

80. *Smith v RSA Insurance Ireland Ltd* UD1673/2013.
81. *Western Excavating (ECC) Ltd v Sharp* [1978] IRLR 27.
82. *British Leyland UK Law v Smith* [1981] IRLR 91.

judged on the information the claimant had within his knowledge at the material time, ie at his resignation. That can only be assessed by looking at the conduct of the employer and the employee prior to the resignation. Knowledge gained after the resignation, which may or may not justify dismissal at some stage in the future, is not relevant. The EAT noted that information subsequent to the resignation may be relevant in assessing compensation if the claimant succeeded in their claim.

The EAT dealt firstly with the investigation process. The EAT accepted the respondent's submission that the process of executing procedures in relation to the investigation of a disciplinary matter does not have to be perfect. The EAT noted that it was well-established in common law that when assessing the reasonableness test one must consider all of the circumstances of the case.

The EAT noted that the first indication that something was wrong was in August 2013 when the claimant was approached by the CFO and was informed that the motor claims reserves were insufficient and would have to be increased by €17 million. The claimant informed the respondent immediately. In September he was informed by his line management that the group had assessed the data and stated that the figure was more likely to be between €20 million and €40 million and the EAT noted it turned out to be the latter. There was a further deterioration in motor claims reserves in October 2013. Around this time an internal audit into the claims function and into large losses on the claims side was carried out. It was noted by the EAT that the internal auditor had raised a red flag in regards to the large claims reserving process, however the Central Bank had just concluded its report on the matter and deemed it to be satisfactory. The EAT noted that a project (Project White) was established at a board meeting in October 2013 to oversee the investigations into reserving points identified by the group and internal audit. The function was also to introduce a new claims-reserving process and draft terms of records for the committee to follow. The EAT noted that it was most unusual that any new processes would be put in place prior to the internal audit being completed and prior to the Project White committee even starting the reviews.

It was noted that as part of the Project White document, reference was made to the fact that the committee had revoked the licences of the CEO, the CFO and the Head of Claims. This decision was not communicated to the claimant until 30 October 2013, despite him having a meeting to discuss these issues in the UK on 23 October; the purpose of which was to put certain questions to him to ensure that no misrepresentations were made to the Central Bank at the next scheduled meeting. It was confirmed that this meeting was not part of an investigation, it was merely a fact-finding exercise to prepare for a meeting in the Central Bank. The EAT noted that the claimant received the questions beforehand. He was invited to attend a subsequent investigation meeting on 5 November in Dublin, which meeting had the status of a formal investigation meeting. The claimant's solicitor requested on 7 November that serious issues be identified in advance of the meeting and a provisional list of questions and supporting documentation be made available to him so he could prepare. However, the respondent was unwilling to do so and responded that he (the claimant) was not under any suspicion of wrongdoing. The EAT noted that in fact one of the questions asked of the claimant in his initial meeting on 23 October was why he did not reserve the full amounts on certain claims identified and this question in the mind of the EAT suggested two things: firstly certain claims did not receive the correct reserve amount; and secondly the claimant was solely responsible for that. The EAT concluded that this question demonstrates that blame was being apportioned. The EAT was satisfied that the claimant was aware of the serious issue that was being investigated and, if he didn't know before the meeting on 23 October, he certainly did afterwards.

The respondent submitted that the claimant was not entitled to the principles of natural justice at an investigating stage and reference was made to *O'Brien v Aon Insurance Managers (Dublin) Ltd*[83] and also the decision of Noonan J in the *Governor and Company of the Bank of Ireland v Reilly*.[84] The EAT found that the claimant was not entitled to all of the information he had requested on 7 November, but he was, at the very least, entitled to know the precise nature of the matters being investigated and how they pertained to him. The EAT noted that this was not a general and broad investigation being conducted by two UK employees; it was a specific investigation into very specific employee roles in the reserving of claims being conducted by two UK employees, but being overseen by the White committee.

The EAT noted that, by 5 November 2015, the claimant's licence had been revoked and two days later he was requested to remain away from the office. While this was not formally a suspension, it had all the characteristics of one. The EAT concluded that, for these reasons, the claimant was entitled to the basic elements of natural justice, ie knowledge of the precise nature of the matters being investigated and how they pertained to him. The EAT was critical of the fact that the final and complete version of the report was dated 28 November 2013 but the claimant had been invited to a disciplinary meeting on 21 November. The EAT noted that despite extensive evidence of documentation being furnished to the EAT, it was not disclosed what the reserving policy was or even if there was one. The EAT concluded from the evidence that there was an informal process in place for the reserving of claims. The EAT noted that at the conclusion of the letter inviting the claimant to the disciplinary hearing, findings of fact were made that the claimant had brought the company into disrepute, breached his duty of trust and confidence and had breached his contract of employment. The EAT noted that one might expect to see such findings following the conclusion of the disciplinary process, but most definitely not at the beginning of it and especially in circumstances when the final investigation report was not yet completed. The EAT noted that it was clear that another investigation was being carried out in the background and a second letter was sent to the claimant on 21 November requesting the claimant to attend an investigation meeting on 28 November to discuss certain issues. The EAT held it was not clear who sanctioned that investigation or what the terms of reference were, but it would seem that the respondent went on a trawling exercise and these issues were what came up. The EAT noted that some of the issues went back as far as 2007 and queried why these issues only came to light at this time.

The EAT noted that the respondent was the largest insurance company in Ireland, having advanced from the fifth largest to the largest during the claimant's tenure as CEO. The claimant was paid a large salary, with generous bonuses, to reflect the level of

---

83.   *O'Brien v Aon Insurance Managers (Dublin) Ltd* [2005] IEHC 3.

84.   *Governor and Company of the Bank of Ireland v Reilly* [2015] IEHC 241. See **[27.21]**.

responsibility that he had. In 2013 the chief actuary had raised issues with the company's reserves, specifically the large loss claims, the reserving generally and claims savings initiatives that had been booked in the accounts. The claimant had a meeting with the chief actuary in July following which the claimant decided to bring in a consultant actuary to look at the numbers and to advise on a course of action. Subsequently in spring 2013, Ernst and Young were engaged by the board to carry out the review of the adequacy of the claims reserves to include incurred but not reported reserves (IBNR). The EAT noted that the conclusion reached was that the claims reserving was reasonable and satisfactory. The claimant asserted that a process (Gateway 50) was set up in late 2011 to formalise the process of setting reserves. The claimant was not involved. The EAT noted that from the minutes from Gateway 50 it was clear that specific claims were discussed, constituting proof that each of the attendees were on notice of the wholly inadequate figures posted. The EAT noted with surprise that no reserve or quantum opinions from solicitors briefed in the matters were produced. From the evidence it appeared that the setting of reserves was done exclusively in-house. Each Gateway 50 attendee was either a manager or a director, and all were experienced enough to know that the figures posted were inadequate. All of them had bosses with whom they could have discussed the matter. The EAT concluded that these individuals were all very experienced and held high ranking posts, with corresponding high salaries and it was thus nonsense to suggest that the claimant somehow bullied or scared all of these individuals into a state of perpetual silence. The EAT held it was nonsense for the respondent to suggest that nobody other than the individuals in Gateway 50 knew about this issue. The EAT found the suggestion that the reason it was not picked up in numerous audits was because the auditors were not put on notice of it to be incredible. The EAT noted that the primary purpose of an audit was to provide an objective independent examination of the company's financial reports. To suggest that auditors only carry out audits on matters that had been disclosed to them was misguided at best. The EAT noted that the Gateway 50 minutes from November 2011 were the only independent evidence in relation to what was involved in the process. However regardless of which set of minutes was relied upon, it was clear that specific cases were discussed, as well as the liability issue, ongoing inquiries, quantum and estimates. The EAT noted that there were three sets of minutes, each different for the same meeting and further noted that the claimant had no involvement in that. It was noted that minutes were sent to London, which led the EAT to conclude that the process was being monitored at Group level.

The EAT noted that at the end of 2012, the Central Bank had carried out an annual prism review, where various risk categories were analysed. The report commented that the respondent's risk reserve margin was low, 5 per cent compared to a peer average of 11 per cent. The board of the respondent was requested to give a commitment to build the reserves. The EAT held it was clear from this report that the 5 per cent margin policy of the respondent was below peer average and not acceptable in the eyes of the Central Bank. This was a Group policy and outside the control of the CEO in this jurisdiction. The EAT further noted that the Central Bank review had taken place in 2012, however between 2007 and 2011 the Group had used €250 million of the Irish company's reserves to prop up under-performing areas of the Group in other jurisdictions. The EAT raised questions whether the respondent would have required such a large capital injection of which a very small portion was allocated to a large claims reserve. The EAT noted that the Irish business was strengthened by receiving a capital injection of €200 million. The large claims issues got €10 million of that; the motor claims issue got €40 million; professional indemnity got €6 million; altogether a total of €60 million. However €1.4 billion was raised to strengthen the Group capital position; of which €200 million was apportioned to Ireland. The EAT concluded that these figures suggested that the Group had a capital issue which was way in excess of the large claims reserving issue and furthermore had the €250 million of Irish reserves not been utilised by the Group, Ireland would not have required a capital injection.

The EAT then considered the question of objective bias. The respondent's chief risk officer was appointed to the Project White subcommittee which, in the view of the claimant, rendered the process fundamentally flawed. The EAT noted the objections from the claimant and others, but that the respondent failed to take any action. The EAT noted that the chief risk officer was a member of the Gateway 50 committee and he was present at the November 2011 meeting; which resulted in three sets of substantially different minutes being produced. He was questioned in relation to reserving practices; therefore it was wholly inappropriate that he be present on any committee task within the investigation, even in the most minor of issues relating to the reserving large claim. The EAT concluded that the chief risk officer should never have been appointed to the committee in the first place and he should have excused himself or should have been removed from the committee immediately following the claimant's letter. The claimant had submitted that, once the motor claims issue was coupled with the large claims issue and the report sent to the Central Bank, he was finished. Originally the issue was one of non-regulatory compliance in relation to reserving a small number of large claims, however the motor claims arm raised totally separate concerns. The EAT noted that it was clear from the figures produced that there was an issue in that area but it would seem from the evidence that the issue had its origins external to the respondent. The EAT noted that how or why this issue was coupled with the large claims issue remained unknown as it was a separate issue and should have been isolated.

The EAT then considered the decision to temporarily revoke the claimant's licence on 30 October and the subsequent request made of him on 7 November to remain away from the offices; to have no contact with staff or interfere in the outcome of the current investigation. The respondent asserted that this was not a suspension, despite having all the hallmarks of one. The EAT concluded that regardless of what the respondent decided to call their request it was for all intents and purposes a suspension. The claimant then received a letter advising him that as issues had become known with regards to the Irish business which would have a material impact on the operating result of the Group, it had to be announced to the London Stock Exchange. He was being formally suspended pending the outcome of an investigation. The EAT noted the decision in *Bank of Ireland v Reilly*,[85] and the fact that only three employees were suspended, including the claimant. The EAT noted that, in circumstances where the claimant had already had his licence revoked and was out of the office and abiding by the respondent's request not to talk to

---

85.   *Governor and Company of the Bank of Ireland v Reilly* [2015] IEHC 241. See **[27.21]**

staff, it was hard to understand why he was suspended when all of the possible risks were covered. The very public suspension of the claimant and his two colleagues on the RTE six o'clock news was no doubt part of the mitigation process. The EAT concluded that suspending the claimant on national television was the equivalent of taking a sledge hammer to his reputation and to his prospects of ever securing employment in the industry again in Ireland, Europe and possibly beyond and it sealed his fate with the respondent. There was no going back from that point. Even if the investigation had turned up nothing, there was no way in which the respondent could have kept the claimant on in employment. The EAT was satisfied that to suspend the claimant in this very public and damaging way was in fact a dismissal disguised as a suspension. Even if the investigation did subsequently find fault, even serious fault, on the part of the claimant, to destroy his reputation and future employment prospects in such a public way could never be acceptable.

The EAT then considered the complaint that the draft report completed post-investigation containing the 'management style issues' relating to the claimant was furnished to the Central Bank and this was outside the scope of the investigation and was furnished without him having an opportunity to respond. The EAT noted that, in dealing with the issue as to how and why any inappropriate reserving practices occurred, the management style issues that were disclosed did form part of the how and why and this information was proffered voluntarily without prompting. The EAT concluded that, while it was satisfied that the management style information did come under the category of how and why, the evidence that it all came about voluntarily was not credible given that all of these individuals were too scared to blow the whistle. The EAT raised the question why all of these individuals would chose to disclose the information in a setting that provided them with no protection from the law and this left more questions than answers. The EAT concluded that, if the information had been proffered voluntarily and had the veracity of those statements been tested, in those circumstances it would have been entirely proper to include them in the report. The claimant was entitled to be informed that such information had been furnished during the course of the investigation and should have been given an opportunity to defend himself against the allegations prior to them going to the Central Bank. The report should have been sent to him. It was a flaw in the process and without the above-stated additional inquiries being made, it was a serious flaw. The EAT concluded that it was well established and that the process does not have to be perfect, but it does have to be fair and objective. The sending of the report in those circumstances must have damaged the claimant's reputation in the eyes of the Central Bank.

The EAT noted the respondent's contention that the claimant did not utilise the internal grievance procedure in his decision to resign. Reference was made to *Conway v Ulster Bank Ltd*[86] where the EAT had come to the conclusion that it was unreasonable for an employee to resign in circumstances where he had not fully pursued the bank's grievance procedures. The EAT noted that, while it was not bound by its own determinations, it did generally follow them, but each case must be assessed on its own facts.

---

86. *Conway v Ulster Bank Ltd* UD474/81.

The EAT held that it must try and establish whether it was reasonable for the claimant not to engage in the company grievance procedures and/or whether there were circumstances existing, at the time the decision to resign was made, that led him to form the opinion that his grievance would not receive a fair hearing. The EAT noted the relevant facts being: (a) the claimant's concerns in relation to the chief risk officer's involvement in the Project White were ignored; (b) his reasonable request for the details of the serious issue being investigated and how it pertained to him was refused; (c) his request for a list of questions to be furnished was refused; (d) his request to be furnished with documentation was refused; (e) his licence was revoked; (f) he was requested to remain away from the office; (g) he was requested not to communicate with staff; (h) his suspension was announced on national television; (i) the report of the investigation in draft form was sent to the Central Bank; (j) he believed the report contained personal information pertaining to him outside the terms of reference; and (k) the large claims reserve issue had been coupled with the motor claims issue. The EAT concluded that, in these circumstances, the claimant was justified in not engaging the respondent's grievance procedure.

In conclusion the EAT was satisfied that, from an early stage in the investigation, the claimant's fate was determined by the respondent. The respondent then went on a fact-finding exercise to justify its predetermined decision. The EAT expressed the view that the decision was probably made to appease the concerns of third parties, ie the shareholders and the Central Bank. The events leading up to and the manner in which the claimant's suspension was announced on television had catastrophic consequences for the claimant personally; the annihilation of his future employment prospects; the respondent's refusal to inform him of serious issues and how they pertained to him; the sending of the draft report without giving him an opportunity to refute the allegations; the secondary investigation for which there was no board sanction or terms of reference; the commencement of a disciplinary hearing prior to the completion of the investigation; and the involvement of the chief risk officer in the process, were all factors that led the EAT to conclude that the claimant was justified in terminating his employment.

The EAT then considered the remedy to be awarded to the claimant. It accepted that, as CEO, the claimant had responsibilities for the day-to-day running of the Irish business and had obligations not only to the board of management but to shareholders and the regulator. There was no doubt that not only the Irish business but also the Group as a whole ran into capital problems in 2013, but these Group capital problems were extraneous to the Irish CEO's position. However, the potential breach of Central Bank regulations in relation to reserving practice within the Irish business was not.

The EAT concluded that the claimant was aware of the reserving practice, as were at least two dozen other employees, most of whom were in Ireland but some of whom were in the UK Group. The EAT was not satisfied that this practice was allowed to continue for so long due to a fear of the claimant. While the CEO did have responsibility to ensure practices which could attract Central Bank criticism did not develop or continue, this reserving practice was one that was known for a very protracted period of time by too many high-ranking company employees to lay the blame solely at the claimant's door. The EAT concluded that suspending the claimant on national television was the equivalent of taking a sledge hammer to his reputation and his prospects of ever securing employment in this industry again in Ireland, in Europe and possibly beyond. The EAT upheld the claimant's complaint of constructive dismissal and awarded him compensation of €1.25 million. This decision was appealed to the Circuit Court.

Non-payment of wages

[27.66] *Kilkerr v Burke Fabrications Ltd[87]—Employment Appeals Tribunal—Unfair Dismissals Acts 1977 to 2015—Organisation of Working Time Act 1997— constructive dismissal—part payment and late payment of wages*

The claimant claimed he had no choice but to leave his employment as he was not getting paid over a period of three years. The respondent maintained that the claimant was not dismissed; rather he voluntarily left his employment.

The claimant commenced employment with the respondent in October 2009. He had no performance issues over the course of his employment and was a good worker. Problems with his pay began on 26 February 2010 when his pay cheque was returned by the bank. The claimant stated that he had regular discussions with a director of the respondent about not receiving his pay since February 2010. Nothing was done about the issue until September 2012, when the respondent replied to the claimant's numerous letters, promising that he would receive all monies due to him.

The claimant took a case to the Rights Commissioner. He was paid €5,000 on the day of the Rights Commissioner hearing. He subsequently left his employment on account, he stated, to the conduct of his employer.

The respondent told the EAT that the business had experienced difficult years but things were now starting to improve. The respondent stated that the claimant had been paid up to date at the time his employment ended. It was accepted that the claimant's hours varied each week during the difficult periods and that issues with his PRSI and PAYE had arisen during the course of his employment.

The EAT held that when an employee provides labour and services to an employer, it is reasonable for the employee to expect to be paid. It noted that, in the present case, the respondent had made part payment of wages to the claimant over a significant period of time. Furthermore, the respondent had requested that the claimant continue to return to his workplace on the mere promise that wages due and owing would be paid. The EAT considered that the reason the claimant did not return to work was that the mutual trust, which is an essential component of the contract of employment, was frequently breached by the respondent's promise to pay his wages and failure or refusal to do so. The EAT concluded that the claimant had been justified in resigning due to the failure on the part of the respondent to pay his wages.

Accordingly the claim under the Acts succeeded and the EAT awarded the claimant compensation of €14,000. Similarly the appeal under the Organisation of Working Time Act 1997 was allowed and the claimant was awarded €1,212 under that Act.

---

87. *Kilkerr v Burke Fabrications Ltd* UD470/2013, WT70/2013.

[27.67] *Lai v Brophy & Co Chartered Accountants*[88]*—Employment Appeals Tribunal—Unfair Dismissal Acts 1977 to 2015—constructive dismissal—where payment of claimant's salary delayed on ongoing basis which resulted in significant back wages owing to him*[89]

The claimant was employed as a senior accountant and auditor from May 2008 to November 2013. He had no written contract of employment and earned €45,000 per annum. His evidence was that, from March 2012 onwards, there were issues with his pay and his salary was delayed on an ongoing basis. The claimant had a number of meetings and engaged in correspondence with his employer in an effort to resolve these issues, without a satisfactory outcome. By email to the respondent on 6 November 2013, the claimant sought payment of back wages totalling €10,105.91 owing as at October 2013. He received no reply to this request and he resigned on 1 November 2013.

The claimant's evidence was that he had no option but to leave his employment after the continued non-payment of wages due to him. He believed he could make no further efforts to secure his outstanding wages. The respondent submitted that it had suffered financially during the recession; clients had not paid the firm and a decrease in business culminated in a lack of cash flow. It was noted that the claimant did not receive any payments throughout that period. The respondent conceded that there were outstanding wages due to him at the time his employment terminated.

The EAT held that due to the conduct of the respondent in not paying the claimant the wages due to him, it was reasonable for the claimant to terminate his contract of employment and his claim succeeded. He was awarded compensation of €36,000.

[27.68] *Lynch v Donegal Highland Radio Ltd t/a Highland Radio*[90]*—Employment Appeals Tribunal—Unfair Dismissals Acts 1977 to 2015—constructive dismissal— fundamental breach of contract—unilateral reduction of salary—attempt to mitigate loss incorrectly restricted to specific area of specialisation—no award for minimum notice in constructive dismissal case where claimant works out his notice period*

The respondent operated a radio station for the North West region of Ireland since 2008. The radio station had been experiencing financial difficulties before and after the respondent had taken ownership. The claimant was employed as a radio presenter from March 2004. The claimant was initially employed on a part-time basis. In order to earn a sustainable wage, an agreement was also reached that the claimant would be entitled to earn commission on sales to boost his income and that he would have use of the company car, Monday to Friday, to assist with this sales role. The claimant used one of the three company cars from Monday to Friday to perform his sales role. The respondent paid the tax, insurance and fuel bills for the car. The claimant had no written contract of

---

88. *Lai v Brophy & Co Chartered Accountants* UD281/2014, RP115/2014, MN105/2015, WT38/2014.

89. It was noted by the EAT that claims under the Redundancy Payments Acts 1967 to 2014, Organisation of Working Time Act 1997 and the Minimum Notice in Terms of Employment Acts 1973 to 2005 were withdrawn during the course of the hearing.

90. *Lynch v Donegal Highland Radio Ltd t/a Highland Radio* UD1599/2013, MN758/2013.

employment but a list of issues relating to hours of employment and salary were drawn up and accepted by the claimant.

In 2009, a 5 per cent cut in salary was agreed to by all staff members, due to the downturn in business of the respondent. The employees were however subsequently informed that a 10 per cent cut would be required to maintain the business. In 2013, the respondent decided that the claimant's customer list would be reduced from approximately 40 or 50 customers to 15 customers, as the claimant was not bringing in sufficient revenue to the station. The claimant's remuneration was reduced as a result. A new marketing manager was employed by the respondent and he was entitled to use the company car. The claimant stated that his entitlement to use the company car from this point onwards was taken away and that his travel expenses increased as a result.

By April 2013, the claimant's customer list had been completely removed by the respondent. On 24 April 2013, the claimant wrote to the general manager of the radio station with concerns regarding his salary, the removal of his customer list, and the removal of his use of the company car during a difficult period in his personal life and informed the general manager that he was giving one month's notice of resignation. The former general manager informed the EAT that he had forwarded the resignation letter to the directors of the respondent and that he had attempted to persuade the claimant to remain at the radio station. The claimant refused an offer made to him by the respondent. The offer did not include an increase in salary. The claimant suggested an increased salary figure to the respondent. The respondent rejected the claimant's proposal and suggested that his resignation be accepted and another sales employee be hired. The general manager gave evidence that he was disappointed that the claimant had to resign but understood that the claimant would be unable to remain in employment if he was unable to supplement his salary by earning commission. The general manager stated that the claimant's use of the company car had also been taken away from him and that he was subjected to ongoing additional pressure from the marketing manager in relation to his level of sales. The general manager stated that a number of other members of staff had not been subjected to such pressure. The claimant informed the EAT that he felt he had no choice other than to resign from his position. The claimant took two weeks' leave and worked out his notice for a further two weeks. The claimant's employment terminated by way of resignation in May 2013. The claimant gave evidence of loss to the EAT.

The EAT found that the respondent's behaviour justified the claimant's resignation and his claim for constructive dismissal succeeded. The EAT found that there was a fundamental breach of contract in allowing an accumulation of losses which led to the claimant's income being significantly reduced without the consent of the claimant. Interestingly, in relation to mitigation of loss, the EAT noted that the claimant's attempts to find alternative employment were limited to seeking employment in the broadcasting sector only, which was too restrictive an approach in the economic climate at that time. The EAT awarded the claimant the sum of €26,000 as compensation. The claim under the Minimum Notice and Terms of Employment Acts 1973 to 2005 failed as it was a constructive dismissal case and the claimant had worked out his notice period.

Removal of duties and failure to pay commission

[27.69] *O'Connell v Melvyn Hanley Solicitors[91]—Employment Appeals Tribunal— Unfair Dismissals Acts 1977 to 2015—constructive dismissal—removal of duties and failure to pay commission—lack of engagement by employer in respect of employee's issues[92]*

The claimant initially joined the respondent as an apprentice solicitor in 1998. On her qualification in 2001, she was employed as a solicitor. From 2002, the claimant received a 30 per cent commission for any new business she brought into the practice. This commission rate was reduced to 15 per cent as of 2007.

Due to the financial circumstances of the practice, the claimant agreed to a 10 per cent pay cut in March 2009 on the basis that a newly-qualified solicitor would not be retained past the expiry date of his contract. In July 2009, commission payments to the claimant were deferred by agreement until the practice's financial situation improved.

The EAT heard that, contrary to what was agreed with the claimant, the newly-qualified solicitor was retained after his contract expired. Furthermore, the claimant gave evidence that she was receiving less work, despite her requests, and that the newly-qualified solicitor was being assigned new work, including work that the claimant had previously been involved in.

As the respondent's financial position began to improve, the claimant raised the issue of her unpaid commission. In May 2012, the claimant again raised the issue of her unpaid commission and the allocation of work. The claimant gave evidence that the principal of the firm told her that her observations were 'unfounded' and 'unhelpful'. The claimant subsequently set out her concerns in writing to the respondent, and it was agreed to discuss the matter in January 2013.

On 4 January 2013, the claimant met with the principal of the firm, who denied knowledge of the agreed deferral of the commission payments, and advised the claimant that he would provide her with a list of work provided to her over the years.

The claimant again raised her two concerns on 8 March 2013, and stated: 'I would like to express my unhappiness at the implicit threats that have been made on several occasions to the effect that if I don't drop the (above) two concerns, this could jeopardize my future employment with the firm'.

Following a number of meetings, the respondent agreed to discharge the outstanding commission on 30 May 2013; but by October 2013 the commission had not been paid. At a meeting on 17 October 2013, scheduled to discuss the issues, the principal asked for verification of the commission. The EAT heard from the claimant that the principal became very aggressive at this meeting, and when the claimant drew this aggression to his attention, the principal responded that no one else in the office thought so.

Following this incident, the claimant went on sick leave and resigned on 11 November 2013. The respondent asked the claimant to reconsider, but accepted her resignation on 15 November 2013.

---

91. *O'Connell v Melvyn Hanley Solicitors* UD75/2014, MN33/2014.
92. The claimant withdrew her complaint under the Minimum Notice and Terms of Employment Acts 1973 to 2005 at the outset of the hearing.

The EAT held that, given the claimant's long service and continued patience and reasonable attitude, and given the respondent's refusal to address the issues raised, the claimant had been unfairly constructively dismissed. The claimant was awarded €55,000 in compensation.

Changes to terms and conditions of employment

[27.70] *McCarthy v O'Shea, O'Lionaird Partnership t/a Bebé Crèche[93]—Employment Appeals Tribunal—Unfair Dismissals Acts 1977 to 2015—Minimum Notice and Terms of Employment Acts 1973 to 2005—constructive dismissal—unilateral change of terms and conditions—no prior consultation—whether change in terms and conditions of employment amounted to demotion*

The claimant was employed as a Montessori teacher with the respondent from July 2008 until her employment terminated on 30 September 2011. She asserted that the respondent had unilaterally, and with no prior consultation, changed her terms and conditions of employment. These changes affected her pay, her hours and her job description. The changes were so significant that the claimant maintained that she was effectively dismissed from her original position and offered a position as assistant to what she deemed to have been her original position. The claimant explained that she had been supported in the performance of her duties as Montessori teacher by an assistant. She maintained that the respondent now appeared to be switching the roles of the claimant and the assistant, who was to assume the 'leader' role.

The changes in the claimant's terms and conditions appeared to be attributable to new regulations which permitted the respondent to claim grants for children attending the crèche. There were two rates which could potentially be granted to the respondent, either €65 or €75 per child per week, depending on the qualifications and experience of the classroom leader. The claimant argued that, although she did not have the level of qualification required in order for the respondent to be granted the higher rate, she did have the requisite experience. Additionally, she was studying for the higher qualification and would soon qualify for the higher rate. The claimant could not definitively say whether the respondent was aware of this fact, as she had not told them directly. She further maintained that the assistant, although being qualified to the higher level, did not have the requisite experience. The claimant told the EAT that she had since opened her own crèche, a process which began after she believed her employment with the respondent had ended.

The respondent's case was that the changes in terms and conditions of employment offered to the claimant were not such that she was being demoted. It was maintained that the new role offered to the claimant was to be an expansion of her previous role. Although the respondent was still going to follow the Montessori framework, restructuring was required in order to qualify for the higher grant. This was why the respondent named the assistant, who had the higher qualification, as classroom leader. The respondent confirmed that the assistant did not have the requisite experience. The

---

93. *McCarthy v O'Shea, O'Lionaird Parnership t/a Bebé Crèche* UD2050/2011, MN2072/2011

respondent stated that the claimant had not objected to her new contract or sought consultation in relation thereto within a reasonable time frame – she had waited a period of seven weeks after being given the new contract before objecting to it. Further, it was maintained that the claimant had resigned of her own volition, as she had already begun the process of opening her own crèche before deciding to resign from her position with them.

The EAT concluded that the claimant was unfairly dismissed from her employment with the respondent by way of constructive dismissal. It was held that it was reasonable for the claimant to conclude that she had no alternative but to resign, given the circumstances leading up to the termination of her employment. The EAT was satisfied that the change in the claimant's terms and conditions of employment amounted to a demotion and reduction in hours per week/pay. A history of difficulties between the claimant and the respondent in respect of pay and other issues was taken into account and it was held that this may have impacted on the claimant's decision to resign. Notwithstanding that possibility, the respondent's actions in unilaterally and significantly changing the claimant's terms and conditions of employment without prior consultation or agreement were so unreasonable as to make it impossible for the claimant to continue as an employee.

The EAT considered the claimant's loss together with her efforts to mitigate that loss, and awarded the claimant €15,000 under the Unfair Dismissals Acts 1977 to 2015. In respect of the claim under the Minimum Notice and Terms of Employment Acts 1973 to 2005, the EAT held that, as the claimant did not give the respondent notice of her intention to resign, there was no obligation on the respondent to pay her in respect of notice and therefore this claim failed.

Affirmation and acquiescence

[27.71] *Adjei-Frempong v Howard Frank Ltd*[94]*—UK Employment Appeal Tribunal— appeal from decision of employment tribunal—constructive dismissal—unilateral variation to terms and conditions of employment—lack of objection from employee— whether employee 'affirms' variation by continuing to work on amended terms— acquiescence—relevance of period of time between employer's breach and resignation—relevance of any period of sick leave taken before resignation— employee's entitlement to time for reflection*

This was an appeal to the UK employment appeal tribunal (the UK EAT) from a decision of the employment tribunal. The appellant had worked as an accounts assistant with the respondent, a small accountancy practice, since July 2006.

Performance issues arose in December 2013. On 17 January 2014 the respondent wrote to the appellant, setting out various concerns in relation to his performance and informing him that his workload was being reduced to bookkeeping and simpler VAT work. The tribunal estimated that this constituted a reduction in the appellant's work of some 30 per cent. This decision to unilaterally alter the appellant's terms and conditions

---

94.   *Adjei-Frempong v Howard Frank Ltd* UKEAT/0044/15/DM.

was confirmed to the appellant by the respondent at a meeting held on 21 January 2014. Various performance issues were also discussed at this meeting. The appellant continued to work for the 10 working days following the meeting of 21 January 2014. During this time he made no objection to working in a reduced capacity. On 4 February 2014 the respondent raised a further performance issue with the appellant. The appellant did not understand the problem identified by the respondent and refused to accept responsibility for it. He did not show up for work the following day, citing work-related stress. The appellant submitted his resignation on 3 March 2014. He refused the respondent's offer to submit a grievance, as he considered the relationship to be 'beyond repair'. He subsequently brought a claim for constructive dismissal.

The tribunal held that the unilateral changes imposed by the respondent amounted to a fundamental and repudiatory breach of contract. However, it further held that, as the appellant had failed to object to the relevant changes between their introduction and his resignation, he had 'affirmed' his contract of employment and therefore could not be said to have been constructively dismissed. The tribunal placed emphasis on the fact that the appellant had failed to engage with the respondent at the meeting on 21 January 2014 in relation to his performance issues. The tribunal relied on the decision of *Western Excavating (ECC) Ltd v Sharp*,[95] where it was held that the complainant in that case:

> ... must make up his mind soon after the conduct of which he complains; for, if he continues for any length of time without leaving, he will lose his right to treat himself as discharged.

On the basis that the appellant had worked for a number of weeks following the change in his terms and conditions without objection, the employment tribunal concluded that the appellant had 'acquiesced' to the breach and was therefore precluded from relying on it as a reason for his alleged unfair dismissal.

The UK EAT considered that the grounds of appeal fell into two categories. The first question was whether the tribunal had erred in holding that the appellant had not objected to the changes imposed on his terms and conditions. The second question was whether the appellant should be taken to have affirmed his contract in the circumstances.

In its determination of the first question, the UK EAT said it was bound to consider the evidence that had been before the tribunal. Although the appellant's evidence had been that he had objected to the changes at the meeting of 21 January 2014, there was no record of such objection contained in the respondent's notes from the meeting. The UK EAT also commented that the making of such an objection had not been included either in the appellant's Form ET1 or in his witness statement. The UK EAT held that, on the basis of the evidence before it, the tribunal had been entitled to conclude that the appellant had not expressed his objection to the amendments to his contract in advance of his resignation. The first ground of appeal therefore failed.

In relation to the second question, the UK EAT commented that 'context is everything' and that cases of this type were 'fact-sensitive'. They commented that the authorities to which the tribunal had regard in reaching its conclusion did not focus on

---

95.   *Western Excavating (ECC) Ltd v Sharp* [1978] ICR 221 CA.

this issue and it was suggested that the tribunal might have been better assisted by relying on authorities such as *WE Cox Toner International Ltd v Crook*,[96] *Buckland v Bournemouth University Higher Education Corporation*[97] and *Chindove v William Morrisons Supermarket plc*.[98] In considering the appellant's delayed response to the unilateral change to his terms and conditions, the UK EAT noted that the changes had taken effect immediately and that appellant had opted not to lodge a grievance. It was considered by the UK EAT that the changes had been understood by the appellant at the meeting on 21 January 2014, if not before.

The UK EAT noted that its concerns in relation to the conclusion reached by the tribunal were as follows:

- the tribunal had failed to distinguish between the period of time when the appellant was working in accordance with the imposed changes (10 working days post 21 January 2014) and the period when he was out of work on sick leave (from 4 February 2014). The case of *Chindove* was relied upon in support of the contention that a claimant's conduct during a period of sick leave may have far less force in implying an affirmation of a breach of contract than his or her conduct when attending work in full health;

- the tribunal had failed to engage with the appellant's evidence that he had been promised, at the meeting on 21 January 2014, that he would be furnished with a written outcome to the meeting. The appellant had stated, before the tribunal, that he had been biding his time until he received such communication. The failure to provide him with such a communication had not been explained to him and he had had no reason to believe that it would not be forthcoming. The UK EAT could not be satisfied that the tribunal took into account the fact that the appellant was still waiting to hear the respondent's final conclusion after the meeting or 21 January 2014; and

- the tribunal did not appear to have regard to the question of the time for reflection which should be afforded to an employee, as per the decision in *Buckland*. The UK EAT placed emphasis on the fact that the employee had been employed since 2006. He had not been provided with notes of the meeting on 21 January 2014, nor was he furnished with written confirmation of the outcome as he had been promised. He was only at work for 10 days after the meeting, following which time he was off work with work-related stress.

The UK EAT concluded that the tribunal's decision was 'unsafe' and allowed the appeal. The matter was referred to the same tribunal for fresh consideration on the issue of affirmation.

---

96. *WE Cox Toner International Ltd v Crook* [1981] IRLR 443.
97. *Buckland v Bournemouth University Higher Education Corporation* [2010] EWCA Civ 121.
98. *Chindove v William Morrisons Supermarket plc* UKEAT/0201/13/BA.

[27.72] *Hart v St Mary's School (Colchester) Ltd*[99]—*UK Employment Appeal Tribunal—unfair dismissal—constructive dismissal—unilateral variation of contract of employment—changes to working days—repudiatory breach*

This was an appeal to the UK EAT from a decision of the UK employment tribunal in a constructive dismissal case. The appellant was employed as a part-time teacher in the respondent school. Following a timetable change in the school, the appellant was required to work part-time over five days as opposed to three. The appellant maintained that this was a repudiatory breach of her contract of employment and resigned as a consequence. She maintained that she had been constructively dismissed.

The appellant had commenced work with the respondent in July 2001, but a written contract of employment was not put in place until March 2003. Although her initial appointment letter stated that she would work two days per week, in reality she worked three days per week. In 2013 the respondent decided to make a policy change, which involved certain core subjects being taught in the mornings. This necessitated a change in timetabling which had an adverse impact on the appellant's working hours. The respondent began a period of consultation with the appellant, inviting her to spread her hours over five days as opposed to the three to which she had become accustomed. The appellant expressed her dissatisfaction to the change and refused to consent to it. The appellant explained to the respondent that she had caring duties to her husband, elderly mother and grandchildren, which meant that she could not work on Fridays. Notwithstanding the fact that agreement was not reached in this regard, the appellant was informed that the change in her hours was to take effect from 1 September 2013. The appellant resigned on 3 September 2013 and brought a claim for constructive dismissal.

The tribunal concluded that the appellant's contract of employment conferred a unilateral power of variation on the respondent. Accordingly, the tribunal held that the appellant had not been constructively dismissed.

In making its case before the UK EAT the respondent relied on two clauses. The first of these was cl 1.4, which provided as follows:

> In the case of the Teacher on a part-time contract the fractional part will be notified separately and may be subject to variation depending upon the requirements of the School Timetable.

The second clause of the contract upon which the respondent sought to rely was cl 2.1, which provided as follows:

> During school term time, except as may otherwise be provided for under Clause 1.4 above, the Teacher shall work all School hours while the School is in session and at any other time … as may be necessary in the reasonable opinion of the Principal for the proper performance of his/her duties.

The tribunal, in holding in favour of the respondent, had placed emphasis on the fact that the respondent had consulted with the appellant in good time, it had provided her with a business document explaining the proposed changes and it had afforded her time

---

99.   *Hart v St Mary's School (Colchester) Ltd,* UKEAT/0305/14/DM.

to put forward proposals in relation thereto. The tribunal also stated that there was no custom and practice in place in the respondent organisation which would have allowed the appellant to work three days per week and that, in fact, the appellant had erred in her interpretation of her own contract. Accordingly, the tribunal held that there had been no breach of a fundamental term of the appellant's contract of employment. It followed that the appellant had not resigned in response to any such repudiatory breach. The appellant appealed this decision to the UK EAT.

On the construction point, it was submitted by the respondent that one should read cls 1.4 and 2.1 of the appellant's contract together, to the effect that the appellant's working days were not contractually fixed.

The UK EAT considered the specific wording contained in the appellant's contract of employment. It was noted that the 'fractional part' referred to in cl 1.4 of the contract was the amount of part-time work provided for by the contract. The UK EAT noted that in these circumstances what had been notified was originally two days, followed by two and half days, and finally three days. The UK EAT then considered the second part of cl 1.4, ie the part that stated that part-time hours 'may be subject to variation depending upon the requirements of the School Timetable'. The UK EAT held that this was merely permissive and that it failed to inform the reader of the circumstances in which the variation may take effect. It was noted that the wording might incline one to think that the variation was more likely to take place at the behest of the respondent. However, the UK EAT did not regard that wording as reaching a standard of being completely unilateral. It was considered possible that the variation could be at the request of the appellant. The respondent may refuse a teacher's request for a variation and vice versa. Furthermore, it was clear that both variations would be subject to the requirements of the school timetable. Even though the reference to the requirements of the school timetable was suggestive, in the UK EAT's opinion, it did not amount to the power to vary unilaterally. The UK EAT concluded that the tribunal had erred in its finding that the wording of the contract was sufficiently clear and straightforward as to confer on the respondent the right of unilateral variation.

Next the UK EAT considered the reason for the appellant's resignation. In doing so, it considered *Wright v North Ayrshire Council*[100] and stated that the correct approach was to ask whether the repudiatory breach played a part in the resignation. The UK EAT quoted the following passage from the judgment in *Wright*:

> Where there is more than one reason why an employee leaves a job, the correct approach is to examine whether any of them is a response to the breach, not to see which amongst them is the effective cause.

The UK EAT concluded that, if the fundamental breach or repudiatory breach was part of the cause of the resignation, then that would suffice to ground the appellant's claim for constructive dismissal, as the law did not require sole causation or predominant effect. The UK EAT concluded that on reading the appellant's letter of resignation, it was at least arguable that the variation was part of the reason for her resignation. The UK EAT held that the appellant's contract contained no power to vary unilaterally.

---

100. *Wright v North Ayrshire Council* [2014] IRLR 544.

Furthermore, it held that the insistence on the part of the respondent that it was entitled to introduce these changes and to require the appellant to work over five days as opposed to three was a breach of her contract of employment. Accordingly the UK EAT overturned the finding of the tribunal and remitted the matter for a rehearing before the tribunal.

[27.73] *Smith v Campbell Wallcoverings Ltd t/a House of Tiles[101]—Employment Appeals Tribunal—Unfair Dismissals Acts 1977 to 2015—constructive dismissal on suspicion claimant was involved in competitive business—unilateral change of terms and change of place of work—failure to investigate complaint of bullying and harassment*

The claimant commenced employment as a store manager with the respondent in January 2005 at the respondent's Sandyford branch. The respondent's head office was in Ballyfermot and the claimant reported to a director, CC. A redundancy process began in March 2013, as a result of a downturn in sales. At that time, the claimant was offered a job by another employer at a more convenient location. He approached PC, the managing director, asking to be considered for any further redundancies but was turned down. It was agreed, however, that he would reconsider in September 2013.

In July 2013, the claimant was preparing lodgements and, on route to the bank, he called to his brother-in-law's (JH) premises; JH was a former employee of the respondent. DC, a director of the respondent company, had parked close by and watched his movements. The claimant was later asked to meet PC at the head office of the respondent; DC was also present.

The claimant was questioned about the other premises and whether JH was opening a business in competition with them. The claimant was of the opinion that it was not his place to inform the respondent of whether JH was opening a tile store. Heated words were exchanged and the claimant felt threatened. He was informed that if JH was opening a tile store, there was a conflict of interest with the claimant working at the Sandyford store. He was instructed to take the remainder of the day off and to report to the Ballyfermot branch the following Monday. He later requested the instruction in writing. The claimant submitted that he had no handbook to refer to in order to lodge a grievance and he had attended his doctor due to the stress and anxiety and submitted a medical certificate to his employer. He returned to work at the Sandyford branch on 12 July 2013 and met CC and PC. He was again instructed to go to the Ballyfermot branch but refused. He was prevented from entering the premises in Sandyford so he left and returned to his doctor and continued to submit medical certificates. The respondent attempted to arrange meetings, however as the claimant was on certified sick leave at the time he felt unable to attend. He tendered his resignation on 19 August 2013.

The claimant denied having any knowledge of JH opening a tile store before July 2013. He denied having any involvement with the establishment of the other business and denied putting up any signage relating to the new store. He claimed his first

---

101. *Smith v Campbell Wallcoverings Ltd t/a House of Tiles* UD1520/2013.

involvement was on 21 October 2013 when JH employed him. At no time was he informed that the relocation to Ballyfermot was a temporary measure.

JH gave evidence of being employed with the respondent up to his redundancy in April 2013. He gained employment soon after and was approached by his new employer to set up a tile business. A number of locations were considered and, in mid-May 2013, a decision was made. JH believed that he informed the claimant in and around 3 July 2013 of his intention to open the store. The claimant had no involvement in the business and did not assist with the setting up of the business. On 21 October he employed the claimant in a general sales role.

DC described having regular day-to-day contact with the claimant and having had a good working relationship. On 5 July 2013, he was at the Sandyford store collecting lodgements. The claimant appeared uncomfortable in his presence and anxious to get him out of the store. DC observed a builder in the store at the time and, when leaving, noticed JH at the other business unit. He continued to observe the claimant, the builder and JH at the new business unit for approximately 30–40 minutes. He reported what he saw to PC and the claimant was requested to meet PC later; DC was also present. The meeting was tense with no shouting and he described the claimant's demeanour as disrespectful. At no time was the claimant told his employment was being terminated he was asked only to report to the Ballyfermot store in order to investigate what was happening. At the time DC had heard rumours from sales representatives that JH was opening a store in competition with their business.

The managing director, PC, explained how business declined leading to redundancies in 2013. The respondent operated seven stores, all of which were performing badly. He had also heard rumours that JH, a former employee, was opening a tile store in the area. DC contacted him on 5 July and explained that he saw the claimant, a builder, and JH at a premises near his in Sandyford. He asked the claimant at a meeting that day what was going on and was told that it was not his business. He took the decision to move the claimant to the Ballyfermot store to investigate if there was a conflict with the claimant working next to his brother-in-law, who was in direct competition with their business. The next contact with the claimant was on 12 July following a period of certified sick leave by the claimant. He prevented the claimant from entering the Sandyford branch and instructed him to report to the Ballyfermot branch. The claimant said he was taking this action as a dismissal. PC denied using threatening abusive language. PC said he was highly suspicious that the claimant was involved in the new business. As well as his suspicion that the claimant was involved in the new business he was concerned that the claimant spent up to 40 minutes in the new store on 5 July while being paid by him.

During the course of the hearing, the respondent accepted that there had been a failure on their part to follow fair procedures or provide an employee handbook to the claimant. Furthermore, it was clear from the evidence that the claimant's allegation that he was bullied and harassed by members of the respondent company had not been investigated and the EAT determined that this, of itself, constituted a serious breach of fair procedures.

The EAT was satisfied that, the respondent unilaterally changed the terms of the claimant's employment when it insisted that he work at the Ballyfermot store, even if only for a temporary period. This is something they were not entitled to do. The contract was quite clear about where the claimant's place of work should be, and that was at the Sandyford store.

The EAT then considered whether the respondent's behaviour in moving/altering the place of work of the claimant was reasonable in the circumstances. The EAT acknowledged that the respondent's concerns over the claimant's involvement with his brother-in-law's new business were reasonable; however the decision to move the claimant to an entirely different store, in breach of his contract of employment was unreasonable.

The EAT was satisfied that the claimant was unfairly dismissed within the meaning of the Acts and awarded him compensation of €5,000 (taking into account the claimant's conduct prior to his resignation).

[27.74] *O'Grady v Kellysdan Ltd t/a McDonalds[102]—Employment Appeals Tribunal— Unfair Dismissals Acts 1977 to 2015—constructive dismissal—request for full-time work declined due to respondent's business requirements—whether request handled reasonably—claimant offered additional hours in another outlet—history of respondent accommodating claimant with respect of changes in working hours*

The claimant contended that she was constructively dismissed from her employment as a junior manager with the respondent fast food franchised restaurant. She explained to the EAT that while she initially worked part time in the restaurant, she progressed to full-time work as a trainee manager after she finished her college course and was eventually promoted to the role of area manager.

After a period of absence due to maternity leave, the claimant requested to work part time. This request was facilitated by the respondent. The claimant stated that she was 'grateful to them that they let me'. She believed that it would not be a problem to return to full-time work if she wanted to. The claimant subsequently decided that she would like to revert to a full-time position. She made enquiries to the store manager in December 2011 but the matter 'dragged on'. The human resources manager advised her to put the request in writing. Accordingly, the claimant sent the respondent a letter dated 17 April 2012. By way of response, dated 27 April 2012, she was informed that due to current business requirements the respondent was not in a position to grant her request. However, the claimant was promised that the situation would be reviewed six months later. She gave evidence that this outcome had disappointed her. She wrote a letter to the franchise head office in order to express her dissatisfaction.

It was the respondent's evidence that the claimant had been offered an extra shift in another outlet of the franchise. She had, however, declined the offer, stating that she was 'happy' with the current situation. The claimant told the EAT that the additional shift had only involved one additional hour of work and that it did not suit her because she would have had to pay for parking. The respondent disagreed, maintaining that the claimant had been offered five extra hours of work.

---

102. *O'Grady v Kellysdan Ltd t/a McDonalds* UD338/2013.

The claimant tendered her resignation on 30 October 2012. She told the EAT that she came to this decision because she had been in the company for eight and a half years and her request to revert to full-time hours had been declined. She further stated that three people had been promoted to her previous position while she had been looking for a full-time position elsewhere. In response to this point, the respondent stated that the new staff had been engaged in roles more junior to that of the claimant.

An informal meeting was held with the claimant in November 2012, after her resignation. The claimant told the general manager of the respondent that she had managed to find a full-time position elsewhere. The general manager wished her well in her new position. The claimant then pulled out a list of prepared questions that she posed to the general manager surrounding data protection issues and a request for CCTV footage of a previous meeting.

The EAT considered the history of changes in the claimant's working hours before her employment with the respondent terminated. The claimant had originally requested to be placed on part-time hours and the respondent had accommodated her. Sometime later she requested to be placed on full-time hours or to be given more hours, and again, the respondent tried to accommodate her. Subsequently she requested to revert to part-time hours and again she was facilitated. Finally she stated that she wanted to work full-time again. The EAT noted that the respondent offered the claimant more hours in another outlet nearby but that the claimant had decided that that didn't suit her for various reasons. The EAT held that when the claimant requested in writing to change her hours, the respondent had replied in a timely manner, stating reasonably that they could not accommodate her at the time, explaining why this was the case and promising to review the situation in future. The EAT considered this to be an act of a reasonable employer. The EAT further accepted the respondent's evidence that the claimant did not want to work more than a certain amount of hours because of the detrimental effect it would have to her welfare entitlements. It was concluded that the claimant had not discharged the onus of proof that she was treated in such a way that was to be construed as an unfair dismissal. Accordingly the claim failed.

Performance management

[27.75] *Young v Bioshell Teoranta[103]—Employment Appeals Tribunal—Unfair Dismissals Acts 1977 to 2015—constructive dismissal—claimant's poor relationship with managing director of respondent—verbal abuse on part of respondent—whether claimant had fallen below standard required by quality management system— demotion of claimant— whether claimant had no alternative other than to resign— whether fair procedures were employed in disciplinary procedure*

This was a claim for constructive dismissal. The claimant had worked for the respondent since 2006. The respondent is a pharmaceutical company that manufactures food supplements, vitamin tablets, mineral tablets and sports nutrition products. The claimant

---

103. *Young v Bioshell Teoranta* UD988/2012.

had been working as a quality assistant manager (QM) from 2008 to 2010 while studying for a masters degree.

The claimant claimed that the respondent had maintained that the claimant had failed the ISO, which is the quality management system. The claimant explained that his relationship with the managing director of the respondent (RE) had deteriorated during 2011 due to the fact that RE had shouted at him and verbally abused him. This was the first time the claimant had experienced this behaviour from RE and he could give the EAT no explanation for it. He told the EAT that he tolerated the abuse because he had a family and he wanted to finish his masters. The claimant explained that the situation had deteriorated when he returned from holidays in August 2011. He had been told that there would be a 7 am start to the working day because the respondent had received notification of an upcoming audit on 10 August. The claimant maintained that from approximately 7 am until 10.30 am on this day, RE shouted at him constantly and called him incompetent. At 3 pm on the same day the claimant was informed that an investigation meeting was to take place.

The claimant remembered that, at some point, he had been told that he had not upheld the ISO standard. He had been asked to admit that he was incompetent. After the investigation meeting he was told that he had breached the respondent's trust, informed that he was suspended and asked to leave the premises. He was told that he would be afforded the opportunity to respond further over the next couple of days. He stated that he felt 'shell shocked' when he arrived home. Subsequently, the claimant received a letter scheduling a further disciplinary hearing. The letter outlined four allegations against the claimant. The claimant attended the meeting on 24 August, accompanied by his sister in law, who took notes. He re-iterated at this meeting that he had consistently disputed the four allegations against him and the accusation that he did not uphold the ISO standards. The claimant stated that RE kept interrupting him and said was verbally abusive. The claimant and his legal representative rejected the minutes of the meeting they received from the respondent, on the basis that numerous comments made by the claimant had been omitted.

By way of letter dated 27 September 2011, the claimant was informed of his demotion from QA manager to QA operative and a resulting pay reduction. He was afforded leave to appeal the decision. Although the claimant returned to work, he refused to accept the demotion. The claimant alleged he was subjected to further verbal abuse from RE. The claimant left the respondent's premises, only to return for his appeal meeting. The appeal was heard by the director/co-owner of the respondent (JR) and lasted a maximum of 15 minutes. The claimant told the EAT that he had spoken to JR on numerous previous occasions in relation to his grievances and requested meetings with him in relation to same. JR had been wholly unsympathetic and basically told him to get on with it. The claimant received an appeal outcome letter dated 21 November, which upheld the decision to demote the claimant and stated that he was not suitable for the role of quality assurance manager. the claimant stated that his poor relationship with RE had created a toxic work environment. He said that he felt the respondent had a responsibility to him to treat him with dignity and respect.

The claimant told the EAT, by way of clarification, that he was familiar with the company handbook. When asked, he stated that there was nothing else he could have done in relation to the grievance and disciplinary procedures available.

RE explained to the EAT that the role of quality manager (ie, the role to which the claimant had been promoted) involves ultimate responsibility for product quality, general upholding of standards and ensuring that the respondent was compliant with regulations. He explained that the ISO standard was the primary responsibility of the claimant and was of crucial importance to the respondent. The respondent was regularly audited to ensure compliance with this standard. Following audits in 2009 and 2010, the respondent's licence had been suspended. RE stated that he had been shocked to receive these notifications, as the implications of same were enormous. The appropriate response to such a notification was for the quality manager to complete action reports, outlining what the failures had been and how they could be fixed. RE explained to the EAT that, during 2010, the respondent had been busy and resources had been stretched. Accordingly, three people were recruited in January 2011 and there were no further requests for staff. Notification of the next audit, which was due in July/August 2011, was received while the claimant was on holidays. When the claimant returned, RE asked him what had been done about the action reports. The claimant told him nothing had been done in this regard and RE expressed his disbelief. RE told the EAT that this was the reason why the disciplinary meeting of 24 August took place. RE agreed that he had not been happy with the claimant's performance but stated that he did not think that he called him claimant 'incompetent'. He denied that he had bullied or harassed the claimant. He explained that he made the decision to demote the claimant because, while he no longer wanted him to work at management level, he wanted to retain him for his expertise.

JR told the EAT that during the appeal hearing he got the impression that the claimant did not want to be there. The claimant did not engage when asked if he had anything new to add. He repeatedly asked to be re-instated. As no new information had been brought to light, JR felt obliged to uphold the original decision to demote. JR added that he had full confidence in RE. He pointed out that the claimant had not used the grievance procedure, nor had he submitted a complaint in writing to the respondent.

The EAT held in favour of the claimant. It was noted that, in order to prove constructive dismissal, the claimant must clearly show that there was no other alternative option open to him, other than leave his employment. It must be demonstrated that all reasonable alternatives had been considered. While the claimant did not adhere to the formalities of the respondent's written policy, the EAT considered it significant that no action had been taken by the respondent on foot of the claimant's complaint to one of the joint owners of the respondent about verbal abuse, amounting to bullying. The original decision to demote the claimant had not been justified. Furthermore, the EAT concluded that fair procedures had not been followed in coming to this decision, nor were they adhered to during the appeal. In light of all the circumstances, the EAT concluded that the claimant demonstrated that he had had no alternative but to leave his employment and was constructively dismissed.

Accordingly, the EAT held that the claimant was dismissed, his dismissal was unfair and that compensation was the appropriate remedy. The EAT awarded compensation of €17,500 in respect of his claim.

[27.76] *Rock v Irish Custom Extruders Ltd*[104]*—Employment Appeals Tribunal— Unfair Dismissals Acts 1977 to 2015—constructive dismissal—poor performance led to multiple warnings—where reasonable alternative role offered*

The claimant worked for the respondent for 13 years. She was given an office promotion following positive reviews of her work on the factory floor. However, it later came to the attention of the managing director that the claimant was prone to making mistakes. The frequency of errors and omissions in her work was a cause of concern for the managing director who feared that these errors could be damaging to other jobs in the respondent's workforce. The respondent began to issue the claimant warnings. After a final written warning had been delivered, the claimant's office job was ended. It was decided that the claimant could go back to her position on the factory floor and that she would not suffer any loss in salary. The claimant found this offer unacceptable and her employment with the respondent ceased.

The claimant argued that her workload had become too heavy for just one person. This was despite the evidence of other employees to the contrary. The claimant also denied being offered any assistance from her supervisor or any other person in the office. She rejected the suggestion that she should have asked for more training, saying that she had not needed it and again stated that her workload was simply too heavy.

Following the termination of her employment and her refusal to engage with the respondent after the fact, and despite attempts by the respondent to re-engage her in her old position with no decrease in salary, the claimant began attending a college course. The claimant denied that her unfair dismissal claim was opportunistic; instead she submitted that she had to go to college in order to optimise her chances of obtaining alternative employment. The claimant submitted that she had asthma, a condition the respondent must have known about as she had three inhalers. She claimed the respondent knew this condition prevented her from being able to take up her previous role on the factory floor.

The EAT found that there was no unfair dismissal in this case. There were clearly performance issues that, despite many attempts, could not be addressed. The EAT found that the respondent would have been within its rights to dismiss the claimant on competency grounds but instead, offered her a reasonable alternative to re-engage in her previous position. The EAT held that the claim must fail.

---

104. *Rock v Irish Custom Extruders Ltd* UD614/2013.

[27.77] *Ojha v Harry Corry Ltd[105]—Employment Appeals Tribunal—Unfair Dismissals Acts 1977 to 2015—constructive dismissal—reasonable letters of warning regarding poor performance—demotion—obligation on claimant when exercising right of appeal—contractual requirement to relocate within respondent's organisation—failure to comply with reasonable requests of employee—claimant resigned unreasonably in response to reasonable request to relocate*

The claimant commenced employment with the respondent in November 2009. He had worked in the retail sector for a number of years prior to his time with the respondent and was well qualified for the position. The claimant commenced employment as store manager and was placed in the respondent's retail unit in the Nutgrove Shopping Centre, one of 22 similar stores owned by the respondent. The claimant was expected to manage eight employees and was responsible for the day-to-day functioning of that store.

In the middle of 2011, the respondent conducted an examination of the performance of the Nutgrove store. The respondent noted that the economic climate was having a negative effect on the respondent's turnover and there was a requirement to prevent the decrease in sales across the board in the respondent's stores. A witness for the respondent informed the EAT that she had become concerned about the claimant's management style and performance having observed his conduct at an interactive training session and at an interview process that she and the claimant conducted in June 2011. The examination of the Nutgrove store linked the poor performance of the store to the management style of the claimant. The claimant was advised, in writing on 15 August 2011 and 16 August 2011, of his under-performance and noted that an improvement in his performance was required. The EAT found that these letters were acceptable in terms of both their tone and direction. The EAT stated that the reference in the letter to the respondent's disciplinary process might have appeared to be overbearing, but, it was noted that the claimant was never referred to a disciplinary process but was merely advised that it was a potential consequence. The EAT did note, however, that the claimant's employment history demonstrated a hardworking and enthusiastic employee. It was noted that sales and commission rates had improved in the Nutgrove store for a three-week period in December 2011 and that the respondent had credited the claimant for this improvement, which came in the aftermath of the examination of the Nutgrove store.

In February 2012, the Nutgrove office was audited and the claimant was subjected to an investigative and disciplinary process, stemming from his time keeping, unauthorised absences and his failure to deposit daily monetary takings. A list of issues was provided to the claimant and the investigation resulted in a disciplinary hearing before the HR manager on 17 February 2012. By letter dated 23 February 2012, the HR manager informed the claimant that he was found to have fraudulently misrepresented his hours on his time sheets and had failed to inform the finance department of lapses and irregularities in making money lodgements. While this conduct constituted gross misconduct, the HR manager chose not to dismiss the claimant but opted to demote him to the role of supervisor. The respondent had proposed to arrange for an occupational

---

105. *Ojha v Harry Corry Ltd* UD848/2013.

psychologist to assist the claimant with his transition into his new position. The EAT noted that the claimant was clearly notified of his right to appeal the findings of the decision. The claimant noted that he had faxed an appeal of the decision to demote him to the respondent. The respondent submitted that notice of the appeal was never received. The EAT found that the obligation to ensure that the appeal reached the respondent lay solely with the claimant and that the claimant should have been alerted to the fact that the respondent had not received the notice of appeal long before he claims he did. It was agreed that the HR department had contacted and informed the claimant with regard to the time frame for making such an appeal. The EAT found that the respondent was not unreasonable in assuming that the claimant had accepted his demotion given that the claimant continued to work in the new position for the following three or four months and where no notice of appeal had been received. On 6 June 2012, the claimant's solicitors wrote to the respondent advising that the claimant 'seeks to appeal every aspect of the disciplinary procedure'. The respondent replied noting that the time period for an appeal had passed, and that both the respondent and the claimant had moved on. No further action was taken. Six months later, the claimant was requested to work at the respondent's store in Blanchardstown for the run up to Christmas, as the Blanchardstown store was one of the busiest in Ireland. The claimant resisted the initial temporary and subsequent permanent re-location to the Blanchardstown premises. He objected to the journey time and the additional expense. The respondent sought to understand the claimant's difficulties and to alleviate same; however, the decision to move the claimant had become irreversible. The EAT noted that the claimant's contract of employment expected him to be flexible in terms of his work location and that the request for the claimant to work at a new location was not unreasonable or onerous.

At the start of 2013, the claimant became increasingly stressed by the interaction between him and management. The claimant did not avail of any mediation or grievance procedure despite being invited to do so. On 13 March 2013, the claimant sent a letter of resignation to the HR department of the respondent. The letter of resignation stated that the claimant had resigned as a result of being 'a victim of racism and harassment within the company'. The EAT accepted that the letter was written in frustration and that there was existed no basis for the accusations of racism and harassment. The EAT found that the reason for the letter of resignation was the alleged unreasonableness of the relocation of the claimant to the Blanchardstown store. The EAT noted that the previous intervention of the respondent, with regard to the claimant's poor performance and the subsequent disciplinary sanctions imposed by the respondent, had no substantial impact on the claimant's decision to resign other than to support a general sense of discontent that the claimant may have felt. The EAT found that the claim failed as the claimant had acted unreasonably by resigning in response to a reasonable request by the respondent and a contractual requirement to relocate the claimant from one store to another.

Failure to deal with complaints

[27.78] *Ogbulafor v Laois County Childcare Committee Ltd*[106]—*Employment Appeals Tribunal—Unfair Dismissals Acts 1977 to 2015—constructive dismissal—resignation of claimant in circumstances where employer on notice of bullying complaint*

A grievance was raised by the claimant in early April 2013 which was put in writing by her by the end of that month. She clearly communicated her further distress in June 2013, however no meaningful action was taken by the respondent employer. The claimant then went on annual leave in July 2013. The claimant resigned and claimed constructive dismissal.

It was noted by the EAT in its determination that the claimant's evidence, that she was bullied in the workplace, was not disputed or contested by the respondent. The EAT noted that the obligation on an employer is to act expeditiously where an allegation of bullying is made. The EAT focused on the period from April 2013 to July 2013 and noted that the respondent had suggested that this was a relatively short time period. However this was not accepted by the EAT which held that such a generalisation was not appropriate in the context of bullying. The EAT framed the question as being: what effect does the passage of such a period of time, without meaningful action on the part of an employer, have on the reasonable employee in such circumstances? The EAT expressed its particular concern that the claimant's clear cry for help in her email of 11 June 2013 did not seem to have solicited any meaningful action on the part of her employer.

The EAT held that the respondent had failed the claimant and noted there was no investigation of her allegations and that the respondent's attention was diverted by the threat of legal action by the party against whom the allegations had been made. This had, in turn, resulted in a failure to act on the claimant's allegations. In the EAT's view the initiation of mediation came too late and was not a substitute for a proper and speedy investigation of the complaints. The Tribunal further noted that the proposed mediator was quickly able to establish that mediation was not an appropriate response in the circumstances.

The EAT held that the respondent had failed in its fundamental duty to the claimant and that the claimant could not have been expected to have faith and trust in the relationship going forward. By a majority view, the EAT held that it was reasonable of the claimant to have resigned her position and to consider herself constructively dismissed. She was awarded compensation of €9,500 which reflected the EAT's view that the claimant might have done more to mitigate her loss.

---

106. *Ogbulafor v Laois County Childcare Committee Ltd* UD1479/2013.

[27.79] *Byrne v Horwath Bastow Charleston Wealth Management Ltd*[107]— *Employment Appeals Tribunal—Unfair Dismissals Acts 1977 to 2015—constructive dismissal—complaints were made by claimant about her manager—attempts were made to address and resolve matter within the team where no formal complaints or grievances initiated by claimant—onus of proof on claimant in constructive dismissal case*

The claimant was employed as a financial planning consultant by the respondent. She submitted that she began to have difficulties with a colleague because of the colleague's conduct and approach to more junior staff members. The claimant's position was that when she asked her colleague to cease her behaviour, the individual acted aggressively and thereafter relations were soured. In May 2012, the colleague was promoted to an associate director and therefore acquired more authority and seniority than the claimant. The claimant was required to report to this manager as well as the managing director. It was the claimant's evidence that the manager's negativity towards her intensified during this period and a specific example was given about an incident where she felt bullied, irritated and harassed by her manager outside of working hours.

The claimant submitted a complaint about her manager's treatment of her and, at a subsequent meeting with Human Resources, the claimant detailed her grievances against her manager. Following another meeting, Human Resources issued a memorandum pertaining to the relationship between the parties. The claimant's evidence was that, despite this she continued to have to report to her manager and felt it was thus pointless to make further complaints. The claimant then continued for the next 12 months, but any efforts to resolve issues with the manager were rebuffed. She did however accept that the manager could be supportive towards her at times and that they had socialised together from time to time. The claimant's evidence was that the manager's conduct towards her continued to cause her difficulty and she began to seek alternative employment. She ultimately resigned from the respondent. In the course of the evidence before the EAT, the claimant conceded that she was aware of the company handbook, which included sections on bullying and grievances, but had lost confidence in utilising these procedures.

A number of witnesses gave evidence on behalf of respondent, all of whom reported that the working relationship between the claimant and her manager was strong and good. It was conceded however that when the claimant's manager was promoted to having managerial control over her, it did negatively impact on the relationship between them. It was noted that there had been an issue in August 2012, where these two colleagues verbally clashed over a work issue following which the manager texted the claimant in an inappropriate way. A subsequent meeting took place with the manager and the claimant and the manager accepted the behaviour was inappropriate and apologised. As a consequence of this, clearer organisational structure was adopted in the office and it was agreed that the claimant was to report both to the manager and the managing director. In evidence, the manager was adamant that she was in no way hostile but, on the contrary, the claimant was aggressive towards her. The manager denied that

---

107. *Byrne v Horwath Bastow Charleston Wealth Management Ltd* UD67/2014.

she had ever bullied, belittled or in any way humiliated the claimant and, aside from the one issue, there was no suggestion that the claimant had any ongoing complaints or grievances against her.

When the claimant gave notice of her intention to resign, one of the respondent directors met with her to discuss the situation and, while the respondent was reluctant to lose her, they were unable to give her the job guarantees sought by her. The respondent's evidence was that the respondent did have an anti-bullying and grievance procedure in place which was available to all staff and furthermore the claimant had never evoked the formal grievance procedure as her complaint was dealt with and concluded using the informal process.

The EAT noted that in a constructive dismissal case, the onus is on the claimant to show that his/her conditions and treatment in the workplace by the respondent are so intolerable that he/she has no other reasonable option but to involuntarily resign. In this case, the EAT found that the onus had not been discharged by the claimant. Before resigning, it was important that the claimant had exhausted all other avenues, in particular any existing procedures, which she had not done. The EAT noted that the burden of proof in such case was onerous, in that the claimant must prove not only that the respondent's behaviour was unreasonable, but that her decision to resign in response was reasonable. At all times, the behaviour of the respondent was reasonable and the EAT noted it had made reasonable and genuine attempts to resolve and defuse the situation. The EAT further found that the version of events in relation to circumstances outlined by the respondent was more credible. While the EAT noted that the claimant may well have had a grievance to a limited extent, it was not sufficient to justify her claim of constructive dismissal; thus the claim could not be upheld.

Unworkable employment relationship

[27.80] *Obst v Bodyblast Fitness Ltd t/a Women's Fitness Plus*[108]*—Employment Appeals Tribunal—Unfair Dismissals Acts 1977 to 2015—constructive dismissal— where claimant began to work with competitor without approval and became unavailable to fulfil her duties for respondent—unworkable employment relationship*

The claimant was employed as a fitness instructor in the respondent's gym which ran various fitness classes and programmes for clients. The claimant did have other jobs working as a fitness instructor at other facilities in the Cork area, which was known to the respondent. She taught a range of classes to include pilates, zumba and personal training. Her part-time role with the respondent allowed her to continue these classes which were only during the academic year in the College of Commerce in Cork. The evidence was that she worked between 24 and 28 hours per week with the respondent. In the course of her employment she was presented with a contract of employment which she did not sign as it made reference to exclusivity of services which was never part of her original conditions of employment.

---

108. *Obst v Bodyblast Fitness Ltd t/a Women's Fitness Plus* UD196/2013.

Issues arose in October 2012 when it was submitted by the respondent that the claimant began to miss scheduled classes and cancel her classes at short notice. The claimant had taken up an instructor role at a competitor without approval from the respondent. The claimant's evidence was that her hours began to reduce in September 2012 and that rostering changes would happen at the last minute. Due to the reduction in hours, she took up an alternate instructor role at another gym. She denied that she had cancelled classes or had phoned in sick at the last minute but conceded that she had not sought approval to take up the alternate role. It was a common case that a meeting took place between the parties at which the respondent made the claimant aware that she was working in another gym without permission. The respondent's evidence of this meeting was that the claimant had requested a reduction in hours, which was not sustainable and which would have had a huge impact on the respondent's business. The respondent's evidence was that the claimant put an ultimatum to it about the required shift changes to suit her work with another employer. The claimant chose to resign by providing him with a handwritten letter of resignation. However, the respondent decided that this letter was illegible and the claimant was provided with a typed resignation letter which she was required to sign the following day.

It was the claimant's evidence that the respondent had originally agreed to her request to change shifts, but on learning that she was taking classes at another gym, the respondent changed its mind. The claimant asserted that she was forced to write a resignation letter and was told she could get a copy the following day. The claimant further asserted that she was forced to resign in circumstances where three options were put to her by the respondent: (i) to continue working with a competitor, which would lead to her dismissal; (ii) to continue working for the respondent with less and less hours; or (iii) to write or sign a letter of resignation.

The EAT accepted that the respondent did not have an issue with the claimant working for a competitor, provided it did not impact on their roster, which had been created around the claimant's availability. The EAT noted however that the arrangements between the parties had become unworkable. The claimant did take up employment at a competitor gym without informing the respondent at a time when she was rostered for work at the respondent's gym. The EAT noted that the claimant did not want to give up her classes at the competitor gym as the rates of pay were considerably better than those of the respondent. However, the respondent could not reasonably be expected to book clients for classes and then have them cancelled at the last minute because of the unavailability of the claimant who was working elsewhere at the same time. The EAT preferred the evidence of the respondent and concluded that there was no unfair dismissal in these circumstances.

Procedural failings in an investigation

[27.81] *Rawski v Callan Bacon Company Ltd[109]—Employment Appeals Tribunal— Unfair Dismissals Acts 1977 to 2015—constructive dismissal—procedural failings in investigation of workplace incident—translation of contracts of employment and policies*

The claimant commenced his employment with the respondent in October 2010, working as a general operative within the factory. The employment appeared to have been uneventful until 19 April 2013.

The EAT heard that employees of the respondent's factory were required to work at least four hours of overtime per week. On the morning of 19 April 2013, the claimant informed the line leader that he was unable to work overtime that day. At the end of his shift he left the line but was instructed to return to the line to carry out overtime. The claimant raised the matter with the line leader reminding him that he had already told him that morning that he was unable to work overtime that day. It was the respondent's case that when the claimant returned to the line he berated and pointed his finger at the line leader and that they pushed each other. The line manager was forced to intervene. It was the claimant's case that he was verbally and physically assaulted by the line leader and that when he complained of this to the line manager he was threatened with dismissal should he pursue a complaint.

The claimant was very upset following the incident and he spoke with a shop steward. It was the evidence of the general manager that he happened upon the claimant and the shop steward in the car park of the factory on 19 April 2013 and that the claimant was upset and in a distressed state. The general manager held a meeting in his office with the claimant in the presence of the area production manager and the shop steward. The claimant made a complaint through English about the matter and the general manager informed him that the matter would be investigated. It was the claimant's evidence that at this meeting a request was made by him to see the CCTV footage but this was not provided to him at any stage.

It was the claimant's evidence that he was very stressed regarding the incident and he attended his doctor on 22 April 2013 as a result. The claimant was prescribed medication and provided with a medical certificate. The claimant continued to be unfit for work thereafter and he provided medical certificates to the respondent via the shop steward.

The claimant's solicitor wrote a letter dated 18 November 2013 asking the respondent to fully investigate the claimant's grievances and noting that the respondent had not contacted the claimant.

The respondent responded by letter dated 22 November 2013 which stated that the matter would first be addressed at local level using the normal union procedure. The claimant's solicitor replied that he was representing the claimant in the matter, not the union, and he again asked the respondent to investigate the claimant's grievances.

---

109. *Rawski v Callan Bacon Company Ltd* UD529/2014.

At a meeting in December 2013 the claimant was informed that he would be referred to the company doctor for assessment. At that meeting, the respondent raised the fact that a number of letters were sent to the claimant but it transpired that the claimant had moved address and the letters had not been sent to the relevant address.

A letter later issued to the claimant's current address asking him to attend the company doctor on 20 December 2013 but he could not attend on that date and his solicitor requested that the respondent re-arrange this appointment. The respondent wrote to the claimant re-arranging the appointment for 10 January 2014. It was the respondent's case that attempts were made on a number of occasions to contact the claimant by telephone for an update in relation to his health. The claimant denied this in his evidence.

The claimant's solicitor wrote a further letter dated 4 March 2014 stating that the respondent had corresponded with a number of incorrect addresses for the claimant despite being aware that he was residing at his current address since March 2013. The claimant stated in evidence that he had never resided at the addresses on those letters. The solicitor's letter further stated that the claimant was resigning his position on grounds of constructive dismissal. The letter noted that the respondent had corresponded with the claimant only in relation to his health but not in relation to his grievance or any investigation.

It was the evidence of the general manager that an investigation was conducted and concluded within days of the incident occurring on 19 April 2013. A letter was written by the operations manager who stated that the line leader had been suspended from his duties as a result of 'pushing' the claimant on the line and that the manager of the line had been dismissed from his duties.

The general manager stated that witness statements were taken from 11 employees in the vicinity of the incident. In reply to questions from the EAT, he confirmed that he wrote the statements of what the witnesses said and they signed them. It was the claimant's evidence that he did not receive this letter despite the fact that it contained his correct address and he further stated that he was not told or provided with the witness statements until February 2014 when his solicitor received copies of them.

In its decision the EAT noted that it must consider, if, in all of the circumstances the claimant was entitled to so terminate his employment and whether it was reasonable for him to do so. There was a serious incident on the 19 April 2013. It was common case that the claimant was in a deeply distressed condition after the incident. The investigation conducted by the respondent was hasty and wholly inadequate, the conclusions drawn were questionable, the documenting of the investigation was poor as was the communication of the outcome to the claimant. The respondent ignored the requests of the claimant's legal representative for a comprehensive investigation.

The communication between the parties at the time was poor and the EAT firmly laid the greater blame for this on the respondent. Irrespective of any informal practices within the place of work, in circumstances where the established line of communication was not proving effective, the EAT could not understand how the opportunity presented for a solid line of communication through the claimant's solicitor was not taken. The respondent's professed frustration at the claimant's failure to engage was totally irreconcilable with the respondent's refusal to avail of the possibility presented to it to engage through the claimant's solicitor.

The EAT determined that, in all of the circumstances the claimant was entitled to resign his position and that it was reasonable for him to do so.

The EAT awarded the claimant compensation of €20,000.

The EAT noted that, while not ultimately relevant to the determination of the EAT in this instance, the peripheral issue of the translation of contracts of employment and supporting handbooks was a source of considerable discussion and debate. The EAT stated that it was simply unacceptable in a workplace where there is a multi-national workforce, that employees would be denied access to copies of documents fundamental to their respective contractual relationship with their employer in their respective native languages. In the view of the EAT, there are very few languages that cannot be easily (and relatively inexpensively) translated.

Lack of support

[27.82] *Hawkins v Arvagh Area Childcare Ltd t/a Busy Bees*[110]*—Employment Appeals Tribunal—Unfair Dismissals Acts 1977 to 2015—constructive dismissal—management inexperienced and unable to effectively manage the claimant—failure to support claimant in employment*

The claimant was appointed to manage a childcare facility. During the course of the hearing, the EAT noted that the claimant had onerous duties, including managing 10 staff, administrative duties and reporting to the Board of the not-for-profit entity that managed the facility, and that this responsibility was not reflected in the claimant's salary. In the determination, the EAT was critical of the Board's management of the facility – in particular in respect of human resources related issues.

The claimant had a difficult relationship with the Board, which became increasingly fraught over time.

The EAT noted that the claimant was placed in a difficult position because she had no obvious superior to make executive management decisions and there was an absence of a disciplinary and grievance procedure in the facility. The EAT heard how certain complaints were allegedly made about the claimant by parents of children who attended the facility, however, no action was taken to investigate these matters.

The EAT also noted the respondent's evidence of the claimant's 'abrasive and uncooperative' behaviour at times.

In August 2012 a former director, PH, rejoined the Board of the facility. PH attempted to conduct investigations into the outstanding complaints against the claimant, which the EAT heard led to a number of letters being issued, which in effect, brought the matters to a close. The claimant was unhappy about the conduct of the investigations, but following the resignation of two of the Board members with which the claimant had difficulty, the claimant told PH that she would be more comfortable in the workplace.

---

110. *Hawkins v Arvagh Area Childcare Ltd t/a Busy Bees* UD638/2013.

Subsequently, a long-serving employee of the facility resigned. This employee informed the Board that the claimant was one of the reasons for her resignation. The EAT heard evidence of the previously difficult relationship between this employee and the claimant. Following the resignation, at meeting in November 2012, PH put it to the claimant that her conduct was the cause of the resignation of the other employee, and during the course of this meeting, PH told the claimant that if she could not cope with the role, she should resign. The claimant went absent and resigned three months later in February 2013.

The EAT held that the claimant was constructively dismissed as she had no support from management during the final months of her employment. The EAT found that PH was not acting with mala fides and was attempting to act in the interests of the facility, but, given the circumstances and the Board's lack of experience in dealing with such issues, proper external advice should have been obtained to manage the issues unfolding between the claimant and the Board. In awarding the claimant €12,500 as compensation, the EAT took into account the claimant's failure to engage in a grievance and mediation process with an external third party as suggested by the respondent.

Flawed recruitment process

[27.83] *Healy v Kerry County Council (formerly Killarney Town Council)[111]— Employment Appeals Tribunal—Unfair Dismissals Acts 1977 to 2015, s 7(1)(c)(ii)— constructive dismissal—informal internal communication of job interview results— fault in recruitment process—claimant forced into accepting retirement package— failure to invoke grievance procedure not fatal due to mental state of claimant—EAT unable to award compensation where claimant permanently medically unfit for work—award of four weeks compensation*

The claimant was a qualified carpenter/joiner who commenced employment as a public servant with Killarney Town Council in May 1978. His initial roles included maintenance duties and carpentry work. Within two years of his commencement, he assumed the role of relief town foreman for six months while the incumbent was sick. He also performed the town foreman's duties when he was absent. The claimant returned to his original role each time the incumbent returned to work. In 2002, the claimant's position changed to temporary clerk of works. Eighteen months later he brought a claim to the Labour Relations Commission as he was unhappy in this role. A new role of assistant town foreman was created and the claimant was appointed to that position in April 2003. The claimant was successful in the running of town's affairs in this position and developed relationships with both statutory and voluntary bodies to the benefit of the town. In December 2009, the claimant assumed the role of acting town foreman on the retirement of the incumbent during the interim period. Evidence was given that the claimant was also successful in this role.

In May 2011, the claimant and a number of other candidates applied for the advertised position of town foreman for Killarney Town Council. The claimant gave

111. *Healy v Kerry County Council (formerly Killarney Town Council)* UD730/2012.

evidence that he had the requisite qualifications, skills, knowledge and experience for the permanent role as he had been performing the role competently and professionally for the previous 18 months. On 9 June 2011, a panel conducted the interviews for the position. The next morning the claimant was informally notified that he had been unsuccessful in his application for the position but would remain in his original position. Shortly afterwards, the successful candidate told the claimant that he was taking over the role of town foreman with immediate effect. The claimant gave evidence that he had expected he would be informed of the selection process results formally in writing. The claimant stated that he had been undermined, badly treated and demoted. He had a health assessment the following Tuesday and was certified unfit for work. He also met with the staff welfare officer and informed her of his complaints and grievances. The claimant stated that he could not remember invoking the formal grievance procedure. The claimant was later informed by management that while he was an exemplary employee, the position had been filled. By letter dated 19 July 2011, the claimant received his interview evaluation. Under the criterion 'knowledge of the role' the panel had judged him 'not qualified' despite him occupying the role for the previous 18 months. He had not at any point been notified that he was not up to the required level.

From 16 June 2011 onwards, the claimant submitted medical certificates certifying him unfit for work and, from late June, the reason provided was depression. He attended a consultant psychiatrist from 23 June 2011. The respondent was unaware of this until after the termination of the claimant's employment. The claimant did not have mental health issues prior to this. The respondent's sick pay scheme expired after 12 weeks but was extended for a further two months until November 2011. The claimant stated that he felt vulnerable when his sick pay ended. The claimant also had a number of personal financial issues at this time. The claimant had attended counselling sessions for which the respondent paid. The end of February 2012 was the deadline for an early and enhanced retirement package. The claimant opted to retire on grounds of ill health, supported by a medical certificate from his doctor dated 29 February 2012 stating that the claimant was 'permanently unfit for work due to chronic illness and depression'. The claimant stated to the EAT that he had retired on health grounds under duress as a result of the respondent's behaviour. The claimant submitted that his application to retire was made under duress as he felt trapped after having worked for the respondent for 33 years. The respondent's only witness was an official from its HR department based in Tralee. He stated that the HR department received the claimant's medical certificates and referred him to the welfare officer. The next interaction the respondent's witness had with the claimant was in relation to his retirement package. The EAT noted that the respondent's witness had very little involvement in the claimant's case.

The EAT stated that, generally, an employer cannot be faulted for not hiring a candidate to a position of employment. However, the EAT noted that the procedures adopted by the respondent in relation to the appointment of town foreman and its behaviour in the immediate aftermath were flawed. The EAT stated that the communication of the interview results was unprofessional and insensitive towards the claimant. The EAT noted that when the claimant obtained his interview evaluation, he discovered that he had lost points in respect of his knowledge of the role, despite acting as town foreman for the previous 18 months and all previous town foremen, for as long as the claimant could remember, had been craftsmen. The claimant was deemed not qualified for the position. The EAT could not determine the best candidate for the position but noted that because various witnesses were not present for the respondent issues could not be explored by the EAT.

The EAT was satisfied that the respondent's behaviour, combined with the resulting financial difficulties the claimant faced, aggravated the claimant's mental health difficulties and resulted in the claimant's resignation and taking an early retirement package at an earlier stage than he otherwise would have done, with resulting financial disadvantage to him. The EAT found that the claimant had been forced into resignation and that this amounted to a constructive dismissal, despite receiving a retirement package. The EAT noted that the claimant's failure to formally invoke the grievance procedure was not fatal in this case, because of the claimant's upset mental state. The EAT stated that the claimant had made his complaints known through communication with the welfare officer and had also met with the town clerk and town engineer and that this sufficed. The constructive dismissal claim succeeded. However, the EAT referred to the claimant's medical certificate dated 29 February 2012 which stated that the claimant was 'permanently unfit for work due to chronic illness and depression'. In the absence of medical evidence that the claimant was fit to work, the EAT could not award compensation. The EAT noted that it could award up to four weeks compensation in such circumstances. The EAT awarded the claimant €5,184.60 under s 7(1)(c)(ii) of the 1977 Act.

Where the fact of resignation is in doubt

[27.84] *Prestige Foods Ltd v Gutauskiene*[112]—*Employment Appeals Tribunal—Unfair Dismissals Acts 1977 to 2015—whether claimant had resigned—language barriers—health and safety issue*

This was an appeal by the respondent employer against a Rights Commissioner's decision. There was a conflict of evidence between the parties over the question of whether or not the employee had resigned from the respondent company. The claimant was employed in the respondent food processing and packaging plant from April 2005 until September 2011. The position occupied by the claimant was general operative for her first two years of employment. Thereafter, she was promoted to supervisor.

The claimant had an operation on her foot, following which she was on sick leave for some time. She was certified fit to work by her doctor on 24 August 2011, who advised her to avoid wearing steel-toed safety boots for six months. The claimant met with a director and the HR manager on this date and furnished the respondent with a brochure in relation to alternative plastic-toed safety boots. After she had been certified fit to return to work, the claimant took 10 days' annual leave to return to Poland. She was due back to work on or around 6 September 2011. While in Poland, she purchased a pair of the afore-mentioned plastic-toed safety boots. On her return from holidays, the claimant expected the director to get back to her in relation to the safety boots. She submitted that

---

112. *Prestige Foods Ltd v Gutauskiene* UD880/2012.

he failed to do so and that the next communication she received from the respondent was when she was sent her P45 in October 2011.

The claimant maintained that she had been unfairly dismissed by the respondent. Contrary to the contention of the respondent, she denied that she had resigned. The claimant's interpreter, her son, corroborated her evidence that she did not resign at the meeting held on 24 August 2011. The claimant had been in receipt of Job Seekers Benefit from September 2011 until it expired. She actively sought employment in Ireland until February 2014, when she returned to live in Poland.

The director present at the meeting with the claimant on 24 August 2011 agreed that the claimant gave him a brochure about the boots at that meeting and that he was to consider the suitability of those boots before reverting to her. After the meeting, the claimant had been granted 10 days of annual leave as per her request. The claimant did not return to work on 6 September 2011, as expected; instead she attended the office on 8 September 2011, accompanied by her son. Another meeting was held with the director and the HR Manager. It was the respondent's evidence that the claimant resigned during the course of this meeting, stating that she no longer needed to work. This had taken the HR Manager by surprise. He had questioned the claimant a number of times as to whether she was sure about her decision, as jobs were hard to come by, but the claimant had been adamant. In summary, the respondent's position was that the claimant was not dismissed but she had resigned of her own volition.

On 14 November 2011, the respondent received a letter from SIPTU on the claimant's behalf. The letter enquired as to the reasons for the claimant's dismissal. The respondent gave evidence that they had phoned the union official and informed him that the claimant had resigned.

The majority of the EAT held that the claimant had not been dismissed, but had resigned of her own volition. The EAT noted the claimant's evidence that she did not realise she had been dismissed until she received her P45 in October 2011. However, it placed emphasis on the fact that the claimant had sought Job Seekers Benefit in September 2011. The EAT found by a majority decision that the claimant had resigned. Accordingly the appeal was upheld and the claim under the Unfair Dismissals Acts 1977 to 2015 failed.

One of the EAT members dissented from the decision of the majority. He noted that health and safety is of paramount importance in the food industry. The claimant could not wear the footwear provided by the respondent due to a foot condition. The fitness to work certificate received by the claimant on 24 August had been conditional upon not wearing the steel-toe cap footwear for six months. At the meeting on 24 August the respondent had said they would refer the brochure about the alternative footwear to the quality department. The option of the claimant working in the packing room was also discussed. The dissenting member concluded that the claimant had not resigned, therefore the appeal should fail and the Rights Commissioner's recommendation should stand. The dissenting EAT member also commented that, in light of the claimant's poor language skills, there was an onus on the respondent to adopt fair and reasonable procedures to make sure that it was clear that a termination of employment was occurring.

[27.85] *Durkin v McSweeney Assets Group Holdings Ltd*[113]*—Employment Appeals Tribunal—Unfair Dismissals Acts 1977 to 2015—examinership process—dismissal— lack of clarity with regard to resignation of claimant from his role of director and/or employee—failure to adopt fair procedures—right to appeal—failure to provide reasons for dismissal for serious misconduct*

The respondent was a group of pharmacies. The claimant was originally employed as a pharmacist in a company in the group in 1993 but later became the manager of all pharmacies within the group and acquired a share in the respondent. In 2008, the recession severely impacted the respondent's business, resulting in half of the pharmacies closing and the subsequent entry of the respondent into examinership in 2011. The claimant was to lead the examinership process on behalf of the respondent as the respondent's owner was based outside of the jurisdiction.

The examinership process was running efficiently until 8 February 2012, the date on which the claimant sought a 24.9 per cent share in the new company that would emerge after the respondent exited the examinership process. Discussions with regard to a new shareholders' agreement had been ongoing between the claimant and the owner of the respondent, but nothing had ever been agreed upon or finalised in writing. The claimant was informed that the shareholders' agreement and related negotiations and discussions had been postponed pending the outcome of the examinership process. The claimant became concerned for his future career with the respondent, and by letter dated 9 February 2012, the claimant apparently resigned from his position. There existed a degree of uncertainty as to whether the claimant resigned from his position as a director, manager or both. It was accepted however on behalf of the respondent under cross-examination that the claimant had resigned from his position as a director but not as an employee. The claimant later stated in evidence that his resignation was only to be used as leverage for the purposes of negotiations regarding respective shareholdings. The respondent's owner ceased all communications with the claimant after 8 February 2012 and all subsequent communications and negotiations thereafter were between the claimant and a partner in KPMG. The respondent noted that negotiations between the KPMG partner and the claimant were conducted solely to ensure that the examinership process was not affected. The claimant did not engage in the examinership process in any way after 9 February 2012. It was noted that the respondent owner was adamant that the claimant would not work for the respondent again.

On 11 February 2012, a colleague of the claimant, who shortly thereafter obtained the position of financial director, contacted the claimant requesting that he reconsider his resignation, as his departure would likely upset the examinership process and the respondent's organisation as a whole. The claimant had previously informed this colleague that he was going to submit his resignation, but at no point qualified this by saying he was only resigning as a director. The respondent's owner was of the belief that the examinership process would fail as a key member was leaving the company. On 13 February 2012, the claimant received a document from the KPMG partner requesting the claimant to sign over all his shares to the respondent as part of an agreement, the

---

113. *Durkin v McSweeney Assets Group Holdings Ltd* UD996/2012.

terms of which the claimant had previously agreed. The claimant's resignation letter was accepted on 16 February. On 23 February 2012, the claimant received the final agreement for the purposes of signing over his shares but the agreement had been altered to provide that the claimant would take mandatory garden leave. The claimant was advised by his solicitor that the provision of mandatory garden leave equated to being removed from the company and the claimant subsequently rejected the agreement. On 24 February 2012, the claimant received a letter stating that an investigation would be commenced into his behaviour and conduct and suggested that he either take garden leave or face suspension. The claimant's solicitors replied, threatening an injunction if the claimant was suspended in these circumstances.

The respondent owner became increasingly worried that the claimant would derail the examinership process and, at a board meeting on 28 February 2012, it was proposed and resolved that the claimant's employment be terminated for serious misconduct. On 29 February 2012 the claimant received a letter stating that his behaviour had amounted to serious misconduct warranting dismissal which was to be effective immediately. The claimant was dismissed as he was a 'threat to the company'. The claimant had not been in contact with the respondent's owner throughout the investigation or disciplinary process and was never informed as to the precise nature of his serious misconduct. The specific reasons for dismissal were never communicated to the claimant.

The EAT found that the claimant had been unfairly dismissed and awarded the claimant €50,000 in compensation. The EAT took into account that the claimant had contributed to his own dismissal. The EAT noted that the respondent's owner did not communicate with the claimant after 8 February 2012 and in particular, did not engage in the disciplinary process. The EAT further noted that, while gross misconduct was defined in the respondent's handbook; serious misconduct, the subject of the claimant's dismissal, was not. The EAT also noted that the employee handbook provided that the respondent was not obliged to apply steps 1 to 5 of the disciplinary procedure for instances of gross misconduct but that 'the express approval of the managing director will be required to effect discharge of any staff member'. The respondent owner did not communicate to the claimant at any stage that he did not want him working for the respondent in the future. The EAT noted that a reasonable employer would have written, as a matter of urgency, to the claimant setting out the severity of the situation and the potential consequences (including dismissal) of the claimant's failure to adhere to his duties and responsibilities. The EAT found it unacceptable that the respondent did not conduct discussions with the claimant in relation to his alleged misconduct, warn and notify the claimant that his position was in danger, advise the claimant that he was entitled to attend a meeting with representation and answer the allegations against him or to allow the claimant appeal the decision. The EAT stated that 'it is not in the gift of the EAT to forgive blatant and flagrant disregard to the claimant's natural and constitutional rights as an employee'. The claimant was not provided with reasons for his dismissal other than what was included in his dismissal letter, such reasons only relating to his resignation as a director during the examinership process. It was noted that a number of further reasons in relation to the allegation of serious misconduct had been outlined by witnesses for the respondent during the hearing of the case but were not put to the claimant in writing prior to this point. The claimant was not offered an appeal; but was instead prohibited from attending at the respondent's premises or otherwise risk removal from the premises by the respondent's security if he did. The EAT noted the claimant had contributed to his dismissal by using the examinership process as leverage to obtain a more suitable agreement for himself and further, disregarding his pivotal role in the examinership process, having previously sworn an original affidavit for the High Court in relation to same and in support of the respondent.

[27.86] *Delaney v The Phone Store t/a Lorat Trading Ltd[114]—Employment Appeals Tribunal—Unfair Dismissals Acts 1977 to 2015—constructive dismissal—whether claimant had formally resigned from her position—whether claimant had discharged burden of proof for unfair dismissal—subsequent failure of claimant to attend work—whether employee can claim constructive dismissal by repudiation of her employment contract—whether respondent's conduct sufficiently grave that a reasonable employee in that same position would have been compelled to resign*

The claimant was employed as a sales assistant in the respondent's phone store in Wexford Town from February 2005 and was promoted to a store manager in 2006. In 2009, she was offered the position of business account manager. The claimant noted that a verbal agreement existed with the respondent's owner that the claimant would revert to the position of manager in Wexford Town if her new position did not work out. The claimant became pregnant in 2010 and informed the store owner. She returned to her position as manager in the Wexford store. The claimant commenced maternity leave and, upon her return, it was agreed that, at her request, she would return to work on a part-time basis. During July and August 2010, the claimant was requested to travel to Dublin to assist with issues in the call centre there and shortly after, was requested to go and work in the Dungarvan store. In September, the claimant was asked to return to the Wexford store. During this time she had relocated, and was residing in Kilkenny. She refused to return to the Wexford store on the basis that her commute would be too long and onerous.

In September 2012, the claimant was contacted by the new area manager who informed her that the employees of the Dungarvan store had complained about her and did not want to work with her anymore. The complaints were formally confirmed to the claimant at a meeting with the area manager in a café on 19 September 2012. The claimant alleged the area manager had acted unprofessionally by conducting this meeting in a public area and that the meeting should have been conducted in more appropriate circumstances. The claimant also noted that her friend had overheard the conversation between the claimant and the area manager in the café. The claimant was upset and did not return to work. The area manager subsequently accepted that the meeting could have been conducted in a more professional manner. On 25 September 2012, the claimant received a call from the area manager asking why she had not returned to work. The claimant responded *via* email but to the store owner. She attended a meeting on 11 October 2012 at which her representative was restricted from attending. The store owner, a different area manager, the claimant and a note taker attended this

---

114. *Delaney v The Phone Store t/a Lorat Trading Ltd* UD373/2013, MN200/2013, WT55/2013.

meeting. It was noted that the claimant requested a copy of the complaints against her but only received copies at the end of the meeting. The claimant activated the grievance policy and the respondent found that sufficient grounds did not exist to substantiate the grievance. The claimant was given seven days to appeal the grievance decision and did so, despite only receiving all relevant statements and meeting minutes one day prior to the appeal deadline. The claimant did not return to work and never received a P45. The claimant noted that she was 'technically' still employed by the respondent after 19 September 2012, as she had not received a P45, but further stated that she had no choice but to leave the company on that date. The claimant alleged that the situation had arisen because she refused to go back to Wexford when requested. The claimant explained to the EAT that she would have considered a position in Kilkenny on a part-time basis or an alternative location on a part-time basis but that she had not informed management of this. She had, however, informed management that she would not return to the store in Dungarvan. The claimant had chosen not to engage in mediation as she had lost all faith in the respondent at that stage.

The EAT first had to determine whether the claimant had resigned and subsequently, whether the claimant had discharged the onus of proof required for a claim of constructive dismissal. The EAT noted that the claimant deliberately absented herself from work on 19 September 2012, after becoming aware that her colleagues had made complaints about her. The EAT further noted that the claimant absented herself on the basis of an ultimatum that she would return to work only if the respondent facilitated her transfer to a location other than Dungarvan, such location being within a suitable travelling distance of her home. The EAT found that by absenting herself from her employment, the claimant had repudiated her contract of employment, but as the respondent had not accepted the repudiation, the claimant's contract of employment had not been terminated. The EAT noted that, despite the claimant considering her employment terminated, she had never informed the respondent at any stage that she had resigned. The claimant had informed the respondent that she would not be returning to work in Dungarvan after 19 September but the EAT found that this did not equate to a notice of resignation.

The EAT noted that to prove constructive dismissal, the conduct of the respondent must be sufficiently grave that a reasonable employee, in the claimant's position, would easily have been driven to leave the job at that particular time. The EAT found that the respondent's conduct did not entitle the claimant to consider herself constructively dismissed and to render the respondent liable for a claim of unfair dismissal. The EAT noted that the respondent attempted to resolve the issue and had offered the claimant the option of mediation. The EAT also found that until the claimant had been informed of the complaints of her colleagues, she was unaware that any issues existed. This indicated to the EAT that her colleagues had not previously presented their concerns to the claimant in the workplace. The EAT found the claimant's claim for constructive dismissal failed.

REDRESS FOR UNFAIR DISMISSAL

Re-engagement

[27.87] *Jones v Bulmers Ltd[115]—Employment Appeals Tribunal—appeal from decision of Rights Commissioner—Unfair Dismissals Acts 1977 to 2015—bullying and harassment investigation—flawed investigation process—bias—no disciplinary hearing—dismissal while on certified sick leave—re-engagement*

This was an appeal of a Rights Commissioner's decision which found that the employee had been unfairly dismissed by the respondent and had awarded compensation to the employee.

The claimant had been employed by the respondent since 2000; had held multiple positions and was also a shop steward. The claimant had a clean disciplinary record and was the chief shop steward with the respondent.

GC, a front line manager in the warehouse department, gave evidence to the EAT that he was the claimant's direct line manager since 2008. The main duty of the claimant was the operation of a forklift within the factory. There were different shift patterns in operation in the factory, one of which paid a shift premium. Operators moved between the different areas of the factory as per work requirements, which varied, depending on the time of year.

The managers met weekly to discuss employee resources required in the different areas of the factory. Operations department interchangeability was provided for in an agreement with the union on flexibility which had been in place since March 2009, as part of a survival plan for the respondent. The deciding factors for interchangeability selection were the number of employees required in each area and the skills of the available employees. One week's notice of the change in shift pattern should be given to the employees who were transferring under the interchangeability agreement but payment in lieu of notice could be provided by the respondent.

An employee resource meeting was held on 2 February 2012 and a decision was reached that the claimant would transfer to the production/canning line as he was a competent employee; albeit he would have required some training specific to the role. Prior to the claimant being asked to transfer, other employees had also been transferred to the production line. There was to be no change in the level of pay.

GC and his colleague AR (front line manager for the production/canning line) met with the claimant on Friday, 3 February 2012 and informed him of the transfer which was to take place the following Monday, 6 February 2012. Conflicting evidence was heard as to what occurred during the meeting. GC gave evidence that the claimant became agitated immediately, stating that he did not have to transfer and querying his selection. GC gave evidence that the exchange escalated and the claimant made gestures and uttered profanities. On foot of this, AR advised the claimant that he was going to contact the human resources department. Following a further verbal exchange GC, put up his hands to restrain the claimant who was coming towards them.

---

115. *Jones v Bulmers Ltd* UD423/2014, UD587/2014.

GC reported the matter to both the production manager (EO'G) and to CE of the human resources department. The claimant was suspended with pay pending an investigation under the disciplinary procedures.

The claimant then made an allegation under the bullying and harassment policy that he was pushed by GC. The disciplinary process was suspended while the grievance process was conducted. The bullying and harassment allegation was not upheld and the respondent then continued with an investigation under the disciplinary procedure.

At the conclusion of the disciplinary process, the claimant was dismissed by EO'G and CE. EO'G gave evidence as to how the decision to dismiss had been taken; he explained that he and CE had felt that the bond of trust had been broken because of the incident that had occurred on 3 February 2015.

The EAT heard further, detailed evidence from the claimant in relation to the ensuing altercation/exchange that occurred between GC, AR and himself which culminated in him being suspended on full pay pending an investigation. The claimant outlined his account in detail to the EAT and challenged the statements of GC and AR, pointing out numerous inaccuracies and allegations made by both. The claimant denied that GC and AR's statements were accurate versions of events and said that he had pointed this out to the investigators. He told the EAT that the issues he raised were never investigated. The claimant stated that he believed that the respondent was only interested in ascertaining his wrongdoing rather than ascertaining what actually happened on 3 February 2012. According to the claimant, both GC and AR had changed their statements, yet nothing was done about this. The claimant gave evidence that GC and AR had colluded in making their statements and their statements were taken at face value.

The claimant stated that he had received a letter dated 9 May 2012 inviting him to a meeting on 16 May 2012 where he was to be informed of the outcome of the investigation under the disciplinary procedure. The claimant forwarded a medical certificate to the respondent confirming his absence on medical grounds from 11 May 2012 to 18 May 2012. The respondent proceeded to hold the meeting in his absence, and he was informed by way of letter dated 16 May 2012 that his employment was terminated with immediate effect from 16 May 2012.

The claimant was given five days to appeal this decision, which he did, and an appeal hearing was held on 18 June 2012. The appeal did not go in his favour and the decision to dismiss was upheld.

The EAT was very critical of the respondent employer in this case. It concluded that the investigation of the incident of 3 February 2012 was fundamentally flawed. The EAT stated that an investigation must be free of bias and be objective and must be seen to be so.

The EAT was of the opinion that the background to the incident of 3 February 2013 was that, following a meeting of managers on 2 February, the claimant was informed as a 'fait accompli' that he was being moved to the canning line at short notice in circumstances that the EAT believed did not comply either with the terms or spirit of the agreement around interchangeability negotiated in 2009 to provide flexibility within the workplace. The EAT was further of the view that it was not entirely unreasonable of the claimant to have concerns, nor was it unforeseeable that the manner in which the decision was delivered to the claimant might prove somewhat provocative.

The EAT was not convinced that the full truth of what occurred during the incident of 3 February was forthcoming from any of the three parties involved, however, it was not the role of the EAT to reinvestigate. The EAT stated that the obligation on the respondent was to carry out a fair, objective and unbiased investigation and to arrive at reasonable conclusions as to what occurred. The EAT found that it was wholly inappropriate for those who conducted the investigation to be members of management where two of the participants in the incident of 3 February were members of management and where there was a complete conflict between the managers involved and the claimant as to what had occurred. Indeed, the two investigators, CE and EO'G, were part of the meeting that made the decision to move the claimant to the canning line, being the decision which upset the claimant and was the catalyst for whatever occurred on 3 February 2012. Further, on the evidence presented to the EAT, it appeared that there was a private discussion between GC and CE and EO'G on 3 February which led to CE and EO'G suspending the claimant without as much as hearing from him.

The EAT found that the clear change of position as to whether GC 'pushed' or 'restrained' and the 'massaging' by both GC and AR of their initial statement on the incident of 3 February should have triggered far more robust and probative questioning had an independent, objective investigator been on the job. There was an inevitability that this would occur where the respondent failed to ensure the independence of the investigative process. The EAT stated that an independent investigator should have been brought on board at this stage.

The EAT found that EO'G and CE should simply have bowed out from the outset as they were simply too close to the overall situation and to a number of the parties involved. Furthermore, the EAT held that:

> The very manner in which the claimant's employment was ultimately terminated by EO'G is suggestive of him being less than independent in a number of respects and would further suggest that other influences were at play during the process …
> it may well be that an independent investigator, following a robust and probative process, might have ultimately arrived at the same conclusions, however, at this point we will never know.

The EAT found that, had there been an independent investigation that arrived at the same conclusions, it would have been reasonable to proceed to a disciplinary hearing. The EAT also stated that it was notable that no disciplinary hearing was held at all. Rather, the investigators, having arrived at conclusions, simply documented their findings and, in so doing, moved to immediate dismissal within the same letter that set out the findings of the investigation. The EAT found that this was 'a further fundamental flaw'.

As a result, the EAT was satisfied that the claimant was denied the opportunity to make representations at a hearing convened to decide sanction and, indeed, to put forward mitigating factors for consideration. Further, the claimant was entitled to such a hearing before a party or parties other than those who conducted the investigation. The EAT stated that 'in a Company with resources and full HR support, this deficiency in the disciplinary process is unacceptable'.

The EAT found it to be inexcusable that, in circumstances where the claimant was on a sick certificate for 'acute anxiety and stress related illness' from 11 May 2012 to 18

May 2012, the claimant was dismissed on 16 May without a disciplinary hearing and in circumstances that indicated undue haste. It was clear to the EAT that the respondent had tired of the process and, further, had allowed its decision to dismiss to be influenced by extraneous matters such as the respondent's desire to improve issues of communication on the ground within the workplace and with the union in circumstances where the claimant's (a shop steward) suspension had disrupted these.

Furthermore, the EAT held that, even if the procedure had been handled correctly, it was of the view that the sanction of dismissal was unduly harsh.

It was clear to the EAT that other forces were at play in the decision to dismiss, specifically, as recounted by the general manager to the EAT, the belief that there would be 'repercussions' for the management team if any sanction short of dismissal was applied and the claimant returned to work.

The EAT further stated that:

> the rights of the claimant as an individual and employee were sacrificed at the altar of corporate exigency. The Tribunal recognises the pressures that exist for industry in a competitive marketplace but, within such a pressurised environment, individual rights must be respected. The claimant was unfairly dismissed.

The EAT concluded that the only appropriate remedy in this case was re-engagement. It was satisfied that the claimant could and would reintegrate into the workplace and the EAT saw no valid reason why that reintegration could not be accommodated.

Accordingly, the EAT determined that the claimant be re-engaged by the respondent within nine months of the date hereof on the production by him of a certificate confirming his fitness to return to work on the same terms and conditions as enjoyed by the claimant prior to his dismissal (save where varied by any general changes made to those terms and conditions during the claimant's absence).

The EAT did not make any compensatory award but ordered that the claimant's continuity of service be preserved.

[27.88] *Mahon v eircom Ltd*[116]—*Employment Appeals Tribunal—appeal to Circuit Court—Unfair Dismissals Acts 1997 to 2015—termination of employment for gross misconduct—order that claimant's payroll be re-engaged with pay*

The claimant commenced employment with the respondent company in 1976. In April 2012 a member of the respondent's HR department (AMS) met with the claimant in the context of an appeal hearing of a disciplinary process. During the meeting AMS became concerned for the health and welfare of the claimant. She gave evidence that the claimant had told her that he suffered from depression and stress. Following the meeting, AMS requested the claimant to attend the respondent's chief medical officer for a medical assessment. The claimant was placed on compulsory sick leave. The claimant told the EAT that AMS's statements concerning his mental state were lies and that he had been in perfect health.

---

116. *Mahon v eircom Ltd* UD477/2014. This case is under appeal to the High Court.

In May 2012, the claimant attended a medical assessment with the chief medical officer but refused to allow the chief medical officer to examine him. The chief medical officer recommended the claimant be placed on compulsory sick leave pending the claimant's attendance at a medical assessment re-arranged for September 2012. The claimant was requested not to attend work, not to contact his line manager and not to drive the company vehicle while on compulsory sick leave. The claimant, however, continued to attend his workplace and use the company vehicle.

POT, the respondent's head of the fixed access build team, gave evidence that the claimant had use of a company vehicle which he was allowed to bring home after his shifts. POT gave evidence that generally if employees were absent from work for a prolonged period of time (more than three or four weeks) the company vehicle should be returned to the respondent and be given to another employee.

POT gave evidence that in September 2012 he was informed by the HR department that the claimant was being placed on compulsory sick leave. On 11 September 2012, POT met with the claimant to inform him of this and also instructed him to return the company vehicle. During this meeting the claimant told POT that he was not going on sick leave and that he was going to work. POT subsequently witnessed the claimant driving the vehicle and wrote to the claimant on 19 September 2012 where he sought to arrange a time to return the vehicle. The claimant did not respond to this letter. On 4 October 2012 another unsuccessful attempt was made to recover the company vehicle. Following this, POT sought help from a professional vehicle recovery company and notified the Garda Síochána that he would be recovering the company vehicle on a particular date. The vehicle was recovered on 5 October 2012 with the help of the professional vehicle recovery company and in the presence of the Garda Síochána.

On 17 June 2013, an agreement was reached at the Labour Relations Commission between the parties in which the respondent agreed that the claimant could come back to work on receipt of a letter from the claimant's GP which would in turn be verified by the chief medical officer. The respondent was working on a process to bring the claimant back to work when the claimant began picketing the respondent on 1 July 2013.

On 2 July 2013 POT wrote to the claimant asking him to desist from picketing and also for an explanation as to why he had refused to return the vehicle. When POT did not receive any response from the claimant he concluded that the claimant's actions constituted a gross misconduct as defined by the respondent's Disciplinary Policy and recommended he should be dismissed. The claimant appealed this recommendation in line with the respondent's Disciplinary Policy, but did not attend the appeal meeting that had been arranged. The person appointed to hear the appeal, AC, confirmed to the claimant that the recommendation to dismiss would not be overturned. A further right of appeal from this decision existed under the respondent's Discipline Code, but the claimant did not avail of this. The decision was subsequently passed to a committee of the respondent's board. The committee recommended the claimant's dismissal to the board, which resolved that the claimant be dismissed. This was communicated to the claimant by way of letter dated 19 March 2014.

The EAT rejected the claimant's argument that AMS was lying about the claimant's mental health and concluded that she genuinely believed the claimant was unwell and so acted appropriately in such circumstances.

On the fifth day of the EAT hearing, the claimant refused to be cross-examined, meaning that the EAT could not consider the evidence offered by the claimant as the respondent was not afforded an opportunity to challenge this evidence under cross-examination.

The EAT concluded that all elements of the dismissal were fair. It was noted that the claimant had been given ample opportunity to appeal his case at the relevant stages and was facilitated when he did not attend appointments concerning medical assessments. It was also concluded that it was reasonable for the respondent to request the claimant to return the company vehicle and the repeated refusal of the claimant to follow reasonable instructions of management throughout the course of these proceedings was a fundamental breach of the contract of employment by the claimant.

The claimant appealed the determination of the EAT to the Circuit Court, the hearing of which took place in June 2015.[117] In October 2015, the Circuit Court delivered its judgment and ordered that the appeal under the Unfair Dismissals Acts be allowed.

In delivering his judgment in the Circuit Court, Hannan J held that he had considered all evidence put forward in relation to the appeal, but he had confined his decision to the claimant's conduct in not returning the company vehicle. Hannan J noted that s 6(4)(b) of the Unfair Dismissal Act 1977 allows for a dismissal to be fair in certain circumstances, but there is also a requirement for an employer to be reasonable (as introduced by the Unfair Dismissal (Amendment) Act 1993). He held that while there were substantial grounds justifying the dismissal, fairness would dictate that the claimant's frame of mind should have been taken into account by the respondent before initiating the disciplinary investigation and it should have impacted on the severity of the sanction given to him. Hannan J held that the failure to consider this was unreasonable in the circumstances.

Hannan J was critical of what he described as the claimant's high-handed and uncompromising behaviour, but he also noted that, from the evidence provided, the claimant had a good work record in the past. Hannan J concluded that the claimant was not unmanageable as alleged. He also concluded that there was not a breakdown of trust which would prevent the claimant's return to work.

It was held that the claimant be reinstated to the post held before his dismissal and that he be re-engaged with pay backdated to 1 January 2015. Hannan J directed that the claimant be classified as employed but suspended from the period of his dismissal for employment record purposes. The Circuit Court order has been stayed pending the outcome of an appeal to the High Court with the claimant to be placed back on payroll effective from 1 January 2015. The appeal to the High Court is listed for hearing in May 2016.

---

117. *Mahon v eircom Ltd* Circuit Court Record No 2015/00085.

Reinstatement

[27.89] *Stapleton v St Colman's (Claremorris) Credit Union Ltd[118]—Employment Appeals Tribunal—Unfair Dismissals Acts 1977 to 2015—whether claimant unfairly dismissed where there were rumours of bullying allegations but claimant not informed of same by her employer and no investigation was carried out and no steps were taken to address the rumours and or any substantive complaints—order of reinstatement*

The claimant worked for the respondent Credit Union without issue since 2005. In June 2011 she had been provided with a copy of the respondent's bullying and harassment policy, which was left on her desk. Later that month she was approached by a member of the public while socialising outside of work and was accused of bullying a fellow employee who was absent on sick leave at the time. In the course of this interaction, the claimant was told that an investigation was going to be conducted by a human resources consultant into allegations of bullying and that she was going to be dismissed.

The claimant subsequently raised this issue with her manager and was informed that the matter would be addressed by a human resources consultant at her annual appraisal, but no such issues were mentioned during that appraisal meeting. Evidence was given that the claimant continued to work and carry out duties as normal and, although a number of meetings took place between herself and the respondent, she was never informed of the allegations against her. The relevant colleague had remained absent on sick leave during this time. A meeting was arranged between the parties to bring about a resolution but this meeting was cancelled and never took place.

The claimant was certified as unfit for work due to occupational stress for a number of weeks in February 2012. She then returned to work and shared an office with her colleague and gave evidence that no attempt was made to bring about a resolution to the purported allegations the details of which were still unknown to her. The claimant was again deemed unfit to work in June 2012 and submitted medical certificates for her absence. A meeting was arranged at her house with the monitoring committee of the respondent and she subsequently received a letter from the respondent stating there were no allegations made against her.

She gave evidence to the effect that she wished to return to work at this stage but made a number of requests before doing. These requests included equality of treatment with other employees, an apology from the respondent's board of directors, arrears of wages, cancellation of sick leave absences, reinstatement of pension entitlements and reimbursement of medical expenses. She further sought that her colleague be reprimanded in line with the respondent's bullying policy. She was formally requested to attend mediation and confirmed a willingness to do so but the mediation never took place.

A meeting took place in September 2012, at which she was legally represented. She was asked in writing to sign a letter withdrawing her various demands and was advised that if she refused she would be dismissed. There was no conclusion to this matter and

118. *Stapleton v St Colman's (Claremorris) Credit Union Ltd* UD1776/2012.

subsequently she was asked to leave the building and return her keys. One month later she received a letter requesting that she engage in a grievance process but she did not receive her P45 and did not resign from her employment. She sought reinstatement as a remedy.

Evidence was given by the respondent which acknowledged that the situation could have been handled differently and that the persons involved in dealing with this matter had no experience of human resources. Further evidence was given that the respondent was unable to accede to any of the claimant's demands. Evidence was given that the dismissal or resignation of the claimant was never discussed by the Board. They wished that she would withdraw her demands and use the grievance procedure.

In a majority determination, the EAT concluded that the dismissal was wholly and substantially unfair and that no procedures had been adopted by the respondent. The majority of the EAT held that reinstatement was the appropriate remedy as the claimant did not contribute in any way to her dismissal, the EAT noted that this was her preferred redress. A minority opinion of the EAT agreed that the dismissal was substantially and procedurally unfair but held that the appropriate remedy was compensation (as opposed to reinstatement) in the amount of €24,500.

See also the reinstatement decision in *The Governor and Company of the Bank of Ireland v Reilly*[119] which is noted at [**27.21**] above.

Mitigation

[**27.90**] *Murphy v Independent News and Media*[120]—*Employment Appeals Tribunal— Unfair Dismissals Acts 1977 to 2015—unfair dismissal—verbal contract of employment in place—lack of fair procedures—failure to fully mitigate loss by searching for further employment only within specific field of expertise*

The claimant was employed as a journalist by the respondent from August 2011. The claimant's role was to write in-depth articles for the respondent's weekend magazine. A net weekly salary of €1,200 was agreed between the claimant and the respondent and it was envisaged that a written contract of employment would be executed; she emailed the managing editor on a number of occasions requesting receipt of a written contract. The claimant also communicated with the magazine editor in relation to the contract that she had allegedly been promised but was informed that she should discuss the situation with the managing editor. Towards the end of 2012, the respondent appointed a new editor. The claimant continued to write articles as before and submitted the articles as usual. In the middle of October, the new editor informed the claimant that he required her to submit more celebrity-based articles in the magazine to which the claimant agreed. The claimant noted that there had never been any issues in relation to her performance.

The claimant soon became increasingly anxious in relation to organisational changes that the respondent was implementing. The claimant discussed the issue with the magazine editor who informed her that she was to continue her work as normal. On 5

---

119. *The Governor and Company of the Bank of Ireland v Reilly* [2015] IEHC 241.
120. *Murphy v Independent News and Media* UD 841/2013.

November 2012, the claimant expected to return to work following a week of paid holidays, but was, in fact, not provided with any work upon her return. She spoke again to the magazine editor who informed her that the respondent was seeking to make cutbacks and that, if she wished, the claimant could speak to the new editor. The claimant chose not to communicate with the new editor. The magazine editor subsequently contacted the claimant again, after having spoken to the new editor and informed her that her employment with the respondent would be terminated. The next day, the claimant met with the magazine editor to discuss the matter but was informed that it was not the right time to discuss her position as the respondent was currently implementing job cuts. A further email dated 21 November 2012 from the managing editor to the claimant stated that the claimant's employment would be terminated and that she would receive her final payment for work performed in the first week of January 2013. The claimant attended a meeting with the managing editor at the start of December 2012 to attempt to re-negotiate her position but was informed that the decision to dismiss her had already been made. The claimant was dismissed on 26 December 2012.

There was no appearance from the respondent at the hearing. From the uncontested evidence given by the claimant, the EAT found that she was employed under a verbal contract and had been paid a net wage of €1,200 weekly into her bank account for a period of 15 months. The EAT noted that no written contract of employment had ever been issued by the respondent despite several requests on the claimant's behalf to have one executed. The EAT found that the claimant was unfairly dismissed. However, in mitigating her loss, the claimant confined her search for employment only to her field of expertise. The EAT awarded compensation of €55,000 to the claimant.

Health and safety

[27.91] See also *Besenyei v Rosderra Irish Meats Group Ltd and Rosderra Meats Group*[121] at **[10.03]**, *Hanlon v Smurfit Kappa Ireland Ltd t/a Smurfit Kappa Dublin*[122] at **[10.04]**, and *Katherine Gordon & Co Ltd v Crowley O'Toole*[123] at **[10.05]**.

---

121. *Besenyei v Rosderra Irish Meats Group Ltd and Rosderra Meats Group* UD37/2014.
122. *Hanlon v Smurfit Kappa Ireland Ltd t/a Smurfit Kappa Dublin* UD388/2014.
123. *Katherine Gordon & Co Ltd v Crowley O'Toole* HSD 155.

Chapter 28

WAGES

PERFORMANCE-RELATED BONUSES

[28.01] *Devlin v Electricity Supply Board[1]—Employment Appeals Tribunal—appeal from decision of Rights Commissioner—Payment of Wages Act 1991—whether non-payment of performance-related bonus unlawful deduction—nature of discretionary bonus*

The claimant asserted that the non-payment of a performance-related bonus was an unlawful deduction contrary to s 5(6) of the 1991 Act. The claimant was employed by the respondent in the power generation division in 1971 and from 1992 onwards he worked as a professional engineer in middle management until his retirement, by way of voluntary severance, in December 2010. Under a 1993 collective agreement between the claimant's trade union and the respondent employer, the claimant opted to have a personal contract of employment which, for his grade, provided for a salary increase of 6 per cent on a point of scale and a performance-related non-pensionable bonus in a range from 0 per cent to 10 per cent of his basic salary.

The collective agreement provided that the bonus would be dependent on the achievement of targets on an annual basis, with such targets to be decided by the respondent following discussions with the individual and senior management. The relevant clause in the claimant's contract of employment stated:

> Under arrangements currently in operation you are entitled to be considered for a performance related bonus (non-pensionable) in a range from 0% to 10% of your basic salary. The bonus is dependent on the achievement of performance targets each year which are decided by ESB following discussions with you. ESB in consultation with your union may vary, amend or withdraw the bonus scheme or introduce other arrangements at any time.

The evidence was that the claimant's bonus was consistently between 8 per cent and 10 per cent, with an average of 9.3 per cent, over the 16-year period since the collective agreement. In November 2009, managers were notified that the 2009 bonus was being deferred. In late 2009, the claimant had applied for voluntary severance with a proposed retirement date of 31 December 2010; this date was later changed to 6 December 2010, for pension reasons. On 25 January 2010, in light of the deferment of the year-end salary and bonus review, the claimant sought to reserve the right to revisit his acceptance of the severance package; however he was informed by the respondent that his acceptance of the package could not be revisited. The claimant had the normal meeting with his manager in January 2010 regarding targets; however the usual 'wrap up' meeting which usually took place in December to review the year did not take place as he had retired on 6 December 2010. The claimant understood that the respondent normally paid a bonus

---

1.   *Devlin v Electricity Supply Board* PW550/2011.

based on average pay if an employee retired before the end of the year. The claimant submitted that there was no evidence that the respondent was in any way dissatisfied with his performance.

The claimant was not paid his 2010 bonus in January 2011 and when he enquired about same he was told that a bonus for 2010 had not been approved. He was then further advised that the respondent had decided not to pay the 2010 bonus. The evidence from the respondent's pension fund was that it was in serious deficit and that the cost base of the respondent had to be substantially reduced for it to remain competitive and survive. In 2009, senior managers had taken a 5 per cent pay cut. Cost savings of €140 million were required to include a payroll saving of €40 million in a €128 million payroll spend. There were constant negotiations with the trade unions in 2009 and 2010 and, as part of the pensions solution, the respondent was trying to introduce pay cuts. The evidence was that there had been constant interaction with very senior union officials whose view, contrary to that of the respondent, was that the payment of bonuses should continue. When the pension negotiations broke down, it was decided to separate pension talks from payroll talks. The pension negotiations ultimately concluded with agreement in mid-2010 and the 2009 bonus was ultimately paid in 2010 under the cover of that agreement.

In December 2010, the respondent decided that the 2010 bonus would not be paid. The union heard about the non-payment of the bonus when various members approached local staff representatives. An urgent meeting was held with the respondent and further engagement took place between the respondent and the various trade unions. This concluded in a payroll agreement in May 2012 which included voluntary severance packages, immediate pay reductions and cessation of all bonus payments. As part of this agreement, the respondent agreed to a settlement payment of €4,500 in respect of each of the managers in employment at that time. As the claimant had retired, he could not avail of this settlement payment. The respondent's position was that only those in employment could avail of this settlement, as they had taken a substantial pay cut due to the pay agreement and the pension calculations were not different. No bonus was paid in 2010.

The EAT noted the provisions of ss 1 and 5(6) of the 1991 Act. In reaching its decision, the EAT held that it must consider the nature of the bonus found in the claimant's contract of employment. The EAT concluded that the bonus was discretionary in nature and was not a contractual entitlement. The fact that any change must be made in consultation with the trade union did not alter this conclusion. A discretionary bonus loses its discretionary character once it is declared.[2]

In this case there was no evidence that a bonus was declared for 2010, indeed the EAT noted that the claimant's manager had not returned to him with his ratings and bonus for the year. A discretion is not unfettered and must be exercised reasonably and in good faith. The EAT was satisfied that, in light of the respondent's financial circumstances, its decision not to pay the 2010 bonus was not an unreasonable exercise of its discretion.

---

2.   *Atrill & Ors v Dresdner Kleinwort Ltd & Anor* [2013] EWCA 134.

The EAT noted that the contractual requirement regarding payment of this bonus was to consult and not to consult and agree. It noted that the evidence before it was that the respondent had advised the union of its decision not to pay the bonus in December 2010, and thereafter discussed it at meetings and during negotiations with the trade union. The EAT was satisfied that consultation had taken place. The EAT noted that, although the parties had prepared a joint statement on the issue of non-payment of a bonus, this was not submitted to the industrial council; this was the final stage of the respondent's internal industrial relations which issued binding recommendations in industrial relations issues. The EAT found that the non-payment of the bonus was not a contravention of s 5 of the 1991 Act and the appeal failed.

The EAT noted that the appellant had agreed to a voluntary severance agreement by email in November 2010. The EAT held that implicit in this agreement was that he could not revisit his severance agreement once accepted. This could be distinguished from a more general type of waiver which referred to other statutory employment rights which an employee may not contemplate at the time of agreeing to the waiver. The EAT found that the waiver also had the effect of precluding the claimant from seeking payment of the bonus.

IS THERE A LEGAL RIGHT TO BE PAID IN CASH?

[28.02] *Britvic Ireland Ltd v A Worker[3]—Labour Court—Industrial Relations Acts 1946 to 2015—Industrial Relations Act 1990, s 26(1)—wages—whether employee who has always been paid his wages in cash had legal right to be paid in cash until retirement*

The claimant was employed by the respondent for 40 years and had always been paid in cash. His trade union sought confirmation that he would be paid in cash for the remainder of his employment and it further asserted that he had a legal right to be paid in cash. The respondent asserted that the claimant was the only employee within the company who was paid in cash and that attempts had been made to accommodate the claimant to make the transition to electronic funds transfer payment. It was further asserted on behalf of the respondent that having to continue to pay the claimant in cash placed a disproportionate burden on the respondent. The Labour Court held that the respondent's proposals were fair and reasonable and should be accepted by the trade union and the claimant.

---

3.   *Britvic Ireland Ltd v A Worker* LCR20966.

DEDUCTIONS AND REDUCTIONS

[28.03] *Earagail Eisc Teoranta v Doherty & Ors[4]—High Court—Kearns P—appeal on point of law—Payment of Wages Act 1991, s 7(3)(b)—whether Employment Appeals Tribunal erred in law in its interpretation of Payment of Wages Act 1991, s 5*

The appellant company supplies premium seafood to a global market and its processing plant employs 200 people. In response to financial difficulties, the appellant introduced a restructuring programme whereby new procedures relating to annualised hours on performance-related pay were introduced. There was a financial rescue of the appellant and it was funded by a number of different banks subject to various conditions and covenants.

As part of a cost-cutting programme, the appellant decided to implement a 10 per cent reduction in payroll costs, which was made to staff wages in May 2011. Kearns P noted that the respondents did not agree with the proposals and initiated complaints under the relevant provisions of the 1991 Act, seeking to argue that the reductions in payroll were unlawful.

The complaints were heard by various Rights Commissioners and, in each case, the complaints were upheld. These decisions were appealed by the appellant to the EAT.

It was submitted by the appellant, before the EAT, that the reduction in pay implemented was not a deduction within the meaning of s 5 of the 1991 Act and reliance was placed on the High Court decision in *McKenzie & Anor v The Minister for Finance & Anor.*[5] *McKenzie* concerned a challenge to the implementation of a Department of Finance Circular on the 'RDF Allowance' providing for reduced rates for motor and travel allowances. It was argued on behalf of the applicant employees in that case that the proposed reduction in the allowance amounted to a deduction of wages under the Act. The respondents contended that the reduction was not a 'deduction' in wages and the 1991 Act was therefore not applicable. Edwards J held that:

> ... the reduction in the RDF allowance is not a 'deduction' from wages payable. It is a reduction of the allowance payable. The Act has no application to reductions as distinct from 'deductions'.

Submissions were made by the respondents setting out the chronology of events and referencing the pressure which was exerted on employees to accept the pay reduction or risk losing their jobs.

The EAT ultimately upheld and reaffirmed the recommendations of the Rights Commissioner and noted that s 5(1) of the 1991 Act stated that an employer shall not make a deduction from the wages of an employee unless, with reference to s 5(1)(c), the employee has given his prior consent in writing.

The EAT interpreted s 5(1) as clearly meaning that an employer:

> ... must receive the explicit written permission of its workforce to allow it to deduct its remuneration. In all of the circumstances of this case the Tribunal

---

4.   *Earagail Eisc Teoranta v Doherty & Ors* [2015] IEHC 347.
5.   *McKenzie & Anor v The Minister for Finance & Anor* [2010] IEHC 461.

cannot accede to the appellant's request that the Tribunal exercise its discretion not to award compensation.

Kearns P noted that detailed submissions had been made by the appellant in relation to the jurisdiction of the EAT to adjudicate on the issue. The appellant asserted that there was a contract of employment and a company handbook in existence setting out the associated terms and conditions governing the relationship of employment, and the matter was not suitable for adjudication by the EAT but instead was a contractual dispute between the parties. It was submitted by the appellant that what occurred in this case was a general, across the board, reduction to salary and not a deduction as captured by the 1991 Act.

It was further submitted that the EAT erroneously interpreted s 5(1) and proceeded on the basis that the provisions of subsections (a) to (c) were to be taken conjunctively; however it was submitted that the provisions were in fact disjunctive and dealt with separate situations where deductions to wages were legally permissible. It was further submitted that, even if the EAT had correctly applied s 5, which was denied by the appellant, it had failed to effectively engage with the appellant and apply the provisions of s 6 of the Act, which conferred a discretion on the EAT not to award compensation in certain cases. It was submitted that the appellant had provided detailed reasons and explanations why the reduction in pay was necessary and had urged the EAT to exercise discretion not to award compensation. It was submitted that the decision of the appellant was made out of economic necessity and that the EAT had failed to have regard to this.

Reliance was further placed by the appellant on the fact that 82 per cent of staff members had accepted the reduction by the time the matter had come before the EAT. The appellant had criticised the EAT for failing to provide any basis for its decision, despite having the benefit of detailed written and oral submissions and reserving its decision for a period of four months. Reference was made to the recent Court of Appeal decision in *Bank of Ireland v Heron*[6] where Kelly J summarised the law concerning the obligations on decision makers to give reasons.

It was submitted by the respondents that the appellant proceeded to unilaterally impose pay cuts when only a minority of employees had agreed, resulting in a number of complaints being made under the 1991 Act. The respondents asserted that both the Rights Commissioner and the EAT have extensive experience in assessing such claims under the 1991 Act. Furthermore, the EAT had the benefit of detailed written submissions regarding interpretation of the Act and did not fall into an error of law in determining that the relevant provisions were applicable in the case.

The respondents submitted that in *McKenzie*, the reduction related to an RDF allowance which covered various expenses incurred by members of the reserve defence forces involved in duties concerning training works. Section 1 of the 1991 Act defines wages and the Court noted that payments in respect of expenses are specifically excluded from this definition. It was therefore submitted that the reduction in expenses or in an allowance that covers expenses could not have formed the basis of a valid claim under s 1 and furthermore the reduction in the allowance was given effect by way of a

---

6. *Bank of Ireland v Heron and Heron* [2015] IECA 66. See [**18.01**].

statutory regulation, so that even if it did fall within the definition of wages, the reduction would have been permissible pursuant to s 5(1)(a).

A preliminary issue in this case was the way in which an attendance note of the EAT hearing, which was prepared by the representatives of the appellant, was brought before the Court. Kearns P noted that it was not necessary to reach a determination in relation to this preliminary issue. The Court was only to determine whether or not the EAT had erred in law in arriving at its decision. Kearns P firstly considered whether or not the complaint was suitable for adjudication by the EAT. Kearns P did not accept that the EAT was not the appropriate body to hear the complaint simply because there was a contract and company handbook setting out terms and conditions. Kearns P noted that the EAT was established as an independent body to provide individuals with a fair and independent means of seeking remedies for infringements of their statutory rights and it had specific expertise in considering industrial relations disputes. The perusal of contract policy documents and terms and conditions of employment was an essential part of the EAT's function.

The High Court was also satisfied that the decision in *McKenzie* was distinguishable from the facts of the present case. Kearns P accepted the submission that the remarks of Edwards J in relation to a reduction as opposed to a deduction were *obiter*. Furthermore, *McKenzie* concerned the reduction in allowance payable in respect of motor and travel subsistence; however the definition of wages in the 1991 Act expressly excludes any payment in respect of expenses incurred by an employee carrying out their employment. Hence, the findings by Edwards J in *McKenzie* that the RDF allowance did not come within the scope of a deduction related entirely to a different situation than the present case, where employees' salaries were reduced. Kearns P was satisfied that the EAT was entitled to proceed to consider the complaints on the basis that the reduction to the employees' wages in the present case may have constituted a deduction in breach of the 1991 Act.

Kearns P then considered whether or not the decision arrived at by the EAT was tainted by any error of law. Kearns P noted that he was required to have regard to the doctrine of curial deference when considering appeals from the decisions of expert administrative tribunals and quasi-judicial bodies as set out by Hamilton CJ in *Henry Denny & Sons*.[7] Kearns P held that he was satisfied that there was a manifest error of law in the EAT's interpretation of s 5 of the 1991 Act. The EAT's determination clearly indicated its view that, pursuant to s 5(1)(c) of the 1991 Act, the written consent of employees was required before the appellant could bring about any changes to salary levels. However, the exception listed at subss (1)(a), (b) and (c) of s 5 were clearly not to be taken conjunctively. Kearns P noted the word 'or' was expressly used in the provision and it is clear that each subsection concerns separate incidences which might give rise to an exception to the rule that an employer shall not make a deduction from wages of an employee.

Section 5(1)(b) states that deductions are allowable where they are authorised by virtue of an employee's contract of employment which is something the EAT should

---

7.   *Henry Denny & Sons (Ireland) Ltd v Minister for Social Welfare* [1998] 1 IR 34.

have considered independently of s 5(1)(c). In treating subss (1)(a) to (c) as conjunctive the EAT erred in law.

The High Court also held that the EAT had failed to provide adequate reasons for a number of other findings. While accepting that previous decisions of the High Court have established that the duty to give reasons does not require extensive analysis of every aspect of a complaint, Kearns P held that, in this case, the brief determination of the EAT was wholly inadequate to meet the low threshold. He noted that it was not clear how the EAT had arrived at its determination and there was not as much as a:

> fleeting reference to vital matters such as the reduction or deduction argument or why section 8.2 of the company handbook is not applicable.

Kearns P noted that there was no engagement, however minimal, with the detailed submissions of the appellant in relation to its financial circumstances at the time and no consideration was given to the circumstances relied on by the appellant for introducing the pay cuts. The Court also noted that the EAT was required to interpret the provisions of the contract of employment and the terms and conditions as set out in the handbook. Aside from briefly stating that s 8.2 of the handbook was not applicable, there was no engagement at all with the provisions of the handbook. In relation to the decision of the EAT not to exercise its discretion in relation to the payment of compensation, the High Court accepted that this was a matter for the EAT based on the facts of the case. As an expert body with experience in this area, the EAT was well placed to make this decision; however, the decision of the EAT was so devoid of explanation as to leave the parties affected by it with no understanding as to how it was determined. The matter was thus remitted to the EAT for fresh adjudication in light of the findings of the High Court.

LAY-OFF WITHOUT PAY

[28.04] *Bord na Móna v Murphy, McKenna, O'Neill, Garrett and Smith[8]— Employment Appeals Tribunal—appeal from decision of Rights Commissioner— Payment of Wages Act 1991—whether respondents lawfully placed on lay-off— whether EAT had jurisdiction to determine this issue under 1991 Act*

It was common case that the respondents had been placed on lay-off. They asserted that there was no provision in their contracts of employment to be placed on lay-off and therefore this was an illegal deduction from their wages. The appellant's position was that these employees had been placed on lay-off and that the EAT had no jurisdiction to decide whether the appellant had a right to do so.

The EAT noted that its function under the 1991 Act was to decide if a particular set of circumstances amounted to an unlawful deduction from wages. The EAT noted this very particular set of facts and held that it was the unanimous decision of the EAT that the appellant's decision to place these employees on lay-off was not a matter which the EAT had jurisdiction to decide upon under the 1991 Act. The EAT was of the view that

---

8. *Bord na Móna v Murphy, McKenna, O'Neill, Garrett and Smith* PW6/PW7/PW8/PW9/ PW10/2014.

the matter had been fully argued before the EAT and therefore overturned the decision of the Rights Commissioner.

Chapter 29

WHISTLEBLOWING

PROTECTED DISCLOSURES ACT 2014

[29.01] The Protected Disclosures Act 2014, which was enacted on 8 July 2014 and came into force on 15 July 2014, has not yet featured in any decisions of the Employment Appeals Tribunal or the Superior Courts. There is, however, one written judgment in the Circuit Court on an application for interim relief under s 11(2) of and Sch 1 to the 2014 Act as to which see para [29.05] below.

The 2014 Act was amended in 2015 by the Workplace Relations Act 2015 and two statutory instruments were made under the 2014 Act in 2015.

The Workplace Relations Act 2015 amended the Protected Disclosures Act 2014 by substituting in respect of the cause of action for penalisation (s 12 of the 2014 Act) the redress provisions (application to an Adjudication Officer and appeal to the Labour Court) created by the 2015 Act. Schedule 2 to the 2014 Act has been amended accordingly.

The 2015 statutory instruments are:

(i)   the Protected Disclosures Act 2014 (Disclosure to Prescribed Persons) Order 2015;[1]

(ii)   the Industrial Relations Act 1990 (Code of Practice on Protected Disclosures Act 2014) (Declaration) Order 2015.[2]

The Protected Disclosures Act 2014 (Disclosure to Prescribed Persons) Order 2015 amends the Protected Disclosures Act 2014 (Section 7(2)) Order 2014[3] which sets out the prescribed persons for the purpose of s 7 of the 2014 Act by deleting the Secretary General of the Department of Education and Skills from the list of prescribed persons, and by amending the description of the matters in respect of which the Secretary to the Standards in Public Office Commission is prescribed. The Director of Commission for Public Service Appointments is added as a prescribed person in respect of all matters related to the setting of standards for the recruitment and selection of public service appointments, including the monitoring and auditing of public sector recruitment and selection activities.

---

1.   Protected Disclosures Act 2014 (Disclosure to Prescribed Persons) Order 2015 (SI 448/2015).

2.   Industrial Relations Act 1990 (Code of Practice on Protected Disclosures Act 2014) (Declaration) Order 2015 (SI 464/2015).

3.   Protected Disclosures Act 2014 (Section 7(2)) Order 2014 (SI 339/2014).

There have been a number of decisions on the equivalent provisions of the UK Employment Rights Act 1996 (as amended) some, but not all, of which are relevant to the interpretation of the 2014 Act.[4]

Disclosure of 'relevant information' or the nature of the necessary belief

[29.02] *Barton v Royal Borough of Greenwich[5]—UKEAT—Employment Rights Act 1996—whether the original referral was a qualifying disclosure and a protected disclosure—reasonable belief*

The claimant, who was employed by the respondent, was advised by a colleague that the claimant's line manager had emailed a large number of documents, which the claimant believed contained confidential or personal data about the claimant, to the manager's personal email and the claimant believed that the line manager's personal email was not part of a secure system or encrypted. The claimant considered that this was a significant breach of the UK Data Protection Act 1998. The claimant did not first report the matter to management but reported his concerns to the UK Information Commissioner's Office (the ICO) (the Irish equivalent of the Data Protection Commissioner) and thereafter to management. Having consulted the ICO website, the claimant telephoned the ICO advice line to clarify his understanding of the UK Data Protection Act 1998. The information that the claimant had provided to the ICO was entirely inaccurate. The manager had emailed 11 documents to her home email, which was password protected, and none of the documents were confidential. Having established that the claimant had referred the matter to the ICO without first referring it to his line manager, the claimant was informed that he should have referred the matter to his line manager before raising concerns with the ICO and he was specifically instructed not to contact the ICO or any other external body in relation to the matter without the prior consent of his line manager. The claimant was told that the respondent would investigate the concerns promptly and it did so. The claimant, having been so instructed, telephoned the ICO to seek advice as to what he should do about the instruction. The respondent regarded the claimant's action in contacting the ICO, despite being instructed not to do so, as a serious breach of duty and he was summarily dismissed. At that time, he was the subject of a final written warning in relation to a different matter and he was also found to have committed gross misconduct by writing an inappropriate letter in the course of his duties to a member of the public. The claimant claimed that he had been unfairly dismissed for

---

4. *Benny v Department for Environment Food and Rural Affairs* [2015] WL537900 UKEAT (relating primarily to employment tribunal rules); *Chesterton Global Ltd v Nurmohamed* [2015] IRLR 614 (relating to the 'public interest' test which does not feature in the Irish 2014 Act); *Sharpe v The Bishop of Worcester* [2015] EWCA CIV 399 (whether an ordained minister was a worker) and *Smania v Standard Chartered Bank* [2015] IRLR 271 (the extra-territorial reach of statutory UK employment law).

5. *Barton v Royal Borough of Greenwich* UK EAT/0041/14/DXA.

whistleblowing and relied on the original communication with the ICO and the subsequent telephone call as protected disclosures.

The employment tribunal concluded that the original referral was a qualifying disclosure but not a protected disclosure because the employment tribunal did not consider that the claimant held the necessary reasonable belief that the information he disclosed tended to show that the respondent had failed, or was failing, to comply with its obligations under the UK Data Protection Act 1998. The employment tribunal held that the subsequent telephone call was not a qualifying disclosure because there was no disclosure of information. The employment tribunal considered that the two disclosures had to be considered separately.

On appeal to the UK EAT, the claimant contended that the two disclosures could be aggregated such that together they constituted a protected disclosure and further contended that the instruction not to contact the ICO was unlawful as contrary to public policy and a breach of Art 10 of the European Convention of Human Rights.

The UK EAT noted that, in order for a disclosure to be protected, there is a two stage test. Firstly, it must be established that the disclosure is a 'qualifying' disclosure; and secondly, if the disclosure is a qualifying disclosure, it must then be found to be 'protected'. The UK EAT referred to the decision of the UK EAT in *Cavendish Munro Professional Management v Geduld*[6] that stated a disclosure, in order to be a qualifying disclosure, must be a disclosure of 'facts' as opposed to the disclosure of an allegation without reference to specific facts. Because the disclosure in this case was a disclosure to a prescribed person, the person making the disclosure must have reasonably believed that the relevant failure that he was reporting was within the description of matters in respect of which the prescribed person was so prescribed and furthermore the person making the disclosure must reasonably have believed that the information disclosed was substantially true. The UK EAT held that the protected disclosure must be a disclosure of information and that one cannot convert a disclosure that does not qualify (for example, because it is not a disclosure of information) into a qualifying disclosure by associating it with another disclosure that does qualify. It noted that the decision in *Bolton School v Evans*[7] was authority for the proposition that disclosure is an ordinary English word and should be given its normal meaning and that a tribunal should look with care at arguments suggesting that a dismissal is because of acts related to the disclosure rather than because of the disclosure itself. The UK EAT concluded that the employment tribunal was entitled, on the evidence, to conclude that the claimant failed to hold the necessary reasonable belief of the truth of the allegations made to the ICO and concluded that the claimant could not create a protected disclosure by aggregating the initial contact with the ICO with the subsequent telephone conversation. It concluded that each disclosure must be considered separately, as neither the initial contact nor the subsequent telephone call was a protected disclosure because they did not involve the disclosure of information.

The UK EAT was not satisfied that the instruction not to contact the ICO was unlawful. The employment tribunal considered it to be a reasonable instruction in

---

6.   *Cavendish Munro Professional Management v Geduld* [2010] ICR 325.
7.   *Bolton School v Evans* [2007] ICR 641, [2007] IRLR 140.

circumstances where there was no blanket ban on contacting the ICO. The instruction was not to take the initiative in contacting them while the respondent's enquiry into the matter was underway. The UK EAT noted that the restriction was not an unqualified restriction because it was a restriction on contacting the ICO without the consent of the line manager and there was no evidence to suggest that a request by the claimant would have been refused, whether unreasonably or at all. The UK EAT could see no basis for finding that public policy should impose a blanket restriction on any limitation of contact between an employee and the ICO in all circumstances. Each case will have to be considered by reference to its own facts as to whether the limitation is reasonable. The instruction in this case would not have prevented the claimant from speaking to the ICO if it were in the context of him being contacted by the ICO. The claimant had already disclosed all relevant information to the ICO and was not seeking to supply further information but was asking for advice and that could not be a protected act.

The UK EAT concluded by noting that the claimant had made serious and wholly inaccurate allegations which were potentially highly damaging. He had contacted the ICO without having taken the trouble to check the accuracy of the allegations or draw the matters raised by his colleague to the attention of his superiors as he did shortly after contacting the ICO. There was no reason why he could not have contacted his superiors before going to the ICO. Finally, the UK EAT noted that an employer needs to show reasonable grounds for its belief in the claimant's misconduct to satisfy the burden of proof in demonstrating a substantially fair reason for the dismissal but it does not need to prove that there actually was misconduct.[8]

Unfair dismissal: onus of proof in a protected disclosure case

[29.03] *Schaathun v Executive & Business Aviation Support Ltd*[9]*—UK EAT— Employment Rights Act 1996—unfair dismissal—burden of proof*

The claimant claimed that she had been automatically unfairly dismissed by the respondent for making protected disclosures within the meaning of s 43 of the UK Employment Rights Act 1996. The respondent contended that the claimant had been dismissed for redundancy or for some other substantial reason, namely the breakdown of her personal and working relationship with the respondent's managing director. The employment tribunal had held that the reason for her dismissal was the breakdown of her relationship with the managing director and the irretrievable destruction of trust which arose from certain events. The claim that she had been automatically unfairly dismissed by reason of a protected disclosure was rejected. The employment tribunal held that it was not necessary to consider whether the reason or principal reason for the dismissal was the protected disclosures because it accepted the managing director's evidence that he did not know of the disclosures. That, in turn, raised for the UK EAT the question as to where the burden of proof lay. Was it for the claimant to establish that the protected

---

8.   *Farrant v Woodroffe School* [1998] ICR 184 and *British Homes Stores v Burchill* [1980] ICR 303.

9.   *Schaathun v Executive & Business Aviation Support Ltd* UKEAT/0227/12/LA.

disclosure was the reason, or the principal reason, for the dismissal or was it for the respondent to satisfy the tribunal as to the reason for the dismissal? The UK EAT noted the decision of the Court of Appeal in *Kuzel v Roche Products Ltd*[10] in which the Court of Appeal emphatically rejected the employer's contention that the legal burden is on the claimant to prove that a protected disclosure is the reason for a dismissal and that where an employee positively asserts that there is an inadmissible reason for the dismissal the burden of proof is on the employee. Although the claimant must produce some evidence supporting her assertions, the claimant does not have the burden of proving that the dismissal was for that reason. The UK EAT in the *Schaathun* case concluded that the legal burden was on the respondent and that the employment tribunal had erred in law in placing the burden of proof on the claimant to show that the reason for her dismissal was that she had made a protected disclosure. Accordingly, the UK EAT set aside the decision of the employment tribunal and remitted the claim to a differently-constituted employment tribunal.

Penalisation: limitation periods

[29.04] Section 12 of and Sch 2 to the 2014 Act prohibit penalisation or threatened penalisation against an employee, or causing or permitting any other person to penalise or threaten penalisation against an employee, for having made a protected disclosure. Schedule 2 provides for complaints to the Workplace Relations Commission. The limitation period in respect of complaints under s 12 is six months 'beginning on the date of the contravention to which the complaint relates'.[11] In *McKinney v Newham London Borough Council*[12] the claimant, who had his grievances rejected at successive stages of the employer's grievance procedure, complained that, by rejecting his grievance appeal, the employer had subjected him to detriment on the grounds that he had made a protected disclosure contrary to s 47(b) of the Employment Rights Act 1996. The facts were that the claimant did not learn of the decision to reject the final grievance appeal until eight days after the date on which the decision was made. The respondent contended that the claim had not been brought within the UK three-month time limit beginning 'with the date of the act ... to which the complaint relates' as prescribed by s 48(3)(a) of the UK 1996 Act. The claim was struck out as being out of time on the basis that the limitation period ran from the employer's decision to reject the grievance rather than the date on which the claimant had received the decision letter. The UK EAT, dismissing the appeal, concluded that the time period within which a complaint might be brought commenced with 'the date of the act ... to which the complaint relates' and that accordingly the time began to run against the claimant from the date of the detriment, whether or not he was aware of it. That in turn meant that the claim was out of time.

---

10.   *Kuzel v Roche Products Ltd* [2008] IRLR 530.
11.   Workplace Relations Act 2015, s 41(6).
12.   *McKinney v Newham London Borough Council* [2015] 1 ICR 495.

Unfair dismissal: interim relief

[29.05] Section 11(2) of and Sch 1 to the Protected Disclosures Act 2014 provide for interim relief in cases where a claim is brought for redress for claimed unfair dismissal by reason of having made a protected disclosure. The Circuit Court is thereby given jurisdiction to grant interim relief where 'it appears to the Court that it is likely that there are substantial grounds for contending that dismissal results wholly or mainly from the employee having made a protected disclosure'.[13] The interim relief could involve reinstatement of the employee or re-engagement of the employee in another position on terms and conditions not less favourable than those applicable prior to the dismissal.

In *Philpott v Marymount University Hospital and Hospice Ltd*[14] the Circuit Court considered an application for interim relief. The applicant had commenced work with the respondent in May 2014 on a five-year fixed-term contract. The applicant was given two months' notice of dismissal in December 2014, such that his employment was to end in February 2015. The applicant claimed that he was dismissed because he made protected disclosures and he lodged an unfair dismissal claim seeking reinstatement and thereafter sought interim relief from the Circuit Court. Specifically, he sought a continuation of his contract of employment pending the determination of the proceedings by the EAT. The Circuit Court approached the matter by examining each of the claimed protected disclosures and alleged wrongdoings set out in a document sent by the applicant to the board of the respondent. The Court, having heard evidence, concluded that each of the claims was false. Specifically, charity funding had not been expended unlawfully, there was no lack of transparency in how the respondent conducted fundraising and how the funds were spent. The Court also noted that the building passed HIQA inspections and that there were no significant issues with the building which posed and continued to pose a critical risk to the health and safety of patients, staff and the public. The Court rejected the assertion that there was mismanagement of financial resources, noting that no financial information was tendered to support the appellant's contention and the Court rejected the applicant's criticism of funding of education for a colleague in circumstances where he had accepted funding for education himself. The Court rejected the interim application on the basis that it could not satisfy itself that the beliefs and disclosures were reasonable. The applicant did not satisfy the evidentiary burden and accordingly the interim remedy was refused.

---

13.   Protected Disclosures Act 2014, Sch 1, para 2(1).
14.   *Philpott v Marymount University Hospital and Hospice Ltd* [2015] IECC 1.

Chapter 30

WORKING TIME

ROAD HAULAGE

[30.01] *Cosgrave Transport (Limerick) Ltd v Bonczak[1]—Labour Court—appeal from decision of Rights Commissioner—European Communities (Road Transport) (Organisation of Working Time of Persons Performing Mobile Road Transport Activities) Regulations 2012 (SI 36/2012), regs 5, 6, 7, 8, 10, 11, 12(f) and 20— maximum working hours—break entitlements—whether period of time during which truck driven by complainant was being loaded or unloaded reckonable as working time for purposes of 2012 Regulations—'periods of availability'—direct effect of European law*

The complainant referred his claim against his former employer, the respondent, to the Labour Court in accordance with reg 20 of the European Communities (Road Transport) (Organisation of Working Time of Persons Performing Mobile Road Transport Activities) Regulations 2012[2] (the Regulations). This appeal against the findings of a Rights Commissioner was heard together with the respondent's cross-appeal in relation to same.

The complainant was employed by the respondent, a road haulage contractor, as a truck driver. He had no regular starting or finishing times. He started work between 4 am and 8 am, depending on the work to which he was assigned. He finished work between 6 pm and 9 pm. He received one break of 45 minutes duration during the course of the day, which was taken when his truck was being loaded or unloaded. He did not receive any other regular breaks. The complainant transported goods in containers. On arrival at a client's premises, the client was responsible for loading or unloading the containers and the complainant did not participate in this work. At the commencement of this loading/unloading process the complainant would take his 45-minute break. The standard arrangement between the respondent and its clients was that the process of loading/unloading the truck would take two hours. One hour after his arrival at a client's premises, the complainant was required to telephone the respondent's office to indicate how much longer the process would take. If the time extended beyond two hours, an additional charge was incurred by the client. The complainant generally remained with the truck during the periods of loading/unloading, though he was not required to do so. The tachograph fitted to his truck was turned off during these periods.

The complainant brought a number of claims against the respondent under the Regulations. The first of the claims related to maximum working time as permitted by reg 5. He claimed that he was required to work in excess of 60 hours in some weeks and

---

1.   *Cosgrave Transport (Limerick) Ltd v Bonczak* RTD158.
2.   European Communities (Road Transport) (Organisation of Working Time of Persons Performing Mobile Road Transport Activities) Regulations 2012 (SI 36/2012).

in excess of 48 hours per week on average. The complainant maintained that the periods during which the truck was being unloaded and loaded constituted working time for the purpose of the Regulations. The respondent contended that these periods were properly classifiable as 'periods of availability', and were not reckonable as working time.

'Periods of availability' are not defined by the Regulations. However, Directive 2002/15/EC, which the Regulations transpose into domestic law, provides that 'periods of availability' are those other than break or rest times during which a worker is not required to remain at his workstation, but must be available to answer calls to start or resume driving or to carry out other work. The Directive specifies that these periods of availability, and their duration, should be notified to the worker in advance.

The Labour Court noted that there is an obligation to interpret and apply domestic law in light of the wording and purpose of a relevant European Union directive. The Court cited *Marleasing SA v La Comercial Internacionale de Alimentacion SA*[3] in support of this contention. The Labour Court also noted that reg 2(2) expressly provides that a word or expression used in the Regulations which is also used in the Directive has the same meaning, unless the contrary intention is evident. Applying the definition of 'periods of availability' as per the Directive, the Labour Court concluded that the loading/unloading times constituted periods of availability and did not constitute working time for the purpose of reg 5. The Court emphasised that these periods were reasonably foreseeable by the complainant, given the standard arrangements in place between the respondent and its clients. The Court also noted that 45 minutes of the loading period was taken by the complainant as a break. It was emphasised that this was not a period of availability but a break entitlement and that this too should be discounted for the purpose of measuring his working time under the Regulations. Taking these factors into consideration and discounting the break periods and periods of availability from the complainant's working time calculations, the Labour Court concluded that the complainant did not work in excess of the periods specified in reg 5.

The complainant also claimed that he had not been provided with sufficient notification, contrary to reg 11 of the Regulations. The Rights Commissioner had concluded that this claim was presented outside the relevant time limit specified under reg 18(4) and as such was barred. The Labour Court affirmed this decision and held that no grounds existed to grant an extension of the time limit under reg 18(5).

In relation to the respondent's cross-appeal of awards made by the Rights Commissioner to the complainant in respect of contraventions of his break entitlements, excessive night work hours and the right to receive records of his hours worked, the Labour Court affirmed the decisions of the Rights Commissioner and found no basis upon which it could justify interference with the awards granted.

---

3.   *Marleasing SA v la Comercial Internacionale de Alimentacion SA* (Case C–106/89), [1990] ECR 1–415.

TRAVELLING TIME

[30.02] *Federación de Servicios Privados del Sindicato Comisiones Obreras (CCOO) v Tyco Integrated Security SL, Tyco Integrated Fire & Security Corporation Servicios SA[4]—CJEU—Directive 2003/88/EC, art 2—reference for preliminary ruling—social policy—protection of safety and health of workers—organisation of working time—concept of 'working time'—workers not assigned fixed or habitual place of work—whether time spent travelling between workers' homes and premises of first and last customers constituted working time*

This determination was a preliminary ruling on the interpretation of point (1) of art 2 of Directive 2003/88/EC concerning the organisation of working time. The matter was referred to the CJEU from the High Court of Spain in the course of proceedings brought by one of Spain's largest trade unions against Tyco, a Spanish company specialising in the provision and maintenance of security systems.

The action was prompted by the closure of Tyco's regional offices in 2011, which resulted in all of its employees being assigned to its central office in Madrid. As a result, technicians employed by Tyco to install and maintain the security systems within the province/geographical area to which they were assigned had no fixed or habitual place of work and had to travel directly from their homes to the places they were to carry out installations or maintenance services each day. In some cases, technicians were spending up to three hours each morning travelling to their first customer. Technicians were provided with company vehicles and received their working day task list and times for appointments daily on their company mobile phones.

The claims arose from the fact that Tyco refused to consider the time spent by these technicians on daily travel between their homes and their first and last customers as 'working time' within the meaning of the Directive. Tyco deemed the working day to start when the technicians arrived at the premises of the first customer and to end when the technicians left the premises of the last customer. Before the closure of the regional offices, however, Tyco used to count the work day as starting when the technicians arrived at those offices to pick up their task list and vehicle.

In considering whether this travel time should constitute 'working time', the CJEU emphasised that the aim of the Directive was to lay down minimum standards for workers and to guarantee better protection of the safety and health of workers by ensuring that they were entitled to rest periods and adequate breaks.

The essential question to be considered was whether the elements of the concept of 'working time' were present during this travel time and therefore whether the time should be regarded as work time or rest time.

The CJEU decided that to exclude travel time from working time was contrary to the health and safety objectives of the Directive in circumstances where it was a necessary means of providing technical services to customers.

---

4.   *Federación de Servicios Privados del Sindicato Comisiones Obreras (CCOO) v Tyco Integrated Security SL, Tyco Integrated Fire & Security Corporation Servicios SA* (Case C–266/14).

The CJEU noted that the definition of working time under the Directive is any time during which the worker is: (i) carrying out his activities or duties; (ii) at the employer's disposal; and (iii) working in accordance with national laws and practice, and the CJEU considered each of these elements in turn.

In relation to the first element, the CJEU placed emphasis on the fact that before the regional offices had been closed, journeys between the offices and customers were categorised as working time and this showed that driving a vehicle from the office to the first customer and from the last customer back was previously recognised as a duty or activity of work. The nature of the journeys had not changed since the closure of the regional offices – only the departure point. For these reasons, the CJEU regarded the workers as carrying out their duties and activities of work while during these travel times.

In relation to the second element, the CJEU held that the decisive factor in determining whether a worker is at an employer's disposal is whether the worker is required to be physically present at a place determined by the employer and to be available to the employer to provide services. The ability to pursue their own interests or manage their time without major constraints are factors which would operate against a finding that the worker is at the employer's disposal. In determining that the workers were in fact at the employer's disposal, the CJEU placed emphasis on the fact that the employer determined the list and order of the customers to be followed and the times of appointments. The workers were subject to the instructions of the employer and were not able to use their time freely or pursue their own interests during this time and consequently were deemed to be at their employer's disposal.

In relation to the third element, the CJEU concluded that it followed that if a worker who has no fixed place of work is carrying out his or her duties and activities during the journey to and from a customer, that worker must also be regarded as working during that journey. Given that travel is an integral part of being a worker without a fixed or habitual place of work, the 'place of work' of such workers cannot be reduced to the physical areas of work on the premises of their employer's customers. The fact that the journey began at the worker's home did not impact that finding, particularly in circumstances where that fact stemmed directly from the decision of the employer to abolish the regional offices.

Accordingly, the CJEU concluded that the time spent by workers without a fixed or habitual place of work travelling each day between their homes and the premises of their first and last customers constituted 'working time' for the purposes of the Directive.

Importantly the CJEU noted that the Directive is limited in scope to the organisation of working time and has no bearing on remuneration, and thus the method of remunerating workers for travel time was a matter to be determined by national law.

ANNUAL LEAVE

[30.03] *Sparantus Ltd t/a Highfield Healthcare v Jemiola⁵—Labour Court—appeal from decision of Rights Commissioner—Organisation of Working Time Act 1997, ss 18, 19(1) and (3), and 21(4)—Directive 2003/88/EC, art 7—whether annual leave continues to accrue while employee on sick leave—direct effect of European law—doctrine of conforming or consistent interpretation*

The complainant maintained that she was not afforded an accrual of annual leave in respect of a period during which she was absent from work on certified sick leave. In making her case, the complainant relied on the decision of the CJEU in *Stringer & Ors v HM Revenue and Customs.*⁶ In *Stringer* it was held that the guarantee contained in art 7 of Directive 2003/88/EC that workers are entitled to four weeks paid holidays per year could not be made dependent on the number of hours worked in a leave year. This led the CJEU to hold that a worker on sick leave continues to accrue an entitlement to annual leave. The worker must be entitled to take this annual leave upon their return to work.

The Labour Court held that the Directive could not have direct effect in a case involving private parties. It considered that there were circumstances in which reliance can be placed on a directive in a dispute to which the doctrine of direct effect is inapplicable by application of the doctrine of conforming or consistent interpretation. The Labour Court cited *Marleasing SA v La Comercial Internacionale de Alimentacion SA*⁷ in support of this contention. However, the Court noted that no submissions had been made on behalf of the complainant upon which the Court could hold that the doctrine of conforming or consistent interpretation applied in this case. The Court held that it was not for the Court to make a case for a party; rather it was for a party who places reliance on a proposition of law to explain to the Court the basis upon which that proposition should be accepted. Due to the lack of submissions on this point made by the complainant, the Court found that it was bound to apply domestic law as it stood. Accordingly, it was held that there had been no contravention of s 19 of the Act in calculating the complainant's entitlement to annual leave in the relevant year.

The complainant also made a claim under s 19(3) of the Act, which relates to times at which annual leave is given. The Labour Court considered that the provision which states that an employee must be afforded an unbroken period of two weeks of annual leave applies only to employees who have worked eight months or more in the relevant leave year. This did not appear to apply to the complainant, who did not present any evidence to challenge the respondent's position on this point. The Court declined to hold that the complainant's argument on the basis of this section was well-founded. The complainant's submission under s 21 of the Act was based upon the complainant's

---

5.   *Sparantus Ltd t/a Highfield Healthcare v Jemiola* DWT14110.

6.   *Stringer & Ors v HM Revenue and Customs sub nom Commissioners of Inland Revenue v Ainsworth & Ors, Schultz-Hoff v Deutsche Rentenversicherung Bund* (Joined Cases C–520/06 and C–350/06).

7.   *Marleasing SA v La Comercial Internacionale de Alimentacion SA* (Case C–106/89).

contention that the respondent was in breach of this provision by failing to provide her with a benefit in respect of certain public holidays that fell in the relevant leave year. The Court considered that the complainant's entitlement in respect of public holidays fell within s 21(4) of the Act. Therefore, it was contingent upon having worked for 40 hours in the five weeks' preceding that public holiday. Accordingly the Court was satisfied that the respondent was not in breach of this section of the Act. The complainant's case in relation to s 18 of the Act (which relates to the zero working hours practice) was that she was not offered work for a period of four weeks, spanning from July to August 2013. Evidence was given by the complainant's former manager, who stated that she had discussed the matter with the complainant and it had been agreed that she would not resume work until the next roster period, which commenced on 23 August 2013. The Court accepted the veracity of that evidence. The Court held that there had been no contravention by the respondent of s 18 of the Act. The Court concluded that the complainant's submissions were not well-founded. The decision of the Rights Commissioner was affirmed and the appeal was disallowed.

See **[31.15]** for legislative changes introduced by the Workplace Relations Act 2015.

HOLIDAY PAY

[30.04] *Bear Scotland Ltd & Ors v Fulton[8]—UK Employment Appeal Tribunal— Langstaff J—Working Time Directive 2003/88—Working Time Regulations 1998— whether Working Time Directive, art 7 provides for non-guaranteed overtime to be included as normal remuneration when calculating holiday pay—whether Working Time Regulations 1998 drafted to conform with Working Time Directive, art 7 and subsequent CJEU guidance—distinction between guaranteed and non-guaranteed working time—whether radius allowances and travel expenses should be included as normal remuneration and included in payment for holiday leave*

The three claimants were each employed by one of the three appellant companies, Bear, Hertel and AMEC, and each of their terms of employment obliged the claimants to work overtime. There was no corresponding obligation for the respondents to provide overtime work to the claimants. In calculating holiday pay for the claimants, overtime hours and overtime pay were not taken into account. In the case of the Hertel and AMEC employees, entitlements to radius allowances and travel-time payments were also excluded from their holiday pay. The claimants brought complaints against their employers in relation to the calculation of the holiday pay received. The employment tribunals in the three cases found that the respondents had unlawfully deducted wages from the claimants by failing to include the non-guaranteed overtime in calculating their holiday pay. The respondents appealed these decisions to the UK EAT. In relation to the Hertel and AMEC employees, the employment tribunal found that the radius allowances and the travel-time payments were not to be included in calculating holiday pay in

---

8.   *Bear Scotland Ltd & Ors v Fulton & Ors, Hertel (UK) Ltd v Woods & Ors, AMEC Group Ltd v Law & Ors* UKEATS/0047/13/BI, UKEAT/0160/14/SM, UKEAT/0161/14/SM.

respect of annual leave. The Hertel and AMEC employees appealed this. As the central issues in the cases raised the same principal issues, the appeals were all heard together.

The right to a paid holiday in the UK is provided for by the Working Time Regulations 1998 (the Regulations) which implement Directive 2003/88.[9] Article 7 of the Directive provides that Member States shall take the measures necessary to ensure that every worker is entitled to paid annual leave of at least four weeks in accordance with the conditions of entitlement to, and granting of such leave set down by national legislation and/or practice. The main issue for the UK EAT to consider was whether or not art 7 of the Directive required that non-guaranteed overtime be paid during an employee's annual leave.

Langstaff J first referred to the decision in *British Airways plc v Williams*[10] where airline pilots sought payment in respect of annual leave consisting of three elements: a proportionate part of their fixed service; a supplementary payment, which varied according to time spent in the air; and an allowance for time spent away from the employee's base. The case concerned the employees' entitlements under the Civil Aviation (Working Time) Regulations 2004 (which was based on Directive 2000/79/EC and contained the same provisions on annual leave as the Directive). In that case, the Supreme Court referred to the CJEU the question as to what extent European law laid down or defined any requirements as to the nature and level of payments to be made in respect of paid annual leave; and what discretion the Member States had to determine how such payments were calculated. The CJEU held that for the duration of annual leave, remuneration must be maintained and that workers must receive their normal remuneration for that period of rest. The CJEU also stated that the purpose of the requirement of payment for leave is to put the employee, during the leave, in a position comparable to periods of work with regard to remuneration. The Supreme Court found that all of the components of the total remuneration that generally related to the personal and professional status of the employee airline pilots had to be maintained during the employees' paid annual leave. Langstaff J noted that it remains to be determined whether he would apply the same principles and approach with regard to the Regulations as was taken by the CJEU in respect of the Civil Aviation (Working Time) Regulations 2004. Langstaff J noted that this case concerned five issues for determination.

The first issue was what art 7 of the Directive required by way of paid annual leave and whether non-guaranteed overtime and other elements of remuneration were to be included in pay for annual leave. He noted that the claimants were contractually obliged to work overtime but that the respondents had no corresponding obligation to provide overtime work. In relation to the Hertel and AMEC employees, there existed a provision to the effect that, while it was not guaranteed, the employees would be required to work overtime and that 'it will not form any part of the calculations on holiday pay entitlement'. Langstaff J noted that 'non-guaranteed overtime' was not specifically at issue in the *British Airways* case and it stood therefore to be decided whether the reasoning in that case could also apply to the current circumstances. Langstaff J noted that there existed no reason not to accept the now settled decisions of the CJEU in the

---

9. Directive 2003/88/EC concerning Certain Aspects of the Organisation of Working Time.

10. *British Airways plc v Williams* [2012] UKSC 43.

British Airways case and in the subsequent decision in *Lock v British Gas Trading Ltd*[11] with regard to the meaning of art 7 of the Directive and it must therefore be viewed as the approved authority on the matter. Upon a close examination of previous authorities, Langstaff J found that art 7 of the Directive requires that non-guaranteed overtime be paid during annual leave and that there was no need to refer the question to the CJEU.

The second issue was whether the domestic legislation could be read in accordance with the interpretation of art 7 as outlined by the CJEU. Langstaff J noted that the Regulations had been developed specifically to implement the Directive and that, if it was necessary to adopt an interpretation that confirmed the intentions of the Directive, this would not do violence to the wording but respect it. He found that the obligation to construe the Regulations 'as far as possible' to conform with the Directive is a powerful obligation. Langstaff J found that the form, nature and purpose of the Regulations made it possible to construe it in line with the Directive and the reasoning of the CJEU with regard to entitlements for holiday pay.

In relation to the third issue, Langstaff J noted that the Hertel and AMEC employees had asserted that sums due to them had been deducted unlawfully from the wages paid. This issue concerned a limitation period with regard to bringing a claim for sums due. In the circumstances, Langstaff J found it unnecessary to thoroughly and retrospectively examine the issue.

The fourth issue concerned the issue of whether the employment tribunal was correct in determining the Hertel and AMEC employees' working hours and that pay in lieu of notice should have been based on the weekly shift patterns that they last worked before their contracts were terminated. Langstaff J noted that the issue was one of contractual construction. The meaning to be constructed concerned a contractual reference to 'overtime' and whether there existed a distinction between guaranteed overtime and non-guaranteed overtime. Langstaff J held that the issue should be construed in accordance with s 234 of the Employment Rights Act 1996. He would approach the matter not by examining what happened after the contract was made but what the agreement was when the parties entered into it, and that the interpretation would accord with the reasonable understanding of the parties concerned at the time of entering into the agreement, assessed objectively and in context. On the basis of his analysis, Langstaff J overturned the decision of the employment tribunal and the appeal on the discrete point of contractual construction succeeded.

The fifth and final issue to be determined by Langstaff J again concerned only the Hertel and AMEC employees. Each of their employees was contractually entitled to certain allowances in the form of radius allowances (payment to employees who travelled daily between home and any site more than eight miles away) and travelling-time payments (payment for time spent travelling between work locations). The claimants claimed that these allowances should be included in the calculation of normal remuneration for the purposes of any payment received in respect of holiday leave. The employment tribunal had found that the radius allowances and travelling expenses were neither 'intrinsically linked' to work performed nor related to the employees' personal or professional status and could not therefore be included in the calculation of holiday

---

11.   *Lock v British Gas Trading Ltd* (Case C–539/12).

pay. The *British Airways* case established that what was to be paid during holidays as 'normal remuneration' were components of pay which were intrinsically linked to work performed; but excluded from this definition were any payments made exclusively to cover occasional and ancillary costs. Langstaff *J* disagreed with the employment tribunal's decision and found that this aspect of the claim against Hertel and AMEC succeeded. Langstaff J found that time spent travelling is not an expense ancillary to travel such as a train ticket or bus fare would be. He noted that it is time spent that is linked to work and the necessity that the time should be spent is indicative of the strength of the link.

DOCTORS IN TRAINING

[30.05] *European Commission v Ireland[12]—Opinion of Advocate General—failure of Member State to fulfil obligations—Directive 2003/88/EC—organisation of working time—concept of 'working time'—doctors in training*

This Opinion of the Advocate General focused on the transposition by Ireland of Directive 2003/88 concerning certain aspects of the organisation of working time into national law by means of the European Communities (Organisation of Working Time) (Activities of Doctors in Training) Regulations 2004,[13] as amended by the 2010 amending Regulations[14] (the Regulations).

The European Commission claimed that Ireland failed to fulfil its obligations under Arts 3, 5, 6 and 17(2) and (5) of the Directive by failing to apply the provisions of that Directive to the organisation of the working time of doctors in training, also known as non-consultant hospital doctors (NCHDs).

The Health Service Executive signed a settlement agreement with the Irish Medical Organisation which represents all practising doctors in Ireland on 22 January 2012, as a result of which, a collective agreement and a standard employment contract came into being between the parties. Clause 3(a) of the agreement states that time spent training, as scheduled in the duty roster and at a time when the NCHD is not on call, is not to be counted as working time. However, the Commission submits that, on the contrary, such time spent training constitutes 'working time' for the purposes of art 2, point (1) of the Directive.

This raised a new point of law regarding the interpretation of 'working time' for the purposes of point (1), art 2 of the Directive. The definition of 'working time' under art 2, point (1) is as follows:

> … Any period during which the worker is working, at the employer's disposal and carrying out his activity or duties, in accordance with national laws and/or practice.

---

12. *European Commission v Ireland* (Case C–87/14).
13. European Communities (Organisation of Working Time) (Activities of Doctors in Training) Regulations 2004 (SI 494/2004).
14. European Communities (Organisation of Working Time) (Activities of Doctors in Training) (Amendment) Regulations 2010 (SI 553/2010).

The Commission also pointed out that the Agreement for Treatment of Training Time, appended to the collective agreement, identifies three categories of training time:

- Scheduled and protected time off-site attending training as required by the training programme;

- On site regular weekly/fortnightly scheduled educational and training activities including conferences, grand rounds, morbidity and mortality conferences; and

- Research, study and so on.

The Commission submitted that, to the extent that the training activities are required by the training programme and take place at a location determined by that programme, they must be counted as 'working time' for the purposes of the Directive. The Commission submitted that this is appropriate for the first two categories of training time. Accordingly, time spent at home in study and research should not be regarded as 'working time' and could therefore be counted as 'rest periods' for the purposes of the Directive. This, the Commission submitted, is appropriate for the third category. The Commission stated the fact that specific hours are reserved in the duty rosters for training activities does nothing to alter the fact that those activities are inherently 'work'. The Commission further pointed out the specific role played by placing limits on working time and imposing minimum rest periods for doctors in safeguarding the health and safety of doctors and their patients.

In response, Ireland contended that the hours of training scheduled in the duty rosters and falling outside on-call periods, which represent protected training time, must not be counted as working time for the purposes of art 2, point (1) of the Directive. According to Ireland, it followed from the judgment in *SIMAP*[15] that the concept of working time is essentially linked to 'the carrying out of, or the availability to and actually carrying out of, the duties and activities of work in the workplace'. Similarly, in the decision of *Jaeger*,[16] to satisfy the definition of 'working time', it is essential that a doctor be available to the employer at a specific location, usually though not exclusively, on site, to provide services and/or to carry out the activities and duties related to his work.

It was Ireland's argument, therefore, that the protected weekly training is time during which an NCHD is not on call and is not engaged in the activities or duties of his work nor available for such activities or duties. The fact that such training time is remunerated is, according to Ireland, merely a reflection of the special status of doctors in training. The essential difference, according to Ireland, is that a doctor on call is available for work and can be called upon to carry out activities or duties, while a doctor in training cannot. The purpose of assigning specific time to training activities within duty rosters, according to Ireland, is simply to make it easier for NCHDs to meet their obligations under the Medical Practitioners Act 2007 and to organise both the NCHD's and employer's time to ensure efficient delivery of services.

---

15. *Sindicato de Médicos de Asistencia Publica (SIMAP) v Conselleria de Sanidad y Consuma de la Generalidad Valenciana* (Case C–303/98).
16. *Landeshaupt stadt Kiel v Norbert Jaeger* (Case C–151/02).

In the Advocate General's analysis, he stated that the aim of the Directive was to harmonise the organisation of working time across the EU to guarantee better protection of the health and safety of workers by ensuring that they are entitled to minimum rest periods and by setting the maximum average duration of the working week at 48 hours, which is expressly stated to encompass overtime.[17]

The Advocate General noted the provisions of the Directive which relate specifically to trainee doctors. In those provisions, there is no particular definition of 'working time'. Therefore, the general definition, set out in art 2, point (1) of the Directive must apply. The Advocate General pointed out that the CJEU has stated that there is no intermediate category between 'working time' and 'rest periods' and that neither the intensity of the work carried out by the employee nor his output are among the elements that characterise 'working time' for the purposes of that Directive. Therefore, the CJEU held that these concepts must be defined in accordance with objective characteristics, by reference to the scheme and purpose of that Directive, which is intended to improve the living and working conditions of workers. Furthermore, art 2 of the Directive is not one of the provisions open to derogation.

The Advocate General stated his belief that the definition of 'working time' is based on three criteria in light of the case law of the CJEU. These are (i) a spatial criterion; (ii) an authority criterion; and (iii) a professional criterion. The exclusion of NCHD training hours from the concept of 'working time' for the purposes of that provision is contrary to the Directive as in the case of a trainee doctor, all three criteria are met. NCHDs must follow a training programme with an appointed body approved for that purpose, and must do so in liaison with their employer, who must organise a duty roster so as to ensure that the training is properly administered. Therefore, the professional training of NCHDs is an integral part of their training and accordingly, they must be considered to be carrying out their activity or duties for the purposes of art 2, point (1) of the Directive when they are following their training programme, including when they are not on call.

It was the Advocate General's opinion that irrespective of whether training takes place at a hospital or on the premises of the training body, what is important is that NCHDs are required to remain during those training hours in a place that they are not free to choose, but which depends on the training programme that they are required to follow. This constitutes a constraint which prevents them from freely engaging in their personal activities. When NCHDs carry out their training outside on-call periods, it does not mean that they have escaped from their employer's managerial authority; and their training is kept under review by their employer.

The fact that the training of the NCHDs is reviewed by the employer is consistent with the finding that under the terms of s 8(b) of the Standard Contract of Employment, the participation of the NCHDs in a training programme is one of the obligations incumbent upon NCHDs under the contract of employment which binds them to their employer. It follows that an employer would potentially be entitled to penalise failure on the part of an NCHD to fulfil their training obligations as specified in their employment contract.

---

17.   Order in *Grigore* (Case C–258/10), para 40.

The training of NCHDs is intended to enable them to adapt to their posts and its purpose is therefore professional in nature. It is not personal time that the NCHDs have independently chosen to dedicate to training; it is intended to satisfy a professional obligation under the control of the employer and, therefore, does not constitute resting time. Rest periods serve to compensate for fatigue arising from periods of work. It would undermine that essential function of rest periods if they were deemed to encompass the time that NCHDs spent in training. The manner in which the CJEU has defined 'rest period' means that Ireland's line of argument can be readily rejected.

The Advocate General concluded by proposing that the CJEU rule that Ireland has failed to fulfil its obligations under Arts 3, 5 and 6 of the Directive by excluding the training hours of NCHDs as scheduled in the duty roster and falling outside on-call periods from the concept of 'working time' for the purposes of art 2, point (1) of the Directive.

[30.06] *European Commission v Ireland—Judgment of CJEU[18]—Directive 2003/ 88—working time—doctors in training*

In its judgment, the CJEU noted that the Commission was not challenging the transposition of Directive 2003/88 by the 2004 Regulations[19] but does contend that the Irish public authorities did not apply the Regulations, which constitutes a failure on the part of that Member State to fulfil its obligations.

In support of its application the Commission referred to the fact that in order to settle a disagreement concerning the working time of NCHDs, the IMO and the HSE signed a Settlement Agreement in January 2010 to which a collective agreement between those parties and a standard contract of employment for NCHDs were annexed. It was submitted by the Commission that cl 3(a) and 3(b) of the Collective Agreement and certain provisions of cl 5 of the standard contract of employment infringed the provisions of Directive 2003/88.

The CJEU noted that various reports concerning the implementation of that Directive and a declaration by the IMO confirmed that there was a failure to fulfil obligations stemming from its implementation in practice. The CJEU noted that the first ground of complaint was that cl 3(a) of the Collective Agreement breached the Directive as it provided that certain training for NCHDs is not to be considered working time. It was submitted by Ireland that the training hours concerned represented a protected training period during which NCHDs were not available to pursue professional activities. Secondly, the relationship between NCHDs and their training organisation was separate from that which existed between an NCHD and their employers. Training requirements for NCHDs do not form an integral part of their employment. Their employer does not direct the conduct of such training nor does it determine the activities

---

18.   *European Commission v Ireland* (Case C–87/14).

19.   European Communities (Organisation of Working Time) (Activities of Doctors in Training) Regulations 2004 (SI 494/2004), as amended by the European Communities (Organisation of Working Time) (Activities of Doctors in Training) (Amendment) Regulations 2010 (SI 553/2010).

which the NCHDs must undertake under that training nor the progression of the NCHD within that training, and it does not determine the place.

The CJEU noted that it was common ground that the training time mentioned in para 1 of annex 1 to the Collective Agreement was not considered working time as provided in cl 3(c) of the Collective Agreement. The CJEU noted that the determining factor for working time is that the individuals are required to be physically present at the place determined by the employer, to be available to the employer, in order to be able to provide the appropriate services immediately in case there is a need. The CJEU noted that in proceedings for failure to fulfil appropriate obligations it was up to the Commission to prove the existence of an alleged infringement and to provide the Court with the information necessary for it to determine whether the infringement was made out.

The CJEU noted that the Commission did not dispute the explanations provided by Ireland to the effect that the training time concerned represented a protected period of training during which NCHDs were not available to provide medical care to patients. However on the other hand the Commission maintained that training activities of NCHDs were an integral part of their employment, in that they must carry out the activities under the terms of their employment contract. The CJEU observed that Ireland had argued, without contradiction, that the relationship between NCHDs and their training organisations were different from that which existed between NCHDs and their employer. The CJEU noted that at the hearing the Commission was unable to substantiate its arguments that the training organisations concerned and the employers of NCHD must all be identified with the State who was the only employer of NCHDs within the meaning of the Directive.

The CJEU concluded that the Commission had not demonstrated that the training times constituted working time within the meaning of the Directive and consequently in relation to cl 3(a) of the Collective Agreement it had not established that the existence of a practice that contravened the Directive and thus the first ground of complaint was rejected.

In its second complaint the Commission argued that cl 3(b) of the Collective Agreement under which 'a reference period of NCHDs whose formal contacts are 12 months or greater shall be extended from 6 to 12 months' infringes the provisions of the Directive. It acknowledged that art 19 of the Directive allows the reference period for the calculation of maximum weekly working time to be extended to 12 months in accordance with the collective agreement. However it was submitted that a provision such as an extension is only possible subject to observance of the general principles relating to the protection of health and safety of workers, and only for objective or technical reasons or reasons concerning the organisation work. However Ireland submitted that the extension of the reference period from 6 to 12 months for NCHDs whose employment contracts were longer than 12 months was compatible with the Directive. It noted that the Collective Agreement referred to the objective reasons concerning organisation of work which necessitated an extension of the reference period, namely the concern of the HSE as to the ability to roster NCHDs flexibly in order to implement fully its statutory obligations. The CJEU noted that the Commission was acknowledging that the reference period may be extended to 12 months pursuant to art 19 of the Directive and had merely pointed out the conditions for such an extension without in any way explaining how, contrary to what Ireland maintains, those conditions were not met in the present case. The CJEU concluded that the Commission had not established in relation to cl 3(c) of the Collective Agreement the existence of a practice which infringes the Directive 2003/88, and the second ground of complaint was rejected.

The third ground of complaint was a challenge to certain provisions of cl 5 of the standard contract of employment for NCHDs. The Commission submitted that there was nothing in the document to show that NCHDs were entitled to minimum daily and weekly rest periods as prescribed in the Directive and to equivalent compensatory rest periods. Further reference was made to cl 5(i) of the standard contract which provided for overtime in addition to the standard 39 working hours per week. It was submitted by Ireland that although it is not set out in the wording of the contract, the protections provided by both the Directive and the 2004 Regulations were an integral part of the document because of the Settlement Agreement that was reached in January 2010. In any event the safeguards were binding on the employers of NCHDs under the 2004 Regulations. The CJEU held that by referencing certain provisions of cl 5 of the standard contract in isolation, the scope of which is moreover subject to discussion between the parties, the Commission had not succeeded in establishing the existence of a practice contrary to the Directive and the third ground of complaint was rejected.

Finally the Commission made reference to various progress reports on the implementation of Directive 2003/88 compiled by the Irish authorities and to a declaration of the IMO which concluded that, even if progress had been made, Ireland had still not fully complied with its obligations. It was conceded by Ireland that it had not been possible in practice to achieve a situation of complete compliance with the Directive in every case but it disputed that this was because of a failure on its part in its obligation to take necessary measures to achieve such a situation. Ireland maintained that it had made constant and concerted efforts to achieve total conformity and practice and that it continued to deal with all instances of non-compliance including the use of financial penalties. It was submitted by Ireland that the Commission's argument was tantamount to saying that the simple fact that the regulation transposing Directive 2003/88 is not respected in all instances was sufficient to justify a finding of failure to fulfil obligations by Ireland under EU Law.

However it was held by the CJEU that it did not suffice for the Commission to refer to the progress report and the IMO declaration to establish that Ireland had not applied the Directive. It was also incumbent on the Commission to show, without being able to rely on any presumption whatsoever, that the practice alleged to be contrary to the Directive can be attributed, in one way or another, to Ireland. The CJEU ultimately held that the Commission had not proved the existence, in relation to Ireland, of practices contrary to Arts 3, 5, 6 and 17(2) and (5) of the Directive in relation to the organisation of working time of NCHDs and therefore the action must be dismissed.

REST BREAKS

[30.07] *Nutweave Ltd t/a Bombay Pantry v Kumar[20]—Labour Court—appeal from decision of Rights Commissioner—Organisation of Working Time Act 1997, s 2(1)— alleged failure to afford complainant breaks in accordance with s 12*

The complainant was employed as a curry chef and alternated in that position with another chef. He gave evidence that he did not have breaks and instead prepared food which he consumed while continuing to work. His evidence was that he rarely received more than a five-minute break during work. It was asserted by the complainant's manager that the respondent's employees generally started work at 3pm and then worked until 10pm or 10.30pm depending on the day of the week. Normally a meal was prepared around 4pm and all employees took a break together at 4.30pm. However, as the premises in which the complainant was employed was a takeaway restaurant, it remained open during that period. Hence, a customer calling to the premises would have to be attended to, which could involve an interruption in the break. The Labour Court was informed by the respondent that if the complainant's break was interrupted he would obtain a compensatory break at the end of his shift. The respondent acknowledged that during the period of the claim it did not maintain working records of breaks in accordance with s 25 of the 1997 Act.

The Labour Court recited the provisions of s 12 of the 1997 Act and noted that, for the purposes of the Act, a break is a period which the worker knows in advance will be uninterrupted; which is not working time; and which he or she can use as he or she pleases. The Court noted the decision of the CJEU in the *Sindicato de Médicos de Asistencia Publica (SIMAP)*[21] that a period during which a worker is required to resume his or her duties immediately if required to do so is to be regarded as working time.

The Court noted s 25 of the 1997 Act and the Organisation of Working Time (Records) (Prescribed Form and Exemptions) Regulations 2001 which prescribed the form of working-time records that are to be maintained under that section. The Court noted that it had been accepted by the respondent that no records in the statutory form were kept during the relevant period in this case.

The Court noted that s 12(1) of the 1997 Act provides that an employee shall not be required to work for a period of more than 4.5 hours without a break of at least 15 minutes. The Court held that, assuming the complainant had a 15-minute break at 4.30pm as asserted by the respondent (the Court did not accept that he had), he was then required to work for a period of at least five hours and 15 minutes without a break. The Court noted that s 12(4) of the 1997 Act makes it clear that a break given at the end of a shift does not meet the requirements of subs (1). The Court held it was also clear that during the purported break at 4.30pm, the complainant was at the respondent's disposal and could be required to resume duties if so required. The Court held that this could not amount to a break within the statutory meaning. The Labour Court concluded that the

---

20. *Nutweave Ltd t/a Bombay Pantry v Kumar* DWT 1537.
21. *Sindicato de Medicos de Asistencia Publica (SIMAP) v Consellaria de Sanidad y Consuma de la Generalidad Valenciana* (Case C–303/98).

claim was well-founded and that the complainant was entitled to succeed in this appeal against the Rights Commissioner's decision. The Court awarded compensation of €2,000.

[30.08] *P&J Security Services Ltd v Chitii*[22]—*Labour Court—appeal from decision of Rights Commissioner—Organisation of Working Time Act 1997, s 12—Organisation of Working Time (General Exemptions) Regulations 1998 (SI 21/1998), reg 3—access to statutory rest break entitlements—whether complainant part of an exempted group within meaning of reg 3*

The complainant was a static security guard for the respondent at its facility in Dunbia. Because of the nature of his work and the fact that he worked alone at a security hut, the complainant did not have allocated break times. Instead he had food and beverage facilities at his work station and was informed that he should close the hut to take toilet breaks by putting a notice on the door saying he would be back in 10 minutes when the need arose.

The complainant brought a claim against the respondent to the Rights Commissioner contending that the respondent was in violation of s 12 of the Organisation of Working Time Act 1997 because he was not allocated a specific break time. The Rights Commissioner concluded that: (1) the issue of toilet facilities was not for consideration under the 1997 Act; and (2) on the balance of probability, the complainant had adequate opportunities to take breaks. The complainant appealed this decision to the Labour Court in accordance with s 28(1) of the 1997 Act.

Section 12 of the 1997 Act provides minimum break periods for employees working over a threshold number of hours. Under the Organisation of Working Time (General Exemptions) Regulations 1998, reg 3(3), the Minister exempted workers engaged in activities of a security or surveillance nature, which require continuous presence, from these set break periods due to the nature of their work. The exemption is not absolute and regs 4 and 5 provide that an employer shall not require an employee to whom the exemption applies to work for more than six hours without allowing him or her a break of such duration as the employer determines; such a break being reasonably regarded as equivalent to the statutory rest breaks.

In dismissing the complainant's appeal, the Labour Court held that the complainant was provided with sufficient opportunity to avail of breaks and that during his four years of employment with the respondent he could and did avail of this opportunity. The Court emphasised that the issue of the location of the toilets was not one that was properly before it, but on the basis that one purpose of a break is to avail of toilet facilities, the Court found that the complainant had reasonable access to toilet breaks and was advised accordingly. The complainant's decision not to close the security hut to take a toilet break was not brought about through the respondent's behaviour but the complainant's own view of what he wished to achieve by so proceeding.

---

22.   *P&J Security Services Ltd v Chitii* DWT 1556.

APPEALS ON QUANTUM

[30.09] *C & F Tooling Ltd v Cunniffe*[23]—*Labour Court—appeal from decision of Rights Commissioner—Organisation of Working Time Act 1997—quantum of compensation—preliminary issue—subsequent amendment of appeal form at commencement of appeal—amendment to appeal form statute barred—excessive award of compensation—penalisation for breach of Directive 76/2007/EC*[24] *with award of compensation*

This was an appeal from a decision of a Rights Commissioner in a claim under the Organisation of Working Time Act 1997. The respondent employer stated in the appeal form that the appeal was limited to a challenge on the quantum of compensation awarded by the Rights Commissioner. At the commencement of the hearing, however, the respondent sought to amend the appeal to include all aspects of the Rights Commissioner's original decision. The Court refused to allow an amendment to the original appeal form, stating that the nature of the appeal that the respondent was seeking to advance would change significantly if the amendment sought were allowed and that the respondent was effectively seeking to present an entirely new appeal at this late stage. The Court further noted that s 28 of the Act allows a party 42 days to appeal to the Court from the date on which the decision of the Rights Commissioner was communicated. The Court noted that this time limit had passed and that the Court would be acting outside of its powers if it were to allow a new appeal. The Court proceeded to hear the appeal in relation to quantum of compensation only.

The Rights Commissioner had found that the respondent had contravened s 14 (Sunday premium) and s 15 (maximum weekly working hours) of the Act and awarded the complainant compensation of €6,500 (s 14) and €10,500 (s 15) in respect of the contraventions respectively. The respondent subsequently submitted that both awards made by the Rights Commissioner were excessive and disproportionate to the contraventions found to have occurred. The respondent also submitted that the awards were inconsistent with previous awards made by the Court in similar instances. The complainant argued that the Rights Commissioner correctly measured the compensation awarded and placed reliance on the decision of the ECJ (as it then was) in *Von Colson v Land Nordrhein-Westfalen.*[25] That case concerned female social workers who had applied for posts at a male prison in West Germany. The authorities appointed two male candidates with lesser qualifications to those posts. The German Labour Court found that there had been discrimination and awarded the plaintiff's compensation under s 611a(2) of the German Civil Code. That provision purported to implement Council Directive 76/2007 on the implementation of equal treatment for men and women regarding access to employment. The ECJ found that s 611a(2) of the German Civil

---

23. *C & F Tooling Ltd v Cunniffe* DWT15125.
24. Directive 76/2007/EC on the implementation of the principle of equal treatment for men and women as regards access to employment, vocational training and promotion, and working conditions.
25. *Von Colson and Kamann v Land Nordrhein-Westfalen* (Case C–14/83).

Code only allowed for an award for reimbursement of travelling expenses incurred by the complainants in pursuing their applications for the posts. The ECJ stated that if a Member State chooses to penalise infringements of the prohibition of discrimination by an award of compensation, such compensation must be adequate in respect of the damage sustained and it must have a deterrent effect. The ECJ pointed out that compensation must be more than merely nominal damages and that the German law had restricted compensation to the reimbursement of travelling expenses which was purely nominal compensation.

In its determination, the Labour Court stated that the decision in *Von Colson* should be confined to its specific facts. While the ECJ referred to instances where a Member State chooses to penalise breaches of a Directive with an award of compensation, the Court, in the current case, stated that this could not be taken to mean that a statutory tribunal, such as the Labour Court, can apply a sanction in the nature of punishment for a contravention of the law. The Court stated that under Irish law, punishment for illegality can only be imposed by the ordinary courts and not by statutory tribunals exercising limited civil jurisdiction. The Court noted that any compensatory redress awarded by the Court must remain within what is capable of being redressed by compensation. The Court noted that this includes any present or future loss suffered by a complainant as well as any loss, damage, inconvenience or expense resulting from the wrong which a complainant suffers. The Court noted, in the context of the instant case, that this included the loss of leisure time and any actual or potential adverse effect that might be reasonably foreseeable on the health and welfare of the complainant arising from the contravention of s 15 of the Act that was found to have occurred.

The Court also stated that the decision in *Von Colson* related to the application of European law in the interpretation of domestic law. Section 14 of the Act was not intended to transpose a provision of European law and the Court concluded that the decision in *Von Colson* does not apply to a case involving the interpretation of s 14. The Court found that the contraventions of the Act that occurred were not of such seriousness as to justify the level of compensation awarded by the Rights Commissioner, and the Rights Commissioner awards went beyond what was fair and equitable in the circumstances. The Court allowed the appeal and varied the Rights Commissioner awards by decreasing the compensation to €2,000 (s 14) and €3,000 (s 15) for each respective contravention.

[30.10] *B Brothers Foods Ltd v Furmanczyk*[26]—*Labour Court—appeal by both parties of quantum awarded by Rights Commissioner—Organisation of Working Time Act 1997*

The complainant worked for the respondent as a store manager and alleged that the respondent had infringed several provisions of the 1997 Act. Both sides appealed against the quantum of compensation awarded by the Rights Commissioner.

The complainant stated that he was regularly required to work in excess of 4.5 hours without a break, contrary to s 12 of the Act. The respondent argued that the complainant

---

26. *B Brothers Foods Ltd v Furmanczyk* DWT1540.

was employed as a supervisor and was responsible for allocating breaks to other staff members and was in a position to schedule his own breaks.

The Court noted that, contrary to s 25 of the Act, the respondent did not maintain records of the complainant's breaks and that the onus of proving compliance with the Act lay with the respondent. The respondent submitted records of the complainant's rosters which disclosed that the complainant was, on occasion, required to work alone for periods in excess of 4.5 hours and, on those days, he could not avail of an uninterrupted break from work.

The Court noted that the Rights Commissioner had come to a similar conclusion and had awarded the complainant €800 in compensation. Having considered the frequency with which the complainant was required to work alone, and the health and safety consequences of depriving workers of access to breaks at work, the Court increased the award to €1,000.

The complainant was often required to work on Sundays. When he commenced his employment, the complainant was paid the statutory minimum wage and he submitted that the requirement to work on Sundays was therefore 'not otherwise taken account of in the determination of his pay', and this infringed s 14 of the Act.

The respondent argued that the contract of employment stated that there was no enhanced rate of pay for overtime and that any day of the week was considered the same. It was argued that this amounted to a requirement to work on Sunday for a flat rate of pay.

The Court found that the complainant was required to work on Sunday and that the requirement was not otherwise taken into account in the determination of his pay. The documentation showed that the complainant had worked on nine Sundays in the relevant period. The Rights Commissioner had awarded the complainant €413.44, however the Labour Court found that the frequency with which the complainant was required to work on Sunday, taken together with the length of his shift on that day, warranted a greater award of compensation and the Court accordingly awarded him €1,000.

The complainant alleged that he was not given 24 hours' notice of his weekly roster, contrary to s 17(3) of the Act. He further alleged that the roster he was given was regularly amended without 24 hours' notice of the changes being given. The complainant also submitted that he was often required to undertake additional hours of work without notice.

The respondent submitted that the complainant was notified in advance of his weekly roster and that the roster did not vary from week to week. The respondent submitted that any changes made, which were rare, could not be reasonably foreseen and therefore came within the scope of s 17(4) of the Act.

The Court noted that, in the absence of the working time records, the onus of proving compliance with the Act lay with the respondent. The Court held that the evidence submitted by the respondent in this regard amounted to no more than assertions and that it was well settled law that mere assertion cannot be afforded the status of evidence.

The Court set aside the decision of the Rights Commissioner and ordered the respondent to pay the complainant €500 for the breaches of s 17.

The respondent did not pay the complainant in accordance with s 20(2) of the Act. It argued that the complainant's holiday pay was incorporated into his basic hourly rate.

The respondent acknowledged that it did not comply with the provisions of the Act but it argued that the complainant was at no financial loss and that, as a consequence, the Rights Commissioner's award of €1,720 had been excessive.

Having considered all of the evidence, the Court found that the complainant was deprived of his statutory entitlements. It stated that the taking of annual leave is an important matter affecting safety and health of workers and that workers must be in a financial position to take annual leave and must not be offered any pressure or inducement to forgo that leave. The Court found that the manner in which the complainant was paid would require him to set aside sufficient monies each week to finance his annual leave and that, if he failed to do so, he would not be in a position to finance himself during his annual leave.

In the circumstances, the Labour Court found that the Rights Commissioner's award was not sufficient. The Court instructed the respondent to pay the complainant €2,500 in compensation for the infringement of his entitlements under the Act, which included all holiday payments due to him.

[30.11] *Zafer Bars Ltd in Liquidation v Csaba*[27]*—Labour Court—appeal from quantum awarded by Rights Commissioner—Organisation of Working Time Act 1997, ss 12, 14, 19 and 21—Directive 93/104/EC*[28]

The complainant was employed as a chef with the respondent from 4 May 2012 until 11 April 2014. The first complaint considered by the Court was the one under s 14 of the Act. The complainant submitted that the respondent was in breach of this section of the Act because he had been made to work every Sunday in the relevant period and this fact had not been taken into account in the determination of his pay. He maintained that he had not been compensated by any of the means set out in the Act for being required to work on Sundays. The finding of the Rights Commissioner was that this complaint was well-founded. The complainant was awarded compensation in the sum of €1,762.50 (comprising €1,462.50 economic loss and €300 compensation). The complainant submitted that this was not adequate compensation and that such a persistent infringement of s 14 of the Act should attract a level of compensation that was both just and equitable in all the circumstances. He added that an element of dissuasion should be encompassed to impede the respondent from infringing his rights in the future. In making his argument the complainant cited *Von Colson and Kamann v Land Nordrhein-Westfalen*,[29] *Lange v Georg Schunemann GmbH*[30] and *Browne v Iarnród Éireann-Irish Rail*.[31] He stated that the *ratio* of these decisions was that courts should make awards of

---

27.   *Zafer Bars Ltd in Liquidation v Csaba* DWT14120.

28.   Directive 93/104/EC, of 23 November 1993, concerning certain aspects of the organisation of working time.

29.   *Von Colson and Kamann v Land Nordrhein-Westfalen* (Case C–14/83).

30.   *Lange v Georg Schunemann GmbH* (Case C–350/99).

31.   *Browne v Iarnród Éireann-Irish Rail (No 2)* [2014] IEHC 117.

compensation that are 'tangible and significant, without being excessive or even generous'[32] and that the compensation he had been awarded did not meet that standard.

The Labour Court noted that the Rights Commissioner appeared to have considered that that the respondent infringed s 14 of the Act on all of the Sundays that fell in the relevant period. The Court further noted the value of the economic loss suffered by the complainant (€1,462.50) and commented that it must decide on an amount that is just and equitable in all the circumstances. However, it found that there was no applicable test available to it in order to arrive at that figure, rather it was a matter of judgment for the Court to apply its expert knowledge in all the circumstances of the case. The Court concluded that the complainant's statutory entitlements were infringed on 26 occasions in the relevant period. It considered the Rights Commissioner's award to be insufficient in the circumstances and upheld the appeal. The Court directed the respondent to pay the complainant compensation in the sum of €2,212.50, which included a compensatory sum of €750.

Next the Court considered the complainant's appeal of the Rights Commissioner's decision under s 12 of the Act. The complainant stated that the entitlement to breaks under s 12 of the Act gave effect to Directive 93/104/EC concerning certain aspects of the organisation of working time. The complainant maintained that this breach of one of his fundamental rights as an EU worker should attract a level of compensation that was both just and equitable in all the circumstances. He argued that the €350 awarded by the Rights Commissioner was not sufficient in that regard and that a sum of between five and 10 weeks of wages would be a more appropriate level of compensation. He drew the Court's attention to the same case law as he cited when making his case under s 14 of the Act. The Court stated that it was hindered by the absence of any evidence of the frequency or degree to which the complainant's rights under s 12 were infringed. The Rights Commissioner's decision was silent on the point and the written submissions to the Court were similarly of little assistance. The Court concluded that it had no evidence upon which it could review the level of compensation awarded, and although the Act requires that the Court make an award that is just and equitable in the circumstances, the Court was not made aware of all of the circumstances by the complainant. In the absence of such evidence, the Court held that it was bound to conclude that the basis for the appeal in relation to s 12 had not been made out. The decision of the Rights Commissioner was affirmed.

The complainant's appeal in relation to s 19 of the Act was based upon his assertion that he was not paid holiday pay in accordance with that section of the Act. The Court considered the following finding of the Rights Commissioner: 'I find that he was not paid the correct rate of pay for the holidays as stipulated in SI 475/1997 and Sec 20. I find that he is owed €200 x 4 = €800 for the economic loss. I award €400 compensation for the breach of his rights under this Act.'

The complainant maintained that the entitlement to annual leave was protected in both Irish and EU law as a fundamental social right and a matter of safety and health. He argued that the infringement of his rights under s 19 of the Act was not adequately compensated by the Rights Commissioner. The Court was presented with evidence that

---

32. Hogan J in *Browne v Iarnród Eireann-Irish Rail (No 2)* [2014] IEHC 117.

one of the former directors of the respondent had confirmed that staff were generally paid to work on bank holidays and during their holidays rather than taking leave at those times. From this the Court concluded that there had been a systemic practice of depriving the complainant of his entitlement to annual leave. It noted that the law did not permit such a deliberate policy to substitute pay for time off. This fact was continuously affirmed by the Court itself and the CJEU. The Court was of the view that, as this systematic practice had not been put in evidence to the Rights Commissioner, a review of the level of compensation awarded was warranted in the circumstances. Accordingly the Rights Commissioner's award of €400 compensation was varied and raised to a sum of €1,600. Together with the economic loss of €800, this meant that the total award made by the Court under s 19 was €2,400.

Finally the Court considered the complainant's appeal under s 21 of the Act. The Rights Commissioner found merit in this claim and held that the complainant was owed €650. The basis of the complainant's appeal was that the Rights Commissioner had failed to make an award of compensation in the circumstances. He argued that the infringement of his entitlement was an offence and that the fact that no award had been made under that heading was not just and equitable. As with the Court's finding in relation to s 19 of the Act, the Court considered that there was a systemic practice in the respondent of depriving staff of their entitlements under s 21. The Court was presented with evidence which indicated that it was the practice in the respondent to pay staff to work on public holidays rather than to allow them avail of the time off. Although the Court saw merit in the complainant's case, it noted that as the respondent was now in liquidation. As a result, the extent to which any potential award the Court could make would dissuade the respondent from repeating such an infringement was limited. The Court held that this was a factor which must be taken into consideration. The Court concluded that, in all the circumstances, the total sum of €1,000 in respect of the infringement of the complainant's rights under s 21 was just and equitable. This amount included €650 for the economic loss he incurred in respect of the four public holidays for which he was not paid a premium for working on those days. The decision of the Rights Commissioner was varied accordingly.

[30.12] *Wicklow Recreational Services Ltd t/a Shoreline Leisure Centre v Marciniuk*[33]—*Labour Court—Organisation of Working Time Act 1997, ss 14, 18, 21 and 26—where multiple claims lodged—claim for penalisation—appeal on quantum—statutory entitlement of employer to contest claim made by employee— delay on part of respondent in paying award recommended by Rights Commissioner*

The Court noted that the facts of the case were not in dispute. The respondent, which operates a leisure centre, employed the complainant as a part-time leisure attendant on a 'zero hours' contract in December 2008. The complainant's remuneration varied each week depending on the hours worked and the nature of the work performed. He was paid between €161.16 and €300 per week. The complainant submitted a series of complaints to the Rights Commissioner over the course of several months. In October 2013

---

33. *Wicklow Recreational Services Ltd t/a Shoreline Leisure Centre v Marciniuk* DWT14123.

complaints were made in relation to ss 14 and 21 of the Act. In February 2014 the complainant submitted a fresh complaint in relation to ss 14 and 21 of the Acts, in addition to complaints under ss 18 and 26 of the Act. Finally, in April 2014 he submitted a further complaint to the Rights Commissioner in which he alleged that the respondent infringed ss 14, 19 and 21 of the Act. The Rights Commissioner ultimately heard all of these complaints together. The complaints under ss 14, 18, 19 and 21 of the Act were found to be well-founded, while the complaint under s 26 of the Act failed. The complainant was awarded €1,249.42 in compensation. This sum was comprised of his economic loss in each case (which in total amounted to €949.42) and compensation 'for breach of his rights under this Act which is to act as a deterrent against future infractions' (amounting to €300).

The Court first considered the complainant's submission under s 26 of the Act. He stated that, as he had originally been employed to work weekends only, he used to work almost every Saturday teaching swimming. This job attracted a higher rate of pay than other jobs with the respondent centre. The complainant alleged that he was penalised after he made complaints about his employer under the Act, an allegation that was denied by the respondent. This penalisation manifested itself in the fact that he was either not scheduled to work on Saturdays at all or rostered to cover for other teachers. The complainant maintained that he suffered financial loss as a result. The respondent submitted that the complainant worked primarily as a lifeguard. This work was rostered on a fair basis by the assistant manager between the six to seven lifeguards employed by the respondent. It was further submitted by the respondent that the assistant manager did not know about the complainant's claims before the LRC and therefore could not have been influenced by them in rostering the complainant for work.

The respondent stated that it had gone to great lengths to accommodate the complainant on several occasions during the course of his employment with them. For example, he had been assigned weekend work when he first commenced his employment, so as to work around his other work commitments (he had a job as a van driver at the time). Subsequently, the complainant informed the respondent that he had taken up social welfare and could therefore only work restricted hours. He was once again facilitated by the employer on this occasion. Contrary to the complainant's assertions, the respondent maintained that he was rostered to work for seven Saturdays in the period from November to December 2013 and in January 2014. The respondent further highlighted that the requirement for lifeguards diminishes in December, when swimming lessons cease. The respondent referred the Court to a graph, which depicted that an average of 16 hours per week were allocated to the complainant. The respondent argued that the complainant had proffered no evidence to substantiate his claim of penalisation. He had failed to establish that his Saturday rosters were less than those of his colleagues or that his hours of work were comparatively less.

The Court noted that the complainant had been invited to set out evidence which proved his assertion that his hours were reduced and that he was denied assignment of the Saturday swimming classes, which attracted the higher rate of pay, as a result of the complaints he made to the Rights Commissioner. He declined to do so. Similarly, he failed to present the Court with other evidence that it had specifically requested, namely, his pay slips; the number of Saturdays upon which he worked prior to the date on which he filed the complaint, and the number in the period after that date; and the number of swimming classes he taught in the period prior to, and subsequent to, the date on which he filed a complaint. The complainant maintained that this information was in the peculiar knowledge of the respondent and that the complainant should not be required to provide evidence of information that was not in his possession. The Court held that in making out a complaint of penalisation the complainant was required to give detail of the detriment suffered by him. It was noted that the complainant's representative had stated that details of his working time and premiums could be read off his payslips and that he had been furnished with his payslips at all times. Therefore the Court did not accept the complainant's contention that the detail regarding the detriment suffered by the complainant was in the peculiar knowledge of the respondent. The Court concluded that the complainant was in possession of all of the information necessary to make out his case and that he had failed to do so and stated that mere assertion did not amount to evidence. Accordingly, the Court concluded that the complainant should fail in respect of his claim for penalisation. The decision of the Rights Commissioner in respect of the complaint under s 26 of the Act was affirmed and the appeal was not allowed.

In his appeal against the level of compensation awarded by the Rights Commissioner under ss 14, 18 and 21 of the Act, the complainant referred the Court to the decision in *E Smith School t/a The High School v McDonnell*.[34] In this case the Court stated that s 27(3) of the Act made clear that a complainant was not limited to recovering the economic or monetary value of any payment withheld by the employer. Jurisdiction existed for a Rights Commissioner or the Court to make an award of compensation which is just and equitable, having regard to the circumstances and to the upper limit of two years' pay. The complainant further argued that the Court was required to set out the essential rationale on foot of which a decision was taken. He referred the Court to the decisions of the Supreme Court in *Meadows v Minister for Justice, Equality and Law Reform*,[35] *Mallak v Minister for Justice, Equality and Law Reform*[36] and *Parhiar v Minister for Justice and Equality*.[37]

The complainant's representative stated that the compensation awarded by the Rights Commissioner was inadequate. However, no submission was made as to an amount the complainant considered adequate in the circumstances of this case. The complainant proceeded to outline what he considered to be aggravating factors in relation to several of his claims. In respect of the alleged breaches of ss 21 and 14, it was submitted that despite the fact that separate claims were issued in October 2013, February 2014 and April 2014, the issues were not addressed by the respondent at any stage. The complainant stated that he had yet to receive his claimed public holiday or Sunday *premia* entitlements. It was further submitted that the complainant had suffered a considerable inconvenience by having to attend two hearings. In respect of s 18 it was asserted that the fact that the complainant was given no or little work in the months of

---

34.   *E Smith School t/a The High School v Mc Donnell* DWT1411. See *Arthur Cox Employment Law Yearbook 2014* at [30.01].
35.   *Meadows v Minister for Justice, Equality and Law Reform* [2010] IESC 3.
36.   *Mallak v Minister for Justice, Equality and Law Reform* [2011] IEHC 306.
37.   *Parhiar v Minister for Justice and Equality* [2014] IEHC 445.

August, September and October 2013 was an aggravating factor. The complainant further asserted that the respondent had tried to justify that fact by alleging that no work had been provided due to some imaginary illness/injury. The complainant alleged that the amount of compensation should take into account the untruths told by the respondent. The respondent submitted that it had accepted the Rights Commissioner's decisions in all cases and had transferred the full amount of the compensation awarded to the complainant. It was conceded that the level of compensation of €300 was reasonable and fair in the circumstances in light of the nature of the breaches. It was further submitted that the compensation awarded was sufficient in order to act as a deterrent against future infractions.

The Court held that an employer has a statutory entitlement to contest a complaint made by an employee. In this case, it was considered that the respondent had taken reasonable steps to establish its obligations under the Act and had taken responsibility for its shortcomings when the case came on for hearing. It had conceded that the complaint under s 21 was well-founded. Although it made out a case against the s 14 complaint, it was unsuccessful in this regard. It was held that the respondent should have been aware of it obligations under s 21 of the Act and should have addressed the matter at the first available opportunity. As a result of its failure to do so, it deprived the complainant of his statutory entitlement for an unjustifiable period of time. The Court concluded that the level of compensation should be adjusted to reflect this failure. The Court further remarked that the respondent had delayed in paying the complainant his entitlement of €225.62 and that the complainant should be proportionately compensated for that unnecessary delay. Accordingly, it was held that compensation in the sum of €100, equating to close to 50 per cent of the total sum owed to the complainant, to be fair and just in all the circumstances of this case. The Court held that the respondent had made out a fair case before the Rights Commissioner in respect of the complaint under s 14 of the Act, as was his entitlement. Although the matter was decided against the respondent, the Court was not minded to penalise a respondent for availing of its statutory right to enter a bona fide defence against a complaint under the Act. The Court concluded that the Rights Commissioner's decision was just and equitable in all the circumstances and determined accordingly.

In relation to the complaint under s 18 of the Act, the Rights Commissioner had awarded the complainant the sum of €318.53. The Rights Commissioner had not specified the amount of compensation he awarded under this section for the infringement of the complainant's rights under the Act. Rather, he had awarded a total of €300 compensation for the combined infringements of ss 14, 18 and 21 of the Act, amounting to €100 for each of the infringements. At this point the Court had already stated that the infringement of s 21 of the Act should be increased by €100, bringing the sum total to €200 in respect of that infringement. The Court took a similar view in respect of the infringement of s 18 of the Act, which brought the total compensation for the infringements of ss 18 and 21 of the Act to €400. As stated above, the Court took the view that the respondent was entitled to defend the complaint under s 14 of the Act and should not be penalised for so doing. Accordingly, it was held that there was no basis for adjusting the compensation of €100 awarded by the Rights Commissioner in respect of that breach. The Court therefore varied the Rights Commissioner's decision by increasing the total award of compensation to €500.

MAXIMUM WORKING HOURS

[30.13] *Andrzej Gera t/a Family Bakery Samo Zdrowie v Krawczyk[38]—Labour Court—appeal from decision of Rights Commissioner—Organisation of Working Time Act 1997, s 15—working hours in excess of 48 hours per week*

The respondent employer appealed the decision of a Rights Commissioner in a claim by the employee under the Organisation of Working Time Act 1997.

The complainant (Mr Krawczyk) commenced his employment with the respondent as a baker on or about 18 January 2013. He contended that he was required to work significantly in excess of 48 hours per week in contravention of s 15 of the 1997 Act. The respondent denied that the Act had been contravened in the manner alleged. It was the respondent's case that the complainant worked no more than 30 hours per week. The respondent accepted that he did not maintain working time records in the statutory form. Consequently, in accordance with s 25(4) of the 1997 Act, the burden of proving compliance with the 1997 Act rested with the respondent.

In his evidence, the complainant told the Court that he was recruited by the respondent in Poland. He was told that he would be expected to work five hours per day over six days per week. He was to be paid €350 per week, he would be provided with accommodation and he would be transported to and from work by the respondent. According to the complainant, when he arrived in Ireland and commenced working, the reality was very different to what he had been told. It was his evidence that he regularly commenced work at 8pm and worked up to 8am or 9am the following morning. The complainant maintained a diary in which his starting and finishing times were recorded. Copies of this diary were put in evidence. These records showed that the complainant worked hours varying from 70 to 98 per week.

The complainant told the Court that an inspection was carried out at his workplace by NERA for the purpose of measuring compliance with the 1997 Act. For the purpose of the inspection he was instructed by the respondent to complete time sheets. He completed these sheets (which were put in evidence) but the working hours recorded were dictated by the respondent and did not accurately reflect his actual working time. According to the complainant, the respondent told him that if he did not complete these sheets as directed he would lose his employment and could be deported. The complainant was referred to pay slips on which hours of work were recorded. His evidence was that these pay slips did not accurately record the hours that he worked.

The respondent gave evidence in which he claimed that the complainant had entered into an agreement whereby he would work seven hours per day. He said that the arrangement was that five of these hours would be paid for and the additional two hours were to offset the cost of accommodation and transport.

---

38.   *Gera (Andrzej) t/a Family Bakery Samo Zdrowie v Krawczyk* DWT 1585.

The respondent referred to the timesheets put in evidence. He said that these time sheets accurately recorded the number of hours that the complainant worked and showed that his average working week was 30 hours (excluding the additional hours worked in respect of accommodation and transport).

The respondent's evidence was that the complainant commenced work at 9 pm and finished working at 4am on the following day. He accepted that the time sheets recorded the complainant's starting time at 2am and finishing at 7am. According to the respondent, the complainant finished work at 4am and remained on the premises until 7am in order to avail of transport home. The respondent accepted that the time sheets upon which he relied did not accurately record the complainant's starting and finishing time. He said that he had been advised that the period between 4am and 7am, when the complainant left the premises, would be regarded by NERA as working time and the times shown on the sheets were adjusted for the purpose of showing compliance with the 1997 Act. He told the Court that while the starting and finishing times were inaccurately recorded the actual working time was accurate.

The respondent accepted that he did not prepare the pay slips and these were created by his accountant.

In evaluating the evidence adduced, the Court found the respondent's testimony was unreliable in all material respects. By contrast, the Court concluded that the complainant gave honest evidence to the best of his recollection. The Court also accepted that this evidence was corroborated by the diary entries maintained by the complainant, the accuracy of which was also accepted.

The complainant was entitled to succeed in his claim and the decision of the Rights Commissioner was affirmed. While no cross-appeal was taken by the complainant, in a *de novo* hearing of the case, the Court was obliged to form its own view on the adequacy of the compensation, having regard to all of the circumstances the Court awarded the complainant €10,000.

WORKING TIME RECORDS

[30.14] *Blue Thunder Fast Foods Ltd t/a Blue Thunder v Oleniacz*[39]*—Labour Court—appeal from decision of Rights Commissioner—Organisation of Working Time Act 1997—preliminary issue—application to extend cognisable period—delay in bringing case due to proximal relationship and lack of legal knowledge—in absence of working time records, employer must prove compliance with Act*

The complainant raised her original complaint under the following sections of the Organisation of Working Time Act 1997:

- section 11 (daily rest periods);

- section 12 (rest and intervals at work);

- section 14 (Sunday premium);

---

39.   *Blue Thunder Fast Foods Ltd t/a Blue Thunder v Oleniacz* DWT15124.

- section 15 (weekly working hours);

- section 19 (annual leave); and

- section 21 (public holidays).

The Labour Court noted that due to the limitation period in the 1997 Act, the cognisable period for the claim was confined to the six-month period ending on the date on which the complaint was presented to the Rights Commissioner. As a preliminary issue, the complainant's solicitor applied for an extension of the cognisable period from 6 months to 12 months, asserting that the delay in bringing the claim was the result of the good relationship between the complainant and the respondent that existed prior to the termination of the employment. It was also asserted that the delay was due to the complainant's lack of knowledge about the Irish legal system. In this regard the complainant relied on the Labour Court determination *G and C Takeaway Ltd t/a Manor Takeaway v Noura Aboutabit.*[40] However, it was noted by the Court that the complainant had relied on this case in error. In agreeing with the findings of the Court in *G and C Takeaway Ltd,* the Labour Court held that the nature of the prior relationship between the parties does not constitute a reasonable cause for a delay in presenting a claim within the statutory time limit. Furthermore, the complainant's ignorance of her legal rights (as opposed to the underlying facts giving rise to those rights) could not excuse the delay.

On that basis, the complainant's application to extend the time period was refused.

In terms of the substantive case, the Court noted that practically all of the material facts were in dispute between the parties. The complainant gave evidence that each of the above provisions of the 1997 Act had been breached by the respondent, which in each case was denied. Both the complainant and the respondent relied on third-party witnesses in support of their position.

The Court heard that it was accepted that the respondent did not make or retain records of working time in accordance with its obligations under the 1997 Act. The Court stated that under s 25(4) of the 1997 Act, the respondent was required to prove, on the balance of probabilities, that it had not breached the 1997 Act in respect of the complainant.

In the absence of reliable records of working time, the Court held that it preferred the evidence of the complainant's witness, as the respondent's witnesses contradicted each other.

The Court held:

In respect of s 11 (daily rest periods), as the complainant was a shift worker, she was entitled to compensatory rest breaks. In the absence of evidence of compensatory rest breaks, it was held the respondent breached s 11.

In respect of s 12 (rest and intervals at work) in the absence of evidence that the complainant was afforded adequate breaks and intervals at work in accordance with the 1997 Act, the respondent was held to have contravened this section.

---

40.   *G and C Takeaway Ltd t/a Manor Takeaway v Aboutabit* DWT14104.

In respect of s 14 (Sunday premium), as there was no evidence that the complainant's pay contained compensation for Sunday work, the respondent was held to have contravened this section.

Both the complainant and the respondent agreed that the maximum working hours required of the complainant was 45 hours; therefore there was no breach of s 15 (weekly working hours).

In respect of the alleged contravention of s 19 (annual leave), the Court noted that the claim related to the period from 18 March 2014 to 19 June 2014. It referred to the High Court decision in *Royal Liver Assurance Ltd v Macken & Ors,*[41] which states that claims regarding the entitlement to annual leave crystallise at the end of the statutory leave year (commencing 1 April and ending 31 March). The Court held that, therefore, the complainant could bring a claim in respect of any shortfall in her full entitlement to annual leave in the leave year ending on 31 March 2014. The Court noted that the complainant appeared to assert that her statutory annual leave should have increased to over 20 days due to the hours worked; however, the Court held that this was not the case under the 1997 Act. The Court held that the complainant did receive her annual leave entitlement and therefore rejected this portion of the complainant's claim.

The complainant also sought pay for accrued but untaken annual leave under the 1997 Act; however, this claim was rejected as the complainant had not made this claim to the Rights Commissioner, and therefore the Court could not hear the complaint.

In respect of s 21 (public holidays), due to the respondent's lack of records, it failed to establish that it compensated the complainant for public holidays and therefore was held to have contravened s 21 of the 1997 Act.

The complainant was awarded the sum of €2,000 for the contravention of s 12; the sum of €750 for the contravention of s 14; and €500 in compensation for the breach of s 21.

---

41.   *Royal Liver Assurance Ltd v Macken & Ors* [2002] 4 IR 427.

Chapter 31

WORKPLACE RELATIONS ACT 2015

INTRODUCTION

[31.01] The Workplace Relations Act 2015, which was enacted on 20 May 2015, mostly came into force on 1 October 2015, with only certain provisions, providing for certain amendments to the Organisation of Working Time Act 1997, coming into force on 1 August 2015. Certain amendments to the 2015 Act were made in the National Minimum Wage (Low Pay Commission) Act 2015 and those amendments also came into force on 1 October 2015.

The 2015 Act has fundamentally reformed the manner in which statutory employment law claims are processed, adjudicated upon and dealt with on appeal. The five former employment fora (namely the Rights Commissioner Service, the Employment Appeals Tribunal, the Equality Tribunal, the Labour Court and the National Employment Rights Authority) have been replaced with a two-tiered structure, with all claims at first instance heard by Adjudication Officers of the Workplace Relations Commission (WRC) and the Labour Court hearing all appeals. Other fundamental changes introduced by the 2015 Act include the introduction of a pre-hearing mediation option for all claims; a uniform time-limit for instituting statutory employment claims; a more effective method of enforcing determinations made and a new regime for ensuring employment law compliance by employers.

The 2015 Act provides that the previous adjudication and appeal regimes continue to apply in respect of complaints or disputes referred to a Rights Commissioner, and to disputes under the Minimum Notice and Terms of Employment Acts and claims for redress under the Unfair Dismissals Acts referred to the Employment Appeals Tribunal, in each case before 1 October 2015. However, appeals from Rights Commissioner's decisions in those cases lie to the Labour Court from 1 October 2015 onwards. Once the existing workload in the old regime is addressed, the EAT and the Equality Tribunal will be abolished, with their functions transferred to the WRC and the Labour Court.

NEW REDRESS PROCEDURE – ADJUDICATION

[31.02] Under Pt 4 of the 2015 Act (ss 38–53) all claims and disputes under all employment law statutes and complaints under the Equal Status Acts 2000 to 2015 will, at first instance, and unless a mediated solution is first reached by a Mediation Officer, be adjudicated upon in private by Adjudication Officers following referral of the complaint or dispute to the Director General of the WRC. In general, claims must be filed with the Director General of the WRC within six months of the date of the contravention to which the complaint relates, but an Adjudication Officer may extend that six-month period by up to a further six-month period if he or she is satisfied that 'the failure to present the complaint or refer the dispute within [the initial six months] period was due to reasonable cause'.[1] This is less onerous than the previous 'exceptional circumstances prevented' test for extending the six-month limit for certain statutory claims, such as unfair dismissal claims.

The Adjudication Officers comprise former Rights Commissioners, Equality Officers and persons appointed following an open competition run by the Public Appointments Service.

Adjudication Officers are required to inquire into complaints and disputes, to give the parties the opportunity to be heard and 'present ... evidence', and to make a decision and have the power to summon witnesses and require documents to be produced. Parties appearing before Mediation Officers, Adjudication Officers and the Labour Court may be represented by solicitors, barristers, trade union officials, officials of recognised employer bodies and by any other person permitted by the Adjudication Officer/Labour Court and by a parent or guardian in the case of complainants who are under 18.

Section 42 of the 2015 Act empowers Adjudication Officers to dismiss complaints if they are of the opinion the complaints are frivolous or vexatious. A decision to dismiss a complaint on such grounds can be appealed to the Labour Court within 42 days and, if successful, the complaint will be remitted to WRC to be reheard by an Adjudication Officer.

Decisions of Adjudication Officers, which have not been appealed, are enforced in the District Court if they have not been implemented within 56 days.[2] Copies of all decisions will be published on the WRC website on an anonymous basis.

WRC ADJUDICATION PROCEDURES

[31.03] The WRC has published non-statutory procedures in relation to the investigation and adjudication of employment and equality complaints. These procedures make clear that it is necessary for the parties to every complaint to be heard by an Adjudication Officer to submit detailed written statements to the WRC in advance of the hearing. Usually, the detailed statement must be furnished by the complainant first and the respondent will be afforded an opportunity to reply in writing to that statement. However, in unfair dismissal cases (not constructive dismissal cases), the statement must be furnished by the respondent first within 21 days of a request by the WRC, with the complainant afforded an opportunity to respond in writing thereafter. Extensions of this timeframe will be granted by the Director General of the WRC in 'exceptional circumstances'. A mere assertion or denial of the compliant in a written statement will not be sufficient to comply with the requirements of the WRC procedures. Any preliminary legal submissions (such as a complaint being out of time) must be raised in the written statement furnished to the WRC. The WRC procedures provide that inferences can be drawn by Adjudication Officers where a statement is not delivered on time. However, the 2015 Act does not empower Adjudication Officers to draw such

---

1. Workplace Relations Act 2015, ss 41(6) and (8). See **[25.01]** and **[25.02]** for case law on reasonable cause.
2. Workplace Relations Act 2015, s 43.

inferences and accordingly serious questions exist in relation to the legality of any adverse inferences drawn by Adjudication Officers in such circumstances.

The WRC procedures envisage hearings being scheduled within six to eight weeks of the complaint being received by the WRC and, in that regard, the late delivery of a statement will not impact on the listing of a complaint for hearing. Once notified, hearings will only be adjourned in exceptional circumstances and for substantial reasons. If a complainant does not attend a hearing, the Adjudication Officer may find the complaint fails for want of prosecution. If the respondent does not attend the hearing, the Adjudication Officer may proceed and make a decision based on the information and evidence available.

Adjudication Officers can ask questions of the parties to a complaint and any witnesses in attendance at a hearing. Adjudication Officers will also afford the parties an opportunity to give evidence and to question the other party and any witnesses in attendance.

After the completion of the investigation by the Adjudication Officer, a written decision will issue within 28 working days or as soon as is practicable.

MEDIATION

[31.04] If the Director General of the WRC is of the opinion that a complaint or dispute is capable of being resolved by mediation, the Director General may refer the matter to a Mediation Officer with the consent of the parties.[3] The Mediation Officer will endeavour to bring about a mediated solution in private. Mediation is voluntary, confidential and without prejudice, but any agreement reached in mediation will be binding on the parties.

APPEALS

[31.05] All appeals from decisions of Adjudication Officers lie to the Labour Court, where the appeal will normally be by way of a full rehearing, with sworn testimony, in public. The Labour Court is the court of final appeal, subject to the right of either party to bring a further appeal from a determination of the Labour Court to the High Court on a point of law only. An appeal must be lodged with the Labour Court within 42 days of the date of the Adjudication Officer's decision but that time limit may be extended without limitation by the Labour Court 'due to the existence of exceptional circumstances'.[4] An appeal on a point of law to the High Court must be filed within 42 days of the decision of the Labour Court.[5]

The Labour Court has jurisdiction to conduct hearings in private on the application of a party to an appeal if there are special circumstances justifying it. The Labour Court can summon witnesses and require the production of documents. Decisions of the

---

3.   Workplace Relations Act 2015, s 39.
4.   Workplace Relations Act 2015, s 44(3) and (4).
5.   Workplace Relations Act 2015, s 46.

Labour Court are enforceable in the District Court if not appealed or implemented within 42 days and are published on the WRC website.

LABOUR COURT RULES

[31.06] The Labour Court has published, under s 20 of the Industrial Relations Act 1946 as amended by s 50 of the Workplace Relations Act 2015, rules in relation to the investigation and adjudication of unfair dismissal and equality complaints, all other statutory employment complaints and appeals against the issuance of compliance notices.[6] The rules also set out the procedure at hearings before the Court.

Investigation of unfair dismissal and equality complaints

[31.07] The rules make clear that an appeal must be lodged within 42 days of the date of the decision being appealed on a form prescribed by the Court. Within three weeks of receipt of the appeal, the appellant must furnish a written submission setting out the factual and legal issues upon which they intend to rely in the appeal. A copy of the appellant's written submission will be sent by the Court to the respondent and the respondent then has three weeks within which to deliver a replying submission.

The appellant's submission and respondent's replying submission must contain the following:

- a concise summary of the factual background to the claim giving rise to the appeal;

- a summary of the evidence to be adduced by, or on behalf of, the party making the submission;

- a summary of any legal arguments that will be relied upon in the course of the appeal;

- the number of witnesses, if any, that the party proposes to call at the hearing of the appeal.

The Court may extend the time for filing the submissions where exceptional circumstances are shown.

The rules provide the Court may, in its discretion, require the parties to attend a case-management conference before a date for the hearing of the appeal is fixed.

Documents required to be served under the rules may be served by electronic means where the recipient of the document has given written consent to the service of documents by electronic means.

The appellant and respondent are required, not later than seven days prior to the hearing date, to send written statements to the Court detailing:

- the names of the witnesses to be called to give evidence;

---

6.   Labour Court (Employment Rights Enactments) Rules 2015.

- a summary of the evidence that each witness is expected to give; and

- any document they intend to rely upon in the course of the appeal.

Appeal against a compliance notice

[31.08] The rules make clear that an appeal must be lodged within 42 days of the date the compliance notice was served. The notice of appeal must be accompanied by a written statement which contains:

- the basis on which the compliance notice is opposed;

- the evidence that will be adduced in advancing the appeal;

- the number of witnesses (if any) the employer proposes to call in support of the appeal;

- an outline of the evidence that the proposed witnesses are expected to give.

A copy of the appellant's statement is sent by the Court to the inspector who issued the compliance notice and he/she has three weeks within which to deliver a replying statement. The replying statement must set out:

- the basis upon which the inspector formed the opinion that the provision in issue had been contravened;

- the evidence that the inspector proposed to adduce at the appeal;

- the number of witnesses (if any) that the inspector proposes to call to give evidence at the appeal;

- an outline of the evidence that the proposed witnesses are expected to give.

The rules provide that the inspector who issued the compliance notice may appear in person or may be represented at the hearing of the appeal. The inspector may give evidence before the Court. Subject to the discretion of the Court, witnesses may give evidence and be cross-examined.

Following the appeal hearing, the Court will affirm the compliance notice, withdraw the compliance notice or withdraw the compliance notice and require the employer to whom the notice applies to comply with such directions as may be given by the Court.

Investigation of statutory employment complaints other than unfair dismissal and equality complaints

[31.09] The rules make clear that an appeal must be lodged within 42 days of the date of the decision being appealed on a form prescribed by the Court.

The appellant and respondent are required, not later than 7 working days prior to the hearing date, to send written submissions to the Court containing:

- a concise summary of the factual background to the claim giving rise to the appeal;

- a summary of the evidence to be adduced by, or on behalf of, the party making the submission;

- a summary of any legal arguments that will be relied upon in the course of the appeal;

- the number of witnesses, if any, that the party proposes to call at the hearing of the appeal.

The rules provide the Court may, in its discretion, require the parties to attend a case-management conference before a date for the hearing of the appeal is fixed.

Documents required to be served under the rules may be served by electronic means where the recipient of the document has given written consent to the service of documents by electronic means.

The appellant and respondent are required, not later than seven days prior to the hearing date, to send written statements to the Court detailing:

- the names of the witnesses to be called to give evidence;

- a summary of the evidence that each witness is expected to give; and

- any document they intend to rely upon in the course of the appeal.

Procedure at hearings

[31.10] The rules provide that the conduct of hearings before the Court shall be regulated by the Chairman of the division of the Court hearing the appeal. Appeals shall be by way of a *de novo* hearing.

Parties to an appeal may be represented by a trade union representative, an official of a body that, in the opinion of the Court, represents the interests of employers, a practising solicitor or barrister or with the consent of the Court, any other person of their choosing.

Except in such cases as the Court considers it convenient to take the written submissions as read, each party shall read their submission and the other party will be afforded an opportunity to comment on the submission presented by the other party.

Witnessed may give evidence and be cross-examined. The Court may curtail witness examination which it considers repetitive or irrelevant and may curtail cross-examination which it considers oppressive. Witnesses may also be questioned by any member of the Court.

The Court may give preliminary rulings on any aspect of a case where it is satisfied that time and expense may be saved by the giving of such a ruling. Whenever it considers it necessary to do so the Court may direct a party to furnish it with further or better information in writing on any matters arising in an appeal and may prescribe the time limit within which the information is to be provided. Any such additional information will be provided to the other party to the appeal, who shall be afforded an opportunity to furnish a response to the information provided. Where a party directed to provide further or better information fails to comply with such a direction or where a party fails to respond to information provided to that party, the Court may draw inferences from that failure as it considers appropriate.

The Court may admit any duly authenticated written statement as prima facie evidence of any fact whenever it thinks it just and proper to do so.

The Court will give a single decision in writing as soon as practicable after the appeal hearing has concluded.

POWERS OF INSPECTION AND ENFORCEMENT

[31.11] Existing authorised officers and Inspectors in the Department of Jobs, Enterprise and Innovation become Inspectors under the 2015 Act and the WRC is empowered, with the consent of the Minister, to appoint additional Inspectors. Inspectors are given extensive powers of entry (save in the case of dwellings where consent of the occupier or a District Court warrant is necessary), inspection of records, removal of records, questioning of persons present, production of records and examination of witnesses under caution and to issue Compliance Notices which can be appealed to the Labour Court and from there to the Circuit Court. Inspectors can also issue fixed-payment notices to a maximum amount of €2,000 where, following inspection of an employer's records, it is established that an employer has contravened a provision set out in the 2015 Act in relation to any of its employees.[7] There is no obligation on the recipient of a fixed-payment notice to discharge it; however, failure to do so within the 42-day time limit will result in a prosecution in respect of the relevant offence on the expiry of the time limit.

The Labour Court is empowered, during the hearing of an appeal, to direct an inspection of an employer's premises and to report thereon to the Labour Court.[8] Provision is made in s 33 of the 2015 Act for information relating to the commission of an offence under the 2015 Act or contravention of an employment law statute to be disclosed to the WRC by official bodies and by the WRC to official bodies and used for the purpose only of the detection, investigation and prosecution of an offence.

ADVISORY AND INFORMATION FUNCTIONS OF THE WRC

[31.12] In addition to hearing statutory complaints, the WRC has replaced the National Employment Rights Authority (NERA) and it is now responsible for discharging the advisory and information functions formerly performed by NERA. The WRC has been tasked with taking proactive steps such as providing advice, information and the findings of research conducted by the WRC to joint labour committees and joint industrial councils and advising and appraising the Minister in relation to the application

---

7. Workplace Relations Act 2015, s 36.
8. Workplace Relations Act 2015, s 30.

of, and compliance with, relevant enactments in order to encourage compliance with employment legislation and relevant codes of practice. The WRC has also been tasked with taking the key mediator role in seeking to resolve material industrial relations disputes.

FEES AND COSTS

[31.13] The Minister is empowered under s 71 of the 2015 Act to introduce regulations to impose fees on users of the services of the WRC and the Labour Court. The Minister introduced the first set of Regulations under s 71 in December 2015[9] pursuant to which an unspecified fee may be payable by an appellant who wishes to appeal the decision of an adjudication officer in circumstances where he/she did not without reasonable excuse, attend the first instance hearing before the adjudication officer. The appeal fee has been fixed at €300 and this fee is refunded if the Labour Court is satisfied there was good cause for failing to attend the first instance hearing.

OFFENCES/PROSECUTIONS

[31.14] The Minister's power to prosecute under employment law statutes is transferred to the WRC by s 37 of the 2015 Act. The 2015 Act creates the following offences:

- Obstruction of, interference with or impeding an Inspector or failing or refusing to comply with a requirement of an Inspector or an accompanying garda or giving of information to an Inspector which the person knows to be false or misleading.

- Failure to comply with an Inspector's Compliance Notice by the specified date.

- Failure to comply with a subpoena issued by an Adjudication Officer of the Labour Court.

- Failure to comply with a compensation order made by an Adjudication Officer or the Labour Court.

- Forgery of, the uttering of a forged document or the alteration of a document issued under the 2015 Act.

- Unauthorised disclosure of confidential information obtained while performing functions under the 2015 Act.

---

9.   Workplace Relations Act 2015 (Fees) Regulations 2015 (SI 536/2015).

SICK LEAVE/ANNUAL LEAVE

[31.15] The 2015 Act[10] amended the Organisation of Working Time Act 1997 with effect from 1 August 2015 so as to provide that annual leave accrues during certified sick leave, but subject to the following limitations:

- the sick leave must be medically certified;

- the delayed annual leave must be taken within 15 months of the end of the leave year (which will be the leave year defined in the Act – 1 April to 31 March – and not the employer's leave year) to which it relates;

- arrears of annual leave paid for on termination of employment are paid at the rate that would have been paid at the time the leave would have been incurred but for the sickness and there is, in those circumstances, a look-back period of up to two previous leave years, depending on when the termination of employment occurs.

See also [**30.03**].

CONCLUSION

[31.16] The introduction of a single point of entry for all statutory employment right claims is to be welcomed; however, concerns have been raised in relation to aspects of the new regime such as the fact that all hearings before Adjudication Officers are heard in private and will not involve sworn evidence. It is very much to be hoped that the new regime will achieve its aim of delivering a world-class workplace relations service which is simple to use, independent, impartial and cost-effective.

---

10.   Workplace Relations Act 2015, s 86(1).

Chapter 32

NORTHERN IRELAND – 2015 IN OUTLINE

INTRODUCTION

[32.01] Northern Ireland employment law is a complex and ever-changing field of law. In Northern Ireland the Department of Employment and Learning for Northern Ireland (DELNI) is responsible for employment law issues such as working time and unfair dismissal. Equality and anti-discrimination matters are the responsibility of the Office of the First Minister and Deputy First Minister (OFMDFM).

Historically, Northern Ireland tended to replicate employment law changes in Great Britain, albeit a year or two later. However, recently the Northern Ireland Assembly has failed to follow Great Britain's reform. Notable examples include the retention of the much-criticised statutory disciplinary and dismissal procedures which were repealed in Great Britain and replaced with a code of practice, produced and managed by ACAS, the introduction of the Equality Act 2010 and other changes designed to reduce 'red tape', such as protected conversations. One of the most significant changes is the introduction of tribunal fees reportedly resulting in a 70 per cent drop in tribunal claims.[1] Despite the dramatic effect that the introduction of tribunal fees has had in Great Britain, there does not appear to be an appetite to introduce similar measures in Northern Ireland.

In practical terms, this means that employers, HR professionals and practitioners operating across the three jurisdictions will face a more complex task in ensuring compliance with ever-diverging employment legislation when dealing with employees in more than one jurisdiction. From a Northern Ireland perspective, employment reform is becoming increasingly interesting as we continue to develop our own path.

This chapter highlights important changes and expected developments in Great Britain which impact upon Northern Ireland and highlights some significant local cases of interest to HR professionals and employers generally.

CALCULATING HOLIDAY AND OVERTIME PAY

[32.02] The Employment Appeal Tribunal (EAT) in Great Britain recently delivered a landmark decision in relation to the way in which statutory holiday pay is to be calculated in order to comply with European law.[2] The EAT decided three test cases against: (1) the engineering company, Amec; (2) the industrial services firm, Hertel; and (3) the maintenance company, Bear Scotland. The workers at these companies said that

---

1. Info available at: //www.gov.uk/government/uploads/system/uploads/attachment_data/file/ 352914/tribunal-statistics-quarterly-april-june-2014.pdf.

2. *Bear Scotland Ltd & Ors v Fulton & Ors* UKEATS/0047/13/BI, UKEAT/0160/14/SM, UKEAT/0161/14/SM, [2015] 1 CMLR 40. See **[30.04]**.

they consistently worked overtime, but that it was not included in their holiday pay, with the result that they received considerably less pay on holiday compared to when they were working.

The EAT held that overtime, including non-guaranteed overtime and other allowances such as travel time payments must be included in the calculation for holiday pay purposes. In essence, the EAT confirmed that holiday pay must be based on 'normal pay' ie, 'that which is normally received'. However, scope for workers to bring backdated claims for underpayment of holiday pay has been limited. In cases where the pattern of work is settled, it should be fairly easy to determine normal pay. Where there is no such 'normal', an average should be taken over a reference period.

In relation to the prospect of retrospective claims, the EAT held that if there is a gap of more than three months, during which there is no underpayment of holiday pay, then any 'series' of unlawful deductions will be broken – meaning that potential claims in respect of earlier underpayments should fall away. Also, importantly, the decision only relates to the 20 days of annual leave under European law. It does not apply to the eight days of additional leave under the Working Time Regulations 1998[3] or any additional contractual holiday entitlement.

[32.03] *Patterson v Castlereagh Borough Council[4]—Northern Ireland Court of Appeal—Working Time Regulations (Northern Ireland) 1998*

In a recent local development, the Northern Ireland Court of Appeal determined in *Patterson v Castlereagh Borough Council* whether voluntary overtime can be included in statutory holiday pay for the purposes of the Working Time Regulations (Northern Ireland) 1998;[5] and held that there was no reason in principle why voluntary overtime should not be included in statutory holiday pay for the purposes of the Working Time Directive.[6] It will be a question of fact for each Tribunal to determine whether or not overtime is 'normally' carried out and whether overtime pay can properly be described as forming part of 'normal remuneration' for these purposes. It should be noted, however, that the Court did not offer any substantive analysis on the circumstances in which voluntary overtime could or should be taken into account. Rather, the Court held that the Tribunal was wrong to conclude that voluntary overtime cannot be included in statutory holiday pay as a matter of principle.

SHARED PARENTAL LEAVE

[32.04] The Work and Families Act (Northern Ireland) 2015 came into force on 5 April 2015. The legislation provides that eligible employees with infants due to be born or placed for adoption from April 2015 will have a new statutory entitlement to shared

---

3.   Working Time Regulations 1998 (SI 1998/1833).
4.   *Patterson v Castlereagh Borough Council* [2015] NICA 47, 2015 WL4041906.
5.   Working Time Regulations (Northern Ireland) 1998 (SR 1998/386).
6.   Directive 2003/88.

parental leave and pay. This change was part of government reform in Great Britain to allow parents greater flexibility in looking after their children in the first year.

Where an eligible mother's baby is due on or after 5 April 2015, she can now elect to end her maternity leave and/or pay early so that leave and pay can be shared with the child's father or her partner, as shared parental leave and pay. The change does not affect existing rules of maternity and ordinary paternity leave/pay, which will remain the same. However, it is important to note that additional paternity leave has now been abolished. Employers can therefore expect eligible fathers and partners to request more leave. However, this will also enable mothers to return to work early as the father or partner may take the remainder of the leave in the mother's place.

Shared parental leave can be taken in discontinuous blocks. This means that leave can be separated by periods of work. Eligible employees are required to inform their employers at least eight weeks in advance of their proposed shared parental leave/pay. Employees are also entitled to submit a further two requests, again with eight weeks' notice, in order to take more leave or to alter the pattern of the leave they wish to take.

In a recent development, the UK government in October 2015 announced its intention to extend shared parental leave and pay to working grandparents. The new rules would allow working grandparents to look after new-borns to enable parents to return to work. It is anticipated that new legislation will be brought forward to enable this change, with the intention of implementing the policy by 2018.

TRAVEL TIME FOR MOBILE WORKERS

[32.05] *Federacion de Servicios Privados del sindicato Comisiones obreras (CC OO) v Tyco Integrated Security SL[7]—Court of Justice of the European Union—whether travel time counts as 'working time'*

The Court of Justice of the European Union (CJEU) has recently ruled on whether travel time is 'working time' under the Working Time Directive (the Directive) in the case of 'mobile' workers who do not have a fixed place of work. The definition of working time is contained in the Working Time Regulations (Northern Ireland) 1998 but is based on the Directive and so the case will have an impact on how Tribunals in Northern Ireland will interpret working time moving forward.

The decision will have implications for employers in Northern Ireland with mobile workforces such as field sales teams, field maintenance staff and care workers. However, its impact is not as dramatic as some press releases have suggested, given that the Directive, to which the ruling applies, has no bearing on employee pay.

The decision is solely about what counts as working time under the Directive. The working time legislation does not govern pay but is concerned with the organisation of working time (such as average weekly working time, rest periods/breaks and minimum periods of paid holiday).

---

7.   *Federacion de Servicios Privados del sindicato Comisiones obreras (CC OO) v Tyco Integrated Security SL* (Case C–266/14). See [**30.02**].

This legislation does not require working time to be paid. This is an entirely separate matter which is governed by the contract of employment and national legislation, namely the UK national minimum wage legislation. Indeed, the CJEU expressly stated in its decision that it is for national legislation to determine whether or not this travelling time or, indeed, any other category of working time, is paid or unpaid.

Under the UK legislation, the general position is that travel from a worker's home to their place of work or assignment does not qualify for the national minimum wage. This has been supported by case law. Recently, in *Whittlestone v BJP Home Support Ltd,*[8] the EAT in Great Britain held that the national minimum wage applied to time spent by a care worker travelling from one client to another, but not to the time she spent travelling between clients and home. Although the national minimum wage legislation will remain unaffected by this recent CJEU decision, it remains to be seen whether trade unions will exert pressure on the government to change its position on this.

The ruling could also mean that employers will have to ask their mobile workers to opt-out of the 48-hour working week under the Directive and the Northern Ireland Regulations (if they have not done so already). Alternatively, it may have an impact on the number of appointments arranged for each working day/week.

NATIONAL LIVING WAGE

[32.06] In July 2015, the UK government announced the introduction of a premium, over and above the national minimum wage, for workers aged 25 and over, known as the national living wage. This new premium is set to be introduced in April 2016 at £0.50p, which will effectively result in a higher national minimum wage of £7.20 for older workers.

On 1 September 2015, a package of measures was also announced which are intended to improve compliance with the National Minimum Wage and the National Living Wage when the latter is introduced in April 2016. Employers in breach of new rules will face higher fines and will potentially be disqualified from holding company directorships. The measures include:

•   Doubling the penalties for non-payment of the National Minimum Wage and National Living Wage. Penalties will increase from 100 per cent of arrears to 200 per cent of arrears but will be halved if employers pay within 14 days. The overall maximum penalty of £20,000 per worker remains unchanged;

•   Increasing the budget for enforcement of the National Minimum Wage and the National Living Wage in 2016; and

•   The establishment of a new HMRC team dedicated to pursue criminal prosecutions in the most serious cases of employers deliberately not paying the National Minimum Wage and National Living Wage.

---

8.   *Whittlestone v BJP Home Support Ltd* UKEAT/128/13, [2014] ICR 275.

It was not initially clear whether these measures would apply across the UK. It is now largely expected that they will. Employers in Northern Ireland should be paying close attention to the changes over the coming months.

Local business leaders have strongly criticised the sharp increase from the current £6.50 for adults. Initial reports however indicate that UK employers will only see their total wage bill increase by 0.6 per cent when the National Living Wage comes into force. Certain industries are likely to feel the changes more than others, with the biggest impact expected in retail and hospitality sectors.

The government has pledged to improve guidance and support available for employers and to work with payroll providers to make sure that payroll software incorporates mechanisms to ensure compliance with the National Minimum Wage and National Living Wage.

'WITHOUT PREJUDICE' COMMUNICATIONS

[32.07] *McKinstry v Moy Park, Maxwell and Johnston[9]—Northern Ireland Court of Appeal—'without prejudice' communications—whether meeting between parties should be excluded from proceedings*

The appellant, Mr McKinstry, had been employed as a production planner and suffered from neuropathy, which affected his feet and legs. On 25 June 2013, the appellant was asked to attend a meeting with two other members of staff, one of whom was a HR manager. The appellant subsequently alleged that he was not made aware of the nature or agenda of the meeting in advance.

At the beginning of the meeting, the HR manager explained to the appellant that they sought to engage in a 'without prejudice' discussion with him. The meaning of the concept was then explained to the appellant, who confirmed his understanding and agreed to continue. The appellant was informed that there were issues with his conduct within the workplace, which he denied. A number of options were then discussed, including a compromise agreement to terminate his employment with the company. The appellant did not accept the compromise agreement and ultimately commenced tribunal proceedings alleging, among other things, discrimination on the basis of his disability.

The industrial tribunal held, at a pre-hearing review, that a meeting between the parties was 'without prejudice' and should be excluded from the appellant's claim against the respondents. The Court of Appeal, setting aside the decision of the employment judge, remitted the case back to the industrial tribunal, before a different employment judge. In essence, the Court of Appeal expressed unease that fundamental issues may not have been sufficiently explored. In particular, the Court was not satisfied that the question of whether there was an extant dispute was ever fully explored by the employment judge. Similar unease was expressed in respect of the appellant's purported agreement to engage on a 'without prejudice' basis. The Court noted that the HR manager who explained the concept of 'without prejudice' to the appellant was not legally qualified. The Court felt it important to ask what exactly had been explained to

---

9.   *McKinstry v Moy Park, Maxwell and Johnston* 01725/13IT.

the appellant and to consider whether any such explanation was legally accurate. It is worth noting that the Court was not suggesting that the explanation was inaccurate, but rather important questions such as this had not been dealt with at the preliminary review hearing. Indeed, the Court suggested that such questions should not have been properly assessed at a preliminary review stage but should, instead, have been considered at the main hearing, where substantial evidence could have been produced. The case has been remitted to the tribunal and a decision is awaited.

Chapter 33

CURIAL DEFERENCE AND THE LABOUR COURT

Tom Mallon BL

[33.01] The Workplace Relations Act 2015 consolidates the determination of all statutory employment law disputes into a single, two-staged process. All disputes will be referred, at first instance, to an Adjudication Officer with an appeal to the Labour Court. The only further appeal available is an appeal on a point of law to the High Court. The Labour Court also has power to refer a question of law to the High Court and the determination by the High Court in such circumstances or pursuant to an appeal shall be final and conclusive.

The courts over the years have had to deal with appeals, on points of law, from a range of expert quasi-judicial bodies. The courts, where appropriate, will exercise curial deference to an inferior body, if that body is regarded as having particular expertise to determine the issues before it.

An appeal on a point of law arises in a number of areas such as the decisions of inferior bodies dealing with matters such as social welfare, income tax and, in recent years, issues considered by the Financial Services Ombudsman (FSO) and the Pensions Ombudsman.

Lengthy consideration was given by Clarke J in *Ashford Castle Ltd v SIPTU*[1] to the level of curial deference which would be afforded to the Labour Court on a point of law appeal from a decision of the Court under the Industrial Relations (Amendment) Act 2001. In his decision, Clarke J referred to a number of the leading Irish cases in this area and quoted from, among others, *Henry Denny & Sons (Ireland) Ltd v Minister for Social Welfare*,[2] where Hamilton CJ made the following observation:

> the courts should be slow to interfere with the decisions of expert administrative tribunals. Where conclusions are based upon an identifiable error of law or an unsustainable finding of fact by a tribunal such conclusions must be corrected. Otherwise it should be recognised that tribunals which have been given statutory tasks to perform and exercise their functions, as is now usually the case, with a high degree of expertise and provide coherent and balanced judgments on the evidence and arguments heard by them it should not be necessary for the courts to review their decisions by way of appeal or judicial review.

---

1. *Ashford Castle Ltd v SIPTU* [2006] IEHC 201.
2. *Henry Denny & Sons (Ireland) Ltd v Minister for Social Welfare* [1998] 1 IR 34.

He also referred to the decision in *Orange Ltd v Director of Telecoms (No 2)*[3] where Keane J quoted, with approval, a judgment of the Canadian Supreme Court (*Canada (Director of Investigation and Research) v Southan INC*)[4] in the following terms:

> ... (an) appeal from a decision of an expert tribunal is not exactly like an appeal from a decision of a trial court. Presumably if parliament entrusts a certain matter to a tribunal and not (initially at least) to the courts, it is because the tribunal enjoys some advantage the judges do not. For that reason alone, review of the decision of a tribunal should often be of a standard more deferential than correctness.

Dealing with the curial deference which should be afforded to a social welfare appeals officer Gilligan J in *Electricity Supply Board v Minister for Social Community & Family Affairs*[5] stated the following:

> I take the view that the approach of this Court to an appeal on a point of law is that findings of primary fact are not to be set aside by this Court unless there is no evidence whatsoever to support them. Inferences of fact should not be disturbed unless they are such that no reasonable tribunal could arrive at the inference drawn and further if the Court is satisfied that the conclusion arrived at adopts a wrong view of the law, then this conclusion should be set aside. I take the view that this Court has to be mindful that its own view of the particular decision arrived at is irrelevant. The Court is not retrying the issue but merely considering the primary findings of fact and as to whether there was a basis for such findings and as to whether it was open to the Appeals Officer, to arrive at the inferences drawn and adopting a reasonable and coherent view, to arrive at her ultimate decision.

In *Faulkner v Minister for Industry and Commerce*[6] Murphy J put the situation in the following terms:

> It is well settled law that, where a quasi judicial function is delegated to an expert administrative tribunal, the decision of such a tribunal cannot be challenged on the grounds of irrationality if there is any relevant material to support it.

All of the foregoing would suggest that the High Court will give substantial curial deference to the Labour Court, and indeed Clarke J in *Ashford Castle* recognised the Labour Court as having particular expertise when he made the following observations:

> The tasks which administrative bodies are given under statute vary significantly. The issues which have to be decided can be of very different types. At one end of the spectrum are issues which involve the same sort of mixed questions of law and fact with which the courts are frequently faced. A person may, for example, be entitled to a social welfare benefit provided that a certain set of facts, as specified by statute, are found to exist. The issue at a hearing within the social welfare system may well, therefore, turn on whether, as a matter of fact, the necessary

---

3.   *Orange Ltd v Director of Telecoms (No 2)* [2002] 4 IR 159.
4.   *Canada (Director of Investigation and Research) v Southan INC* (1997) 1 FCR 748.
5.   *Electricity Supply Board v Minister for Social Community & Family Affairs* [2006] IEHC 59.
6.   *Faulkner v Minister for Industry and Commerce* (25 June 1993) HC, Murphy J.

qualifying requirements have been established or disqualifying requirements have been shown to exist. In such cases the findings of fact will be very similar to the facts which will be found by a court should a comparable issue arise in judicial proceedings. At the other end of the spectrum, expert bodies may be required to bring to bear upon a situation a great deal of their own expertise in relation to matters which involve the exercise of an expert judgment.

Clarke J then having considered the level of expertise required in a number of areas dealt with by the Labour Court in the following terms:

> In those circumstances it seems to me that the Labour Court, when exercising its role under the Act, is very much towards the end of the spectrum where it is required to bring to bear its own expert view on the overall approach to the issues. It, correctly in my view, identified that its decision must be one which is fair and reasonable to both sides. Precisely what is fair and reasonable in the context of terms and conditions of employment is a matter upon which the Labour Court has great expertise and, in my view, the Labour Court is more than entitled to bring its expertise to bear on the sort of issues which arise in this case ...

> For those reasons it does seem to me that a very high degree of deference indeed needs to be applied to decisions which involve the exercise by a statutory body, such as the Labour Court, of an expertise which this court does not have. Similarly in assessing whether a decision could legitimately have been come to by the Court, it is necessary to consider all of the materials which were properly before the Court and to identify whether those materials could reasonably have led to the conclusion reached, taking into account the legitimate exercise by the Labour Court of its own expertise in the matter.

In recent years the courts have given considerable curial deference to Ombudsmen. In *Willis & Ors v The Pension Ombudsman*[7] Kearns P expressed the following views:

> A high threshold must be crossed by any appellant from a decision of a financial/ pensions ombudsman. The court has no difficulty in accepting that the relevant test for a statutory appeal against a decision of the Pensions Ombudsman should be the same as that provided for in respect of the Financial Services Ombudsman as laid down by Finnegan P in *Ulster Bank v Financial Services Ombudsman* [2006] IEHC 323 where it was stated at p 9:

>> To succeed on this appeal the Plaintiff must establish as a matter of probability that, taking the adjudicative process as a whole, the decision reached was vitiated by a serious and significant error or a series of such errors. In applying the test the court will have regard to the degree of expertise and specialist knowledge of the Defendant. The deferential standard is that applied by Keane CJ in *Orange v The Director of Telecommunications Regulation and another* and not that in *The State (Keegan) v Stardust Compensation Tribunal*.

---

7.   *Willis & Ors v The Pension Ombudsman* [2013] IEHC 352.

It is however extremely important to note that later in the same judgment Kearns P made the following observation:

> I accept, as I must, that in this context the Pensions Ombudsman could not, regardless of the merits of the case, legitimately make a decision which the law did not permit. But subject only to that consideration he enjoys a significant discretion to allow and achieve a fair outcome in relation to a complaint.

The new procedure under the Workplace Relations Act in effect replaces the former jurisdiction of the Employment Appeals Tribunal (and both the Circuit Court and the High Court in claims under the Unfair Dismissals Acts) with a single appeal to the Labour Court. It is respectfully submitted that the Labour Court, in applying legal principles pursuant to the Unfair Dismissals Acts and/or pursuant to any other statutory provision, is not exercising some particular expertise. Nothing in the legislation requires that Adjudication Officers and/or members of the Labour Court have any particular legal skill and whilst no doubt they will continue to enjoy a level of deference in relation to the determination of facts, that deference in my view cannot be extended to decisions of law.

In *Dunnes Stores v Doyle*[8] Birmingham J had to deal with a point of law appeal from the Employment Appeals Tribunal pursuant to the provisions of the Payment of Wages Act 1991. Birmingham J stated that 'in essence' the issue upon which the Employment Appeals Tribunal had to adjudicate was whether the employee was employed to work a 37.5-hour week or a 40-hour week. He then said that: 'The immediate question that arises is whether the decision of the Tribunal involved a question of law or a question of fact or a mixed question of law and fact.'

He dealt with the curial deference point in the following terms:

> Identifying the contractual entitlement of an employee of course involves legal determinations. Where such legal determinations are made by a tribunal then there is the option of having the conclusions reviewed in the High Court through the appeal on a point of law route. When that occurs, and the High Court is asked to consider whether the Tribunal correctly applied the law, there is no scope for the doctrine of curial deference. Here though, as appears from the determination and the record of the proceedings, the Tribunal was concerned to decide what was essentially a question of fact. When engaged in that task, the Tribunal's view, given its composition, representative as it is of both sides of industry, is entitled to great respect.

The issue was also recently covered by Kearns P in *Earagail Eisc Teoranta v Doherty & Ors*[9] in the following terms:

> Having found that the Tribunal was entitled to adjudicate on the matter, the Court must next consider whether or not the decision arrived at is tainted by any error of law. In doing so, the Court is required to have regard to the doctrine of curial deference when considering appeals from the decisions of expert administrative tribunals and quasi-judicial bodies as set out by Hamilton CJ in *Henry Denny &*

---

8.   *Dunnes Stores v Doyle* [2014] 25 ELR 184.
9.   *Earagail Eisc Teoranta v Doherty & Ors* [2015] IEHC 347. See **[28.03]**.

Sons. This Court must confine itself to a consideration of a point of law only and may only interfere with a finding of fact when it is entirely unsustainable based on the information before the Tribunal. However, as was made clear in *National University of Ireland Cork v Ahern and others* [2005] IESC 40, [2005] 2 IR 577, the process by which certain findings of fact were made is often a question of law. McCracken J stated at paragraph 9:

> … matters of fact as found by the Labour Court must be accepted by the High Court in any appeal from its findings. As a statement of principle, this is certainly correct. However, this is not to say that the High Court or this court cannot examine the basis upon which the Labour Court found certain facts. The relevance, or indeed admissibility, of the matters relied on by the Labour Court in determining the facts is a question of law. In particular, the question of whether certain matters ought or ought not to have been considered by account by it in determining the facts, is clearly a question of law and can be considered on an appeal under [the relevant section].

In *Earagail Eisc Teoranta* Kearns J went on to refer to the decision of Birmingham J in *Dunnes Stores* and determined that in the case before him there was a manifest error of law in the Tribunal's interpretation of the relevant Act. He also referred to the failure on the part of the Tribunal to provide adequate reasons for a number of its findings and he stated that the brief determination of the Tribunal was 'wholly inadequate to meet even this low threshold'.

CONCLUSION

[33.02] In summary it seems to me that the very high level of curial deference referred to by Clarke J in *Ashford Castle* is not the appropriate level in determining questions which arise pursuant to, *inter alia*, the Unfair Dismissals Acts and/or the Employment Equality Acts. The Industrial Relations (Amendment) Act 2001, whilst leading to a legally enforceable decision on the part of the Labour Court, called on the Labour Court to exercise its expertise in relation to the assessment of terms and conditions of employment. It is respectfully submitted that the Labour Court has no particular expertise in determining the fairness or otherwise of a dismissal or in interpreting the law pertaining to employment equality. The Adjudication Officers and the Labour Court are quasi-judicial bodies exercising important functions pursuant to a whole range of statutes and determining questions of great value and great importance to both employers and employees. In performing their duties they will be required to interpret and apply the law and will not be entitled to any level of curial deference from the superior courts in performing that part of their duty.

INDEX

[All references are to paragraph number]

B

Bonuses

performance-related, non-payment, 28.01

Breach of cash-handling procedures

dismissal, 1.93

Breach of company procedures

dismissal, 1.101, 27.44–27.45

Breach of confidentiality

dismissal, 1.94, 27.33–27.34

Breach of trust/dishonesty

dismissal, 1.92, 27.25–27.30

criminal convictions, 27.35

Budget 2016

pensions, 20.01

benefits increase, 20.04

pension levy, 20.02

public servants, 20.06

sustainability concerns, 20.05

USC exemption on employer PRSA contributions, 20.03

Bullying *see* **Employment related torts**

C

Capacity

dismissal, 1.86, 27.15–27.18

Children and Family Relationships Act 2015 (No 9 of 2015)

adoption, 17.04

generally, 17.03

maternity leave, 17.05

parental leave, 17.06

Civil partners

discrimination, pensions case law, 20.20

Collective agreements

dispute resolution clauses, 1.41, 13.28

trade union recognition, 1.43

transfer of undertakings, 26.04

Commission

failure to pay, constructive dismissal 27.69

Companies Act 2014

appointment of directors, 3.03

background, 3.02

compensation for loss of office

new law (s 251), 3.20

old law, 3.19

directors' duties, 3.05

breaches, liability to account and indemnify, 3.13

anticipated claims, 3.15

exclusion of liability and indemnities, 3.16

power of court to grant relief, 3.14

compliance statement, 3.08

disclosure of interest in contracts, 3.12

ensuring compliance with Act, 3.06

ensuring secretary has necessary skills or resources, 3.17

fiduciary duties, 3.09

other interests, 3.10

power to act in professional capacity for company, 3.11

regard to employees' interests, 3.07

introduction, 1.09, 3.01

removal of directors, 3.18

service contracts and remuneration of directors, 3.04

Companies (Amendment) Bill 2015 (No 10 of 2015)

generally, 17.37

Company procedures

breach of, dismissal, 1.101, 27.44–27.45

Company vehicles

installation of GPS vehicle management system, 1.42, 13.28

Conditions of employment *see* **Terms and conditions of employment**

Confidentiality

breach of, dismissal, 1.94, 27.33–27.34